Learn OS X Lion

Scott Meyers and Mike Lee

Apress®

Learn OS X Lion

ISBN-13 (pbk): 978-1-4302-3762-4

ISBN-13 (electronic): 978-1-4302-3763-1

Trademarked names, logos, and images may appear in this book. Rather than use a trademark symbol with every occurrence of a trademarked name, logo, or image we use the names, logos, and images only in an editorial fashion and to the benefit of the trademark owner, with no intention of infringement of the trademark.

The use in this publication of trade names, trademarks, service marks, and similar terms, even if they are not identified as such, is not to be taken as an expression of opinion as to whether or not they are subject to proprietary rights.

President and Publisher: Paul Manning
Lead Editor: Michelle Lowman and Douglas Pundick
Technical Reviewer: Joe KissellEditorial Board: Steve Anglin, Mark Beckner, Ewan Buckingham, Gary Cornell, Jonathan Gennick, Jonathan Hassell, Michelle Lowman, James Markham, Matthew Moodie, Jeff Olson, Jeffrey Pepper, Frank Pohlmann, Douglas Pundick, Ben Renow-Clarke, Dominic Shakeshaft, Matt Wade, Tom Welsh
Coordinating Editor: Kelly Moritz
Copy Editors: Damon Larson and Kim Wimpsett
Compositor: MacPS, LLC
Indexer: BIM Indexing & Proofreading Services
Artist: SPi Global
Cover Designer: Anna Ishchenko

Distributed to the book trade worldwide by Springer Science+Business Media, LLC., 233 Spring Street, 6th Floor, New York, NY 10013. Phone 1-800-SPRINGER, fax (201) 348-4505, e-mail orders-ny@springer-sbm.com, or visit www.springeronline.com.

For information on translations, please e-mail rights@apress.com, or visit www.apress.com.

Apress and friends of ED books may be purchased in bulk for academic, corporate, or promotional use. eBook versions and licenses are also available for most titles. For more information, reference our Special Bulk Sales–eBook Licensing web page at www.apress.com/bulk-sales.

The information in this book is distributed on an "as is" basis, without warranty. Although every precaution has been taken in the preparation of this work, neither the author(s) nor Apress shall have any liability to any person or entity with respect to any loss or damage caused or alleged to be caused directly or indirectly by the information contained in this work.

Contents at a Glance

Contents

About the Authors

 **Scott Meyers** is the founder of SquareLike LCC, a technical services company specializing in the development and distribution of content across a wide range of platforms and mediums. Beyond mentoring writers and content creators, Scott has 15 to 20 years of experience providing consulting, training, and development services for Mac OS and the Web, with significant expertise in developing and maintaining secure, distributed systems for multiplatform computing environments.

Scott lives in Carmel, Indiana, with his wife, two kids, a cat, a dog, and other assorted critters (currently various mice and goldfish). When not working or writing, Scott likes building and modifying tube amplifiers and then making loud guitar noises through them, traveling, photography, coaching soccer, and watching FCB beat Real Madrid.

Scott can be contacted at scott@learnmacos.info. Answers, updates, and errata for this book can be found at www.learnmacos.info.

 **Mike Lee**, the world's toughest programmer, is the founder and CEO of United Lemur, a philanthropic revolution disguised as a software company. Mike has had a role in creating many popular iPhone applications, including Obama '08, Tap Tap Revenge, Twinkle, and Jott.

Prior to the iPhone, Mike cut his teeth—and won an Apple Design Award—at the Seattle-based Delicious Monster Software. Mike is a popular blogger and occasional pundit, and has been seen on Twitter as @bmf.

Mike is originally from Honolulu but currently lives in Silicon Valley with two cats. Mike's hobbies include weightlifting, single malts, and fire. Mike can be contacted at mike@unitedlemur.org.

About the Technical Reviewer

 **Joe Kissell** is senior editor at TidBITS, a web site and weekly e-mail newsletter about Apple and the Internet, and the author of numerous print and electronic books, including *Mac Security Bible* and *Take Control of Upgrading to Lion*. He is also a senior contributor to Macworld, was the winner of a 2009 Neal award for Best How-To Article, and has appeared on the MacTech 25 list (the 25 people voted most influential in the Macintosh community) since 2007. Joe has worked in the Mac software industry since the early 1990s, and previously managed software development for Nisus Software and Kensington Technology Group. He currently lives in Paris, France with his wife, Morgen Jahnke, their son, Soren, and their cat, Zora.

Acknowledgments

A great deal of love and thanks go out to my family: Sara Beth, Ethan, and Isabel—writing sucks away a lot of time and often has the side of effect of making me a bit cranky, and I couldn't have done this without their support (and I often wonder why I still get it).

Also, a book like this takes a lot of people to make it successful. With that in mind, a big thanks to everyone who worked on this book with me. First, thanks to Mike Lee, who coauthored the first two editions of this book, but who was busy with a little thing called Appsterdam (`www.appsterdam.rs`) this time around. His wisdom (as well as many of his words) still permeate this book. Thanks to Joe Kissell for catching numerous errors and providing wonderful advice along the way, Kelly Moritz for making sure everything got moved along where it needed to go, Doug Pundick, Michelle Lowman, Damon Larson, and all the others at Apress who helped make this book possible.

Thanks also goes out to the folks at Apple who continue to amaze us with great products and great support for their products.

Scott Meyers

In addition to the teams at Apress and Apple without whom this book could not exist, I have to acknowledge three groups of people who have accompanied me on this ride. First, I have to thank the mentors who have given so freely of their time and knowledge to make me the engineer I am today. I can only hope to live up to your lessons. Second, I have to thank the trail of broken engineers and designers who have followed me into the madness in which great software is forged. You've earned your success. Finally, I have to thank the crazy people who should know better than to set aside their perfectly adequate lives to pursue their passions armed with little more than a book and a dream. You are the reason we write.

Mike Lee

Introduction

If you're new to the Mac or just new to Lion, this book is for you . . .

Wait, I didn't say new to computers!

That's where this book differs from many others. This book assumes that you have used computers before—maybe not a Mac and probably not Lion—but you have some experience with what a computer is and how to use it. With that understanding, this book can talk to you, without talking *down* to you.

Learn OS X Lion is divided into nine sections to help you not only get up to speed using OS X Lion, but also delve into Lion's nooks and crannies so you can get the most out of it.

Part 1 begins by providing you with a quick tour of OS X Lion, describing unique features of the operating system and how to take advantage of them.

Part 2 then builds on the first section to show you how applications generally behave with OS X Lion, and how to work with documents. This includes a discussion of common applications that are included with OS X.

Part 3 provides information about connecting to the Internet and how to use Safari, Mail, and other Internet applications included with Mac OS X Lion.

Part 4 provides a quick introduction to the iLife application suite, including iPhoto, iMovie, and GarageBand. While not specifically included with OS X, these apps are included with every new Mac.

Part 5 starts our move away from the basics to look at a wide range of administration tasks in OS X. Here we provide a tour of the System Preferences, as well as important information on backups, security, and disk maintenance.

Part 6 provides a solid introduction to OS X's command-line environment and Darwin subsystem.

Part 7 shows how to take advantage of the advanced networking features of Mac OS X, including sharing resources and joining corporate networks.

Part 8 provides solutions to working with non-Apple environments from your Mac.

Part 9 concludes by providing an introduction to workflow automation and development on and for OS X.

By the time you finish this book, you should not only have a solid understanding of how to use and maintain your Lion, but you should be well poised to continue into a wide range of computing topics including networking and development if you so choose.

Introducing Mac OS X 10.7 Lion

In part I of Learn Mac OS X 10.7 we have three primary goals: Provide an overview of Lion's interface including essential interface components and applications such as the Finder, the Desktop, the menu bar and the Dock. Provide the big picture of how Mac OS X is organized, where files and applications are stored, and the purpose of essential files and folders found in Mac OS X. Give a quick look at a few tools and features that are backed into Lion to help you be as productive as possible.

Welcome to Lion

Our journey to learning all the ins and outs of Mac OS X 10.7 (a.k.a. "Lion") begins now. To begin with, this chapter is going to cover a large swath of fundamentals that you will need to get the most out of Mac OS X. This includes:

- An introduction to the Aqua interface and common elements in Mac OS X

- A look at the menu bar and the Dock

- Using the Launchpad

NOTE: If you are upgrading from a previous version of Mac OS X, or for whatever reason you need to reinstall Lion on your Mac, you may want to quickly take a detour to Appendix A for a look at installing and setting up Lion.

The Aqua Interface and the Desktop

The overall interface (Figure 1–1) of Mac OS X is referred to as "Aqua." Apple defines Aqua (with a Capital "A") as "The graphical user interface and visual theme of Mac OS X." If you have been a longtime Mac user you may have noticed that Aqua has evolved with each major release of Mac OS X. Elements have been refined, often sleeker, sometimes darker, but still recognizable from version to version. This evolution has continued with Lion.

Aqua is defined by a number of common elements: windows, toolbars, icons, files, folders, and the desktop. Aqua elements, combined with the Finder, the menu bar, and the Dock provide the key pieces for using your Mac computer.

NOTE: The Finder is the primary application in Lion that allows you to move around and work in Mac OS X. The application is automatically launched when OS X starts and generally remains running. We will cover the Finder in depth in Chapter 2.

Figure 1–1. *A screenshot of Mac OS X Lion showing the menu bar (at the top), the Dock (at the bottom), a Finder window (in the foreground), and the desktop in the background. Folders, files, and various other icons, as well as the Finder's toolbar and window, are all Aqua elements.*

As you move along in the book you will be introduced to many specific interface elements and shown what purpose they serve. You will also learn that while there is a lot of variability in the interface from application to application, and even from computer to computer (Mac OS X offers a great deal of personal customization), Aqua is designed in such a way that amidst all the differences, things pretty much work consistently.

Before you move on to the rest of the book there are a few general interface elements that are worth taking a look at beginning with the desktop.

The Desktop

The desktop metaphor has existed in Mac OS since the very first Macintosh computers hit the market more than 25 years ago (the first Macintosh computer was introduced to the press in October of 1983, though its noted public introduction occurred on January 22, 1984 with the famous, perhaps somewhat ironic, Super Bowl advertisement. The desktop in Mac OS X refers to the background area on the screen (see the background in Figure 1–1). By default the desktop is empty (except for the desktop wallpaper) until you plug in (or insert) an external disk, CD, or DVD that will then show up as an icon on the desktop. That said, many people use the desktop to place files or folders just like one would on the actual surface of one's desk or table.

The desktop is technically an extension of the Finder with some unique twists; as such you will learn more about the desktop later in this chapter.

> **NOTE:** A number of the Personal System Preferences as well as some of the Finder Preferences have a direct effect on the desktop's appearance and behavior. The Finder Preferences are covered later in this chapter. All of the System Preferences are covered in Chapter 18.

Windows

Windows (not to be confused with Microsoft Windows) are basic elements that "float above" the desktop and generally contain either a document, an application, or occasionally views of other files folders, and applications. According to Apple interface documentation, all windows must at least contain a functional close button in its title bar. This little tidbit separates windows from dialogs. Figure 1–2 shows a typical document style window with common window elements including the window control buttons, title, versions button, full screen toggle button, and a scrollbar.

The window title bar resides at the top of every window (with a few notable exceptions where applications work outside the normal UI guidelines). Usually, at a minimum the window title bar will contain the window control buttons and the window title. The version button and full-screen toggle button are both new in Lion and will appear when supported. One other important window element shown in Figure 1–2 are the scrollbars that allow you to scroll through a document when its size exceeds the window view area.

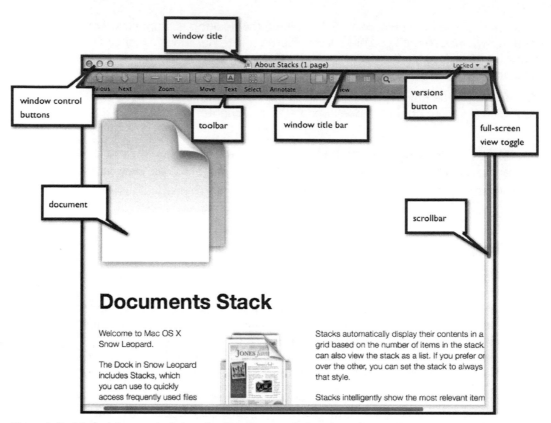

Figure 1–2. *A typical document window showing common window elements*

WHY DOES EVERYTHING SEEM TO BE SCROLLING BACKWARD?

In Lion, Apple, by default, made scrolling behave similar to swiping on iOS. This effectively reverses the direction of scrolling. Now down is up and up is down (or was it that way, and now up is up and down is down?) No matter how you look at it, coming from older versions of Mac OS X, or any other computer OS, everything seems backward. Now you could continue to work like this, and after three to seven days you might totally accept this and everything else will suddenly seem backward, or you can go to the mouse or trackpad system preference (covered in Chapter 18) and unselect the "When using gestures to scroll or navigate, move content in the direction of finger movement" option at the very top of the preference pane. If you decide to change this back (for opposite day, to just mess with a friend or co-worker, or when Apple releases a touchscreen Mac where this would make more sense) just reselect the option.

The Window Control Buttons

Each of the window control buttons has a specific function. The left-most window control button (denoted by an "X" when you hover over it) closes the window (but does not necessarily quit the application). The middle window control button denoted by the minus sign (-) is the minimize button. The minimize button will send the window to the dock, and depending on your dock preferences this will either create a separate window icon on the right side of the dock (just to the left of the trash), or it will minimize the window into the application icon. To reactivate a minimized window, click on the dock icon representing the window; or, if the "minimize windows into application icon" preference is selected, click on the application icon in the dock to reactivate all minimized windows belonging to that application. The right-most window control button, denoted by the plus sign (+) when hovered over, is the zoom button. This will toggle the window size between a maximized size and the current size.

> **NOTE:** Some applications, particularly certain noted Apple applications (i.e., iTunes), don't exactly follow these rules. In fact, iTunes doesn't have a proper window title bar at all. In moments like this feel free to join one of two camps of people: those who curse Apple for dictating specific rules and then breaking them (most developers fall into this group) or those who marvel at Apple's skill at breaking the mold and building new inventive interface paradigms (caused by excessive exposure to reality distortion fields emanating from Cupertino). Picking a side can be fun. Most people, however, just learn to accept these little things.

The Versions Button

Versions is a new feature introduced in Lion that will work behind the scenes to keep track of previous version of documents. The Versions button on the window title bar will only appear on the document windows of applications that support this new feature. We will explore Versions in more depth in Chapter 5.

The Full-screen Toggle

The ability to run full-screen applications is another new feature introduced in Lion. For applications that support this feature, the full-screen toggle will expand the window to full-screen mode. To toggle out of full-screen mode, hover the mouse pointer at the top of the screen until the menu bar appears and select the full-screen toggle button that appears on the far right of the menu bar.

> **TIP:** One notable control that is missing from many windows in Lion is the resize control that once appeared in the lower-right-hand corner of most windows allowing you to alter the size of a window. In Lion you can resize any window by clicking on the edge of any window. Upon clicking on the edge of a window, your mouse pointer should change into a small icon with two arrow heads indicating the direction that you can resize your window. Clicking different edges (and on the corners) will allow you to resize your window much more effectively than in the past.

A THIRD TYPE OF WINDOW

When we talk about windows here we are generally talking about application and document windows. In common Apple terminology there is a third type of window that Apple describes as "windows that contain controls and options that affect the active document or selection." Examples of such windows include: floating pallets and toolbars, Inspector and option windows, and Apple's Fonts window. While from a user perspective these are simply special windows, from a developer perspective these are called panels. When looking at these things from the user perspective we will continue to use the term window in describing these (as long as there is a close button in the menu bar). If we are looking at these from the developer perspective we will refer to these as panels. In user space, panels without close buttons are referred to as dialogs.

Dialogs

Another common window-like element that is common in Mac OS X is the dialog. A dialog is a special pop-up element that prompts you for additional information. Upon selecting the proper information the box will automatically close. Common dialogs that you will encounter include print dialogs and the shutdown dialog (shown in Figure 1–3).

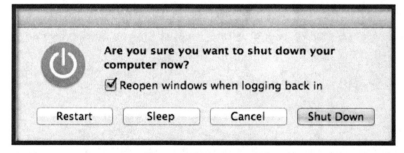

Figure 1–3. *A dialog, such as the shutdown dialog shown here, is a standard way that Mac OS X prompts you for additional information before proceeding with a task.*

Shortcut Menus

One final reoccurring element to touch on up front is shortcut menus (otherwise referred to as contextual menus). Shortcut menus are menus that pop up when you control-click on many other elements in Mac OS X. These shortcut menus (Figure 1–4) provide shortcuts to many common options, and we will take advantage of these throughout the book.

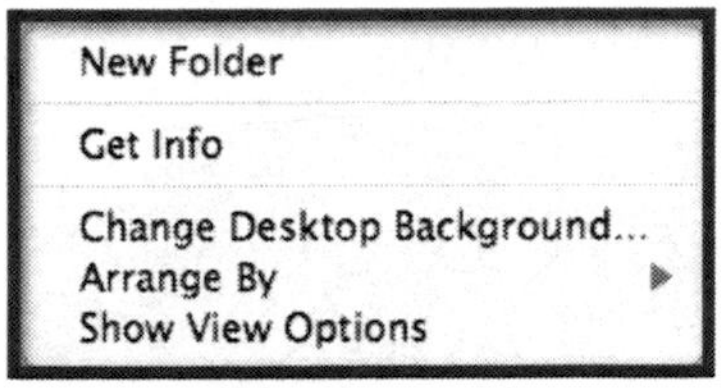

New Folder

Get Info

Change Desktop Background...
Arrange By ▶
Show View Options

Figure 1–4. *Shortcut menus, such as the desktop shortcut menu shown here, provide an easy way to access common context-aware options in Mac OS X.*

NOTE: Control-click (i.e., hold the Control key and click the mouse) is generally synonymous with the right-click on a two button mouse (Mouse Click 2) or a two-finger click on the trackpad. While control-click may seem a bit of an anachronism with most computer mice available today offering at least two mouse buttons (real or simulated), as opposed to the days when Macs only had one mouse button, we will be using the term throughout the book.

Now that we have had a quick look at some essential reoccurring interface elements, let's take a look at a few specific interface elements beginning with the menu bar.

The Menu Bar

As we take a look at the Finder, we often reference the Finder's application menu that resides in Mac OS X's menu bar. The menu bar (Figure 1–5) is one of the most important user interface elements in Mac OS X (and has been since the very first Macintosh OS). The menu bar is arranged into three areas: the Apple menu, application menus, and status menus. We will look at each of these one at a time.

 Finder File Edit View Go Window Help   Tue 5:06 PM

Figure 1–5. *The menu bar is an essential element of Mac OS X.*

The Apple () Menu

The Apple menu, on the far-left side of the menu bar (shown expanded in Figure 1–6), is a special menu containing a number of system-level commands and resources that are particularly handy to have easily accessible. These include the About This Mac command; links to Mac OS X's Software Update; the Mac App Store; System Preferences; Dock preferences; the Recent Items command (including shortcuts for applications, documents, and servers); the Force Quit; the Sleep, Restart, and Shutdown commands; and the Log Out *User* command. Most of these are fairly obvious as to what they do; however, some additional information about some of these items may be helpful.

Finder	File	Edit	View	(

About This Mac
Software Update...
App Store...

System Preferences...
Dock ▶

Recent Items ▶

Force Quit Finder ⌥⇧⌘⏏

Sleep ⌥⌘⏏
Restart...
Shut Down...

Log Out Scott Meyers... ⇧⌘Q

Figure 1–6. *The Apple menu on the menu bar provides access to a number of system commands.*

The About This Mac command opens a window (shown in Figure 1–7) that gives you some basic information about your computer. Clicking the light gray text under the large Mac OS X that reads Version 10.7 will cycle through additional information, including the exact operating system build number and the computer's serial number (this is a much easier way to get your serial number than searching around for it on your actual computer).

Figure 1–7. *About This Mac window in Lion*

The More Info... button in the About This Mac window will launch the new System Information application (which replaces the System Profiler) along with a new enhanced

About This Mac information window (Figure 1–8). The System Information application's About This Mac view provides useful information about both your Mac hardware and software ranging from detailed information about connected storage devices (and what kind of data is stored on them) to links to support and warranty information about your specific Mac.

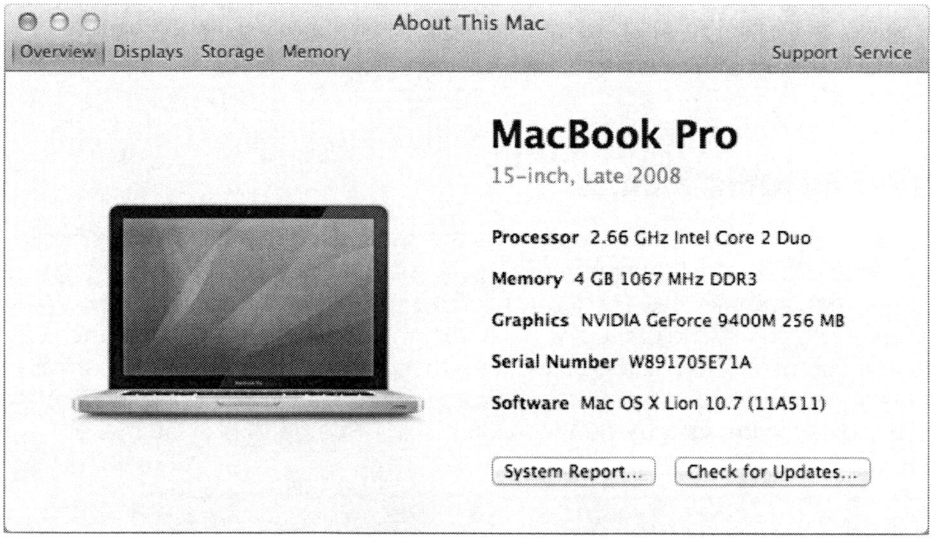

Figure 1–8. *The enhanced About This Mac information window is part of the new System Information application (which replaces the System Profile application in Lion).*

The Recent Items command opens a sub-menu that by default shows you the last ten applications, documents, and servers you accessed. You can adjust these defaults in the Appearance panel in System Preferences. You'll also see an option here to clear all items if for whatever reason you don't want that information to display.

The Force Quit command opens a new window that shows all the currently running Mac OS X applications. From this window you can select any of those applications to quit immediately. By immediately, we mean right away—no saving files or anything. The application will just quit. About the only time you may find yourself needing this is if an application freezes up (or in Apple lingo "stops responding") or if you need to "relaunch" the Finder.

> **TIP:** You can also Force Quit any item from the dock by Control-Option-Clicking on the desired item in the dock and selecting "Force Quit" from the shortcut menu (If you apply this to the Finder instead of Force Quit you will see "Relaunch"). One other option, if all else fails: holding down Command-Option-Shift-Escape for a few seconds will force quit the foreground application.

NOTE: You may notice that some menu items have an ellipsis (…) after them and some don't. According to Apple's Human Interface Guidelines, items with the ellipsis will require some additional user interaction to complete a task. In general, this means it will either present you with a dialog or open a window with additional options. Other items common in menus are the sideways triangle on the far right, which indicates the menu Item will open a sub-menu, and of course keyboard shortcuts are viewable for a number of menu items.

Application Specific Menus

Moving just to the right of the Apple menu begins the application menus. This is where people new to Macs tend to get thrown off; you see, in OS X there is only one application menu bar, and this is it. The application menus, however, are dynamic in the sense that the information in one menu bar will reflect the application running in the foreground. So if Microsoft Word is the active foreground application the menu bar will provide the menu items provided by Microsoft Word (Figure 1–9). If you bring the Finder or another application to the foreground the menu bar will change to provide menu items for that application.

Figure 1–9. *The menu bar's application menu presents Microsoft Word's menus when you're using Microsoft Word.*

NOTE: While Mac OS X runs many applications concurrently (i.e., it multitasks), it assumes that the user is generally actively using one application at a time. The application that is currently being used is referred to the foreground application; any other applications are referred to be running in the background. Sometimes the foreground application is also called the application that has focus.

In keeping with standard Mac User interface guidelines, many of the menu items are similar from one application to another; additionally, the general arrangement of the menus should be fairly consistent from one application to another (however, developers can create applications that deviate from this in sometimes minor and sometimes major ways). The first menu to the right of the Apple menu, called the application menu, should always reflect the name of the current foreground application. In addition to the application menu, almost all proper Aqua applications have at least the following additional menus: File, Edit, Window, and Help. Everything between the Edit and Window menus tends to vary from application to application.

The five most common menus tend to serve the following purposes:

Application Menu: This menu identifies the application and usually contains the About application option to access the application's preferences and the Quit application command. This also contains the Services menu item, one of the most overlooked features of OS X.

> **TIP:** The Services menu is a powerful way to leverage the power of external services provided by other applications inside any application. By default Apple provides a number of services. However, many applications also make some of their features available through the Services menu. We encourage you to play around with this; because it's a powerful feature that too few people take advantage of.

File: This is the menu where you generally create new documents or open, save, and print existing application documents.

Edit: The Edit menu contains standard menu items such as the Cut, Copy, Paste, Select All, Undo, Find, and Replace commands as well as Spelling and Grammar sub-menu items. The actual list of items here will vary from application to application, as some of the default items are commonly removed from certain types of applications, and some applications will add a few items of their own.

Window: The Window menu manages multiple open windows from an application. Certain applications are designed to run in only one window and may therefore remove this menu.

Help: The Help menu (Figure 1–10) contains a list of help documentation for the application and OS X in general. The help search feature, introduced in Mac OS X Leopard, provides an immediate dynamic contextual help system to help you find just the right help or item you need to find.

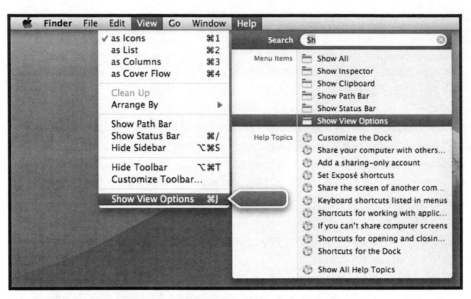

Figure 1–10. *Lion's help system can help find an application's menu items.*

NOTE: One unique feature of OS X applications that relates to the menu bar is that since the menu bar is separate from the application window, the application can (and usually does) run even if no windows are open. This is one of those big WTF (Wow That's Fascinating) moments that people have when coming to the Mac from Microsoft Windows. With Windows, when you close the last open window (usually by clicking the X button on the far-right side of the title bar), the application closes along with the window. This is not so for many applications in OS X. In OS X if you close a window (usually by clicking the X button on the far-left side of the title bar), then the window closes, but the application itself is probably still running. To actually close an application in Mac OS X, you generally must explicitly quit it from the application menu (or by using the Command-Q keyboard shortcut or selecting "Quit" from the applications Dock item shortcut menu).

NOTE: Contrary to the previous note, sometimes applications do quit when you close the window. This is one of those further head-scratching moments in OS X. The reason is that in OS X there are different application types. There are document-based applications, which usually follow the previous rules, and then there are other applications that don't (always). The general rule is that if you can have multiple windows open, then you can have none, even while the application is running. However, if your application provides only a single window, then when that window is closed, the application usually quits. Examples of default Apple applications that quit when the windows are closed are System Preferences, Dictionary, and Font Book.

Status Menus (a.k.a. Menu Bar Icons, Menu Bar Status Icons, Menu Bar Items)

On the far right of the menu bar is where you may find any number of status menus. These are special menus that are available at all times that can provide information as well as quick access to certain functions. The magnifying glass icon on the far right is the Spotlight icon where you can access the Spotlight search feature of Mac OS X; this icon is ever-present and immovable. Some status menus, however, can be reordered by Command-Dragging them with your mouse. If you drag an icon out of the menu bar, it will be removed from it. Most of the status menus that are available by default in Lion are tied to System Preferences, so if you accidentally remove one, you can usually add it again in the appropriate System Preferences panel.

> **NOTE:** Many third-party applications provide options for including status bar menus; this can either be helpful or can cause excessive clutter in your menu bar. If an application you frequently use offers an option to add a status menu item it's generally worth trying it, but if you find you don't use it, don't hesitate to turn it off.

Besides the status menus available from System Preferences, additional status menu items are available from various applications and third-party utilities. A couple of examples included with Lion are the Script menu that can be added from within the AppleScript Editor and an iChat menu available from the iChat preferences.

> **NOTE:** The Script menu makes a large number of useful pre-written AppleScripts available from the menu bar (and of course you can add your own AppleScripts to the menu). This is a wonderful menu to include if you use even a few AppleScripts on a frequent basis. We will touch on AppleScript in Chapter 30.

The Dock

The next interface element we'll look at in this chapter is the Dock (shown in Figure 1–11). The Dock allows you to keep your favorite applications a click away, manages the applications you have running, provides a place to access your favorite folders and documents, and holds your Trash can for deleting Finder items you are done with.

Figure 1–11. *Lion's default dock position and icons*

Dock Icons

The items on the Dock are completely customizable; the only three elements that are bound to the Dock are the Finder item, the Launchpad item, and the Trash item. The Dock is divided between application icons and other items by a faint dashed line resembling a crosswalk (called the *abbey road graphic*). We cover the types of items on the Dock next.

Favorite Applications

Beginning on the far left of the Dock are the application icons. The first two on the far left are always the Finder icon followed by the Launchpad icon, but the ones that follow are entirely customizable. To add one of your favorite applications to the Dock, just select the application in the Finder, and then drag the icon onto the Dock where you'd like it to be. You can also click and drag any icon already on the Dock to another location on the Dock or off the Dock entirely. To launch any of the applications on the Dock, just click them. Control-clicking any Dock icon will open a shortcut menu with useful options that vary on the application and whether it's running or not.

> **NOTE:** You can't remove the icon of a running application from the Dock; if you try, it will spring back to the Dock. This, however, will cause the item to leave the Dock when the application quits.

Open Applications

Anytime you open a Mac OS X application, the icon for that application will be added to the Dock just to the right of your other docked applications (provided that it is not in the Dock already). By clicking any open application icon on the Dock, you will make that the active application. Additionally, if that application has no open windows, then usually a new window will open when you make that application active. Upon closing any application not normally found in the Dock, the icon on the Dock will disappear.

> **NOTE:** In previous versions of Mac OS X a small indicator light would always appear under open applications in the Dock (indicating they are in fact running). In Lion this is no longer the only behavior, as there is an option in the Dock's preferences to toggle the visibility of the indicator light.

Folders and Stacks

In versions of OS X prior to Leopard (Mac OS X 10.5), you could add a folder to the Dock so that its contents would be easily available. In Leopard, Apple introduced stacks to Mac OS X, and while you could still add folders to the Dock, the folders on the Dock were turned into *stacks*.

Stacks, as they were originally released in Leopard, received mixed reviews. In many ways they were seen as a step backward from the old folder on the dock behavior; however, with subsequent point releases of Leopard stacks were refined and improved. With Apple's next Mac OS X release, Snow Leopard (Mac OS X 10.6), stacks had matured to the point where they had become a clear improvement to Mac OS X.

> **NOTE:** The term stack originated from an idea that stacks would represent piles (or stacks) of papers such as the ones that people would traditionally keep on their desk, and in some earlier experimental releases of Mac OS X they were essentially stacks of documents that you could collect on the desktop. The reality is that in computer terms there was very little difference between a stack and folder, just the metaphor, and thus appearance, changed. Today stacks are in fact actual folders that are found in the Finder. When you move a folder onto the dock you can apply some special ways of viewing the contents of the folder, thus making it a stack.

To create a stack, just select the desired folder from the Finder and drag it into the area between the abbey road graphic (to the right of the application icons) and the Trash (being careful not to actually drag them into the Trash). Upon adding the folder to the dock, it will, by default, change from a folder to what appears to be a stack of items that were contained in the folder. Clicking this stack in the Dock will expand it, making all its items accessible to you. By default, depending on the number of items in the stack, the stack will either expand to a single column of items, called the Fan view (Figure 1–12), or expand to a row of items, called the Grid view (Figure 1–13).

From the contextual menu of any stack you can make a few changes in how a stack looks and behaves. First, alter how the items in the stack are sorted when they are expanded (this may also alter what item is "on top" of the stack). These Sort By options are the same options available to sort items in the Finder (by Name, Date Added, Date Modified, Date Created, and Kind). Next you choose if you'd like the Dock icon to appear as the default stack of items or as a Folder. Finally you can override the default behavior of how a stack expands by setting each stack to open explicitly in Fan view, Grid view, or the List view (Figure 1–14), which is very similar to the original Folder behavior prior to Leopard.

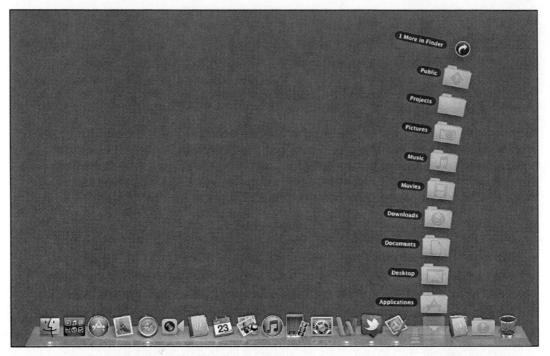

Figure 1–12. *A stack opened in the Fan view*

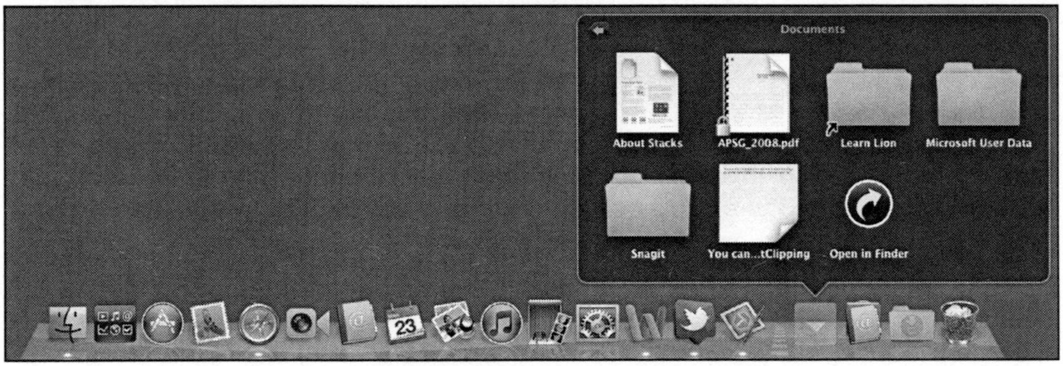

Figure 1–13. *Traversing a stack in the Grid view with parent menu in upper-left corner*

Figure 1–14. *A stack opened in the List view*

NOTE: One of the biggest issues people had with stacks when they were first introduced was that you could not traverse through sub folders in stacks as you could in the old folder listings. Instead, selecting a sub folder in a stack would just open up that folder in the finder. Later Apple added the List view to stacks that would allow one to browse through folders recursively. Today the ability to traverse folders in stacks is kicked up another notch, for now you can browse through folders in the Grid view as well (shown in Figure 1–13). In Lion, when you click on a folder in a Grid view, the new folder will open up in the Grid. A small arrow icon in the upper-left-hand corner of the Grid view will allow you to go back to the parent folder.

NOTE: The Grid view has the ability to utilize scrollbars to scroll through a large number of items, while the Fan view will only show up to nine items. The Automatic view option will default to Fan view but switch to Grid view when more than nine items are in a stack.

TIP: In Lion, if you hold your pointer over an item in a stack and press the Space key, a quick view window will pop out showing you the contents of the item.

By default, OS X starts you out with your Download folder and your Documents folder placed as stacks on your Dock.

Minimizing Windows

Occasionally you may get overwhelmed with the number of windows open at one time. You may at first decide to close some; however, you may be frequently referencing or working with some of these windows so you don't want them closed, just out of the way. Mac OS X provides a few ways of dealing with window clutter; the most common of these is to minimize windows. Clicking the minimize button in the upper-left corner of any window (that's the middle window control button that will reveal a minus symbol (-) when you mouse over it), the window will shrink into the Dock and out of the way. Depending on the Minimize windows into application icon setting in the Dock's preferences the minimized window will either shrink into the Dock as its own icon (Figure 1–15), or the window will shrink into the application icon.

Minimized Window

Figure 1–15. *If the Dock's Minimize windows into application icon option is unselected, minimized windows will appear as icons on the right side of the Dock.*

To reactivate a window minimized to the Dock, just click on the minimized window icon in the Dock and the window will spring back up. If you have your windows minimizing into the application icon, then you may reactivate the window from the applications Dock icon (the shortcut menu from any active application's Dock icon will list all application windows, and a grey diamond icon will appear next to any minimized windows).

CLOSE VS. HIDE VS. MINIMIZE

There are three ways to deal with windows that you wish were out of your way. The first, most obvious thing you can do is close the window. When you close the window it ceases to exist (though often the application is still running). One problem with closing many windows is that when you close the window you also lose the *state* of the window. *State* in this context is the ability to remember what the window was presenting at the time you closed it. For example, if you were working on an important Word document and closed the document window without saving your document first, all unsaved changes are lost! (Word, and most other sane applications, will prompt you to save any changes when you attempt to close a window of this nature.) Minimizing a window preserves the state of the window, so when you reactivate it, it will reactivate just how you left it when you initially minimized it.

One other option is the ability to hide an application. This option is available in most application menus and it comes in two flavors: **Application > Hide Application** and **Application > Hide Others** (these generally have the keyboard shortcuts of Command-H and Option-Command-H, respectively). The **Hide Application** option will hide all the windows belonging to the selected application. The **Hide Other** option will hide all the windows of every application except the selected application. State is preserved in hidden applications, and bringing any hidden application to the foreground will reopen any hidden windows.

> **NOTE:** Some applications can actually preserve the state when you quit them. For example, in Lion, if you have a number of windows open in Safari when you quit it, when you reopen Safari it will reopen all the windows open when you quit the application. This behavior is not universal, so it is a good idea to assume that when you quit an application, you will lose any unsaved changes.

The Trash

The final item on the Dock is the Trash. Rather than immediately deleting Finder items, in Mac OS X you generally move an item to the Trash when you are done with it. Then when you are ready, you empty the Trash to permanently delete items. This two-step process adds an extra precaution to keep you from accidentally deleting a file. You can drag any item into the Trash (or use Command-Delete), where it will remain until you empty the Trash. To empty the Trash, you may select Empty Trash from the Trash's shortcut menu, or you can select **Finder > Empty Trash** from the Finder's application menu.

> **TIP:** One old feature that resurfaced in Snow Leopard is the "Put Back" feature. If you select Put Back from the shortcut menu of any item in the trash, the selected trash items will automatically be returned to the Finder location that they were in before being dragged into the Trash.

One advantage of emptying the Trash from the Finder menu is that it also gives you the option to securely empty the Trash. This option actually overwrites the data on the storage device making it very difficult to recover even using some fairly sophisticated recovery tools.

One other somewhat strange use of the Trash is that if you drag any removable media, external hard drives, or network resources on to it, rather than delete those items it will actually eject, unmount, or disconnect the resource. This is actually the traditional way to do this, though it's especially odd for people new to Macs.

Using the Dock

As you may have guessed from the preceding discussion, the Dock is very useful for putting your favorite items a click away, as well as helping to manage running applications. The Dock has some very powerful features that may not be immediately evident that we can take a look at.

Dock Item Shortcut Menus

Like most items in Mac OS X, the Dock takes full advantage of shortcut menus. One thing to pay attention to, though, is that the shortcut menus of Dock items are highly variable and not only present many options unique to the application responsible for the item but also present different options depending on what the application is doing.

There is no room to go over every option for even the default Dock items; however, we can take a look at some common options available to specific types of Dock items.

Dock Shortcut Menus for Application Items

The shortcut menus for application dock items are the most variable because each application can place its own useful shortcuts in its shortcut menu. That said, there are a number of common items (which may vary slightly depending on whether the application is running or not and whether it is permanently placed on the Dock or just present because the application is running).

Open | Quit: Depending on whether the application is running or not an option to Open or Quit the application will be present in an application Dock shortcut menu. The exception to this is the Finder, which is always running (some special options for the Finder will be discussed in the next chapter).

Show | Hide: For running applications the option to Show or Hide the applications will show up (depending on whether the application is currently hidden or not). Since clicking on a hidden applications dock icon will show the application, this is mostly useful for hiding an application.

Options ➤ Keep in Dock: This option will toggle whether an icon will remain in the Dock when the application is not running

Options ➤ Open at Login: This option will toggle whether or not an application will automatically start when you log in to your computer. This option is not the only way to make this happen, so whether or not this option is selected from the Dock is not an absolute indicator of whether an application will start or not at login.

Options ➤ Show in Finder: This option will open a Finder window at the location of the original item represented in the Dock.

Shortcut Menus for Stacks

The shortcut menu for each stack (we introduced stacks earlier in this chapter) is where you set up all options for that stack. The primary options available from a stack shortcut menu are:

Sort by: The Sort by options determine how items are sorted in a stack. The options available are: Name, Date Added, Date Modified, Date Created, and Kind.

Display as: The Display as options let you choose whether you would like the stack to appear as a stack or a folder in the Dock.

View content as: The View content as options determine if the stack expands into a Grid, Fan, or List view.

Open "*Folder*": The Open "*Folder*" item will open the stack in a normal Finder window.

The remaining options available are similar to those already covered.

The Trash Shortcut Menu

The shortcut menu item for the Trash has only two items: Empty Trash and Open. The Open option will open the Trash in a Finder window.

Launchpad

One new tool we should cover before we move on is the Launchpad. When Apple announced Lion it mentioned that it would bring to Mac OS X features originally designed for iOS devices (iPhones, iPods, and iPads). Launchpad is a prime example of this.

Launchpad is an application launcher that enables you to organize, view, and launch applications in the same way as you would with an iOS device (Figure 1–16). If you have used an iOS device, using Launchpad should be immediately familiar.

Figure 1–16. *Launchpad is an application launcher based on the interface of Apple's iOS. Users of Apple's iPhones, iPads, or newer iPods should find this very intuitive.*

Launching Apps from Launchpad

To launch an application from Launchpad, you must first trigger the Launchpad interface by clicking on the Launchpad icon in the Dock (it is the second icon from the left). Once the Launchpad view is active you can launch an application by clicking on its icon. That is it, easy!

Organizing Apps in Launchpad

With the Launchpad view you can also organize your applications in a very iOS fashion. To reorganize application icons simply select and drag it around to where you want it. You can move it before or after other icons and move over to a new screen.

> **NOTE:** Just like iOS devices, Launchpad is capable of having multiple screens of icons. To go to another screen simply scroll there using your mouse or trackpad, or click on one of the dots at the bottom of the Launchpad view.

In addition to sorting the order of your icons, you can group related icons together into folders. Dragging one icon on top of another will create a folder of icons that will appear as a single icon in the Launchpad view until you click on it at which time it will expand to reveal all the individual icons in the folder. To continue to add icons to a folder just drag new icons onto the folder icon. You can also drag icons out of a folder if desired.

Once you have a folder created, you can rename it by opening the folder, clicking on the name at the top (which should highlight the name), and then typing in your chosen name (Figure 1–17). By default Mac OS X will attempt to guess a name for a new folder based on the perceived category of applications you are initially grouping together.

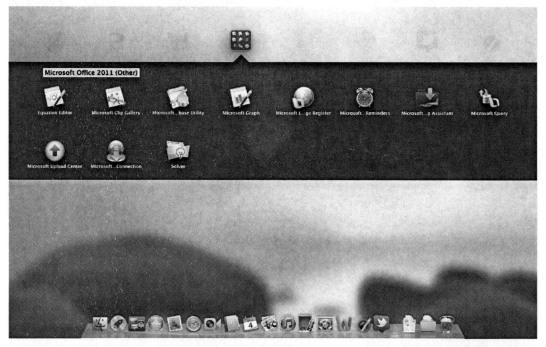

Figure 1–17. *Just like iOS you can group application icons into folders. To rename a folder, open it and click the name at the top and replace it with one of your choosing.*

Deleting Apps from Launchpad

Not only does Launchpad provide a handy way to organize and launch applications, but you can also delete certain applications from within Launchpad (specifically Apps installed from the OS X App Store). To delete an application click and hold the desired icon until all the icons start to wiggle. Apps that can be deleted will have a small "x" in the top-left corner of the icon. Clicking the "x" will prompt you to delete the application.

> **NOTE:** By default all applications will appear in Launchpad, and there is no way to remove an App from Launchpad without deleting the actual application. If there are Apps listed in Launchpad that you don't want to see, the best solution is to create a folder for all the extra apps and just stick all the extras there.

Summary

With this chapter we wanted to provide you with a taste of the essential elements of Mac OS X that you will be using frequently in your Mac life. One element (actually an application, and a very special one at that) that we have briefly mentioned here that deserves much more attention is the Finder, so that is what we will discuss next.

Chapter 2

Using the Finder

The Finder is an application that provides the interface for navigating your file system, managing files and folders, opening applications, and many more essential tasks that are required to use on your computer. It is elegantly designed to find whatever you are looking for on your computer and then get out of your way so you can work (or play, or create, or whatever you choose to do on your Mac). In this chapter we will give you a proper introduction to the Finder and how it is used including:

- A tour of the Finder window

- How to navigate around your system using the Finder

- Managing Finder items such as documents and applications

- Searching in the Finder

- Using the Finder to get information about files

- Customizing the Finder

While the Finder is an application, it is not just any application; it is a key piece of Mac OS X, one that your Mac generally expects to be running at all times any user is logged in to the Mac. One immediate difference is that there is no evident way to quit the Finder, and if you do force quit the Finder it will immediately relaunch. (If you control-option-click the Finder's Dock icon, which is pinned to the far left position on the Dock, the resulting option that would say "Force Quit" for any other application will instead say "Relaunch").

QUITTING THE FINDER

Mac OS X is designed to have the Finder running at all times a user is logged into the Mac computer, and generally this expectation should be adhered to. That being said, it is possible to quit the Finder.

To do this you simply need to invoke the following command in the Terminal:

```
defaults write com.apple.Finder QuitMenuItem 1
```

After entering this command, the next time the Finder starts (you may issue the "Relaunch" command by using option-control-click on the Finder's Dock icon and selecting "Relaunch" from the resulting shortcut-menu), a "Quit Finder" option will appear in the Finder menu allowing you to quit the Finder just like any other application. You can then launch the Finder from the Dock when it is needed again.

To return the Finder's start menu back to its default state, issue the following command in the terminal:

```
defaults write com.apple.Finder QuitMenuItem 0
```

This will return the Finder to its intended unquitable state.

> **NOTE:** The only time one can log into Mac OS X without the Finder launching is by logging exclusively into your Mac's command line interface. This is most common when a user accesses their Mac remotely using SSH. We will delve into the command line interface later in this book.

Anatomy of the Finder Window

Most of the work done with the Finder is done in a Finder window (Figure 2–1). Before you jump in to looking at tasks the Finder can perform, you will take a look at the Finder window, explore the options available, and look at the different ways in which it allows us to look at our files.

> **NOTE:** The word "files" has multiple contexts in Mac OS X. Generally when you refer to a file you are referring specifically to a file that is created by an application; for example, a .doc file, a text file, or an image file would all represent these types of files. However, in a broader sense everything contained on a computer is also considered a file. We will touch on this time and time again as we progress through the book. For now, just be aware that occasionally when we refer to files, we are including folders and applications in that group.

By default the Finder window consists of three main elements: the toolbar, the sidebar, and the main view area. Let's take a look in more detail at each of these beginning with the toolbar.

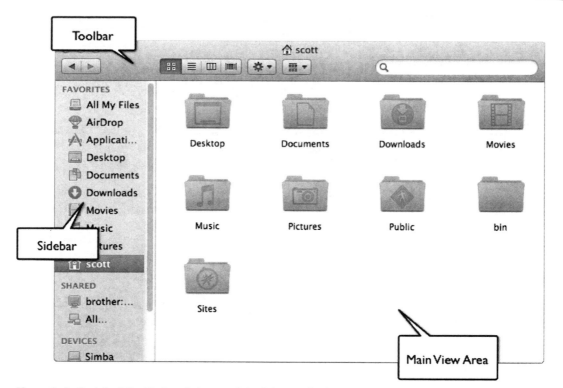

Figure 2–1. *By default the Finder window consists of three main elements: the toolbar, the sidebar, and the main view area.*

The Toolbar

The Finder's toolbar (Figure 2–2) in Lion has undergone some subtle changes since Snow Leopard. For example, the view options that previously appeared as buttons, now take on the appearance of a slider. Also by default the Quick Look button is gone and the Arrange button is added.

> **NOTE:** Most toolbars for most Mac OS X applications can be customized and the Finder is no exception. Later in this chapter we will discuss customizing the toolbar including how to add back the Quick Look.

> **NOTE:** If you upgraded Lion over a previous version of Mac OS X, your Finder's toolbar (as well as other items) may appear differently then what is shown in this book. This is because Lion has picked up preferences from the older version of Mac OS X and has altered its default state to your past preferences.

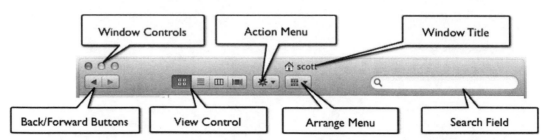

Figure 2–2. *By default the Finder's toolbar contains just a few navigation, view, and search controls. The standard application window title bar containing the window controls and the window title are also shown here.*

Looking at the default buttons, the Back/Forward buttons will navigate you forward and backward through the Finder window's history, just like the forward and backward button on most web browsers. The View control will allow you to select how you'd like to view the items in the main view area: icon view, list view, column view, or Cover Flow view. We will look more closely at the different views later in this chapter. The Arrange menu allows you to select how items are grouped together in the main view area. This is similar but different from the other Arrange by options. Finally, the Search field provides a powerful search capability of all the files on your computer (and beyond). Searching is also covered later in this chapter.

The Sidebar

The Finder's sidebar (Figure 2–3) is a customizable area that provides easy access to specific folders, devices, network resources, and saved searches. The sidebar divides these into three categories:

Favorites: At one time Favorites was a special toolbar in the Finder that contained your favorite directories for easy access. While the concept survived, the term "Favorites" was missing from Leopard and Snow Leopard. In Lion Favorites returns, replacing "Places" and "Search For" in the sidebar. Favorites is a highly customizable place where you can quickly access any folder as well as your saved searches. A few special items in Favorites are "All My Files", which is a predefined search, and Air Drop, a special location for peer-to-peer file sharing (which we will cover more in Chapter 26). If you would like add a folder to your Favorites just drag it onto the sidebar. You may also rearrange the items in your Favorites by dragging them up or down. To remove an item, select "Remove from Sidebar" from the item's shortcut menu (control-click the item to bring up the shortcut menu).

Shared: The shared area will show any network devices or volumes that you have access too. By default any network devices that Mac OS X detects automatically will show up here. Additionally any network resources you connect to manually will appear here also (as long as you maintain a connection). This will not appear if you aren't connected to a network or if no shared network resources are detected.

Devices: Any connected volumes included internal and external hard drives, disk media (i.e., CDs and DVDs), memory cards, thumb drives, digital cameras and camcorders with shared storage, and others will show up under Devices for easy access. If you are a MobileMe subscriber your iDisk will show up here as well.

Figure 2–3. *The sidebar allows easy Finder access to important locations and searches on your computer.*

Views in the Finder

The View control on the Finder toolbar changes how items will appear in the Finder main view area. There are four primary views available: Icon view, List view, Column view, and Cover Flow view.

Icon View

The Icon view (Figure 2–4) is the default view. In it items appear as large icons that represent the type of each item. Folders appear as folders, files appear as files (generally with some indication of what the file contains or which application is responsible for the file). Applications appear with their own custom icon, and other various file types appear in various ways.

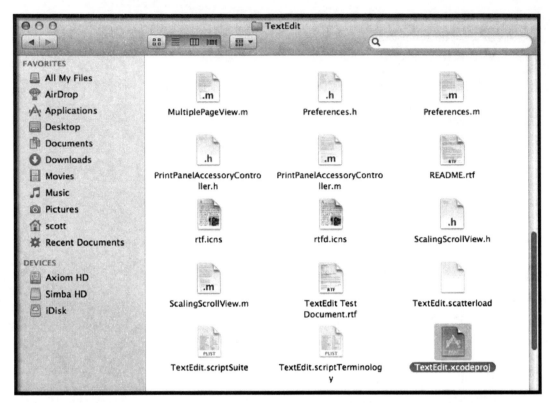

Figure 2–4. *The Finder Icon view presents items in the Finder by large icons representing the file type.*

List View

The List view (Figure 2–5) presents items in the Finder as a list. While the icon presented is smaller, the List view readily provides additional information about each item in the Finder (by default this includes the date last modified, the size, and the kind of file; however, other options are available). One additional feature of the List view is that folders have a disclosure triangle allowing you to view their contents without navigating away from your current location.

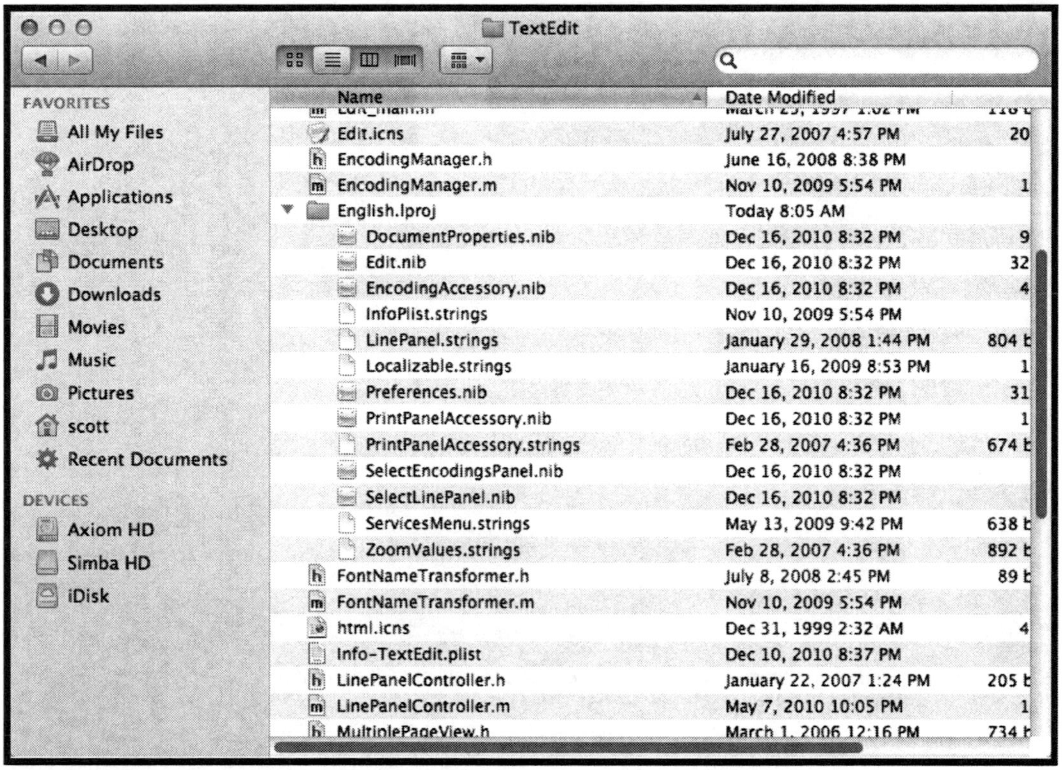

Figure 2–5. *The Finder's List view not only provides additional information about Finder items, it also allows you to view the contents of folders without changing your location.*

NOTE: *Disclosure triangles* are small triangle elements found to the left of certain interface elements that can be toggled to reveal or hide additional information about an item. A disclosure triangle pointing to the right indicates that it is closed; you may click on the triangle to reveal the additional information. *Disclosure buttons,* similar to disclosure triangles, can be clicked to reveal additional options in many dialogs and utility windows. In the case of disclosure buttons, a downward facing triangle indicates that additional options are hidden, when revealed the buttons triangle will face up.

Column View

The Finder's Column view (Figure 2–6) was introduced in the first version of Mac OS X and is the descendent of the File Viewer used in NeXTSTEP and later OpenStep (from which Mac OS X descends). The columns in Column view represent the folder hierarchy of your current location (the columns to the left represent parent folders). The columns on the right will either provide a list of enclosed items (if a folder is selected) or information about the selected item (if it's a non-folder item), including a preview of the item.

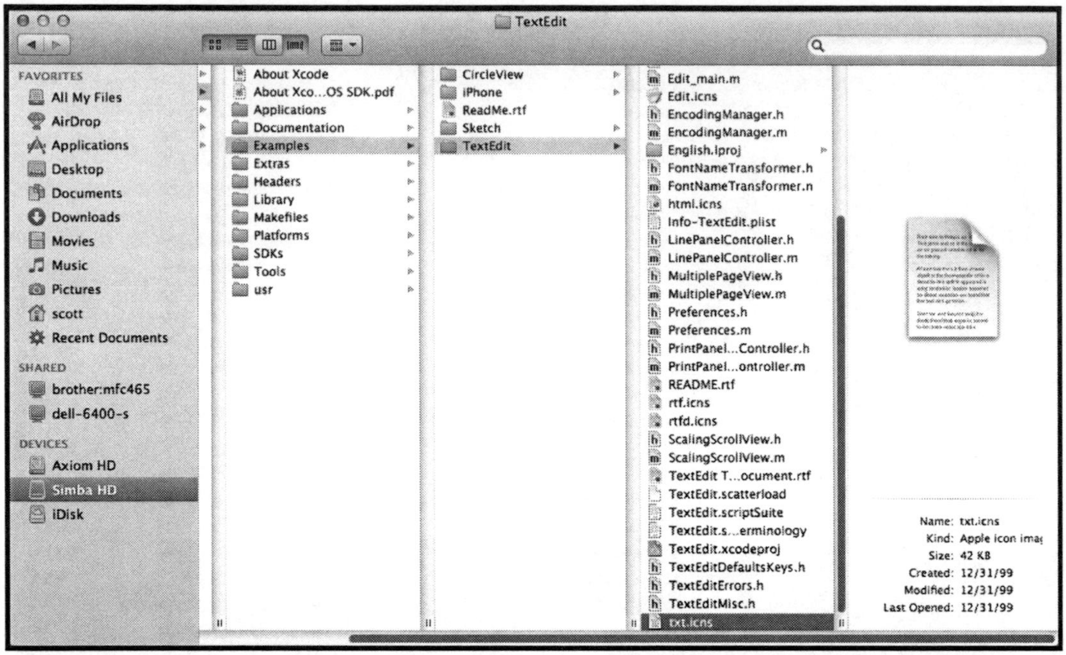

Figure 2–6. *The Finder's Column view provides a hierarchical view of your current location and provides selected information and a preview of selected Finder items.*

> **TIP:** The Column view is very nice for browsing media files. When a media file is selected, the right-most column will allow you to preview the item. This includes full playback of any supported audio or video file right from the Finder.

Cover Flow View

The fourth Finder view is the Cover Flow view. The Cover Flow view (Figure 2–7) presents a split window with a standard List view on the bottom; the top, however, provides a scrollable display that allows you to "flip through" previews of the items in your location. This view can be extremely useful for helping you to visually identify a particular file in a crowded folder, such as when you want to fine a particular image file in a folder of many image files.

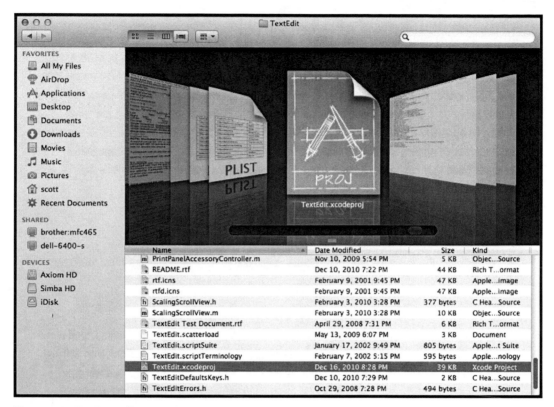

Figure 2–7. *The Cover Flow view is useful for visually identifying files.*

Common Finder Tasks

Now that we have had a brief tour of the Finder, it is time to learn how to accomplish a number of common computing tasks that take place in the Finder. We will begin with some basic navigation tasks and then move on to a series of file management tasks.

Navigating in the Finder

Navigating in the Finder is generally pretty straightforward. To open a new Finder window either select **File >New Finder Window** from the Finder's menu bar or with the Finder as the foreground application use the Command-N (⌘N) keyboard shortcut.

NOTE: Like most modern Operating Systems, Mac OS X is multitasking. It can run multiple applications and processes (a.k.a. tasks) concurrently. While there are numerous benefits to a multitasking environment, in practical terms people tend to direct their attention to one task at a time (i.e., people are not wired together to multitask, though we quite often *multi-switch* or quickly move from one task to another sometimes so rapidly that it seems to have the same effect). To build an effective interface around a multitasking environment, the concept foreground and background applications was introduced. In traditional terms, the foreground application is the application that has focus. All user input is directed toward that application, while the background applications whirl away behind the scenes.

TIP: In Mac OS X the active foreground application is the one whose name appears in the menu bar.

NOTE: If no Finder windows are open, clicking on the Finder icon in the Dock will also open a new Finder window. If other Finder windows are already open, clicking on the Dock icon will just bring those windows to the foreground. One caveat here is that minimized windows will stay minimized unless all current Finder windows are minimized, in which case the last window minimized will become active.

When you open a new Finder window, it will by default show the location or items that are set in the Finder preference's "New Finder windows show:" option (covered later in this chapter). In Lion this option is initially set to "All My Files," which displays all of the visible documents in your home directory.

TIP: There are a few ways to open a new Finder window in locations other than the default location set in the preferences. For example, stacks on the Dock have an "Open in Finder" option that will open a Finder window in that folder location. Also, if you have chosen to display hard drives or other devices on your desktop, double-clicking on the desktop icon will open a finder window at the root of the selected device.

One thing you may notice looking in the "All My Files" Finder location is there are no folders and the back button is grayed out, so it seems for all practical purposes there is nowhere to navigate to. At this point if you have a good idea of where you want to look for a file you can select its nearest location from the Finder's sidebar.

Once you come to grips with where you are in Lion's file system, moving around in the Finder is pretty easy. In order to move down into a folder, simply double-click on it and the Finder will descend into that folder. Moving up to a parent folder is less obvious. If you started out in a parent folder you can use one of the Back buttons on the Finder toolbar, otherwise you can either use the **Go >Enclosing Folder** menu option or the handy Command-Up Arrow keyboard shortcut.

> **NOTE:** Chapter 3 is dedicated to providing you with a solid understanding of Lion's files structure, which is a much bigger discussion than we have space for here. For now you are just trying to learn the basics of the Finder.

By selecting an appropriate location from the sidebar and navigating up or down a folder or two, you should be able to find what you are looking for with minimum amount of fuss. If, however, you wish to open a Finder window at a specific location (including locations that may normally be hidden by the Finder), you can use the Finder's "Go to Folder..." command.

The Go to Folder Command

The **Go > Go to Folder...** menu item is a very useful option if you know specifically what folder you want to open. For example, as we uncover more about Mac OS X, you will soon learn about a whole range of folders that, by default, are hidden from the Finder. To access one of these folders simply use the **Go >Go to Folder...** Finder menu option (or the Command-Shift-G keyboard shortcut) to open the "Go to the folder" dialog (Figure 2–8). Then just enter the Folder path in the text field and select Go to immediately open a Finder window in that location.

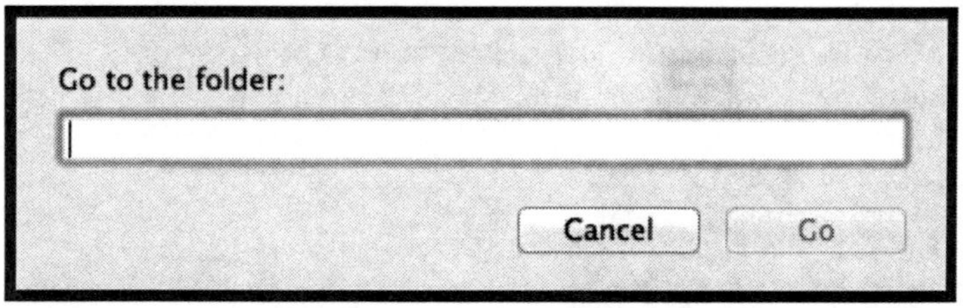

Figure 2–8. *The Go to the folder dialog (Command-Shift-G from the Finder) allows you to enter a desired folder location to be opened immediately in the Finder.*

For example, if you would like to go to your Library folder (which, as of Lion, is now a hidden folder). You could type "**~/Library**" in the text field and click Go to be taken there.

> **TIP:** While we will discuss file paths later in the book, it is worth mentioning that the "~" in a file path is a shortcut to your Home directory. So "~/Library" is the same as "/Users/your username/Library".

Searching

Occasionally you may need to find a file that you have no idea where it's located (or you have an idea but you need to sort through a lot of clutter to find it). Luckily the Finder has a powerful search technology called Spotlight to help you find what you are looking for.

Spotlight, introduced with Mac OS X 10.4 (Tiger), is a system-wide search tool that locates items on your computer that match your search criteria. Spotlight not only allows you to search for items on your computer, it also allows you to save your searches by creating Smart Folders, and will even allow you to search other computers and resources on your network (provided these resources allow such access).

> **NOTE:** When you first install Mac OS X, Spotlight is not immediately available. Before Spotlight is ready, it must index your entire system. This can take several hours to complete. While Spotlight is indexing, your hard drive will spin a lot, your system will get hot, and the computer's fan (if it has one) will probably start running full speed. There will also be a pulsing black dot inside Spotlight's magnifying glass icon in the upper-right corner of the menu bar that indicates Spotlight is indexing.

Performing a Basic Search

To perform a Spotlight search, you can either click the magnifying glass in the upper-right corner of your screen or use the Command-Space keyboard shortcut. This will open a simple drop-down text field for you to type in your search (Figure 2–9). As you begin to type, the drop-down field will expand to reveal possible matches for your search (Figure 2–10). As you refine your search, the matches will dynamically change to the most appropriate choices.

Figure 2–9. *Spotlight's search field*

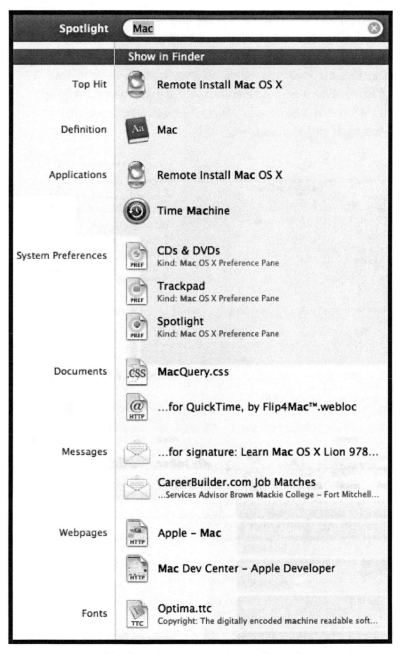

Figure 2–10. *Spotlight reveals top matches for your search as you type.*

Once you have finished typing your search phrase, the top results matched will be revealed for you, organized by type. Depending on how specific your search is, there could be only a few possible matches; however, often there are more matches than fit in the simple drop-down menu. Selecting the Show in Finder item will open a special

Finder search window containing all the results from your search (Figure 2–11). This window will also allow you to further refine and save your search.

> **NOTE:** Figure 2–11 also represents the results that you will get if you start your search in the search field on the Finder's toolbar. Where you choose to enter your search depends, but using the Spotlight search field has a few unique features and it's readily available even when an application other than the finder is in the foreground.

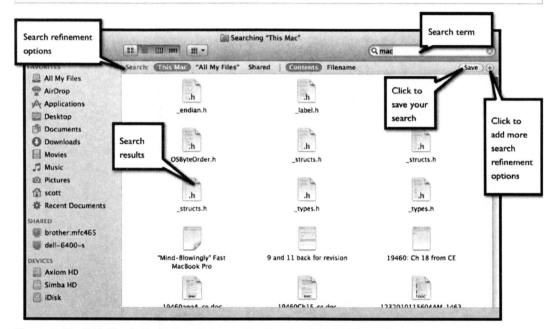

Figure 2–11. *Searching in the Finder allows you to refine your search and save it.*

SPECIAL SPOTLIGHT FEATURES

There are a few interesting features available when you search from the Spotlight search field as opposed to the Finders search field. A couple of interesting spotlight features include:

- When an item is selected in Spotlight's results window, if available a preview window will appear to show you the contents of the item. This includes the Definition type, making Spotlight a super quick way to lookup the meaning of any word.

- You can type mathematical formulas into Spotlight, which then uses its calculator function to present you with the result.

Refining and Saving Your Searches

Whether you start with a simple Spotlight search and, as discussed earlier, choose the Show in Finder option or you start a search directly in the Finder's search field, you will be presented with a special Finder search window (shown above in Figure 2–11) that will allow you to refine and save your searches. The Finder search window and regular Finder window are different in two ways. First, since you are dealing with search results, the items shown are not necessarily located in a single folder but rather may be collected from all over your hard drive and attached file systems. Second, there are one or more special search toolbars present at the top of the Finder view area that allow you to refine your search.

There is always one primary search toolbar at the very top of every Finder search window that will allow you to generally refine the scope of your search. Specifically it allows you set the search for your entire computer (This Mac), or to limit the search to the specific folder from which the search began (if the search was initiated from the Spotlight menu icon this option will read "All My Files"). Furthermore, it allows you to choose whether to search just the File Name of Finder items or if it should search the Contents of individual files to match the search term. Occasionally you will have other search options listed here; for example, shared or network resources on which you have permission to perform searches may appear.

To the far right of the topmost search bar is a Save button that will allow you to save your search for future use (as a Smart Folder), and then there is a + or - button that will allow you to add or remove additional search criteria. Each time you add criteria, a new bar will appear that will allow you to refine your search from a series of drop-down lists (Figure 2–12).

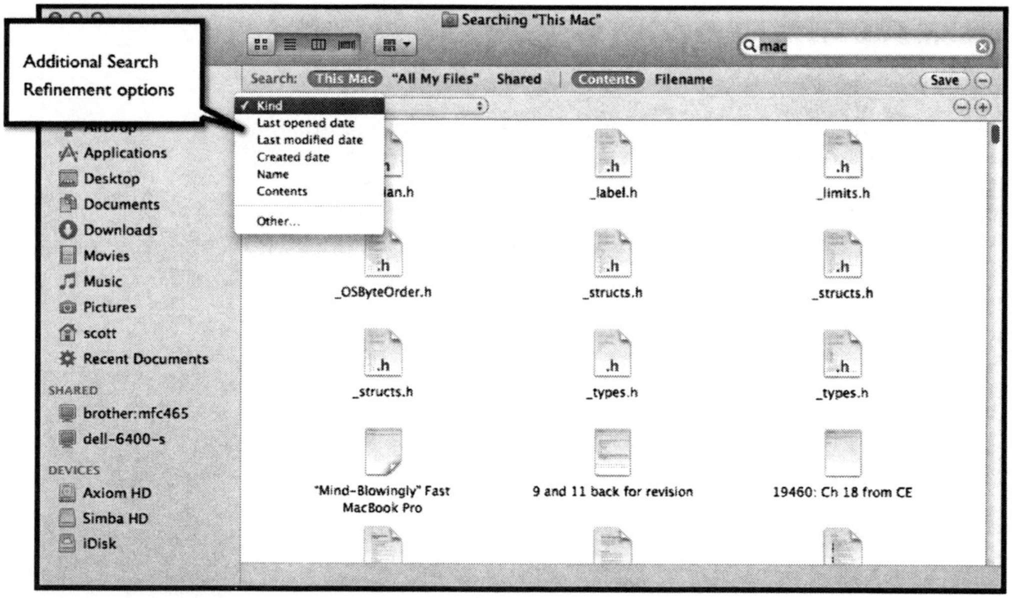

Figure 2–12. *Refining a search using search criteria*

Table 2–1 describes the general search criteria.

Table 2–1. *Search Criteria to Refine Searches*

Criteria	Description
Kind	This can help narrow down your search to a specific kind of file and includes the following options: Applications, Documents, Folders, Images, Movies, Music, PDF, Presentations, Text, and Other. Certain options will allow you to further refine the kind; for example, Images will allow you to narrow search results to specific image formats.
Last opened date	This will allow you to narrow search results to a date, or range of dates, when the item was last opened.
Last modified date	This will allow you to narrow search results to a date, or range of dates, when the item was last modified.
Created date	This will allow you to narrow search results to a date, or range of dates, when the item was created.
Name	This will allow you to match additional search strings against the name of the file.
Contents	This will allow you to match additional search strings against the contents of the file.
Other	This option will open a window with a number of additional search criteria that can be added to your search (Figure 2–13); many of these items are common metadata items or other common possible search criteria. Your actual list may change because of third-party applications that add their own options.

Once you have your search criteria set, you can select the specific item you are looking for in the Finder's Search view.

If you want to save your search, click the Save button in the top-left side of the view area. This will open a Save dialog (Figure 2–14) that will let you save your search and if desired add it to your Finder sidebar (it will then appear under "Favorites").

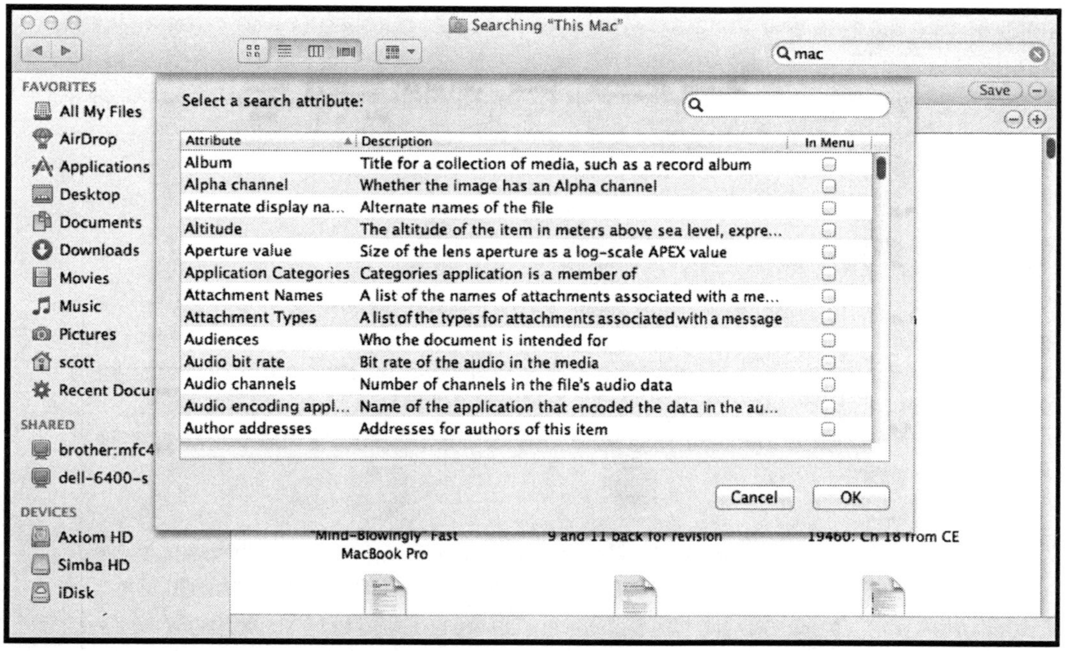

Figure 2–13. *The Other search option opens a window that contains a large list of other common metadata and search criteria.*

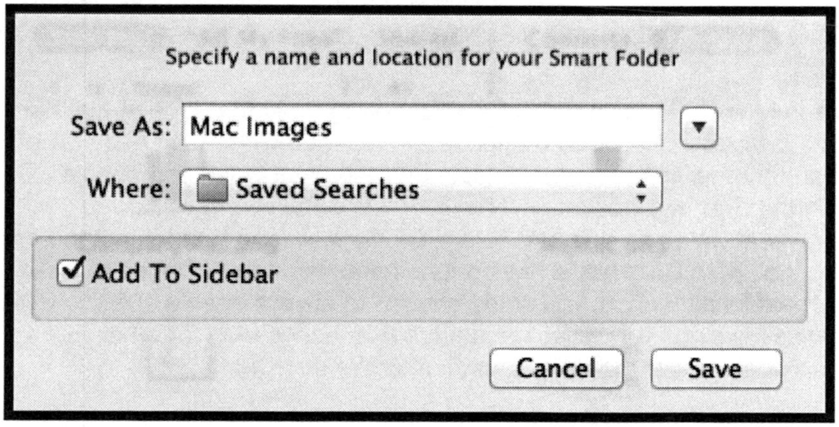

Figure 2–14. *The Smart Folder Save dialog box*

Setting Up Smart Folders

The default locations for saving a search is in your ~/Library/Saved Searches folder. If you look there, you will see that saved searches are nothing more than a collection of Smart Folders. There is one subtle difference between the Smart Folder created out of a search and when you create a Smart Folder from the Finder's **File >New Smart Folder...** (Option-Command-N). When you start with a search, the results will always reflect the initial search term, and when you create a Smart Folder from the Finder, there is no initial search term so you can build your search based purely on other criteria (like file type and creation date).

At this point you should have a pretty good understanding of how to find things in the Finder. As you progress through the book you will learn a few more tricks , but for now let us move on to what you do once you find what you are looking for.

Opening Files and Applications

Opening a file or application is quite easy. From the Finder find the desired file or application and double-click on its icon. (If you are opening a file or application from the Dock or from Launchpad, a single click will open the item.) When you open (or *launch*) an application, that application will open. Opening a file is a bit more interesting since it is possible (even likely) that you may have multiple applications that could open a particular file type.

> **NOTE:** File types are mostly determined by the file extension they are given. For example, files that end in .pdf are assumed to be PDF documents, files that end in .doc are assumed to be Microsoft Word documents, and files that end in .app are assumed to be applications (more on that later). Depending on your Finder preferences, certain file extensions may be hidden, so unless the Finder's "Show all filename extensions" option is selected, "About Stacks.pdf" may appear as "About Stacks" in the Finder. The ability to show or hide an extension may be set on a file-by-file basis within many applications when you save a file.

Each document type in Mac OS X has a default application to open that type of file. For example, Preview (a full-featured file viewing application included with Mac OS X) will be the default application for most image and PDF files. So by default when you open a PDF file it will open in the Preview application. However, suppose you have Adobe Reader installed and would like to open a particular PDF file in Adobe Reader instead of Preview, what do you do? Mac OS X has a few options here: you could choose to open a specific PDF in Acrobat Reader once; you could choose to always open a specific PDF in Acrobat Reader while keeping Preview as the default PDF application for other PDFs; or you could make Acrobat Reader the default application for all PDFs.

Temporarily Opening a File in a Non-default Application

To open a document in its non-default application simply select "Open With" from a document's shortcut menu. Open With will reveal a sub-menu that provides a list of all applications identified as being able to open the selected file with the default application listed at the top (Figure 2–15). If a specific application you are looking for is not listed, you may select the Other... option and browse to your desired application.

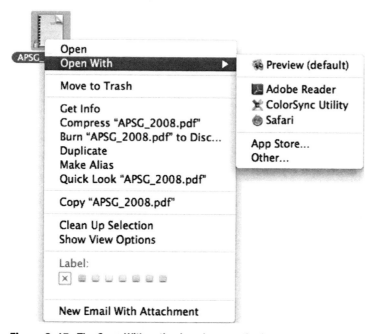

Figure 2–15. *The Open With option in a document's shortcut menu will allow you to choose which application you wish to open a document with.*

Always Opening a Specific File in a Non-default Application

A file's Info window (Figure 2–16) provides information and options about a particular Finder item. We will explore the Info window in detail later in this chapter. For our purposes here, first open Info window by selecting "Get Info" from an item's shortcut menu, then look at the Open With area in the window (if not expanded click on the disclosure triangle to reveal all the Open With options). The Open With area of the Info window has a single menu, which when expanded shows a list of available applications much like the Open With option from the item's shortcut menu. The difference here is when you choose an application, rather than immediately open the item in that application, it will instead remember the selected application and then, by default, always open the selected item in that particular application even if it isn't the default.

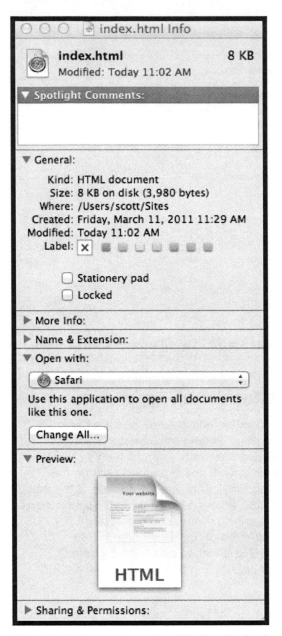

Figure 2–16. *You can change the default application for a specific file of all files of a specific type in a files Info window.*

Changing the Default Application for a File Type

The default application for files of a certain type can be changed in the Info window of any file of that type. To make this global change, simply open the Info window and select the desired default application under the Open With area and then click on the

"Change All..." button. This will cause a dialog to appear asking you to confirm this action. Clicking the Continue button in the dialog will make the change active.

Occasionally when you install a new application, or open a file in a non-default application, you will be prompted with a dialog asking if you would like to make that application the default application for all files of that type. For example, the first time you open a PDF file in Acrobat Reader it will ask if you would like to make Acrobat Reader the default application for all PDFs (Figure 2–17).

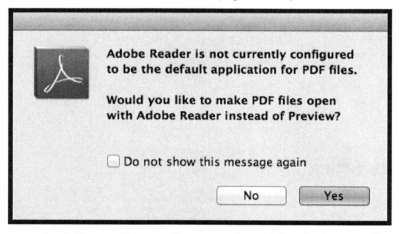

Figure 2–17. *Many applications will prompt you to make them the default application for a specific file type when you install or first open them.*

QUICK VIEW

Occasionally you just want to quickly view a file on your computer without launching any application. Mac OS X will allow you to do this with most file types using Quick View. Selecting an item in the Finder and pressing the Space key will open a Quick View window (Figure 2–18) displaying the item you selected. Using the arrow keys on your keyboard you can continue to scroll through items in the Finder and the Quick View window will change to display the selected item.

Quick View has some nice uses. For example, if you have a folder filled with images, you can select all the images in the folder, then press the Space key to start a slide show of the images in Quick View (go full screen for the best effect).

Quick View uses a filter system to display files. If an appropriate filter is available then the file will be displayed. Occasionally Quick View will be unable to display the contents of a file, either because a proper filter is unavailable, or the item itself is not viewable (an application, for example). In this case the Quick View window will display some basic information about the item.

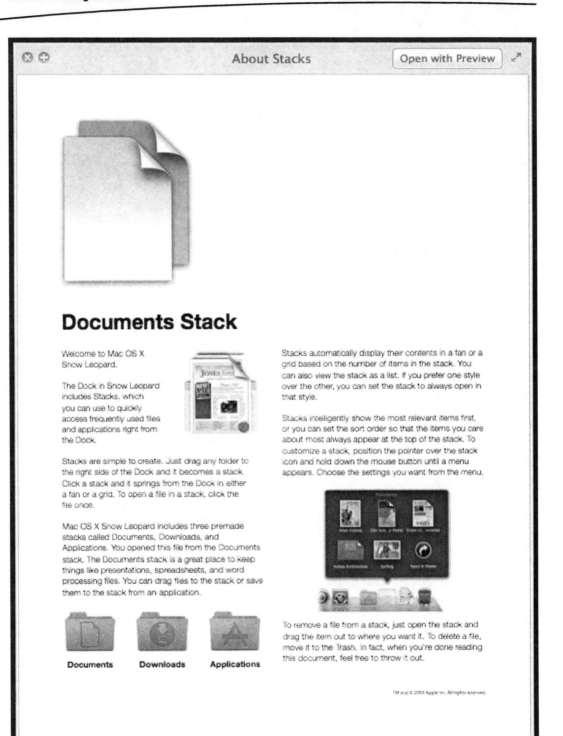

Figure 2–18. *Selecting an item in the Finder and pressing the Space key will open a Quick View window allowing you to view the contents of the selected item.*

Moving, Copying, and Creating Aliases of Finder Items

Besides opening and viewing files, the Finder is also used for managing your documents and applications. Management is done in the Finder by simply dragging and dropping items where you want them.

If, rather than just moving a file, you want to make a copy of the file, you can do this by using the Option-drag keyboard-mouse shortcut. (You should notice a green button with a plus sign appear while you are dragging to indicate you are making a copy.) Command-Option-drag will create an alias of the Finder item you are dragging.

> **NOTE:** An *alias* is like a copy of an item, but rather than actually copying the item the alias just points to the original file. In Windows these are called *shortcuts* and in Unix terminology these are *links*.

> **NOTE:** If you are moving a file from one volume to another, the Finder will, by default, create a copy rather than simply moving the file. You can override this behavior by holding the Command key while moving the item.

If you want to create a copy of an item in the same folder as the original, you can use the **File** >**Duplicate** command from the Finder's menu or use the Command-D keyboard shortcut (or select Duplicate from the item's shortcut menu). You may also create aliases by selecting **File** >**Make Alias** or pressing the Command-L keyboard shortcut. One final way to create a copy of a Finder item is to use a standard copy-paste operation; select **Edit** >**Copy** (or press Command-C) to copy an item, and select **Edit** >**Paste** (or press Command-V) to paste it wherever you want.

> **NOTE:** Aliases are the OS X equivalent of shortcuts in Microsoft Windows. Rather than creating a copy of an item, OS X creates a link that points to the original Finder item. This is used when you want to keep one original Finder item yet you want to access it from different places in the file system.

Renaming Finder Items

To rename a Finder item, you need to first select the item and then click the name of the Finder item. If you do this too quickly, though, the system may recognize this as a double-click and open the item. Once the item is selected for editing (the name will become highlighted in a rectangular edit field), you can edit the text as desired. Alternately, you can just select a Finder item and then press the Return key; this will toggle the name for editing without the need to time your second click.

> **CAUTION:** When the name is selected for editing, the entire name minus the file extension is selected, so any typing will immediately overwrite the original name. If you want to just tweak the name, you can use the arrow keys or your mouse to position the cursor where you want to insert or delete text without overwriting the whole name.

You can also rename Finder items in the Info window, which we will talk about very shortly.

> **CAUTION:** Certain Finder items, such as applications and default system folders, should not be renamed. Renaming the default folders can cause all sorts of unexpected and undesirable results, and renaming applications can cause them to stop working correctly. As a general rule, you can rename any of your files and any folders you create, but you may want to think twice about renaming other items. If you do happen to make a mistake, you can use the Undo command (Command-Z) to reset the name to its previous state.

Creating New Folders and New Smart Folders

Sooner or later it's likely you'll want to create new folders to help organize your files or other Finder items. The easiest way to create a new folder is to select **File >New Folder** from the Finder's menu or use the Shift-Command-N keyboard shortcut (or the shortcut menu item). This creates a new folder with a rather generic name, so you'll probably want to rename it right away, and then it's ready to go.

To create a smart folder (which is really just the result of a saved search), select **File >New Smart Folder** from the Finder's menu, or use the Option-Command-N keyboard shortcut. This will open a New Smart Folder window ready for you to fill in the search criteria.

BURN FOLDERS

Besides regular folders and Smart Folders, the Finder also has an option to create a Burn Folder. A Burn Folder is one where you can collect Finder items that you would like to "burn" to a CD or DVD (provided your Mac has a SuperDrive or a suitable alternate writable media device).

Burning items to CDs and DVDs is not as popular as it once was; there are easier, cheaper, and generally better means of backup these days. And if you want to share a file usually you can send it across the Internet or network much easier then burning and physically passing on a CD or DVD. Still, if you find the need to burn data to a CD or DVD, the Burn Folder is a good way to do so. (There are actually a few ways to create CDs and DVDs in Mac OS X, and we will cover some others later in the book.)

To use a Burn Folder, copy the data you wish to burn to the Burn Folder (the Finder will not actually copy or move the data you wish to burn, rather it will create an alias to the original data). Once you have collected all the items you wish to burn, select the Burn "*Burn Folder*" to Disc... option from the Burn Folder's shortcut menu and follow the steps in the resulting dialogs.

Once you are finished you can safely *trash* the Burn Folder (the data will still remain on your computer in its original location).

If you were intending to burn a music CD, this is better handled from iTunes. We will talk about that later.

Getting (and Altering) Information About Finder Items

If you want to get more information about a particular Finder item, then the Info window (Figure 2–16) is the place to go. The Info window allows you not only to view information about a Finder item, but it will also allow you to add or alter information and attributes about the item. To open an Info window, select an item in the Finder, and then select **File >Get Info** from the Finder menu (or use the Command-I keystroke or the Get Info shortcut menu item). Table 2–2 describes the basic structure of the Info window.

> **NOTE:** Depending on the file type, the content of the Info may vary. A document, for example, would present different information than an application.

Table 2–2. *Sections of the Get Info Window*

Section	Description
Spotlight Comments	This is a text field that allows you to add any comments about the item. These comments are searchable in Spotlight.
Kind	This tells the item's type: Folder, Application (for applications, it will let you know whether the application is universal, Intel or PowerPC), or Document.
Size	This gives the size of the item (including the number of items in folders).
Where	This gives the directory path of the item's location (including the original location for aliases).
Created	This is the date when the item was created.
Modified	This is the date when the item was last modified.
Label	This shows the item's label, which is editable, allowing you to set the label of an item to one of seven predefined Finder labels (discussed later in this chapter).
Share Folder	This check box allows you to share a folder and its contents with other users of your computer and network (appears only if Kind is Folder).

Section	Description
Open in 32–bit mode	This check box is available when an application has the ability to run either as a 64-bit application or a 32–bit application. All recently released Macs are capable of running in 64-bits (which allows them to access large amounts of memory). As such most applications that support it are fine running in 64 bit mode, and unless you are having a conflict with a specific application it is best to just leave this box alone.
Stationery Pad	This check box for documents causes a selected document to always open as a copy of itself. This essentially sets up the document as a template.
Locked	This check box locks a file so it cannot be modified in any way as long as it remains locked.
More Info	Occasionally additional information about the file will appear here. For example, this will occasionally reveal when an application was last opened.
Name & Extension	This is an editable text field that shows the item's full name (including the extension), which is immediately editable. OS X uses the file's extension as one way to choose what application can open a file, so changing the extension may change how a document is opened (possibly making it unreadable). A check box allows you to choose whether to show or hide the file extension in the Finder.
Open With	Discussed earlier in the chapter, this allows you to change the default application of a document from one application to another application.
Preview	This shows a preview of the item (this will play back supported audio and video files).
Sharing & Permissions	This allows you to view and alter the abilities of any users and groups to access the item. The ability to view and alter this information depends on the permissions you have. In general, you must be the file's owner or an administrator to edit this information.

TIP: If you want to replace the icon of any Finder item, you can do this by selecting the icon at the top of the Info window and then pasting any graphic on your Clipboard over it. Should you ever change your mind, you can delete the custom icon, which will cause the item to return to its default icon.

Compressing (Zipping) Finder Items

Often, especially when you want to send files via e-mail to someone else, you may want to compress or archive a file. OS X allows you to create .zip files from within the Finder. You can do this easily by selecting the item (or items) you want to compress and selecting **File** >**Compress "***Item Name***"** from the Finder's menu or using the Compress shortcut menu item. If you want to create an archive of multiple items to be compressed into a single .zip file, just create a folder containing all the desired files and then compress the folder.

> **NOTE:** These days many files and media formats are already compressed, so compressing, say, a single .jpg or .mp3 file won't cut down on the file size much, if any (in fact, some will actually be larger). Still, if you are sending many files, even if they are already compressed, it's a good idea to "zip them up" together. Even though the total file size might not decrease much, it may leave more free space on your computer because of the nuances of how files are stored on your disk. Plus, a single archive is easier to manage than a bunch of separate files.

By double-clicking a .zip file, the Finder will automatically expand the compressed item.

> **NOTE:** By default the Finder uses the included Archive Utility to create and open compressed items. By default Lion can handle many types of compressed items via Archive Utility; however, there are some compression and encoding types that require third-party software to open. This includes the SIT format, which was once the most popular compression format for Macintosh systems prior to OS X Tiger. .sit files will require StuffIt Expander, which is available through the Mac App Store.

Labeling Finder Items

For many years Mac OS has had the ability to label Finder items, and that tradition continues. Labels allow you to colorize Finder items as a way to sort them in the Finder; additionally, labels can have names associated with them (setting the names and colors for labels is covered later in this chapter) that may help you organize special items in the Finder. To label a Finder item, you can select it in the Finder and then select the appropriate label from the **File** >**Label:** item in the Finder menu.

In Icon and Column views, the label color will highlight the item's name with the selected color; in List view, it will highlight the item's entire row. Items in the Finder can then be sorted by label, and labels are an additional search parameter for smart folders and Spotlight.

> **NOTE:** When sorting items by label in the Finder, the sort order is determined alphabetically by the label name, not by the color. This may be something to keep in mind when naming labels.

Customizing the Finder

Now that you have seen some of what can be done in the Finder, let's take a look at some of the options available to you to customize the Finder. We will begin by looking at options for customizing the Finder's toolbar, and then move on to learning about the Finder's preferences, and finally we will look at display options for the Finder's various views.

Customizing the Finder's Toolbar

Earlier in the chapter we introduced the Finder's toolbar (Figure 2–2). We mentioned that there are a number of available options for customizing the buttons on the Finder's toolbar. To add or remove items on the Finder's toolbar, select Customize Toolbar... from the toolbar shortcut menu (Control-Click on the toolbar to bring up the shortcut menu). This will open up a dialog presenting you with a number of items (Table 2–3) to customize your toolbar with (Figure 2–19). To change the items or the order of the items on your toolbar simply drag the button on or off the toolbar and move them around as desired. To return to the default toolbar simply drag the default toolbar from the bottom of the dialog up to the toolbar.

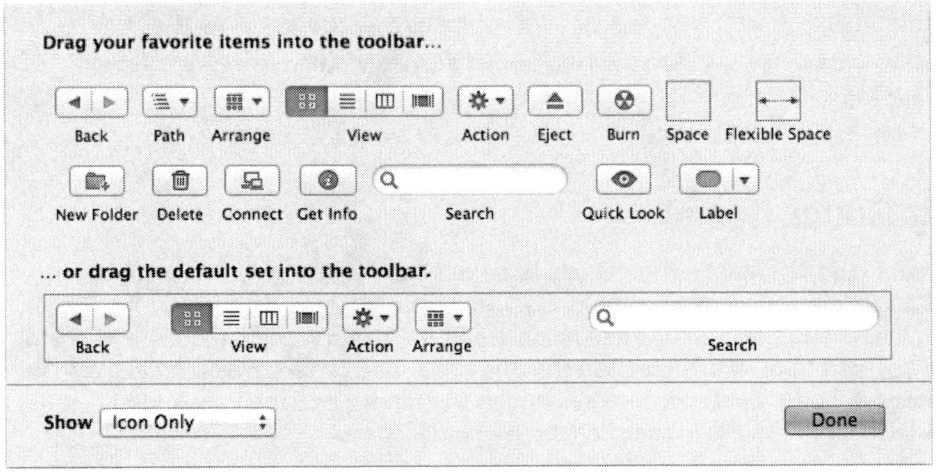

Figure 2–19. *Select Customize Toolbar... from the toolbar's shortcut menu to open a dialog presenting you new items and options to customize your toolbar.*

Table 2–3. *Toolbar Items Available for the Finder's Toolbar*

Button	Function
Back	The Back button allows you to navigate up and down to previously visited Finder locations, just like the Back button on a web browser.
Path	The Path menu provides you with hierarchical lists of parent directories for your current Finder location. You can move to a parent location by selecting it from this menu.
Arrange	The Arrange menu allows you to select an option to group items in the Finder's view area. The grouping of items with this option is different from the sorting options selected by the traditional Arrange by: view option.
View	The View control allows you to select how items will appear in the main view area.
Action	The Action menu provides a list of common actions that you may wish to perform on Finder items. In general, this menu is less useful than using the various shortcut menus.
Eject	The Eject button ejects selected media when applicable.
Burn	The Burn button will open up a dialog to guide you through the process of burning selected Finder items to an appropriate removable media format.
Space	The Space item simply places a fixed size empty space on your toolbar, useful for separating groups of toolbar items.
Flexible Space	The Flexible Space item places an area of empty space on your toolbar. Unlike the Space item, Flexible Space will expand and contract depending on the width of the Finder's toolbar.
New Folder	The New Folder option will create a new folder in the current Finder location.
Delete	The Delete Item will move the selected Finder item(s) to the Trash.
Connect	The Connect item will open up a window prompting you for information to connect to a remote server. We will discuss this more in Part VII of the book.
Get Info	The Get Info item will open an Info window for the selected Finder item(s).
iDisk	The iDisk item will open up the top level of your iDisk (provided you have configured your system with a valid MobileMe account).

Button	Function
Search	The Search field provides an area to initiate a text-based search.
Quick Look	The Quick Look button will open up the selected Finder items in a Quick Look window.
Label	The Label menu will allow you to provide a Finder label to the selected Finder item(s).

Beneath the list of available toolbar items are two other toolbar options. The Show option allows you to select how the toolbar items are presented, by icon only, text only, or icon and text. The Use small size option will slightly decrease the size of the items in the toolbar.

Once you have customized your toolbar, click the Done button to dismiss the dialog and save your toolbar options.

View Options

One of the key controls available on the default toolbar is the view control, which allows you to select which view Finder items will be presented in: icon view, list view, column view, or Cover Flow view (we introduced these Finder views earlier in this chapter). Depending on the view, there are a number of options available for customizing how items appear in the Finder. To present these options select **View >Show View Options** from the Finder's application menu (or use the Finder's Command-J keyboard shortcut). This will open one of four view option windows (Figure 2–20) with various view options for each Finder view.

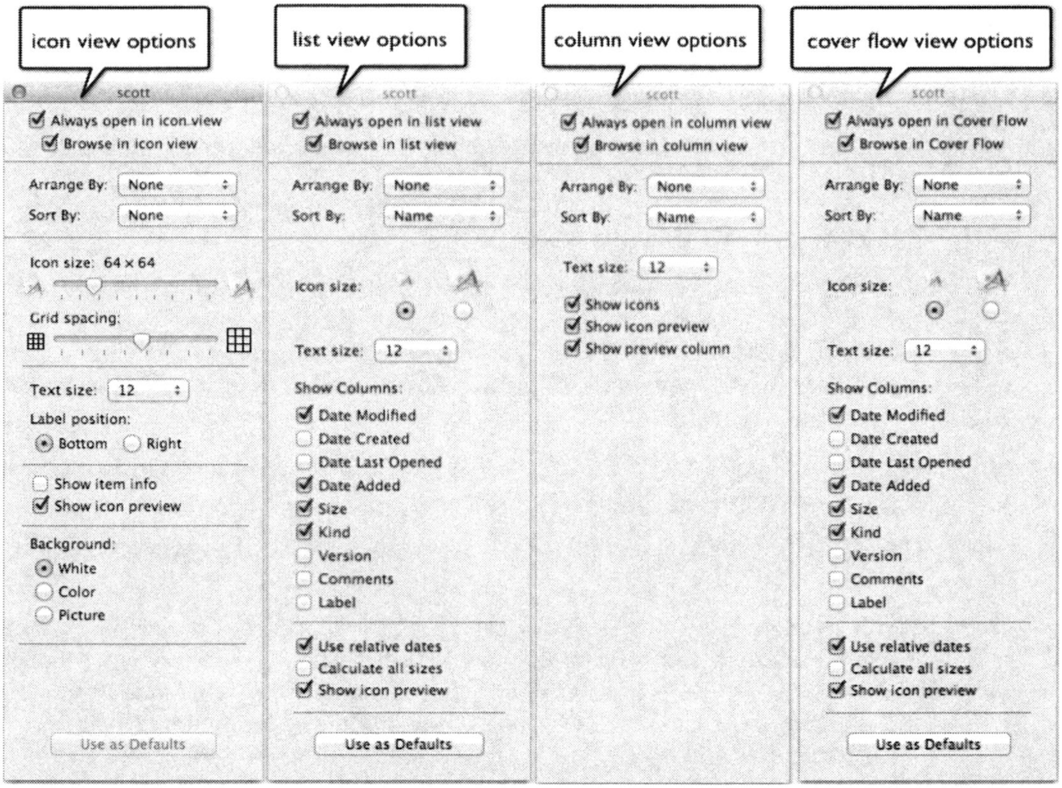

Figure 2–20. *The view options available from View >Show View Options in the Finder application menu will vary with each view.*

Descriptions of each of the various view options are as follows:

Always open in *icon view, list view, column view, Cover Flow*: Selecting this check box will set the default view for when you open the particular folder.

Apply to sub-folders: If the Always open in ... option is selected, selecting this will make all sub-folders open in the same view.

Icon size: In Icon view this will allow you to scale the size of the icons from 16x16 pixels all the way up to 512x512 pixels (the default is 48x48 pixels). In List view and Cover Flow this will allow you to display small- or medium-sized icons in the list.

Grid spacing: In Icon view, this option allows you to determine how close icons will be spaced to one another when arranged on an invisible grid.

Text size: In each view this will determine the point size of the text, the default is a 12–point font size.

Label position: In Icon view this determines if the text label is below or to the right of the icon.

Show Columns: The Show Columns section in List and Cover Flow view determines what information about each item will appear in the list. The selected columns also determine how you may sort the items (by clicking on a column header).

Use relative dates: The Use relative dates option will affect how dates appear in the List view. When selected rather than absolute dates (as selected in the Language & Text System preference) relative dates such as "Today" or "Yesterday" will be displayed where appropriate.

Calculate all sizes: Normally the sizes will only be calculated for non-folder items in a directory. When the Calculate all sizes option is selected the size of folders will also be calculated (which entails discovering the size of all items included in the folder). For certain folders with many items this option can cause the system to slow down while it calculates.

Show item info: When this option is selected in the Icon view additional information will appear for certain Finder items.

Show icons: The Show icons option determines if icons will be displayed in column views.

Show icon preview: When the Show icon preview option is selected, when possible (generally with document items) Finder icons will be a rendering of the items content. For example, icons of images will be thumbnails of the image, and Text documents will appear as small thumbnails of the actual text document. When this option is unselected or the system is unable to create a preview, default icons will be used (for documents this will usually be chosen by the default application for a given file type).

Show preview column: When this option is selected for Column views, a preview column will appear for any non-folder item.

Arrange by: Arrange by will group items together in the View area based on menu selections.

Sort by: Determines how file types are sorted based on menu selection. Sort by option may vary based on Arrange by options.

Background: The Background option allows you to determine the background of the view area in Icon view. You may choose White (the default), Color (which will allow you to toggle a color picker to choose a background color), or Picture, which will allow dragging and dropping an image to display in the background.

Use as Defaults: This button allows you to select the current settings as the default settings for all Finder views. (The Finder will remember custom options, so this only affects viewing folders in which you have not previously customized the Finder views.)

Finder Preferences

Besides altering the view options for each of the Finder's views, you can apply a number of additional preferences that affect the Finder as a whole. The Finder preferences (like most application preferences) are in the main application menu. In the case of the Finder, that's **Finder >Preferences** (the default keyboard shortcut to open the preferences of any application is the Command-comma (,) shortcut). The Finder's preferences are divided into four sections: General, Labels, Sidebar, and Advanced.

The Finder's General Options

Table 2–4 describes the Finder's General preferences (shown in Figure 2–21), which cover a few general Finder behaviors.

Table 2–4. *Finder General Preferences*

Preference	Description
Show these items on the desktop	This offers three check boxes to determine what sort of devices will automatically show up on the desktop.
New Finder windows open	This is a drop-down list that determines where a newly opened Finder window will start by default (this is where you begin when you open a new Finder window from the Finder's File menu or when you click the Finder icon in the Dock).
Always open folders in a new window	This check box, if checked, will cause all folders clicked in the Finder to open a new window rather than to open the contents of the folder in the existing window.
Spring-loaded folder and windows	This is a nice feature in OS X that helps in moving Finder items. When activated, if you drag and hold a Finder item over a folder for a period of time, that folder will spring open to reveal its contents. This way, you can move an item into a deep folder structure without first having to open the destination folder beforehand. The Delay bar indicates how long it takes for the folder to spring open.

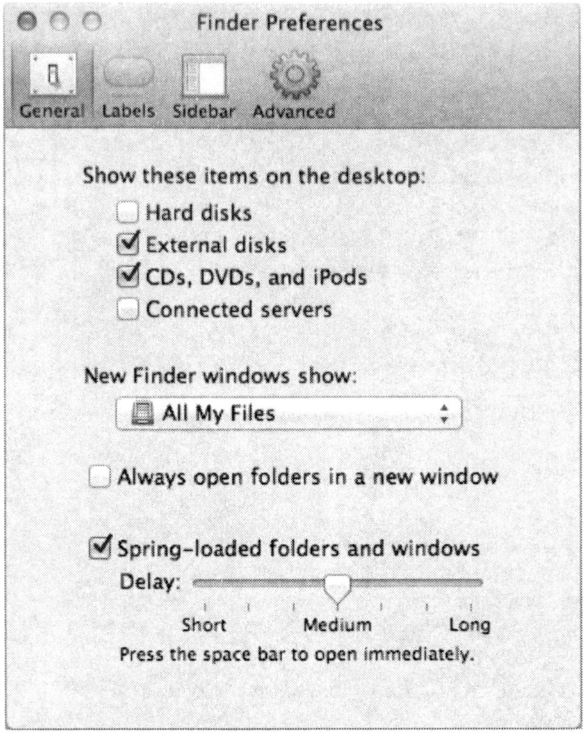

Figure 2–21. *The Finder's general preferences*

Customizing Labels

The Labels tab in the Finder preferences (Figure 2–22) allows you to customize the names of the various colored labels. To change a label's name, just edit it in the text field next to the appropriate color.

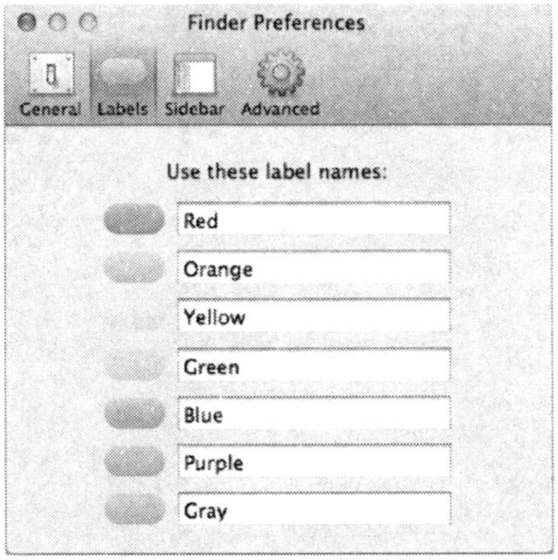

Figure 2–22. *The Labels settings in the Finder*

Customizing the Sidebar

The Sidebar preference tab (Figure 2–23) allows you to select what items automatically show up in the Finder's sidebar. This includes most user-oriented folders and locations, common shared resources, and connected devices.

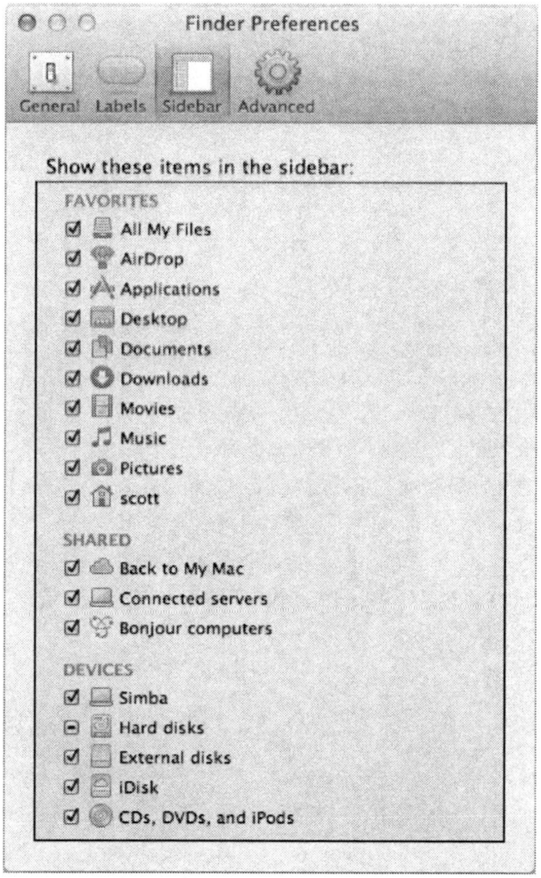

Figure 2–23. *The Finder's Sidebar option determines what items will appear in the sidebar.*

Setting Advanced Options

The final Finder preferences tab are advanced options (Figure 2–24) of which there are four fairly self-explanatory check boxes:

- Show all file extensions
- Show warning before changing extension
- Show warning before emptying the Trash
- Empty Trash securely

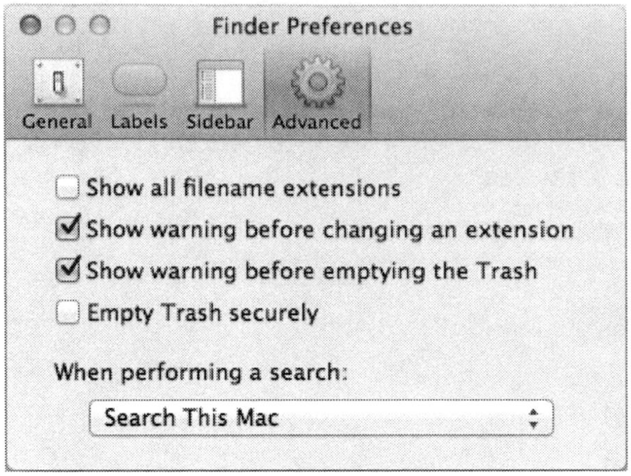

Figure 2–24. *The Advanced Finder preferences*

NOTE: The "Empty Trash securely" option actually writes over the disk space where the Trash items are located, making it nearly impossible to recover the items once they are deleted. This differs from a normal Trash empty procedure, which just lets the computer know that the space where the file exists is available for writing over. Until something overwrites that same area on your disk, that data could be recovered with the right software. The "Empty Trash securely" option takes more time to complete, especially if you are deleting a large amount of data. If you want to selectively use this command, you can select **Finder >Secure Empty Trash…** from the Finder's application menu, or select Secure Empty Trash from the Dock Trash icon shortcut menu using the special Control-Command-click.

Summary

With what you have learned about the Finder here you should have all the knowledge you need to start working with files and applications; however, before you get too far you should first take a close look at the file system and learn how files and applications are organized in Lion. In the next chapter we will explore the files system and learn how and why things are organized the way they are. We will also take a peek at some stuff that the Finder hides from you.

## Chapter 3

The Mac OS X File System

In this chapter, we are going to step back and take a tour of Mac OS X's file system to discover what items exist in what folders and why (and also what you can but shouldn't change, and why). We'll the following cover in depth:

- The overall file structure of Mac OS X

- Your personal home folder and its contents

- The top-level folders, including the System folder, Library folder, and Application folder

- Other common folders

- Hidden folders

The Overall File Structure of Mac OS X

Moving around the file system in Mac OS X is a bit like moving around a city on a subway. You start at one central station and choose a location to head toward. Once you get to the next station you may transfer trains and head to another station. You continue along your path, switching trains as needed, until you either reach your destination or reach the end of the line. In Mac OS X all local paths begin at the root of your primary hard drive (the one you boot Mac OS X from). From there a series of paths move downward, each with its own purpose. A basic map (like a subway map) outlining the paths of file system is shown in Figure 3–1.

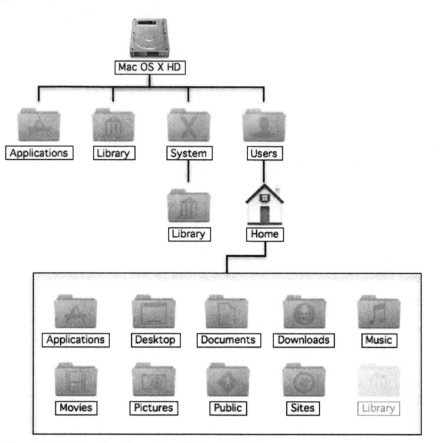

Figure 3-1. *A simplified view of Mac OS X's default file system*

> **NOTE:** Figure 3-1 describes roughly what is visible by default from the Finder. As you will see later in the chapter, there are a number of paths normally hidden from the Finder.

The file system is devised so that certain items belong in certain folders. For example, most of your applications go in an Applications folder, and most of your documents created by these applications go in the Documents folder within your home folder.

It's common to use *path* to describe where something is located in the file system. A path consists of folder names separated by forward slashes (/), which indicate that one folder contains another. A path beginning at the root, or top level, of a file system will actually begin with a /. A path beginning in your home directory will begin with a tilde (~). For example, the path to my Documents folder in my computer folder could be written either as /Users/scott/Documents or ~/Documents.

> **NOTE:** The actual name of your home folder is the account name (or short name) chosen when you set up an account in Lion. When I set up my account, I chose "Scott Meyers" as my full name, and "scott" as my account name, so my home folder is named `scott`.

> **NOTE:** All these slashes and tildes may seem arbitrary at the moment, and it's possible that you will never even have to type in a / or ~ to get where you need to go on your computer. The path notation you're learning here, however, is necessary to access and utilize a lot of the features hidden beneath the surface of Mac OS X.

The Users Folder and Your Home

The Users folder, located in the root (top level) of the file system in every Mac OS X installation, is where each user's personal folder resides. This personal folder is usually referred to as the user's home folder (or just home). Inside the Users folder will be a home folder for each of the system's users (named after the short name chosen when the account was created) and a Shared folder. The Shared folder is a place where files that are shared among all users may be kept. Your home directory is where you generally keep all of your documents, and where all of your personal settings are stored.

Your home folder, by default, starts out with ten subfolders: Applications, Desktop, Documents, Downloads, Library, Movies, Music, Pictures, Public, and Sites. Each of these folders has a specific purpose, as explained in Table 3–1.

> **NOTE:** Beginning in Lion, user Library folders are hidden. There are some reasonable justifications for this; however, we feel this is still an important folder to discuss, so we are still going to discuss this as if it were still visible.

Table 3–1. *Default Home Folders and Their Descriptions*

Folder	Description
Applications	This folder contains applications that are installed for a specific user; most applications are shared, however, and are therefore stored in the main `/Applications` folder.
Desktop	The contents of this folder are the items that appear on your desktop.
Documents	This is the primary folder for you to store all your document files. When you go to save or open a document from within an application, this is usually where you will start out.

Folder	Description
Downloads	This is generally the default location for files that are downloaded from the Internet via Safari or other applications. This folder was not present by default in Mac OS X prior to Mac OS X 10.5 Leopard.
Library	Most of your personal system and application settings are stored in this folder, including application preferences and data files, as well as a host of other items, such as plug-ins, caches, preference panes, and much more. In general this is a place where all that extra stuff that your computer and applications need to function properly gets stored. In Lion, this folder is hidden to prevent users from accidentally removing files that could affect the performance and stability of applications.
Movies	This is the default folder where imported videos and iMovie files will be stored. It's worth pointing out that movies and videos that you buy from the iTunes Store are stored in the Music folder!
Music	This is where your iTunes, GarageBand, Logic, Logic Express, and other music files are stored by default.
Pictures	This is the default folder for most of your images. This is where iPhoto and other photo applications will store their files by default.
Public	This is a special folder where you can store files that you wish to share with others on your computer or network. Inside of this is a Drop Box folder where others can leave you files as well. To share files with users on your network, file sharing must be enabled on the Sharing Preference pane.
Sites	This is the default folder for your personal web pages if web sharing is enabled on the Sharing Preference pane. Web sharing is covered in depth later in this book.

These default folders cover most of you personal folder needs (though subfolders are common in each of these). Occasionally you may want to add another folder for a specific need, and that's fine; this is, after all, your home.

The Applications Folder

The Applications folders, as you may have guessed, is the recommended folder for installing and keeping applications. Most users have two primary Applications folders of significance: the main /Applications folder, where applications available to all users are located; and ~/Applications, where applications available only to a specific user are kept. (A third /Developer/Applications folder is created if you install the Xcode tools; this is where development applications may be stored.) Keeping all your applications in these folders makes things fairly easy to find and manage. If, however, you find that you have many applications and this folder starts to get cluttered, it's common to create your own subfolders to organize types of applications. For example, you may create

/Applications/Games for any games you install or /Applications/Graphics for any graphics apps you install. This sort of organization makes it easy to find what you are looking for.

> **NOTE:** With the introduction of Launchpad, I find I rarely move any application into subfolders in the Applications folders; rather, I organize my applications into groups within Launchpad for quick and easy access.

> **TIP:** You may want to drag any critical or frequently used applications on to the Dock so that they will always be a click away.

> **CAUTION:** Some applications don't like to be moved from where they are installed. For the most part, any moved application will function just fine; the problem is that sometimes, when it comes time to update your application, the update utility expects the original application to be in a specific location. This is especially true of Apple's default applications, which are frequently updated with the Software Update utility. If you do move an application into a subfolder and something strange happens when you try to update it, you can usually move the application back to its original location and redo the update with no harm—it's just a bit inconvenient. As a general rule, if an installer installs the application, it's best to leave it where it installs (though often installers have an option to install in subfolders). If you install an application manually by just dragging it into the Applications folder (as you can do with many apps), then it's probably safe to put it wherever you want.

The Library Folders

One thing you may notice about the file system is that there are multiple Library folders. This is by design, and while there are many similarities between the contents of the Library folders, they are scoped differently.

> **NOTE:** There are actually four Library *domains*, though generally you only see three Library folders. Some applications can contain their own application-specific Library folder to contain plug-ins or other information that only they use.

The Library folders each contain the necessary support items for the applications on your system, as well as key system items. These include things like preference settings, cache items, scripts, and screen savers. In practice you almost never need to fuss with the contents of any Library folder; however, there are times when it may benefit you to do so (especially the Library folder in your home directory). That said, for each Library folder there are certain rules. We'll look at each of the three primary Library folders in general first, and then we'll explore common subitems contained in Library folders in general.

The Library and System Library Folders

The primary Library folder (/Library) has a *global scope*, as does the Library folder contained in the System folder (/System/Library). That is, their contents support every aspect of the system. Specifically, the System Library folder contains items necessary for the system to operate, and the primary Library folder contains the items necessary for most applications, third-party hardware, and other items that affect every user on the system.

As a general rule, the System Library is sacred. Only necessary system-level items should be installed there, and only system-level events should affect them. As such there is almost no reason for you (or me) to touch anything in there unless you are 100 percent sure you know exactly what you are doing and that doing it here is the only way to solve your problem. Changing anything here can cause very bad things to happen (or even worse . . . cause nothing at all to happen . . . ever).

On the other hand, there are times where it may benefit you to make a few changes to items in the main Library folder. This could be anything from installing a screen saver that you want to make available to all users of your computer to uninstalling some old items left over from an old application or hardware device. That said, you should still be 100 percent certain of what you are doing before you do it. While errors you make here might not render your system unusable, they could certainly make it less usable.

> **CAUTION:** Though sometimes you may want to clean out old, unnecessary files that tend to build up in your Library folder, make sure that these items are no longer being used before you remove them. Sometimes an item installed by one item is used by another item as well (this is especially true with certain common frameworks and components). Often it's better to err on the side of keeping an unnecessary item rather then accidentally deleting a necessary one.

The Personal Library Folder

The Library folder inside your home directory (~/Library) is your own personal Library folder. This is where settings that affect individual users are kept. This includes your personal system and application preferences, your mail settings (and actual mail), your Safari bookmarks, your iCal data, and much more. This Library folder is the preferred one for adding personal items such as screen savers, desktop backgrounds, and add-on scripts. This Library folder also is in most need of an occasional cleaning; however, all the cautions mentioned previously still apply.

> **TIP:** As mentioned earlier, in Lion user Library folders are hidden; as such, they will not by default show up in the Finder. In Chapter 2 you learned about the Finder's Go to Folder… command (Go > Go to Finder… from the Finder's menu), where you can enter **~/Library** to go to you user Library folder. An easier way to access your Library folder is directly from the Finder's Go menu. If you hold the Option key down when you select the Go menu, Go > **Library** will appear as one of the selectable options.

Common Library Items

Each of the Library folders tend to share a number of subfolders that typically contain the same type of items. Some of the Library folders also contain unique subfolders that have special significance. Table 3–2 points out a few common Library subfolders and explains their purpose.

Table 3–2. *Common Library Subfolders and Their Purposes*

Folder Name	Purpose
Application Support	This is the primary folder for applications to store any necessary support files, usually in a subfolder named after the application. Additionally, some companies (such as Apple and Adobe) will store information that may be shared among different applications here. Some of these files contain registration information, and even saved data, so it's a good idea to include these files in any backup scheme you have. In general, if you delete an application, then the support files contained here are safe to delete. Additionally, some application folders will contain subfolders themselves where users may add plug-ins, scripts, or other features.
Audio	The Audio folder contains subfolders for audio plug-ins (Audio Units, VST, Digidesign, etc.) and other support items for audio applications (this includes all of your GarageBand loops and plug-ins).
Automator	The Automator folder in /System/Library contains many default Automator actions that are used within the Automator to build more complex workflows. Additional Automator actions may be installed in either /Library/Automator or ~/Library/Automator (however, these folders will need to be created, as they don't exist by default—either you create them manually, or some installer package may create them).
Caches	The Caches folder exists in each of the Library folders. This is where the system or an application may store data that it refers to often, and rather than re-forming the data from scratch, it can use the data from the cache, saving time and system resources. Some people routinely clean out their Caches folders since the data there will be restored. However, some of the data stored there could take some time and resources to regenerate (and it will be regenerated), so unless a cache file has grown to an excessive size or has become corrupted, there is little use in doing this, except for deleting caches for applications that no longer exist on your system.

Folder Name	Purpose
Calendars	This folder, located in ~/Library/, is where calendar information is stored. This is mostly used by iCal, but the info is available to other apps that may utilize iCal information.
CFMSupport	This folder contains shared libraries that are used by Carbon-based applications (Carbon was the most framework for Mac OS applications prior to Mac OS X and the Cocoa frameworks). The CFMSupport folders in general should be left alone unless you get specific instructions to add or remove an item.
ColorPickers	The ColorPickers folders are where color picker plug-ins go. Color pickers are the various color selection windows available to you when an Aqua application (a standard Mac OS X Cocoa application) allows you to select a color. Snow Leopard includes a few different color picker plug-ins: Color Wheel, Color Sliders, Color Palettes, Image Palettes, and Crayons. Other third-party color pickers are available for increased functionality or personal taste.
ColorSync	The ColorSync Library folders contain ICC profiles and support files. These files are used by ColorSync to allow color devices (monitors, printers, scanners, digital cameras, etc.) to be calibrated for specific situations and so that color remains consistent from one device to another.
Components	Components are special bundles that provide added capabilities to the system or to individual applications (similar to plug-ins). The components located in the Components folder are generally used by the system; other components are located in other folders (e.g., QuickTime components are in the QuickTime folder and often provide audio and video codices).
Compositions	Items in the Compositions folder are movies or Quartz Composer files that provide the animated backgrounds in applications like PhotoBooth and iChat. In general, if you wish to add additional files for this purpose, you can create them and add them to ~/Library/Compositions to make them available for you to use.
Cookies	The Cookies folder in ~/Library/ is where Safari (and perhaps other web browsers and WebKit-enabled applications) store cookies that are presented from web sites. The proper way to manage the contents of this folder is through Safari (the Show Cookies button in Safari's Security Preferences).
CoreServices	The CoreSevices folder, which resides in /System/Library, contains a number of interesting utility applications that are used by the system. Things like the Dock, the Finder, and even Spotlight are in here (yes, they are all just individual applications). Obviously it's strongly encouraged not to remove any of these items.

Folder Name	Purpose
Documentation	This is where many applications store their documentation files, including interactive help documents.
Extensions	Extensions are items that add functions to the system. Extensions generally enable specific hardware features. Warnings about not messing with /System/Library/ items apply doubly here!
Favorites	The Favorites folder contains saved searches and aliases of folders that you have displayed in the Favorites section of the Finder's sidebar.
Filesystems	Mac OS X has a architecture that allows file system plug-ins. These items provide OS X with the ability to read and write to various file system formats.
Filters	This folder contains Quartz filters. These filters provide various means of manipulating an image's appearance.
FontCollections	Font Book allows you to group fonts into various "collections"; that data is stored in this folder.
Fonts	These folders are where all your fonts are stored. /System/Library/Fonts/ stores all the primary system fonts that your system absolutely needs. /Library/Fonts/ contains most other fonts that you wish to make available to all users and applications. Any fonts stored in ~/Library/Fonts are available to you, but not other users.
Frameworks	Frameworks are the essential building blocks of most applications in Leopard. Most applications rely on a number of the native OS X frameworks in /System/Library/Frameworks. Additionally, some third-party applications and utilities will require additional frameworks, which will be installed in /Library/Frameworks.
Graphics	Like the Audio folder, the Graphics folder contains Image Units and Quartz plug-ins that provide additional graphics capabilities to many Quartz-enabled graphic apps.
Image Capture	This folder contains plug-ins and support devices that allow for the acquisition of images from external sources (scanners, digital cameras, etc.).
iMovie	This folder contains iMovie plug-ins and sound effects.
Internet Plug-Ins	The Internet Plug-Ins folder contains the plug-ins for Safari and other applications. These allow the browser to display specific types of content inline, such as Flash, Java, Quick Time, and more)
iTunes	This folder may contain iTunes plug-ins, such as visualizer plug-ins and audio plug-ins. It may also contain other files, including iPod and iPhone updates.

Folder Name	Purpose
Java	The various Java folders contain the various core Java runtime libraries and extensions.
Keychains	The Keychains folder in ~/Library contains your keychains. These provide the system's built-in technology for storing passwords and authentication information. These files are highly encrypted. The way to open and manage a keychain file here is through the Keychain Access utility.
LaunchAgents	This directory contains launchd files that cause applications or services to activate when a user logs into the computer. Keep in mind that the items stored in your ~/Library/LaunchAgents folder will only be launched when you log in.
LaunchDaemons	The contents here are similar to those in the LaunchAgents folder; however, items in LaunchDaemons will activate when the system starts, whether or not a user logs in.
Logs	Many of the applications and services in OS X generate log files that keep track of important events that occur during the execution of a particular service. These files are stored in the various Logs folders. All of these logs are accessible (to those who have proper permissions to read them) via the Console utility.
Mail	~/Library/Mail stores most of your mail account info and your actual mail folders for OS X's Mail application (this includes all locally stored mailboxes and messages).
Modem Scripts	The Modem Scripts directory contains a number of files that initialize various brands of modems.
PDF Services	This folder contains that various PDF workflows available from the PDF submenu of the Print panel.
Perl	The Perl folders contain the required and additional libraries for the Perl scripting language.
PreferencePanes	This folder contains the individual preference panes that appear in the System Preferences window.
Preferences	The Preferences directories contain all the saved preference data for every application and system component. The preferences in /Library/Preferences/ contain system-wide settings, while the files in ~/Library/Preferences/ contain all of your personal settings for your environment to operate correctly. Deleting a preference file usually causes an applications to revert to its default state, with all your personal settings gone (certain applications that require registration codes for activation will often need to be reactivated as well). Almost every application you launch will create a preference file, so you tend to acquire a large number of them. Feel free to clean out preference files from applications you no longer use.

Folder Name	Purpose
Printers	This folder stores information about your selected printers, as well as other important printing system files.
PrivateFrameworks	This directory contains a number of frameworks that are, as the folder indicates, private. In this case, these are frameworks used by Apple that are specific to OS X or an application, and aren't generally available to other programs.
Python	This directory contains additional Python libraries. (Unlike Perl, Python is compiled as a Framework in Mac OS X, so the core libraries are stored in the /System/Library/Framework/ directory.)
QuickLook	This directory contains Quick Look plug-ins that are placed here by Apple or other third-party developers to add viewing capabilities to Quick Look.
QuickTime	The QuickTime folder contains QuickTime components (including third-party drivers) that enhance the capabilities of QuickTime.
Receipts	The /Library/Receipts folder contains records of applications installed using Apple's standard installer. OS X uses the contents of this folder as sort of an odd package management system. This is used by the system in many ways, so it's best to leave this alone. The exception is removing any receipts of applications you have removed.
Recent Servers	This folder keeps track of recent servers you've connected to through the Finder.
Ruby	This directory contains libraries for the Ruby programming language, including any "gems" you have installed.
Safari	The ~/Library/Safari/ folder keeps track of Safari information, including your bookmarks, history, values for forms, and more.
Saved Searches	This folder contains the saved searches you perform from within Spotlight.
Screen Savers	This folder contains your screen savers.
ScriptingAdditions	This folder contains items that enhance the capabilities of AppleScript.
ScriptingDefinitions	This folder contains dictionary documents that are available from within the Script Editor. This provides information about AppleScript syntax and usage.
Scripts	This folder contains AppleScripts that are accessible from various sources. If you plan on utilizing your own scripts, you should create a ~/Library/Scripts/ folder to contain them. Occasionally, individual applications will install application-specific scripts in a subfolder of Scripts.

Folder Name	Purpose
Services	This folder contains service applets that are available to most Cocoa applications from the *Application* > Services submenu. Many of the services the system provides are kept here, while other applications may store services with the application bundles.
Speech	This folder contains items that are used by the OS X speech system, including the various speech voices.
Spotlight	This folder contains some Spotlight plug-ins that add to the search abilities of Spotlight.
StartupItems	This is an old mechanism for starting up applications and services in OS X. This has been replaced by the launchd system, so most of the items that once went here have been moved to the LaunchAgents or LaunchDaemons folders.
Tcl	Like Perl and Python, Tcl is a scripting language that is used by the system, as well as some other common third-party add-ons. The Tcl folder is where the Tcl (and Tk) libraries are stored.
User Pictures	This folder contains user images that are used as the default login icons that are selectable when you add an account.
WebServer	/Library/WebServer is a folder used by the Apache web server installed on Mac OS X. This folder contains the default Apache root Document folder, as well as the CGI-Executables folder. This is one Library folder that we will talk more about later in the book.
Widgets	The Widgets folders are where all your Dashboard widgets are stored.

While there are other folders in your various Library folders (and often third-party applications will install their own), that covers many of the default ones. We'd just like to add one more caution that, as a rule of thumb, if you are unsure of what an item in one of your Library folders is, just leave it alone.

Other Common Folders

We've covered most of the default folders you'll interact with in Lion, but there are some other common folders you may encounter as well. One of the most common is the /Developer folder, which is present if you install the Xcode tools during or after your Mac OS X installation. Contained in this folder are all the developer applications, documentation, and other items necessary to develop your own Mac OS X applications.

Another common folder that may present itself is the /opt folder. This folder is used by MacPorts (which we will talk about later in the book).

Hidden Folders

The folders we have talked about are really only a small subset of folders actually contained in Mac OS X. A majority of folders and contents are actually hidden from the Finder. These hidden files are mostly the UNIX parts of Mac OS X; this is largely referred to as the *Darwin subsystem* of OS X. Later, in Chapters 23 and 24, we will discuss Darwin and the UNIX underbelly of Mac OS X in greater depth.

If you are curious as to these hidden files, the following AppleScript can toggle the visibility of hidden Finder items:

```
tell application "Finder" to quit
try
        do shell script "defaults read com.apple.finder AppleShowAllFiles"
        set OnOff to result
on error
        set OnOff to "0"
end try

if OnOff = "0" then
        set OnOffCommand to "defaults write com.apple.finder AppleShowAllFiles 1"
else
        set OnOffCommand to "defaults write com.apple.finder AppleShowAllFiles 0"
end if
do shell script OnOffCommand
delay 1
tell application "Finder" to launch
```

To run this script, open the AppleScript Editor (found in the Utilities folder in Launchpad), type the script into the editor, and then click the Run button. Then have a look in the Finder and relish all the other folders and items that appear. Run the script again to rehide the hidden items. Feel free to create a Scripts folder in your ~/Library/ folder and save this little file there under "Toggle Hidden" or some such name so it will be available to you later.

> **NOTE:** Most hidden files are there for a purpose, and are likewise hidden for a purpose. Usually this purpose is to protect the files from accidental disturbance by casual users. It's generally best to leave hidden files alone, at least until you learn what they do and how to work with them properly (some of which will be covered in this book).

Summary

Now that you've had a glimpse of how everything is organized on your computer, and you know how to move around it, we're going to take a brief sidetrack in the next chapter to point out a few of the unique features in Mac OS X, including the new Mission Control app.

## Chapter 4

The Extended Desktop: Mission Control, Spaces, and Dashboard

Over the years, Apple has refined how users are able to view and manage multiple windows and applications. In Lion, a number of these technologies have come together in an extended desktop metaphor that melds the best from previous versions of Mac OS X with some iOS flavor. These technologies, which are now all seamlessly part of this extended desktop metaphor, include:

- Mission Control
- Spaces
- Dashboard

The Extended Desktop

In Lion, Apple has introduced Mission Control, which ties Spaces and Dashboard together into a seamless extended desktop (Figure 4–1) and replaces the Exposé features. Using keyboard shortcuts you can easily navigate from view to view; however, this extended desktop metaphor really comes together through the use of a multitouch trackpad or touchscreen device, which lets you scroll from one view to another using (by default) the three-finger scroll.

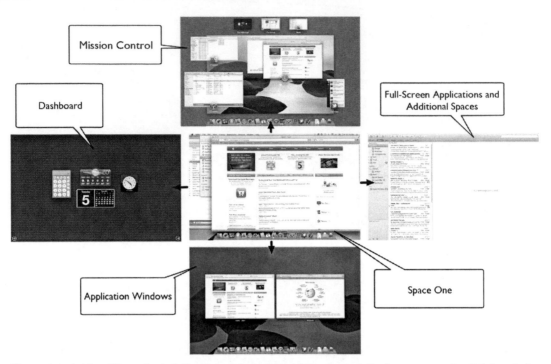

Figure 4–1. *In Lion, Misson Control, Dashboard, Spaces, and full-screen applications are seemlessly integrated into an extended desktop.*

While these are all tied together, each technology has its own unique purpose and features, so we will look at these one by one beginning with Mission Control.

> **NOTE:** We will not specifically be discussing any full-screen applications in this chapter, other than to mention that when an application is being run in full-screen mode, the application will occupy its own space.

Mission Control

Exposé was introduced in Mac OS X 10.3 Panther to help users more easily work with windows. It allowed users to move, shrink, and highlight windows in ways that are incredibly useful, especially when working with many open windows at once. When Spaces was introduced in Mac OS X 10.5 Leopard, Exposé was tweaked to reveal spaces as well as windows.

Originally, Exposé provided three distinct views: All Windows view, Application Windows view, and Desktop view. In Lion, among other changes, most of these views and the functions they provided have been simplified into the new Mission Control app.

Mission Control (Figure 4–2) can be accessed a number of ways: by pressing the F9 key, pressing the dedicated Mission Control key (the F3 key on modern Apple keyboards), or swiping up on the trackpad with three fingers. Across the top of the Mission Control view will be small windows representing all of your current spaces and full-screen applications (including Dashboard). Below the spaces, all the open windows on your current desktop will be shrunk down and arranged by application for easy viewing. Clicking any application window or full-screen application will immediately bring that window and application to the foreground. Clicking an active space will alter the Mission Control view to present the open windows in the selected space.

> **NOTE:** On Apple keyboards, the F keys (aka function keys) are often used for controlling things such as the brightness of the screen, the volume, and other features. This is especially true with MacBooks and MacBook Pros that by default have the F keys set to control these features. In such cases, you must use Fn-[F key] to activate the desired F key. If you would rather have the F keys work as the F keys by default, you can set this behavior in the Keyboard Preference pane.

> **NOTE:** Three-finger swiping is only available on trackpads that are multitouch capable and when the Swipe for Mission Control & Spaces option is selected for Three Fingers in the Trackpad preferences.

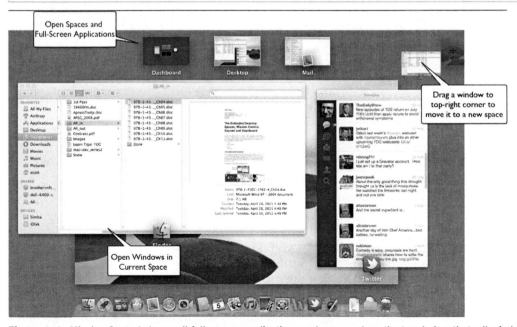

Figure 4–2. *Mission Control shows all full-screen applications and spaces along the top; below that, all windows currently active in the current space are reduced and arranged by applicaiton for easy selection.*

Mission Control enables a couple of other views as well. First is the *Desktop view* (Figure 4–3). The Desktop view slides all the currently open windows off the screen, making the entire desktop visible so you can access any items located on the desktop that may have been blocked by the windows. This is especially nice for people who tend to collect a large number of items on their desktops. The other view is the *Application Window view*, which reveals all the open windows of the currently running application; this has a view and behavior just like the Application Window view that existed in Exposé.

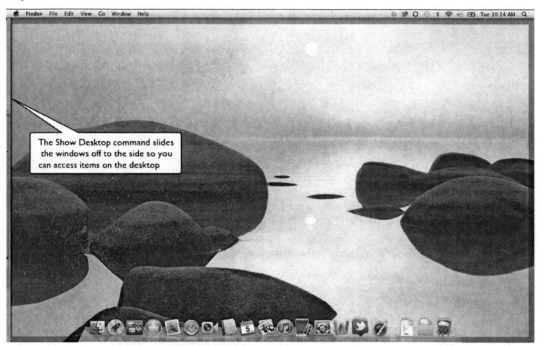

Figure 4–3. *The Desktop view moves all the open windows to the side to reveal the entire desktop. The edges of the open windows remain slightly in view along the darkened edge.*

NOTE: The keys to activate the various Mission Control, Spaces, and Dashboard commands can be set in the Mission Control System Preference pane (covered in Chapter 18).

Spaces and Full-Screen Applications

Spaces allows you to set up multiple working environments, or desktops, and switch between them. This is commonly referred to as creating and managing *virtual desktops*.

Like much of Mac OS X, Spaces has been refined in Lion. In the past you would set the number of available spaces you would want available, and they would be immediately available to use. In Lion there is no predetermined number of spaces; rather, they are created (and removed) as needed. Also, instead of being organized in a grid pattern, the spaces in Lion extend horizontally, with space 1 being the leftmost space and each subsequent space being located one space to the right.

There are a couple ways to move an active window from one space to another. First, you can always select your desired space from Mission Control to be taken right to it. Second, you can activate any application to be immediately taken to the space where the selected application is running. Last, but certainly not least, you can scroll from space to space using mouse and trackpad gestures.

> **TIP:** To quickly activate any running application, use the Command-Tab keyboard shortcut to bring up a list of all running applications.

One special full-screen application that is always present to the left of space 1 is Dashboard.

Dashboard

Dashboard (Figure 4–4) is a special application that is designed to run widgets. A *widget* is a miniapplication that can do various things. Mac OS X ships with a number of widgets installed that can display the current time, give you the latest movie schedule for your area, give you the local weather forecast, and much more.

By default, you activate Dashboard with the F12 key (or, on newer Macs and Mac keyboards, you can use the dedicated Dashboard key [F4]). Alternatively, you can just access Dashboard from Mission Control or using the Spaces commands to move one space to the left of space 1.

To add a widget to Dashboard, you can click the + sign in the lower-left corner of Dashboard. This will open the widget bar across the bottom of the screen, which contains all the Dashboard widgets currently installed (Figure 4–5). To add any of the installed widgets, select them and drag them off the bar onto the desktop. To remove a widget, click the *X* on the top left of any widget when the widget bar is open. To move a widget, just click it and move it around to wherever you want, and it will reappear in your selected location each time you activate Dashboard.

> **NOTE:** Holding the Option key while mousing over a widget will also reveal its Close (*X*) button.

In addition to the widgets included with Mac OS X, many other widgets are available to download and install. A good place to look is www.apple.com/downloads/dashboard/. If you download a widget in Safari, it will usually recognize the file as a widget and ask you whether you'd like to install it. To manually install a widget, just stick it in your ~/Library/Widgets folder (you may need to create this folder if it doesn't exist). Once it's installed, it will be available from the widget bar. You can uninstall widgets by moving them out of the Widgets folder. You can also deactivate widgets using the Manage

Widgets widget, which presents a list of all the installed widgets with check boxes that can be unchecked to deactivate any widgets.

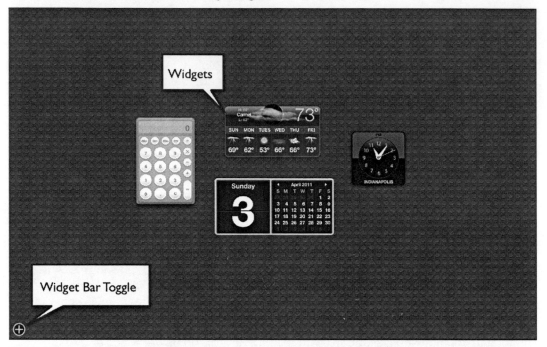

Figure 4–4. *Dashboard with the default time, weather, calculator, and calendar widgets. The + sign in the lower-left corner toggles the widget bar, allowing you to add more widgets to Dashboard.*

NOTE: Double-clicking a Dashboard widget in the Finder will also install the widget. If you are an administrator, it will ask you whether you'd like it installed for yourself or for everyone. If you are a regular user, it will install it in your ~/Library/Widgets folder.

Widget features vary from widget to widget; however, many widgets have settings hidden in them. To check a widget's settings, mouse over the widget to see whether a small *i* appears (usually in one of the corners). Clicking this *i* will cause the widget to flip over, revealing the widget information and settings.

Figure 4–5. *Dashboard with the widget bar open at the bottom and the Manage Widgets widget open in the middle of the screen*

Summary

This chapter wraps up the first part of this book. By now you should have learned the basics of Mac OS X and should be ready to get to work. Next you are going to start learning about and using various applications in Mac OS X. We'll begin with a brief introduction to applications.

Part **II**

Working with Applications

Learning how to use Mac OS X well requires not only knowledge of the core features of the Operating System, but also a knowledge of how applications work, after all, applications are what really makes an computer fun, useful, or whatever is it you computer is and does for you. In Part II we are going to learn the basics of using applications: We will explore common features that will be present in the majority of Mac OS X applications. We will look at how to find, install and manage new and updated applications. Finally, we will take a look at a handful of interesting applications included with Mac OS X Lion.

## Chapter 5

Mac OS X Application Basics

We have already looked at a couple specific applications, but what exactly are applications and how do they work? In this chapter, we will begin to discover what applications are and take a look at some common features found among many standard Mac OS X applications. Some things you will learn about in this chapter are

- Opening, closing, and quitting applications

- Opening and saving documents from an application

- Managing documents with Versions

- Running applications in full-screen

- Using the Services menu

In official Apple nomenclature, an application is "a computer program that performs a specific task, such as word processing, database management, and so on." We also learn that the use of the word *application* specifically applies to a computer programs with a graphical interface. A computer program without a graphical interface is just a *program*.

> **NOTE:** Mac OS X is capable of running different types of applications, including Java applications, AIR (Adobe Integrated Runtime) applications, web applications, and with the right software, even applications written for other operating systems. These types of applications may look or behave different from native Mac OS X applications (and each other). Unless otherwise specified, we will generally be talking about native Mac OS X applications.

> **NOTE:** Most Mac OS X applications are written using Cocoa, Apple's object-oriented application framework. Applications utilizing Cocoa gain many of the distinct looks, feels, and features that Mac OS X applications are know for.

Opening and Quitting Applications

There are a few common ways to *launch,* or open, an application in Mac OS X, each of them quite simple. The traditional way is to locate the application icon in the Finder (usually in the Applications folder) and double-click it. Single-clicking the application Dock icon can launch any applications that you have chosen to keep in the Dock. Double-clicking a document in the Finder will also open that document's default application (and should also open the actual document). Finally, Lion introduces Launchpad, which we introduced in Chapter 1 as a new way to launch applications.

> **NOTE:** If you're a command-line enthusiast, you can also launch an application using the "open" command. We will discuss this more in Part 6 of the book.

Quitting applications in Mac OS X is a bit interesting; while not difficult, it is different from what many people familiar with other operating systems, like Microsoft Windows, are used to. For one, clicking the window control button (the red button located where the *X* button is traditionally located for the majority of Microsoft Windows applications) does not always quit an application; usually it just closes the window, leaving the application active in the background. To assure an application actually quits in Mac OS X, it is best to explicitly quit the application. There are three common ways to do this: use the **Application** > **Quit Application** command from the application menu, use the Command-Q keyboard shortcut, or select **Quit** from the application's shortcut menu on the Dock.

> **NOTE:** It is possible for an application to quit when you close the application windows. Apple's own Address Book and iCal application are example of this. A general rule of thumb is that if an application can have multiple windows open at once (e.g., a word processor), it can have no windows open and still be running, while if an application only has one window (e.g., iCal or Address Book), then when that window closes the app may quit. In reality, application developers have to go out of their way to make an application quit when the windows are closed, so often this behavior is not utilized.

Documents and Files: Opening, Creating, Saving, and Using Versions

We looked at launching and quitting applications, but what about opening and saving the documents that we create in our applications?

Opening a Document

There are two primary ways to open a document; the first is directly opening the document from the Finder, as we discussed back in Chapter 2. The other way to open a document is to use the File > Open... command found in most application menus. The Open command (Command-O) will present you with the Open dialog (Figure 5–1). The Open dialog provides a Finder-like view, allowing you to browse the system and select the item you want to open. Once you've selected the desired file(s), click the Open button in the lower-right corner of the dialog to open the item(s) in the current application.

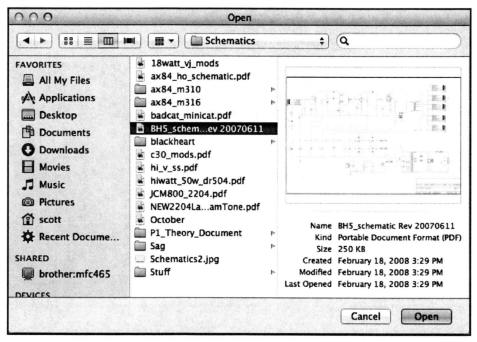

Figure 5–1. *An Open dialog (in this case from the Preview application) provides a Finder-like interface for selecting the file(s) to open.*

TIP: Most applications will allow you select multiple files in the Open dialog and open them all at once. To select multiple documents, hold the Command key down as you select additional files.

> **NOTE:** Most applications are only able to open certain types of documents. While the Open dialog presents most files visible in the Finder, many files may be grayed out, signifying that the current application is not recommended for opening them. Occasionally there will be an option in the Open dialog to highlight and open additional file types that the current application is capable of opening. Some applications will even allow the user to force open file types that the current application may not be able to open properly, which often results in gibberish appearing onscreen.

Creating a New File

Often you will want to create a new file from scratch in an application. Generally this is done by selecting the **File** > **New** command in the application's menu bar (or using the Command-N keyboard shortcut). Depending on the application, things may not be this simple. Some applications, for example, are able to create different types of documents. In many of these cases, selecting **File** > **New** will open a dialog for selecting the specific type of document you want to create. In other applications there is no explicit **File** > **New** option; rather, there are multiple **File** > **New** *something* options. Some applications even have a submenu attached to **File** > **New** that presents a number of new options.

This variation should not be taken as a bad thing, as it is indicative of the many amazing things you can do with Mac OS X applications. As a rule, no matter what the options are in the File menu, I find the Command-N keyboard shortcut almost always results in the desired effect, and in the few cases where it does not, then I can usually find what I am looking for in the File menu.

Saving Files (Without Versions)

With the introduction of Versions in Lion, saving files in Mac OS X has changed, at least for applications that support Versions. Since most existing (pre-Lion) applications do not yet support Versions, it is still important to understand the traditional methods of saving files, though.

SAVE VS. SAVE AS...

In applications that do not support Versions, which include most applications written prior to the release of Lion, there are two distinct save options in the File menu: Save and Save As.... The difference between these options is that Save is intended to overwrite an existing version of the document with the same name and in the same location. Save As..., on the other hand, will always prompt you for a new name and location, and is designed for creating an entirely new saved document. In practice, if you are working on a new, unsaved document and click Save instead of Save As..., you will be presented the Save dialog as if you had clicked Save As....

In the past when you clicked Save in some applications, the new file information would get stuck onto the end of the existing file, so after a number of saves the file would grow unnecessarily large. Back then, it was recommended to occasionally use Save As... to create a fresh file without the bloat. This is no longer the case. Still, Save As... has its uses; for example, if you want to save a file in a different format, the options in the Save dialog will often allow you to do this.

For applications that do not support Versions, a user can save a new file by selecting **File > Save As...** from the menu bar. This command will bring up the Save dialog, which differs in a number of ways from the Open dialog discussed previously. First, while the Open dialog generally opens in it own window, the Save dialog usually drops down from the current document's toolbar. Second, even the simplest Save dialogs tend to have both a condensed view (Figure 5–2) and an extended view (Figure 5–3).

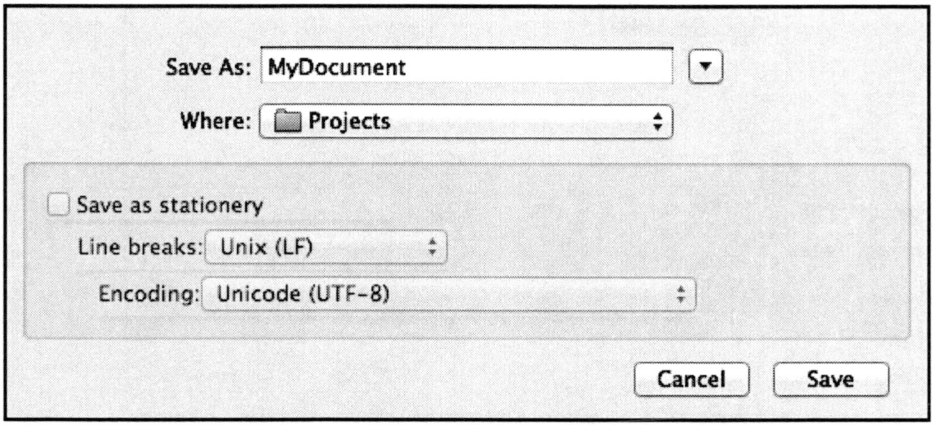

Figure 5–2. *The condensed view of a Save dialog from Bare Bones' TextWrangler*

The condensed Save dialog asks what you would like to name the file to be saved and provides a drop-down menu of common and recent folders into which to save the file. Beneath that is an area with application-specific save settings, which, depending on the application, can be very simple or quite complex. Clicking the disclosure triangle to the right of the Save As text field will expand the Save dialog into an expanded Finder view and may occasionally show additional save options not available in the simplified view.

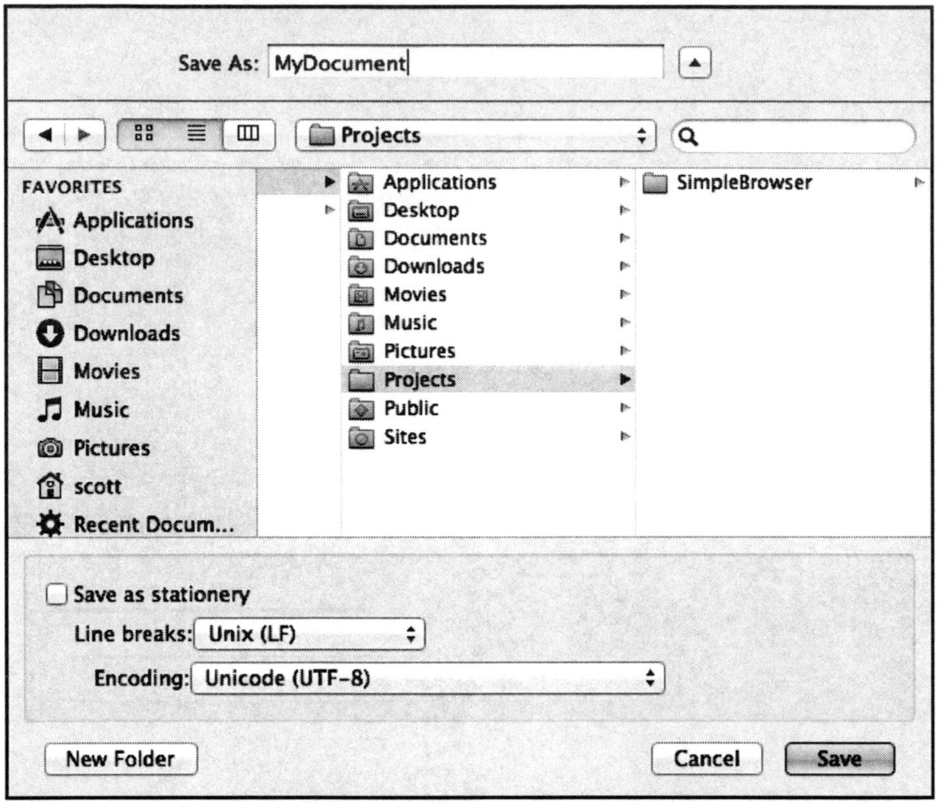

Figure 5–3. *The expanded view of the Save dialog shown in Figure 5–2*

> **NOTE:** Some applications will also offer Import... and Export... options, which are similar to the Open... and Save As... options. However, these generally provide additional options, including opening or saving a file that is in a format other than the application's native format, and changing a file from one format to another. A good example of this is when you wish to change an image file of one type to another; for example, saving a RAW image file from your DSLR (Digital SLR) camera as a JPEG for viewing on a web site.

Working with Versions

Versions is a new technology introduced with Lion that maintains a historical record of changes to a document. The concept (and much of the interface; see Figure 5–5) is very similar to that of Apple's Time Machine backup utility, introduced in Mac OS X 10.5 Leopard. (We will cover Time Machine in Chapter 20.) However, rather than keeping snapshots of your system on an external storage system, Versions keeps a record of previous versions of a document stored locally.

Versions changes the way documents are saved in Mac OS X. Rather than overwriting the old file when a new version of a file is saved, Versions saves the newest file while retaining the previous versions of the file in the background. This not only affects how files are saved on the disk, but also alters the act of saving a file. Instead of making you choose between Save and Save As..., it provides a single Save option, which will appear either as Save... or Save Version (both share the keyboard shortcut associated with the traditional Save option: Command-S). Save... will appear for any new, unsaved document, while Save Version will appear for any existing or previously saved document. Whether or not a Save dialog appears when you save a document depends. If you are saving a new, unsaved document, the Save dialog will appear, and if there are file type changes (e.g., if you change a document from rich text to plain text in TextEdit), the Save dialog will appear. Outside of these situations, Save Version will save a new version on top of the old version.

> **TIP:** Applications that support Versions will also save a new version of a document automatically when you close the document or quit the application. So, forgetting to save a revised document before you close it can become a thing of the past. Still, until all the applications that you use support Versions, it's probably best to stay in the habit of frequent saving before quitting.

The Versions menu (Figure 5–4) allows you to browse all previous versions of your document, revert your current document to the last opened version, or lock your document so that no new changes can be made to it.

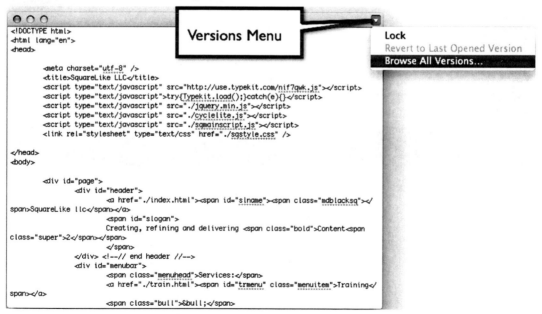

Figure 5–4. *The Versions menu (on the right side of the window bar of supported applications) allows you to access Versions features.*

> **NOTE:** The Versions menu will change to notify you about a document's status. If the document is locked, then "locked" will appear next to the menu. If the document has been edited since last opened (or saved), then "edited" will appear.

To access previous versions of a file, select **Browse All Versions...** from the Versions menu. This will take you to the Versions interface (Figure 5–5), where you can view past versions of your document and compare them to your current document. Using the timeline on the far right of the screen you can zoom backward to view past versions of your document. If you would like to restore a past version, select it on the right and click the Restore button. When you restore an old document, the current version simply becomes the last archived version, so nothing is ever lost.

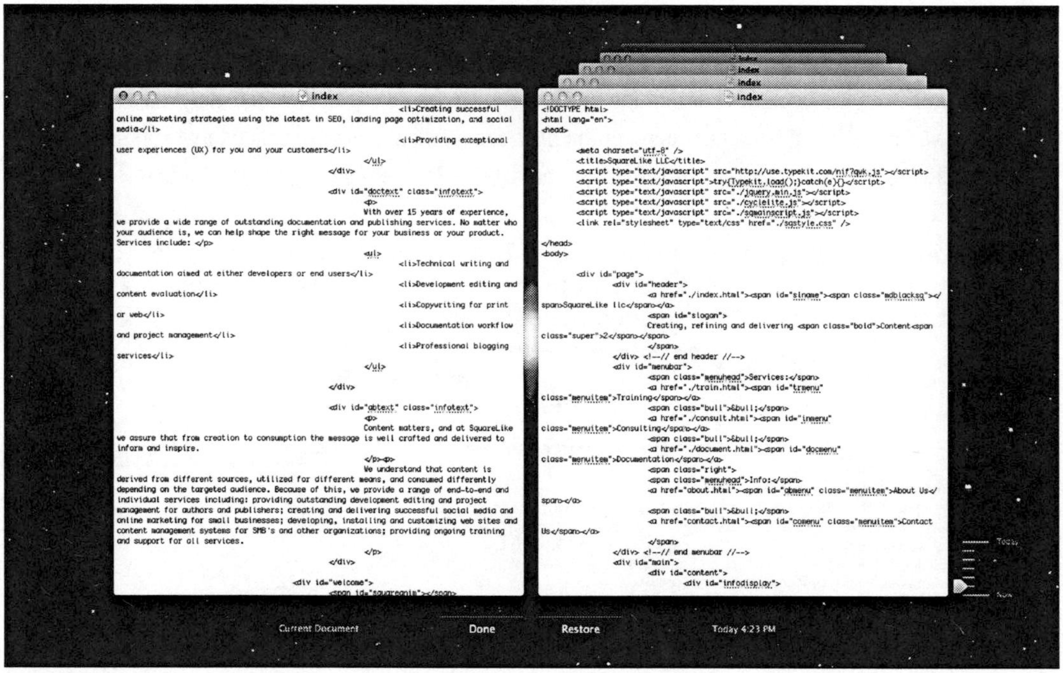

Figure 5–5. *The Versions browser presents the most recent document on the left and each of the previous document versions on the right. The past versions are browsable through a timeline.*

> **TIP:** Versions is an excellent resource for developers wanting to just try something out. If it works great but doesn't really suit you, can always revert back to a previous state.

Full-Screen Applications

Mac OS X 10.7 Lion also introduces the ability to run an application full-screen in its own space. Application windows capable of running full-screen will have a full-screen toggle button on the right side of the window's title bar (Figure 5–6). Clicking the toggle will expand the window to run full-screen inside of its own space (you can use the keyboard and swipe shortcuts that apply to Spaces to move from a full-screen application back to your desktop space).

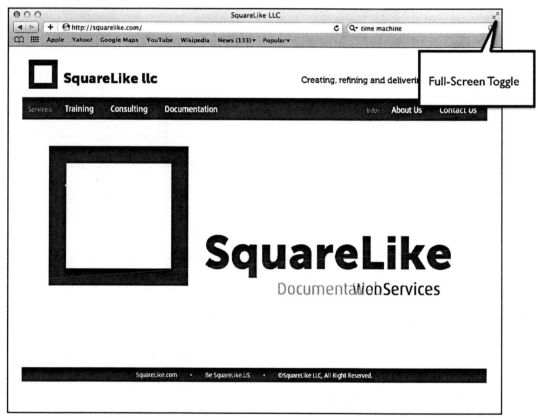

Figure 5–6. *Application windows that are capable of running full-screen will have the full-screen toggle button displayed in the window's title bar.*

> **NOTE:** Lion does not introduce the ability to run an application in full-screen. Many applications, ranging from Apple's own Aperture to Mozilla's Firefox web browser, have had the capability to run in full-screen for a while. However, Lion makes significant advances in not only the way full-screen mode is handled, but also in the ability to move full-screen applications into their own space. This allows for easy switching between applications, whether they are running in full-screen or not, without first having to switch out of full-screen mode.

By default, an application running in full-screen will hide the menu bar. However, by holding the cursor over the top portion of the screen, you can make the application's menu bar slide into view, presenting you with full access to the menu bar, including the toggle button to exit the full-screen view (Figure 5–7).

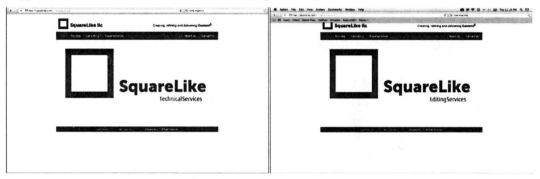

Figure 5–7. *The image on the left shows Safari running in its default full-screen view with the menu bar hidden. The image on the right shows the menu bar slid into view.*

Other Common Application Features

Besides what we've covered previously in this chapter and elsewhere in the book, there are a few other useful things to know about when working with applications in Mac OS X.

Using the Services Menu

Services are some of the most powerful features in Mac OS X. They are also some of the most overlooked. Services provide a way for users to utilize selected features and abilities of one application from within another.

Services are available from the **Application** > **Services** menu in most applications. The services available at any given time depend on a number of contextual factors. For example, selecting any text in an application will provide you with a number of available services, such as Look up in Dictionary and Search with Google. Selecting specific text may provide additional options; for example, selecting a web address will reveal the Open URL service. A number of these services even have system-wide keyboard shortcuts. For example, if you are reading some text in an application, you can select a word or phrase from that text and press Shift-Command-L to automatically open a Google search on that phrase.

> **NOTE:** The Shift-Command-L Services shortcut is the default shortcut set up in the System's Keyboard Shortcuts preferences in the Keyboard & Mouse preference pane. This is fully customizable and apt to change. In fact, in previous versions of Mac OS X the default shortcut for this command was Shift-Control-F. Also, in the event that there is an overlap of keyboard shortcuts between services and an application, the application's shortcut should take precedence.

While there are a few stand-alone services that are part of Mac OS X (such as Summarize), most services are associated with applications (e.g., the Open URL service is associated with Safari). As such, the types of services available to you will depend on the specific applications you have installed. A list of all the currently available services on your system (as well as the ability to toggle each specific service on and off) is located under the Keyboard Shortcuts tab in the Keyboard System Preferences pane (covered more in Chapter 18).

> **NOTE:** Even though the Services menu is present, Services may not be available from all applications. In general, Cocoa applications support the Services menu out of the box; however, Carbon apps (of which a few still are prevalent) don't. If you find yourself using one of these applications and missing this feature, you should let the developer know how you feel, and perhaps they will someday update their application.

Using AppleScript and Automator

Most OS X Aqua applications expose at least some of their abilities to AppleScript and the Automator to allow savvy users to extend the functionality of the application or to utilize the features of the application in an automated workflow. This ability can be put to some very powerful uses and is covered in much depth in Chapter 31.

Summary

Most of what we have covered in this chapter applies to most of the applications you will use on your Mac. That said, developers have a lot of freedom to change the behavior of any of the features covered in this chapter in their applications (in fact, Apple has notoriously altered many of its applications to behave a little differently).

Speaking of applications, the next chapter will discuss how find, install, and manage applications.

## Chapter 6

Installing and Removing Applications

Mac OS X Lion comes with a wide variety of standard applications for many common computer tasks, including applications for using the Internet (including Mail and Safari), applications for viewing media (including iTunes and DVD Player), and more. If you recently bought your Mac new, then it likely included some additional bundled software, including iLife. No matter what software your computer came with, there will likely be a time when you wish to add to your collection of applications. This chapter will show you how to find and install new applications, and how to manage the applications once they are installed.

This chapter will cover

- Using the App Store application
- Installing application packages
- Removing installed applications

> **NOTE:** In this chapter we'll dig into many nuances of installing and managing the applications on your Mac. This isn't meant to confuse or complicate the process, but to provide a solid understanding. In general, installing an app on your Mac is exceedingly easy, and the process is self-explanatory; we just want to make sure that you are prepared for the rare cases when it isn't.

Introducing the Mac App Store

Finding software for the Mac has not always been easy. In the past, if you walked into a software-selling retailer, you might easily miss the small section of Mac software hidden among the rows of Microsoft Windows software (if there was any Mac software at all).

Seasoned Mac users did not fret, however; long ago they learned that there is an abundance of Mac software for most every need. It often required a bit of digging on the Internet to research, locate, and download or order the software you were looking for, but the software was there, much to the chagrin of many Windows user who say, "Well, a Mac can't do this." Only to have the savvy Mac user respond, "Well actually, this application does that quite well, even better I think."

Even aided by web sites such as VersionTracker (which today is just another part of CNET's download.com service) and MacUpdate, which provide a running list of new and updated applications, it hasn't always been easy to discover the full extent of Mac software available. Prior to the release of Lion, Apple decided to help demystify Mac software with the unveiling of the Mac App Store and the App Store application (Figure 6–1).

Figure 6–1. *The App Store application provides an easy way to browse and buy a wide range of applications for your Mac.*

The App Store application is your window to the Mac App Store. You can access this application from Launchpad, from the Applications folder in the Finder, by Selecting **App Store...** from the Apple menu, or by clicking the App Store icon in the Dock or from Launchpad.

When you first launch the App Store app, you will be asked to either enter your Apple ID or create one. Not only will the account you create store payment information (App Store credit, credit card, and PayPal are all accepted), but it will also be used to register your applications to your computer.

NOTE: In order to utilize the App Store, you will need an Apple ID. Your Apple ID is used not only for the App Store, but also for iTunes and a number of online features. If you have a MobileMe account, your MobileMe account info can be used as your Apple ID; however, you can set up a separate Apple ID if you like. Once you choose your Apple ID, all your purchases will be associated with that ID, so you want to pick one and stick with it. You will also need to store payment info with your Apple ID to purchase applications. If you don't have or don't wish to use a credit card, and you don't want to register with a PayPal account, you can use a prepaid iTunes or App Store card and use that to initially set up your account.

NOTE: If you have multiple computers—say, an iMac and a MacBook Air—you can use your Apple ID to install applications from the App Store to both computers without needing to repurchase an application.

Once you have signed in with your Apple ID, you will be taken to the App Store's Featured Apps page (notice that the Featured button on the App Store's toolbar is highlighted). The Featured Apps page calls attention to new or popular Mac OS X applications.

The Featured view is only one of five main views in the App Store application. Moving across the toolbar, there is also a Top Charts view, which presents the most-downloaded applications, broken down by categories and whether the application is free or not. (Paid apps have two categories: most downloads and highest grossing.)

After the Top Charts view is the Categories view (Figure 6–2), which allows you to browse applications based on their category. Some categories are even further broken down; for example, under the category for Games there are a number of subcategories (Action, Adventure, Arcade, etc.).

Figure 6–2. *If you are browsing for an application of a specific type, the Category view is a good place to start.*

NOTE: Some applications may be listed in multiple categories; for example, many Productivity applications may also be listed under Business.

Selecting an application listing in any of the first three views will open up a page detailing the application, along with screenshots and customer reviews (Figure 6–3).

Figure 6–3. *Selecting an application in the App Store application will give you information about the application, along with screenshots and reviews. There will also be a button to purchase or download the application.*

Installing an Application from the App Store

If you discover an application you want to buy or download from the App Store, simply click the Buy button (shown in Figure 6–3). If the application costs money, the purchase price will be shown on the Buy button, and if the application is free the button will say "Free." Once you click the Buy button, you may be asked to confirm your Apple ID and password (if you recently signed in, this step may be bypassed); then, if the application costs money, you will be prompted again to confirm your purchase. Once you are signed in and confirm any purchases, your application will begin to download immediately. Upon completion of the download, the application will be installed in the Applications folder in the Finder, and the application will be added to Launchpad. That's it.

Checking Your App Store Purchases

The fourth tab on the App Stores toolbar is called Purchased. When selected, the App Store application will present a view containing all your App Store purchases (Figure 6–4). Not only does this view present a list of applications purchased from the Mac App Store, but it will also allow you to install or reinstall any such applications that aren't currently installed on your computer.

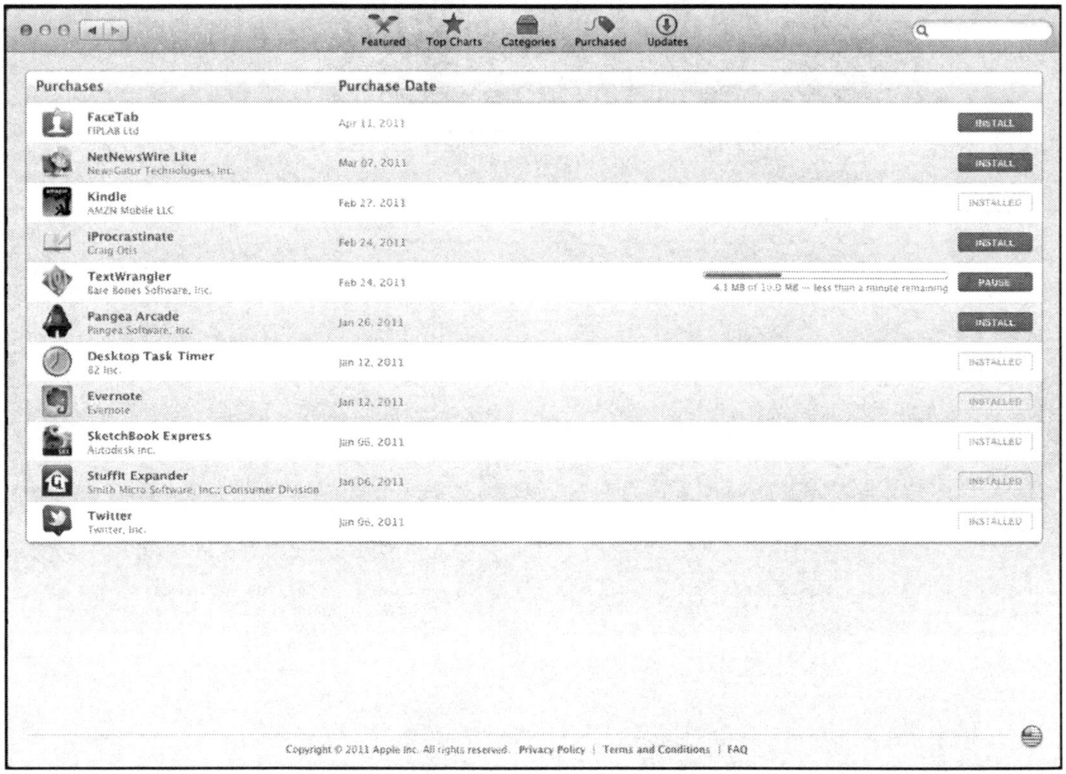

Figure 6–4. *The Purchased view in the App Store application will let you view and reinstall any previously purchased or downloaded applications.*

Keeping Your App Store Purchases Updated

The App Store application, in addition to keeping track of all of your purchases, will also keep track of any updates to your purchased applications. When you launch the App Store application, if any of your purchased applications need updates, the Updates icon on the toolbar will change, adding a number to it (this overlay is referred to as a *badge*). The badge number represents the number of applications with available updates. Clicking the Updates icon will take you to the Update view (Figure 6–5), which provides details about available updates and presents you with the opportunity to either update each outdated application individually or update all outdated applications at once.

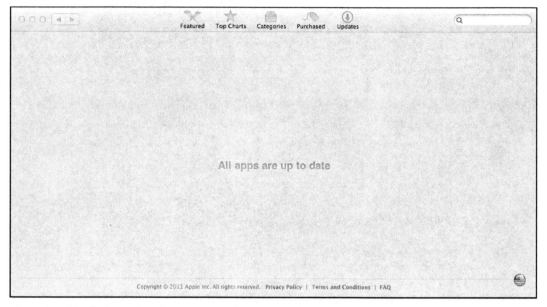

Figure 6–5. *The Updates view allows you to easily keep track of and apply updates to your App Store purchases.*

THE PROS AND CONS OF THE APP STORE

While the App Store has a number of advantages—ease of use, centralized management of applications and updates, behind-the-scenes registration so you don't have to futz around with serial numbers and registration steps—there are currently a number of limitations evident when using the App Store. First, applications must conform to certain rules to be allowed into the App Store. Following are a few of the restrictions that Apple outlines for Mac App Store applications:

- Applications must not change the user interface or operation of Max OS X.

- Applications must comply with the Mac OS X Human Interface Guidelines (though one could point out that Apple's own apps seem to be excluded from this requirement).

- Applications must not duplicate functions in any currently shipping Apple software.

- Applications must not duplicate functions of existing approved App Store applications.

- Applications must not use registered trademarks or copyrighted material without explicit permission from the rights holders.

- Applications must not be beta or trial software.

- Applications may not install additional software components along with the software. (In other words, the App must be single, self-contained App.)

Beyond the restrictions imposed by Apple about what applications may be carried in the Mac App Store, there are a number of other issues with the Mac App Store. For example, there is no upgrade path from previously purchased software to App Store versions.

Because of these restrictions, some of the most popular Mac OS X applications from companies like Microsoft and Adobe, as well as applications by many other software developers, are not offered in the Mac App Store.

Overall, the Mac App Store provides a great service to users of many applications; however, it should not be considered the only source of Mac OS X software.

> **NOTE:** One common developer complaint about the App Store is that some of the rules for items in the App Store are somewhat loosely enforced. Sometimes apps that should seemingly be included are rejected and apps that should be rejected are included. Overall the process seems somewhat subjective.

Getting Applications Outside the App Store

While the App Store is a great place to find a wide range of applications, it is not the only way to get applications for your Mac; in fact, many popular applications are not even available in the Mac App Store. In other cases, you may have previously purchased an application from a web site or directly from the developer, and they may offer updates or upgrades not available from the App Store.

> **NOTE:** The Mac App Store uses its own system to manage applications, so while it may recognize applications that have been installed outside the App Store, it will not be able to manage them, or provide updates or upgrades to them. If you purchase an application outside the Mac App Store, yet later wish to utilize the App Store features with that application, then you will need to repurchase that application through the App Store.

As mentioned earlier in the chapter, there are a number of resources outside the Mac App Store for discovering and purchasing new applications. MacUpdate (http://macupdate.com) is an excellent web site that tracks a wide range of software releases for Macintosh computers, usually providing links back to the developer's web site so that you may purchase the software directly from the developer (though recently, many developers have been directing users to the Mac App Store to purchase their applications). Like the App Store, MacUpdate provides information about the application, as well as customer reviews to help you make decisions about software.

> **NOTE:** Many developers provide trial versions of their software for download from their web sites. Trial versions of software allow you to try an application before you buy it so you can be sure the application works the way you want it to before you take a financial plunge. Trial software is currently not available in the App Store.

When you acquire software outside the Mac App Store, you are on your own installing it. The most common way to distribute an application outside the App Store is on a downloadable *disk image* (or occasionally an actual CD, DVD, or USB flash drive). A disk image is a virtual storage device (usually containing a `.dmg` or `.img` extension). Double-clicking a disk image will cause the disk image to *mount*, causing it to appear as a new attached storage device in the Finder.

> **NOTE:** Often, when you download a disk image from the Internet, the web browser will recognize the file as a disk image, automatically mount it, and open up the virtual disk in the Finder.

Many disk images simply contain the application on them, along with any supplementary documentation or readme files. To install them, you simply need to drag the application from the disk image into an Applications folder. Other applications, especially those that are fairly complex or contain more than one application (e.g., Microsoft Office), may contain an installer application to help you register and install the application.

Installing an Application Package

Installer packages make installing complex applications fairly easy; however, if you just click through the installer, you may miss some important options. Although every package you install will be slightly different, the general process is similar, so the best way to show how this works is to walk you through some of what you may encounter.

Starting the Installer

An installer package is usually distributed on a disk image, or even a CD or DVD. Upon opening the disk (image), you will usually see one or more packages (Figure 6–6). Double-clicking the package will begin the installer.

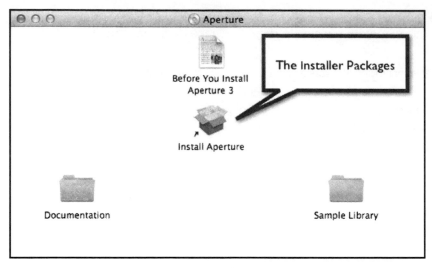

Figure 6–6. *Most standard installer packages, like the Aperture 3 installer shown here, look like little boxes.*

NOTE: There are two similarly appearing types of package files; some have the .pkg extension, and others have the .mpkg extension. The .mpkg files are special metapackages that generally contain a number of smaller .pkg files. The installation of both types will be similar; however, the .mpkg file often will have more available options.

When you double-click the installer package, Mac OS X's Installer application will start the installation process. One of the first things the Installer may do is check your system to verify it is suitable for installing the application (Figure 6–7).

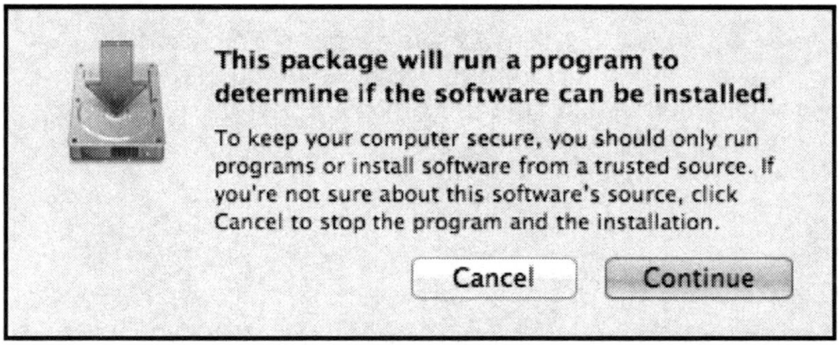

Figure 6–7. *Some packages must check your system before they can begin the installation.*

After the system check (if necessary), the Installer will generally present you with a few screens of information about the application. This generally includes up to three items: an Introduction screen, a Read Me screen, and a Software License screen.

The Introduction screen generally just welcomes you to the installation application and summarizes the software you are installing. The Read Me screen contains more in-depth information about the application(s) you are installing. Often readme files will contain some important last-minute information about the software, so they're worth the read. Following that, you may be presented with a software license that, when you click Continue, will prompt you with a sheet asking whether you agree or disagree (you have to agree if you want to install the software). Depending on the software, before you continue your install, you will occasionally be prompted to enter registration information along with a serial number or license key (Figure 6–8). If you purchased a physical software package, then this key is usually included with the documentation; if you downloaded that application, then the key is usually e-mailed to you separately.

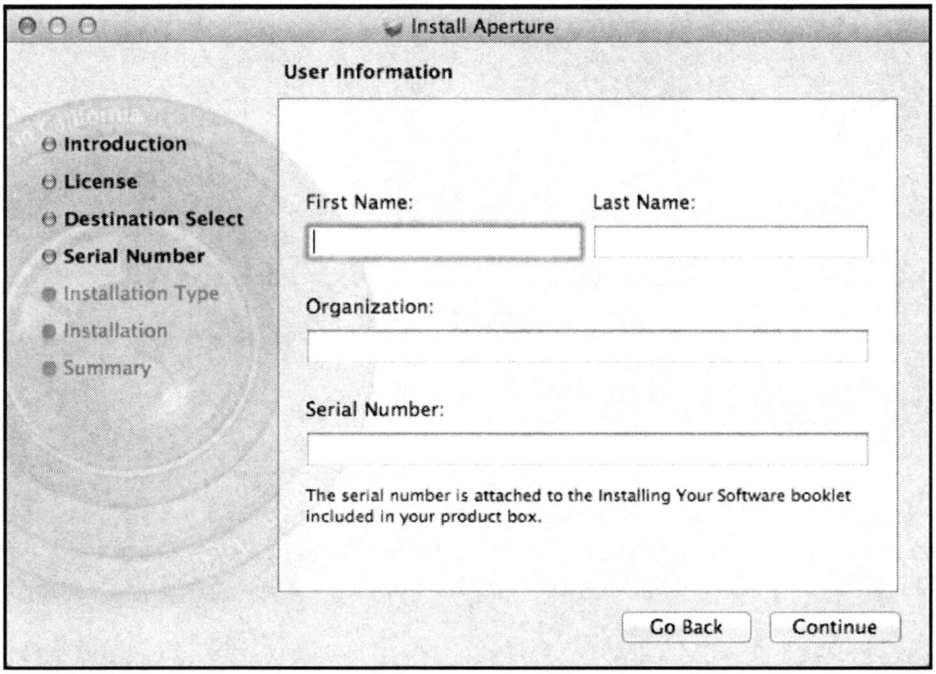

Figure 6–8. *Some software requires that you enter a serial number or license key before you can continue.*

Customizing Your Installation

After you've clicked through the informational screens and accepted any licensing agreements, you will be presented with the Standard Install screen (Figure 6–9). Some applications at this point will offer you the opportunity to customize your installation.

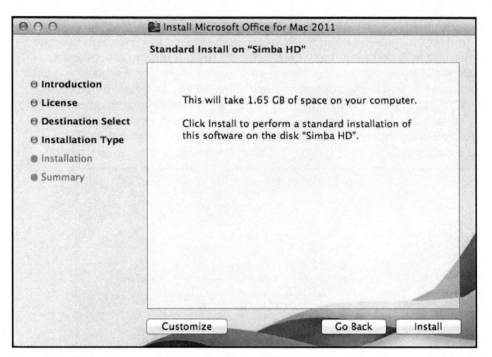

Figure 6–9. *The Install screen in Microsoft Office for Mac 2011 allows you to either proceed with the standard install or choose to customize your install.*

NOTE: Most of the time, a standard install (which used to be called an easy install) will install the application along with the most popular options in the Applications folder (occasionally in a special subfolder just for the particular application and components).

NOTE: Many applications that use an installer, rather than allowing you to simply copy the application in place, do so because they require more than a simple application bundle or have special install options. Many times these applications require additional components to be installed in locations other than the Applications folder, and the installer does its best to simplify this process for the user. However, this also means that unless an uninstaller application is also included, removing all the components manually will require more than just dragging the installed application into the Trash.

If you choose to customize your installation (or are at least curious about what customization options are available), click the Customize button, which will take you to a screen providing you with the ability to fine-tune your install (Figure 6–10).

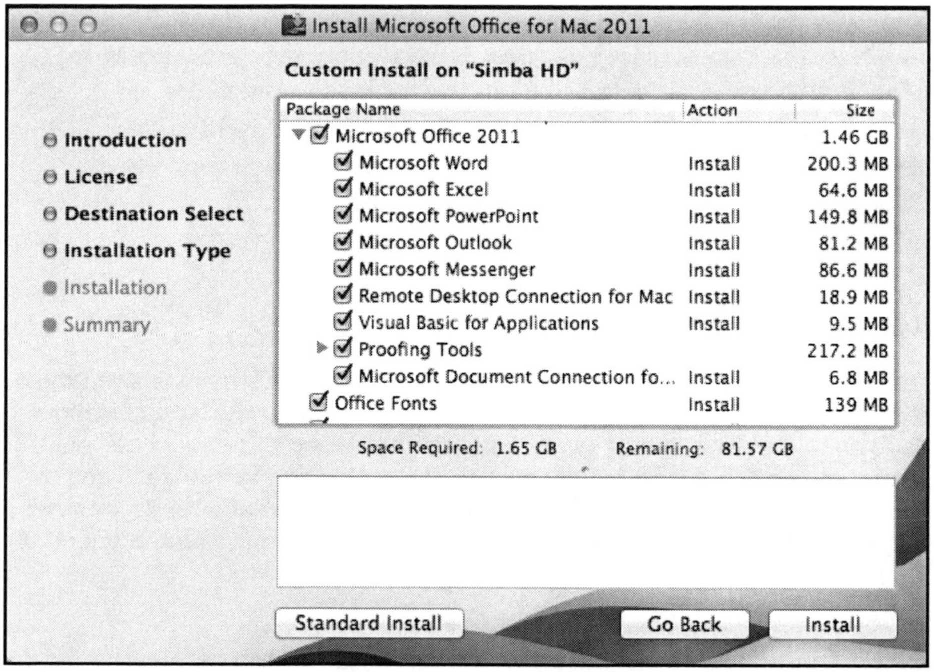

Figure 6–10. *The Custom Install screen allows you to manually select which components of your software will get installed.*

> **NOTE:** Many applications, such as Microsoft Office 2011, are actually a combination of a few separate applications, so it's not unexpected that these kinds of apps offer lots of options on the customize screen. This is not uncommon even for "applications" that we might at first assume are just single applications. In general, if given the option, I always like to click the Customize option just to see what's getting installed and what my options actually are.

Depending on the package, the custom options available to you will vary greatly, but generally the Custom Install screen will let you add/remove optional components to/from your install, and may also provide a column to customize the installation folder on the selected install volume (otherwise, the default install will be either directly in the Applications folder or in a subfolder in the Applications folder).

Whether you choose the standard install or a custom install, once you click the Install button, the installation will begin (though often you will be prompted to enter an administrator password before the install will begin).

When the installation is complete, you will often be presented with a screen letting you know that your installation was successful (and depending on the install, you may be asked to restart your computer).

> **NOTE:** An application package, like many applications, is actually a bundle of various pieces. To look inside a package, select **Show Package Contents** from the contextual menu. One particularly interesting file you will find inside is the BOM file (usually called `Archive.bom`). What's interesting about this is that it contains a listing of all the application parts and where they go. To view this information, use the `lsbom` command-line tool.

Removing Applications

Completely uninstalling applications is often a bit more complicated than installing them. Certain applications include an uninstaller application (and certain installer applications likewise include an uninstall option). If this is the case, then using this should be your first step. Otherwise, the first step is simply moving the application to the Trash and emptying it. Either of these steps generally removes the application effectively; however, applications tend to leave behind some additional traces that you may want to get rid of.

> **NOTE:** AppZapper (`http://appzapper.com/`) and CleanApp (`www.syniumsoftware.com/cleanapp/`) are two applications that can help remove applications completely. When you wish to uninstall an application, simply drag the application file into AppZapper or CleanApp, and let them scour your system to automatically remove all (or most) traces of the application.

> **NOTE:** Applications that were installed through the App Store can be deleted from Launchpad or the Finder. To delete an App Store application from Launchpad, you can either drag it into the Trash from Launchpad or click and hold the icon in Launchpad until a small *X* badge appears over the icon (the icons will all begin to wiggle as well). Clicking the small *X* badge will delete the application. The *X* badge will only appear on applications installed from the App Store.

> **CAUTION:** Removing an App Store application from Launchpad will delete the application.

CAUTION: Once the application file is removed, the application is gone. There is no immediate need to scour through your system to remove all the remnants of all deleted applications, and when you start digging around in Library folders there is always the risk of deleting the wrong file. Accidentally deleting an important file in one of the Library folders can result in bad things that range from a minor inconvenience to your computer failing. If you have any doubt about what you are deleting, it may be best not to do it.

Cache Files, Preferences, and Support Files

The first place to look for leftover files is in your ~/Library folder, particularly in the Caches folder, the Preferences folder, and the Application Support folder.

The Application Support folder is a common place for applications to store all sorts of items that help them function. This should be stop one. Just take a look and see if the application you are removing has a support folder here (it will usually have the same name as the application itself). If so, you may delete it.

NOTE: Before you delete support files, make sure you have any information that the application was storing for you backed up.

NOTE: Some applications will create their own support folder in your ~/Library folder rather than in the Application Support subfolder.

After you clean out any application support files, check the ~/Library/Caches folder. Here, many applications (especially network-enabled apps) store temporary cache files. These can take up lots of space, so you don't want to leave any unused cache files lying around.

NOTE: While cache files can provide a significant boost in application performance and are generally something you want keep unaltered for applications you plan to keep around, occasionally a cache file will cause some issues for an application. Because of this, deleting an application's cache is often one of the common troubleshooting steps in attempting to resolve application errors. While cache files are useful, they are rarely necessary, and if you delete one, the application will recreate it next time it's running.

> **CAUTION:** It's never a good idea to remove a cache file while the application that it belongs to is still running.

The next place to look is your ~/Library/Preferences folder. This folder keeps track of all your personal preferences for all your applications and many other system features; and every application, even if just launched once and closed, is likely to have created a file here. Finding the appropriate preference file is a bit tricky. Traditionally, there was no specific naming convention for preference files, so they were usually named after the application. Additionally, certain software developers would (and still do) create a folder here to store the preferences for all their applications (because some applications share preferences among similar applications). Today, however, there is a specific naming convention for most preference files that uses a reverse top-level domain for the developer, followed by the name of the application, followed by some subinformation if needed. So, for example, all the preference files for Apple products would follow the format com.apple.*appname*.*subpref*. Usually, these will end with a .plist extension, indicating the type of file is a property list. Once you locate the appropriate preference for your deleted application, you may likewise delete it.

> **NOTE:** Preference files are interesting to take a peek at. Xcode, if you installed it, makes browsing and editing these .plist files easy. Most .plist files are written in XML, which can be viewed in any text editor as well. While you should exercise some caution with preference files, you may discover preferences for certain applications that aren't otherwise accessible (hidden preferences).

> **NOTE:** While it's not recommended that you regularly delete preference files, if you do mistakenly delete one, it essentially resets the application back to the first time you used it. With some apps, this may cause no noticeable difference; with others, you may need to go through the setup or registration process again. While this may be inconvenient, it's rarely a big problem.

> **NOTE:** Occasionally, an application may create some of these files in the /Library folder as well. Feel free to delete these.

Frameworks, Components, and Receipts

Besides the extra items mentioned previously that are installed and created by applications, a number of applications may install some additional support files. These include special development frameworks, special components, and contextual menu items. Most of these items can be safely deleted; however, you should use care when doing so.

Components (found in the Components subdirectory of a Library folder) are generally not needed when you remove the application they are associated with either. The only problem is that these items are often named in such a way that it's hard to determine what component is attached to what application, and deleting the wrong one can cause an existing application to fail. In general, if in doubt, leave it alone. If, however, you are sure that you no longer need a component, you may remove it.

Frameworks are trickier. One application may install a third-party framework, and a subsequent application you install may also use that framework, so even if you delete the initial application that installed the framework, by removing the framework you could damage another application. As such, I generally recommend against uninstalling any frameworks unless you are absolutely sure that it's safe. Other than taking up some disk space, an unused framework won't interfere with your system in any way.

Finally, most installer packages leave behind a *receipt* (which is a copy of the package file) in the /Library/Receipts folder. When you delete an application, it's safe to delete any package files here associated with it. Removing receipts for existing applications could, however, affect the ability to upgrade the application in the future—and many update packages use receipt data to determine the necessity or eligibility for an upgrade.

Other Hidden Application Files

The last types of files that may be installed along with the application are hidden or obscure files. These files are installed for one of two reasons. First, some applications install files that are accessible from the command line—while these files are not normally viewable from the Finder, they are not specifically hidden from you (often applications will check with you before installing command-line tools). The other reason applications install hidden or obscure files is specifically so you don't find them; this is usually for licensing reasons and to prevent you from pirating the software or reusing timed-out demo versions of software.

The "hidden" command-line tools (which really aren't hidden; they just aren't immediately visible) can easily be removed from the command line (this is covered later in the book, beginning in Chapter 23). The other files—the ones that are actually intentionally hidden—are problematic. While they generally don't affect your system in any way (other than restricting the use of a particular application), the idea of them lying around bothers people.

While there are no specific instructions for finding and removing all of these intentionally hidden files, there are some suggestions:

■ Look around your file system using the command line. Lots of files that are hidden from the Finder are easily revealed from the command line. If you find files in a Library folder or subfolder at the command line that you don't see in the Finder, they are probably being hidden.

■ If you are really stumped, have an extra hard disk that you can use, and some time on your hands. Create two partitions on the disk and install a clean system on each. Then install the suspected application on one partition and compare the resulting file systems. If you do this correctly, then any additional files on the application partition belong to the application. (There are a number of ways of creating directory lists, including all files, and then comparing the lists using a variety of command-line and text-based tools.)

■ Finally (and this should probably be the first step you try), search the Internet for information about the application and hidden files. As with most things, it's unlikely that you're the first person to encounter this situation, and perhaps the answers you are looking for are already out there.

NOTE: Even though you might not want these hidden files around once you remove the associated application, if you are currently using the application, it's likely that you need these files for it to work correctly, so use caution here and don't delete hidden files just because they are hidden—you probably won't like the results.

Summary

There are thousands of Mac OS X applications available for most computer tasks you can conceive of, but before you start filling up your computer with every application you can find, let's take a look at what you already have. In the next chapter we will look more closely at a few of the applications included with Lion.

Chapter 7

Lion's Applications

Depending on how Lion found itself on your computer, the applications you will find installed on said computer will vary. If you upgraded your computer from a previous version of Mac OS X, then all of your existing applications should be present and accounted for. If you purchased a new Mac that came with Lion, then it should also have iLife installed, plus any optional software you chose to have preinstalled. If you installed Lion on a clean, formatted volume, then you will only get the software that comes with Lion. Beyond essential operating system applications such as the Finder, Launchpad, App Store, and so on, Lion includes a useful collection of additional software including Mail, Safari, FaceTime, Address Book, iCal, iTunes, Photo Booth, Dictionary, and more. In the next section of this book we will cover the contact, communication, and Internet applications, and beyond that we will cover many of utilities and development tools, but that still leaves us with some fun and useful applications to cover. In this chapter we will provide an introduction to these applications, including

- iTunes
- QuickTime
- Preview
- Photo Booth

iTunes

iTunes (Figure 7–1) was originally designed as a simple music library and playback application. It has since moved beyond just music, and today, combined with the iTunes Store, iTunes can download and play back Internet streaming radio, movies, and TV shows, and it can even be used to purchase and download applications for installation on your iPhone or iPod touch. Combined with an Apple TV or one of many Apple AirPort products, you can even use iTunes to stream music and video around your network.

While iTunes is feature rich, it's still easy to use. The iTunes toolbar provides the basic controls to start, stop, and control the media playback, while the main window area is designed to select and manage your media.

The main window provides a column along the left side to select your media libraries (sorted by type) and your playlists, along with sections for the iTunes Store and Ping (a new social networking feature), and the Genius feature. The main view area to the right is where you can view your media in a number of different views (selectable via the view toggle in the toolbar): List view (Figure 7–1), Album List view (Figure 7–2), Grid view (Figure 7–3), and Cover Flow view (Figure 7–4). This area also allows you to work with the other features. Finally there is a new optional sidebar that provides your most recent Ping activity.

> **TIP:** With List view you can also display a media browser by selecting **View > Column Browser > (Show/Hide) Column Browser** (Command-B). The Column Browser makes it very easy to find the music you are looking for by allowing you to search by artist, genre, and album at the same time. The version of iTunes that ships with Lion allows a great deal of flexibility with the Column Browser. Not only do you have control over what columns to show, but you can adjust the position of the columns to be located to the left of your media list or in the traditional top view.

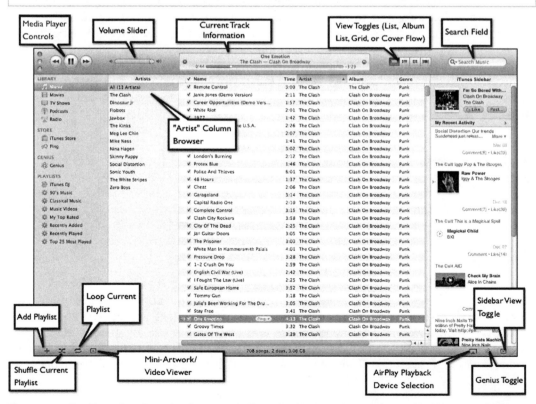

Figure 7–1. *The iTunes interface showing a music library in List view with a single "Artists" Column Browser*

Figure 7–2. *Viewing your iTunes library in Album List view groups songs by "Album by Artist."*

Figure 7–3. *Grid view presents a view of all of your albums.*

Figure 7–4. *Cover Flow view lets you "flip through" album covers to find what you are looking for. Also, in certain modes, like iTunes DJ mode, it can provide visual cues to what artists are coming up next.*

NOTE: The views, while not exactly the same, are similar for all types of iTunes media (movies, TV shows, podcasts, radio, etc.).

Importing Media into iTunes

In order to take advantage of iTunes, you must first import your media into it. The way this is done depends on what sort of media you are starting with. If you already have a collection of supported digital media files (including MP3, AAC [Advanced Audio Coding], and MOV), then you can use the File > Import... command from the menu bar (though drag and drop is often easier).

NOTE: The Advanced tab in the iTunes preferences contains a number of options that are relevant to importing media. For example, you may want to select the "Copy files to iTunes Music folder when adding to library" and "Keep iTunes Music folders organized" options prior to importing any media.

iTunes will also let you import music directly from CDs into your music collection. When iTunes is running, if you insert a music CD into your SuperDrive, iTunes will ask if you'd like to import the CD to your collection. When importing, iTunes will take the music files from your CD and convert them to a new digital format. By default iTunes will convert your music to high-quality AAC files, which are not only suitable for iTunes playback, but also compatible with most modern mobile audio devices, including iPads, iPods, and iPhones. From the General tab in the iTunes preferences, you can adjust the behavior of iTunes when you insert a CD, and you can click the Import Settings... button to open a dialog that will allow you a great deal of flexibility in choosing what digital format iTunes will import your music into. Depending on your needs and desires, you can import CDs in various AAC, MP3, AIFF, WAV, and Apple Lossless (an uncompressed format for maximum sound quality) formats.

> **NOTE:** Which settings are best for importing your CDs is mostly a personal choice. If you are a true audiophile with lots of hard drive space, then of course Apple Lossless format is your best choice (it makes an exact copy of the audio with no loss in quality whatsoever, yet still occupies only half the space as a CD audio file). For everyone else, it becomes a space, quality, and compatibility issue. AAC and MP3 are both compatible with most digital media players; however, MP3 supports many older audio devices that AAC does not. Many people feel that AAC provides better playback quality at the same compression over MP3 (and at higher compression I tend to agree). I find that 256 Kbps AAC (the default iTunes Plus file format) provides excellent audio files while saving considerable disk space over uncompressed (or lossless) formats, while 128 Kbps AAC provides good enough sound quality for most situations and allows you to cram lots of music onto your iPod.

> **NOTE:** When you insert your CD, if you are connected to the Internet, iTunes will seek out information about the CD you inserted and automatically fill in the CD and track details (unless you turned this feature off in the iTunes preferences). If for some reason the details are wrong, or you'd like to change them, then select the track (or tracks) you wish to alter, and select **Get Info** from the shortcut menu. The Get Info box will not only reveal more information about the tracks and album, but will allow you to freely edit the information.

A third way to get music into your iTunes library is to buy it from the iTunes Store (Figure 7–5) (formerly know as the iTunes Music Store before Apple started selling videos and mobile applications there).

The iTunes Store, which now ranks as one of the leading music retailers in the world, provides a huge selection of music new and old, along with an ever-increasing selection of movies, TV shows, music videos, and audio books. Most of this is for sale, although there are occasionally freebies available for download.

Figure 7–5. *The iTunes Store in iTunes*

To buy music from the iTunes Store, you must first sign in with your Apple ID (if you have a MobileMe account, that info is also your Apple ID unless you've previously registered using some other information).

ITUNES STORE FILES, DRM, AND ITUNES PLUS

In the past, all the files you purchased from the iTunes Store were "protected" using a method of digital rights management (DRM) called FairPlay. As far as DRM goes, FairPlay is fairly lenient, allowing any purchased files to be transferred and played on five different computers (the same five for all purchases, and each computer must be authorized). It also allows a playlist with a particular song to be burned to seven audio CDs, it allows unlimited syncs to iPods and iPhones, and it allows the ability to stream the items to Apple AirPort Expresses and Apple TVs.

However, over time, Apple has started distributing some items not only free of DRM, but also of a higher quality than traditional iTunes music files. These files are called iTunes Plus files, and are common 256 Kbps AAC files. Today, all music (but not video) purchased from Apple's iTunes Store is distributed in the iTunes Plus format. Also, Apple has made it possible (for a small fee) to upgrade your old FairPlay Files to iTunes Plus, though if you choose not to, the FairPlay files will continue to work as they always have.

By the way, the iTunes Plus files do contain embedded information about who purchased the file, which should not bother anyone who wishes to use the files legitimately, but could be used to help identify people who are taking their purchases straight to BitTorrent or some other file-sharing system.

> **NOTE:** While you can easily export your own iMovies and other QuickTime movies so that they will appear in iTunes (and sync with your iPod/iPhone), Apple doesn't provide a way to import DVDs into iTunes. This could be because Apple sells movies on the iTunes Store, but it's unlikely. More likely is that importing movies from DVDs is somewhat legally ambiguous. From a technical standpoint, it's perfectly legal to make a copy of a movie you own—however, to make a copy of a DVD, you must decode the content that is actually encrypted on the disk, which may run afoul of the Digital Millennium Copyright Act (DMCA, which makes it illegal to circumvent access control mechanisms protecting copyrighted works except under certain circumstances). Many people may justify that making a copy for personal use falls into the exemption category, but the movie industry and some others tend to disagree. Either way, if you wish to do this, it's usually a two-step process: ripping the DVD (or converting the files on the DVD for use on your hard drive), and then converting the files into a format more suitable for playback on other devices. To rip a DVD, I currently recommend RipIt (`http://ripitapp.com/`), but only you can decide if the $18.99 licensing fee is worth it to you. HandBrake (`http://handbrake.fr/`) is another excellent tool for converting a DVD file to the iPhone-ready M4V format; however, the newest version removes that ability to rip DVDs natively.

Creating Playlists

Once you have some music in your iTunes library, you may want to create playlists of your favorite tunes for specific occasions. iTunes provides a number of interesting ways to create playlists. The most basic playlist is one you create yourself by selecting each song from your library and then adding it. To create one of these playlists, simply click the + button in the lower-left corner of the iTunes main window; this will create a blank playlist for you to name and add any songs you wish (using drag and drop).

iTunes also has the ability to create *smart playlists*. These are like smart folders in that you select some search criteria, and iTunes will automatically populate the smart playlist with songs that match the criteria. iTunes comes with a number of common smart playlists already (Recently Played, Recently Added, My Top Rated, and more). To create your own, hold down the Option key, and the + button you would use to add a regular playlist will turn into a gear icon. Clicking this gear button will open up a dialog box for you to name and define your own smart playlist.

One final way to create a playlist is using iTunes Genius feature. The iTunes Genius feature attempts to analyze your music collection so that you can pick any song to base a playlist on. iTunes, using the Genius feature, will attempt to create a playlist of songs that mesh well with the song you started with. Additionally, upon analyzing your music library, the Genius feature may create its own Genius mixes based on the songs in your library. (This feature will also be used to provide you with a lit of music in the iTunes Store that you may want to purchase.)

> **NOTE:** iTunes Genius doesn't just create playlists, it analyzes your entire library. This information is also used by the iTunes Store to help make recommendations for music you may wish to buy, and also to help feed the data that devises the Genius results in the first place. This means two things: first, you will need an iTunes Store account for this to work (you'll also need an account if you want iTunes to automatically attempt to download album covers for you); and second, the information you send will be used to help sell you stuff. Now, since the personal data is restricted to your own account, there really isn't an immediate privacy issue here, but if you don't want people collecting marketing information about your music likes and dislikes and then using it to try to sell you stuff (though really in a noninvasive way), then you may not want to activate this feature. (Personally I use it and find it fairly interesting).

Sharing and Streaming iTunes Media

iTunes allows you to share your iTunes library with others on your network. You can enable this from the Sharing tab in the iTunes preferences. This will allow your library to show in the iTunes libraries of other people on your network. Likewise, you can view and play songs from other users on your network who are sharing their libraries.

> **NOTE:** DRM-protected iTunes Store files can't be shared unless the receiving computer is one of the five computers authorized to play back your iTunes DRMed files. In fact, if you attempt to play one from an unauthorized computer, the music will stop.

Besides sharing your files, you can also stream your files. Music files can be streamed to other devices that utilize Apple's AirPlay protocol, such as AirPort and AirPort Expresses equipped with speakers, as well as Apple TV systems. Video can be streamed to Apple TV systems. To stream your files, select the output source from the drop-down menu in the lower-right corner of iTunes.

To fully take advantage of Apple TV with iTunes, you must also set up Apple TV in the Apple TV iTunes preferences.

> **NOTE:** AirPlay (formerly known as AirTunes) is a protocol that allows you to stream music from your iTunes library to other devices. Current receiving devices include AirPorts and AppleTVs, as well as a growing number of third-party devices.

Syncing iPods and iPhones

When you connect an iPod or iPhone to your computer, the device will show up as a device in your iTunes library. Selecting the device will allow you to configure the settings, which will range from simple for an old iPod shuffle (Figure 7–6) to more complex for an iPhone (Figure 7–7). After you set your settings, click the Apply button to resync your device with the new settings.

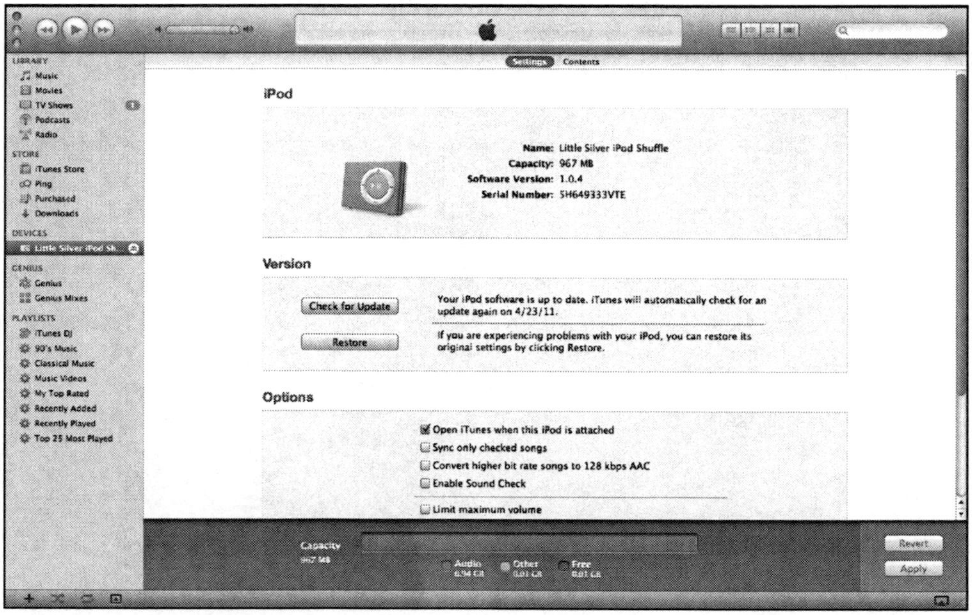

Figure 7–6. *Device settings allow you to update and apply settings to iPods and iPhones. For an iPod shuffle, there aren't too many options.*

Figure 7–7. *Due to its enhanced capabilities, iTunes displays quite a few more options when an iPhone is connected to it.*

If you use an iPod touch, iPhone, or iPad with iTunes, you can take advantage of iTunes to help manage the applications on your device directly from iTunes. Clicking the Apps tab will present you with a listing of all available mobile apps on your computer, along with a view of the apps installed on your "i" device (Figure 7–8). From this view you select which apps you want installed, as well as arrange how they will appear on the device. The changes will take effect when you sync your device with iTunes.

Figure 7–8. *iTunes provides a very nice interface for managing mobile apps on iPod touches, iPhones, and iPads.*

QuickTime Player

QuickTime itself falls into two general areas: there are all the QuickTime technologies that exist behind the scenes in the system that make the music play and the videos go, and there's QuickTime Player (Figure 7–9), which provides an application for viewing QuickTime media.

By default, QuickTime Player is simply a viewer for various media types, including, of course, QuickTime movies, but also a wide range of other video, audio, and image formats. Generally, when you double-click a media file that QuickTime Player is set to play back, QuickTime Player will open automatically and start playing the file.

> **NOTE:** QuickTime Player is only one way to play back QuickTime media. QuickTime can also be embedded in web browsers and integrated into other applications (e.g., iTunes is essentially a special-purpose media player based upon QuickTime).

QuickTime also provides the means to extend its capabilities with special plug-in files (called codecs) that allow it to play back other media formats.

Figure 7–9. *A video playing in QuickTime Player*

Beyond media playback, QuickTime Player enables you to create and record new media files right from QuickTime Player by choosing **File** > **New Movie Recording** (Option-Command-N), **File** > **New Audio Recording** (Option-Control-Command-N), or **File** > **New Screen Recording** (Control-Command-N) from QuickTime Player's menu bar This will open a record window to record the media. The screen-recording option, the newest to find its way into QuickTime Player, is especially handy for creating simple screencasts directly from your computer.

> **TIP:** QuickTime certainly isn't the only game in town. While it is an excellent product that works well with a wide range of formats, many popular formats are incompatible with QuickTime. QuickTime itself provides a plug-in API so third parties can create plug-ins that will playback nonnative formats; however, many people who deal with a wide range of different media formats will opt for more professional tools that will handle a wider range of formats. For many users without the budget to invest in professional media tools, the open source VLC Media Player is a simple, well-supported alternative to QuickTime Player. For more information about VLC Media Player and to download it, visit www.videolan.org/vlc/.

Preview

Preview (Figure 7–10) is to PDF and image files what QuickTime Player is to video. It provides an excellent alternative to Adobe's Acrobat Reader for viewing PDF files, complete with support for performing text searches, copying and pasting text from a PDF, viewing encrypted PDFs, creating bookmarks, previewing pages, and using annotation capabilities. Beyond that, it's a multiformat image viewer that allows you to quickly open a wide range of image formats.

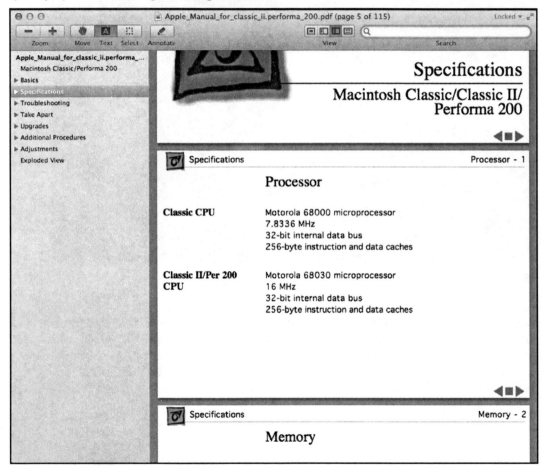

Figure 7–10. *A PDF document open in Preview*

Besides viewing images, Preview also gives you the ability to do some minor image editing, including image color adjustments, cropping, resizing, and saving in an array of image file formats.

Photo Booth

Photo Booth is a fairly silly yet highly entertaining application that takes advantage of the iSight camera (aka FaceTime camera) that is attached to most new Macs (except Mac Pros and Mac minis), as well as built into Apple's line of LED Cinema Displays. When you launch Photo Booth, it will automatically fire up the camera built into your computer and allow you to capture photos or videos.

Once Photo Booth is launched, you can switch between a single picture, four quick pictures (just like a real photo booth!), and a video mode, using the button on the left below the preview area. You can also apply effects to the images or video by clicking the Effects button and scrolling through the effect previews. All the images and videos shot with Photo Booth will scroll across the bottom. Selecting an existing image will open it up in the preview area (Figure 7–11), allowing you to send the image to someone through Mail, add the image to iPhoto, or use the image as your iChat or Account icon.

Figure 7–11. *Photo Booth displaying a snapshot using the Comic Book effect*

Other Default Lion Applications

Lion comes with a number of other applications for various purposes that aren't covered elsewhere in this book. These applications are described in Table 7–1.

Table 7–1. *Other Applications Installed with Lion*

Application	Description
Calculator	This application provides not only a simple calculator mode, but also advanced scientific and programming modes. It also provides conversions to and from many systems of measurement.
Chess	This application provides a 3D chess set that pits you against the computer. It also supports voice recognition, which makes it interesting to play around with.
Dictionary	This is a handy application that provides dictionary, thesaurus, and Wikipedia references for a word or term, either individually or together.
DVD Player	This application provides a great experience for watching DVDs on your Mac.
Stickies	This application allows you to create sticky notes that will appear on your desktop.
TextEdit	This is a simple text editor with some basic word-processing features.

Summary

Besides these basic applications, which range from indispensable to at least sort of interesting, Apple provides a number of other common applications, many of which we talk about in other areas of this book. In the next chapter we will look at connecting to and working on the Internet. There we will introduce a number of additional applications that are included with Lion.

Part **III**

Mac OS X and the Internet

Many of today's most common computer activities revolve around the Internet. Not only does Lion make it easy to connect to the Internet over wired or wireless networks, but it also includes a host of excellent applications for surfing the Web, checking your e-mail, and more. This part of the book will walk you though connecting to the Internet, and then provide you an overview of the included applications and technologies that help you take advantage of it.

## Chapter 8

Connecting to the Internet

One of the first things most people will want to do when they set up a new computer is get it connected to the Internet so they update their Facebook or Twitter status to something like, "Playing with my new computer." In most situations, getting connected to the Internet in Lion is pretty easy, but the steps to do so may differ depending on your situation. In this chapter we will cover

- A brief introduction to networking
- Connecting to the Internet over a broadband connection using Wi-Fi or Ethernet
- Other ways of connecting to the internet
- Setting up Location profiles

By the time you reach the end of this chapter you should be ready to start using Safari, Mail, and other Internet-enabled applications and technologies.

Networking and the Internet, an Introduction

> **NOTE:** Networking technology these days is mostly plug-and-play (or select-and-play, since much networking doesn't even use plugs anymore). In reality you need to know very little to get connected. If you are comfortable with just jumping right in, feel free to jump ahead in this chapter for just the info you need to move on. If you run into trouble or decide to learn more about the process, come back and start reading from here. We will be covering networking in more depth in Part 8 of this book. There we will discover that, while accurate, in most cases, our description of networking here represents a fairly simple network architecture that applies to many common home and small business networks, but is often an oversimplification of many larger networks. The Internet itself is in fact a highly complex collection of servers and networks, the scope of which exceeds the range of this book.

Today most people connect to the Internet either through a wired Ethernet connection, or more often through Wi-Fi. In most situations when you make such a connection from your computer you are joining a local network or *local area network (LAN)*. To complete the connection to the Internet there is usually a network device called a router or some other device that takes date from your LAN and passes it up to a *wide area network* (WAN), which in many cases is the Internet (Figure 8–1).

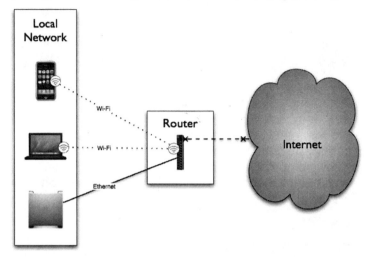

Figure 8–1. *In most situations you will be connecting your computer to a router. The router will then pass data from your local network to and from the Internet.*

NOTE: Figure 8–1 represents the router as a single unit. Many Internet access providers provide subscribers a single such unit that provides all the necessary pieces: Wi-Fi, a wired hub, a firewall, and so on. There are many situations where this unit will be made up of many different individual components.

In today's world of high-speed Internet, the connection that rests between your router and the Internet is referred to as a broadband connection. Table 8–1 covers some of today's prominent broadband technologies.

Table 8-1. *Common Broadband Networking Technologies*

Technology	Description
DSL	Digital Subscriber Line (DSL) is, along with cable, one of the most popular broadband technologies used today. DSL sends a digital signal over copper phone lines, making it easily available to many existing phone customers. There are a number of variants of DSL; the most common today is Asymmetric DSL (ADSL). The big drawback to ADSL is that its speeds start to diminish over distance, making this technology less effective for rural areas. ADSL also provides fast download speeds while limiting its upload speed; this makes it suitable for most home users but less useful for businesses. Symmetric DSL (SDSL), on the other hand, provides the same upload and download speeds. ADSL is commonly referred to as residential DSL, while business DSL is usually SDSL.
VDSL	VDSL is a newer, "very-high-speed" DSL technology that is beginning to be rolled out all over the world. This DSL technology is currently able to provide up to 100 Mbps upload and download speeds over traditional POTS copper wiring. As with DSL, this speed diminishes over distance; still, VDSL provides higher speeds and longer distances than earlier versions of DSL (in the United States, AT&T is rolling out VDSL as U-Verse, and Verizon calls its implementation FiOS).
Cable	Cable broadband is another big broadband technology used today. This provides access over existing cable TV lines. Unlike DSL, cable broadband does not lose its effectiveness over distances, and traditionally has been able to provide faster data speeds than DSL; on the other hand, cable is also generally more expensive, most cable companies provide cable broadband only to cable TV subscribers, raising the costs associated with cable even higher, and also most cable services are shared over an area, so your access speeds may be affected by high usage of others in your area.
ISDN	ISDN is one of the original broadband technologies available to consumers. It provides faster-than-dial-up speeds; however, there are lots of higher costs associated with it. ISDN has for the most part been replaced with other less expensive, faster technologies today.
T1	T1 lines (also called DS1 and E1) are broadband, high-speed connections that are common in many commercial offices. Originally, T1 connections were special telephone lines designed to carry voice communications for large organizations; however, early in the expansion of the Internet, digital T1 lines were used to provide high-speed Internet connections. T1 lines are still in use in many businesses for both voice and data. The downside to T1 lines is that even today they are regulated and require special lines to be run to connect the provider with the user. This makes their costs high. There are also T2 and T3 lines, which are similar yet faster than the T1 lines.

Technology	Description
SONET	Synchronous optical networking (SONET) technologies are slowly replacing T1 as the commercial data connection of choice. Using fiber-optic lines to carry the digital information allows OC-x technologies to provide extremely high-speed data throughput over long distances (though at a very high cost).
Wi-Fi	Wi-Fi is a blanket term that covers wireless 802.11 technologies, including Apple's AirPort technologies. Although the range of Wi-Fi is relatively low, in high-density and commercial areas it is quite popular. (Being short range, Wi-Fi is usually used in conjunction with a hardwired broadband technology such as DSL, cable, T1, or OC-x.)
WiMAX	WiMAX is a new emerging wireless broadband technology that attempts to provide faster speeds and greater range than Wi-Fi.
LTE	LTE (Long Term Evolution) is another emerging contender for high-speed wireless networks. Many mobile phone companies, including AT&T, T-Mobile, Vodafone, and Verizon have announced plans for or are currently testing LTE as their next generation (4G) of mobile technology.
Satellite	Satellite broadband provides high-speed access utilizing satellites to provide the communication over great distances. Satellite broadband is generally slightly more expensive and slightly slower than other methods of broadband; it is a viable alternative especially in rural areas where other technologies are unavailable or prohibitively expensive. The disadvantage of satellite broadband is a latency problem where a delay of 500 to 900 milliseconds is added to any other network latency transmitting the signal into space and then back again. Although this is not a big deal for casual Internet usage including web browsing and e-mail, it's a burden for real-time Internet activities such as VoIP (and it's a real killer for online gaming).

Besides the technologies listed in Table 8–1, a range of other technologies are available, and new ideas and technologies are constantly being developed. What's interesting about almost all of these, though, is the following:

■ They all carry IP packets from point A to point B.

■ In a broadband environment, most of these technologies (except in most cases wireless technologies) usually just bridge a gap between the Internet and a router on your end.

Because of this, the actual broadband technology has little to do with how you set up your computer to take advantage of it. When the broadband connection enters your home, office, or company, it is usually run into an Ethernet or Wi-Fi router, which in turn you connect to with your computer using standard TCP/IP networking.

TCP/IP NETWORKING

TCP/IP networking consists of a collection of networking protocols collectively known as the Internet Protocol (IP) suite. In very general terms, Transmission Control Protocol (TCP) is responsible for application data carried over the Internet, and Internet Protocol (IP) is responsible for communication data. So although TCP carries the message, IP makes sure the message gets where it needs to go. When you configure your networking, you are essentially setting up your computer as a uniquely identifiable destination on the Internet for IP to successfully deliver TCP data to your computer.

The most common IP protocol used today is version 4. IPv4, in theory, addresses each computer on the Internet with a unique address made up of four series of numbers, called *octets*, that range from 0 to 255. A typical IP address may look like 153.29.250.112.

For those of you keeping count, this means IPv4 can address, in theory, only a bit more than 4 billion devices. When this was conceived in the early 1980s, a device was a computer, and 4 billion seemed like a lot. Today not only are there a lot more computers, but there are other devices such as phones, watches, automobiles, and more, that use TCP/IP. In addition, a significant chunk of those 4 billion address are reserved for special uses, and you may notice a problem . . . we have run out of unique IPv4 addresses.

Although there are a number of ways to extend IPv4 (IP Masquerading, NAT, and other technologies that are common today), a new version of IP, IPv6, has been defined and is currently being deployed. (The US government was pushing for deployment for all civilian and defense vendors by the summer of 2008, clearly that has past and IPv4 is still very much in use.) For comparison, IPv6 supports approximately 3.14 undecillion addresses (undecillion is 10 to the 36th power (or add 36 0s) . . . either way it's a big number).

Configuring Your Mac for a Broadband Connection

For your Mac to function on the Internet, it must have the following information:

A qualified IP address: IP addresses are discussed in the "TCP/IP Networking" sidebar; this is a unique address that identifies your computer on the Internet so that all information being sent to your computer actually makes it there. You cannot (usually) just make up an IP address; it must be assigned, or else it may not work.

A subnet mask: A subnet mask is used to separate the network address from the host address. This can be further used within a network to create subnets; breaking up a host address into subnets allows more effective routing of IP traffic. An example of an IPv4 subnet mask is 255.255.255.0, and any IP address that shares the first three octets in the IP address is part of the same subnet. If all that sounds foreign to you, don't worry, just use the subnet mask your ISP or network administrator gave you.

A gateway address (or router): The router address (also known as a gateway address) is the IP address of the next upstream router.

A DNS server address: The DNS (Domain Name System) server is usually the primary server for your subnet that is responsible for providing DNS services. A DNS server is responsible for translating a domain name (that is, apple.com) into an IP address (in other words, 17.254.3.183). You can list multiple DNS servers if you would like, and if the first one is unable to resolve a domain name, then the next one listed will be consulted.

Search domains (optional): Search domains are an optional list of domains to search if a domain address cannot be resolved by any of the DNS servers. This can provide a shortcut on some networks as well, since it will allow you to address a computer by the host name alone.

While this seems like a lot of information, most routers and networks these days utilize DHCP (Dynamic Host Configuration Protocol) that will automatically assign each of these pieces of data with no necessary input or additional configuration needed from you the user.

> **NOTE:** IPv4 has set aside a number of IP address blocks as private addresses (10.x.x.x, 172.16.x.x, and 192.168.x.x). These private IP addresses are for the creation of private networks that utilize IP. Many routers (and firewalls) take advantage of these private IP addresses to perform network address translation (NAT, aka network masquerading). This allows the router to be assigned a valid Internet IP address yet assign all the computers behind it private IP addresses. The router can then act as a gateway between the private network and the Internet, providing each computer connected to the router with full Internet access without a dedicated IP address. Most current implementations of NAT provide Internet clients with complete functionality. Server processes running behind NAT, however, need special considerations and are limited. This can be used advantageously from a security point of view, and in fact, many firewalls use NAT combined with port forwarding to hide the actual server from the Internet.

> **NOTE:** Port forwarding allows the router or firewall facing the Internet to masquerade as a server while server requests are actually being passed along to other systems on the private network. This can be set up so specific services, which use specific ports, can be passed to specific systems. So, all e-mail traffic using ports 25 (SMTP), 110 (POP3), and 143 (IMAP4) could point to one server behind the router, while all web traffic using port 80 (HTTP) would be directed to another.

There are two primary ways to connect your Mac to a broadband connection: Ethernet and Wi-Fi. Today all shipping Macs include Wi-Fi, and with the exception of the MacBook Air they all include an Ethernet port as well. Provided you are connecting to a network that utilizes DHCP, for an Ethernet connection all that should be required is to plug your computer into the network using an Ethernet cable. For a Wi-Fi network you will need to select the proper Wi-Fi network you are connecting to and, depending on the security, you may need to add a Wi-Fi password. Let's look closer at connecting to a Wi-Fi network.

> **NOTE:** Apple does provide a USB Ethernet device for the MacBook Air if an Ethernet connection is a necessity for you.

Connecting to a Wi-Fi Network

While configuring a network (or not provided DHCP is present) is the same whether you are connection to an Ethernet or Wi-Fi network, the connection process differs. "Plugging in" to an Ethernet connection is a simple as plugging the network cable into your computer (we are of course assuming that the other end of this cable leads to an active router of some sort). Because of the physical nature of an Ethernet connection, access control and security can be controlled by physically controlling the "wire." Wi-Fi on the other hand is much more complex, since there are no wires, presumably anyone with a Wi-Fi-enabled device could connect to the Wi-Fi network. Because of this, additional security standards have been implemented in most Wi-Fi networks to both control access and secure wireless data. This added security makes connection to a Wi-Fi network a two-step process that we will walk through here.

CONNECTING TO A WI-FI NETWORK

1. The first step is to assure that your Wi-Fi network is turned on. From the System Preferences Network pane (Figure 8–2) make sure Wi-Fi is selected from the Interface List on the left, and select Turn Wi-Fi On from the box on the top right.

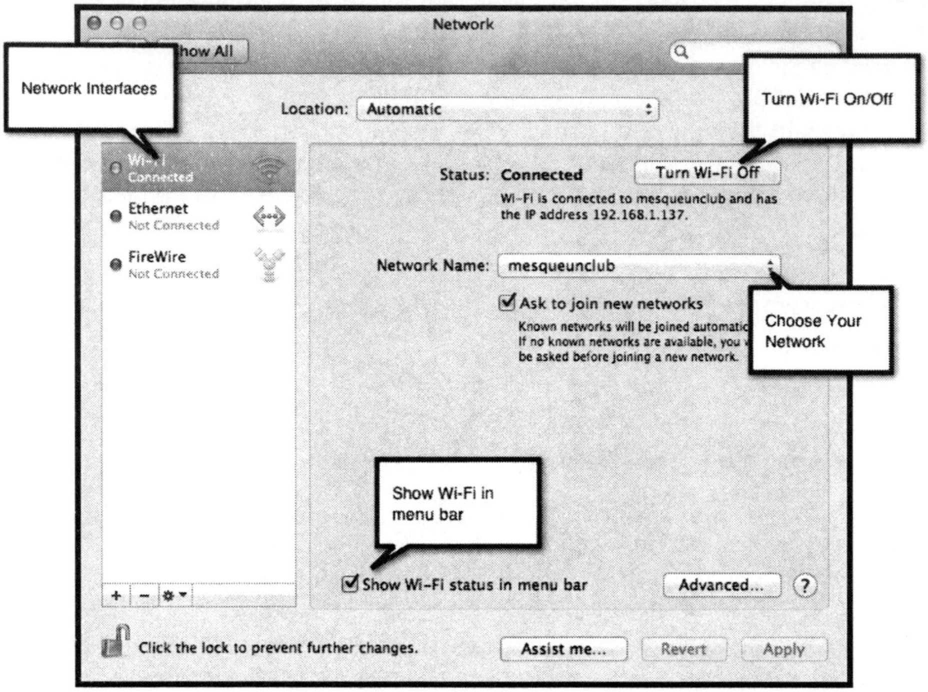

Figure 8–2. *You can access all the Wi-Fi options from the System Preference Network pane.*

   2.   Once Wi-Fi is turned on, clicking the Network Name menu will reveal a list of all
            visible Wi-Fi networks reachable by your computer (Figure 8–3). Select the name of
            the network you wish to join.

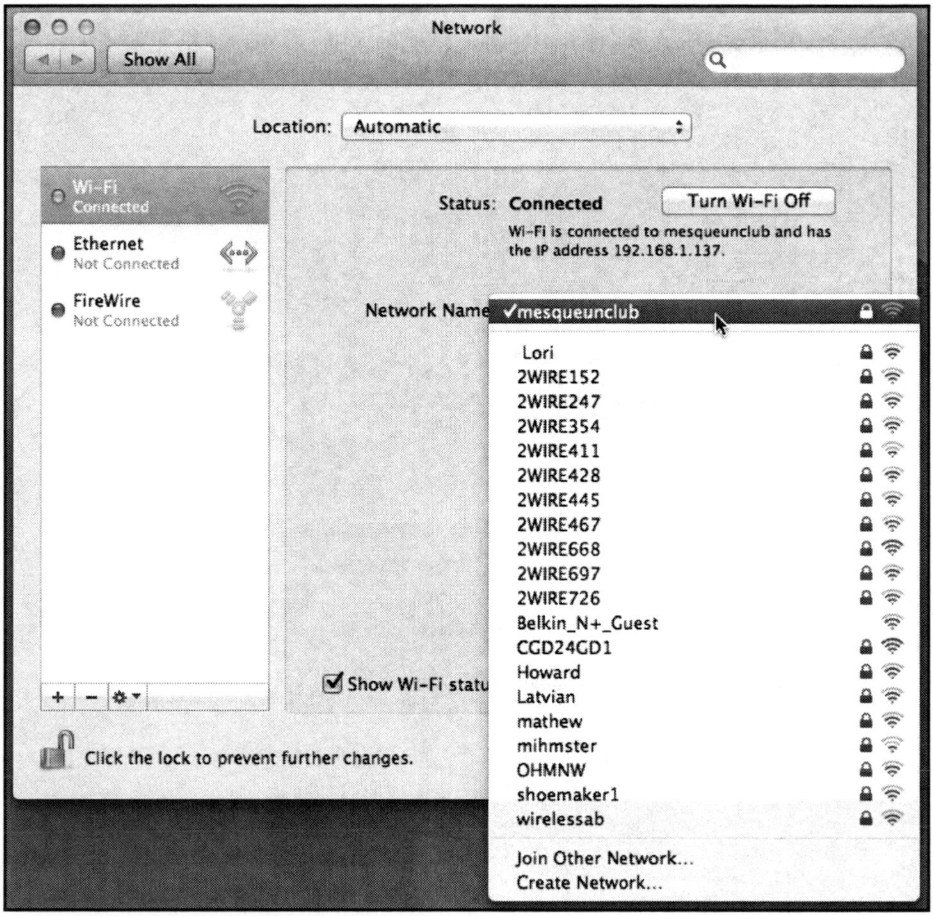

Figure 8–3. *The Network Name menu will show you all the visible Wi-Fi networks in your area.*

NOTE: To the right of the network name (also known as the *SSID*), two icons may appear. The first is a lock signifying that the network is protected and will require user authorization to connect to it. If there is no lock, then the network is an open Wi-Fi network. The second icon signifies the signal strength of each network; the more dark bars the stronger the signal.

3. If you select a secured network (one with a lock next to the name), then when you select the network a dialog will appear asking for your credentials (Figure 8–4). In most cases this is a simple password, but some networks require additional credentials and/or certificates. Table 8–2 lists the most common security protocols used for Wi-Fi networks.

The Wi-Fi network "mesqueunclub" requires a WPA2 password.

Password: [   ]

☐ Show password
☑ Remember this network

Cancel   Join

Figure 8–4. *When you attempt to join a secured network, a dialog will appear to walk you through the authentication process; usually this just requires entering a password.*

TIP: WEP passwords are generally hexadecimal strings 10 digits long for 40-bit and 26 digits long for 104-bit keys. Apple, however, tends to use common "password" strings for passwords (which are then converted to hexadecimal strings). The thing is, if you are connecting to a WEP-secured WLAN and are given the hexadecimal key, when you type it into the Password text box, Mac OS X will assume you are entering a text password and convert the string you enter from a normal text string to a hexadecimal string. To prevent this from happening, you must start the hexadecimal string with a $ character. So if you are given 3B-2D-98–AA-32 as a hexadecimal string, you should enter $3B2D98AA32 in the Password box.

Provided your authentication was verified in the last step, at this point you should be connected to the network.

Table 8–2. *Common Wi-Fi Security Protocols*

Security	Description
WEP	Wired Equivalent Privacy (WEP) was written as part of the 802.11 standard to provide access control and data security to WLANs. Standard 64-bit WEP uses a 40-bit encryption key; however, today 128–bit WEP is prevalent and supports a 104-bit encryption key. Although WEP is quite popular and does provide at least some protection from casual eavesdropping, from a security standpoint it is considered broken. Not only are the keys vulnerable (a WEP key can be cracked in a few minutes using readily available software from the Internet), but there are other inherent flaws in WEP that makes it unsuitable for situations where security and data integrity are a priority.
WPA/WPA2	Wi-Fi Protected Access (WPA) was created in response to flaws discovered with WEP, and it was quickly implemented and is based upon the IEEE 802.11i standard (WPA2 fully implements 802.11i, while WPA implements most of it). WPA uses an improved encryption key, making cracking the key significantly more difficult than cracking a WEP key, and improves data integrity checks lacking in WEP. WPA2 further increases the strength of the encryption key. WPA and WPA2 offer two modes of use: a Personal mode and an Enterprise mode. Personal mode works similarly to WEP in that there is a single preshared encryption key (PSK) used. In Enterprise mode a user must first log into a RADIUS server that assigns a dynamic key to that user. Not only does this provide excellent user access control, but by providing a unique key for each user, it provides excellent data security as well.
802.1X	This is an IEEE standard that is part of the same group as 802.11 (though it is not directly related). It is a method of authentication often used in conjunction with WPA2 Enterprise mode when authenticating the user to the RADIUS server.
LEAP	Lightweight Extensible Authentication Protocol (LEAP) was developed by Cisco for Cisco wireless routers. This requires the user to first log in with a username and password to receive a WEP key. Beyond the login, this operates similarly to WEP; as such, it is not used much anymore.
None	It is of course possible to have no security on a WLAN. This is referred to as an *open network*. Most public Wi-Fi access points are open networks (though some require registration and perhaps fees to access the Internet). The most important thing to keep in mind about using an open network is that there is no wireless encryption, so everything you send over the network is potentially viewable by those around you. As such, it's important to use encrypted connections to services you are accessing whenever possible.

ALL WI-FI NETWORKS ARE NOT THE SAME

There are different types of security available for Wi-Fi networks, and while each of these standards falls under the 802.11 standard, they are not all compatible with each other. The current batch of Wi-Fi versions in use today include

802.11b: This was what the original AirPort technology was based on and what most people associate with Wi-Fi. It provides reasonably fast transfer speeds over a reasonably large area. It operates in the 2.4 GHz radio frequency range.

802.11a: 802.11a came out about the same time as 802.11b, provided faster transfer speeds, and used radio frequencies in the 5 GHz range, which cut down on interference from cordless phones, Bluetooth devices, and microwave ovens. However, 802.11a products started shipping late by which time the industry was already implementing 802.11b. As such, 802.11a never really caught on to the extent of 802.11b. (An ironic twist on this is that although Apple has never supported 802.11a, the current AirPort chips included with Intel-based Macs do support 802.11a.) 802.11a is not compatible with 802.11b or 802.11g.

802.11g: 802.11g is 100 percent compatible with 802.11b, but when used with 802.11g devices at both ends, it provides much faster transfer speeds and a slight boost in distance. Apple's AirPort devices (both in computers and base stations) quickly switched from 802.11b to 802.11g (Apple called this AirPort Extreme). The downside with 802.11g is that it still operates in the crowded 2.4 GHz radio frequency range.

802.11n: 802.11n is the newest version of 802.11. 802.11n increases transfer speeds five times (or more) over 802.11g, and doubles the range of 802.11g when used in 802.11n mode with other 802.11n devices. It can work in either the 2.4 or 5.0 GHz radio frequency range. 802.11n devices also can operate in three modes: Legacy, which supports 802.11b/g and 802.11a; Mixed, which supports 802.11b/g, 802.11a, and 802.11n; and then a pure 802.11n mode, which is necessary to take advantage of the increased speed and distances offered by 802.11n. All of Apple's current products use this version of 802.11.

Today most computers as well as many newer Wi-Fi routers support multiple versions of 802.11 to provide maximum speed for supported devices, while still maintaining compatibility with older Wi-Fi devices.

To make viewing and joining Wi-Fi networks faster and easier, a Wi-Fi status menu item is available for your menu bar. To use this, first make sure "Show Wi-Fi status in menu bar" option is checked in the System Preferences Network pane (Figure 8–2). When the Wi-Fi status menu is visible it will provide you with a constant view of the signal strength of your current Wi-Fi network. Clicking the Wi-Fi status icon will open up a menu allowing you to toggle on and off your computer's Wi-Fi radio as well as provide a list of currently available Wi-Fi networks in your area (Figure 8–5).

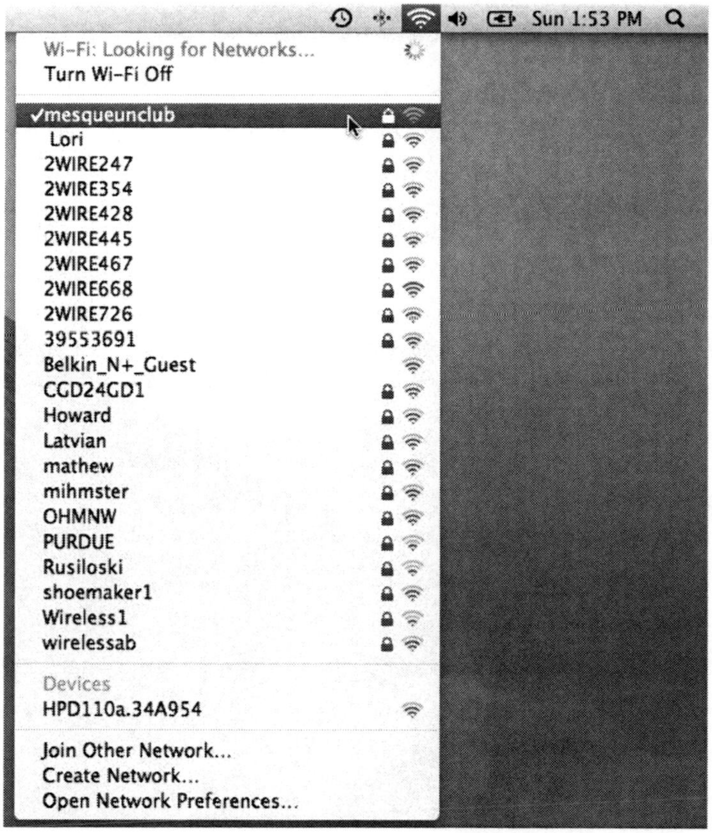

Figure 8–5. *The Wi-Fi status menu on the menu bar provides you with the information and tools to connect to a Wi-Fi network without using the System Preferences.*

TIP: Clicking the Wi-Fi status menu while holding down the Option key will reveal additional information about the Wi-Fi network you are currently connected to.

CAUTION: It is advisable to only connect to Wi-Fi (or other) networks you trust. Many times what appears to be an open Wi-Fi network is actually a *honeypot*, a tempting network that in reality is used to collect information about you, your computers, and your Internet accounts. These types of shady networks are frequent in public places and should be avoided.

Manual Network Configuration

Suppose you plug in your computer to an Ethernet connection or connect to a Wi-Fi network successfully, but for whatever reason you are still not connected to the network or the Internet. What's wrong? There are actually a number of things that could be wrong, but the problem usually comes down to one two things: a problem on the network, or a problem on your computer. Network problems are, unfortunately, outside the scope of this book, but if the network is working fine then the problem may be in your network configuration.

Most often the first sign something is wrong is when you attempt to surf the web of check your e-mail. If you try to browse the Web with Safari it will generally let you know when you are not connected (Figure 8–6).

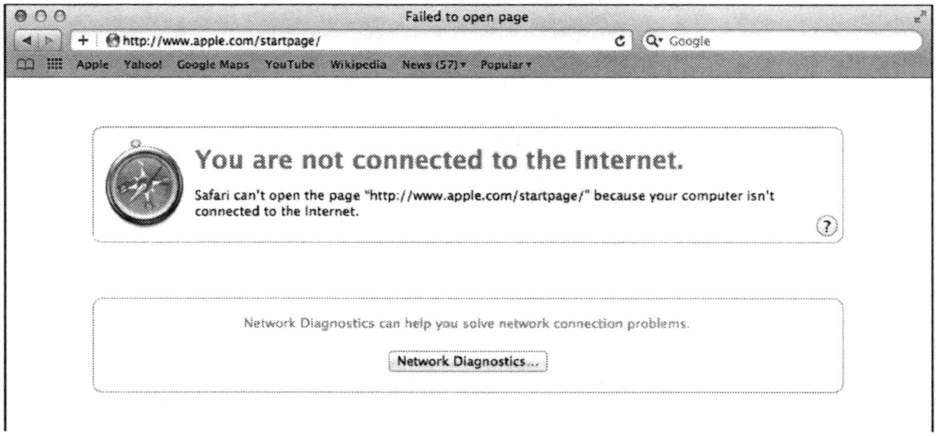

Figure 8–6. *Safari will tell you if it cannot reach the Internet. Clicking the Network Diagnostics... button will launch Mac OS X's Network Diagnostics tool, which will walk you through some steps to repair your network connection.*

When things are wrong with your network connection and Network Diagnostics can't isolate the problem, the next step is to usually go to the System Preferences Network pane. Sometimes just a glance at the System Preferences Network pane can provide a clue as to what's wrong (Figure 8–7).

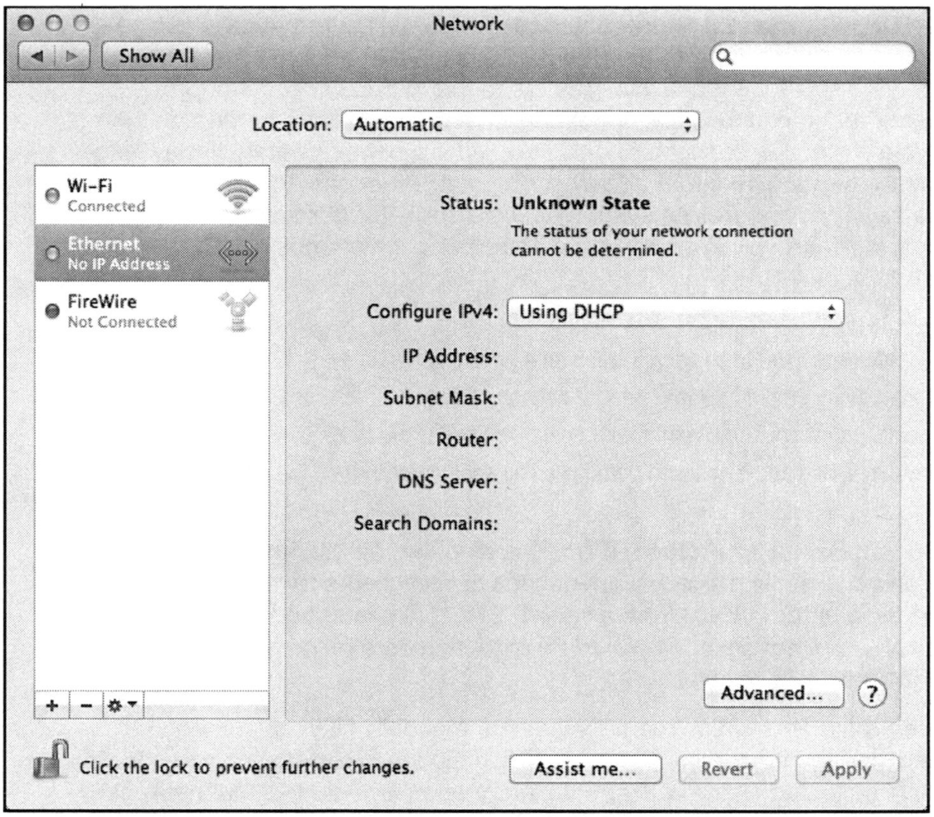

Figure 8–7. *The yellow circle next to the Ethernet interface indicates the computer is connected to a live Ethernet cable, but something is wrong. In this case it tells us "No IP Address"—a clear sign that DHCP isn't working.*

NOTE: After a moment of not detecting an IP address assigned from a network connection, Mac OS X will automatically assign one to the network interface in the 169.254.x.x range, which is used for Apple's Bonjour technology (more widely known as Zeroconf). This would, for example, allow you to connect a number of Macs together, either directly or through a hub to form a small private network.

Once you select the interface you're attempting to configure, you must determine how you wish to configure the network interface. When configuring IPv4 (which is still used most frequently today), you are presented with the following configuration options from the Configure IPv4 drop-down menu:

> **DHCP:** Dynamic Host Configuration Protocol (DHCP) is more and more common these days in almost every environment. Not only does it make setting up a system incredibly easy from the user end, but it also allows reuse of IP addresses and increased manageability from the administrative perspective.

DHCP with manual address: Usually DHCP will automatically assign a computer that connects to it the next available IP address that it has at its disposal. It will lease this address to that particular system for a period of time (and usually continue to renew that lease as long as the system remains connected); however, after a period of time, it may issue the system a different IP address. For most situations, this is fine; however, occasionally a system needs a static (or permanent). This option allows you to pick a static IP address, which most DHCP servers will honor.

> **NOTE:** IP addresses need to be unique; even on a private network, every IP address needs to be different from every other IP address on that network. Because of this, when you manually assign an IP address, you should be careful that it doesn't belong to the block of IP addresses being dynamically assigned and that it isn't being used by another system on the network.

BootP: Bootstrap Protocol (BootP) is an older technology that was created to allow diskless workstations or thin clients to receive an IP address automatically from a server. DHCP is based upon BootP but is much more advanced. It would be extremely rare these days to encounter this option.

Manually: This option requires that you manually fill in all the required networking information. If a manual connection is necessary, you should have collected all the appropriate information (IP Address, subnet mask, router, and maybe DNS information) ahead of time.

Off: This turns off the interface.

Create PPPoE Service: This will prompt you to create a new PPPoE (Point-to-Point Protocol over Ethernet) interface for configuring the PPPoE service. If this is required, your service provider will give you the necessary information for this (username, password, and perhaps a service name).

> **NOTE:** The TCP/IP configuration options are visible from the System Preferences Network pane for many interfaces including Ethernet and Bluetooth, however to access them with others (for example, Wi-Fi), you must click the Advanced... button, which will bring up a dialog box with a number of tabs across the top. Selecting the TCP/IP tab will present you with these configuration options as well. If you must configure DNS, you must click the Advanced... button and select the DNS tab for any interface.

NETWORK DIAGNOSTICS

The Network Diagnostics tool (Figure 8–8), hidden away in the /System/Library/CoreServices folder, can help you troubleshoot and resolve some network issues. It will do this by walking you through a series of steps appropriate to the selected interface, prompting you for information along the way. Usually (but not always), if you work your way through this tool and your connection issues are still not resolved, then the issues you are having are either occurring outside of your computer, or you have entered improper information somewhere along the way.

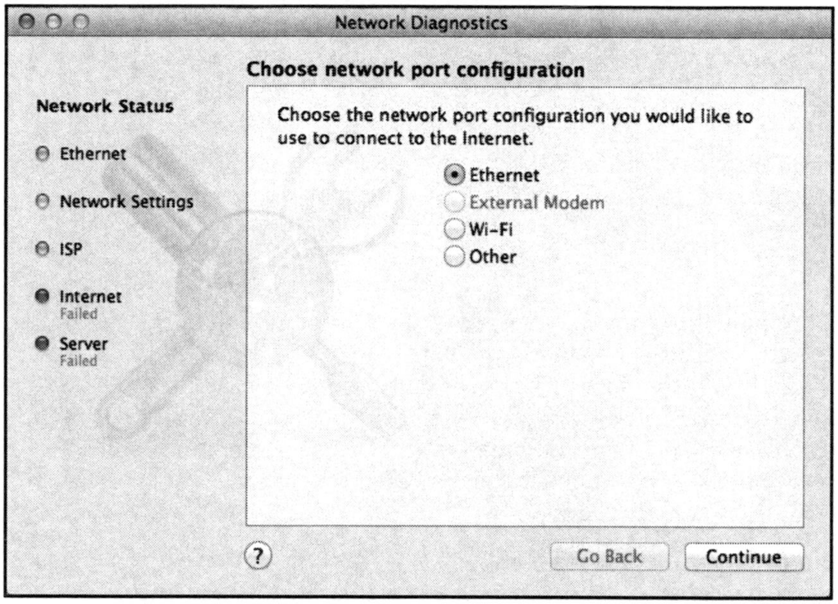

Figure 8–8. *The Network Diagnostics tool can help you troubleshoot a faulty Internet connection.*

TIP: Occasionally when you try to connect to an Internet connection, you are initially connected to a private network and many services won't work. To complete the connection you must first open your web browser and follow a series of steps to connect to the Internet. This is common in hotels, and many public Wi-Fi hotspots.

Other Network Connections

Besides the broadband connections listed previously, there are many other ways that you may connect to the Internet with your Mac. Many mobile wireless providers (including AT&T, Verizon, T-Mobile, Vodafone, and so on) provide various capabilities to connect to the Internet using their networks. These include dongles that plug into your USB port that serve as modems, or tethering your mobile phone either through a cable or through Bluetooth so your computer can utilize your phones network connection. The various instructions for setting up each of these connections should be provided by your wireless carrier.

> **NOTE:** Many phones these days (including the newest iPhones) can actually provide Wi-Fi service to your computer. This makes connecting to a mobile wireless network from your Mac as easy as connecting to any other Wi-Fi network.

One type of networking that is gone from Mac OS X Lion is dial-up networking. The current versions of Lion no longer have the built-in capability to dial in using a modem (in fact, when you try to connect an Apple USB modem to a Lion computer, you get a dialog stating, "Unsupported You cannot use an Apple USB Modem with this computer."

Creating Separate Networking Profiles for Different Locations

If you rely on DHCP for everything or you never move your computer around, then you really don't have to futz around with networking much (lucky you). However, if you are using a portable computer and you need to connect multiple networks that use different settings, then you may want to take advantage of the Location feature. At the top of the Network System Preference pane, there is a drop-down list that by default is set on Automatic. While Automatic is selected, any changes you make to any of your network interfaces are saved in the Automatic location.

If you need to have multiple network configurations—one at home that is basically the same as the Automatic setting and one for work where you are assigned specific networking information—then you can add a location from the Location drop-down list at the top of the Network System Preference pane and configure the networking for any specific locations as needed. Once you have multiple locations set up, a Location item will appear in your Apple menu that will allow you to switch your networking preferences from one location to the next.

Summary

This chapter covered what you need to get your Mac connected to the Internet. We attempted to skirt around some of the more complex networking issues, saving most of those for Part 6 of this book, which is dedicated to networking. The point of this chapter was to get you up and running so you can follow along with the next chapters, which cover Safari, Mail, and other Internet-related applications.

## Chapter 9

Browsing the Web with Safari

Lion includes the latest version of Apple's own web browser, Safari. Safari is a fast, standards-compliant web browser loaded with lots of useful features for getting the most out of the Web. This chapter will take a look at Safari and its capabilities, including the following:

- Safari basics
- Adding and managing bookmarks
- Tabbed browsing
- Downloading content from the Web
- Viewing PDFs
- Auto-filling form data
- Security
- Advanced browsing features
- RSS and syndication feeds
- Plug-ins and inline content
- Web clippings

Safari Basics

Safari is Mac OS X's default web browser, but you can install and use any other available Mac web browser as well including Chrome, Firefox, Camino, OmniWeb, Opera, and others. (Later in the book you'll see how you can even whip up your own in Xcode without writing a single line of code!) However, most people who start using

Safari tend to stick with it. Like most Apple software, Safari packs in a lot of useful features while still providing a clean, easy-to-use interface.

The Basic Interface

Safari (Figure 9–1) appears and works like most other popular web browsers, with a few twists that set it apart from most other browsers (even previous versions of Safari). By default, its toolbar is sparse yet functional, with only a handful of items (Back, Forward, and Add Bookmark buttons; an address field; and a web search field). Below the toolbar is the Bookmarks bar, which provides easy access to your favorite bookmarks or bookmark collections. It also provides buttons to open your Collections (Figure 9–2) and Top Sites (Figure 9–3). Below the Bookmarks bar is the Tab bar (when it is shown), and below that may be the Find Banner (which only appears when you use the **Edit** > **Find** > **Find...** (or Command-F) command). Finally, at the very bottom is the Status bar (if enabled, which by default it is not), which provides information about the progress of loading pages as well as displaying the location of links in a page.

> **NOTE:** The Find command searches for content within the current page. This is not to be confused with the Search field in the menu bar that will utilize your default search engine to search the entire Web.

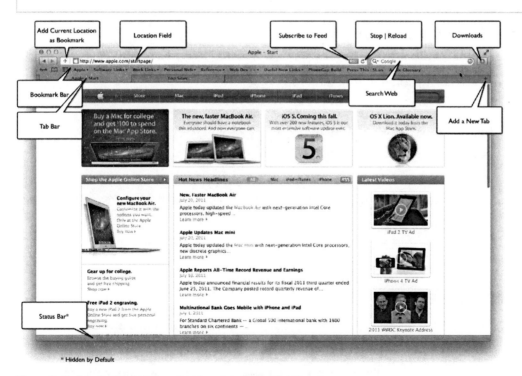

Figure 9–1. *A typical Safari view showing open tabs and web pages*

Figure 9–2. *Safari's Collections view is where you can view and manage your browsing history, bookmarks, and more.*

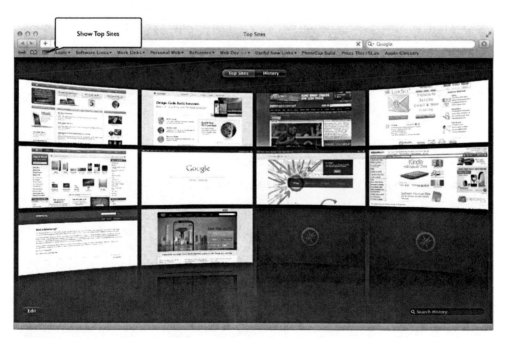

Figure 9–3. *The Top Sites view dynamically presents small representations of the web sites you visit the most. (Clicking one of the small windows loads the site.) Clicking the History tab will present you with a Cover Flow–like view of your recent browsing History.*

> **NOTE:** By default, only the toolbar and Bookmarks bar are shown. You must select **View > Show Status Bar** (or Command-/) to activate the Status bar. The Tab bar will open automatically when more than one Tab is open. Many of these default behaviors can be overridden by the options in the View menu.

Like many applications we have seen so far, Control-click the toolbar and select **Customize Toolbar...** from the shortcut menu to open a dialog containing other buttons and items that you can drag to your toolbar (Figure 9–4). Some popular items that users add are the Home and Print buttons. From the Customize Toolbar dialog, you can add, remove, or reorganize any of these items on your toolbar. At the bottom of the Customize Toolbar dialog is a default toolbar, which you can use to return your toolbar to its default state.

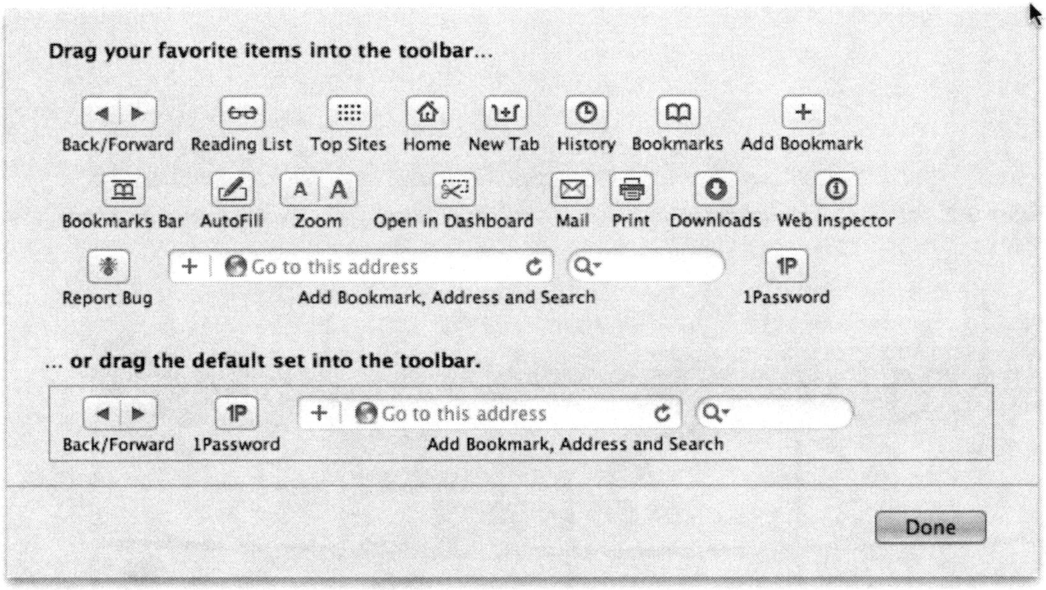

Figure 9–4. *You can customize your Safari toolbar in a number of ways to suit your needs.*

Besides the options viewable in the window, like most applications, there are many menu items in the various menus provided. Table 9–1 provides a list of Safari menu items that are unique or particularly useful to Safari.

> **NOTE:** Many menu items (as well as their keyboard shortcuts) are common among all Mac OS X applications. Occasionally, though, even common items have unique behavior in for specific applications and situations. For Safari, we will go over all the default options, but as we progress through the book, we will only cover options that are unique to the product or that haven't been covered previously.

Table 9–1. *Useful Safari Menu Items*

Menu/Submenu Item	Keyboard Shortcut	Description
Safari		
Block Pop-Up Windows	Shift-Command-K	Toggles Safari's ability to block those mostly unwanted pop-up windows that spring up automatically when you load some web pages. This doesn't prevent pages that you initiate by clicking a link from displaying.
Private Browsing...		Toggles Private Browsing. When Private Browsing is activated, none of the pages you visit are added to your browser history, and items are removed from your browser cache and downloads.
Reset Safari...		Allows you to selectively reset (clear) a number of items that Safari stores all at once. These include the history, cache, cookies, and AutoFill information.
Empty Cache...	Option-Command-E	Empties your browser cache.
File		
Open Location...	Command-L	Highlights the Location text field in the toolbar, allowing you to type in a URL of a web resource you wish to open. (Pressing Return will then take you there directly, without needing to move your hands from the keyboard.)
Open in Dashboard...		Allows you to select a region of the current web page to be added as a web clipping to your Dashboard.
Import Bookmarks...		Allows you to import a bookmark file from another location on your computer (including bookmarks from some other browsers).
Export Bookmarks...		Exports your Safari bookmarks into a separate file for archiving or for importing into a different browser. The bookmark file you export will be a properly formatted HTML file, so you can use it in various interesting ways.

Menu/Submenu Item	Keyboard Shortcut	Description
Edit		
AutoFill Form	Shift-Command-A	Attempts to fill in a web form using data from the AutoFill feature in Safari. This feature is sometimes triggered automatically when you begin to fill out a form.
Find >		Opens a submenu of the following items (i.e., the items from Google Search to Jump to Selection).
View		
(Show|Hide) Toolbar	Command-| (Shift-Command-\\)	Toggles the visibility of the main toolbar.
Customize Toolbar...		Opens the Customize Toolbar sheet as described previously.
(Show|Hide) Bookmarks Bar	Shift-Command-B	Toggles the visibility of the Bookmarks bar.
(Show|Hide) Tab Bar	Shift-Command-T	Toggles the visibility of the Tab bar. This only has an effect when no tabs are currently open (or if there is only one tab).
(Show|Hide) Status Bar	Command-/	Toggles the visibility of the Status bar.
Show Reader	Shift-Command-R	Shows the Reader, which presents a list of pages you have saved to read at a later time.
Reload Page	Command-R	Reloads the current page. This causes the page to fully reload, overwriting any information in the cache.
Actual Size	Command-0 (zero)	Adjusts the browsing area to display its contents at its normal size.
Zoom In	Command-+ (Command-=)	Zooms into the web page, making its contents bigger (by default, this does more than just increase the text size; it increases the size of all the elements and graphics).
Zoom Out	Command--	Zooms out, decreasing the size of all the elements in the web page.

Menu/Submenu Item	Keyboard Shortcut	Description
Zoom Text Only		When this option is selected, the Zoom Out command only impacts the text on the web page.
View Source	Option-Command-U	Opens the web page's source in a separate window.
Enter Full Screen		Will open the current Safari window in a full-screen view in a new space.
History		
Show Top Sites	Option-Command-1	Opens the Top Sites view in the current browser window or tab.
Show All History	Option-Command-2	Opens up your browser history in the Bookmark Collection view.
Home	Shift-Command-H	Takes you directly to your home page as configured in your preferences.
Search Results SnapBack	Option- Command-S	Returns you to your last Google web search results page. This feature even works with searches performed directly from the Google web page.
Reopen Last Closed Window		Reopens the last window you closed. The window opens with any tabs that were closed with it as well.
Reopen All Windows From Last Session		Reopens all previously opened windows from the last session (and returns Safari to the state it was in the last time you closed it).
Clear History		Clears your browser history.
Bookmarks		
(Show|Hide) All Bookmarks	Option-Command-B	Toggles open the bookmark window in the main viewing area. This is the same view as the Show All History view. This view allows you to view and organize all of your bookmarks.
Add Bookmark...	Command-D	Opens a small sheet that allows you to add a bookmark to the current web page to any of your bookmark folders.

Menu/Submenu Item	Keyboard Shortcut	Description
Add Bookmark For These [*n*] Tabs		Allows you to add bookmarks for all the open tabs in a window at once.
Add Bookmark Folder	Shift-Command-N	Creates a new unnamed folder selected in the Bookmarks view.
Bookmarks Bar >		Opens a submenu containing the bookmarks that you have on your Bookmarks bar (this may be turned off in Safari's preferences).
Window		
Select Next Tab	Control-Tab	Cycles to the next tab.
Select Previous Tab	Control-Shift-Tab	Cycles to the previous tab.
Move Tab to New Window		Opens the active tab in a separate window.
Merge All Windows		Consolidates all open browser windows into one window using tabs.
Downloads	Option-Command-L	Opens and brings to the foreground the Downloads window.
Activity	Option-Command-A	Opens and brings to the foreground the Activity window.
Bring All To Front		Brings all to foreground.
Help		
Installed Plug-Ins		Opens a window listing all of the browser plug-ins currently active in Safari.

That covers the basics of the interface, including the menu items. Now we'll take a closer look at how to perform certain tasks in Safari.

Setting Your Home Page

Your home page is the default web page that Safari goes to when it is initially launched. Out of the box, this is set for the Apple Start page (www.apple.com/startpage), which provides Apple news and links to other Apple products and features. If, however, you'd like to open a different page (or no page) when you start Safari, then open the Safari preferences (**Safari > Preferences...** [Command-,]), and with the General tab selected (Figure 9–5) set a few options:

New windows open with: This drop-down list allows you to select what will initially appear in new Safari windows. The options include Top Sites, Homepage (set below), Empty Page, Same Page (i.e., the page that was last opened in Safari), Bookmarks (will show you book mark collection), Tabs for Bookmark Bar (will open every bookmark in you Bookmark Bar collection in its own tab), or Choose tabs folder (this option will let you select any folder in your collection and have each bookmark contained within open in its own tab).

Homepage: This text field allows you to enter the URL of any web page that you'd like to use as your homepage.

Set to Current Page: Clicking this button automatically enters the URL of your current web page into the Homepage text field.

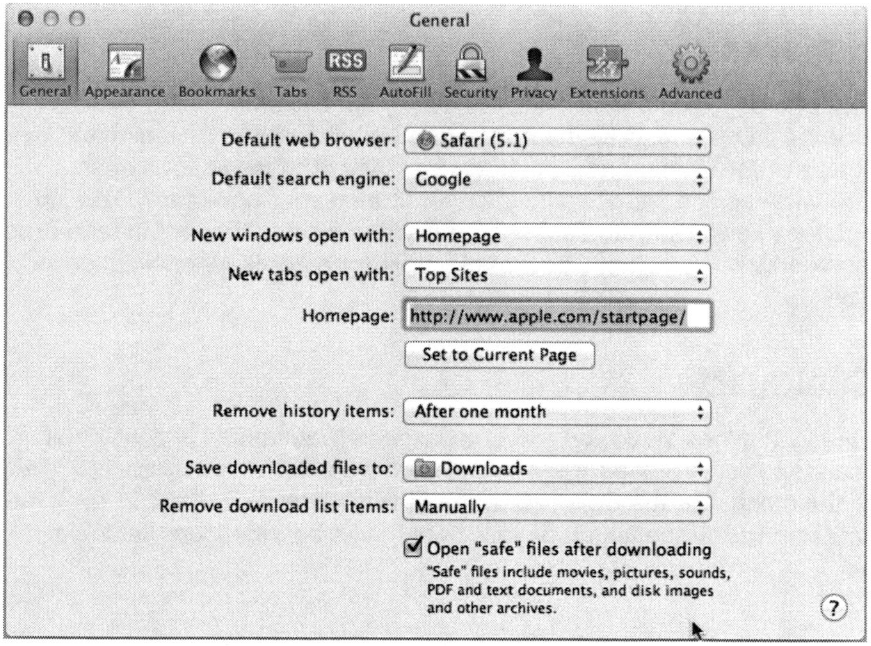

Figure 9–5. *You can select your own home page on the General tab of Safari's preferences.*

Searching the Web

If you are searching for something on the web, Safari provides a Web Search field on the right hand side of the toolbar where you can directly enter your search. By default Safari will perform your search using Google, however under the General tab of Safari's preferences you can choose to use Bing or Yahoo as alternates to Google as your default search engine.

> **NOTE:** Clicking the magnifying glass icon on the left side of Safari's Web Search field will provide a menu that will allow you to alter your default search engine without going to Safari's preferences. It will also display a list of possible refinements of your current search and a list of previous searches.

Bookmarks

Bookmarks provide a way for you to keep track of the web sites you visit that you'd like to return to (or keep track of for some other reason). Safari has a very nice bookmark system in place that allows you to keep an extensive collection of bookmarks well organized in folders and collections.

Adding Bookmarks

To add a bookmark of a page you are visiting, you can select **Bookmarks > Add Bookmark** from the menu, use the Command-D keyboard shortcut, or click the Add Bookmark button on the left side of the location field in the toolbar. Any of these actions open a dialog allowing you to name and choose a location for storing your bookmark. You can also add a bookmark by selecting the URL from the Address field in the toolbar and drag it down to the Bookmarks bar, a specific bookmark folder, or a bookmark collection in the Collections view.

Managing Bookmarks

When you are in the Collections view, you can organize your bookmarks in a way that makes the most sense to you. To enter the Bookmarks view, select the **Bookmarks > Show All Bookmarks** from the menu, use the Option-Command-B keyboard shortcut, or click the Show All Bookmarks button on the far left of your Bookmarks bar (the icon that looks like an open book).

> **NOTE:** When viewing the items in the Bookmarks Bar collection, you may notice a column called AutoClick, which contains a check box next to each folder item. When the Auto-Click feature is selected, rather than providing a drop-down list of bookmarks contained in that folder, all the bookmarks contained in the folder open in individual tabs when you select this item in the Bookmarks bar.

In the left column of the Collections view, there are two areas: Collections and Bookmarks. *Collections* are special groupings of bookmarks or other related items. The

Bookmarks Bar and Bookmarks Menu collections provide a place for you to store bookmarks so they are easily accessible from Safari; the contents in these two collections are fully customizable. Other collections provide access to links that are collected automatically. The Address Book collection contains all the URLs associated with contacts in your Address Book. The Bonjour collection contains a list of web sites on your network that take advantage of Bonjour. The History collection provides links to your browsing history. All RSS Feeds is a collection of links that lead to RSS feeds rather than traditional web pages.

Below the collections are your primary Bookmarks folders. Here you can add, remove, and move around folders, and store any bookmarks within them. This is a great way to store large amounts of bookmarks in an organized manner. It's important to note, though, that the bookmarks stored here are only accessible from this view. If you need quicker access to particular bookmarks, it's best to store those in the Bookmarks Bar or Bookmarks Menu collections.

> **NOTE:** The Bookmarks Item under the Collections column will not show up until you add bookmarks to Bookmarks Menu that are not contained in the Bookmarks Bar. This provides a mechanism to archive bookmarks that you use infrequently but want to keep around just in case.

Bookmark Preferences

The Bookmarks tab in Safari's Preference window (Figure 9–6) provides a few to customize how Bookmarks are handled in Safari.

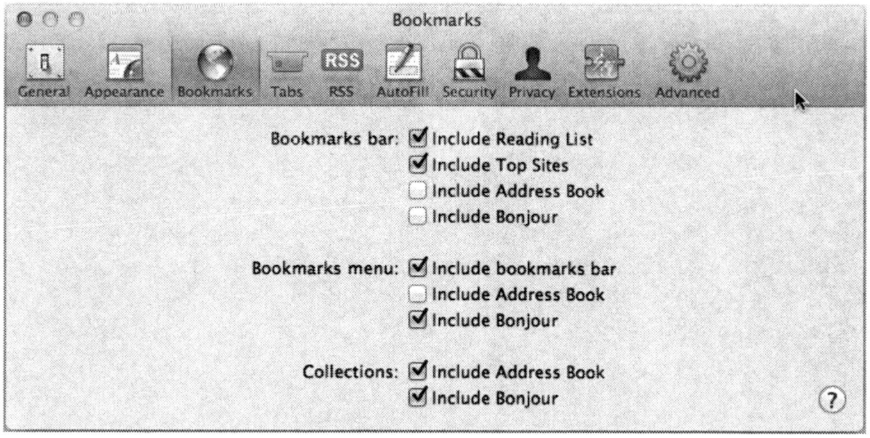

Figure 9–6. *The Bookmarks options in Safari's Preference window*

The Bookmarks bar and Bookmarks menu options allow you to select from a list of collections. Any selected collections then appear as items in the selected element. The Collections options let you choose whether to include the Address Book or Bonjour collections at all.

Tabbed Browsing

Safari fully supports tabbed browsing, which allows you to open up and view multiple web pages at one time all in one window. For those of us with a history of browsing many sites at once, this is a massive improvement over shuffling around many separate browser windows.

The ability to use tabs is always present in Safari—however, setting a few options in the Tabs tab in Safari's preferences (Figure 9–7) can make using tabs more convenient.

> **NOTE:** When you adjust the Tabs preference options, the actions associated with common keyboard shortcuts also change. At the bottom of the Tabs window, a list of the keyboard shortcuts and their resulting actions updates dynamically, depending on your selections.

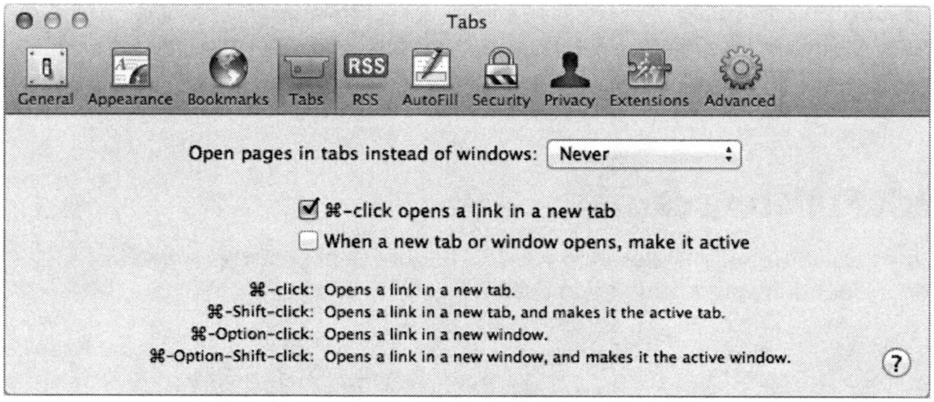

Figure 9–7. *The Tabs options in Safari's preferences*

Initially Safari's Tabs preferences are set up to open all new pages in a new window rather than a new tab (or to never open pages in tabs instead of windows), you can adjust this behavior by choosing a different option on the "Open pages in tabs instead of windows" menu. Other options include Automatic, which will open new pages in a tab unless the page is specifically formatted to open in a new window; and Always, which will cause all new pages to open in a new tab. If you enjoy using tabs, then Automatic is probably the best option.

Creating New Tabs

To create an empty tab in a Safari window, select **File > New Tab** from the menu (or use Command-T). Otherwise, depending on your preferences, new tabs can be created when you Command-click a hyperlink in a web page or when you click a link in an external application.

Moving Tabs

Occasionally you may want to move the tabs around into a different order in the title bar (or even into a different browser window). To move a tab, just grab (click and hold) the tab, and then drag the tab across the Tab bar to reorder it. If you drag the tab out of the Tab bar, though, the tab will change into a thumbnail of a browser window. If you release the window in this state, you will have moved the tab into a new window. This works the other way around too; if you grab the shaded corner of a stray browser window, you can drag it into the Tab bar of another window to convert it into a tab. (And yes, you can use this to move a tab from one browser window into another as well.)

> **TIP:** To quickly consolidate any number of open browser windows into tabs in a single browser window, use the **Window > Merge All Windows** menu item.

Closing Tabs

To close a tab, you can either click the small x located on the left side of any tab or use the **Close Tab** menu option in the File menu (or the Command-W keyboard shortcut).

Downloading Content from the Web

Besides browsing the Web, Safari can also download content that it encounters on the Web. When you click a link in Safari that leads to a file that Safari doesn't display, Safari will automatically start to download the selected item. When the download begins, a small progress bar will appear on the Downloads button on the toolbar to track the download progress.

> **NOTE:** Safari doesn't support all the popular protocols used today to download files, including BitTorrent, Gnutella, and others. If you wish to utilize this type of file download, you will need to get a third-party application like Acquisition (www.acquisitionx.com) or Transmission (http://transmission.m0k.org).

> **NOTE:** The first time you attempt to launch an application or open a file that you have downloaded from the Internet, Mac OS X will always warn you that you are about to open an application you downloaded from the Internet and that you should do so only if you downloaded it from a trusted source.

On the General tab of Safari's preferences, a few options affect how Safari downloads items:

Save downloaded files to: This option allows you to choose a folder to save all downloads in. By default, this is the Downloads folder in your home directory.

Remove download list items: This option allows you to choose whether downloaded items remain listed in the Downloads window until you remove them manually (using the Clear button), or whether this list should be cleared automatically when the download is complete or you quit Safari. Private Browsing overrides this option. Additionally, failed or canceled downloads are never cleared automatically.

Open "safe" files after downloading: When this option is selected, items deemed safe will launch automatically when they have completed downloading. When this option is selected, archives will be uncompressed and disk images will be mounted automatically. This will not in any situation cause a newly downloaded application to launch automatically, though (that would be considered unsafe).

Web Forms and AutoFill

Many functions of many web sites require that you fill out forms with data ranging from simple web site login information to shipping information and other contact info. Filling this information in time and time again can be very tedious. To help, Safari provides a feature called AutoFill.

The AutoFill options are located under the AutoFill tab in Safari's preferences (Figure 9–8). Here you can select what type of information you would like Safari to save and fill in when you access many forms in a web site.

Figure 9–8. *The AutoFill options in Safari's Preference window*

Checking the "Using info from my Address Book card" option enables you to use the contact information about you stored in your Address Book card to fill in that information when it is requested in an online form. This detects fields like "Address," "email," and so on, and fills in the appropriate information. Clicking the Edit... button next to this option opens up the Address Book application to your Contact information.

The "User names and passwords" option, which is off by default, stores usernames and passwords for various web sites. It ties a specific username/password combination to a particular web site and only fills in the specific username/password combo for that specific site. This data is stored safely in your keychain so that it would be difficult for someone to discover your password using devious means. However, if this is active, any user who has access to your account will be able to access any web sites protected by information stored here (unless you do not unlock your keychain). The Edit... button allows you to view and edit web sites and usernames associated with those web sites that are stored in AutoFill. Passwords are not shown (however, you can view them in your keychain with the Keychain Access utility).

> **TIP:** While Apple's keychain is an excellent tool for securely storing important information, there are a number of third-party applications that are available specifically for managing passwords. 1Password (available from the Mac App Store) is one such application that provides tight integration with Safari (and other popular browsers), as well as the ability to sync your password data from your computer to a number of other devices, including iPhones, iPads, Android devices, and even Windows PCs. Applications like 1Password make it easy to effectively utilize strong, unique passwords for web sites, which helps keep your online information protected.

If you check the "Other forms" option, data will be collected from forms on various web sites, and that information will be stored for reuse the next time you visit those sites. You can view what web sites AutoFill is storing data for by clicking the Edit... button.

> **CAUTION:** While AutoFill is convenient, it also could allow someone to access you online accounts by visiting sensitive web sites from the account you have AutoFill associated with. If you use AutoFill you should probably be careful to disable auto login from your system and to log out of your account when you are away from your computer or enable the "Require password [*immediately*] after sleep or screen saver begins" in the Security & Privacy System Preferences.

Security and Privacy

As more and more services and activities shift over to taking place on the Internet, and particularly on the Web, browser security becomes more and more important. Since its inception, Safari has proven to be one of the more secure browsers out there, and the version of Safari that ships with Mac OS X seems to uphold that level of security.

> **CAUTION:** Safari is not without security flaws. Throughout Safari's evolution there have been a number of known security issues uncovered, and it is probable that others, unknown or outside of public knowledge, exist. While there are no reports that any of these things actually resulted in a security breach, it underlies the importance of keeping your software up to date, as issues like these are usually quickly resolved after they are discovered.

Secure Browsing

To support a secure environment, Safari has built-in support for an array of protocols that assure the information you send and receive from a web site is encrypted. Safari supports the standard Secure Sockets Layer (SSL) versions 2 and 3, as well as Transport Layer Security (TLS, a newer, potential replacement for SSL). Whenever you have a secure connection between your browser and a web site, Safari will display a small lock icon on the right side of the title bar. Clicking the lock will provide information about the security being used, as well as the certificate information assuring that the web site is indeed what it claims to be.

> **CAUTION:** It's not advisable to send any information you deem private or important over the Web unless you know who is on the receiving end and the connection is secured. This rule generally applies beyond the Web as well, and should be followed for all network communication. A secure connection doesn't guarantee the information you submit will be secure once it reaches its destination.

Blocking Web Content

Safari can also block certain types of web content, specifically any pop-up windows that are not only annoying but may contain undesirable content. To enable pop-up blocking, you can select Block Pop-Up Windows from the Safari menu (or use Shift-Command-K). Safari tries to block only non-requested pop-ups, but if for some reason Safari blocks a desirable pop-up window, then you may need to toggle off this protection temporarily.

Besides blocking pop-ups, you can block other web content as well. On the Security tab of Safari's Preference window (Figure 9–9), you can disable JavaScript, Java, and plug-ins to further block potentially harmful content. Also, at the very top of the Security Preference tab, an option warns you when you are visiting a potentially fraudulent web site. This option will notify you if you are about to visit a site that may be used in phishing scams. *Phishing* refers to when one site pretends to be another site to acquire personal information such as credit-card information or usernames and passwords to sensitive sites. (Banks, eBay, and PayPal are common sites that phishers attempt to mimic.)

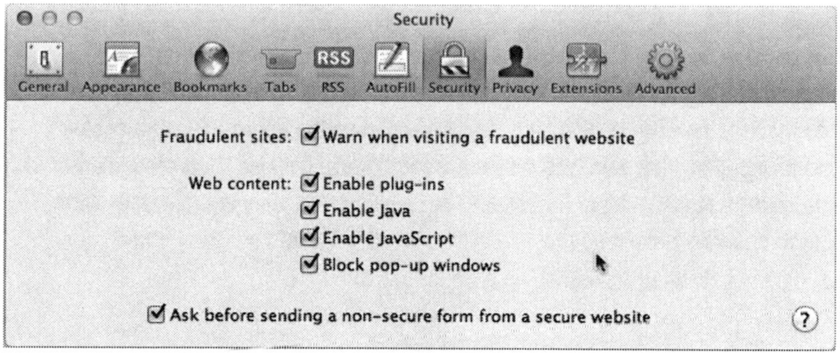

Figure 9–9. *The Security options in Safari's Preference window*

> **NOTE:** Disabling plug-ins, Java, and JavaScript may make for a safer and perhaps less distracting web browsing experience, but by disabling these things, you will also be losing a great number of features, and some web sites may become unusable. It comes down to your own personal security vs. hassle priorities.

Private Browsing

Another way to protect your information when browsing is to utilize the Private Browsing feature of Safari. When Private Browsing is enabled (by selecting **Private Browsing...** from the Safari menu), Safari will not save any of your browsing activity in the browser history or cache. This assures that people can't go into your computer and poke around at places you've been and items you've been browsing.

> **CAUTION:** Private Browsing may overlook items in your Downloads window, specifically any canceled or incomplete downloads, as well as any data cached by plug-ins (i.e., Flash).

Controlling Cookies

HTTP is a stateless protocol, which means that generally when you load a web page there is no common mechanism to remember anything about your last visit. There are, of course, many ways to work around this, but the most popular method today is to use a cookie to keep track of session data as well as other data (web site preferences and other information can be stored in cookies as well). As such, cookies are an important part of using the Web today, and while you can disable them, you will be losing out on a great deal of web functionality doing so.

NOTE: Since cookies became popular, there has been a large amount of paranoia about them, most of which is unfounded. Cookies can track your movement around a web site, and they can contain personal information, however, cookies are location based so the information in a cookie is only useful to a single location. That said, you may not want to leave cookies lying around on a computer in a user account that others have access to—but beyond that, they are generally safe and make the Web a much more interesting place to visit. Like plug-ins and so many other computing features, it comes down to a security vs. ease issue.

NOTE: While cookies are only relevant to a specific location that doesn't mean that they can't follow you around the web. Google's AdSense, for example, is a popular addition to many sites wishing to generate revenue through advertising. Since other web sites embed a piece of AdSense into their web site, the information AdSense (or Google) gets from one site, can be used on other sites using AdSense.

Safari has a number of options available to you regarding the accepting of cookies. In the Privacy tab of Safari's Preference window (Figure 9–10), you can select how you want to deal with cookies by blocking cookies in certain circumstances. Your options for blocking cookies include "From third parties and advertisers" (the default and suggested option), Always (no cookies allowed), and Never (accept all cookies).

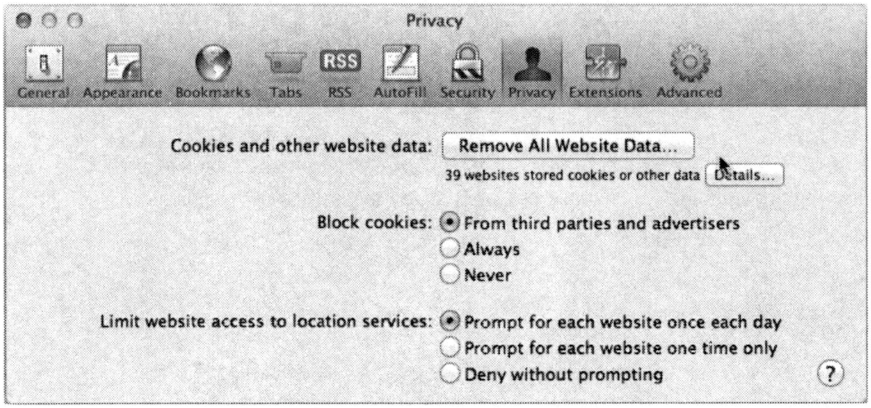

Figure 9–10. *The Privacy tab in Safari's preferences allows you to control what sort of data is collected and shared with Safari. The options here allow you to determine what cookies you would like to block and how location data may be used. You can also remove selected or all data Safari has collected from here.*

Removing Cookies and Other Stored Data

In addition to storing cookies Safari also maintains a cache of most of the content you encounter on the Web locally to help improve the browser's response time when revisiting a web site. While this is fantastic from a performance point of view, you might not want to leave all the items you were browsing lying around in your computer, as they may contain sensitive or private information (they can also take up a good amount of disk space, although that's not as big of a problem today as it was a few years ago).

In the Privacy tab of Safari's preferences you can view and manage not only the cache files, but also any stored cookies. To simply wipe out all stored data (cache, cookies and offline application data) Click the Remove All Website Data… button next to "Cookies and other website data:" This will bring up a dialog asking you to confirm that you want to erase all of this data and clicking the Remove Now button will wipe it all away. To selectively delete data, or to view what data is being stored from what web sites, click the "Cookies and other website data:" Details… button. This will open a dialog allowing you to browse by web site and see what data is being stored, you can then remove the data for any individual web site.

> **CAUTION:** One place that Safari data may still exist, even after you use Remove All Website Data…, is in your `~/Library/Caches/com/apple.Safari` folder. Here a special `Cache.db` file and Webpage Previews folder exist. The Webpage Previews folder contains `.jpg` image files of many web sites you have visited. These files are used in the various Top Site and History cover flow views. If you are really trying to cover your tracks (and didn't select Private Browsing to begin with) you will want to manually delete these items.

Occasionally you may want to just clean out Safari's cache files without erasing cookies. To do this, just select the **Safari > Empty Cache…** from the menu or use the Option-Command-E keyboard shortcut. This opens up a dialog to confirm you want to empty the cache. Click the Empty button to empty it.

> **TIP:** It is possible to disable the cache entirely. To do so, you must first select the "Show Develop menu in menu bar" option on the Advanced tab of Safari's preferences. Next, select **Develop > Disable Caches** from the new Develop menu.

> **CAUTION:** The Develop menu has lots of fun and useful options (launching the Web Inspector is awesome for debugging web sites), many of which can be useful if used in the proper context. However, used poorly, these options can cause all sorts of problems with Safari and have an unfortunate effect on your web browsing experience. If you don't know and understand what you are doing here, it's best to leave these options alone.

Advanced Safari Features

Safari has a few advanced options located in its preferences (Figure 9–11) that are useful in certain situations.

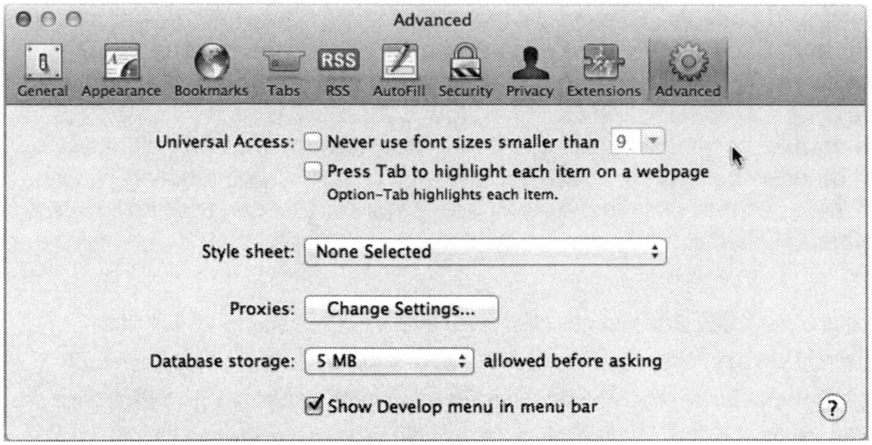

Figure 9–11. *The advanced Safari preferences*

Universal Access

The Universal Access options on the Advanced preference tab allow you to adjust the minimum font size for readability and to select between using Tab or the default Option-Tab to cycle through links *and* form items on a web page.

> **NOTE:** The difference between the default Tab and Option-Tab is that, unless you set the "Press Tab to highlight each item on a webpage" option, Tab will only cycle through form items (as well as the address field and search field on the toolbar), while Option-Tab will cycle through form items and hyperlinks.

Setting a Default Style Sheet

The Advanced Safari preferences also include the ability to use a specific style sheet that will affect every web page you visit. It's important to note that only text settings are imported from this style sheet to help improve readability, so the layout of each web site shouldn't be affected—unless large text settings cause items to wrap funny, which is really the fault of an inflexible web design(er), not Safari or the style sheet.

Database Storage

Database storage is a new feature in Safari that is also part of the emerging HTML 5 standard. This enables web applications to store application data in a local database so you can continue to work with a web application even if you are offline. The Database storage option in the Advanced preferences allows you to set the maximum size of data that you allow in your web database. By setting this value to something very low (or none) will not prevent the use of web Database, however; you will be prompted if you reach the limit as to what you would like to do.

> **NOTE:** Two other options on the Advanced tab of Safari's preferences are an option to change proxy settings, which will take you to the proxy settings of the active network device on the Network pane of the System Preferences, and a check box to "Show Develop menu in menu bar," which we touched upon previously.

RSS Feeds in Safari

RSS is a way for web sites to syndicate their content. This allows users to subscribe to a web site's RSS feed, which contains any updates to the web site. This is great if you like to visit a large number of web sites frequently, because with RSS, instead of going to each site to see what's new, you can get a list of new items from all of the web sites and filter out what items interest you.

> **NOTE:** When is RSS not RSS? When it's some other type of syndication standard. RSS has always had a few things that others found as weaknesses. This has resulted in two things: first, people adding content to RSS feeds that weren't covered by the RSS standard (Apple, for example, does this for iTunes podcast feeds); and second, people getting together and inventing new syndication standards, like ATOM. Most RSS clients, including Safari and Mail, support ATOM along with RSS—however, they still tend to refer to it all under the blanket of RSS.

> **NOTE:** Occasionally, a particular web site will have more than one RSS feed available. This is especially true of larger web sites, like news sites or even Apple. This allows subscribers to only receive information that they find interesting (for example, a sports site may allow you to subscribe to an RSS feed that only relays stories about a particular sport or a specific team).

Safari contains the ability to subscribe to RSS feeds as easily as adding a bookmark, and it makes a suitable RSS reader with some nice features.

NOTE: Apple has also added the ability to handle RSS in Mail, which provides a nice alternative to Safari's RSS feature. While some items referring to this will come up here, we will focus on how Safari handles RSS here, and how Mail handles RSS in the next chapter.

NOTE: Even though Apple provides a couple of good options for viewing RSS feeds, a number of other third-party applications specifically handle RSS feeds (called news aggregators) that add some additional or unique features or that help you organize a large number of feeds in a more suitable way. One such reader is NetNewsWire (http://netwirenewsapp.com). NetNewsWire is a free, full-featured RSS aggregator that makes managing and reading a large number of RSS feeds a snap. If you manage lots of RSS feeds, NetNewsWire is definitely worth checking out.

Adding Feeds

When you are browsing the Web in Safari, whenever you visit a site with an RSS feed, a blue RSS icon will appear on the far right side of the Address field in Safari's toolbar (Figure 9–12).

| + | http://www.apple.com/startpage/ | RSS | C |

Figure 9–12. *A web site that has an RSS feed associated with it will display a blue RSS box in Safari's address bar.*

Clicking the RSS icon either opens the RSS feed in your browser or opens a list of all the feeds available if more than one feed is available. Select the feed you wish to subscribe to from the pop-up, and the news feed will open up in Safari (Figure 9–13).

NOTE: When you select an RSS feed from within Safari, the RSS feed opens up in the default RSS newsreader. If your default newsreader is not Safari (e.g., Mail or a third-party RSS reader), then something else will happen than what is described here.

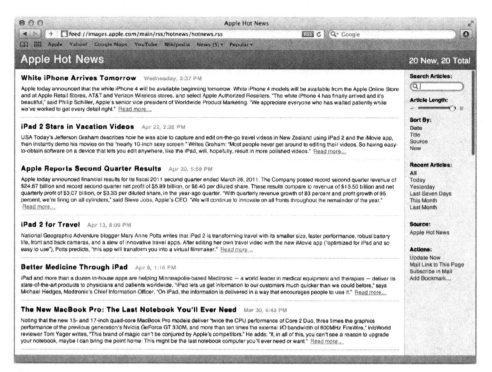

Figure 9–13. *An RSS feed open in Safari*

Once the feed is open, you can add the feed just as you would any bookmark (Command-D). Adding a feed saves the feed's location but doesn't necessarily update the feed automatically (which is usually the desired result). Depending on your RSS options, you must add the bookmark to either your Bookmarks Bar collection or your Bookmarks Menu collection for the feeds to update automatically. (You may want to create an RSS folder in one of these locations to store your favorite RSS feeds.)

> **NOTE:** The Bookmarks view provides an All RSS Feeds collection that contains all the RSS feeds you have bookmarked. You can use this to view all your RSS feeds in one place.

> **NOTE:** When you go to add the bookmark, you will notice an option to add the bookmark to Mail. This is provided if you wish to subscribe to the RSS feed in Mail as well.

Reading Feeds

Reading RSS feeds is pretty straightforward in Safari. If you select a specific feed, all of the current articles will appear in the Safari view area. If you select a collection of feeds by clicking View All RSS Articles in the Bookmark menu or from a folder list in the Bookmark bar, then all the articles from all the feeds will be displayed.

On the right side of the view area are some RSS options that apply to the feed(s) you are viewing. The Search Articles text field allows you to search for specific strings within all the visible articles. Below the Search Articles text field is the Article Length slider. This limits how much of the feed summary to show. (RSS feeds themselves vary in how they summarize articles. Some feeds give no summary at all, while others send the entire article.) The Sort By options adjust the order in which the articles appear in Safari. The Recent Articles option adjusts which articles appear in the view. For example, if you select Today, then only the articles that were updated today will be shown. The Source item shows where the feeds come from: if you select an individual feed, then the feed's name will be shown (and will open the source site if clicked); if you select a collection of RSS feeds, then the name of that collection will be shown. Finally, there are some actions available: Mail Link to This Page opens up a new mail message in Mail containing a link to the news feed or feeds being shown; Subscribe in Mail subscribes to all the feeds in Mail (which is handy if you use Mail as your primary RSS reader).

Feed Options

The Safari preferences include an RSS tab containing some options for RSS feeds (Figure 9–14).

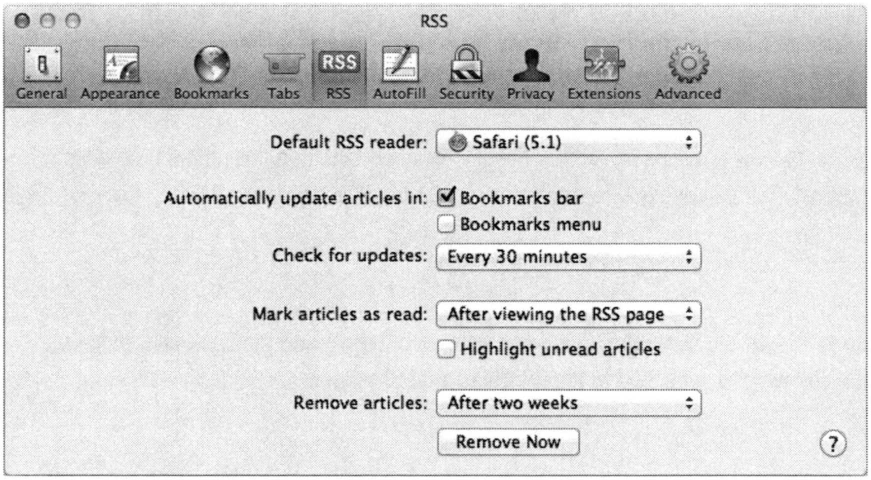

Figure 9–14. *The RSS options in Safari's Preference window*

The "Default RSS reader" option provides a list of all the known RSS readers installed on your system. The application chosen here is the primary one that Safari will use to open RSS links in.

The "Automatically update articles in" options allow you to select whether you would like all the RSS feeds in your Bookmarks bar, Bookmarks menu, or both to be updated automatically. The "Check for updates" list determines how often these feeds get updated.

The "Mark articles as read" option allows you to choose if an article should be counted as read when it's opened in a page or only after it's been clicked on. You can also select to highlight unread articles.

Finally, while RSS feeds themselves often limit the number of articles that are contained in the actual feed, Safari will keep track of all the articles once downloaded until they are removed. The "Remove articles" list allows you to determine when Safari should automatically remove older articles.

Safari Plug-Ins

Browser plug-ins are special add-ons that typically enable a web browser to view a special type of file or application that the browser itself would not display natively. Safari in Lion comes equipped with only two browser plug-ins: a Java applet plug-in that will allow Java web content to display in the browser, and a QuickTime plug-in that will allow a wide range of multimedia to display properly in the browser. Occasionally, however, you may come across some content on the Web that requires some other type of plug-in (for example, an Adobe Flash based application or media player). Depending on the web site, you may be prompted to download and install the plug-in, or you may just be told that you are missing the required plug-in (and usually told which one you are missing). Two common plug-ins not installed by default are plug-ins for Adobe Flash and for Windows Media. To get the Adobe's Flash Player, visit www.adobe.com and follow the links to download Flash Player (or just go straight to http://get.adobe.com/flashplayer/). Microsoft doesn't develop a plug-in for Windows Media for the Mac, however they make a free version of Telestream's Flip4Mac available that will add the ability to playback certain .wma and .wmv files in QuickTime. You can get this component from http://windows.microsoft.com/en-US/windows/products/windows-media-player/wmcomponents.

Beyond that, there are some other infrequently used plug-ins. Often when you encounter these, there will be information about what is necessary to view the content. Luckily, though, the days of plug-in madness have passed (i.e., the dot-com days when every wannabe tech company had its own plug-in for its own proprietary format). With the advent of many new features in HTML 5 perhaps a day will soon come where plug-ins are no longer necessary.

> **NOTE:** Safari posses the ability to natively display a wide range for common web content ranging from image files to PDFs without the need for any plug-ins.

Extensions

The ability to add extensions to Safari was added with Safari 5. Extensions provide a way for developers to add new features to Safari including UI features such as custom toolbar buttons and bars, inject scripts and style sheets into web pages, and much more.

To discover what extensions are available, take a look at the Safari Extension Gallery (Figure 9–15). To visit the Safari Extension Gallery select the **Safari > Safari Extensions...** menu option to open the gallery in a new tab or window. Once there you can browse through the various extensions and install them by clicking the Install Now button associated with the desired extension.

Figure 9–15. *The Safari Extension Gallery provides a list of available Safari extensions.*

Once you have some extensions installed, you can set them up, check for updates, turn them on or off, or uninstall them from the Extensions tab in Safari's preferences (Figure 9–16).

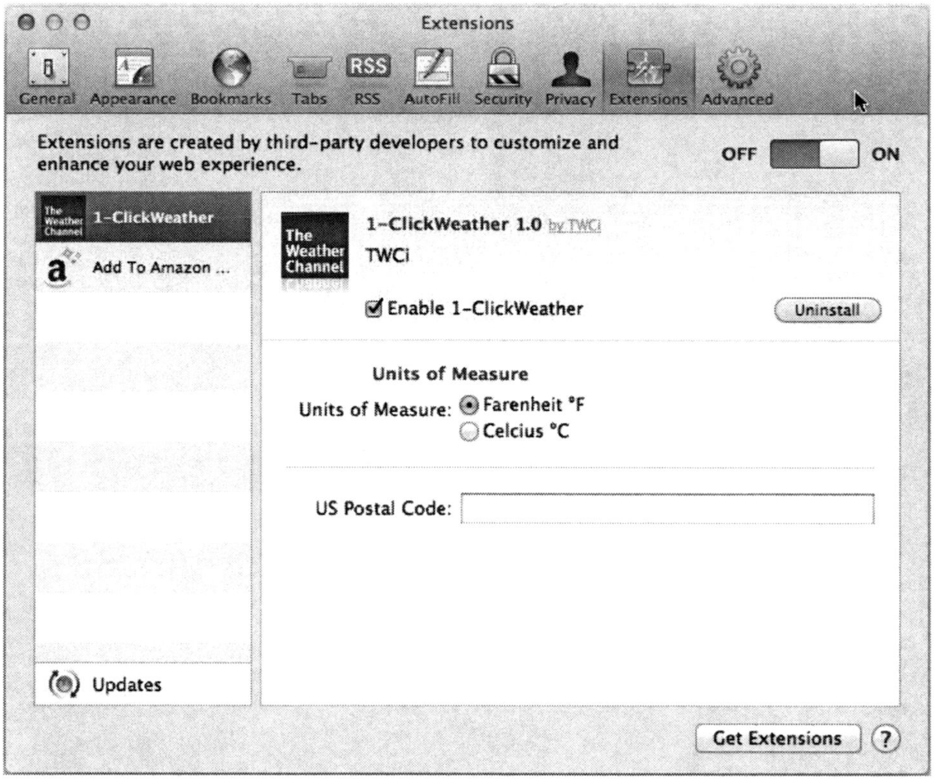

Figure 9–16. *The Extensions tab in Safari's preferences allows you to manage all of your installed extensions.*

Summary

Since Apple introduced Safari, it has been a quite capable web browser, but with the latest version of Safari, Apple has introduced what is clearly one of the best (and fastest) web browsers available on any platform today. Combined with its tight integration with Mac OS X, it's a clear winner. Of course, there is much more to the Internet than the Web—in fact, for many people, e-mail is the most important feature of the Internet—so next, we'll talk about Mail, along with iCal and Address Book, which now all work together to provide a seamless way to manage your e-mail, news feeds, to-do lists, notes, and more.

## Chapter 10

Working with Mail

Mail is Apple's e-mail application, and has been part of OS X from its start. With each new release of OS X, Apple refines the Mail application a bit. With Lion, Mail not only picks up a few features, but gets a facelift in the process. This chapter will walk you through this latest version of Mail, showing you the following:

- How to get around the new Mail interface

- How to add and configure e-mail accounts

- How to compose new messages

- How to set up mail signatures

- How to deal with junk mail

- How to manage mail and mailboxes

- How to use other Mail features like Notes and RSS

Introducing Apple's Mail Application

Up until Lion, most of the changes to Mail, at least as far as the interface, have been evolutionary. In Lion, not only has Apple added new features, but it has given Mail's interface a rather significant upgrade (Figure 10–1).

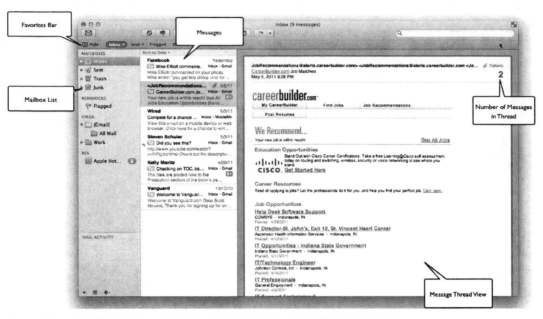

Figure 10–1. *Mail's main Message Viewer window has a new look in Mac OS X 10.7.*

One of the first new things users who have used Apple's Mail application before will notice is that the layout has changed. The new layout presents three columns side by side: the mailbox list is in the first column; the messages in the selected mailbox are displayed in the second column; and finally the message view, which displays the selected message (or message thread), is prominently displayed in the third column.

Besides the new layout, elements within the layout have changed as well. The toolbar has been streamlined with new icons (Figure 10–2), and offers the new ability to flag messages with different flags (similar to labels in the Finder). Also, the message view can now display entire threads in one single view, and provides additional options in the message header, including a small toolbar that appears when you hover your cursor over the header separator (Figure 10–3). Finally, beneath the toolbar, there is a new Favorites bar. Mailboxes from the mailbox list can be dragged up to the Favorites bar for easy access. Then you can click the Hide button on the Favorites bar to hide the mailbox list for a cleaner two-column view.

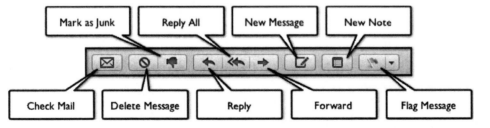

Figure 10–2. *The new default toolbar in Mail. Like most toolbars this can be customized to your needs or desires.*

Figure 10–3. *A small toolbar is available from the message view in the separator between the header and the message.*

Besides the options provided by the interface, Mail provides a number of additional commands and options on the menu bar. Interesting commands that may not be obvious are covered in Table 10–1.

Table 10–1. *Select Menu Bar Items for Mail*

Item	Keyboard Shortcut	Description
File >		
Add Account...		Opens a window to walk you through adding a new mail account.
Import Mailboxes...		Aids you in importing e-mail messages from other Mail mailboxes or even other e-mail clients.
Add RSS Feeds...		Opens a dialog box to add URLs of RSS feeds you want to subscribe to in Mail.
Edit >		
Complete	Option-Esc	Opens a list of possible words for the word you are typing.
Paste as Quotation	Shift-Command-V	Pastes the text in the clipboard into a new mail message formatted as quoted text.
Paste and Match Style	Option-Shift-Command-V	Pastes any text on the clipboard into a message matching the currently selected message text style.
Append Selected Messages	Option-Command-I	Appends any selected e-mail messages to a new message.
Attachments		Opens a submenu, allowing you to select one of three options for dealing with attachments in mail messages.
Attachments > Include Original Attachments Reply		Includes in replies any attachments that are included with an original message.
Attachments > Always Send Windows Friendly Attachments		Creates attachments that work with most Windows mail clients.

Item	Keyboard Shortcut	Description
Attachments > Always Insert Attachments at End of Message		Always inserts attachments at the end of the message rather than allowing attachments to be inserted inline.
Speech		Opens a submenu, allowing you to have the default system voice start and stop reading your mail message aloud.
View >		
Message Attributes		Opens a submenu containing a list of message elements that will be displayed for each message in the Message List column.
Bcc Address Field	Option-Command-B	Toggles the visibility of the Bcc address field for a new message.
Reply-To Address Field	Option-Command-R	Toggles the visibility of the Reply To address field in new messages. The address entered here will be the default address any replies are sent to.
Select		Opens a submenu of options for easily selecting messages that are part of the same thread.
Select > All Messages in this Thread	Shift-Command-K	Highlights all the messages in a specific e-mail thread.
Select > Next Message in this Thread		Selects the next message in the current e-mail thread.
Select > Previous Message in this Thread		Selects the previous message in the current e-mail thread.
Message		Provides a submenu containing view options for individual messages. Some of these options are only available when a message contains alternate formats (i.e., some messages contain both rich text and plain-text versions).
Message > Long Headers	Shift-Command-H	Reveals additional header information about each e-mail message.
Message > Raw Source	Option-Command-U	Reveals the entire contents of an e-mail message in plain text, including all header information and all formatting.

Item	Keyboard Shortcut	Description
Message > Plain Text Alternative	Option-Command-P	Displays a message in plain text if it's sent with a plain-text alternative message.
Message > Previous Alternative	Option-Command-[	Displays the previous alternative format for the selected e-mail message.
Message > Next Alternative	Option-Command-]	Displays the next alternative format for the selected e-mail message.
Message >Best Alternative		Selects the best alternative text format for viewing the message in Mail (this is the default).
Display Selected Messages Only		Hides all messages in the message list except those that you have selected (which is useful if used in combination with Select > All Messages in this thread).
Mailbox >		
Synchronize All Accounts		Synchronizes all IMAP and Exchange accounts, updating both remote and local mailboxes with any changes.
Online Status		Displays a submenu allowing you to view and toggle the online status of each account individually.
Get New Mail		Displays a submenu allowing you to choose a specific account to check for new mail messages.
Synchronize		Displays a submenu allowing you to choose a specific account to synchronize.
Erase Deleted Messages		Displays a submenu that presents options for removing deleted (trashed) messages permanently, including removing each individual account separately.
Erase Deleted Messages > In All Accounts...	Command-K	Erases all deleted items in all accounts, including expunging messages from IMAP and Exchange servers (though server settings may override this).
Erase Deleted Messages > On My Mac		Deletes any trashed messages stored in the local trash; this won't erase any message stored on remote servers (such as IMAP and Exchange).

Item	Keyboard Shortcut	Description
Erase Junk Mail	Option-Command-J	Permanently removes any junk e-mail messages stored in the Junk mailbox. For this option to be available, you must activate the "When junk mail arrives: Move it to the Junk Mailbox" option in Mail's preferences.
New Mailbox...		Opens a dialog box allowing you to name and choose a location for a new mailbox.
New Smart Mailbox...		Opens a dialog box to allow you to name and configure a new smart mailbox. Smart mailboxes are similar to smart folders for searching and sorting e-mail.
Edit Smart Mailbox...		Opens a dialog box allowing you to alter the selected smart mailbox's rules.
Export Mailbox...		Saves an archive file of the selected mailbox, allowing you to import the mailbox and data back into Mail at a later date. This is useful both as a way of creating emergency backups when moving old mail from one computer to another, and as a way of creating archives of old mail prior to cleaning out your mailbox.
Use This Mailbox For		Opens a submenu that allows you to designate the specific purposes of mailboxes, such as storing mail drafts, trash, junk, and sent messages. This is nice if, for example, your IMAP server has a Junk mailbox named Spam. With this command, you can tell Mail to use the Spam folder for junk mail to keep all of your junk mail in a single folder (and so Mail won't create an extra Junk folder).
Rebuild		Rebuilds your selected mailboxes. This can help with a number of performance and reliability issues; it's good to use this every once in a while.

Message >

Item	Keyboard Shortcut	Description
Reply With iChat	Shift-Command-I	Allows you to start a chat with the sender of a message if the sender has a known iChat (or AIM) account (i.e., it's in your Address Book or buddy list) and is currently available online.

Item	Keyboard Shortcut	Description
Redirect	Shift-Command-E	Redirects a selected message to another recipient. This is useful if you were sent an e-mail by mistake and you wish to forward it to the intended receiver. Using this option causes replies to go back to the original sender as opposed to you.
Mark		Opens a submenu to provide options for marking or labeling e-mail messages in your mailboxes.
Mark > As (Unread|Read)	Shift-Command-U	Toggles selected messages as being unread/read.
Mark > As (Not) Junk Mail	Shift-Command-J	Toggles the current message as junk mail or not junk mail.
Mark > As Low Priority		Marks the selected message as low priority.
Mark > As Normal Priority		Marks the selected messages as normal priority.
Mark > As High Priority		Marks the selected messages as high priority.
Flag >	Shift-Command-L	Opens a submenu to flag the selected message with one of seven colored flags. The keyboard shortcut Shift-Command-L will apply the default red flag to a message.
Archive		Moves the selected message into a mailbox called Archive, which will be created under the existing account.
Apply Rules	Option-Command-L	Applies your mail rules to selected messages.
Add Sender to Address Book	Shift-Command-Y	Adds the e-mail address (and name if available) of the sender of selected messages to your Address Book.
Remove Attachments		Removes the attachments of a selected message.
Format >		
Make (Plain|Rich) Text	Shift-Command-T	Toggles the formatting of the text in a message from plain text (which has no formatting) to rich text (which is actually formatted using HTML and allows formatted text and images). Traditionally, e-mail was all plain text, and today some people and e-mail clients still prefer it that way.[a]

Item	Keyboard Shortcut	Description
Window >		
Message Viewer		Selects or opens the Message Viewer window (Mail's default window).
Photo Browser		Opens Mail's Photo Browser window, allowing you to browse iPhoto libraries for images to include in your messages.
Address Panel	Option-Command-A	Opens a window containing an abbreviated view of contacts from your Address Book, displaying only their names and e-mail addresses.
Previous Recipients		Opens a window to keep track of all your previous message recipients. Whenever you start to type an e-mail address in a To, Cc, or Bcc field, the Mail application uses this list to attempt to autocomplete the name.
Activity	Command-0 (zero)	Opens the Activity Viewer window, showing any background activity taking place in Mail.
Connection Doctor		Opens a window that checks all the network connections used by Mail. This helps determine whether a network failure is on your end or on one of your mail servers. This also helps verify that all of your accounts are set up and working properly.

[a]*When sending a message using rich text from Mail, the Mail application will also include a plain-text version of your message for people who prefer plain text, or can't or won't accept rich text.*

Of course, before you start digging into Mail, the first thing you need to do is add an e-mail account (or accounts).

Adding E-mail Accounts

The easiest way to add a new e-mail account to Mail is to select **File > Add Account...** from the menu. This will open up a dialog that will guide you through the steps needed to add your new account. You can also access this account setup walkthrough when you add an account from the Accounts tab in Mail's System Preferences. The information you'll need to know varies with the type of account and the mail service you use.

NOTE: There are a number of ways to add an e-mail account for Mail in Mac OS X. When you first set up Mac OS X, you are prompted for your MobileMe account information if you have a MobileMe account, so that account may already be present when you launch Mail the first time. Also, the System Preferences contains a new Mail, Contacts & Calendars preference pane where you can set up accounts that may be recognized by Mail. We are only covering how to add accounts from Mail here; other methods will be covered elsewhere in the book.

The first bits of information you will need to know for all e-mail accounts are your e-mail address and your password (Figure 10–4). Once you enter this information, Mail contacts the server and attempts to autoconfigure the e-mail account. This is effective for a large number of e-mail services, including Gmail, Yahoo, and MobileMe, and even many Exchange 2007 servers that have their autoconfigure options set. If you get the option to set up an account automatically, select that option, and let Mail do the rest.

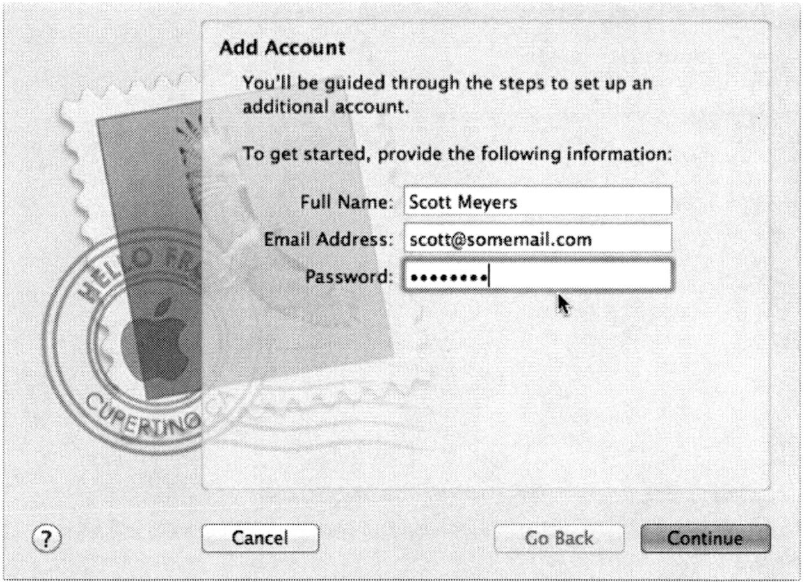

Figure 10–4. *The first step in setting up a new e-mail account in Mail is to enter your name, e-mail address, and password.*

If your account isn't set up automatically, then you'll need some more information to set up both your incoming and outgoing mail servers. To configure your incoming server (the one you receive your e-mail from), you'll need to know the following information (Figure 10–5):

- The type of server or protocol you are using: POP, IMAP, Exchange 2007, or Exchange IMAP.

- The address of your incoming mail server.

If you are configuring an Exchange IMAP server, you'll also be asked for the address of the Outlook Web Access (OWA) server. You'll also be asked for a description, which will be the name by which Mail refers to this account.

> **NOTE:** There are two options here for Microsoft Exchange support. For Exchange 2007 and newer Exchange servers, Mail offers native support and the Exchange option should work fine (and will also allow you to add contacts and calendar support). For older Exchange servers, however, you must use the Exchange IMAP option, and the Exchange server in question has to be set up to support IMAP. If you are setting your access for a company exchange server, the specific information you need should be available from your IT department or person.

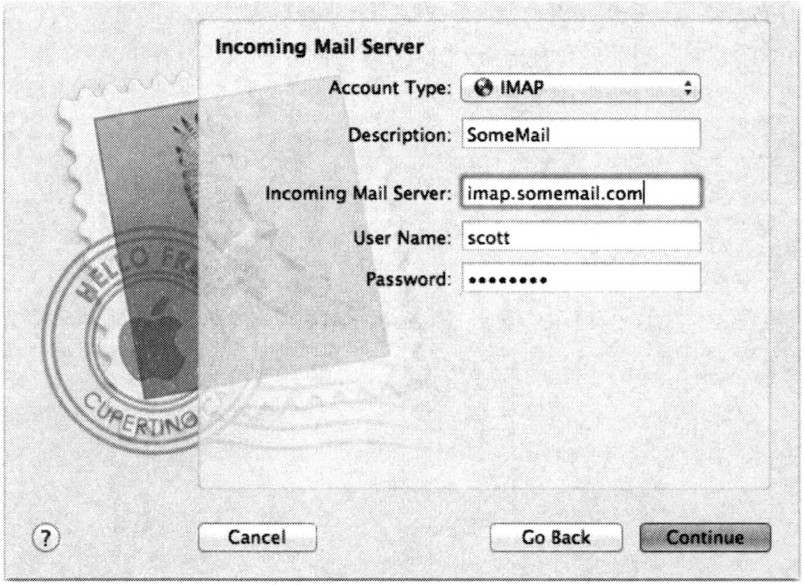

Figure 10–5. *If Mail cannot automatically fill in your mail settings based on your e-mail address, it will first prompt you for information about your incoming mail server.*

> **NOTE:** Figure 10–5 shows the configuring of an IMAP account. This dialog box will look the same when you configure a POP account, but for an Exchange server, it will appear a bit different. For an Exchange 2007 and newer servers, it will provide a couple of check boxes asking you if you'd like set up your Exchange contacts and calendar. If you check these, you will be able to access your Exchange contacts in Address Book, and your Exchange calendar items in iCal. For an Exchange IMAP connection, you will need to know the web address of your OWA server.

Once you enter all your information and click the Continue button, Mail will try to contact the server and determine the best means of connecting to it. If this fails, then you will get a message warning you that Mail was unable to connect to the mail server. This usually means something was entered incorrectly, the mail server is down or not accepting connections, or the server is unreachable (perhaps behind a firewall that requires a VPN connection). If you get this warning you may want to double-check that all the information is correct and fix any mistakes. If you are sure everything is correct, you can click Continue again to move on.

At this point, depending on what happened when Mail contacted your incoming server, you may or may not be prompted to select your security settings (Figure 10–6). If you are, you should enter them here. We strongly encourage you to select SSL encryption.

> **NOTE:** When Mail first attempts to contact your account, if it connects successfully and discovers that an SSL connection is available, it will automatically utilize that.

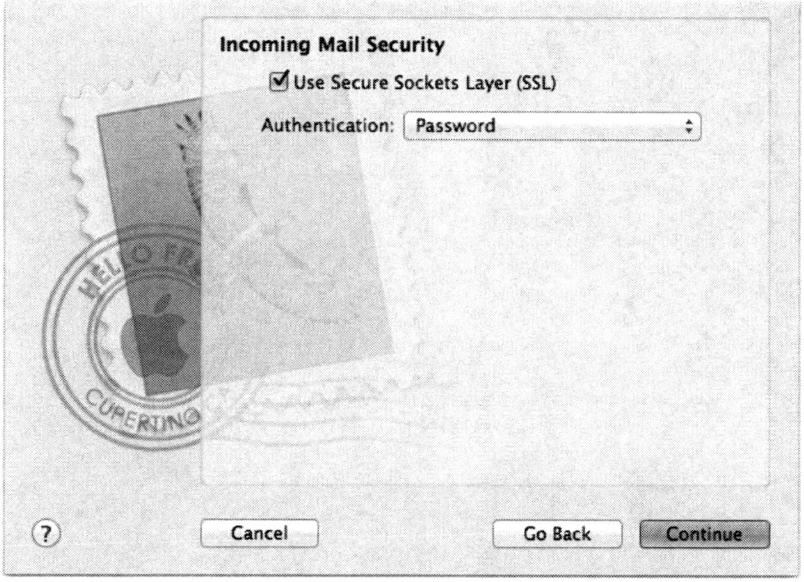

Figure 10–6. *If prompted to choose an SSL connection, you should do so.*

The next step is selecting your outgoing mail server for this account (Figure 10–7). Here you can either choose an existing outgoing mail server (one from an existing account) to use when sending mail from this account or enter the details of a new one. Usually you will want to enter the outgoing account information associated with the account you are setting up.

NOTE: SSL encryption encrypts the data being passed between your computer and the server at the other end. Some services, for whatever reason, don't accept SSL encryption (or any other encryption) for e-mail. If this is the case, we strongly urge you to find another e-mail provider and not use the account lacking encryption. Checking your e-mail over an unencrypted connection and sending your username and e-mail address across the Internet in easy-to-read plain text that anyone with a little know-how can intercept is very, very bad. For Mac users, Apple provides free iCloud e-mail addresses, and you can always get a free, permanent, secure Gmail account at www.gmail.com (which may redirect you to Google—it's OK, Gmail is synonymous with Google Mail), so you have no excuses.

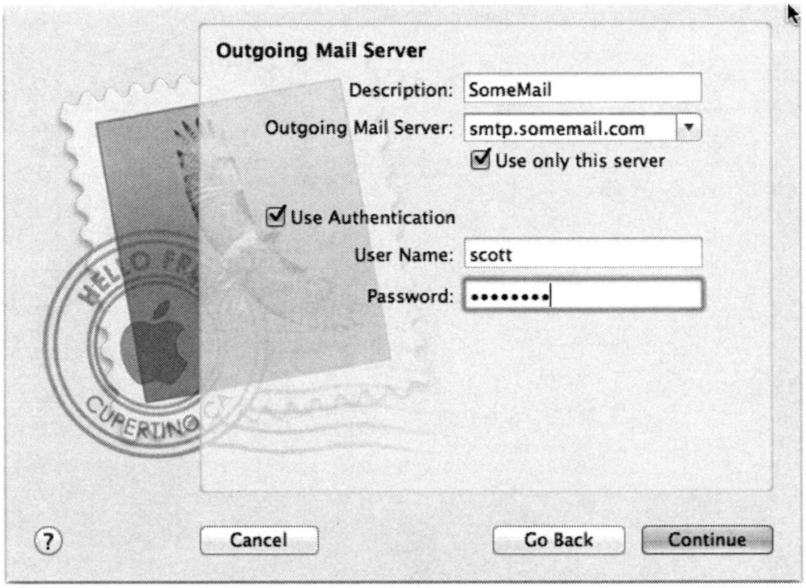

Figure 10–7. *Configuring your outgoing (SMTP) server*

NOTE: Almost all outgoing servers will be Simple Mail Transfer Protocol (SMTP) servers. SMTP is what makes e-mail work by moving your message from SMTP server to SMTP server until your message reaches its destination. Unfortunately, as the name implies, it is very simple, but it is also very old. It was written for a day long ago when the Internet and e-mail were used mainly by educational, government, and research institutions. Spam wasn't a problem. Today, most SMTP servers have evolved to provide some checks in an attempt to limit spam, but the fundamental design of SMTP is to accept and route all e-mail as quickly and effortlessly as possible. As such, spam gets through. This presents some issues for non-spammers (well, spammers too, but the more "issues" they have, the better, right?). Certain public Internet connections routinely block SMTP traffic, so if you find yourself attempting to send an e-mail from a public place or even from work or a hotel room, you may find it doesn't work. In some cases, there is a special SMTP server you can gain access to (Mail will present you with the opportunity to change or add an SMTP server when it fails to connect to the default SMTP server tied with a particular account); other times, it's just not going to work. About the only real solution we've found in some of these situations is to send messages through a web mail interface.

TIP: Since many service providers block the standard SMTP ports, many e-mail services offer up port 587 as an alternative SMTP port. Mail by default will try both the standard port 25 and common alternates (465 and 587).

Just like when you configure your incoming account, when you enter new outgoing account information, Mail will attempt to contact the server to acquire additional information about the server and to verify the connection when you click the Continue button. If Mail can't connect to the server, you will get a warning asking whether you'd like to continue. After you click Continue, you may or may not get the Security Options screen to set up a secure connection for outgoing mail.

Upon completion of entering your outgoing mail information, you will be presented with a summary of your new account information (Figure 10–8). If everything is correct, click the Create button to create your new account.

Figure 10–8. *Preview your e-mail account information, and click Create to create your new account.*

Once your accounts are set up, you can edit or delete an account in Mail's preferences under the Accounts tab (Figure 10–9). By selecting an account on the Accounts pane, you can edit that account using one of the three subtabs: Account Information, Mailbox Behaviors, or Advanced. The Account Information pane allows you to edit the server information, username, and password (essentially the same stuff you used to set up the account, unless your account was autoconfigured). The Mailbox Behaviors pane allows you to select how messages are stored and how Mail should deal with specific types of messages (including notes, trash, and suspected junk mail). The options provided here, as well as the specific behavior, will vary depending on the account type. The Advanced tab contains a number of other options for your account, including the ability to disable the account in Mail or to toggle SSL for connecting to the incoming server.

Figure 10–9. *Mail's Accounts preferences allow you to revisit the configuration of your mail accounts, plus make a few additional choices about how Mail will work with a specific account.*

NOTE: If you configure an IMAP account manually (or sometimes even if it's autoconfigured), and everything connects OK, but you notice a number of strange mailboxes popping up in Mail (and possibly no mail), it's likely that you will need to set the IMAP path prefix under Mail's Advanced Accounts preferences. What specifically needs to be set here will vary with your account, but if one of those strange folders that pops up says something like "Mail," that's a good place to start. (Of course, the most effective thing would be to contact the server's support people or administrator and ask.)

> **TIP:** If you have more than one e-mail account in Mail, the order in which the accounts are listed in the Accounts preferences is important. Mail considers the account listed first as the default mail account. When you create a new message, it generally associates that message with this account. To reorder your accounts, you can simply select and drag them up or down in the Accounts pane.

Receiving and Managing E-mail

Receiving, reading, and managing e-mail messages are the main tasks that most people are occupied with when using their mail clients. Mail provides some nice features for this, whether you deal with a few messages from a single account every day or hundreds from multiple accounts.

Checking and Reading New E-mail

Mail is set up, by default, to automatically check for new e-mail in each of your active, online accounts every 5 minutes. This interval is adjustable on the General tab of Mail's System Preferences (Figure 10–10) from the "Check for new messages" drop-down list. Of course, you are always free to check your e-mail manually by clicking the Get Mail button in Mail's toolbar or by using one of the Get Mail options on the Mailbox menu.

By default, when Mail discovers new messages for one of your accounts, the new messages are downloaded into the inbox associated with the account, and the "new mail" sound will play, notifying you of new mail. Additionally, the number of unread messages in your inbox will appear on the Mail icon in the Dock (known as a *badge*), as well as next to your inbox. Unread messages in the message list area of the Message Viewer window will be flagged with a small blue dot, which will go away when you select the message to read.

> **NOTE:** In the mailbox list in Mail's Message Viewer window, Mail provides a single inbox that expands into separate inbox folders for each account. This allows you to view your messages from different accounts either together by selecting the inbox item or separately by account by selecting one of the subitems under Inbox.

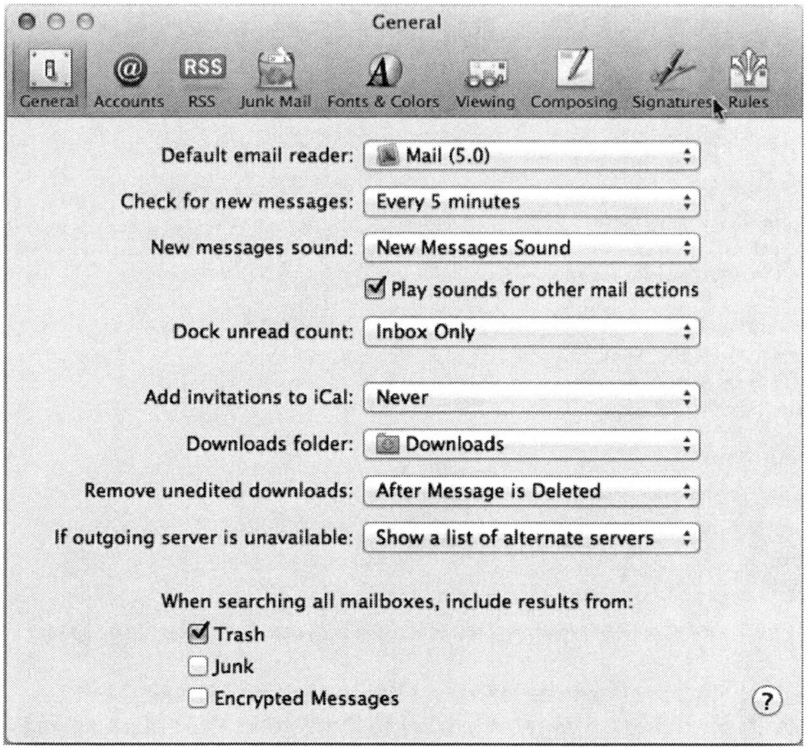

Figure 10–10. *The General tab of Mail's preferences provides many of the common options you may want to adjust.*

When you select a message, its contents appear next to the message list area in the message view area of the Message Viewer window. You can scroll through it there, or if you double-click the message item in the message list area, the message will open in a separate window.

Dealing with Junk E-mail

Mail has a built-in system to help you identify and deal with junk mail, or spam. This system is actually quite good, and with proper training, should be sufficient for most users. For the best results, however, the Junk mail filter must be trained. By default, Mail's junk filter is pretty average as far as filters go, but as you mark missed messages as Junk and mislabeled good mail as Not Junk, Mail will learn over a fairly rapid period of time what you consider to be junk and what you don't.

Most of the configurable options regarding how junk mail works are contained on the Junk Mail tab of Mail's preferences (Figure 10–11).

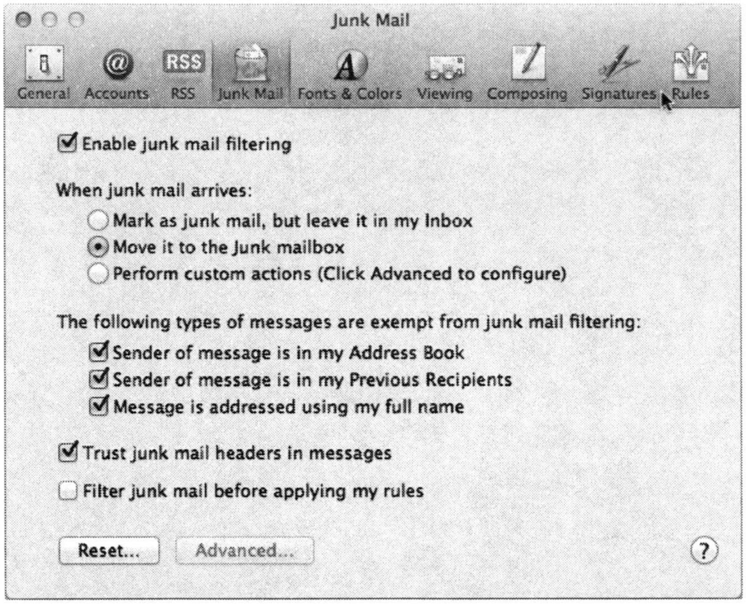

Figure 10–11. *The Junk Mail tab provides options regarding how Mail deals with mail it considers to be spam.*

The first option on the Junk Mail preferences tab is to enable junk mail filtering. Below that are options for what Mail should do with e-mail it considers junk. The "Mark as junk mail, but leave it in my Inbox" option is the best choice when you are first training Mail as to what you consider junk and what you don't. When you think Mail is identifying junk mail at a good rate, you can alter this setting. The "Move it to the Junk mailbox" option creates a new mailbox called Junk where, when this option is activated, Mail will store junk mail rather than in your inbox. The final option, "Perform custom actions," allows you to set up a custom mail rule for dealing with junk mail when you click the Advanced... button. We cover setting up mail rules in the "Creating Mail Rules" section of this chapter.

> **CAUTION:** The Erase Junk Mail menu item on both the Mailbox menu and the shortcut menu available from the mailbox area of the Message Viewer window causes any messages stored in your Junk mailbox to be immediately deleted—not stored in the Trash, but gone. This is both a handy way to rid yourself of trash and an easy way to accidentally rid yourself of an important message that was flagged as Junk by mistake.

Next, you can choose certain criteria for messages that should never be marked as Junk. You can exempt mail from people in your Address Book or people in your Previous Recipients list, or e-mail that is addressed using your full name. Exempting people listed in your Address Book and Previous Recipients list is usually safe; however, we find that for whatever reason, lots of junk mailers tend to know our full names, so this option is questionable.

The "Trust junk mail headers in messages" option allows Mail to look at certain e-mail headers that are commonly used by ISPs and mail servers to rate the probability that a message is junk. The results of using this option are mixed depending on your mail server.

> **NOTE:** We leave this option checked since it covers all our accounts; however, if one of your e-mail accounts has its own junk mail quarantine, when a message is released, Mail may still flag it as Junk when it hits the inbox, since the headers that identify it as Junk on the mail server may still be intact.

The "Filter junk mail before applying my rules" option identifies mail as junk before looking at any other rules. This option could prevent rules from running on messages that Mail considers junk. If this option in unchecked, then, unless you specify a custom junk mail action, the junk filter will work after your mail rules are run, thus allowing them to affect all messages.

The Reset... button resets all of your junk mail options and resets all the junk mail training you have done.

Creating Mailboxes to Store E-mails

Besides your inbox and other special-purpose mailboxes and folders that Mail creates for you, it's likely you'll want to create your own to organize any saved messages, as well as notes you store in Mail.

> **NOTE:** In Mail, folders are synonymous with mailboxes. Mailboxes you create will actually appear as folders, and although you can store both mail and notes in them, they are still generally called mailboxes in Mail.

To create a new mailbox, simply select **Mailbox > New Mailbox...** from the menu bar or select **New Mailbox** from the menu that appears when you click the + button in the lower left of the Message Viewer window. This opens a dialog box with a text field to enter the name of your new mailbox and a drop-down list for you to choose where you want the mailbox to be created. In general, new mailboxes are stored On My Mac (that being your Mac), which means they are kept locally. If you have access to an IMAP or Exchange mail account (which includes MobileMe and Gmail), then you can also create folders on the remote mail server this way (since IMAP stores your mail remotely). This makes those mailboxes and the items stored within them accessible from any computer you have set up to access that account.

Once you create a mailbox, if you want to change its location, you can do so by selecting and dragging the mailbox where you'd like it. To further add to the flexibility, you can nest mailboxes (i.e., mailboxes can reside in other mailboxes).

In addition to your standard mailboxes, you can also create *smart mailboxes* in Mail, which will dynamically contain messages based on rules you define. Setting up a smart mailbox in Mail is similar to setting up a smart folder in the Finder. It's good to know that like smart folders, messages added to smart mailboxes aren't moved there; the messages will still remain in their regular mailbox as well.

Creating Mail Rules

Mail rules can help you deal with large amounts of e-mail by automatically performing tasks on individual messages that meet certain specified criteria. To view your rules, go to the Rules tab in Mail's preferences (Figure 10–12).

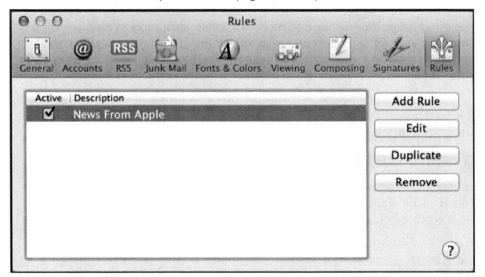

Figure 10–12. *The Rules tab shows your existing rules and allows you to edit them or create new ones.*

The Rules preference tab allows you to view your existing rules, activate or deactivate each of them, and reorder them. The four buttons on the right allow you to create new rules (Add Rule), edit an existing rule (Edit), create a copy of a rule as a starting point for a new rule (Duplicate), and delete a rule (Remove), respectively.

The activated rules will be applied in the order they are listed on either each new message as it arrives or selected messages when **Message > Apply Rules** (Option-Command-L) is applied. The order of the rules is significant since the last-run rule will have precedence over previously applied rules. Additionally, each rule has the option of preventing further rules from being executed. To reorder your rules, simply drag to put them in the order in which you want them executed.

> **NOTE:** Rules are generally applied to mail in a certain folder, so if one of your rules happens to move a message into a different folder, the following rules will not be processed for that message.

To create a new rule, click the Add Rule button, and a sheet will open for you to begin creating the rule (Figure 10–13).

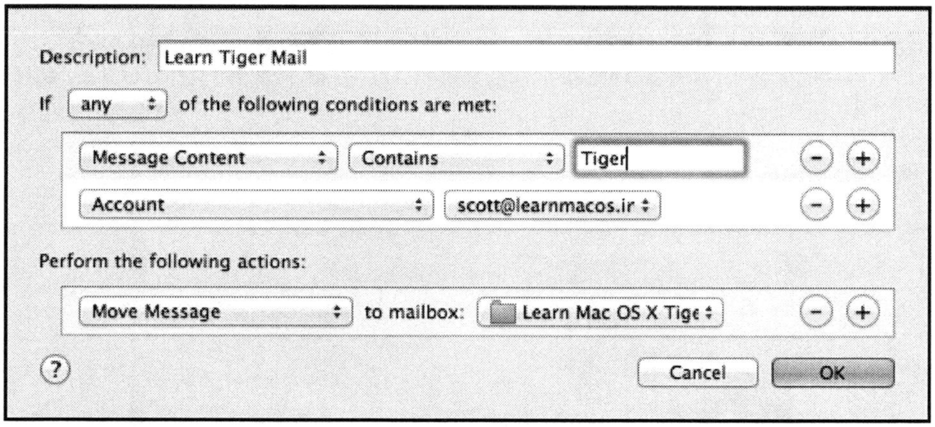

Figure 10–13. *The rule sheet allows you to fill in the criteria for new rules and edit existing rules.*

A rule has three parts: the description (or name), the conditions when the rule's actions are applied, and the actions that will occur when the conditions are met. The description can be any name you want to use to identify the rule.

You can set the conditions so that the actions will trigger when any of the conditions are met or all of the conditions are met. To add a condition, click the + button next to any existing condition, and a new blank condition will appear below. To remove a condition, click the – button next to the condition you want to remove.

You can add and remove actions the same way that you add and remove conditions (using the + and – buttons). Some special actions available are Run AppleScript, which allows you to run any AppleScript, making the possibilities of what you can do here rather immense, and "Stop evaluating rules," which immediately halts running all further rules for the current message.

ADDING ICAL EVENTS FROM MAIL

Often people will e-mail you important dates that you'll want to add to one of your iCal calendars. Mail makes this easy.

You can receive an event in two ways. First, if the event is sent to you as an iCal event attachment, just double-click the attachment, and iCal will open the event and ask you which of your calendars you'd like to add the event to.

Mail can also recognize dates in the text of a message. If you hold your mouse over a date listed in a message, the date will become outlined and act as a small drop-down menu, allowing you to add the date to iCal (Figure 10–14).

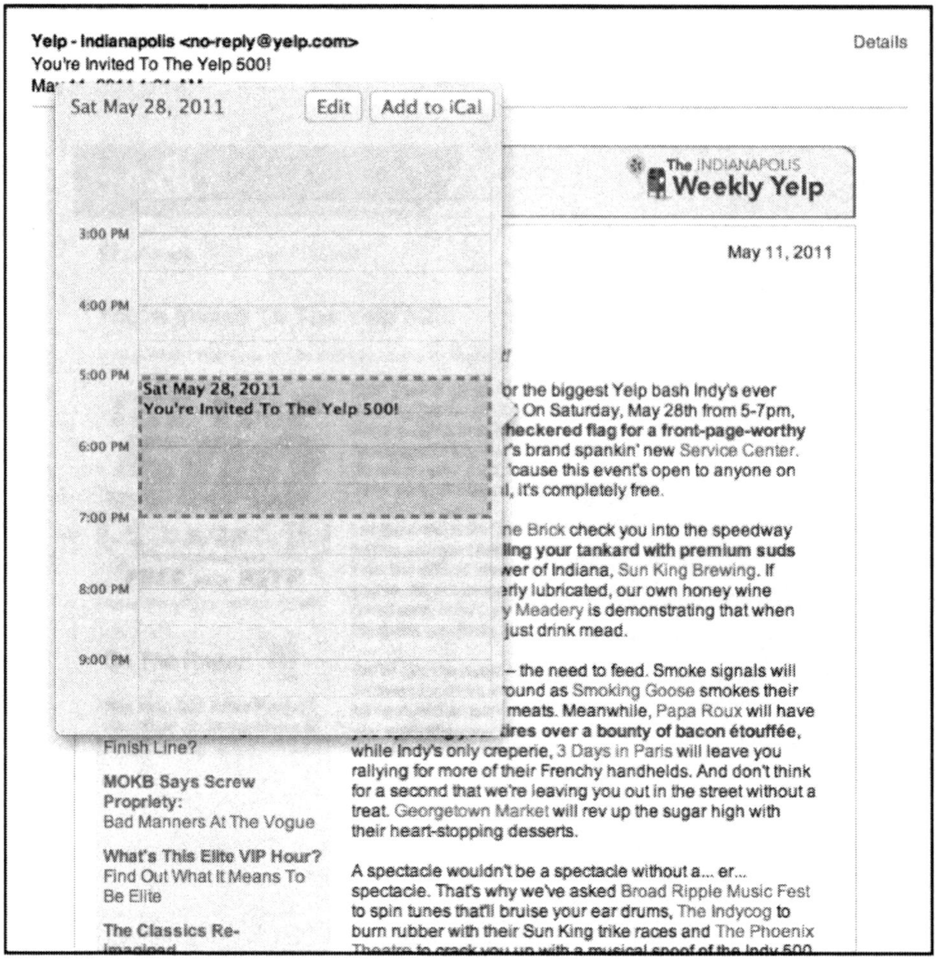

Figure 10–14. *You can click any date in a message's text to add a new iCal event.*

Once the date is selected, you can either click the Add to iCal button to add the event as is, or click the Edit button (Figure 10–15) to fill in any additional information about the event before adding it (Mail will try to fill in some information based on the information it can get from the message).

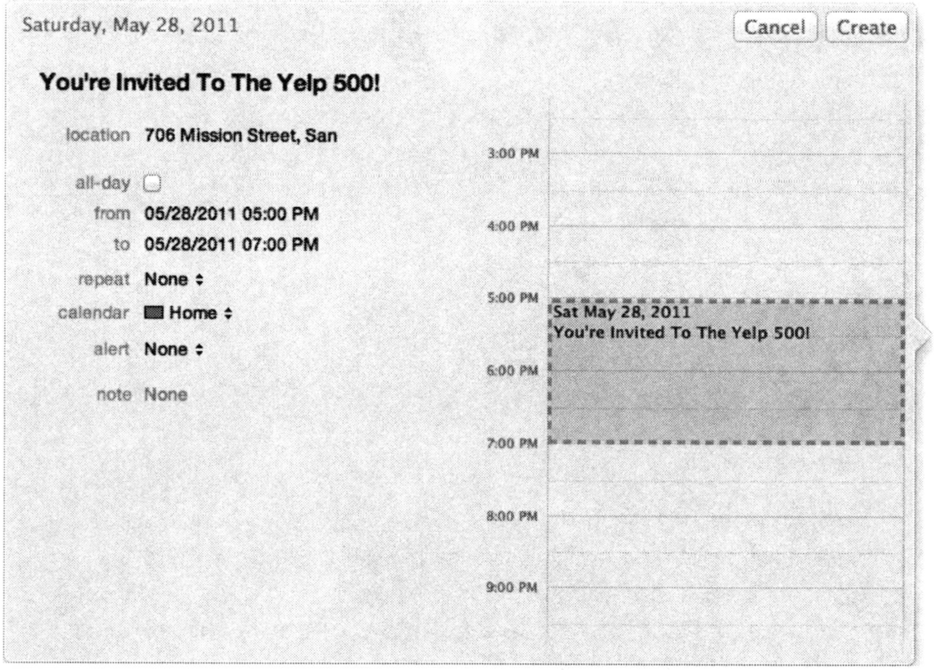

Figure 10–15. *Clicking the Edit button expands the event right in Mail to allow you to make additions to the event's data.*

If you edit the event details, when finished click Create and your new event will be added.

Sending E-mail

Sending e-mail is a pretty straightforward task: you create a new message; type your recipients, subject, and message; and click Send. Mail adds a few options that you can take advantage of, such as the ability to use stationery to apply a theme to your message.

Creating a New Message

To start a new message, select **File > New Message...** (Command-N) from the menu bar, or click the New Message button on Mail's toolbar. This opens a blank New Message window (Figure 10–16).

To start, you must first fill in the To and Cc (and/or Bcc) fields with the names of your recipients and fill in the Subject field with the subject of the message. Also, if you have multiple accounts set up, make sure the message is being sent from the proper account.

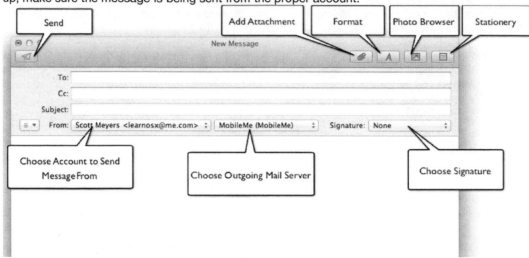

Figure 10–16. *Mail's New Message window*

> **NOTE:** The To field is traditionally for the primary recipients of a message. The Cc (which stands for *carbon copy*) field is for including anyone else you want to keep in the loop. The Bcc field (which stands for *blind carbon copy)* is where you can add recipients that will be unknown to all other recipients, including other Bcc recipients.

> **NOTE:** By default, certain fields, including Bcc, Reply-To, and Priority, are hidden. The small drop-down menu to the left of the From field allows you to reveal these fields, as well as any other header information you'd like to add (via the Customize option).

As you fill in the recipient information, Mail will attempt to autocomplete the names or addresses you are typing using information from your Previous Recipients list, your Address Book, and any LDAP or Exchange address books that are configured and connected. If Address Book has multiple e-mail addresses for a name that you enter in one of these fields, you can click the name to select which e-mail address(es) you'd like to use. Additionally, if you click the Address button on the New Messages toolbar, you will get a list of all the names and e-mail addresses contained in your Address Book.

The From field allows you to select from which of your accounts you'd like the message to be sent. The initial account listed will be the one belonging to your default e-mail address. However, if you are viewing e-mail in a mailbox other than the default mailbox, then selecting New Message will cause that account to be used instead of the default. This has the effect of ensuring that any message you reply to will come from the account to which it was sent. You can alter this behavior in the Composing section of Mail's System Preferences.

After you have filled in the required fields, you can start typing your message in the large text area. By default, the message text is formatted using rich text (which in Mail is HTML). This allows you to style your text using different font styles, colors, and sizes (accessible from the Fonts and Colors buttons on the toolbar or from the various options in the Format menu bar's submenus). Additionally, you may include inline images in your message.

To add an image to your message, you can drag and drop the image file from the Finder into your message, or you can use the Photo Browser built into Mail to browse your iPhoto library for an image to insert.

To add an attachment to your message, you can drag and drop the file in your message, or you can select the files you want to be attached from the dialog that appears when you click the Attach button on the toolbar (or you can select **File** > **Attach File...** or press Shift-Command-A).

> **NOTE:** There is a preference for using Windows-friendly attachments. This option is selected by default, and it is likely that you will want to keep it selected unless you are 100 percent sure the person you are sending an attachment to is using a Mac.

When you are done with your message and are ready to send it, just click the Send button on the toolbar, or select **Message** > **Send** (Shift-Command-D) from the menu bar, and your message will be sent using the outgoing server set up for the chosen account.

If, for some reason, your outgoing mail server is unreachable, Mail will prompt you to either try again later or try sending the message using one of the other outgoing mail servers you have set up for other accounts. If you want to try again later (maybe you have limited Internet access or SMTP is being blocked), the message will be saved, and Mail will attempt to send the message later.

If you are working on a message and you aren't ready to send it, when you close the message, Mail will ask you whether you'd like to save the message as a draft. If you select Yes, the message will be saved in your Drafts mailbox (if one doesn't exist, it will be created). You can select the message from your Drafts mailbox later to finish and send it or delete it.

Using Mail Stationery

The Mail application in Lion has the ability to apply themes to your e-mail messages using what Apple calls *stationery*. When you are creating a new message in Mail, if you click the Show Stationery button on the toolbar, a special area will slide open between the header fields and the message text to reveal a selection of stationery.

As you select specific stationery, the stationery will be previewed in the message area. Usually stationery consists of a background, image area, and text area. The text area is where you type your message. In general, the photo areas may be replaced with your own images. To replace the placeholder image with your own image, just drag a new image from the Finder or the Photo Browser into the image area, and the placeholder image will immediately be replaced with your chosen image. Besides the images, some of the backgrounds (such as Birthday Daises) have different options that are available by clicking the background.

> **NOTE:** Stationery items are really just bundles of specially formatted HTML documents and images. Therefore, it's possible to create your own. However, the exact process of packaging them is a bit complex. Mail does allow you to save new messages as stationery so that you can use them as the basis for future messages.

Replying to and Forwarding a Message

Besides creating a new message from scratch, you can also send mail by replying to or forwarding existing messages. The primary difference between a reply and a forward is that a reply will be, by default, directed to the initial sender (and other original recipients if you choose Reply All), whereas a forward is usually addressed to someone not part of the initial e-mail thread.

When you reply or forward a message, the original message is usually included (or quoted) in the reply. The original messages are usually indented and formatted in a special way (as quoted text), leaving room at the top of the message for you to add your own text to the e-mail thread.

> **NOTE:** When you redirect a message, you are not adding to or continuing the thread so much as just passing the message on to someone else as you receive it.

Creating Notes

Mail also has the ability to store notes. Notes are a fantastic way to keep track of just about anything and can be stored right alongside your mail in any mailbox.

To create a new note, just click the Note button on the Mails toolbar, or select **File > New Note** (Control-Command-N) from Mail's menu bar. This opens a New Note window (Figure 10–17), which is ready for you to start entering your information.

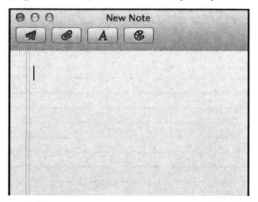

Figure 10–17. *A New Note window in Mail waiting for information*

In Lion there is no need to save notes, as notes are continuously saved in the background.

Reading RSS Feeds in Mail

Another feature in Mail is the ability to subscribe to and read RSS feeds. If you set your default RSS reader to Mail (either in Mail or in Safari's RSS preferences), then whenever you select an RSS link, you will be prompted to add the news feed in Mail. Otherwise, you can use options in Safari to subscribe to a feed in Mail or add the URL of an RSS feed in the dialog box that appears when you select **File > Add RSS Feeds...** from Mail's menu bar.

When you initially subscribe to an RSS feed in Mail, it will appear in the RSS area in the Mailbox column; however, depending on your preferences, when you select a feed, an arrow will appear to the right of it that will bump the feed up to your inbox. This will not only add new RSS items to your inbox but will also notify you when new RSS items are downloaded.

In general, feed items appear and behave as messages, while feeds behave as individual mailboxes. You can even sort your feeds into separate mailboxes to help keep them organized (and read many feeds at once).

If you want to unsubscribe to a feed, you can select **Mailbox > Delete Feed...** from the menu bar (or **Delete Feed** from the feed's contextual menu), which will delete the feed and remove any items.

Summary

For many people, e-mail has become a key communication medium for work and play. Apple's Mail application provides a wide range of features and tools for users to get the most out of e-mail, and provides a central hub for contact and event management. With that in mind, in the next couple chapters we will cover Address Book and iCal.

Address Book

Address Book (Figure 11–1) is Mac OS X's primary tool for managing contact information. It allows you to add contact information about individuals and organizations, create groups, and even access networked directory services.

The latest version of Address Book that ships with Lion has received an entirely new look vs. previous versions. Instead of the old three-column view, Address Book in Lion provides a new book-like interface with two primary views: a List and Card view (Figure 11–1) and a Groups view (Figure 11–2).

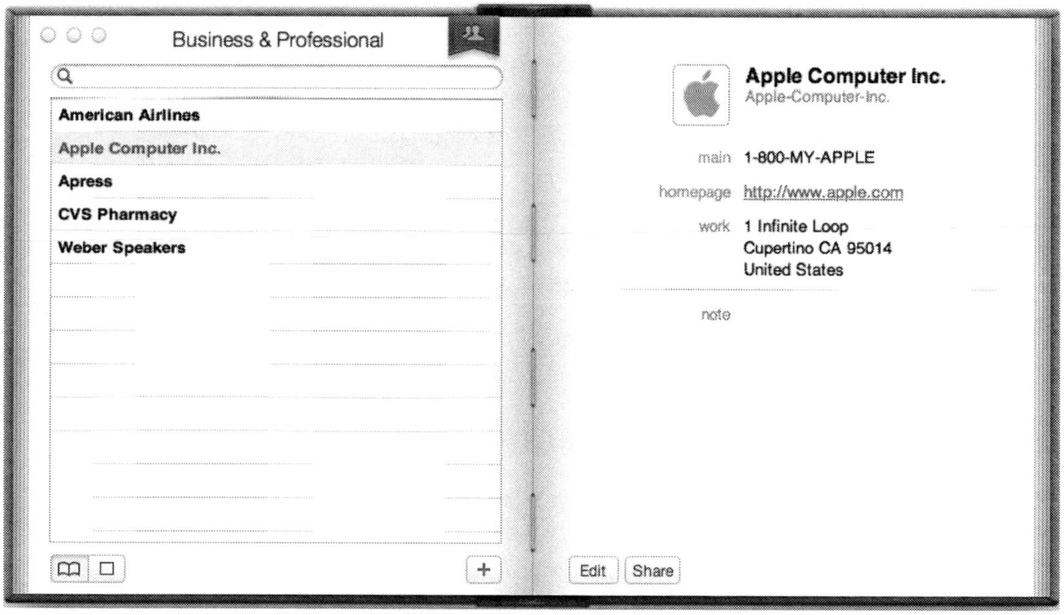

Figure 11–1. *The Address Book List and Card view shows a list of all the contacts in a group on the left side and details for the selected contact on the right.*

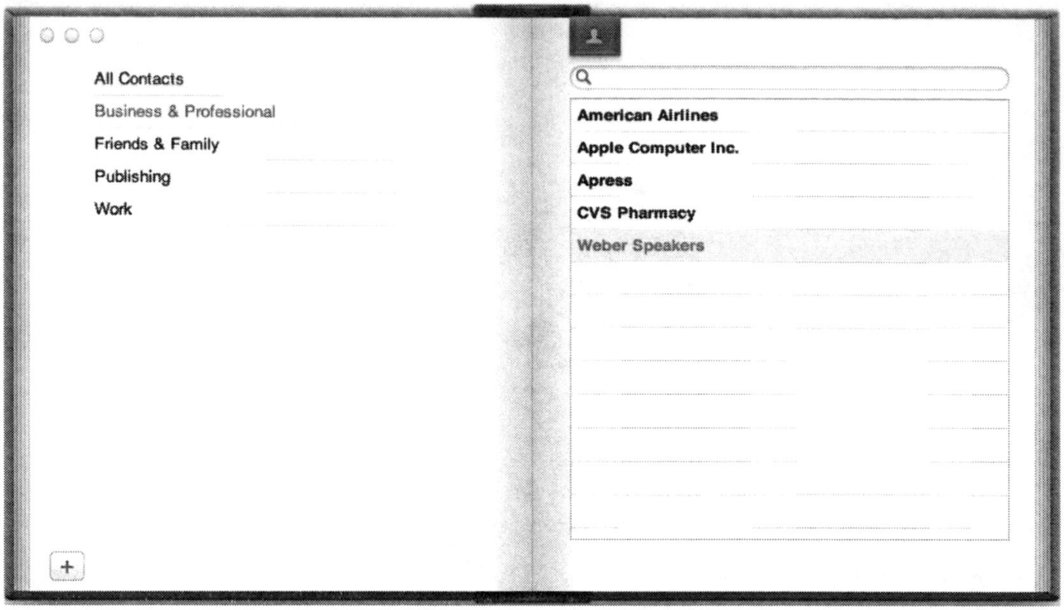

Figure 11–2. *The Address Book Groups view shows a list of all your groups and shared directories on the left side and a list of contacts in the selected group on the right.*

TIP: By default, Address Book sorts contacts by first name. You can change how the contacts are sorted and displayed on the General tab of Address Book's preferences. (I generally prefer my contacts to be sorted by last name, but displayed first name first.)

NOTE: Address Book also has a Card Only view for simply viewing a single contacts information at a time.

Adding and Editing Contacts

You can get new contacts into Address Book in a few ways. The most common are importing or syncing them from another device or file, using data detectors in Mail, and entering them manually.

If you have contacts stored on another Apple device (such as an iPad, iPhone, or iPod touch), you can sync your existing contacts using iCloud (covered in Chapter 15) or when you sync your device using iTunes (covered back in Chapter 7).

If you use an Exchange server (Exchange 2007 or later) for your e-mail, when you set up that account in Mail you were given the option to set up Contacts and Calendars at the same time. If you selected Contacts at that time, your Exchange contacts should already show up as a separate group in your Group view.

The latest version of Address Book also allows you to sync your Google and Yahoo contacts with Address Book. You can add these accounts from the Accounts tab in the Address Book preferences (Figure 11–3). To use this feature, simply select the appropriate check box, and fill in the account information from the resulting dialog box.

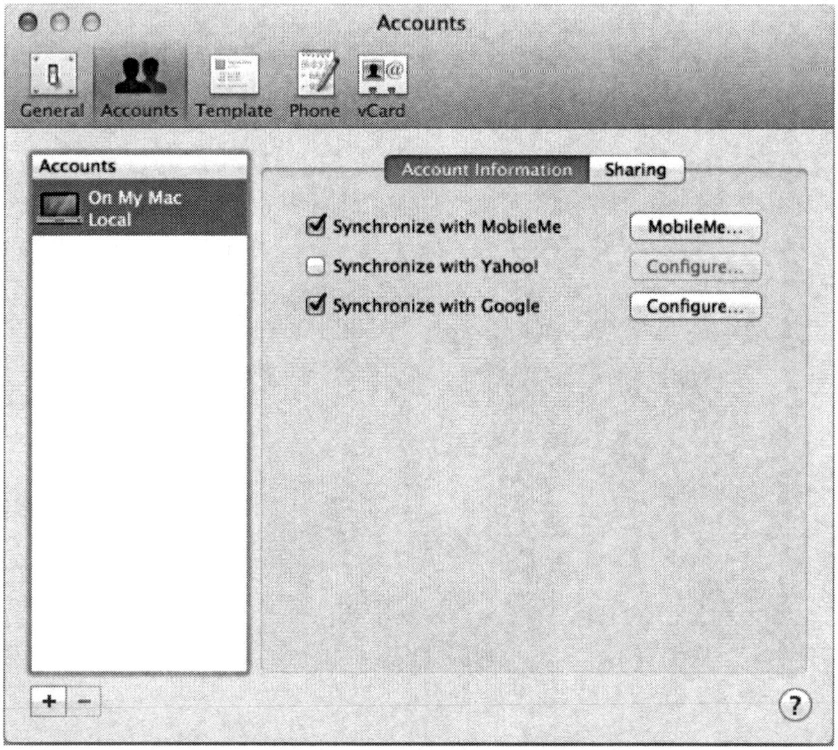

Figure 11–3. *From the Accounts tab in the Address Book preferences, you can choose to sync your contacts with Google or Yahoo.*

NOTE: When you sync your contacts with other systems, some information may be lost on the other end. For example, when you sync your contacts with a Google account, it will sync all of your local contacts into a singe My Contacts group rather than any groups you have set up on your Mac.

SETTING UP YOUR GOOGLE AND YAHOO ACCOUNTS FROM SAFARI

If you usually check you Gmail or Yahoo mail from Safari, the first time you try to check it in Lion, you may get a little surprise. A dialog box will pop up in Safari (Figure 11–4) asking you if you would like to use Mail, iCal, and iChat with the account you're checking. If you'd like to go ahead and do this, simply click the Add Account button, and the dialog will change, asking you which apps you'd like to use with this account (Figure 11–5). Once you select the apps you'd like to use and click the OK button, the account will be set up and ready to go.

Figure 11–4. *The first time you try to check your Yahoo or Gmail e-mail from Safari, you will be asked if you'd like to set up that account so it will be accessible from Mail, iCal, and iChat.*

Figure 11–5. *If you choose to add the account, you will be asked which apps you'd like to set up the account to use.*

One important app that is not automatically configured this way is Address Book, to sync your Contacts from your Gmail or Yahoo account to your Address Book, you will need to manually select that option as detailed above.

You can also import contacts from various files, including vCards (which provide a standard way of sharing contact information among many contact management clients), LDIF files (which provide a standard format for exchanging LDAP data), and even comma-separated value (CSV) or tab-delimited text files. Finally, you can also import contact data from Address Book archive files. Any of these can be imported using **File > Import...** on the menu bar; additionally, you can drag vCard files into Address Book to import them, or simply double-click them in the Finder, provided that Address Book is the default application for dealing with vCards. (If you drag a contact from Address Book, it will be exported as a vCard.)

If you need to add a new contact from scratch, either click the + button at the bottom of the Name column, or select **File** > **New Card** from the menu (Command-N). This will create a new empty contact card ready to edit in the card view area (Figure 11–6).

> **NOTE:** When you add a new card, it will be added to the currently selected group. If no group is selected, the card will only be visible from the All Contacts group.

> **NOTE:** The card view area has two modes: an edit mode and a view mode. By default, Address Book opens with cards in view mode, which will hide empty fields and restrict the editing of the contact fields (clicking a field name in view mode will generally open a menu with options pertaining to the type of field it represents). Address Book will switch to edit mode when you create a new contact. In edit mode, clicking a field will select it for editing; additionally, all default template fields will be visible even if they are empty, and you will be able to add new fields. To toggle between the modes, click the Edit|Done button beneath the card view area.

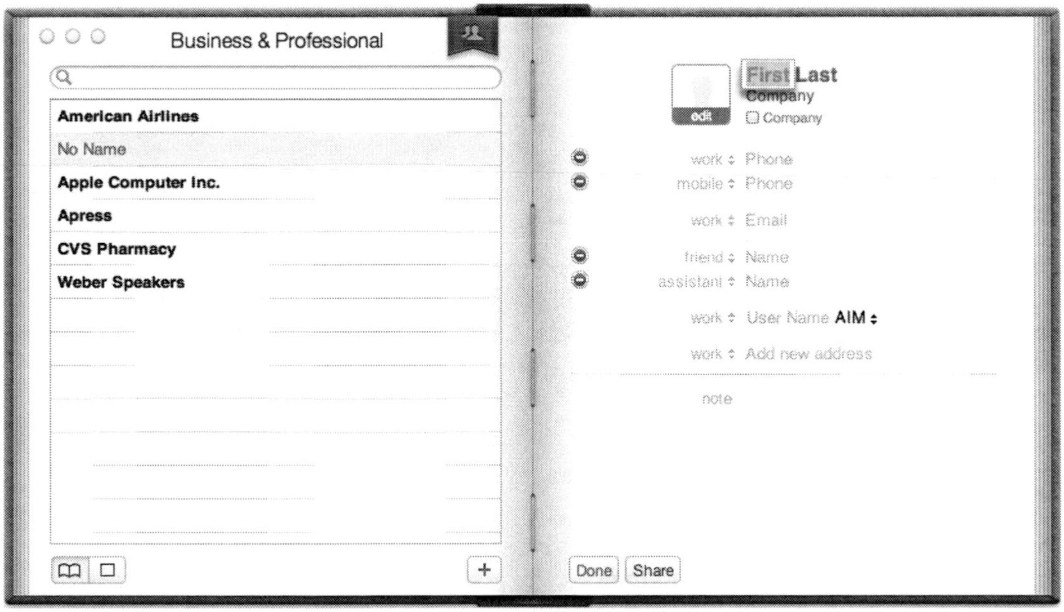

Figure 11–6. *Address Book with a new contact card waiting to be filled in*

When the new card is created, it will reveal all the fields set up in the template. To fill in a field, simply click the gray text describing the field, and type the proper information.

Many fields include a drop-down list that describes the nature of the field—generally whether the information is associated with home or work and other descriptive information that can help differentiate between similar information. To delete an entry in edit mode, just click the red "–" button to the left of the field. When you add fields in edit mode, a blank field will be added as you fill in preceding fields.

If you are looking for a specific field that is currently not listed on the card, you can add a number of fields from the **Card > Add Field** menu. This includes fields such as birthdays and other dates (which can be added to iCal) and other common contact fields.

If you find you are consistently adding information fields that are available but aren't listed in the default contact card template, then you can change the card template on the Template tab of Address Book's preferences.

If you'd like to associate an image with a contact, you can drag an image into the image field of a contact (the gray shadow of a head next to the name).

If the contact is primarily a business or organization, selecting the Company option will list the company name in the Name column rather than the person's name associated with the card (if there is one).

> **TIP:** While Address Book has a lot of predefined fields, including a number of IM fields that when you click them will automatically open an iChat window, there is no field for Skype. While you can create a custom Skype field, by default it doesn't do anything when you click it. To work around this, create your custom Skype field as a URL and then prefix the contact's Skype ID with "skype:" (e.g., "skype:sdmeyers"). This will create a link that will open up the contact in Skype if Skype is installed on your Mac.

Setting Up Your Own Card

One special card in the Address Book is the card that represents you and your information. This information is used for all sorts of things in the system and various applications, so it's good to keep it up to date. If you'd like to set a different card, for whatever reason, as My Card, select the desired contact and click **Card > Make This My Card** from the menu.

Creating Groups

You might want to create contact groups for several reasons: to create mailing lists, to make it easier to find particular contacts, or to just keep things organized. To create a group, just click the + button under the Group list in the Groups view, and a new group will be created. To add contacts to the group, you can drag existing contacts from the Contacts page to the group item on the Group page, or you can create new contacts from within the group.

Once you create the group, you can right-click the group name to export the vCards of the group, send an e-mail to each member of the group, or edit the group distribution list, which determines which e-mail addresses are used when you send a group e-mail.

Sharing Contacts

Address Book allows you to share your contacts with specific people through iCloud. To enable this feature, you must turn on sharing on the Accounts tab of Address Book's preferences (click "Share your address book" under the Sharing tab), and then you must select which other iCloud members you are allowing to view (and optionally edit) your contacts.

Viewing Shared Contact Lists

If you have permission to view a shared Address Book through iCloud, select **File >** **Subscribe to Address Book** from the menu, and then enter the iCloud member information of the person whose Address Book you'd like to share. If you have permission to view these contacts, then they will show up as a group in your Address Book.

Besides allowing iCloud address sharing, Address Book can also display contact information being shared through CardDAV, LDAP, Yahoo, and Exchange, provided you have access to these services. You can add these accounts on the Address Book preferences Accounts tab (Figure 11–3). Under the accounts list, click the + button to add a new account, which will bring up a dialog that will walk you through configuring you account.

> **NOTE:** Names for directory services will appear only in response to a search string (occasionally a very specific search string). Ideally, if you find you need to contact certain people listed in a directory service often, drag their information from the directory service section into a group or the All item to add that person to your local address book.

Printing Labels and Envelopes

One nice feature of Address Book is the ability to print labels or envelopes for a specific contact or group of contacts. To find this feature, select the contact or group you want to print labels or envelopes for, and then select **File > Print** (Command-P).

Make sure to expand the Print dialog (Figure 11–7), and select Address Book from the Print Options menu. This reveals a number of options, not only to print labels and envelopes, but also to print nicely formatted contact lists or small Address Book pages.

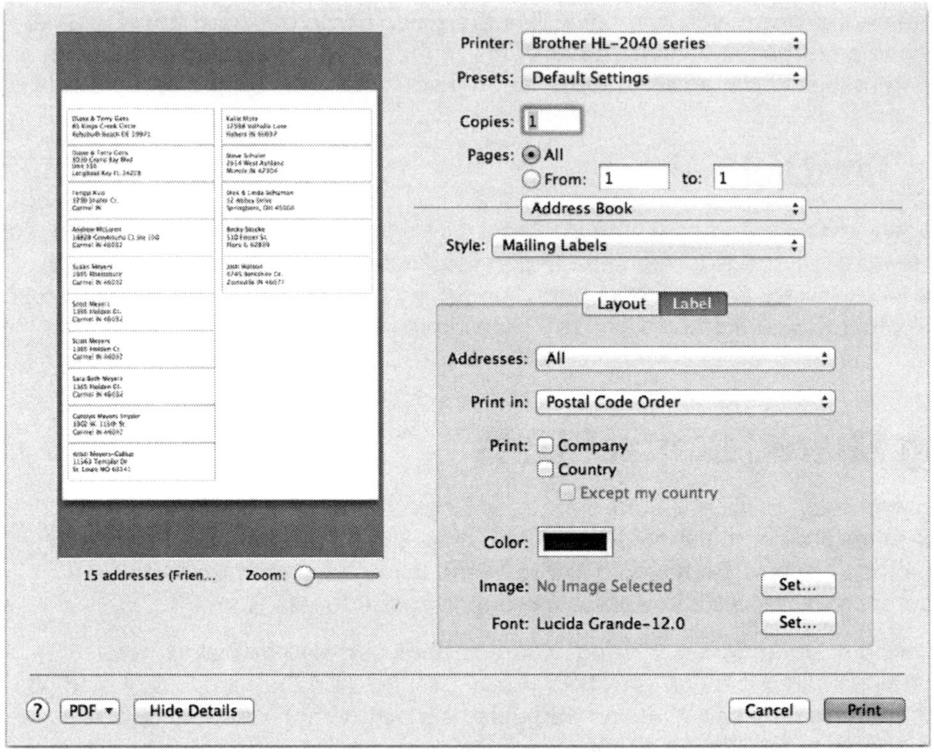

Figure 11–7. *Address Book has print options that automatically print envelopes, labels, and contact lists.*

Summary

Address Book is an easy-to-use contact management application with enough features for most users. There are of course a number of more powerful contact management and CRM applications available to Mac users, but for the majority of people Address Book works well.

Next we will cover iCal, which does for calendaring what Address Book does for contact management.

## Chapter 12

Using iCal

iCal is the Calendar application Apple includes with Mac OS X. Like Address Book, iCal's look (Figure 12–1) has changed significantly in Lion. The new look has no columns, and instead presents a unified look with four views selectable from the toolbar: Day, Week (Figure 12–2), Month (Figure 12–3), and Year (Figure 12–4).

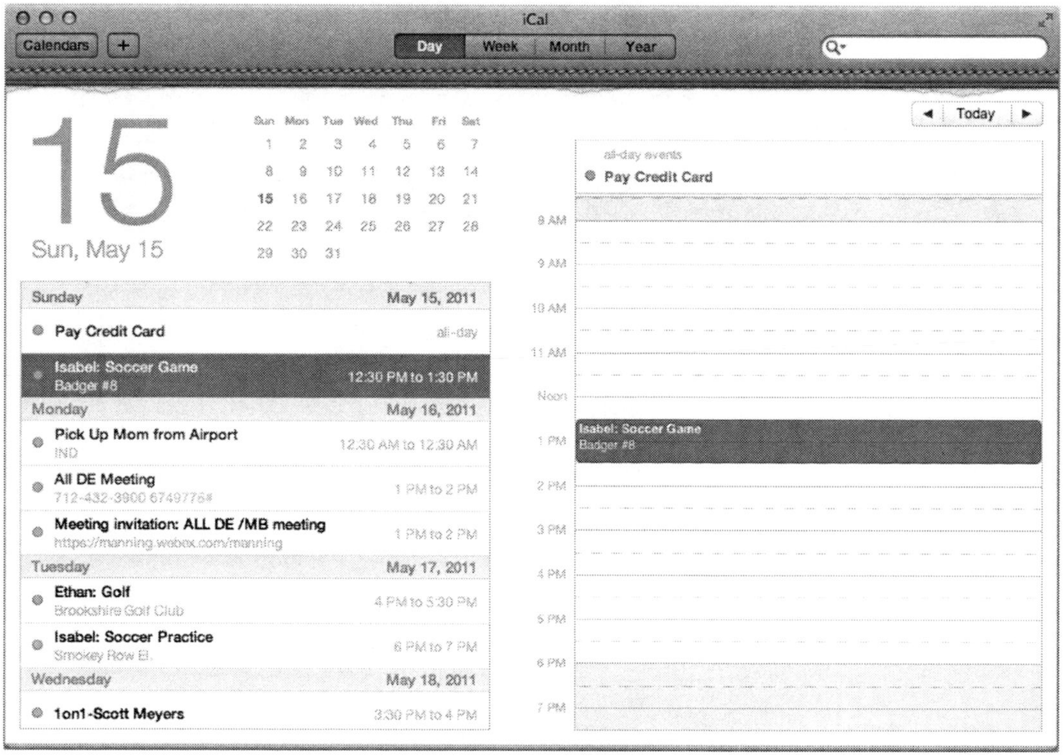

Figure 12–1. *In addition to the day's schedule, the Day view in Apple's iCal provides a small monthly calendar, as well as a list of upcoming events.*

Figure 12–2. *The Week view in iCal provides a look at all the events for a given week.*

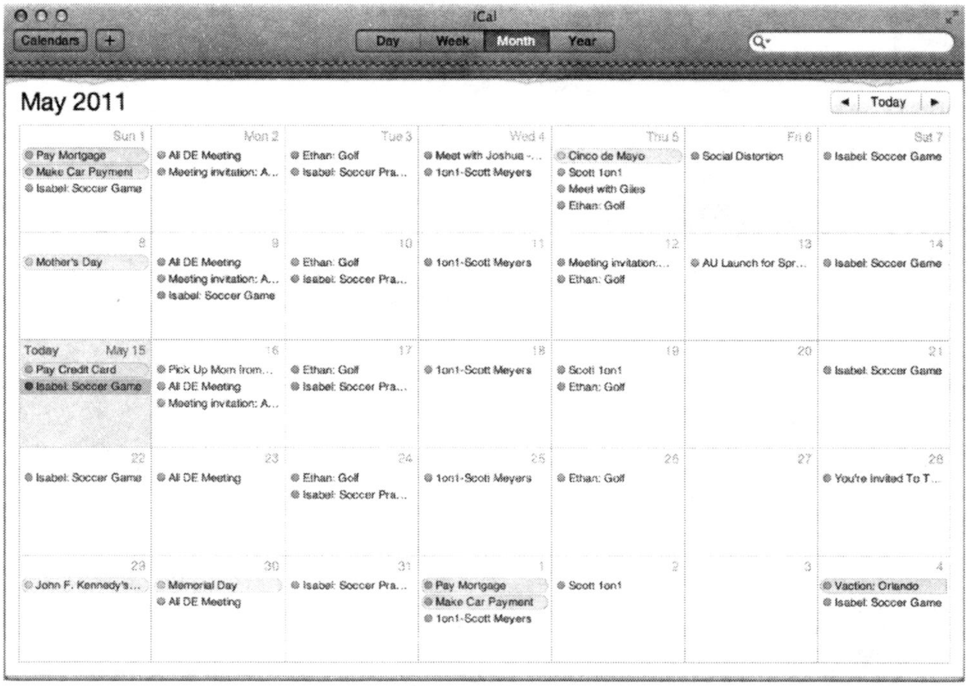

Figure 12–3. *The Month view in iCal provides a traditional view of a month, with notes for a day's events.*

Figure 12–4. *The Year view is a new view that shows that whole year in a single view. Busier days have different colors from lightly scheduled days.*

Managing Calendars in iCal

iCal organizes events into calendars accessible from the Calendars menu on the left side of the toolbar (the menu appears as a button). Each calendar can not only be viewed separately, but can have its own sharing options as well. This helps you manage your events and who has access to them all at the same time.

By default, iCal starts you out with two calendars: Home and Work. To add an additional calendar, select **File > New Calendar** from the menu. If you have multiple calendar accounts, a submenu of possible accounts will open with all of your calendar accounts (e.g., "On My Mac" and "Google"). Select the account you wish to create a new calendar under, and a new untitled calendar will be created and highlighted in the Calendar menu on the toolbar. You can now rename you new calendar as you wish.

Control-clicking a calendar on the Calendars menu will open a shortcut menu with a few options. Selecting the Get Info option will open up a dialog allowing you to add a description and change the highlight color of events belonging to the selected calendar.

In addition to creating different calendars to group together events, you can also create calendar groups to group together related calendars. To create a calendar group, select

File > **New Calendar Group** (Shift-Command-N) from the menu; this will create a new group that you can individual calendars to by dragging them into that group.

Adding and Editing Events

You can add an event in a number of ways. Selecting **File** > **New Event** (Command-N) or clicking the + button next to the Calendars menu will open a Create Quick Event dialog. To create your event, type in a name for your new event, the date, and the start and end times, and press the Return key, and iCal will add the event. For example, if you type "Dentist Appointment at 8-9:30am 5/21," iCal will create an event called Dentist Appointment from 8:00 to 9:30 a.m. on May 21st. Alternatively, you can click and drag on a time in Day or Week view to create a new event at the time, or double-click a date in Month view to add an event on that day.

> **TIP:** The Create Quick Event text field will not only recognize specific times and dates, but will also recognize general terms like *Friday* or *Tomorrow*, so "Lunch at Noon Tomorrow with Sara Beth" will create a new event for tomorrow at noon. Events without a designated time will be added as all-day events, so you could add an event like "Disney World Vacation 6/4 to 6/12."

When you first create an event, a popover may appear next to the event so you can make edits if necessary.

> **NOTE:** By default, new events will be created in your default calendar. If you wish to create an event in a specific calendar, click and hold the + button and a popover will appear allowing you to select the calendar you wish to add your new event to. You can change your default calendar on the General tab of the iCal preferences.

Once your event is created, if you want to edit it or view all the information contained in it, double-click it to open the Event Information pop-up. There you can view all the event's information or click the Edit button to put the window into edit mode (Figure 12–5) so you can make changes. In edit mode, you can change the date and times associated with an event, change the calendar the event is associated with, set an alarm to go off reminding you of the event, and make the event repeatable.

This mode also allows you to tag the event as an all-day event, which will list the event differently in the calendar view and allow the event to span multiple days. Finally, you can add attachments, notes, and URLs to the event to help you keep associated files and information tied to the event. When the event information is complete, just click Done.

If an event gets rescheduled or needs to be moved for any reason, rather than having to go into edit mode, you can change the date and time of the event by dragging the event from one time slot in the calendar to another.

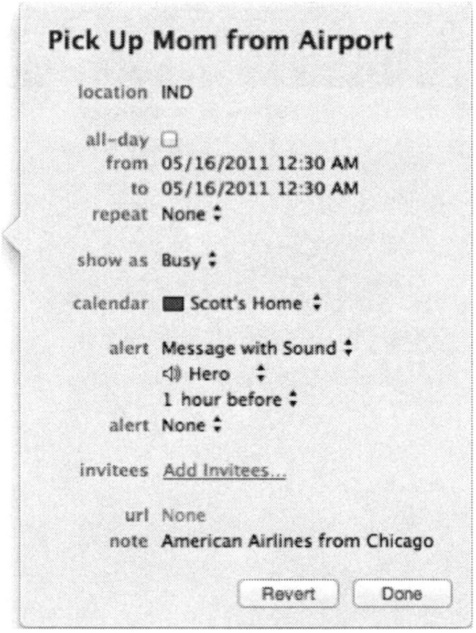

Figure 12–5. *You can add and edit event information from the Event popover dialog.*

Adding Reminders

Besides events, iCal also provides the ability to keep track of reminders (formerly know as To-Dos). To view reminders in iCal, select **View** > **Show Reminders** (Option-Command-T) from the menu, and the Reminders column will appear along the right side of the iCal window (Figure 12–6).

Control-clicking a reminder will open a shortcut menu that will allow you to add some details to your reminder, such as its priority and what calendar the reminder belongs to. Selecting Get Info from the shortcut menu will open a dialog with additional details, allowing you to add additional information such as a due date, and set alarms associated with the reminder.

Figure 12–6. *iCal's Day view with the Reminders column shown*

Inviting Others to Events and Appointments

In an event's edit mode, you are able to invite additional people to an event. By clicking Add Invitees, you can add any number of people you want to add as attendees for your event. Any attendees who are listed in your Address Book are automatically sent an invitation to the event.

NOTE: If an attendee isn't in your Address Book, you can still type in an e-mail address to send an invitation.

TIP: When you add invitees to an event, a new Available Meeting Times... hyperlink appears in the event. If you have access to the invitees' shared calendar, you can access each of the invitees' calendars to find a time when everyone is free.

Adding Time Zone Support

iCal has a nice time zone support feature that is not activated by default, but if you often travel or deal with people in other time zones, then this is a fantastic feature to use. Activating time zone support is as easy as selecting the "Turn on time zone support" option on the Advanced tab in iCal's preferences. Once the support is turned on, you will notice that a small time zone drop-down list will appear in the upper right of iCal's main window above the search field. You can alter this field to reflect the time zone that iCal is in. Additionally, events will gain a time zone setting. With time zone support enabled, iCal will automatically alter event times based on the time zone of the event and the time zone of iCal.

Subscribing to Public Calendars

Sometimes you may want to subscribe to a calendar other than your own. For example, you may want to subscribe to a calendar that provides the schedule of your favorite basketball team, or you may want to subscribe to a calendar that contains all the common UK holidays.

To get a taste for what calendars are available, choose Calendar > Find Subscriptions... from iCal's menu. This opens your web browser to an Apple web site where Apple makes available a number of common shared calendars (including many sports teams' schedules and cultural holidays).

Besides the calendars available from Apple, organizations often post calendar links on their web sites that will allow you to subscribe to their calendars. Finally, If you know the location of a shared calendar on the Web, you can use the Calendar > Subscribe... menu command (Option-Command-S), which opens a dialog box and allows you to enter the URL of a calendar you wish to add.

You can unsubscribe from a calendar by selecting Delete from the shortcut menu of the calendar from the Calendars menu.

Sharing Your iCal Calendars

Occasionally you may have an iCal calendar that you would like to share with others. To share one of your iCal calendars, you must either use iCloud or have access to a private CalDAV server.

If you are sharing a calendar that is already being stored on iCloud, then select the iCloud calendar you wish to share and select Calendar > Share Calendar... from the menu bar. This will open up a dialog (Figure 12–7) asking you what name the calendar should be shared as, and whether you would like to share the calendar with "Everyone" or "Only the people you invite." Publishing the calendar for everyone will create a public shared calendar that anyone with the URL can subscribe to. If you choose the "Only people you invite" option, a field will open where you can add the e-mail addresses of the people (or names of people in your Address Book) you wish to invite to share your calendar. Next to each person you add, a menu will allow you to select whether that person should have read and write access to the calendar (i.e., they will be able to add and edit events), or read-only access.

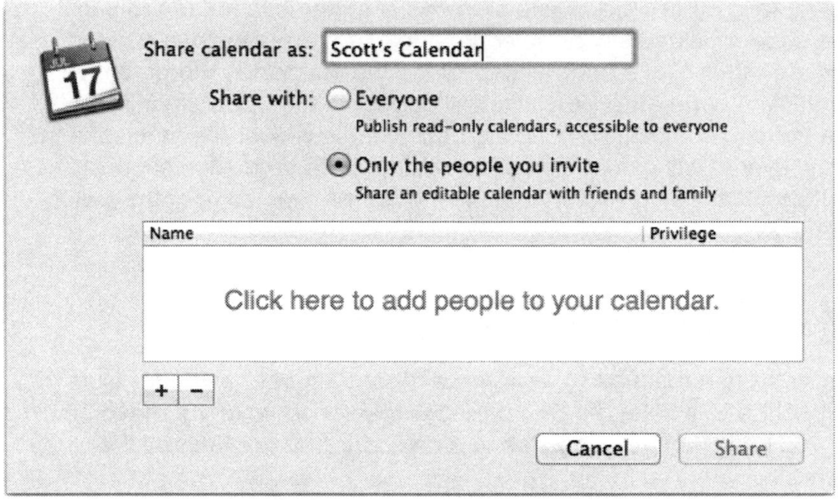

Figure 12–7. *When you choose to share a calendar through iCloud, a dialog will appear to help you choose how you wish to share the calendar.*

When you click the share button for "Everyone" calendars, you will be presented with a URL that leads people to your calendar; for "Only the people you invite" calendars, the individuals you are sharing the calendar with will be sent an e-mail telling them what they need to know to access the shared calendar.

If you wish to share a non-iCloud calendar, then select **Calendar > Publish...** from the menu bar. This will open a different dialog (Figure 12–8), asking you to choose a name you would like to share the calendar as and whether you want to publish the calendar on "iCloud" or "A private server." If you choose a private server, you must enter the server's URL and your login credentials. Next, there are a series of check boxes to choose what information will be shared. When everything is filled out, click the Publish button and you will be given the URL to the shared calendar.

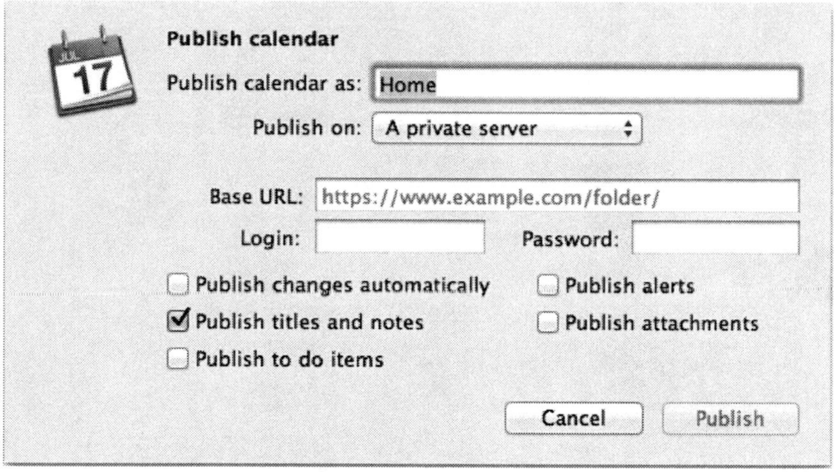

Figure 12–8. *You can publish a calendar to be shared through any CalDAV server.*

> **NOTE:** If you wish to share your iCal calendars using the private server option, then you must have access to a CalDAV server. CalDAV is a standard supported by Apple and other companies in which calendar data is stored on a server and shared over the Web (usually over a secure SSL connection for nonpublic calendars). Apple's own calendaring server included with Mac OS X Lion Server is a fully compliant CalDAV server.

Managing Calendaring Accounts in iCal

As we touched upon earlier in this chapter, iCal is able to access calendars that are hosted on other systems, including Exchange 2007 and later, Google Calendars, Yahoo Calendars, Private CalDAV servers, and of course iCloud. You can add and manage these accounts from the Accounts tab in the iCal preferences (Figure 12–9).

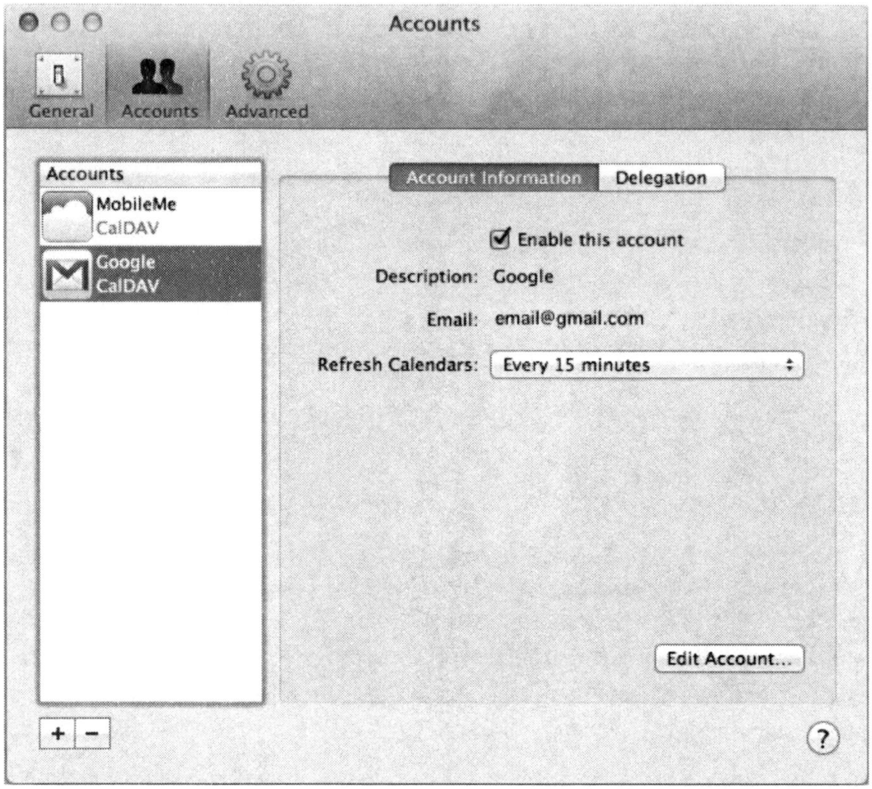

Figure 12–9. *The Accounts tab in the iCal preferences allows you to add and manage different calendaring accounts.*

To add an account, click the + sign at the bottom of the Accounts list and follow the steps presented in the dialog. You will be guided though adding a CalDAV, Exchange, Google, Yahoo, or MobileMe-type calendar account.

> **NOTE:** Many of the details of adding accounts is now better handled from the Mail, Contacts & Calendars pane of the System Preferences. This will be covered later the book.

Once an account is added, you can access some information about the account here as well. The options here will vary with account type.

One interesting option under the Accounts tab is the Delegation subtab. Delegation is similar to sharing (in fact, they are often used synonymously), in which a calendar owner can "delegate" others to access their calendar and act on their behalf. For certain accounts (including Google and Exchange), you will find any calendars you have access to on that system located under this tab. You can select any of these calendars and they too will appear in iCal.

> **TIP:** In general, different calendaring systems have different ways of sharing calendars, and they aren't always entirely compatible. iCal makes the best of these inconsistencies and generally does a good job of smoothing out the differences, but there are still a number of oddities. For example, Google Calendar only maintains only one primary calendar per account. You can of course add other calendars in Google Calendar, but to iCal these additional calendars will show up as delegates under the Google account, so this doesn't provide the same out-of-the-box experience that you get with, for example, MobileMe. Also, certain features of other calendaring systems (sharing is a big one) are best utilized through their native interface rather than iCal.

Summary

Just like the holy trinity of onions, bell peppers, and celery in Cajun cooking (you can substitute carrots for peppers for a more French flair), e-mail, contact management, and calendaring form the traditional backbone of "getting things done" in many people's personal and professional lives. These last three chapters, on Mail, Address Book, and iCal, should have provided you enough information to be proficient with these tools. As technology continues to move forward, however, new ways to communicate are constantly being introduced. In the next chapter we will look at some different ways to communicate using iChat and FaceTime.

## Chapter 13

Instant Communication with iChat and FaceTime

Beyond Mail, Apple includes a couple of additional applications that are designed for communications: iChat and FaceTime. Unlike Mail, iChat and FaceTime are generally intended for real-time communication, much like talking on the telephone. Unlike the telephone, these applications and the technologies behind them can go far beyond just real-time voice communication. FaceTime, which is a relatively new Mac OS X application (though it has been included with many recent iOS devices) provides real-time video communication between your computer and other computers and supported mobile devices (such as recent iPhones and iPads). iChat on the other hand has been part of Mac OS X since version 10.2, and today can be used for text, voice, or video chat over a number of popular instant-messaging (IM) protocols. In this chapter we will cover

- Getting set up with iChat
- Adding and managing iChat "buddies"
- Text-based IM
- Voice and video with iChat
- iChat file transfers
- Using FaceTime

Using iChat

IM is the Internet communication method of choice for many people in many situations. iChat is Apple's default IM client on Mac OS X and has lots to offer. First, it's compatible with Yahoo, AIM (AOL Instant Messenger), and Google Chat systems, three of the biggest IM networks out there. Second, it adds lots of cool features that go beyond simple text chat, including voice and video chat. Finally, it's easy to use and well integrated with other Mac OS X applications.

Getting and Setting Up an iChat Account

First of all, if you already have a MobileMe account that you have set up prior to this (e.g., to use with Mail), then your MobileMe account should already be set up and active in iChat when you first launch it.

> **NOTE:** If you were a .Mac account holder and had a *user*@mac.com account that you used for iChat, you will need to manually enter this account on the Account tab of the iChat preferences, even if you have set up MobileMe previously. This is because on AIM (the chat service that MobileMe uses), *user*@me.com and *user*@mac.com are separate accounts, even though they are the same for most other MobileMe services.

If you haven't previously set up a MobileMe account and want to add or create an account for iChat, you can do so from the Account tab of the iChat preferences (Figure 13–1). To begin, click the + button below that account's list. This will open the Account Setup dialog (Figure 13–2), which will ask you for your account type, username, and password. The account type options are

- **AIM**: For using an AOL account name on the AIM network

- **me.com**: For using your MobileMe account on the AIM network

- **mac.com**: For using an older .Mac username on the AIM network

- **Jabber**: For using a Jabber account on any Jabber server

- **Google Talk**: For using your Google account on Google's talk server (which uses Jabber as well)

- **Yahoo**: for using your Yahoo account on Yahoo's IM server

For the first three account options (AIM, me.com, and mac.com), there is an option to get an iChat account if you don't already have one. Choosing this option will take you either to AOL's sign-up page (for AIM) or the iCloud sign-up page for me.com or mac.com. For Jabber, Google Talk, and Yahoo, you must already have an account set up.

> **NOTE:** Getting a new iChat account under both the AIM and mac.com options will take you to a form to sign up for a free account. The me.com accounts are part of Apple's iCloud service.

Once you've selected you account type, enter your username and password and click Done, and you should be ready to go (unless you are setting up a Jabber account, in which case you will need to enter the server information for the specific Jabber server you are using).

NOTE: There is one other type of account that iChat can use that does not need to be configured: Bonjour. The Bonjour account will automatically use your Lion account info to identify you and will find any other iChat users on your LAN who have their Bonjour account activated. Bonjour is a great way to instant-message people in your organization a few offices away, or one of your children upstairs in their room blaring music loudly with their door closed.

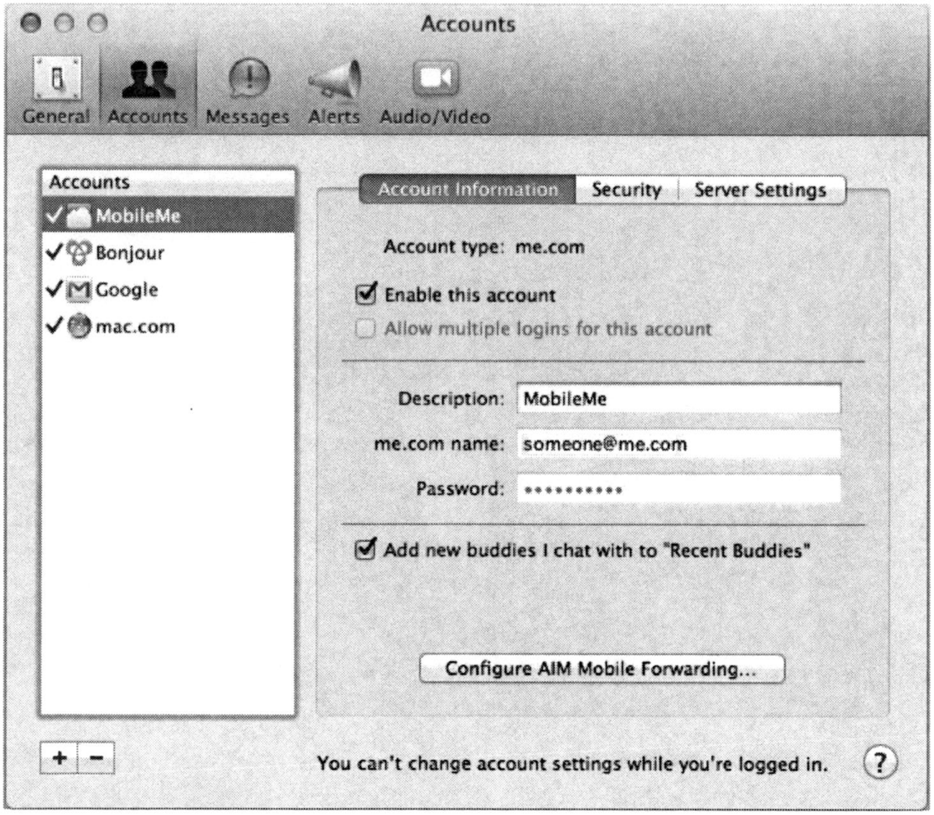

Figure 13–1. *You can add and manage your IM accounts from iChat's Accounts preferences.*

Figure 13–2. *The Account Setup sheet used to add new iChat accounts*

Depending on the account type for each account listed in your Accounts column, there will be some additional configuration options. The key option you'll want to know about is the "Enable this account" option. "Enable this account" enables the account and lists it on the **iChat** > **Accounts** submenu, and will attempt to connect to the account when iChat starts.

Some accounts also have security options associated with them; these options generally enable you to restrict how other people view your status when you are online.

Logging Into Your iChat Account and Setting Your Status

Logging into your iChat account(s) is a fairly easy process. Obviously, if you have selected the option to have your account automatically log in when iChat launches, then you really don't have anything to do. However, to manually log in and log out, all you have to do is toggle your account in the **File** > **Accounts** submenu.

When you log in, your iChat Buddies window opens up, which allows you to access all available IM features and view your buddy list, as shown in Figure 13–3.

Figure 13–3. *The latest version of iChat allows you to combine all your buddies from various accounts into a single iChat Buddies window.*

> **NOTE:** The version of iChat that ships with Lion defaults to a single buddy list that will display the buddies from each of your accounts in a singe view. If you prefer to have separate buddy lists for each account (which is how past versions of iChat displayed things), you can uncheck the "Show all my accounts in one list" option on the iChat preferences General tab.

The top of the account window provides your account status. The top line provides your name (or the name associated with your accounts). You can toggle between the two by clicking the name/handle. To the left of your name is your online status: a green dot means you are online and accepting instant messages, a red dot means you are online but not accepting incoming instant messages, a faint gray circle means you are online but invisible (people can't see that you are online), and no dot means you are offline.

Below the name is your online status message. Your status message and current online status will be visible to anyone (unless you limit the visibility of your status in the account's security preferences). To change your status message, click the status message and select a new status from the pop-up menu. You can set a custom status message by selecting Custom Available... or Custom Away... from the menu, and then typing in anything you want. Selecting Edit Status Menu... opens a dialog where you can create, edit, or delete the status messages that appear in the pop-up, and change whether and how iChat remembers your custom status messages. Below that is the Use Same Status for All Accounts option. If this is selected (the default setting), people viewing any of your accounts will all see the same message. Unselecting the Use Same Status for All Accounts option will add additional status menus for each account you have set up in iChat.

To the right of your name is your picture, also known as your buddy icon. Your initial picture is the same icon you have associated with your account and your contact info in Address Book. To change your picture, drop an image on the current picture, or click it to bring up a list of recent pictures. From the Recent Pictures sheet, you can also select Edit Picture... for more options, including taking a snapshot with iSight.

If you have audio or video chat enabled, a green audio or video icon will also be visible. A stacked video icon means that you (or a buddy) can use iChat Theater (a feature that allows videoconferencing with multiple iChat users).

Adding and Managing Buddies

Most IM accounts maintain buddy lists to keep track of friends, family, and associates who have related IM accounts. These buddies (or friends) can be managed from within iChat. To add a buddy, click the + button at the bottom of the iChat Buddies window and select the Add Buddy... option, or select **Buddies** > **Add Buddy...** (Shift-Command-A) from the menu bar. This opens up a dialog for you to fill in information about your new buddy, as shown in Figure 13–4.

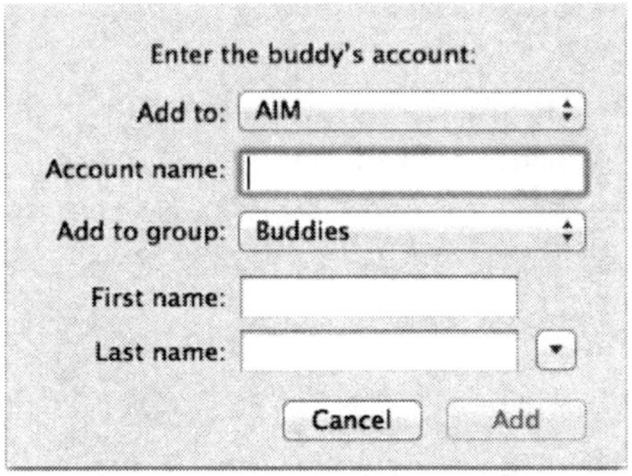

Figure 13–4. *Adding a Buddy in iChat*

Address Book is integrated with iChat. If your buddy is already listed in your address book, iChat will autocomplete the Add Buddy form as you type. Clicking the disclosure button to the right of the Last Name field expands the sheet into a people-picker that displays all the groups and contacts you have in your address book. Selecting an Address Book card associates it with that buddy. You can also drag contacts from Address Book into your buddy list to add them.

To help you keep track of your buddies, you can organize them into groups. To create a group, click the + button at the bottom of the account window to open a menu, and select the Add Group... option. A small sheet will open up and ask for the name of your new group. Enter the name and click Add to add the group. To change or delete groups, select the Edit Groups... option from the + buttons menu.

When you add a buddy, you are asked what group you'd like that person to be in. If you'd like to change the group, simply select and drag your buddy into a new group. If you'd like to rearrange the order in which your groups appear, grab their headers and drag them around.

On iChat's View menu, there are a number of options about how to display offline buddies. You can hide them, display them in their regular groups, or coalesce them into a special offline group.

The View menu also lets you choose whether to use groups at all; whether to display your audio or video status; whether to display buddies by full name, short name, or handle; and whether to sort buddies by name or availability, or not at all.

Communicating with iChat

While iChat started as a specialized version of AOL's Instant Messenger client, it has evolved into a multiprotocol communication powerhouse. The traditional features are still there, but they are joined by advanced audio and video chat modes, and are augmented by integration with other programs on the system. Control-clicking a name on your buddy list reveals a long list of options, each one representing a different method of communicating.

> **NOTE:** In addition to the buddy list's contextual menu, you can also initiate communications with selected buddies from the Buddies menu on the menu bar, or by the menu items' associated keyboard shortcuts.

Text Chat

Invite to Chat... is the first option. Selecting this opens a new chat window. Typing a message and pressing Return cause a window to pop up on your selected buddies' screens inviting them to chat. If they accept, you will be able to type messages back and forth, forming a conversation, as shown in Figure 13–5.

The chat window displays your conversation as it happens, with the users' buddy icons and text balloons indicating who said what. To enter a message, just type your text in the text field at the bottom of the window. When someone is typing, a gray thought balloon appears next to their buddy icon, so you know they're formulating a response and not just ignoring you.

> **NOTE:** The thought balloons only appear in one-on-one chats. It would be entirely too annoying if a ten-person chat window were constantly full of thought balloons.

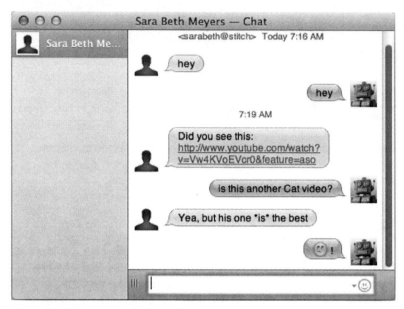

Figure 13–5. *Having a text chat in iChat*

That the chat option is first on the list suggests it's iChat's preferred method of communication. This is a not a coincidence, as the chat mode offers several conveniences over traditional IM.

Chats can involve more than two people. Selecting multiple buddies when initiating a chat will send invitations to everyone. Anyone who joins that chat will be able to participate in the conversation.

Chat mode uses a chat room metaphor, similar to Internet Relay Chat (IRC). That means people can be invited to join at any time and leave as they please. As long as one person remains in the chat room, the conversation will remain open.

Even if you're only talking to one person, chat is still a good mode because you always have the option of inviting more people—more like a natural conversation. Imagine if you were in a coffee shop talking to a friend when another friend came in. How silly it would be to have to leave the coffee shop and come back for them to join you?

> **NOTE:** You can chat without using your buddy list. To start a chat with someone who isn't on your buddy list, select **File > New Chat...** (Command-N) from the menu bar and fill in the information in the pop-up dialog box. To join a chat room by name, select **File > Go to Chat Room...** (Command-R) and type the name of the room. If a room by that name does not exist, it will be created.

IM VS. CHAT

In iChat, selecting Send Instant Message... works almost identically to Invite to Chat...; in fact, the window will still say you are "chatting with" your buddy. Don't be fooled; IM has fewer options than a true chat. While you can hold multiple IM conversations, you can't have three or more people talking at a time, nor can you add participants as you can with a chat.

To add to the confusion, if you try to send an instant message to multiple buddies at once, you will actually start a chat session, even though you selected Send Instant Message..., not Invite to Chat...!

Audio and Video Chats

Like you, people in your buddy or chat participant lists with video chat enabled will display a camera icon. Clicking this icon invites them to video chat and present you with a video preview window, giving you a last chance to get the spinach out of your teeth. If they accept, you will see a picture-in-a-picture video screen.

> **NOTE:** Video chat is not always available. Whether or not video chat is available depends on a couple of things, including the type of account you are using and the type of setup being used (client and hardware). Your iChat Buddies list provides you with information about what types of services are available for each of your online buddies. A phone icon indicates your buddy is only available for text chat, a single video icon indicates they are available for one-on-one video/audio chat, and a stack of video icons indicates they are available for multiuser video chat (or iChat Theater).

As with text chat, video chat can support multiway conferencing, as shown in Figure 13–6. Depending on the speed of your computer's processor, you can video chat with as many as three people simultaneously. Chat participants can be selected when you start the chat, or they can be invited late by pressing the + button at the bottom of the window.

Figure 13–6. *Three-way videoconferencing in iChat*

Adjacent to the + button is a mute button, which disables the audio portion of the chat. To the right of the mute button is a button for going into full-screen mode. To the far left is the Effects button, which toggles a menu of real-time effects you can apply to your video, as shown in Figure 13–7.

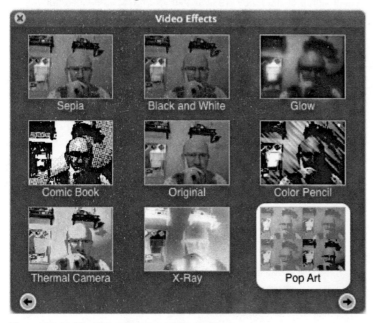

Figure 13–7. *The Video Effects window in iChat*

You can also summon the Video Effects window by selecting **Video** > **ShowIHide Video Effects** (Shift-Command-E) from the menu bar. To select an effect, click it. To remove the effect, click the original effect in the middle of the page.

There are a few pages of effects, which you can navigate by using the arrow buttons on either side of the panel. There are also several blank spots on the last page where you can insert your own effects by dragging pictures, videos, or Quartz Composer compositions into the blank spots.

Background Effects

Video effects that have an outline of a person in them are background effects. If you select one, iChat will ask you to step out of the frame while it analyzes the background. It will then replace the background with full-motion video. When you step back into the frame, it will appear that you're standing in front of the new background, as shown in Figure 13–8.

For best results, select an even, neutral background. If you happen to have a high-tint green or blue chroma-key screen, use that. Otherwise, a white wall works well. Make sure your clothes have sufficient contrast from the background (unless you want to look like a floating head). If you see spots where the background shows through, select **Video** > **Reset Background** (Option-Command-R) from the menu bar and try again. It also helps if you don't move around too much.

All in all, the background effects are probably not going to convince your boss you're hard at work at the office while you sip margaritas on the beach, but it may certainly add a fun flare to your Friday meetings.

Figure 13–8. *The results of applying background effects in iChat*

Variations on Video Chat

Clicking a buddy's video icon always launches video chat, even if all you want is audio chat. Fortunately, there are several other ways to launch audio and video chats, the most obvious of which is to select Invite to Video Chat or Invite to Audio Chat from the buddy list's contextual menu, or from the Buddies menu on the menu bar.

If a buddy does not have audio or video chatting enabled, these menu items will become Invite to One-Way Video Chat and Invite to One-Way Audio Chat. That means, for example, you can still originate a video chat with them, and they will be able to see you, but you won't be able to see them.

You can also click the telephone and camera buttons on the bottom of your buddy list to launch that type of chat with the selected buddies. Clicking the text button is equivalent to double-clicking: it will launch some kind of text-based communication, depending on context.

iChat also works with other AIM video chat clients, most notably AIM for Windows, assuming the users have the appropriate hardware.

Mobile Text Messaging

Most mobile phones support text messaging via the Short Message Service protocol, also known as SMS, or simply *text messaging.* iChat has two ways to participate in text messaging. First, you can send a text message to a buddy by selecting Send SMS... from the buddy list contextual menu, or **Buddies > Send SMS...** from the menu bar.

In order for the Send SMS... command to be enabled, you must have a phone number set for your buddy in Address Book, and that number must be labeled as "mobile." If the number is labeled as anything else, including home, main, pager, or a custom label, it will not work in iChat.

> **CAUTION:** Support for SMS only works on phone numbers from the United States, Canada, and other members of the ten-digit North American Numbering Plan. The same is true for AIM mobile forwarding (discussed following).

Sending an SMS message launches a chat window, just like sending an instant message. If your buddy sends a response, it will show up in the chat window, as expected. If you have since closed the window, iChat will open a new one. However, this is not a true instant message, so if your buddy tries to respond after you've closed iChat or logged out, that person will receive an error message.

Another way to communicate with iChat from your mobile phone is to enable mobile forwarding on your AIM account. This is done online, but you can get to the appropriate web page by clicking the Configure AIM Mobile Forwarding... button in iChat's account preferences. The process is simple: you enter your phone number and AOL sends a confirmation code to your phone. Enter the code on the activation page, and you're done.

With mobile forwarding enabled, you will never go offline. If anyone sends you an instant message, it will be converted to an SMS text message and sent to your phone. Your responses will be returned in the chat window, much like the Send SMS feature.

In iChat, buddies who are receiving their messages via mobile forwarding will have a gray "broadcasting" symbol next to their names. Their availability dot will be clear to light-gray in color, and they will have the status message they had when they logged out.

> **CAUTION:** Most mobile plans limit the number of SMS text messages subscribers can send and receive, and some even charge a fee for each message. Keep this in mind before using mobile messaging features from iChat.

File Transfers

One nice feature of iChat is the ability to send a file to someone you are chatting with. If you'd like to send a file, select **Buddies > Send File...** (Option-Command-F), which will open a file dialog to select the file you wish to send. Once the file is selected, the person you are sending the file to will get prompted to accept the file. When that person accepts, the download will begin.

Likewise, if you are being sent a file, you will be prompted in your chat window to accept or decline the item. If you accept, the file will be downloaded to your system.

You can also drag files from within the Finder to names in your buddy list, or into the input field of an open chat. Certain types of files, such as images and PDFs, will be rendered in place.

To save the image, drag it from the chat window to the Finder. If the image is large, it will be scaled down in the chat window; but when you drag it, you will save the original file as if you had just transferred it.

Since moving files around in iChat has become so common, iChat has a File Transfers window, much like the one found in Safari. This window contains a list of files, their transfer status, and a magnifying glass icon you can click to jump to the file in the Finder. The File Transfers window will launch automatically as needed, but you can also summon it from the menu bar by selecting **Window > File Transfers** (Option-Command-L).

> **CAUTION:** While Mac OS X doesn't have the vast virus problem that plagues other computing environments, Mac users are not immune to Trojans and other malicious files. If you open unknown files from unknown sources, you are you are inviting trouble, so don't do it.

Screen Sharing

Screen sharing allows you to view and control another user's computer from a window on your own machine, or conversely, show them something on your screen. It's a great way to show something to a friend, collaborate with a colleague, or provide technical support for a family member.

You can initiate screen sharing from within iChat by selecting Share My Screen... or Ask to Share Remote Screen... from the buddy list contextual menu or the Buddies menu bar item. You can also click the Screen Sharing button on your buddy list. That's the one on the right side that looks like one rectangle overlapping another.

> **NOTE:** The Share My Screen... and Ask to Share Remote Screen... menu items will change to reflect the buddy you have selected, so don't be surprised if you actually have to click Share My Screen with Alice... or Ask to Share Bob's Screen....

Integrating with Mail

Mail and iChat represent two different ways of communicating that are nevertheless complementary. You might start writing an e-mail message and realize it would be better said over iChat. Or you might want to iChat someone, but that person isn't online.

For situations like these, iChat and Mail both make it easy to use the other. In iChat, selecting Send Email... from the buddy list context menu or the Buddy menu bar item will launch Mail with a new message to that buddy, assuming you have that person's e-mail address in Address Book.

If you are reading mail from or composing mail to a buddy who is available in iChat, that person's name will display a green availability dot. Mail includes Reply With iChat among the options available from the message contextual menu, the menu bar, and an optional toolbar icon.

Advanced Status Messages

Despite their name and original purpose, iChat's status messages have become a handy way to announce things to your friends without having to specifically address them. Since status messages can't be too long, it's often handy to just set your status to a link, which your friends can follow if they want to know more.

In iChat, friends with URLs in their status messages will display a small gray circle with an arrow on it. Clicking the arrow launches the URL in Safari. You can also launch the URL by selecting Open URL from the buddy list contextual menu.

Another popular use for the status message is displaying the current song you're listening to in iTunes. You can set this to update automatically by selecting Current iTunes Song from the status message pop-up menu. If your buddy is taking advantage of this feature, his or her status message will have the same gray circle and arrow as with a URL, except clicking it will take you to that track in the iTunes Store.

Using FaceTime

Back when Apple introduced the iPhone 4, it also introduced a new application along with it called FaceTime. FaceTime allowed iPhone 4 users to video chat over their phones. Since its introduction, Apple has been adding FaceTime to all devices with forward-facing cameras, including the iPad 2 and of course Mac OS X.

Beginning with Mac OS X 10.6.6, FaceTime for Mac OS X (Figure 13–9) has been available as an additional purchase from the Mac App Store (as well as included with newer Macs); however, it is now included as part of Lion, and provides an excellent way to communicate face-to-face with other iOS users.

Figure 13–9. *FaceTime is presented in a single window with a video view on the left and an information view on the right.*

NOTE: When FaceTime was announced by Steve Jobs in September of 2010, he promised that Apple would work with standards bodies to make FaceTime an open standard. While things like this often take time, this has not yet occurred; however, it is possible that devices other than Apple-branded ones will soon support FaceTime as well.

Logging In with FaceTime

When you first launch FaceTime, FaceTime will walk you through a series of steps to log in and start using FaceTime (Figure 13–10). First, you will be asked to sign in with your Apple ID or create a new account. If you have more than one Apple ID, use the on that you would like people to use to contact you. Next, you will be asked for your region, or the country you live in (unless you use your MobileMe ID). Next, you will be presented with a screen asking what e-mail address you would like others to use to contact you through FaceTime (if you choose an e-mail address other than the one used for your Apple ID, you will have to verify the e-mail address before continuing). Once your e-mail address has been verified, the informational screen will change to your contact list from Address Book, and you'll be all ready to go.

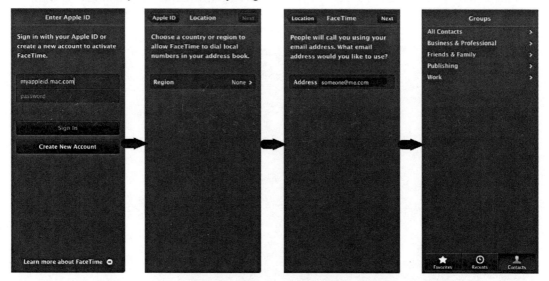

Figure 13–10. *When you first start FaceTime, you will need to follow a few steps to get started.*

Once you have logged on initially, you can you go to FaceBook's preferences to change account information including adding additional e-maill addresses.. You can also turn on or off FaceTime from the preferences or from the menu using **FaceTime** > **Turn FaceTime Off/On** (Command-K).

Making and Receiving FaceTime Chats

To initiate a FaceTime chat with someone, simply select the person you wish to contact from your contacts list, and then select the appropriate phone number (if you are calling their iPhone) or e-mail address (if you are calling their computer or other iOS device), and FaceTime will initiate the call.

If someone is attempting to reach you through FaceTime, the FaceTime window will pop up and your computer will start to ring. The top of the FaceTime window will display who is trying to call you, and the bottom will present buttons to accept or decline the call (Figure 13–11).

Figure 13–11. *When someone is trying to reach you, your computer will start to ring, and the FaceTime window will appear, asking if you would like to accept or decline the call.*

While FaceTime is fairly simple, it does a good job of providing a videophone-like experience, and its compatibility with iOS devices makes a great way to communicate with others on the go. When given the option to choose between FaceTime and iChat, the decision is really yours; iChat has more features, but for video chat with someone on a mobile iOS device, FaceTime is hard to beat.

OTHER OPTIONS FOR CHAT, VOICE, AND VIDEO

Besides iChat and FaceTime, which come with Mac OS X Lion, there are numerous other applications and services available for real-time communication over the Internet.

In the IM game, AIM, Yahoo, and Google each provides its own clients for its services, which provide some unique features that may or may not work with iChat. Also, Microsoft has its own popular messaging system and makes a Mac client available, and new chat services such as Facebook's are popping up all the time. There are also other third-party IM clients, such as the excellent Adium client (http://adium.im), which works with a wide range of IM services.

For voice and video chat, there are a number of other options, the most popular being Skype (www.skype.com), which not only provides Skype-to-Skype video and audio conferences, but also provides VoIP (Voice over IP) services so you can use it to call and receive calls from standard mobile and landline phones.

Finally, for group text chat in real time there is always IRC, which, while almost 20 years old, is still running strong. To check out IRC, you'll first need an IRC client, such as Colloquy (http://colloquy.info), and then you'll need to discover an appropriate network (try www.irchelp.org for more info).

Summary

In this chapter we discussed a number of ways to reach out and communicate with others using text, voice, and video in real time. While there are a number of different ways to do this, usually you will find that most of the people you wish to chat with tend to hover around one or two services.

Communicating over the Internet, which we've covered so far in this part of the book, is one of the most popular uses of the Internet today. One that is more popular, however, at least in terms of bandwidth used, is file sharing—something we will be covering next.

## Chapter 14

From MobileMe to iCloud

Leading up to Apple's WWDC (World Wide Developers Conference) in 2011, Apple announced its new iCloud service, and during WWDC Apple provided some additional information about iCloud (and MobileMe). iCloud will provide many of the features that are currently available with MobileMe. Unlike MobileMe, iCloud will be free. In this chapter you will learn

- What iCloud is and what services it provides

- How to set up your Mac to use iCloud

- Getting an `@me.com` e-mail address for use with iCloud

- Transitioning from MobileMe to iCloud

> **NOTE:** At the time of this writing, iCloud is not generally available, so details here are based on prerelease announcements and early beta software features. We feel that including this material here will be relevant and useful once the final version of iCloud is unveiled. Up-to-date details as they emerge will be posted at `www.learnmacos.info`.

What Is iCloud

iCloud is Apple's answer to cloud computing for Mac and iOS users. It enables users to store music, photos, documents, contacts, appointments, and more "in the cloud," and then pushes that information to any registered devices wirelessly. Most of this happens automatically without any user interaction, assuring that all of a user's up-to-date content is available across computing devices.

From the user perspective, iCloud is not really a single thing, but rather a blanket term for a number of cloud services that utilize Apple's iCloud infrastructure. Because of this there is no single iCloud application or control panel; rather, parts of iCloud are built into various system preferences and applications. Upon launch Apple has broken down the services provided by iCloud into the following features:

- iTunes in the Cloud

- Photo Stream

- Documents in the Cloud

- Apps, Books and Backup

- Mail, Contacts and Calendar

iTunes in the Cloud

There are two main services provided with iCloud's iTunes in the Cloud feature: syncing your new and existing iTunes purchases, and iTunes Match. Syncing of existing iTunes purchases is fairly straightforward: from within iTunes, click iTunes Store and select the Purchased link from the Quick Links menu. This will take you to a screen (Figure 14–1) where all of the items you've ever purchased from iTunes will be listed, allowing you to download (or redownload) the purchased items. This feature allows you to purchase an item at one location (another computer or iOS device) and download it to another without having to physically sync devices or manually transfer the purchased files.

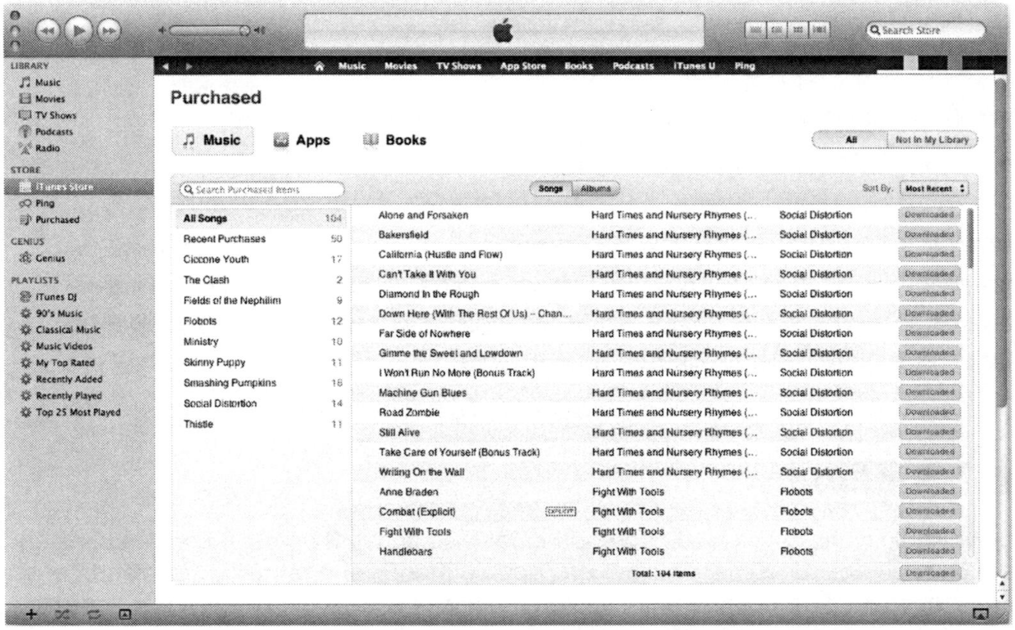

Figure 14–1. *From the Purchased view in the iTunes Store you can view and download any of your previous iTunes store purchases, no matter what computer or device you originally purchased them from.*

Besides downloading past purchases from the iTunes Store, you can also have new purchases automatically downloaded by selecting the appropriate option under the Store tab in the iTunes preferences. When selected, if you purchase a song, book, or app from any other devices, it will automatically be downloaded to your computer(s).

iTunes Match

One extension to this service is an addition called iTunes Match. For $24.99 a year iTunes Match, will keep track of your iTunes library. Every song in it, no matter how it ended up in your library, will be available to download on any computer running the latest version of iTunes or any iOS 5 devices, provided that the song in question exists on the iTunes Music Store. If any song isn't available in the iTunes Music Store, the service will still work, but first you must upload any songs not already available in the iTunes Music Store (iTunes will handle all of this automatically, though).

> **NOTE:** No matter the type or quality of the music in your original collection, the music that is downloaded from iTunes Match will be 256Kbps iTunes Plus–formatted audio files.

Photo Stream

Photo Stream is another feature of iCloud that stores and streams photographs to all your iCloud-enabled devices. On OS X, Photo Stream works primarily with iPhoto (covered in Chapter 15); however, it is possible that other applications may emerge that take advantage of this.

Photo Stream will store the last 30 days of photos in the cloud and immediately make them available to any Photo Stream–enabled software or devices. For example, a photo you take with your iPhone with iOS 5 or higher will immediately be uploaded up to iCloud's Photo Stream, where it will be immediately available in iPhoto on your Mac. The photo will remain on iCloud for 30 days, which should give you plenty of time to move it into an album if you so desire.

> **NOTE:** A photo may appear in your stream-viewing application even after it has been removed from iCloud. For example, the Photos app on iOS 5 will store the last 1,000 photos from your stream in a rolling Photo Stream album.

> **CAUTION:** Photo Stream is not a photo-backup feature. Your photos will be deleted from the iCloud after 30 days. You should plan on backing up any important photos elsewhere (in fact, for those special photos you may want to make two or three backups). If you wish to keep photos permanently backed up "in the cloud," then you may want to look in to some other photo-sharing services, such as Smugmug (www.smugmug.com), Flickr (www.flickr.com), or Photobucket (www.photobucket.com)

Documents in the Cloud

Documents in the Cloud allows applications to store files on iCloud so they are available from the same app on any other device. Currently this feature is built into the latest version of iWork, so a keynote presentation you create on your Mac can be edited on your iPad and then presented from your iPhone.

> **NOTE:** Initially, only iWork on OS X and iOS had full support for Documents in the Cloud; however, any application developer can utilize this feature from with in their application, so others are soon to follow.

Apps, Books and Backup

The Apps, Books and Backup feature is predominately geared toward iOS users. In OS X, apps and books are backed up and accessible through iTunes under the Purchased link in the iTunes store, in the same manner as iTunes-purchased music. The backup feature here is exclusively for backing up all your iOS data. This is significant in that going forward, all of your iOS data will be stored in the cloud, so while you still are able to, it will be unnecessary to sync your iOS device to a Mac or PC for updates (or for anything at all).

Mail, Contacts and Calendar

Most of the contacts, calendar, and mail features that were previously handled through MobileMe will now be handled through iCloud. These features are all set up in the Mail, Contacts & Calendars System Preference (Figure 14–2). (We will cover the details of setting up an iCloud account in the Mail, Contacts & Calendars System Preference pane later in the chapter.)

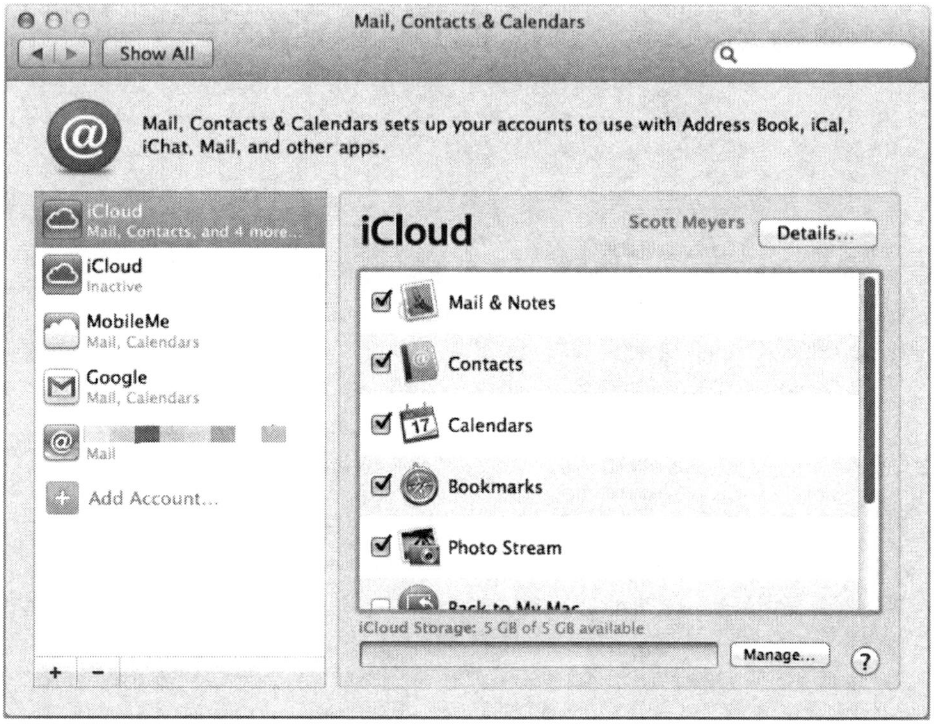

Figure 14–2. *Many of the features that iCloud provides mirror features that were available in MobileMe.*

Other iCloud Features

Some other features available from iCloud include Back to My Mac and Find My Mac. Back to My Mac is a feature introduced as part of MobileMe that allows you to not only share files with a remote Mac, but actually share the screen of a remote Mac as well, allowing you to work on the remote Mac from far away. (This will be covered more in Chapter 26.) Find My Mac allows you to locate your Mac if it gets lost or stolen.

How Does Find My Mac find my Mac?

Unlike mobile phones, Macs today don't have GPS for exact location tracking. Because of this, Find My Mac uses known wireless access points to locate your Mac. For this to work, your Mac must be on and connected to a Wi-Fi hotspot. If your computer or its Wi-Fi is off, then Find My Mac will not be able to find a current location, but it may be able to identify its last location.

How does Apple know where a computer is through Wi-Fi? Good question. All Wi-Fi routers have a unique identifying code, known as a BSSID, that is broadcast along with the wireless network name. While you can change the name of your device, the BSSID remains the same. By driving around, one can access the BSSID information of every Wi-Fi hotspot that one comes in contact with. By mapping out the location and strength of the Wi-Fi hotspot, one can create a map with the location of all available Wi-Fi hotspots. When you use Find My Mac, the current BSSID is sent up to iCloud where the location of that hotspot can be determined. Countless Wi-Fi routers have been mapped thanks to companies like Google, who has collected vast amounts of Wi-Fi information while creating its street view imaging.

Conspiracy theorists aside, there is no real need to freak out about this. The BSSID that your computer is connected to at any given time isn't floating around the Internet unless your computer specifically sends that information through a software application. So, unlike your cell phone, you can only be tracked by your computer if you allow it.

NOTE: How do I know if information such as the BSSID of the Wi-Fi device I'm connected to is being sent to someone? The most direct way is to monitor your network traffic. While there are many options for doing this, Little Snitch (www.obdev.at/products/littlesnitch/index.html) is a very good option. Little Snitch can be configured to let you know whenever any application attempts to send any information over the network. It will then let you choose to let the application continue or to stop the transmission.

Setting Up iCloud on Your Mac

Before you can use iCloud, you must have an Apple ID. If you've purchased anything from the App Store or iTunes Store, then you already have one. If you have used MobileMe in the past, you can use your MobileMe e-mail address as your Apple ID. If not, you will be prompted along the way to create one.

CAUTION: As of this writing there is no way to consolidate existing Apple IDs, so if you have one, then it's probably best to use that one, and not create another. If you end up buying items using different Apple IDs, or store information under one ID and want to access it with another, you are out of luck.

Once you have your Apple ID (or have decided which one you want to use), you can activate iCloud in the Mail, Contacts & Calendars System Preference pane (shown in Figure 14–3).

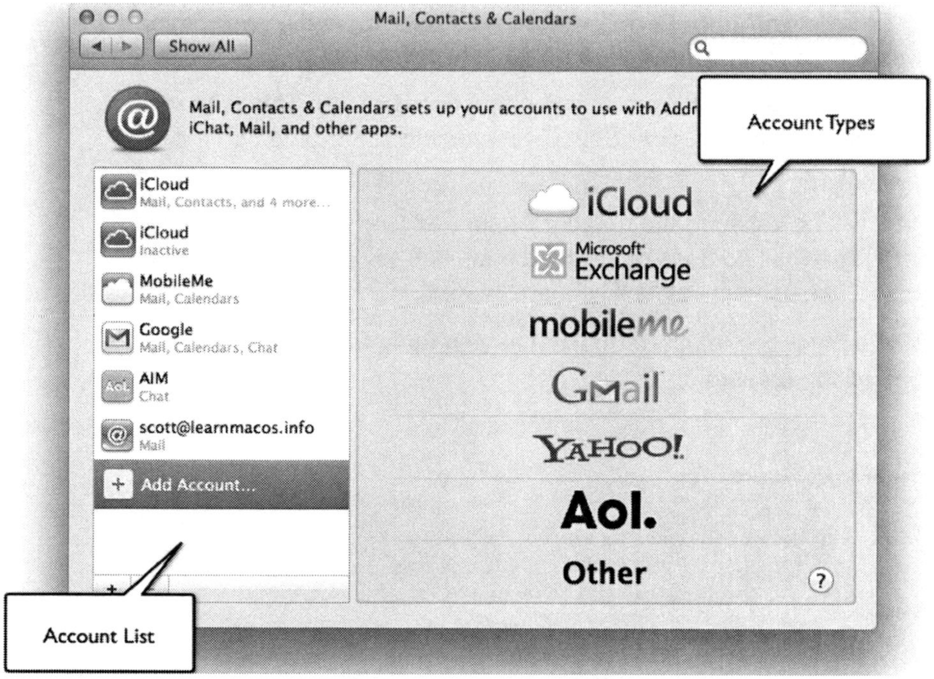

Figure 14–3. *When Add Account... is selected in the Mail, Contacts & Calendars System Preference pane's Account List column, a list of available account types will appear in the information area.*

To begin, select the Add Account... option in the Account List column, and select iCloud from the list on the right. This will present you with a simple dialog asking you for your Apple ID and password (Figure 14–4). If you have an ID, enter the information, and an iCloud account associated with the entered Apple ID will be created.

Figure 14–4. *To add an iCloud account, just enter the Apple ID and password you want to have associated with your iCloud account.*

If you haven't created an Apple ID yet, select the Create Apple ID... button, and the dialog will walk you through a three-step process to create one:

1. First you will be asked for your location and date of birth. This is to verify that you meet the minimum age requirements in your location (in the United States it's 13 years old).

2. Next you will be asked to create your Apple ID. Here you can either use any existing e-mail address or create a new, free @me.com iCloud e-mail address to use as your Apple ID (Figure 14–5).

3. Finally you must accept the terms-of-use agreement, and your iCloud account will be created.

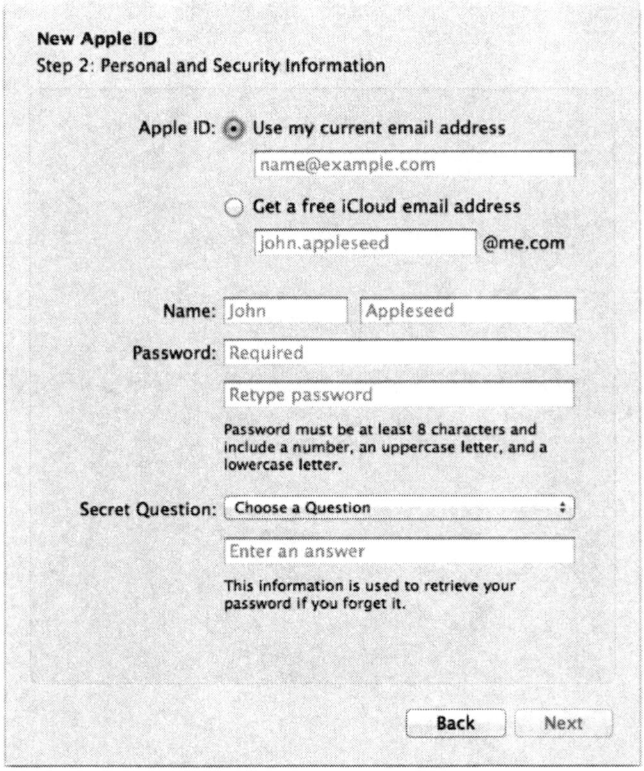

Figure 14–5. *If you don't have an Apple ID, you can create one either by using an existing e-mail account or by creating an @me.com e-mail address to use.*

Once your iCloud account has been created, you can select your account from the Account list, and select some of the options you'd like to turn on for use (see Figure 14–2 again). Options include

> **Mail & Notes:** This sets up Mail to use your @me.com e-mail address. If you used a non-@me.com e-mail address as your Apple ID, you will be prompted to create an @me.com e-mail address when you select this.

Contacts: This will store your contacts on iCloud so they will stay in sync across devices.

Calendars: This will allow you to store calendar data on iCloud.

Bookmarks: Selecting this option will keep your Safari bookmarks synced between devices.

Photo Stream: This will enable the Photo Stream feature. To use this on your Mac you will need iPhoto 9.2 or later.

Back to My Mac: This will enable Back to My Mac for your computer. To gain full access you will need to turn on Sharing on the Sharing System Preference pane.

Find My Mac: This will enable you to locate your Mac if it is missing or has been stolen (providing it is connected to a known Wi-Fi network).

If any additional information is needed when selecting any of these options, you will be prompted for it; otherwise it should just work.

Moving from MobileMe to iCloud

With the announcement of iCloud, the fate of MobileMe became clear: going forward, it will cease to exist. Existing MobileMe users have had their MobileMe services extended to June 30, 2012, at which time the switch will be thrown and MobileMe will cease to be. In the meantime, MobileMe users will have between fall 2011, when iCloud officially launches, until that time to transition from MobileMe to iCloud. When you transition, you will be able to move your mail (including your @me.com and @mac.com e-mail addresses and aliases), contacts, calendars, and bookmarks from MobileMe to iCloud.

What we are currently unsure about, though, are other MobileMe services such as photo/file sharing, web sharing, and iDisk. It looks extremely likely that web sharing (common with iWeb users) will cease to exist. iDisk could easily be transitioned to iCloud, but details about such a move are currently unavailable. Whatever happens, MobileMe will still be around until June 2012, so it seems that there will be plenty of time to adapt.

Summary

iCloud provides transparent cloud services to OS X and iOS, which will help make the management of data and information across multiple devices seamless and effective. Additionally, it provides an infrastructure that any application can utilize to provide integrated cloud services across the OS X and iOS platforms. Some applications including iPhoto already have iCloud abilities built into them.

Next we will look at iPhoto, followed by the other two key iLife applications: iMovie and GarageBand.

iLife

iLife is Apple's bundle of digital lifestyle applications. While not part of OS X, the iLife applications iPhoto, iMovie, and GarageBand are included with every new Mac, and at $14.99 a pop on the OS X App Store, it's likely that a few more of these applications will come in handy. This section includes that latest versions of these three applications. What isn't included is a discussion of iWeb and iDVD. While these applications are included as part of the iLife '11 DVD, they are not available on the OS X App Store and weren't actually updated for iLife '11.

## Chapter 15

iPhoto

iPhoto has always been one of the best consumer photo management tools available on any computer platform. Unlike simple photo editors, iPhoto is a complete photo workflow tool, allowing you to import and organize your photos, edit them, and then export and share them in a number of ways. In this chapter we will

■ Introduce iPhoto

■ Explore iPhoto's image management features

■ Discuss how to edit images in iPhoto

■ Share and print photos with iPhoto

Photo Management

When you connect a digital camera to your computer and launch iPhoto (you can set iPhoto to launch automatically when you connect a digital camera in iPhoto's general preferences), your camera will show up as a device in iPhoto and give you a number of import options (Figure 15–1). By default, iPhoto will import all the images into a single event (an *event* in iPhoto is one method of categorizing photo collections, sort of like folders; we'll give more details next). However, if you select the Split Events option, iPhoto will autosplit your images into separate events based on the date and time they were taken. If you are undecided, don't worry, you can rearrange your photos into different events at any time.

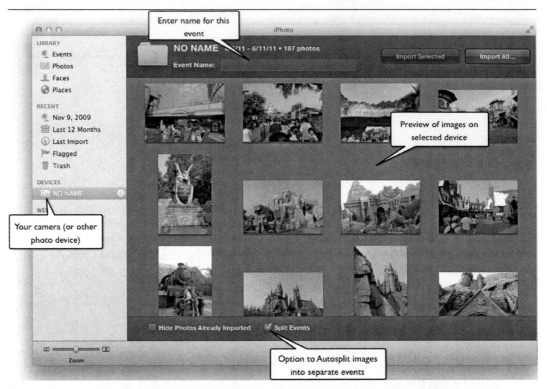

Figure 15–1. *One of the first things you'll want to do is import images into iPhoto. By selecting the device or location where your images are, you can choose which images to import.*

NOTE: The exact method iPhoto will use to autosplit events is set with the Autosplit into Events menu in iPhoto's general preferences.

Events are the primary way that iPhoto divides and organizes your photos. Upon import, each image is stored in an event. Once imported, you can move images from one event to another by dragging and dropping an image from one event to another. An image can only be in one event at a time. If you would like to create a new event, select the images you want to put in a new event and drag them onto the Events Library item. A new untitled event will then be created with the selected images.

While events provide one way to organize photos, iPhoto offers many others, including the standard methods of creating albums and slideshows, as well as using Places and Faces.

TIP: While an image can only belong to a single event, a singe image can appear in multiple albums.

Places

Places organizes your photos by the location that the picture was taken, using GPS data embedded in a photo's metadata or location data you enter manually. A wave of new cameras that include GPS systems (including, of course, many mobile phone cameras) can add this GPS data automatically. If your images aren't geotagged—that is, embedded with the location data—out of your camera, then you can add the location data automatically from within iPhoto.

Just select a photo (or select a collection of photos) and open the info column by clicking the info tool button that appears in the lower-right corner of iPhoto.

At the bottom of the Information view, Click the Assign a Place... text field and start typing in the location you wish to assign to the photo. As you type, the Location area will expand and possible suggestions will begin to appear. Your previous locations will appear first followed by suggestions derived from Google Maps. Once you have typed in your location, if it is a previous location or identified by Google Maps it will appear on a map (Figure 15–2).

If the location is not known (or mislocated), you can add or move the pin on the map to assign a specific location.

Any geotagged photos from a defined location will be added to that location automatically.

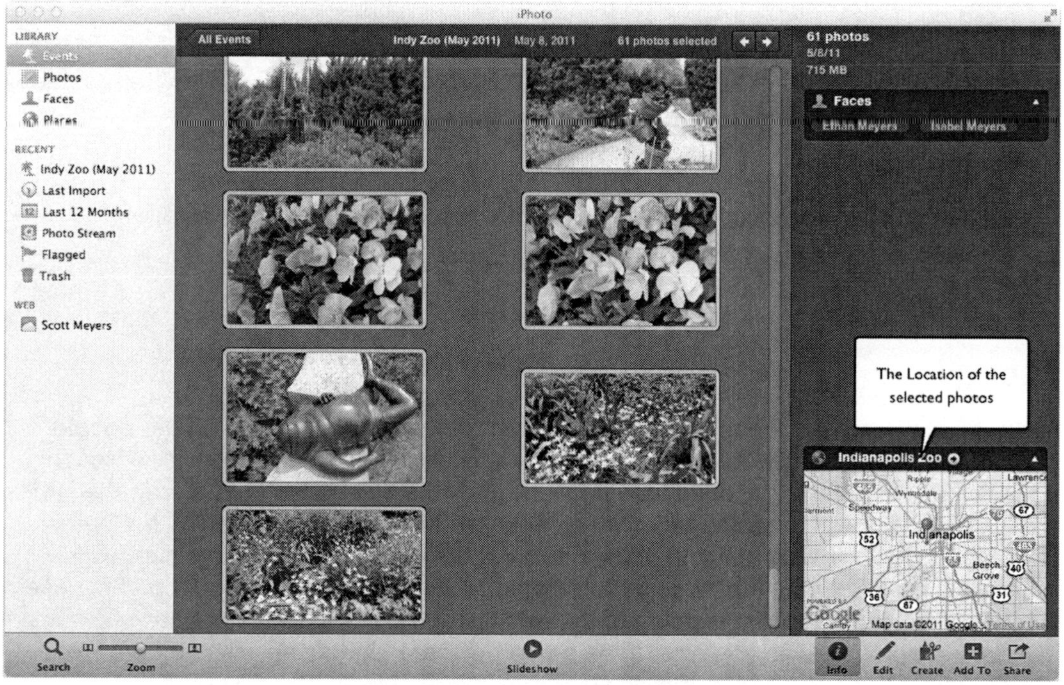

Figure 15–2. *The location of any selected photos will be shown in the info view. You can add locations to photos here as well.*

Once you have locations assigned to your photos you can view photos based on location by selecting a location on a map presented when Places is selected under Library in the Library column (Figure 15-3).

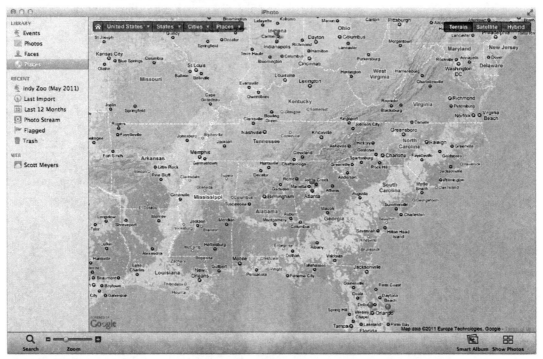

Figure 15-3. *Places will allow you to view photos based on their location.*

> **NOTE:** You can manage your selected places and add custom locations from the window presented when you select **Window > Manage My Places**.

Faces

Faces is another great feature to help you organize your photos based on the people captured in your photos. To take advantage of this, first select the photo or photos that you wish to add names to, open the Info view, and click the Faces area. When the Faces area is selected, any detected faces will appear on the photo (Figure 15-4). If iPhoto thinks it already knows the name of the people in the photo, it will make a suggestion; otherwise, it will identify the faces as "unnamed." Clicking the unnamed face text makes it editable for you to enter the name of the person. (A list of possible matches shows up in a drop-down menu as you type. If the person you are identifying is listed here, you should select their name from the list so iPhoto knows this is the same person.)

Figure 15–4. *iPhoto's Faces feature allows you to identify people's faces in photos. iPhoto then tries to find all the photos in its library that belong to that person.*

Once you've identified a face or two in iPhoto, iPhoto automatically attempts to find the identified faces in every photo in your library. When you are viewing an individual in the Faces view, if iPhoto thinks that there may be additional photos of the person that have been unverified, it will let you know (Figure 15–5).

> **NOTE:** The Faces feature is quite sophisticated in identifying people's faces in your library. However, it's not foolproof and often misses a number of photos of an identified person. It also occasionally identifies the wrong face as an identified person (with occasionally bizarre and often entertaining results).

Figure 15–5. *The faces view allows you to view all the photos of a specific individual. Additionally, iPhoto can help identify photos that may contain the selected individual automatically.*

> **TIP:** When you first begin identifying faces, you may want to start by selecting Faces in the Library column and then selecting the Find Faces button from the tools in the lower-right corner of iPhoto. This will bring up an interface that will quickly identify all the detected faces in all of your photos and allow you to assign a name to them (a few at a time).

Other Ways to Manage Photos

Albums and *smart albums* provide another way to organize your photos. While every image is stored in a particular event, Albums provides you with another way to manually organize photos. For example, if your events are organized by days, and you went on vacation to Florida for three days, you could collect all of the photos from all three events into a single album. Additionally, you may want albums for all pictures of family members in a "Family" album.

> **TIP:** Folders are created to organize albums. For example, if we, as suggested above, created an album for our Florida 2011 vacation, then we may want to keep that album in a folder called Vacations.

Another feature included in iPhoto is the ability to tag individual photos with titles, ratings, and keywords. Titles allow you to provide easily recognizable names to images without renaming the actual image file. This is very useful for those who use specific naming schemes for files (such as time and date information) that may not be very descriptive of the image content. Ratings simply allow you to quickly rate your photos from zero to five stars, allowing you to find your very best (four- or five-star) photos quickly at a later time. (You could even create a smart album that would automatically contain all your five-star images.) Keywords allow you to add searchable words that help describe your images; they can range from very specific names to general categories.

KEYWORD TIPS

Keywords aren't very useful if you aren't somewhat consistent with them. If you use different words for every photo, then they quickly become out of control. However, if your keywords aren't specific enough, then they don't serve much purpose either. One suggestion is to jot down some general keyword categories (e.g., you can start out with People, Places, and Things as your top-level keywords), and then add some subcategories (e.g., under People, you might have Family, Friends, Celebrities, etc.), and then add some more-specific information under that (specific names of people). The most important rule is to be consistent.

As a general rule, keywords should be no more than 64 characters long. This length is based on the maximum length for IPTC (International Press Telecommunications Council) data. This is a standard format of transmitting image data along with digital images.

---

iPhoto keeps track of all your keywords. To view them, open the Keyword window (Shift-Command-K). You can use this window to add keywords to selected photos by clicking the keyword. You can even set up common keywords with their own keyboard shortcut to apply them quickly to any photo. This not only makes adding popular keywords easy, but is also a good way to keep keywords consistent.

Once all the data (titles, ratings, and keywords) is set up for your images, you can really take advantage of the search and smart album tools in iPhoto to find just the right image or images you are looking for.

Photo Editing

iPhoto includes a range of easy-to-use image-editing tools. To switch into edit mode, select an image to edit and click the Edit icon in the lower-right corner of iPhoto. iPhoto provides three sets of tools for editing photos:

- Quick Fix
- Effects
- Adjust

Quick Fix

The Quick Fix tools provide image correction tools that are both quite easy and commonly used. The Quick Fix tools include:

- **Rotate**: Rotates the image 90 degrees counterclockwise (or clockwise if you hold the Option key). You may need to use this more than one time to rotate an image that needs it.

- **Enhance**: Provides some automatic image adjustments to attempt to improve the image.

- **Fix Red-Eye**: Provides a tool that can help eliminate red-eye in photos. When the autofix red-eye option is selected, iPhoto will attempt to automatically remove red-eye.

- **Straighten**: Allows you to slightly rotate a photo where the subject is slightly skewed.

- **Crop**: Allows you to select and crop an image.

- **Retouch**: Provides tools that can help mask blemishes or strange anomalies in photos (including dust specks).

Effects

The Effects tools provide a number of filter effects you can apply to you images. Each of these effects are cumulative, so each time you click an effect it will increase the effect on the image. The options include:

- **Lighten**: Will lighten the entire image

- **Darken**: Will darken the image

- **Contrast**: Will add contrast to the image (note that using the Levels feature in Adjust is much more effective)

- **Warmer**: Will add a reddish tint to the image

- **Cooler**: Will add a bluish tint to the image

- **Saturate**: Will increase the color saturation of the image

- **B&W**: Will create a black-and-white image from your photo

- **Sepia**: Will create a sepia-toned image from your photo

- **Antique**: Will create an interesting "antique" color effect

- **Matte**: Will create a white circular matte around your image

- **Vignette**: Will create a dark circular vignette around you image

- **Edge Blur**: Will blur the edges of you image

- **Fade**: Will cause the colors to appear faded

- **Boost**: Will boost the colors and contrast

- **None**: Will remove effects

> **TIP:** If you find you have horribly ruined your image, you can always use the Revert to Original button to remove all editing effects.

Adjust

The Adjust tools (Figure 15–6) provide a number of very high-quality image enhancement tools that give you precise control over levels, contrast, exposure, color, sharpening, and other sophisticated image-editing features.

Figure 15–6. *The image-editing tools in iPhoto are easily accessible in full-screen mode, which provides an uncluttered way to view and edit your images.*

Printing and Sharing Your Photos

Taking and organizing your photos is nice, but ultimately you'll likely want to share them with others, and iPhoto provides a number of ways to do this, both digitally and physically.

If you just want to share some photos with a minimum of fuss, you can select the desired images in your library and e-mail them to the desired recipients, print them from your own printer, or order professional prints directly from within iPhoto.

> **NOTE:** The first time you order prints, you will need to set up an account for yourself. This is fairly easy, as iPhoto will walk you through the process.

For those who wish to share photos with a bit more flair, iPhoto has a number of ways to satisfy this desire. Using the Share button, you can publish photos directly to your MobileMe web galleries (while they last), your Facebook account, or your Flickr account. Also, your iPhoto library is accessible from many other applications, including iWeb and iMovie; they provide a number of other ways to view and share your photos.

For those who wish to add a bit more flair to your photo presentation you can use the Create button to create slideshows that can be exported in QuickTime format or if you prefer a non-digital interesting hard copy of your images, you can create an order amazing photo books, cards, and even calendars from your photos.

PHOTO STREAM

Photo Stream was announced as part of iCloud. This service streams your most recent images from all iCloud-connected devices to each other. While this is not (at least initially) a method of sharing images with others, it does allow you to always keep your most recent images close at hand. For iPhoto users this means that if you also have an iPhone iPad or other iOS 5 devices, any images you capture with you iOS device will automatically be added to your Photo Stream and available in iPhoto. Likewise, any images you import into iPhoto will be immediately available on any or you iOS devices.

Photo Stream will only keep images for 30 days, so if you want to keep an image that was streamed from you iPhone into you Photo Stream, you should move the image from your Photo Stream in iPhoto to a new or existing event.

Summary

iPhoto seems to strike that perfect balance between ease of use and power, while providing powerful editing tools that most professionals would be happy with. It also provides a simple method to manage all you digital photos. In the next chapter we will look at iMovie, Apple's attempt to do for video what iPhoto has done for photos.

## Chapter 16

iMovie

iMovie (Figure 16–1) is Apple's consumer-level application for managing video and creating movies. Like iPhoto, iMovie is designed to easily allow people like you and me to quickly create great-looking movies from our video collections. This is especially useful now that the ability to shoot video is everywhere from our phones to our digital cameras. While entire books are written on creating movies with iMovie, in this chapter we will cover the basics, including

- Importing videos

- Managing your clips with events

- Creating new iMovie projects

- Building movies from your clips and photos

- Adding text, transitions, and music to your movie

- Exporting your movie

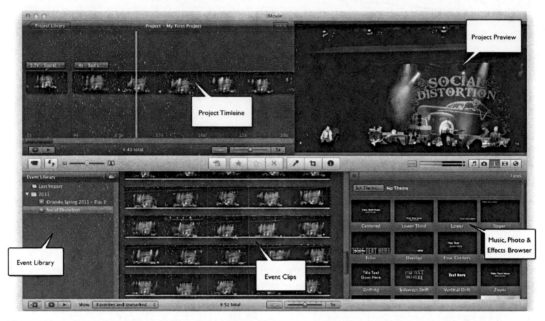

Figure 16–1. *iMovie provides a single window divided into areas that help you quickly assemble and edit a movie.*

Importing Video into iMovie

The first step in creating a movie in iMovie (or any video application) is to import video. When iMovie is running, it will automatically detect any camera, camcorder, or even phone with digital video files on it when it is connected to your computer.

> **NOTE:** If for some reason your device isn't detected or you are importing video from some other device or location, you can manually begin to import using either **File > Import from Camera...** (Command-I), **File > Import > Movies...**, **File > Import > Camera Archive...**, or **File > Import > iMovie HD Project...**, depending on the source. We will be assuming you are importing from a camera here.

When new videos are detected for import, the Import window will appear (Figure 16–2). Depending on how the videos are stored on your camera (either on linear media like MiniDV tapes or on nonlinear media like hard drives or flash media), you may be able to select individual video files (nonlinear media) to import, or you may be able to control the camera to stream the video into iMovie (linear media). Either way, when you go to import the video, you will be prompted about where you want to save your video and whether you want to add it to an existing or new iMovie event (Figure 16–3). iMovie also provides you with an option to analyze and apply video stabilization after the import is complete. This is a feature of iMovie that attempts to detect and remove camera shake from videos.

Figure 16–2. *iMovie's Import From: Camera window allows you to view and select videos to import.*

Figure 16–3. *Before you import the video, you must choose a location and event to save the movie into. You can also select from options for stabilizing and optimizing your video.*

> **NOTE:** If you anticipate creating a lot of video, it may be a good idea to think about getting an external hard drive for your video. Digital video can consume a large amount of disk space. This is especially true of raw DV or HDV, but even new digital video formats such as AVCHD, which manages to significantly compress video while still retaining high quality, can fill up disk space fairly quickly.

Making a Movie

Once you have your video imported, you can start the task of taking your video clips and putting them together into a movie. This usually involves a few steps: creating a project; assembling your video clips (and photos if you want to add them to your movie); adding any text, transitions, and additional audio; and finally saving your movie.

Creating a Project

Creating a movie in iMovie begins by creating a project. To create a new project, select **File > New Project...** (Command-N) from the menu. This will bring up the new project dialog, which presents you with a number of Project Themes and Movie Trailers templates (Figure 16–4).

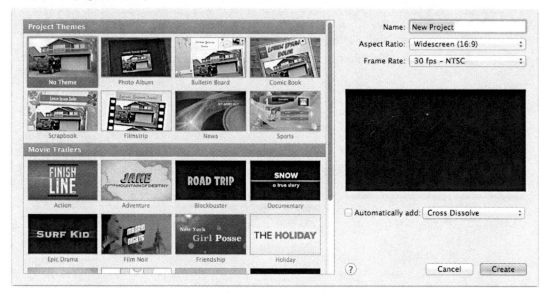

Figure 16–4. *When you create a new project, you can select a theme or movie trailer to help you create a compelling movie.*

Project themes allow you to just add clips and let iMovie add text effects and transitions automatically (you will of course still need to edit the text). If you don't wish to use a theme, select the No Theme theme. If you choose to use No Theme, you can still include elements from other themes in your movie.

Movie trailers are movie templates introduced in iMovie '11 that have predefined outlines and storyboards that when assembled will create a professional-looking movie trailer. To create a movie trailer, choose a trailer you'd like to create (some trailers are designed for individuals while others are designed for groups), fill out the outline (Figure 16–5), and then add clips that match up to the storyboard requirements (you can also add clips directly to the Shot List tab). When everything is filled out and the appropriate clips are added, iMovie will assemble all the pieces into a finished work.

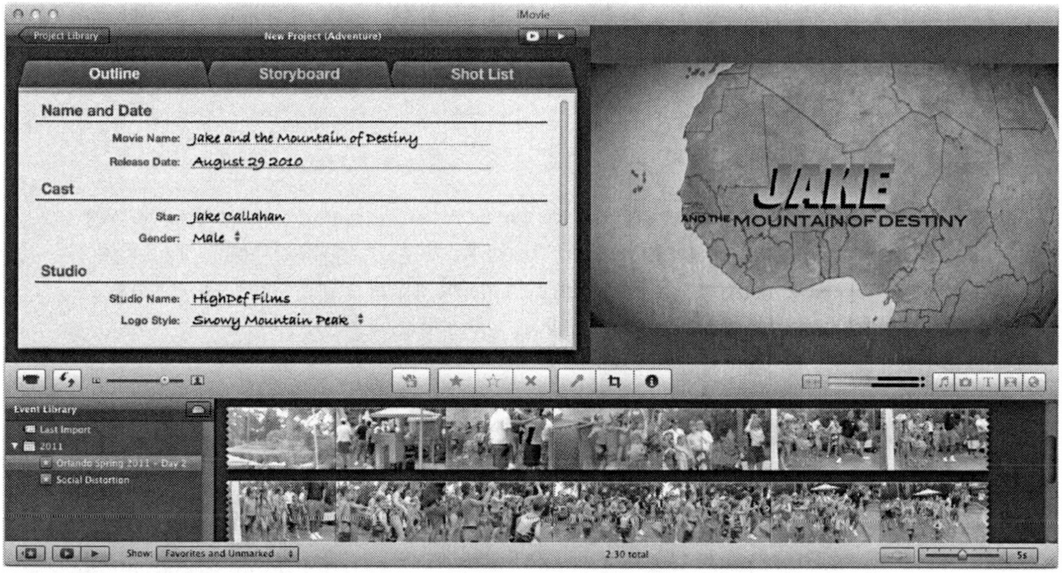

Figure 16–5. *To create a movie trailer, just fill out the outline provided and add the suggested type of movie clips.*

Working with Clips

To add an imported video clip to a movie, drag the clip from the event clip view to the project timeline. Sometimes, however, you may wish to work only with part of a clip. If this is the case, you can select just the part of the clip you would like to use. To do this, simply click and drag over the area of the clip you wish to use. This will surround the selected clip with a yellow box that you can expand or contract on either end by grabbing the edge and dragging. To preview just the selected video, select Play Selection from the shortcut menu. You can then drag just that selection to your project.

> **NOTE:** When working with clips in iMovie, iMovie retains the original imported video so any edits, cuts, or crops can be reversed.

Beyond cropping a clip, you can make various audio and video adjustments to a clip by selecting it and opening the inspector by clicking the inspector button (it has an *I* on it) or simply pressing the I key on the keyboard.

> **TIP:** iMovie has a number of keyboard shortcuts that use a single key to perform actions. For example, to start or stop a video from the current position, press the spacebar. To open the inspector window, press the I key. To view all the shortcuts, select **Help > Keyboard Shortcuts**.

> **TIP:** The clip-editing tools are available for both event clips and project clips.

> **TIP:** Besides adding video clips to a project, you can also add still photos from your photo library. To do this, open the photo browser to view and select an image from your iPhoto or Aperture library, and then just drag the image to the project timeline where you would like to place it. You can then use the inspector to select how long the image will be displayed and to add video effects to the image so it appears to move.

Adding Text and Transitions

Once you have your video clips set up in the timeline, you can then add transitions between clips, as well as text (referred to as *titles* in iMovie) that floats above a clip.

To add a transition between two clips, open the Transitions Browser, choose the transition you'd like to use, and drag it between two clips on the project timeline. Generally, that's all you have to do; however, you may use the inspector to tweak the transition if you'd like.

> **TIP:** While transitions, used properly, can make a movie look very nice, if you use lots of different transition styles in a movie, the results will look amateurish. For a more professional look, it's best to pick a simple transition you will use throughout the whole movie and use it sparingly.

Adding titles to a movie is similar to adding a transition. First select the title style you wish to use from the Title Browser, and then drag it over the clip in the project timeline where you would like it to appear. Once you have added the text, you may edit it in the project preview view.

Adding Music and Sound Effects

To add additional background sounds or music to your movie (or foreground music if you are creating a music video), open the Music and Sound Effects Browser, select the audio file you would like to add, and drag it onto the timeline where you would like the audio to begin.

Once the audio file is added to the project timeline, you can adjust the overall volume or create fade-ins and fade-outs (called *ducking*) so the audio flows well with any audio already on the video track.

If you would like to add voiceovers directly to the video, click the voiceover button (the button that looks like a microphone), select your audio input device, and then click the timeline where you'd like to add your voiceover. iMovie will then begin a countdown and start recording where you selected. The recoding will continue until you click the timeline again to stop it.

Finishing Up

Once you have finished your movie masterpiece, you'll want to save it. To do this, select **File > Finalize Project** from the menu. This will cause all the movie to be re-rendered in your selected format (based on your project properties). For even a short video, this can take a long time, even with a super-fast computer, so you may want to consider finalizing your video when you are ready to take a break from using your computer. Once your movie is finalized, you can export it to other formats.

Exporting Your Movie

Once you have finalized your movie, it's likely that you'll want to share it. iMovie provides a host of export options under the Share menu item. While the options may differ depending on the destination, many of the share options ask you what size you will want to export your movie as. The size options include Mobile, Medium, Large, HD 720p, and HD 1080p. iMovie makes suggestions on which format to choose based on its destination. Whatever you choose, keep in mind that larger sizes result in significantly larger file sizes.

Besides choosing the size depending on the export location, you may need to provide account information. If, for example, you wish to export your movie directly to Facebook, choose your account (or add you account information) and iMovie will do the rest.

Summary

Hopefully this chapter provided a good starting point for learning iMovie. As you explore and use it, you will discover that there are quite a number of interesting features lurking beneath the surface. However, iMovie does have limitations, and if you reach them you may wish to look to Final Cut Pro X for more features (and of course more complexity).

Next we will move on to the final of iLife's three principal applications: GarageBand, iLife's music creation application.

## Chapter 17

GarageBand

GarageBand (Figure 17–1) is Apple's entry-level DAW (digital audio workstation). GarageBand allows you to record, mix, and edit multiple audio and MIDI tracks together and then save them as audio files in a variety of formats. While GarageBand lacks some features of Apple's other DAWs (Logic Express and Logic Studio), it provides a number of professional-quality software instruments and effects coupled with reasonable track-editing abilities (including volume, panning, and track automation abilities) that can easily create professional-sounding recordings. Additionally, GarageBand includes a few other features for fun and learning. In this chapter we will

- Create a new GarageBand project
- Build audio tracks with loops
- Work with MIDI tracks
- Record a live instrument or vocals
- Edit an audio track
- Export a song

Figure 17–1. *GarageBand's main window here is divided into tracks, track information, and the track editor with the toolbar at the bottom.*

Creating Projects in GarageBand

Before you can do much with GarageBand, the first thing you must do is select the type of project that you will begin with. To begin, select **File > New** (Command-N) from the menu. This will open up the GarageBand's Project Chooser window (Figure 17–2). With New Project selected in the list column on the left, the view area on the right will display a number of new project templates. Depending on your goals, you may select any of these project templates—the only differences are the number and initial setup of the tracks you begin with; however, you can add any type of track to any project and delete or change any exiting tracks you don't want or aren't using.

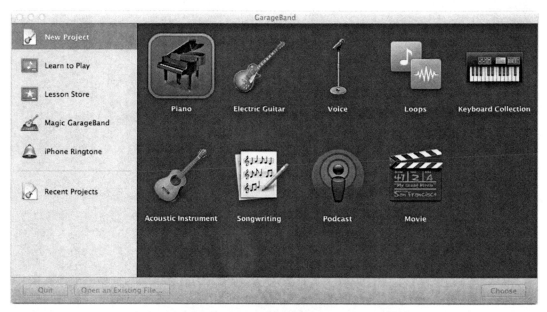

Figure 17-2. *The Project Chooser provides a starting point for all GarageBand has to offer.*

> **NOTE:** The Podcast and Movie selections are a little different. The Podcast selection adds a special track to drop an image that will be displayed during the podcast. The Movie option adds a movie track to the top, where you can drop the movie onto the timeline and record or play along with the movie.

No matter which project type you choose, you will next be taken to the track view, where you can begin to create your audio work.

LEARN TO PLAY, LESSON STORE, MAGIC GARAGEBAND, AND IPHONE RINGTONE

Besides creating new projects, the Project Chooser provides some additional options: Learn to Play, Lesson Store, Magic GarageBand, and iPhone Ringtone. While we won't be going into too much detail on these here let me explain each of them real quick:

- *Learn to Play* will provide you with a number of interactive lessons that will teach you how to play either guitar or piano. Initially, Intro to Guitar and Intro to Piano lessons are included, but you can add additional lessons from the Lesson Store (some for free; others for a fee).

- The *Lesson Store* allows you download additional Learn to Play lessons. The lessons not only include ones that build upon the intro lessons that are included in GarageBand, but also add artist lessons, in which an artist will personally teach you how to play his or her song. The current selection includes lessons from artists ranging from Norah Jones to Squeeze. While many of the basic lessons offered are free to download, the artist lessons usually run to $4.99 each.

- *Magic GarageBand* provides a virtual band for you to play or record with. Here you can choose one of several types of music ranging from reggae to rock, and have the computer control various instruments while you play along. While the options are sometimes limiting, the result are fun to practice to.

- *iPhone Ringtone*, as the name implies, creates a track for you to create you own ringtone that can be downloaded to your iPhone.

While most people use GarageBand just to record new music, these extra features are fun and are worth checking out.

Working with Tracks

Tracks are the individual parts of music that when put together form a song. Traditionally, each track would represent an instrument or voice in the final song. By keeping each part in a separate track, you can add, remove, or edit a singe track without affecting the rest of the song. In GarageBand, each track can contain either a software instrument track or a real instrument track. The software tracks contain MIDI information that is translated into sound based on the software instrument associated with it. Real instrument tracks contain actual sound files that can come from prerecorded music or loops, or can be recorded on the fly in GarageBand through an audio interface (including the built-in audio inputs if necessary).

> **NOTE:** If you are serious about recording, you should probably look into purchasing an audio interface for your computer. A decent two-channel USB2 or FireWire audio interface can cost less than $200 and will provide you with much better sound quality than using your Mac's built-in audio port. Obviously, there are more expensive audio interfaces as well that include more features. Some companies that make good audio interfaces include Apogee, TASCAM, Mackie (or TAPCO), M-Audio, Digidesign, PreSonus, and MOTU (Mark of the Unicorn).

Using Loops

One of the easiest ways to start building a track is using a loop. A loop is small audio clip that can be used as building block for a track and a song. GarageBand comes with a large selection of built-in loops and many more available for download.

To view your available loops, click the Loop Browser button in the lower-right corner of GarageBand to open the Loop Browser. The Loop Browser has three views modes: Column, Button, and Podcast Sounds. Each view provides a split screen that allows you select the type of loop you are looking for at the top, and then to browse and preview the actual loops at the bottom (Figure 17–3).

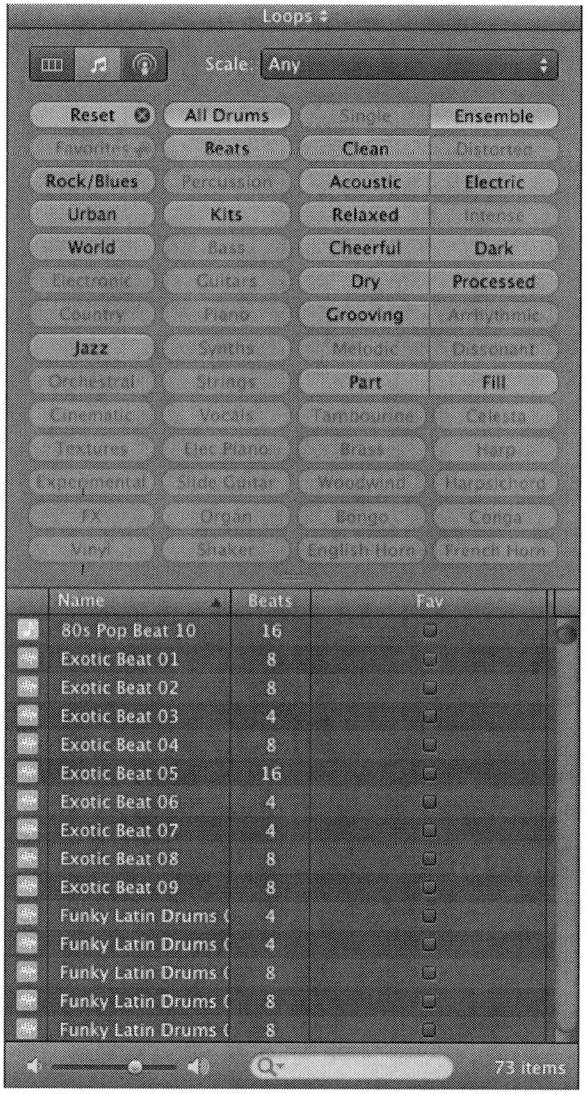

Figure17-3. *The Loop Browser (shown here in Button view) allows you to select the type of loop you are looking for at the top and then preview actual loops at the bottom.*

NOTE: Loops can either be real audio loops (loops with a blue icon) or preprogrammed MIDI loops (loops with a green icon). When the loops are part of your project, you may edit them in the Track Browser according to their type. However, an edit to a single loop segment will affect all the subsequent instances of that particular loop.

When you've identified a loop you'd like to use, drag it from the Loop Browser either onto the track you'd like to add it to or below the tracks to automatically create a new track.

Once a loop is in a track, you can cause the loop to repeat itself over and over again (or *loop*) by holding the holding the cursor over the edge of the loop until the traditional arrow cursor changes to a loop cursor. Then just drag the loop out on the timeline to loop as required.

> **NOTE:** There are numerous loops available for GarageBand beyond the loops that come with it. Not only does Apple sell add-on loop packs, but many third-party vendors also sell loops for almost any occasion.

> **TIP:** Even if you intend to record live instruments for all your tracks in a song, it's not uncommon to begin setting up a few background tracks built from loops just to provide some backing guidance as you lay down your initial tracks.

Adding MIDI Tracks

When you are done working with loops and ready to start recording you own music, the first step is to create a new track; this can be done by clicking the New Track button in the lower-left corner of GarageBand (the one with the + icon on it), or by selecting **Track > New Track...** (Option-Command-N) from the menu. This will open the New Track dialog (Figure 17–4). To create a MIDI track, select the Software Instrument option and click Create.

> **NOTE:** If you have a MIDI keyboard or other MIDI instrument connected to your computer that you'll be using to create your MIDI track, you may click the Instrument Setup disclosure triangle and make sure the appropriate device is selected. If you don't have a MIDI instrument, you can use your computer keyboard as a makeshift MIDI keyboard. You can always change this later.

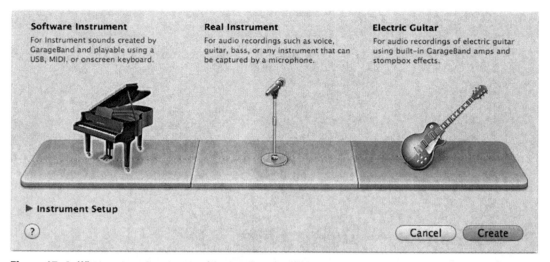

Figure 17–4. *When you create a new track, you must select if the track will be a software instrument (a MIDI track), a real instrument (usually recorded through a microphone; this includes vocals), or an electric guitar (which uses GarageBand's built-in software amps and effects).*

When you select a MIDI track, one of the first things you may want to do is select an instrument from the Browse tab in the Software Instrument Track Info view. GarageBand includes a wide range of software instruments, from traditional piano sounds and drum kits to far-out synth textures.

> **TIP:** if you don't have a MIDI instrument, select **Window > Musical Typing** (Shift-Command-K) from the menu. This will not only provide an onscreen window where you can control the sound, but will also activate you computer keyboard to be used as a MIDI input device.

When you have the instrument you wish to use, you can begin to play or record your music.

> **NOTE:** MIDI is really just a series of values from 1 to 127 that control everything about the music, including pitch, modulation, and volume (or *velocity*). When combined with *samples* (which are the basic sounds of a particular instrument) or synthesized sounds, you get your software instrument. Because of the way this is set up, it's very flexible. For example, you can change the instrument without affecting the other values, so if you create a MIDI track using a piano sound, you may later change the piano to a violin by just changing the instrument.

Once your MIDI track is recorded, you can make a number of adjustments to it in the Track Editor (Figure 17–5). Here you can actually click and edit every note, as well as change almost any other MIDI parameter. For a more classical composition–oriented view, if you click Score you can edit the music using a traditional music score. You could in fact entirely recreate the MIDI track in this view if you desired to.

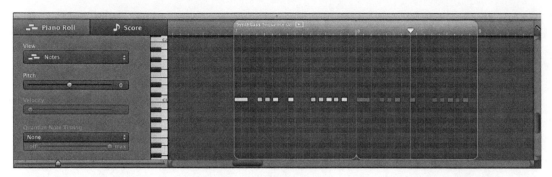

Figure 17–5. *The Track Editor showing a MIDI track in Note view. You can also view this as a traditional music score, or view other MIDI parameters such as modulation and velocity.*

Recording Real Instrument Audio Tracks

To add a traditional audio track into GarageBand, create a new track as discussed previously, but select Real Instrument. This will create an audio track ready for recording. To record, select the audio input device (this can be set up in the New Track dialog by clicking the Instrument Setup disclosure triangle or in the Track Info view on the Input Source menu).

With the track selected, GarageBand will start to record through the selected input device when you click the record button.

> **NOTE:** The Monitor menu in the Track Info view will determine if the audio you are recording will be played back through the output (or *monitor*) during recording. By default this is off, but if you'd like to hear what you are playing through the output as you are playing, select On from the menu. If you are not worried about feedback, you may also select "On (no feedback protection)" from the menu; however, if you start getting feedback, this may not be the best option.

> **NOTE:** GarageBand provides a number of track effects, such as compression, equalization, and reverb. You can select some predefined effect setups based on the type of track you are recoding from the info window. Since these effect are applied post-processing (i.e., they are added over the raw audio) so any selections you make can be altered at any time without affecting the original audio track.

Recording a Guitar Track

Traditionally, recording a guitar track is difficult. To begin with, guitar amps are generally large and heavy to haul around, and then add to that dealing with guitar effects and cables, and the chore of just getting everything set up. But that's the easy part; the hard part is recording an electric guitar through a traditional amp > microphone > input setup. Guitarists love things to be loud, and often the sweet overdriven amp sound doesn't start kicking in until an amplifier is at an ear-shattering volume. This makes recording . . . difficult.

To help solve these problems, guitarists have been turning to digital effect processors for direct recording without the issues. Initially, some these solutions sounded less than real, but modern digital effects are often undistinguishable in recordings from a real honest tube amp. The latest version of GarageBand has digital guitar amplifiers and effects built right in, so by just plugging in your electric guitar you can play around and record with a wide range of amplifiers and effects (Figure 17–6).

Figure 17–6. *In additional to the handful of amps that emulate a range of classic amplifiers, you can choose from a number of different effects for your guitar.*

Beyond setting up your amp and effects, recording is pretty much the same as recording any other type of track.

> **NOTE:** When recording using the built-in guitar amps and effects, you will want to turn on monitoring. Depending on how you have your audio set up, it can be tricky to avoid feedback. This is when a good pair of headphones comes in real handy.

> **TIP:** Almost all guitar presets have noise reduction turned on, which can cause low volumes to cut out. I generally turn noise reduction off across the board to avoid this, unless working with extremely high gain setups where such a thing would be impractical.

> **TIP:** If you do choose to record an electric guitar traditionally, here a few tips. First, use the smallest wattage amp you can find; a small 6-watt tube amp will sound very big when recorded (Jimmy Hendrix did a lot of studio work using a Fender Champ). Second, record it cleaner than you would normally play, which will add definition to the final recording. Finally, keep effects to a necessary minimum; you can always add them later.

Post-Processing

Once you've recorded your tracks, you can add post-processing to individual tracks or to the master track (which affects all the individual tracks). Common effects include compression, visual equalizer, and reverb, though there are many additional effects available. These effects are managed under the Edit tab of the Track Info view (Figure 17–7). To add an effect, click an empty effect space and select the effect you'd like to add. Clicking an effect will allow you to adjust the effect'sparameters.

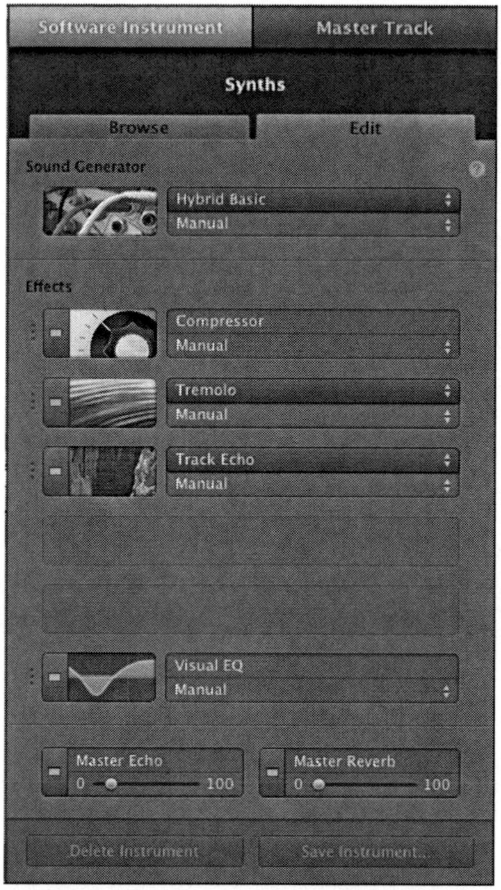

Figure 17–7. *Post-processing by working with track effects allows you to fine-tune your audio tracks before saving and exporting your song.*

Saving and Sharing Your Song

Once you have completed your song, you can export the finished song to disk for sharing (or directly into your iTunes library); however, there are also different ways to share your project.

If you are simply wanting to save your song so it's available through your iTunes library, select **Share > Send Song to iTunes...** from the menu. This will open a dialog that will allow you to add meta tags to your song, as well as select the output quality of your song. You can select what playlist you'd like to send your song to. If you'd like to simply export your song as a file on your disk, select **Share > Export Song to Disk...** Once again, you'll be able to choose the export quality of your song, as well as a file name for it.

Besides simply exporting your song, though, you can export your whole project. By selecting **File > Save As...** from the menu, you can save an archived project (which you may choose to compress or not) that you can then share with others. This is nice if you are working on a song where you may want a friend or bandmate to add a track to the song you are working on. By sending them the archive, they'll have everything they need to open the project in GarageBand and continue to work on the song.

Summary

Like the previous chapters on iLife applications, this chapter (hopefully) provides enough to get you started with GarageBand, yet there are many more features in GarageBand than we have time for here.

GarageBand, iMovie, and iPhoto provide a wide range of incredibly useful media applications for computer users. Of course, each of these apps has limits (though many people never reach them), so Apple provides a range of professional apps that build upon each of these, including Logic Pro (Apple's professional DAW software), Aperture (Apple's professional photo management software), and Final Cut Pro (Apple's professional video application).

Next we will move away from applications and go back to OS X specifically, moving from the using–OS X phase of the book to the administering–OS X phase, beginning with an in-depth tour of System Preferences.

Lion Taming: Customizing and Administering OS X

While OS X Lion is generally fairly well behaved upon installation, there will likely come a time where the default settings don't work for you and you'd like to change something. There are also a few things that any OS X user should know about basic system maintenance and backup. In Part 5, we will take a close look at Lion's System Preferences and all the options hidden there, from customizing alert sounds to adding new users. We'll then move on to adding external devices to your Mac, including setting up printers. Finally, we will discuss a number of routine tasks that will help keep your computer and your data safe and in good working order.

## Chapter 18

Exploring System Preferences

Many of the configuration and administration options for OS X are located in System Preferences (Figure 18–1). System Preferences is an application that presents a collection of individual items called *preference panes*. Each preference pane presents configurable options for one specific facet of the OS.

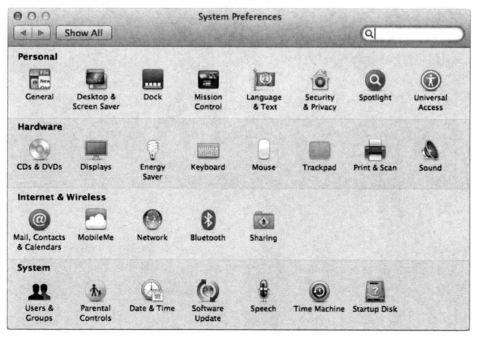

Figure 18–1. *Lion's default system preferences*

This chapter will give an overview of each of these preferences and explain what they all do. We will discuss them according to how they are categorized in System Preferences:

- Personal preferences
- Hardware preferences
- Internet & Wireless preferences
- System preferences

> **NOTE:** Many third-party applications, utilities, and hardware devices install their own *PrefPane*, which will be added to your System Preferences, so you may find additional preference panes toward the bottom of your System Preferences. In general, we will only be covering Apple's default system preferences.

Personal Preferences

The first row of preferences in System Preferences contains the Personal preferences (Figure 18–2). These preferences together largely affect your personal environment and can be set differently for each user on your system.

Figure 18–2. *The Personal preferences in System Preferences*

General

The General preference pane (Figure 18–3) contains a number of options that control how certain aspects of your environment will not only look but also behave.

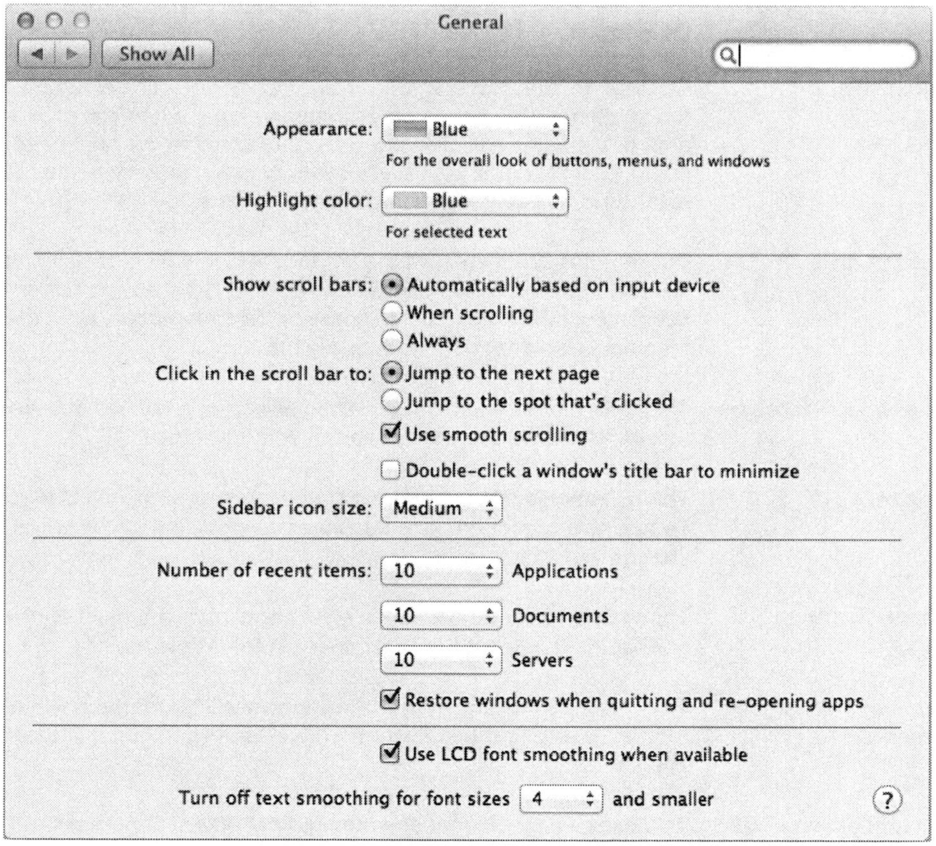

Figure 18–3. *The General preference pane in System Preferences*

Table 18–1 lists each of the appearance options and describes them.

Table 18–1. *Appearance Options*

Option	Description
Appearance	This option allows you to change certain visual elements from blue to graphite (i.e., gray scale). These elements include the window widgets in the top left of the title bars (switching from blue to graphite causes the red, yellow, and green buttons to each change to become the same graphite color). The scroll bar handles and some other UI elements (e.g., the edges of the drop-down option menus) also change from blue to graphite.
Highlight color	This option allows you to change the highlight color of selected text in most applications.
Show scroll bars	This option selects when the new scroll bars in Lion will be visible.

Option	Description
Click in the scroll bar to	This option affects the scroll behavior when you click an empty part of the scroll bar. Depending on your setting here, when you click an empty area of the scroll bar, the view will either scroll to the next page up or down (depending on where you click) or scroll directly to the relative location in the view where you clicked in the scroll bar.
Use smooth scrolling	Clicking this box increases the smoothness in which items scroll by. Because this forces the content to refresh on the screen faster, smooth scrolling comes at the cost of some system resources. On most newer machines, the effect of this is negligible.
Double-click a window's title bar to minimize	This option does what it says. When selected, it causes any window to minimize into the Dock when you double-click the
Sidebar icon size	The "Sidebar icon size" option selects the size of the icons in sidebars. To see how this works, open a Finder window and see how the icons change with this setting.
Number of recent items	These three drop-down menus select how many items of each type will appear in the Recent Items submenu in the Apple menu.
Restore windows when quitting and reopening apps	When this option is checked, all windows will be restored when you reopen an app to the state they were in when you last quit the application.
Use LCD font smoothing when available	This option controls font smoothing. Font smoothing rounds off fonts so the edges don't look jagged on the screen. Occasionally this can alter the font's appearence and at very small font sizes it can cause them to become blurry—in which case, there is an option to turn off font smoothing for smaller fonts. worth pointing out that this option may vary if you are using an external display.

NOTE: Font smoothing (and onscreen font displaying in general) in Mac OS X is fundamentally different than in Microsoft Windows, and there are definitely proponents of each. In Mac OS X, the priority is preserving the look and spacing of the font so that the printed and onscreen text look identical. In Windows, the priority is placed on making the font most readable on the screen, even though that may mean that the onscreen font will be altered in unintended ways. As a result, the fonts in Mac OS X appear more accurate (in respect to their printed counterparts) but can seem a little soft or fuzzy, while the fonts in Windows look crisper, but the spacing and layout often don't appear necessarily as intended and might not match the final output.

Desktop & Screen Saver

The Desktop & Screen Saver preference pane is where you go to change your desktop picture or alter your screen saver and its settings. This pane is divided into two tabs: one that sets the desktop image (Figure 18–4) and one that contains all of your screen saver options (Figure 18–5).

Figure 18–4. *The Desktop tab of the Desktop & Screen Saver preference pane sets your desktop background image.*

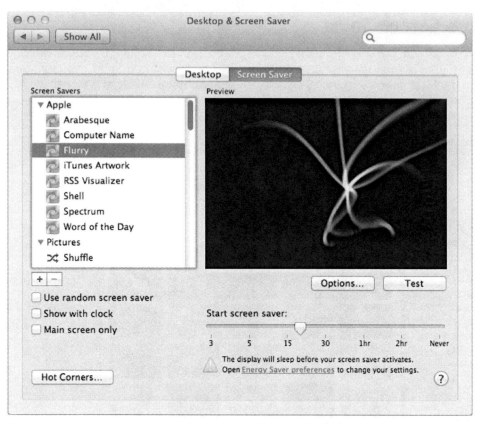

Figure 18–5. *The Screen Saver tab of the Desktop & Screen Saver preference pane*

The Desktop tab presents you with a selection of images to use as your desktop background. By default, Apple provides a wide selection of attractive backgrounds, classified into general categories. Clicking one of the folder items in the left column presents you with a preview of all the images in the right viewing area. Selecting an image in the viewing area automatically sets the image as your desktop background and puts the preview image in the top image space with the image's name besides it.

The default background images are set with preselected shape, position, and scale; however, if you choose one of your own images, a drop-down menu will appear that will allow you to alter the aspect of the image you choose. These aspects are described in Table 18–2.

Table 18–2. *Desktop Image Aspect Selections*

Aspect	Description
Fill Screen	This option scales your image so that it fills the entire screen. Rather than fill the difference with empty space, it scales the image up to fill the empty space (possibly clipping off the edges of your image).
Fit to Screen	Fit to Screen scales the image so that the entire image fits your screen. This option doesn't alter the image's height or width, so empty space may appear above and below your image (the color of the empty space may be selected in the color swatch next to the Aspect menu).
Stretch to Fill Screen	Stretch to Fill Screen scales the image to fill the screen, too. This option, however, adjusts the aspect ratio so that the entire image fills the screen. This may stretch your image's content oddly.
Center	This option doesn't on the screen. If your image dimensions are smaller than your screen dimensions, then empty space will appear around the image. If your image dimensions are larger than your screen dimensions, then the image will extend beyond the screen, effectively cutting off the edges. (You can select the background color that will be shown along the edges if visible.)
Tile	Like Center, this option doesn't the top-left corner of your image with the top-left corner of the screen. If the dimensions of the image are smaller than the dimensions of the screen, then the image will repeat itself to the right of and below itself over and over until it fills the entire screen.

This preference pane automatically reveals any top-level images in your Pictures folder; additionally, it shows items from your iPhoto and Aperture libraries so you can select images from them. You can also add your own image folders by clicking the + button and selecting the folder you wish to add. Also, if you'd like, you can set your preferences so that your background image will change at regular intervals.

The "Translucent menu bar" option at the bottom, toggles the appearance of the menu bar from translucent to opaque.

> **TIP:** The translucent menu bar allows you to view parts of your desktop background that were previously hidden behind the menu bar. If you wish to keep the menu bar translucent, keep in mind that high-contrast areas of images behind the menu bar can make the menu bar items difficult to read. Keep this under consideration when selecting your desktop backgrounds.

> **NOTE:** If you have multiple displays set up on your computer, a Desktop window will appear on each of them so you can independently set the background on each display.

The Screen Saver tab presents a list of available screen saver modules on the left side of the window with a Preview area to the right. In addition to the individual modules, you can also select groups or libraries of images to be used as a screen saver.

To set up your screen saver, first choose the module you'd like to use. Some modules have settable options; if the selected module has options, the Options button will be active. Once you have chosen the module and set its options, you can test it by clicking the Test button. This activates the screen saver with your chosen module. To return, just wiggle the mouse or press a key.

Below the Preview area is the "Start screen saver" slider, which determines how long your system must be idle before the screen saver starts.

> **NOTE:** All Macs can power down their screen after a certain amount of idle time. If this time is shorter than the screen saver start time, then the screen saver will never start. If this is the case, you will receive a warning to this effect in the Screen Saver preference pane, along with a link to the Energy Saver preference pane, where you can control the sleep setting.

The following are some other screen saver options:

- **Use random screen saver***:* This option randomly chooses a screen saver module when the screen saver starts.

- **Show with clock***:* This provides an overlay that presents the current time over the screen saver.

- **Main Screen Only**: This option appears if you have multiple displays attached to your computer, when checked the screensaver will only appear on your main display.

- **Hot Corners...**: This button brings up the Hot Corner dialog, which allows you to assign certain functions to occur when the mouse cursor is moved into one of the corners of your screen. Two of the available options are Start Screen Saver and Disable Screen Saver (which prevents the screen saver from starting if the mouse cursor is in the selected corner).

While the screen saver modules included in Lion are nice, there are many third-party screen savers also available for download (www.apple.com/downloads/macosx/icons_screensavers/ is a good place to start looking). To install a new screen saver, just download the screen saver file and then double-click it. This brings up a dialog box asking if you'd like to install the screen saver for just yourself or for all the users of your computer. If you select the option for just you, the screen saver file will be installed in ~/Library/Screen Savers/; if you choose to install it for everyone, it will be installed in /Library/Screen Savers/.

Dock

The Dock preference pane (Figure 18–6) presents options for configuring your Dock behavior. Table 18–3 describes the preferences available for the Dock.

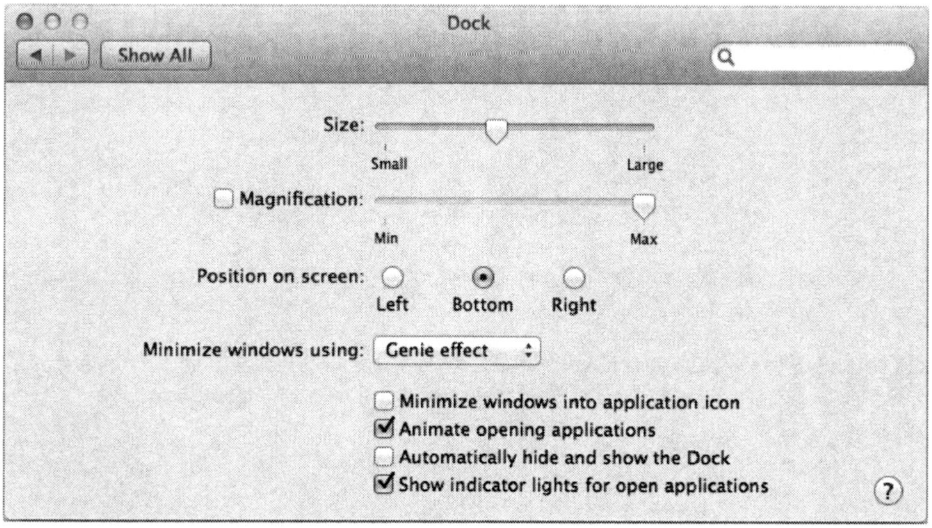

Figure 18–6. *The Dock preference pane*

Table 18–3. *Dock System Preferences*

Preference	Effect
Size	This affects how big the Dock icons and the Dock will be.
Magnification	If selected, this affects how big Dock items will magnify to when the cursor moves over them. This is useful if you have many small items in the Dock. (You can trigger the magnification effect with the preference unselected by mousing over the Dock with the Control-Shift keys held down.)
Position on screen	This allows you to position the Dock on either side or the bottom of the screen. When the Dock is on either side, its appearance will change from the glass appearance (the default, translucent appearance where it appears as if the icons are sitting on a glass shelf) to a flatter appearance.
Minimize windows using	This allows you to choose between two different effects—the Genie Effect and the Scale Effect—when you minimize items onto the Dock. This really has no effect on anything practical and is purely an aesthetic thing.

Preference	Effect
Animate opening applications	When selected, the application icons bounce up and down in the Dock while the application is starting up. (Some people count the bounces as a metric for how fast an application launches.)
Automatically hide and show the Dock	When selected, this causes the Dock to disappear and remain hidden until you move the mouse down to the area of the screen where the Dock would normally appear, at which time it will slide back into view to perform any regular Dock functions. This is nice in certain applications where you want to use the entire screen for the application and the Dock would normally get in the way.
Show indicator lights for open applications	In past versions, a small light would always appear underneath the application icon in the Dock for all running applications. In Lion you now have the option to turn these indicator lights off.

NOTE: You can select many of these Dock preferences by choosing the Dock item in the Apple menu, by right-clicking the space just to the right of the application icons on the Dock, or by clicking and dragging the Dock itself.

TIP: If you prefer the appearance of the Dock while it's on either side (without the glass appearance), but still want the Dock located on the bottom, you can change its appearance by entering the following commands in the Terminal application (if command-line stuff intimidates you, you may want to read Chapter 23 before you do this): `defaults write com.apple.dock no-glass -boolean YES`, followed by `killall Dock`. To reverse this, repeat the previous commands but change YES to NO.

Mission Control

The Mission Control preference pane (Figures 18–7) provides options for configuring OS X's new Mission Control (which replaces/enhances Exposé & Spaces).

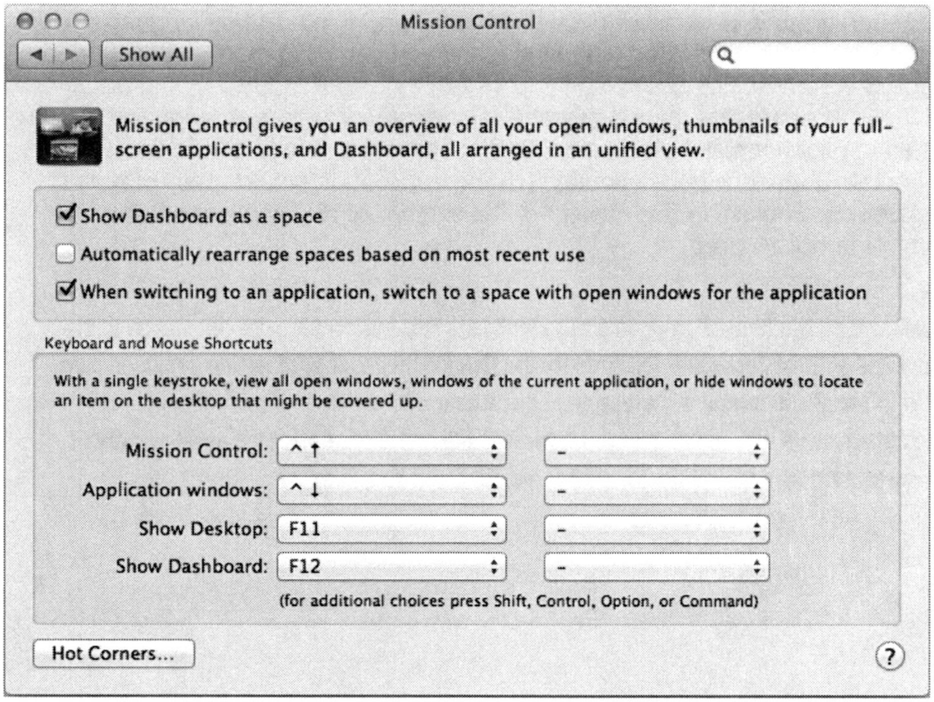

Figure 18–7. *The Mission Control preference pane in Lion replaces the Exposé & Spaces preference pane.*

The Mission Control preference pane provides a few ways to tweak the behavior of Mission Control, and also provides a way to customize the keyboard shortcuts for activating the various Mission Control features (Mission Control is covered earlier in Chapter 4).

NOTE: Many Apple keyboards have dedicated keys for controlling Mission Control that override the traditional F-keys. The Mission Control keyboard and mouse shortcuts here do not affect these keys.

TIP: On many Apple keyboards, the F3 key that would once trigger Exposé now will open Mission Control.

Language & Text

The Language & Text preference pane controls the language and regional display settings of your computer, as well as default text handling in OS X. This preference pane has four tabs that control various settings: Language, Text, Formats, and Input Sources.

The Language tab (Figure 18–8) allows you to set your preferred display language. The column on the left lists the activated languages, and you can drag them in the order of your language preference. For example, if you switch the order of English and Japanese so that Japanese appears first, then Japanese will become the default language for your system and all applications. If, however, an application weren't localized in Japanese (i.e., didn't contain Japanese translations), then the application would attempt to find your second choice (English, in this case). For the system or any application, the first available language will be used.

> **NOTE:** *Localization* is a term referring to adding language information for a specific region in the world. Saying that an application is localized for the Ukraine means that Ukrainian language data was added to the application and is available to those who wish to use it. If you encounter an application that lacks a localization that you favor, you may want to contact the developer about this. You could even help implement the proper localization if you so desire.

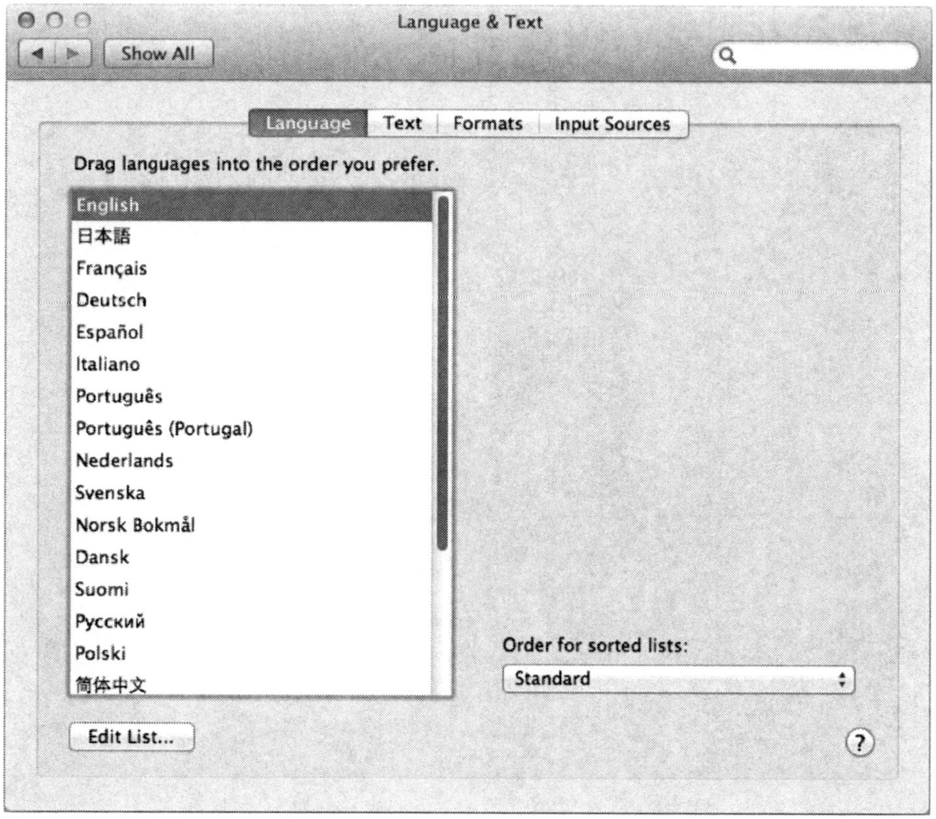

Figure 18–8. *The Language tab of the Language & Text preference pane sets your default display language.*

You may notice that while the default list of languages covers many languages, many more are not covered. To add or remove languages from the list, click the Edit List... button. This brings up a dialog box with many more languages to choose from. Checking the box next to any of these languages will include that language in the default list.

The other option on this tab is an "Order for sorted lists" drop-down list. This selection determines the language used for sorting items in the Finder when you choose to sort items by name.

The next tab in the Language & Text preference pane is the Text tab (Figure 18–9). Here you will find a number of options for dealing with text, including a number of features to automatically substitute certain text with symbols, and options for smart quotes. All of these options are similar to AutoText features found in many word processors.

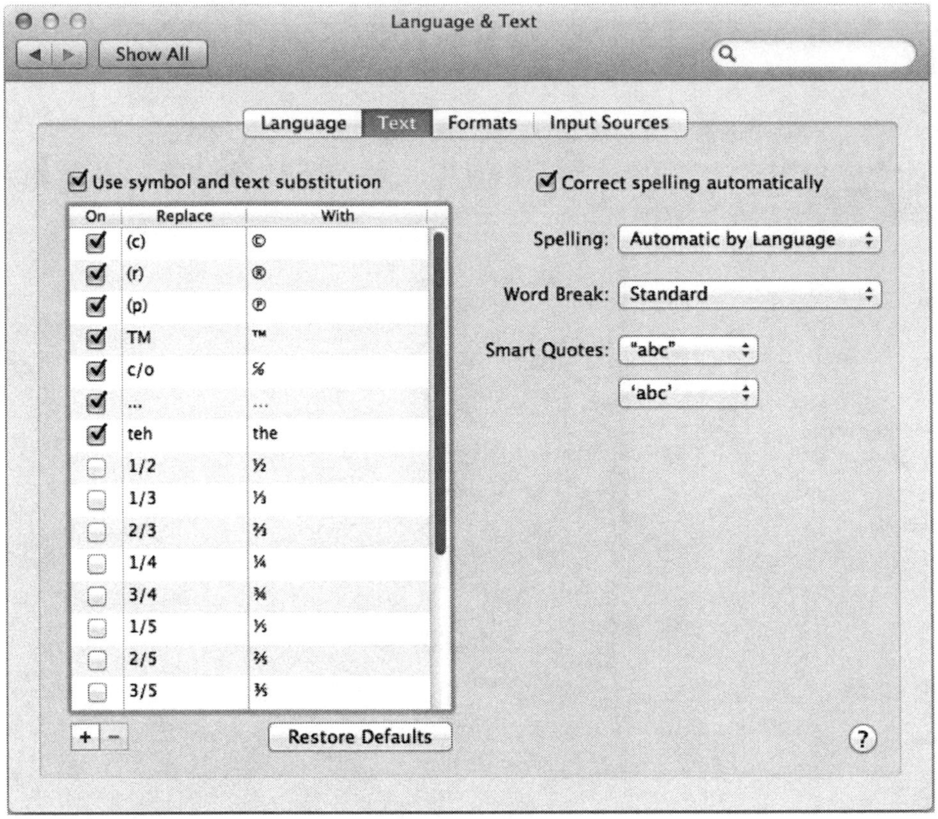

Figure 18–9. *The Text tab of the Language & Text preference pane includes some system-wide options for dealing with text.*

NOTE: Computer programmers may be interested in the "English (United States, Computer)" option under the Word Break list. This selection causes the computer to react more favorably to words in computer programs, specifically when it comes to common naming practices of variables. For example, if you have words separated by a colon (such as setName:aName), it will understand that these are separate words when selecting text.

The Formats tab (Figure 18–10) sets up default date, time, number, currency, and measurement unit settings for your computer. Selecting your region from the Region drop-down list generally sets these items accurately. For example, switching from United States to United Kingdom alters the order of the date, switches to a 24-hour clock, changes the currency from US Dollars to British Pound Sterling, and changes the measurement units to metric. If, however, the default settings for your region aren't exactly what you want, you can alter or customize most of them. If you don't see the region that you want in the Region menu, try checking the "Show all regions" selection.

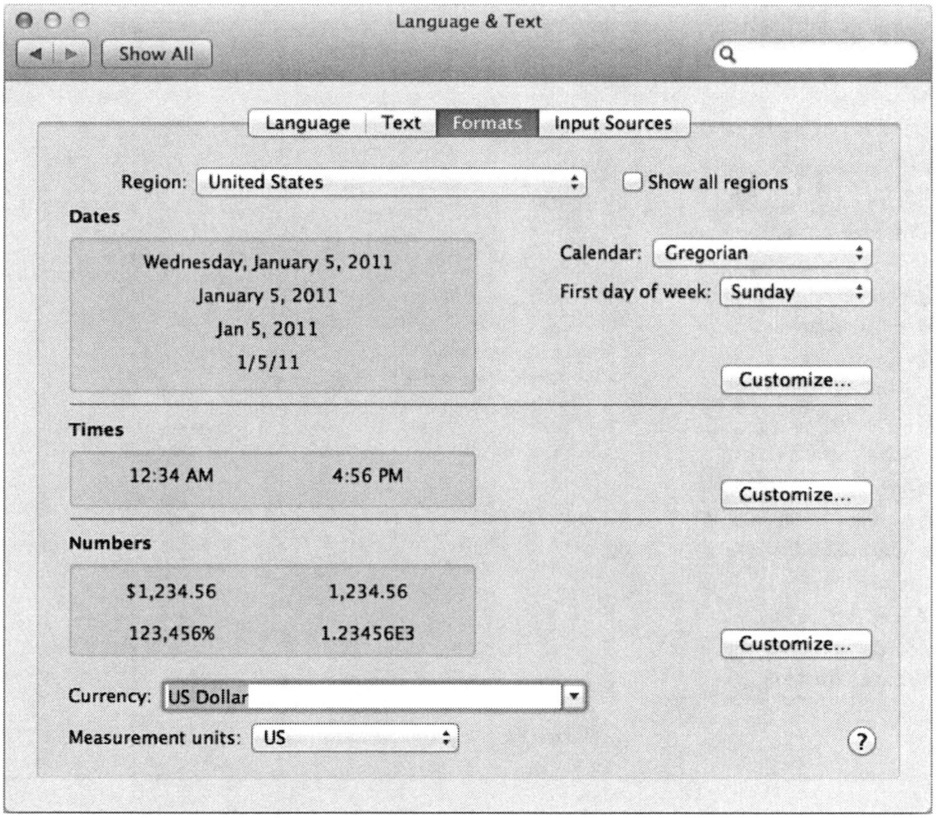

Figure 18–10. *The Formats tab of the Language & Text preference pane sets how dates, times, numbers, currency, and measurements appear.*

NOTE: It seems that whatever region you choose, the Calendar setting will stay set to Gregorian, so if you wish to use a different calendar system, you will need to set that manually.

The Input Sources tab (Figure 18–11) is where you set up your input language and devices. It contains a long list of various items with check boxes. Each item represents an input palette, an input method, an input device (specifically, a keyboard), or a keyboard mapping. These items combine to allow a large number of languages to be used to input text in Mac OS X. Using the check boxes, you can select any number of languages and input devices that you commonly use. If you select more than one item, the "Show Input menu in menu bar" option will automatically be selected, allowing you to easily switch between inputting different languages at any time from the menu bar.

Figure 18–11. *The Input Sources tab on the Language & Text preference pane sets the language input options for your systems.*

The input palettes in the list provide the ability to open up a couple of special Input Source dialog windows (Figure 18–12) that allow you to input characters by clicking them. The Keyboard Viewer (which becomes available from the menu bar if you select the Keyboard & Character Viewer option under the Input Sources tab) is particularly interesting, since it shows how your keyboard is mapped and responds dynamically as you type on the keyboard. For example, if you press the Option key, the Keyboard Viewer will change to reflect the symbols available with the Option-*key* combinations. Paying attention to changes while playing around with this can teach you new tricks. For example, if you look at the changes while you hold the Fn key, you may notice a number of interesting functions (e.g., Function-Delete deletes the characters in front of the cursor rather than behind). The Character Viewer provides a way to browse and input a wide array of symbols and characters as well as input text from complex languages such as Chinese and Japanese.

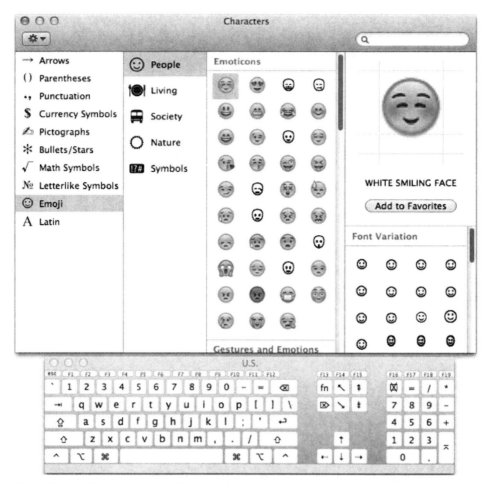

Figure 18–12. *The Character and Keyboard viewers*

The input methods in the list affect the behavior of inputting text, primarily for languages with very large character sets. For such languages, you will commonly enter two or more keystrokes to input a single character. These varying input methods facilitate this.

Finally, the keyboard items affect the keyboard layout and language. In general, this is to accommodate different languages and the keyboards designed for them; however, you can use these options to remap any keyboard (even though in doing so, the letters on the keys will no longer match the inputted character). While some of the remappings are extreme, others are subtler—for example, switching to a Spanish key map will alter only a few symbol keys (making common Spanish symbols easier to access). In addition to changing the input character maps of your keyboard, changing to certain languages will alter the direction of input—for example, switching to Arabic or Hebrew will cause the input to flow from right to left rather than left to right.

In general, if you need to enter text, characters, or symbols and you are not quite sure how, selecting either the Keyboard Viewer or the Character Palette is a good place to start to help you find what you are looking for.

Security & Privacy

The Security & Privacy preference pane seems oddly placed in that many of its options affect the entire system rather than just your personal preferences. The Security & Privacy preference pane provides four tabs: General, for general system security options; FileVault, for encrypting your personal home folder and all of its contents; Firewall, which can help secure your system from network intrusion by limiting access to computer network services; and Privacy, which will allow you to set certain privacy option on a per-application basis.

Chapter 21 is dedicated to system security, so these preferences and more will be covered there.

Spotlight

The Spotlight preference pane (Figure 18–13) helps you customize what types of items Spotlight will index and in what order you want the results of a search to be returned to you.

The Spotlight preference pane has two tabs: Search Results and Privacy. The Privacy tab allows you to select folders that you want to prevent from being indexed. This can prevent information that you'd like to keep private from showing up in any searches of your system, or it can save system resources by indexing only the items that you are interested in indexing.

The Search Results tab provides a few more customization possibilities. First of all, it allows you to block certain types of files from appearing in a Spotlight search result. So, if you'd like to exclude mail messages from being returned in a Spotlight search, you can uncheck the Mail Messages item (this affects only system-wide Spotlight searches; messages will continue to be searchable from within Mail). Additionally, you can arrange the items in the Search Results list in the order that you'd like those items to be returned to you, so if you'd like all the matched images to appear before the matched contacts, just move the Images item above the Contacts item.

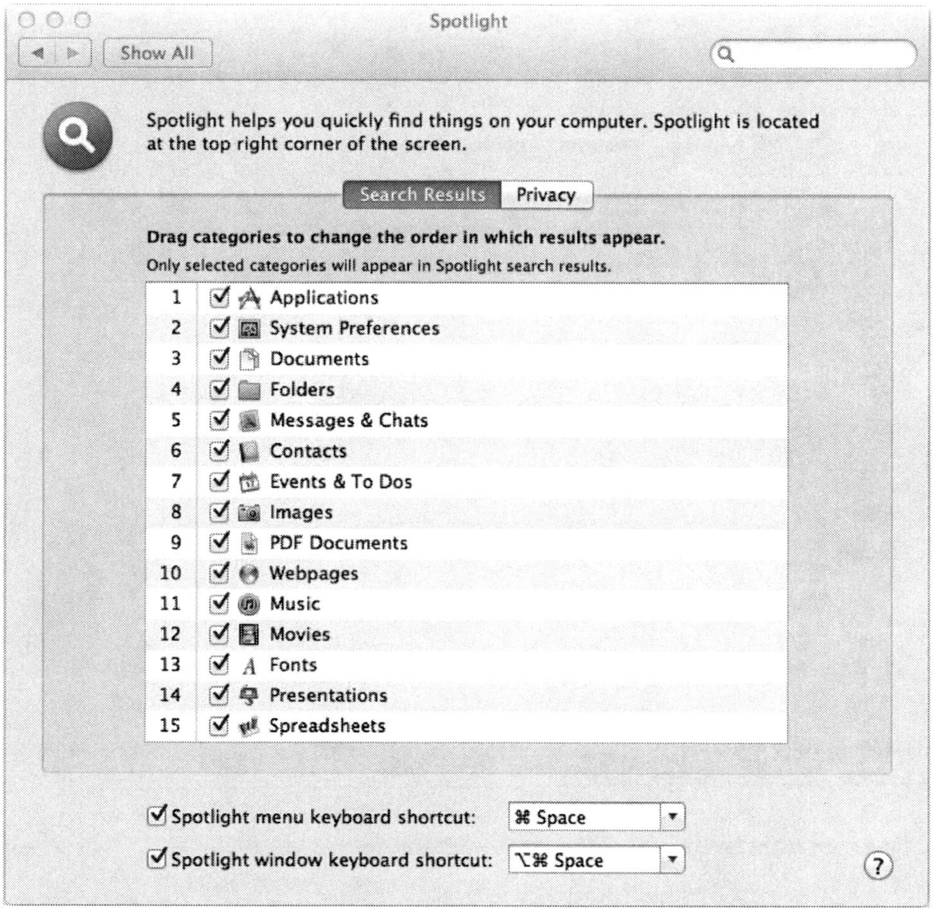

Figure 18–13. *The Spotlight preference pane with the Search Results tab showing*

The options below the window allow you to alter the keyboard shortcuts for activating Spotlight. Should you decide to change these, consider that while most applications are aware of the default settings, custom settings may overlap with some applications' built-in shortcuts, so there may be times when the keyboard shortcuts you set do something unexpected.

Universal Access

The Universal Access preference pane provides settings to assist people who have difficulty hearing, seeing, or otherwise working with their computer. This preference pane is divided into four tabs: Seeing, Hearing, Keyboard, and Mouse & Trackpad.

The Seeing tab (Figure 18–14) provides a number of options to assist people who have trouble seeing things on their computer screen.

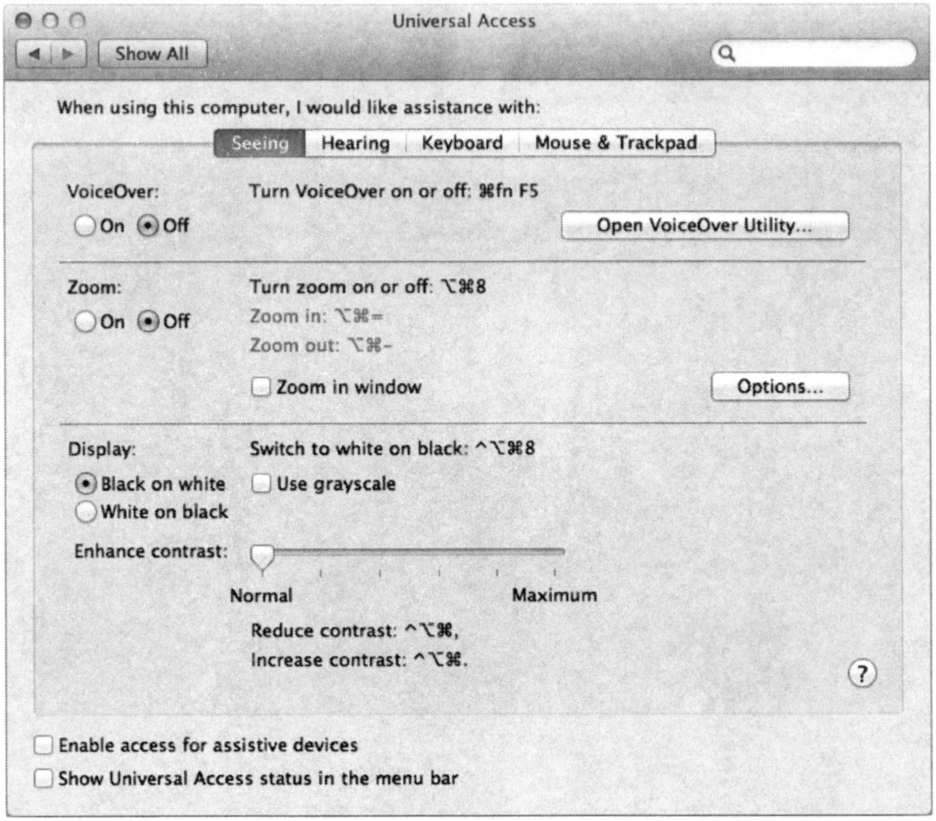

Figure 18–14. *The Seeing tab of the Universal Access preference pane*

VoiceOver, when activated, speaks out selected regions of the computer interface. First, it identifies the selected window, and then it allows you to tab through interface features, speaking the name of each as you tab through. VoiceOver itself has many options and can be fully customized via VoiceOver Utility (Figure 18–15), accessible in the Utilities folder from Launchpad or by clicking the Open VoiceOver Utility... button on the preference pane.

> **NOTE:** VoiceOver is a sophisticated piece of software, providing options for everything from minor audio assistance to full Braille output for the blind (and many options in between). VoiceOver Utility provides many options to customize this to whatever your needs are, and we encourage anyone needing this level of assistance to fully explore it.

Zoom allows you to zoom in and out of the screen. This is an extension of the zoom functions for the mouse and trackpad discussed earlier, but it provides a few additional options and methods of zooming.

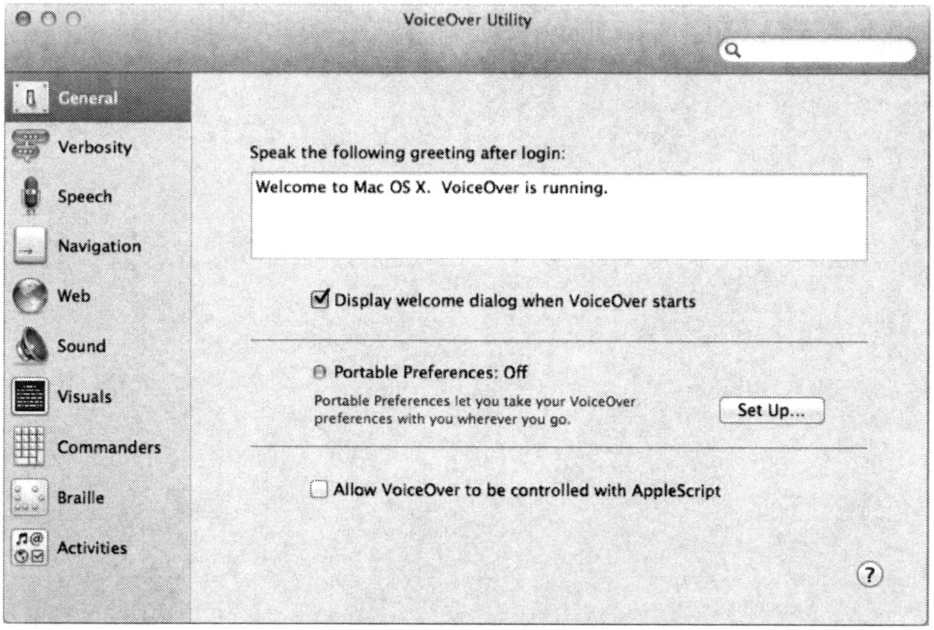

Figure 18–15. *VoiceOver Utility provides many options for customizing VoiceOver's capabilities.*

The Display section provides options that allow you to alter the display. This includes switching the display output to gray scale or color, adjusting the display's contrast, and even inverting the color scheme of the display (try Command-Option-Control-8).

The Hearing tab (Figure 18–16) provides a few options to aid people with hearing issues. The primary option here allows you to flash the screen when an alert occurs. This option can also come in handy if you work in a very loud (or very quiet) environment.

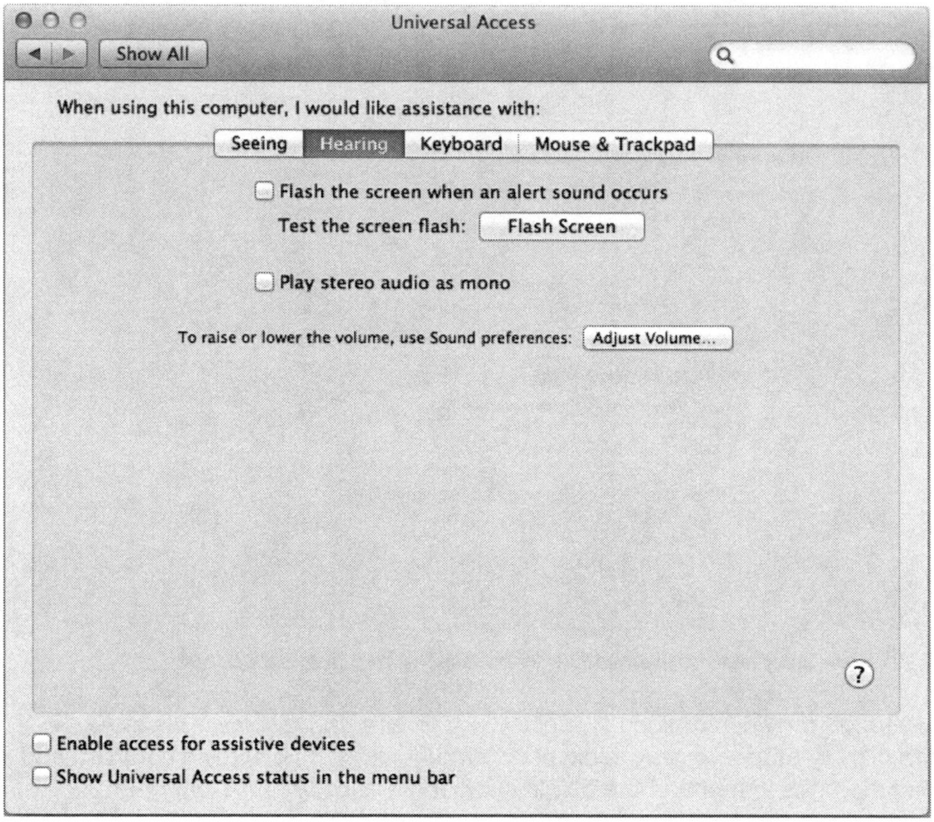

Figure 18–16. *The Hearing tab of the Universal Access preference pane*

The Keyboard tab (Figure 18–17) builds upon the keyboard options on the Keyboard preference pane (covered below). Sticky Keys provides options for people who may have trouble holding multiple keys at once, so that they can more easily use keyboard combinations and shortcuts. The Slow Keys option helps the system ignore accidental key input.

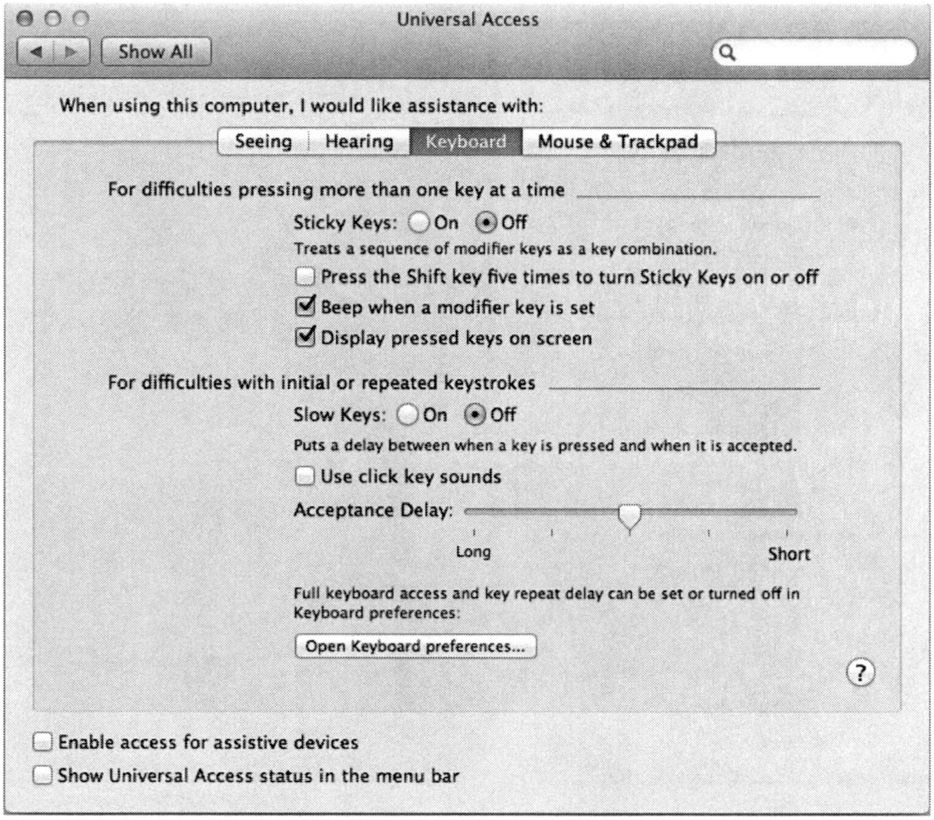

Figure 18–17. *The Keyboard tab provides some additional keyboard options.*

The Mouse & Trackpad tab (Figure 18–18) provides options for people who have trouble using the mouse or trackpad. Mouse Keys allows you to use the keyboard's keypad to move the cursor around on the screen instead of the mouse. There is also an option to increase the size of the mouse cursor so that it's easier to track on the screen.

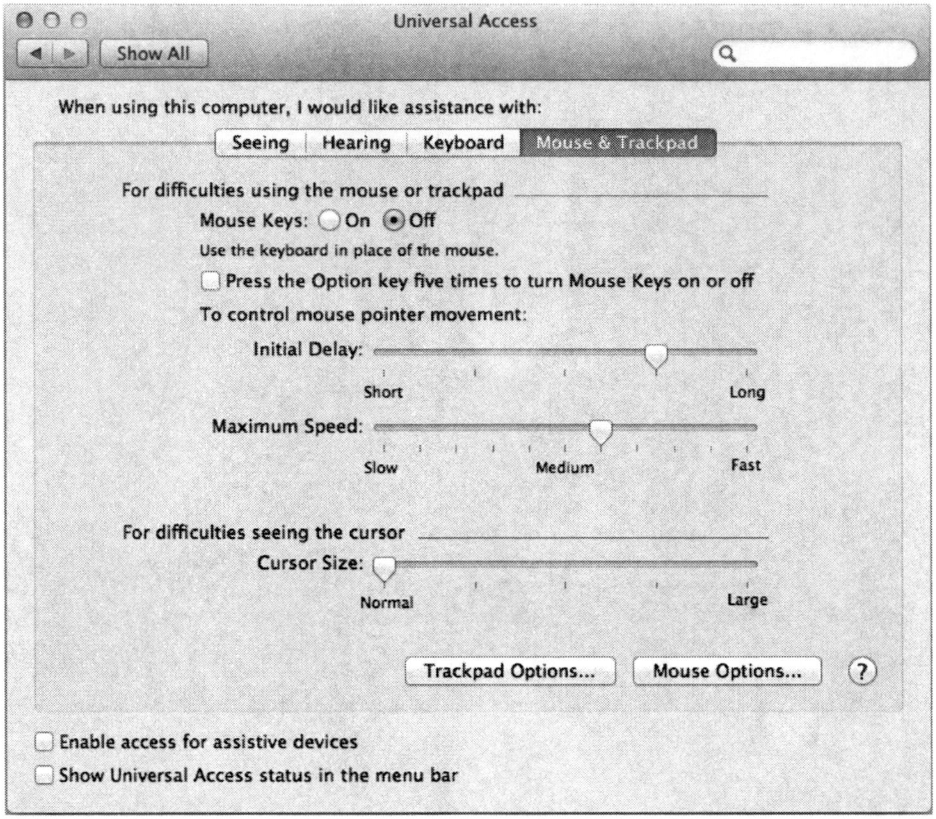

Figure 18–18. *The Mouse & Trackpad tab on the Universal Access preference pane adds additional mouse and trackpad options.*

NOTE: Two options that are available under all four tabs are "Enable access for assistive devices" and "Show Universal Access status in the menu bar." "Enable access for assistive devices" enables additional tracking features in the UI that may be necessary for some software and special hardware devices. "Show Universal Access status in the menu bar" adds a status menu to the menu bar that shows the status of various Universal Access settings.

Hardware

The row of preference panes below the Personal preferences contains the Hardware preferences (Figure 18–19). Here you will find settings for most of the hardware devices included with your computer.

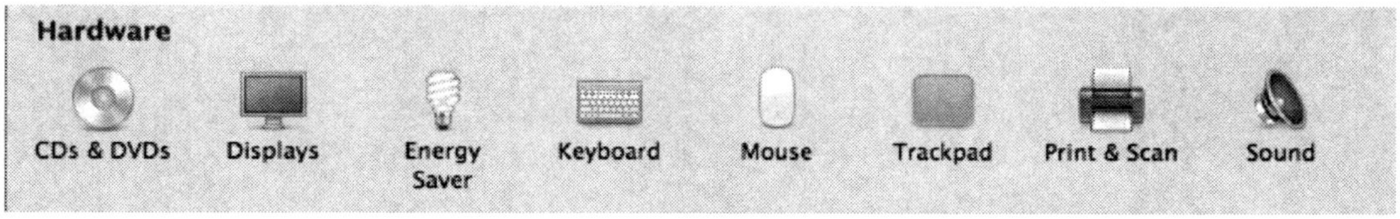

Figure 18–19. *The Hardware preference panes*

CDs & DVDs

The CDs & DVDs preference pane (Figure 18–20) allows you to select what will happen when you insert certain media formats in your computer. The media formats that you can assign actions to include blank CDs, blank DVDs, music CDs, picture CDs, and video DVDs.

Figure 18–20. *The CDs & DVDs preference pane*

NOTE: This preference pane will only appear if you have a CD/DVD drive attached to your computer, so by default this will not show up on a MacBook Air.

Displays

The Displays preference pane allows you to make adjustments to your computer displays. By default, there are two tabs on this preference pane: Display and Color, but if you have more then one Displays attached to your computer an additional Arrangement tab will be there as well.

The Display tab (Figure 18–21) allows you to set the display resolution for your display. Additionally, depending on the monitor additional options may appear for Brightness, Refresh Rate, and Rotation. If your computer has ambient light sensors (as some Apple laptops do), you can set an option that will automatically adjust your screen's brightness according to the brightness of your environment.

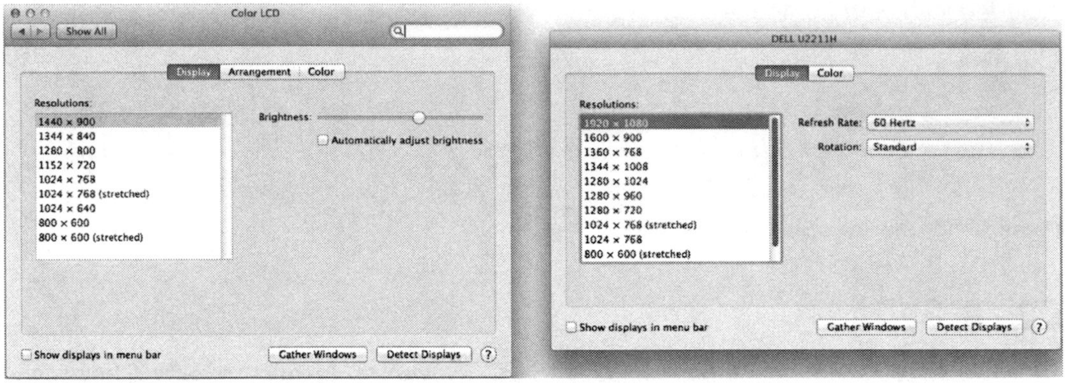

Figure 18–21. *Two slightly different panes of the Display tab of the Displays preference pane are shown here. If you have more then one display, each display will have its own independent controls.*

NOTE: The Gather Windows button will appear if you have more then one display attached it will gather together all independent Display Preference Windows on the main screen.

The Color tab (Figure 18–22) allows you to manage the display's color profiles. A *color profile* is a data file that contains color information about a device or color standard. ColorSync uses these data files to match up colors so that an item appears consistent from one device to another. All this allows an image from your digital camera to appear on your screen the way the camera intended and then allows the image you print out on your printer to match what you see on the screen. The trick, however, is to assure that your screen has the proper profile.

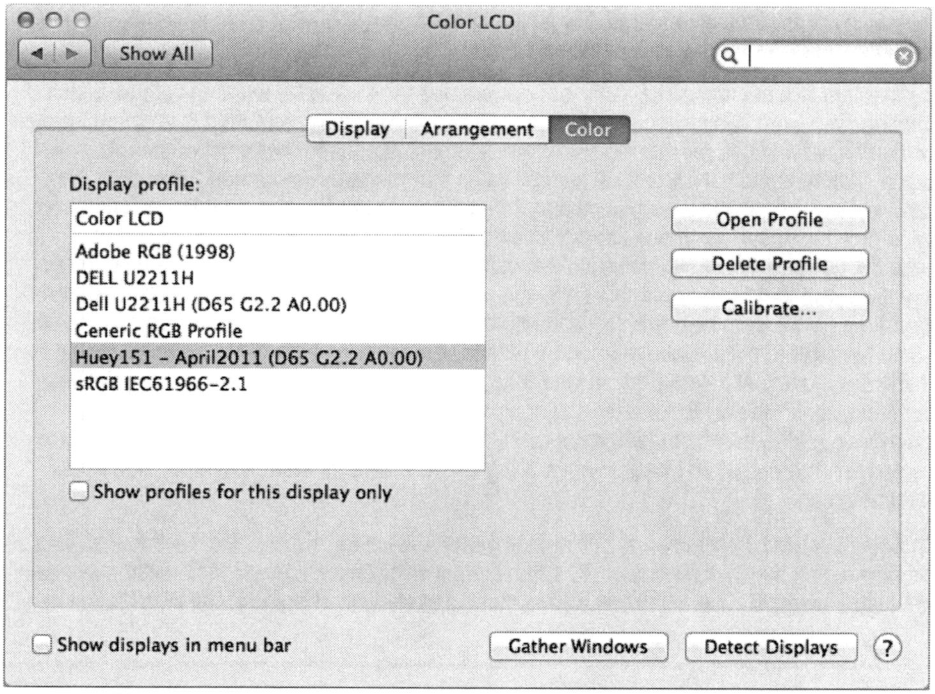

Figure 18–22. *The Displays preference pane's Color tab helps you manage your display's color profiles.*

Mac OS X comes with some generic color profiles for Apple displays as well as some others; however, it's likely that you will want to calibrate your monitor, creating a custom profile for your display.

> **NOTE:** Why calibrate your display? Because the generic color profiles that ship with Mac OS X are just that—generic. They are a decent average, but in reality each display is slightly different, so it's highly unlikely that the generic profile will match reality. Also, the generic profiles don't take into account your ambient lighting situation, which can have a big impact on how colors appear on your screen. Also, calibration allows you to adjust your display's gamma.

GAMMA AND OS X: WHY ARE THINGS DARKER?

Gamma (or gamma correction) is a numerical value that determines the overall value, or brightness, of an image being displayed. The details of gamma could quickly divert into a discussion of complex algebraic equations and light physics, but in general terms, gamma represents a nonlinear relationship between the pixels of an image and the brightness of the monitor. This results in the variation of the brightness, contrast, and dynamic range of an image that appears onscreen. Lower gamma values create brighter images, and higher gamma values result in darker images. In general, the goal of adjusting gamma is to find a balance in the dynamic range of the display device, where whites are white, blacks are black, and all shades in between are accurately rendered. For a computer display, the ideal gamma number to make the best of the lights and darks usually falls between 1.8 and 2.5.

Once all Macs defaulted to a gamma of 1.8. This was determined to be ideal for working with all things destined for printing. Microsoft Windows computers, meanwhile, traditionally defaulted to a gamma around 2.2 (this really didn't have much to do with Microsoft per se; it just happened that most of the CRT monitors of the day happened to have a natural gamma value that ranged from around 2.2 to 2.5). This was a throwback to TVs (2.2 gamma is also known as TV gamma). As computer output transitioned from paper to digital, a problem occurred: images designed on a Mac looked dark and ugly on Windows computers, while things designed on Windows looked washed out and ugly on Macs. (There were other color space issues as well, but the gamma thing was the big elephant in the room.) Ultimately, the World Wide Web Consortium (W3C) (with help from HP and Microsoft) declared that the standard color space for the Internet would be sRGB (a color space devised by HP and Microsoft) and the default gamma would be 2.2. Now it's fairly easy to adjust the gamma on your Mac, but it's just not something most people would intuitively know to do, so in the past there were still imaging conflicts on the Web between Macs and Windows machines. To add to this mismatch, most digital imaging devices, such as digital cameras and digital video recorders, also outputted images with a 2.2 gamma. Sooner or later, it seemed that Apple would have to come around.

Beginning with Snow Leopard, Apple changed its default gamma value for displays from 1.8 to 2.2. As a result, if you've been using an older version of OS X, the default color space on your Mac today may seem a bit darker and higher contrast. Overall, this is a good thing, and viewing images on the Web should be a bit better.

To create a basic profile, click the Calibrate... button on the Color tab. This opens up the Display Calibrator Assistant (Figure 18–23), which walks you through the process of manually calibrating your display.

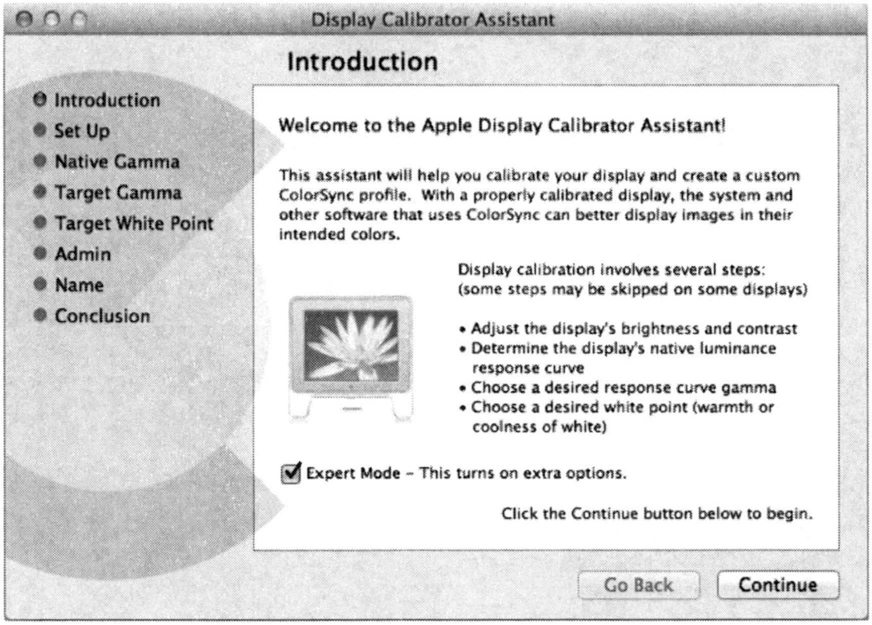

Figure 18–23. *The Display Calibrator Assistant*

Once the Display Calibrator Assistant is open, you can start calibration your displays color by clicking the Continue button.

> **NOTE:** You may notice that an expert mode offering extra options is available. If you are calibrating an older CRT, then the expert mode might work for you reasonably, but many of the expert tests are extraordinarily difficult to get right if you are using a flat-panel display (since color shifts as your angle of view changes). If accurate color matching is really important to you, we recommend picking up a hardware device that will calibrate your monitor for you. Something like the Pantone Huey will do an excellent job for less than $100.

Clicking the Continue button takes you to the screen where you select your target gamma (Figure 18–24). There are only two options in basic mode: Gamma 2.2 (Standard) and Gamma 1.8. As stated previously, we generally recommend the 2.2 gamma option.

> **NOTE:** Clicking Continue skips two steps: Set Up and Native Gamma. Certain displays (predominantly CRTs) require extra steps to create a baseline for the calibration. If you find yourself confronted with these steps, just follow the onscreen instructions to work through them.

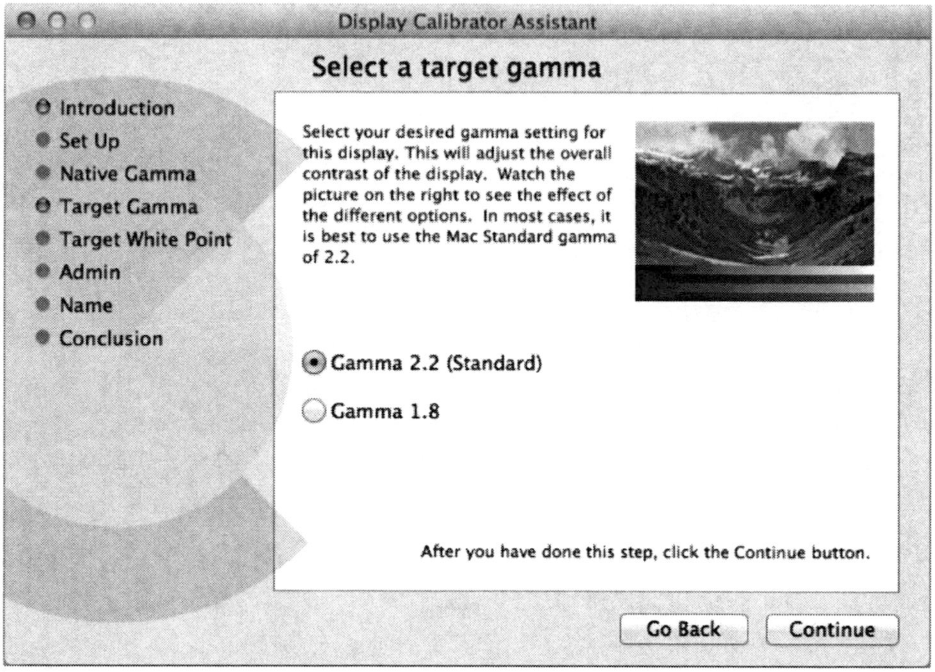

Figure 18–24. *Selecting the target gamma in the Display Calibrator Assistant*

Continuing on from the gamma selection, you're taken to the screen where you can set the display's white point (Figure 18–25). *White point* is the strangest and most difficult-to-grasp concept in color matching. Your eyes generally compensate for ambient light so that things that may not be white appear white. This makes setting the white point of your monitor a bit tricky to do manually. In general, depending on the ambient light surrounding your computer, you will find a comfortable white point around 6000 to 7500 K (Kelvin, which is how white point is measured). For most modern displays, this should be right about where the native white point is, so unless you really know you don't want to use your native white point, we recommend using it.

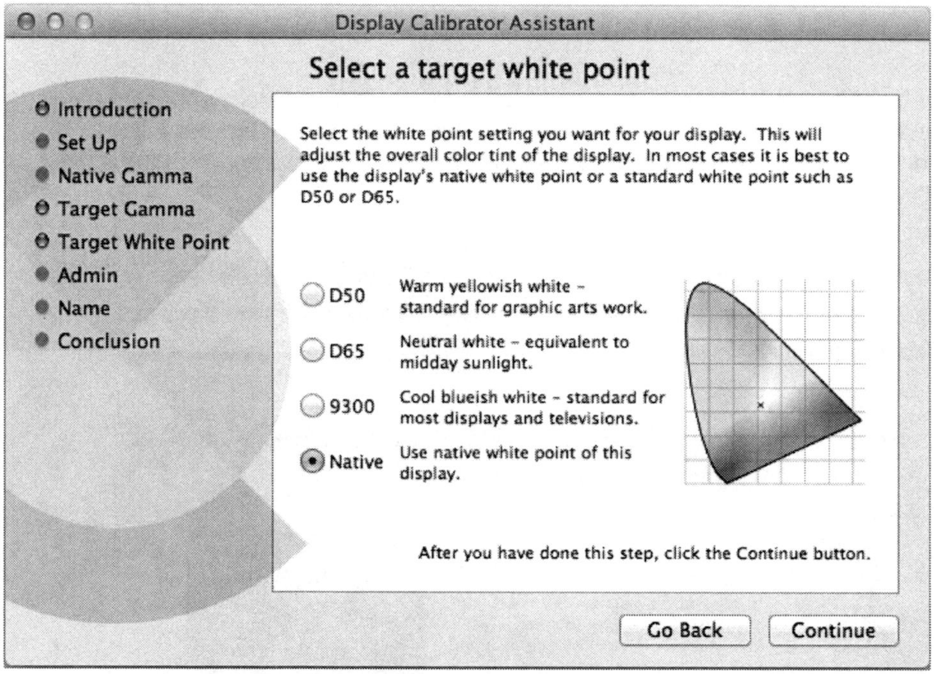

Figure 18–25. *Selecting a target white point for your display*

NOTE: Besides measuring white point in Kelvin (commonly referred to as the *correlated color temperature),* there are other common names given to certain white points, such as D50 or D65. D65 is also known as the television white point and is the default sRGB color space white point.

NOTE: If you use a hardware device to calibrate your monitor, it may initially seem to have a weird effect on the white point of your display—even though it's likely spot on. This is your eyes playing tricks on you again (this is temporary and lasts only until your eyes adjust to the new white point setting).

After you set the white point, click the Continue button. If you are using an account with administrator status, you will be prompted to choose if you'd like this profile to be available to users other than yourself; if not, you'll jump straight to the Name step, where you'll be asked to name your new profile. You can call your new profile anything you want, but we recommend using something sensible.

Once you are done, click Continue. You will be presented with one last screen, essentially telling you that you're done. Click the Done button. When the assistant goes away, you will see your new profile as an option in the Display Profile area, along with any other profiles.

If you happen to have two or more displays hooked up to your computer, a third Display tab called Arrangement will appear (Figure 18–26). This provides a view area that lets you arrange your monitors next to each other and a check box that allows you to mirror your displays. If the Mirror Displays option is checked, then both displays will have the same information on them. If the Mirror Displays option is unchecked, then the displays will act together as one large work area.

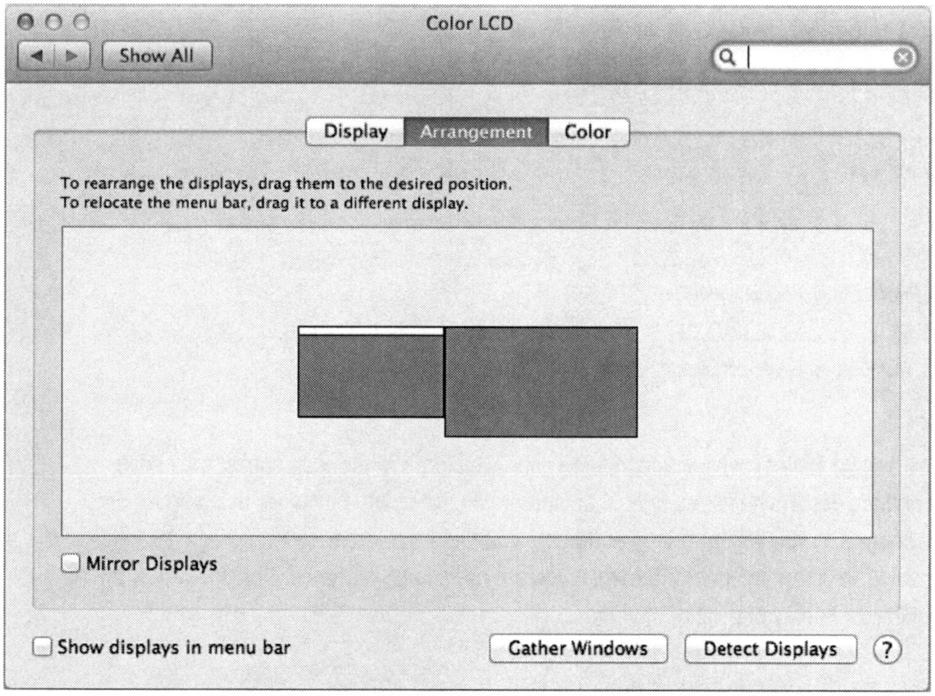

Figure 18–26. *When you have multiple displays attached to your computer, the Arrangement tab allows you to arrange the monitors into one large workspace.*

Energy Saver

The Energy Saver preference pane (Figure 18–27) allows you to adjust some power-saving features for your computer. It does this by causing certain functions of your computer to sleep after a short idle period and by throttling overall performance of your system to conserve energy consumption.

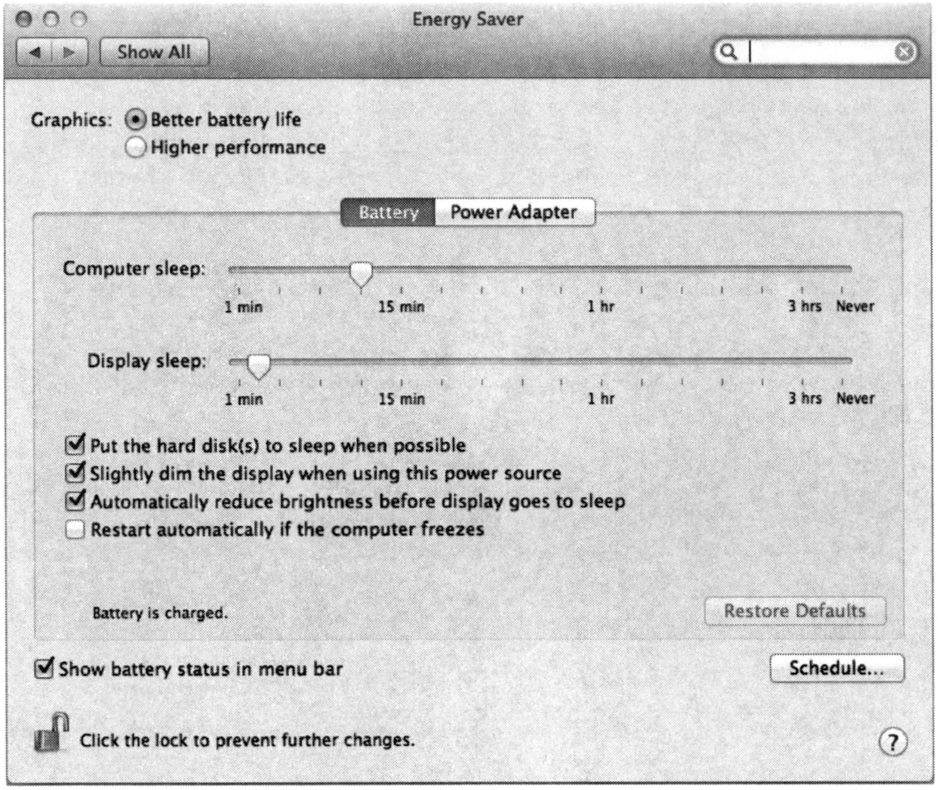

Figure 18–27. *The Energy Saver preference pane*

> **NOTE:** The Energy Saver preference pane, like many System Preferences panes, may have different options depending on the type of computer you are using. If you are using an Apple notebook computer, you will have tabs at the top to set your preferences individually for when you are using the power adapter or for when you are running on batteries. Desktop Macs, on the other hand, provide only one set of options.

Table 18–4 lists the general options available in this preference pane and their effects.

Table 18–4. *Energy Saver Settings*

Setting	Description
Graphics: Better battery life | Higher performance	Many Professional Apple laptops come equipped with two graphics chips: an integrated graphics chip and a more powerful, dedicated graphics processor. Selecting "Better battery life" will enable the integrated graphics card, which, while less powerful, uses less power. Selecting "Higher performance" will enable the dedicated graphics processor for highest performance. You may need to log out to activate this change. Some newer Mac products now allow automatic graphics switching, which will choose which processor to use based on the current activity.
Computer sleep	This slider allows you to set a value for how long the computer should remain idle before it automatically sleeps. (A computer is idle whenever it is not actively receiving user input. Even while it is processing some data or playing back a movie, the computer can be idle unless you are actively typing or moving the mouse around.) In sleep state, most computer processes stop, and most hardware is powered down (or placed in a low–power consumption mode). A minimal amount of power is consumed to keep the current state of the computer in memory so that it can quickly resume where it left off when it is woken up.
Display sleep	This mode is similar to the Computer Sleep setting, but it affects only the display (which is traditionally one of the most power-hungry components of a computer). Even when you have reasons not to sleep the computer, it's not a bad idea to turn off the display, as displays are usually the most power-hungry components of a computer.
Put the hard disk(s) to sleep when possible	This check box tells the computer to power down the hard drives when it determines they are not being used. Powering down hard drives can save a bit of energy.
Wake for network access	This mode allows incoming network connections to wake up your computer. This option is not available when running under battery power.
Automatically reduce brightness before display goes to sleep	As it says, this mode dims the display before it actually puts it to sleep. This comes in handy if you are, for example, watching a movie on your computer; since you are not actively interacting with your computer, it will consider itself idle. By dimming the screen, you will be able to react to let your computer know you are still there before it just shuts down your screen.
Start up automatically after a power failure	This option is useful if you are running on a power adapter without a battery backup (primarily when using a desktop computer). If this option is selected, in the event of an unexpected power loss, your computer will restart automatically when power is restored.

Restart automatically if the computer freezes	This option will cause your computer to restart if it ever happens to freeze, which while rare, can happen.
Schedule...	This button opens up a dialog box that allows you to set a schedule for your computer to shut down or start up automatically at a predetermined time. For example, if you arrive at work every day at 8:30 a.m., you could have your computer start up and be ready for you at 8:15 a.m. every weekday morning.
Show battery status in the menu bar	This option adds a menu icon in your menu bar that indicates if you are running on the power adapter or battery power. It also tells you how much charge remains in the battery. This option is available only for notebook computers with a battery.
Slightly dim the display when using this power source	This setting is available under the Battery tab on notebook computers. It causes the brightness of the display to drop a few levels to conserve energy when running on battery power.
Restore Defaults	Clicking this button resets all preference options back to the default state.

NOTE: One final option is the lock in the lower-left corner of the preference pane. If you are an administrator on your computer, clicking this lock will lock the preference pane so that changes cannot be made to it until it is unlocked. Clicking the locked icon presents a standard authentication dialog box asking for your administrative password to unlock the preference pane. In general, if other people use your computer and you don't want them monkeying around with important settings, lock them.

Keyboard

The Keyboard preference pane controls the options for your keyboard. It is divided into two tabs: Keyboard and Keyboard Shortcuts.

The Keyboard tab (Figure 18–28) provides options for your keyboard. The basic options are the following:

- **Key Repeat rate**: This slider controls how fast a letter will automatically repeat if you hold down a key.

- **Delay Until Repeat**: This slider controls how long you must initially hold down a key until the letter starts repeating.

- **Modifier Keys...**: This button opens a dialog box that allows you to remap the modifier keys (e.g., to switch the behavior of the Command and Control keys for a more Microsoft Windows–like experience). You can also turn these keys off (such as the Caps Lock key).

- **Show Keyboard & Character Viewers in menu bar**: This option will turn on the Keyboard & Character Viewer along with the Input Method menu item in the menu bar.

Other hardware-specific options include the following:

- **Use all F1, F2, etc. keys as standard function keys**: On many Apple keyboards, the function keys control features such as volume, screen brightness, and other aspects of hardware by default. To use these function keys as standard function keys instead, you must hold down the Fn key. Selecting this box reverses the default behavior.

- **Automatically illuminate keyboard in low light**: This is for special Apple keyboards (like those found on many Apple notebooks) that allow the keyboard to light up. Selecting this box will cause the keys to light up in low-light conditions. You can use the slider to turn off the keyboard lights after a designated period of idle time.

- **Set Up Bluetooth Keyboard...**: If you have Bluetooth available on your computer, this button will appear at the bottom of the preference pane. Selecting it will open a dialog box (Figure 18–29) that will walk you through the process of connecting a wireless Bluetooth keyboard to work with your computer.

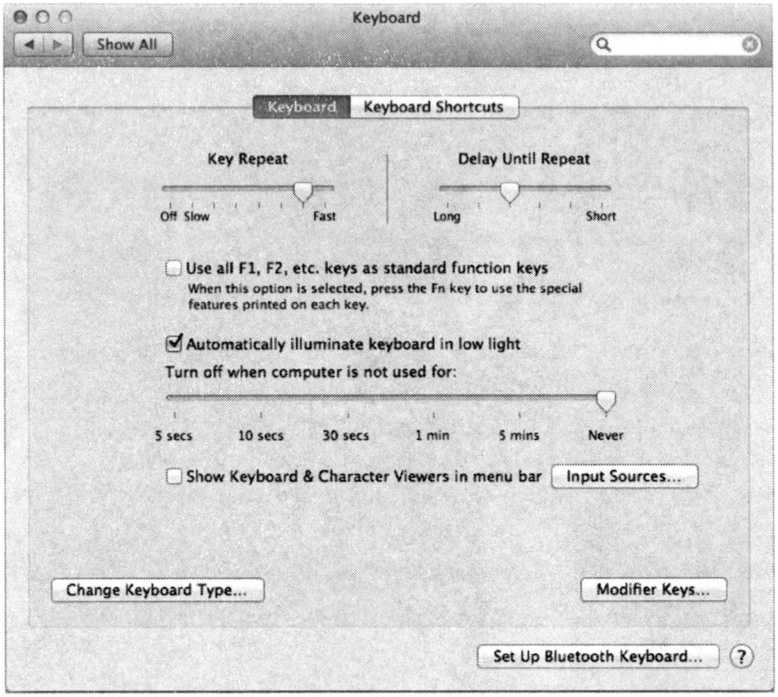

Figure 18–28. *The Keyboard tab on the Keyboard preference pane controls your keyboard.*

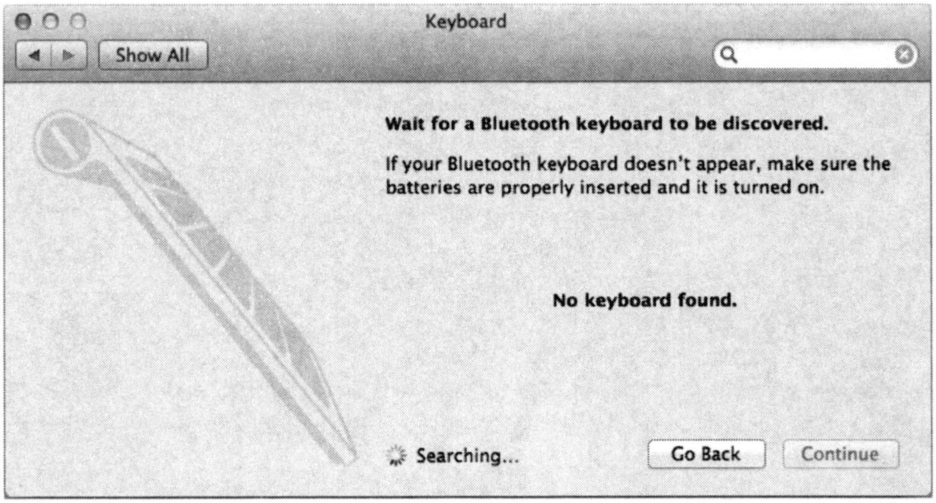

Figure 18–29. *Clicking the Set Up Bluetooth Keyboard... button will open a dialog box that will walk you through the steps needed to set up your wireless Bluetooth keyboard to work with your Bluetooth-enabled computer.*

Many years ago, one of the biggest fears we heard from people about Macintosh computers was that they felt they needed to use the mouse for everything, while with Windows there tended to be a keyboard shortcut for just about everything. (Ironically, the other big fear was people wrongly assumed that Macs work only with one-button mice.) The reality is that on a Mac there are keyboard shortcuts for all common tasks, along with some things you may not have thought of. The Keyboard Shortcuts tab (Figure 18–30) lists all the system-wide keyboard shortcuts, organized in useful categories, in one place. You can also change the default shortcuts here as well (although we recommend against this). Additionally, by clicking the + button at the bottom of the list, you can add a keyboard shortcut to any menu item in many applications.

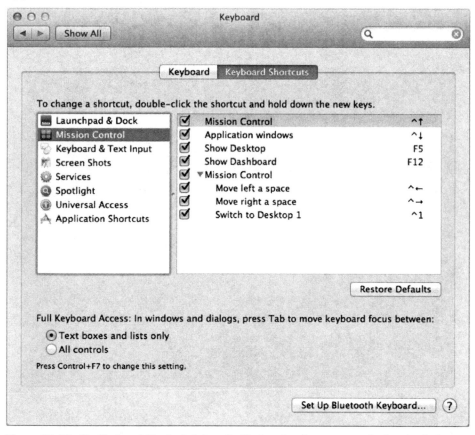

Figure 18–30. *The Keyboard Shortcuts tab on the Keyboard preference pane displays (and allows you to remap) a wide number of system-wide keyboard shortcuts.*

CAUTION: The ability to add a keyboard shortcut for any menu item in any application is a powerful feature. It can, however, cause all sorts of messiness if used haphazardly. Feel free to take advantage of this—however, be careful not to override existing, common keyboard shortcuts.

TIP: One item contained here that isn't specifically keyboard shortcut related is the Services item. Not only can you select keyboard shortcuts for individual services here, but you can also turn individual services on and off. Browsing through the list of available services, you may find one of particular interest to you that is toggled off; as such, it might be useful to take a quick look here to see what's available.

Mouse

The Mouse preference pane provides different options depending on the mouse you have attached to your computer (provided you have a mouse attached at all). For most mice, it will provide a number of standard mouse options (Figure 18–31). These options include setting the mouse's tracking speed, double-click speed, scrolling speed, and depending on the mouse whether the left or right button is the primary click (which is nice for left-handers). The pane also includes options to use the scroll wheel to zoom (magnify) the screen.

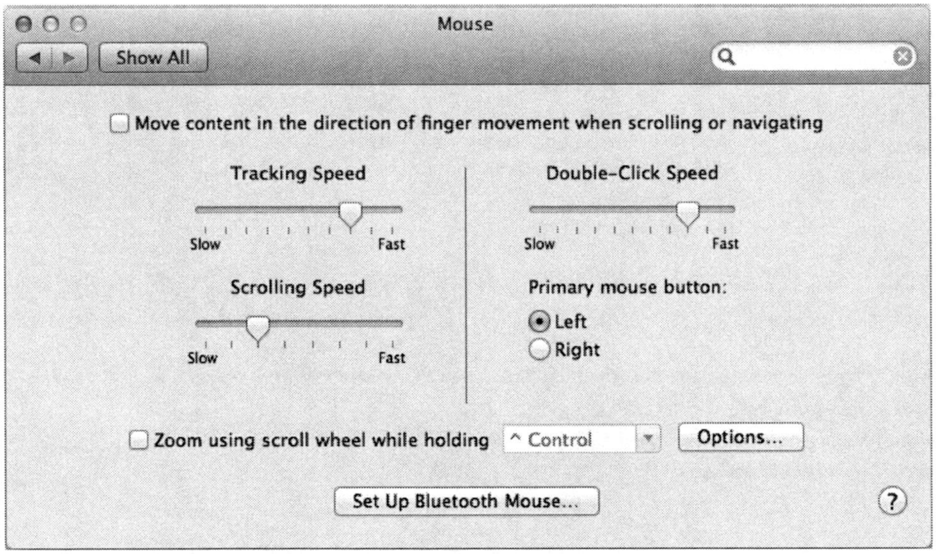

Figure 18–31. *The default Mouse tab on the Mouse preference pane*

If you happen to have an Apple Magic Mouse connected to your computer, the Mouse tab will be quite different and provide different options tailored specifically for the mouse (Figure 18–32). This special preference pane allows you to select special actions for the different features available on this mouse.

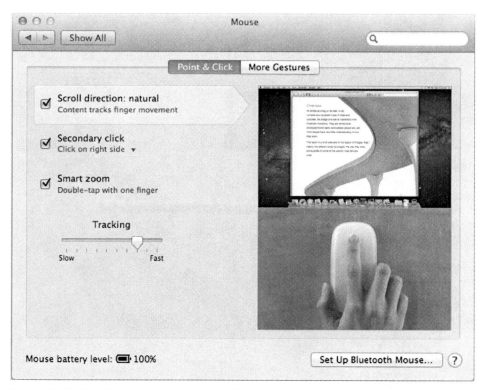

Figure 18–32. *The Mouse preference pane for Apple's Magic Mouse provides a number of different options allowing you to enable and customize gestures.*

Trackpad

The Trackpad preference pane is available on Macs that have a built-in trackpad or those with the Magic Trackpad attached. Like the Mouse preference pane the options provided for your trackpad may vary depending on how old your laptop is.

For most recent Apple Laptops, as well as computers using the Magic Trackpad, the preference pane (Figure 18–33) will present three tabs allowing you customize a large number of options and gestures.

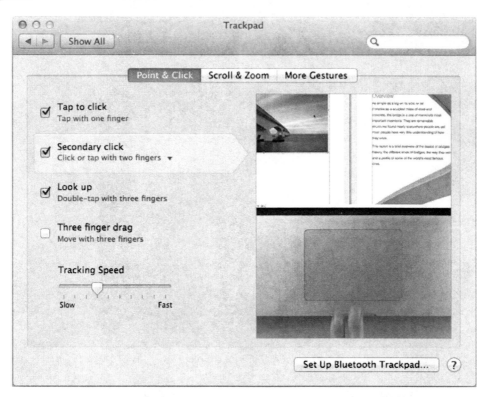

Figure 18–33. *The new Trackpad preference pane for the new multitouch glass trackpads*

> **TIP:** Under the More Gestures tab of the Trackpad System Preferences pane is one of the last mentions of Exposé in OS X. Here you can set up a gesture (swiping down with three fingers is the default) to provide the current app's Exposé view (showing all open windows).

Print & Scan

The Print & Scan preference pane allows you to add and manage local and network printers and scanners. Setting up printers and scanners will be covered in detail in the next chapter (Chapter 19).

Sound

The Sound System Preference pane controls your sound input and output devices, and provides options for system sounds and effects. The Sound preference pane has three tabs: Sound Effects, Output, and Input.

The Sound Effects tab (Figure 18–34) allows you to set your alert sound (the sound your computer plays when it tries to get your attention).

The Output tab (Figure 18–35) allows you to select your primary output device (if more than one is available) and set the setting for the selected devices. At the bottom of the Sound preference pane is the "Output volume" slider, along with an option to show (and control) the volume in your menu bar.

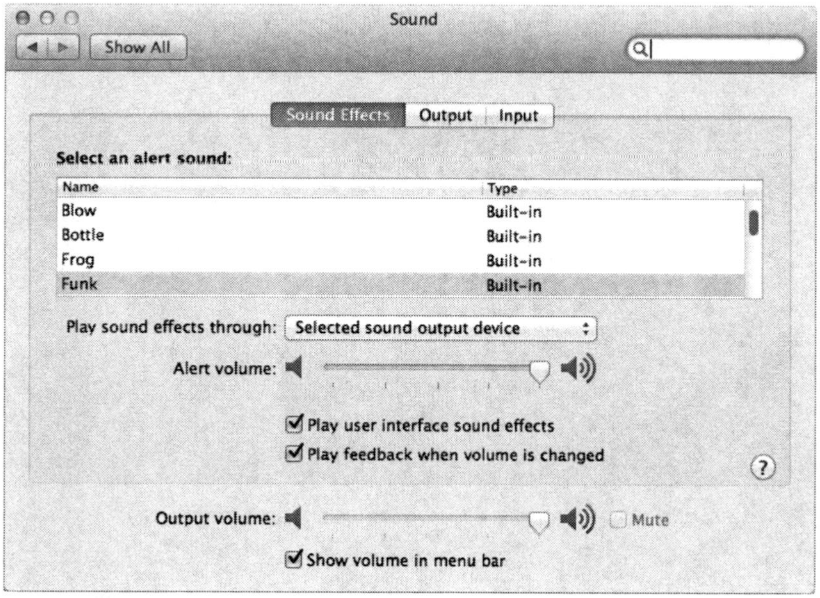

Figure 18–34. *The Sound Effects tab lets you choose your system alert sound and provides a few options for audio feedback.*

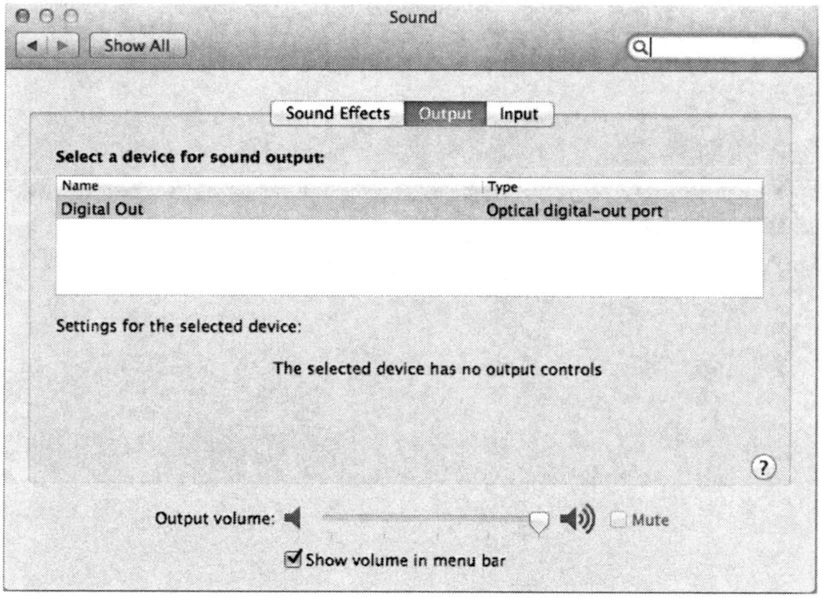

Figure 18–35. *The Output tab on the Sound preference pane*

The Input tab (Figure 18–36) on the Sound System Preference pane lists each of your available input devices and allows you to make level adjustments for the selected input device. Ambient noise reduction may help eliminate excess background noise; however, in some cases, it could also adversely affect the input sound quality.

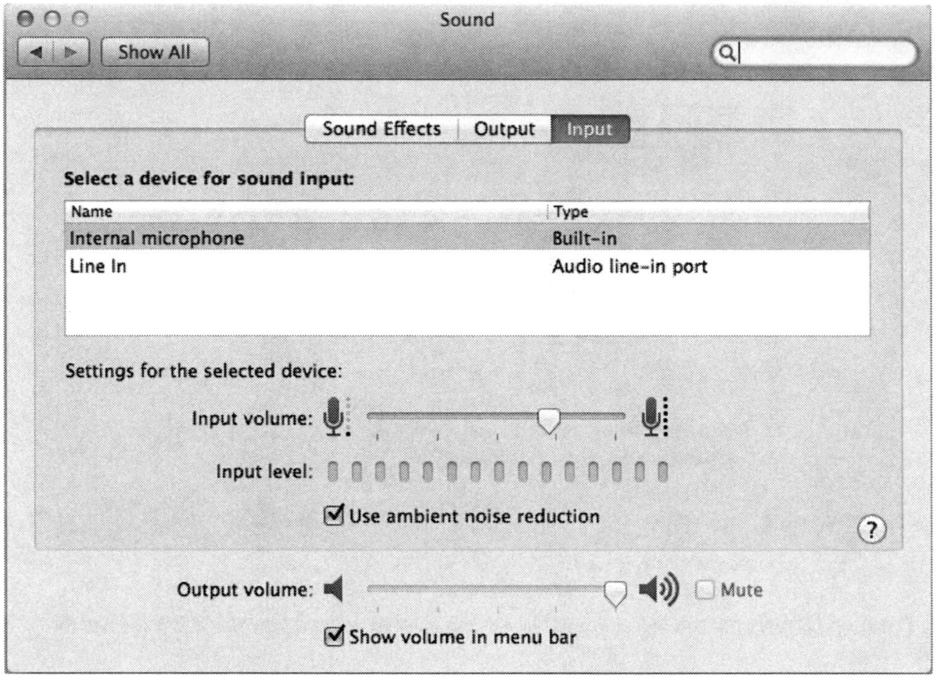

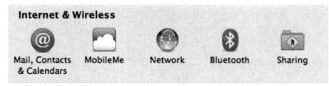

Figure 18–36. *The Input tab on the Sound preference pane controls your sound input devices.*

Internet & Wireless

The next section of System Preferences deals with Internet and network preferences (Figure 18–37). This contains your Mail, Contacts & Calendars; Bluetooth; MobileMe; Network; and Sharing preference panes.

Figure 18–37. *Internet & Wireless system preferences*

Mail, Contacts & Calendars

The Mail, Contacts & Calendars preference pane (Figure 18–38) is a new Preference pane added in Lion that borrows from the Mail, Contacts, Calendars setting in iOS. This Preference pane provides a single location where you can set up and manage various online accounts. Much of this is covered in various places in Part III of this book.

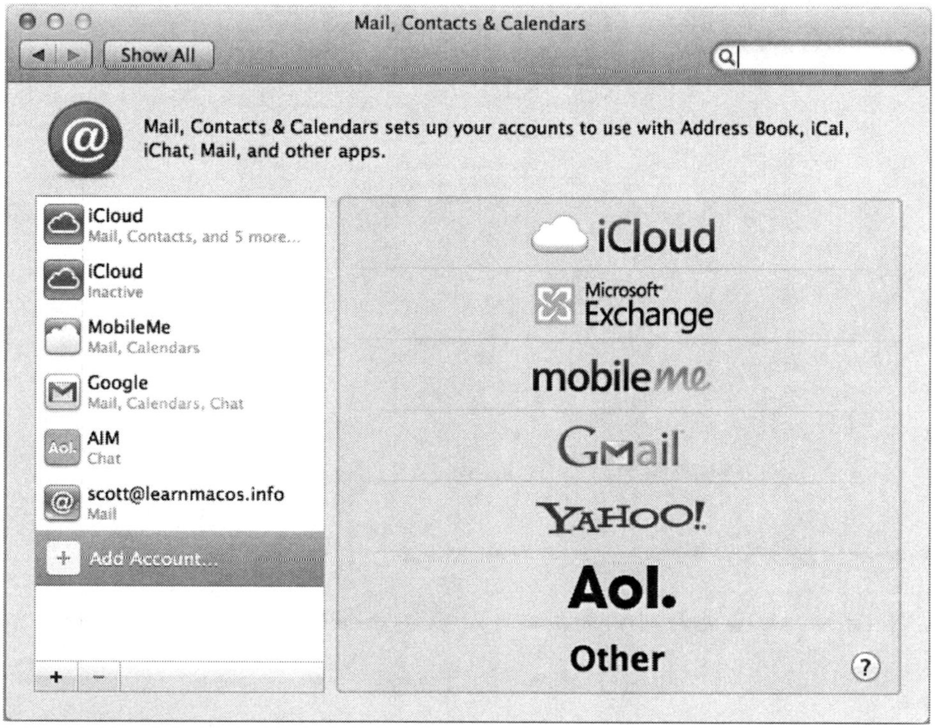

Figure 18–38. *The Mail, Contacts & Calendars preference pane provides a single location to manage many of your online accounts for use with various OS X applications.*

MobileMe

The MobileMe preference pane allows you to set up and manage your MobileMe account. If you have used MobileMe in the past, not much has changed here from previous versions of OS X, and since Apple has signaled the end of MobileMe in June of 2012, we won't go into any detail here.

Network

The Network preference pane (Figure 18–39) allows you to add and configure all of your network connections. Setting up a basic network connection was covered in Chapter 8 and later in Chapter 25 we will cover some additional network configuration.

Figure 18–39. *You can add and configure all of your network interfaces on the Network System Preferences pane.*

Bluetooth

The Bluetooth System Preferences pane (Figure 18–40) is where you can manage all of your Bluetooth wireless connections. The basic options here are to enable Bluetooth (by checking the On option) and Making Bluetooth discoverable. Making Bluetooth discoverable allows other Bluetooth enabled devices to detect you computer. Pairing other Bluetooth devices with your computer is covered in the next chapter.

Figure 18–40. *The Bluetooth preferences allow you to enable Bluetooth and manage paired devices.*

NOTE: Making you computer discoverable via Bluetooth allows other computers and devices to discover your computer. By leaving this option unchecked your computer will still be able to detect other (discoverable) Bluetooth devices, even if they cannot discover your computer.

Sharing

The Sharing preference pane (Figure 18–41) enables you to activate and configure various methods of sharing data or computer resources with other devices over a network. The details of most of the available shared services are covered elsewhere in the book (especially in Chapter 26).

Figure 18–41. *The Sharing preferences allow you to enable and configure various sharing services, including file sharing, printer sharing, and remote access.*

TIP: The Computer Name field at the top of the Sharing preference pane allows you to give your computer a name that it will be identified with over the network. Feel free to be creative (I've named all my computers after Disney characters, ranging from Axiom (the ship in *WALL-E*) to Simba (from *The Lion King*).

System

The System section of System Preferences (Figure 18–42) contains the remaining preference panes that are installed with Lion. The preference panes in the System section are Users & Groups, Parental Controls, Date & Time, Software Update, Speech, Time Machine, and Startup Disk.

Figure 18–42. *The System preference panes in System Preferences*

Users & Groups

The Users & Groups preference pane (formerly called Accounts) manages all the system's users, including some of their settings and their login options. When an existing user is selected, you will see two tabs—Password and Login Items—each containing information about that specific user.

The Password tab (Figure 18–43), as the name suggests, allows users to change their password by clicking the Change Password button. It also allows you to do the following:

- Change your user icon by clicking the icon image and selecting a new image from the drop-down list (or use the Edit Image selection to create a custom image)

- Change your user name by typing in a new name (this, however, doesn't change your short name)

- Add your Apple ID so the account information can be used for iCloud and other services

- View and edit your address book card in the Address Book application

- Allow the user to reset their password using their Apple ID (This will verify account information on Apple servers before allowing them to reset their password)

- Grant (or remove) administrator rights on the computer, provided that you are an administrator (you cannot remove administrator rights from yourself)

- Enable (or disable) parental controls for the user (provided that you have administrator rights)

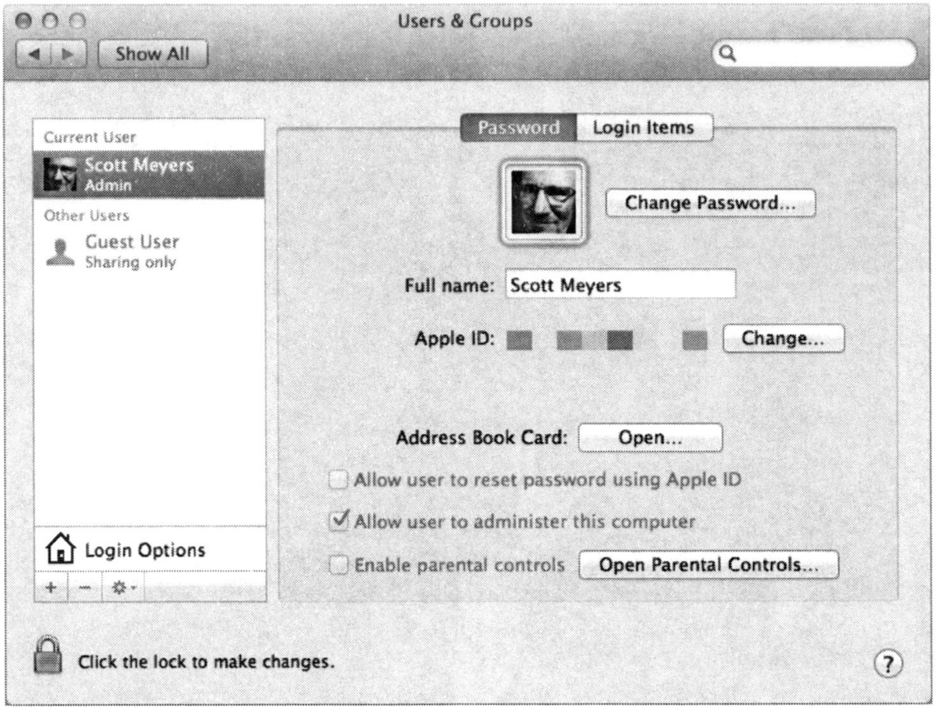

Figure 18–43. *When a user is selected, the Password tab allows that user to change his or her password and other user information.*

The Login Items tab (Figure 18–44) lets you manage applications, scripts, other executable items that you want to start, and even folders or documents you want to open automatically when you log into your computer. In general, what you will find listed here are background tasks that certain applications use to provide some sort of feature. You can, however, add your own items. For example, if you want the Mail application to start up immediately when you log into your computer, you can add it to this list by clicking the + button and selecting Mail from the resulting dialog box.

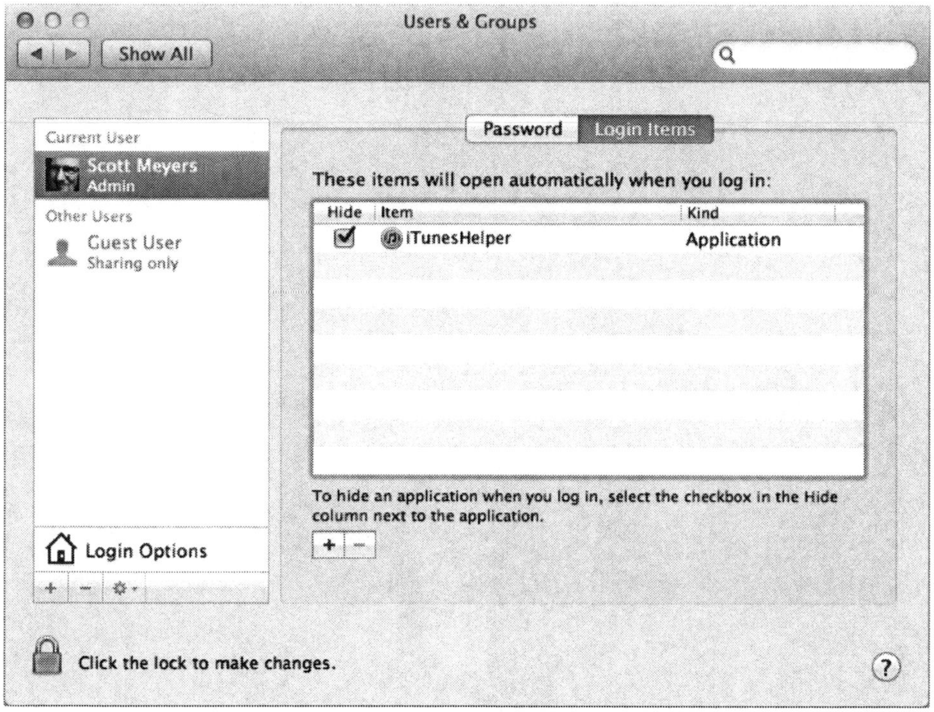

Figure 18–44. *The Login Items tab allows you to manage scripts and applications that will run automatically when you log in.*

Selecting Login Options (Figure 18–45) allows you to set options that govern login behavior. They are listed and defined in Table 18–5.

Table 18–5. *Login Options*

Option	Description
Automatic login	This option allows you to select a user who will be logged in automatically when the computer starts up. This is handy if you are the only user on a particular system. Disabling this option requires users to log in whenever the computer starts up. If "Automatic login" is set, a user can still log out, allowing others to log in.
Display login window as	This sets what a user sees at the login screen. The "List of users" option provides a list of all the users of the system. Clicking one of the user's names or icons prompts for a password. The "Name and password" option prompts for the user's any of the usernames. The "List of users" option is faster and more user-friendly, but the "Name and password" option provides slightly better security.
Show the Restart, Sleep, and Shut Down buttons	This shows the Restart, Sleep, and Shut Down buttons on the login screen, allowing these options to be used when no user is logged in.

Option	Description
Show input menu in login window	This option provides a list to set different language or input options prior to logging in.
Show password hints	This shows the user's password hint after a failed login. Obviously, there are security implications with this option.
Show fast user switching menu as	Checking this option adds a user-switching menu to the right side of the menu bar, allowing you to switch from one user to another without logging out first. You can then select from the option to Menu to choose what information appears in this menu.
Use VoiceOver in the login window	This option enables VoiceOver at the login window. VoiceOver causes any text under the mouse to be spoken through the computer. This is useful for the visually impaired.
Network Account Server	Clicking the Join... button allows you to select and open Directory Server, Active Directory Domain, or Mac OS X Server. These servers provide directory and network security services that allow organizations to manage users centrally across a wide array of computer and network services.

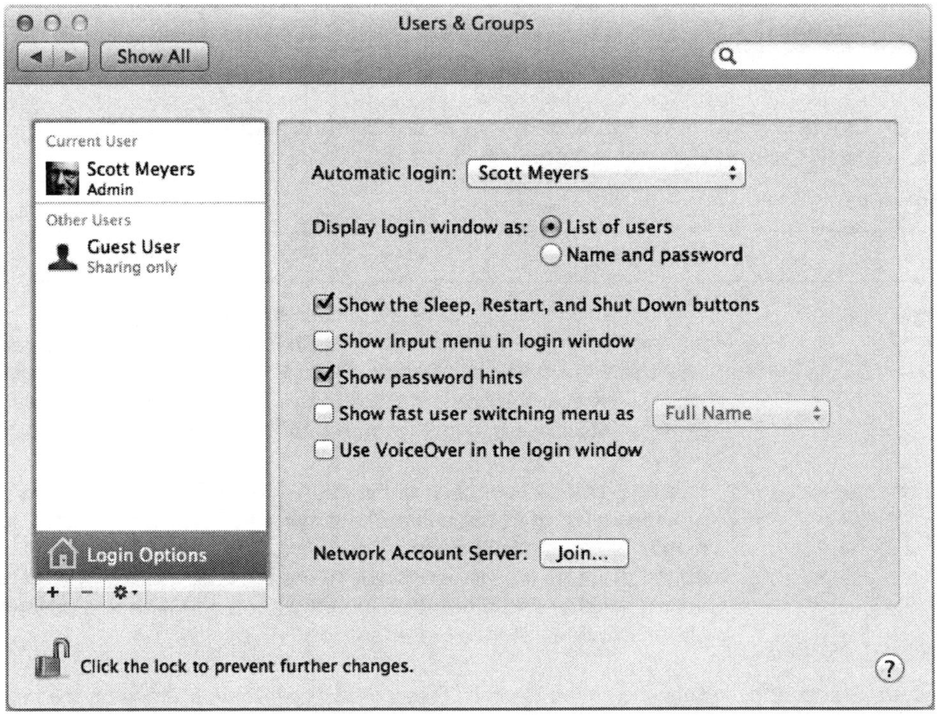

Figure 18–45. *Selecting Login Options from the bottom of the user list allows you to customize the login process.*

Adding New Users to Your System

To add a new user to your system from the Accounts preference pane, first make sure that the preferences are unlocked, and then click the + button at the bottom of the user list. This brings up a window (Figure 18–46) to enter the basic information for your new user.

Figure 18–46. *Information needed to add a new user*

This window requires some basic information. To the right of New Account is a drop-down menu prompting for what type of account you are creating. Options include the following:

- **Administrator**: This grants users the ability to do just about anything they want on the system.

- **Standard**: This allows users to work fairly normally on the system but won't let them perform any tasks requiring administrator access.

- **Managed with Parental Controls**: This allows the administrator to restrict users in various ways using parental controls (covered later in this chapter).

- **Sharing Only**: This only allows access for remote file sharing; these users cannot actually log in through the login window.

- **Group**: This is a special option that, rather than creating a new user, creates a group that existing users can be part of. You can allow access to files, folders, applications, and other system services based on the groups a user belongs to.

After you select the account type, just enter the name of the account, the short name, the password (twice), and a password hint if you'd like. If you are having trouble coming up with a password, you can access a random password generator (Figure 18–47) by clicking the key icon.

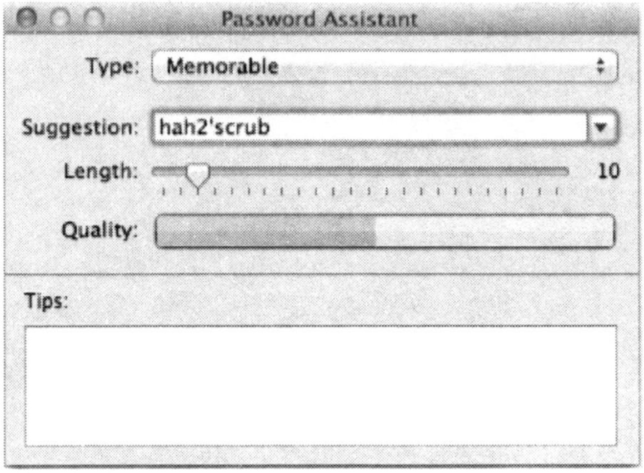

Figure 18–47. *Password Assistant helps you create a reasonably strong password for new accounts.*

NOTE: The short name, once selected, shouldn't be changed. For all practical purposes, the short name is your actual username for the system, and the full name is just a familiar alias to it.

TIP: As an administrator, if you Control-click any username on the Accounts preference pane and select Advanced Options..., an Advanced Options dialog will appear that will allow you to edit some user information used by the system. These options largely define user information that is stored in various system configuration files and provide basic information that is used throughout Mac OS X for many things, including file ownership and permissions. If you come from a UNIX/Linux background, many of these items may be familiar and even useful to you in some situations (especially when setting up special accounts). You can even change the short name (account name) here, but as the warning points out, this could damage the account.

By default, a Guest account will automatically be added to your user list. The Guest account is a limited account with its own options (Figure 18–48).

The Guest account can be configured in various ways. Selecting "Allow guests to log into this computer" enables the Guest account and allows guests to log in and use your computer as a sandbox of sorts. They will have access to most applications—however, all settings and files they create will be wiped out when they log off (unless they save them to a shared location). "Allow guests to connect to shared folders" allows guests to access any shared folders on your system over the network. It's important to note that guests never need a password, so by allowing a guest access, you are essentially allowing anyone access to your system.

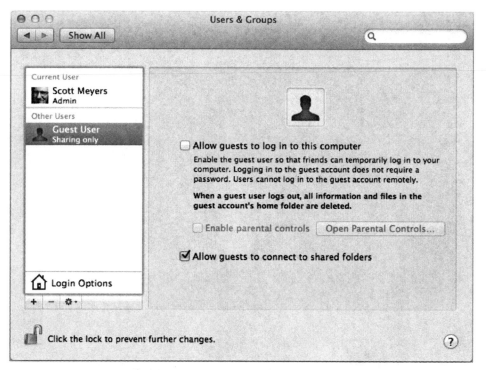

Figure 18–48. *Guest account options*

Parental Controls

Parental controls allow an administrator to put in place a number of restrictions upon a user. These are generally thought of as a way for parents to limit the computing activities of their children but could be used in any situation in which you want to restrict or monitor a user's activity on the computer. The Parental Controls preference pane lets you tailor the controls for any user account that has parental controls enabled. To set the controls, first select the desired user from the user list (if the list is empty, then you have no accounts with parental controls enabled, and you will be asked if you want to enable them), and then work through the five tabs presented to configure them. The five tabs on the preference pane are Apps, Web, People, Time Limits, and Other.

The Apps tab (Figure 18–49) provides options that control how a user can interact with the system itself as well as what Apps are available for use. The Use Simple Finder option alters the Finder's appearance (Figure 18–50), removing many options and directories, and providing access only to a user's allowed applications and his or her documents. For old-school Macintosh users, this is similar to what At Ease used to provide.

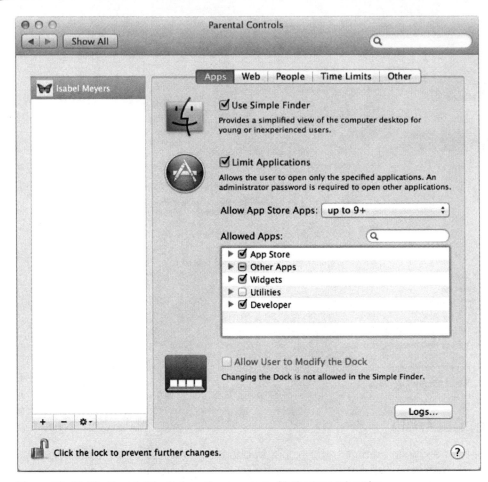

Figure 18–49. *The Parental Controls preference pane with the Apps tab active*

Figure 18–50. *The Simple Finder*

The Limit Applications option allows access only to the applications (or groups of applications) selected in the following list. If you are using the Simple Finder, then only the selected applications will show up; otherwise, the user will be prompted for an administrator's password before launching an unselected application. Applications from the App Store can be set automatically based on the App's age restriction.

The Web tab (Figure 18–51) allows you to attempt to limit the content that the user has access to. The Website Restrictions options offer three choices for attempting to manage web content:

- **Allow unrestricted access to websites**: Does not block any web sites.

- **Try to limit access to adult websites automatically**: Tries to filter out adult web sites using a variety of methods. While somewhat effective, this is not foolproof, and it may both block sites that you don't find objectionable and let some objectionable content through. The Customize button allows you to fine-tune this behavior a bit by manually entering acceptable and unacceptable web sites.

- **Allow access to only these websites**: Allows you to specifically enter the addresses of acceptable web sites. Only those entered will be accessible. Obviously, this will likely block lots of valuable information, while at the same time this is really the only way to block objectionable content with some certainty.

NOTE: Content filtering has proponents and detractors from both political and technical points of view. As a parent of two I have mixed feelings about this sort of technology—currently I don't use any content filtering, but I reserve the right to change this if I notice the kids doing something that really concerns me. That said, these filtering technologies are not foolproof and should not be relied upon to protect your children or anyone else from unsavory elements of the Internet. The best advice we know of is to be honest with your kids about things they may encounter on the Internet, and explain what your values are and why. Most kids will get it.

TIP: Logs are kept on most online activity that occurs with protected accounts. To view the various logs, click the Logs... button that is found at the bottom of most Parental Controls tabs; this will bring up a list of all related activity.

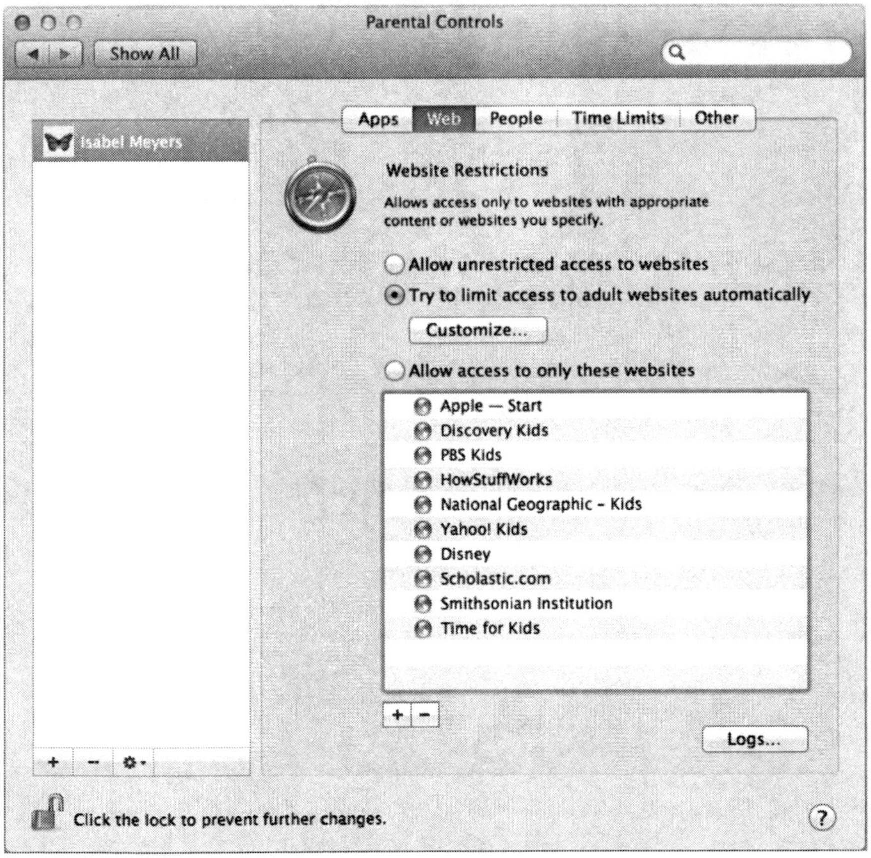

Figure 18–51. *The Web tab on the Parental Controls preference pane*

The People tab (Figure 18–52) allows you to specify addresses of select people who you allow the user to interact with through Mail and iChat. There is an option at the bottom that can be set to send a message to you every time the user attempts to contact someone who is not preapproved for permission. This is a decent way to attempt to keep track of people who a user is interacting with online—however, this has no effect on web-based chats, or any other e-mail or messaging applications. As such, this is really only effective in combination with other controls.

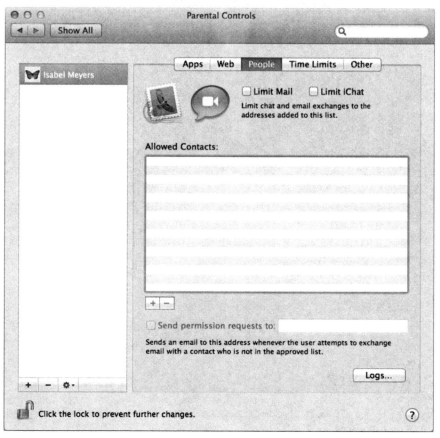

Figure 18–52. *The People tab of the Parental Controls preference pane attempts to control what people a user is in contact with online.*

> **TIP:** While online content won't jump out of your computer and cause any physical harm, people are a different thing altogether. It's important to discuss, especially with children, that people on the Internet are not always what they seem and are not all harmless. Personal information should not be shared with strangers, whether in chats, in e-mails, or on web sites. In my experience, knowledge and understanding are better at protecting our children and ourselves than depending on computer systems and blocking technologies.

The Time Limits tab (Figure 18–53) allows you to limit the time a user spends in front of the computer. It allows you to set daily limits for weekdays and weekends, as well as set specific times when the computer is off limits.

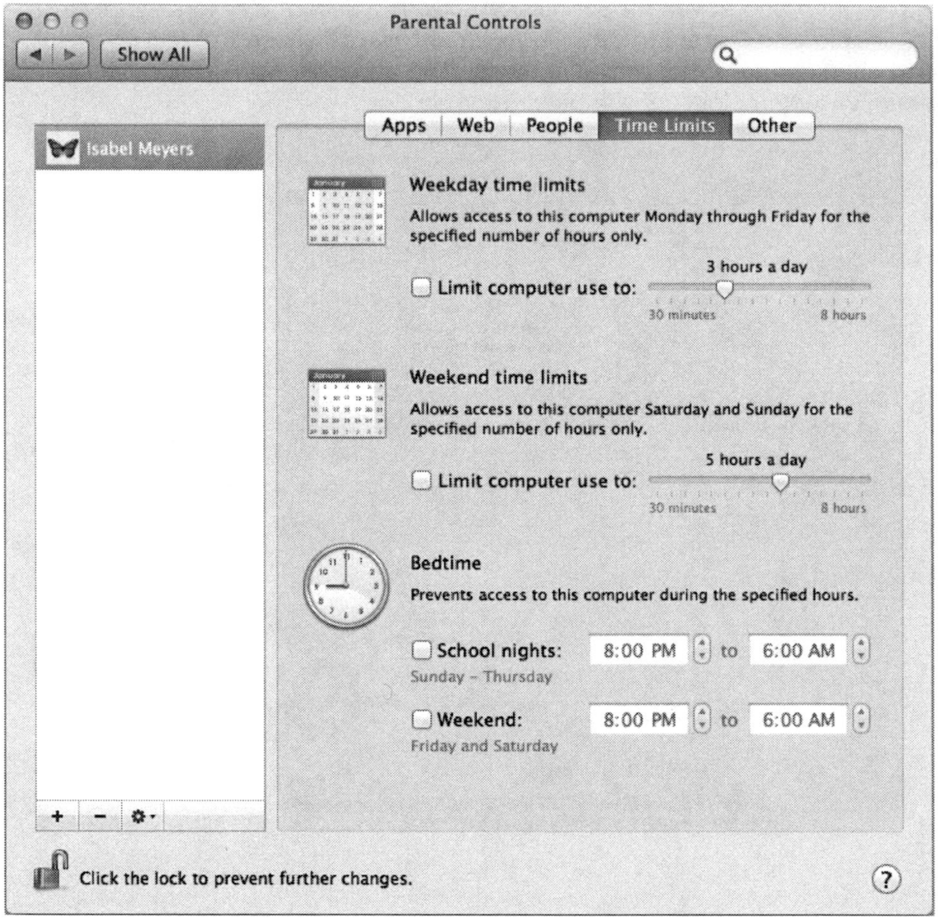

Figure 18–53. *The Time Limits tab on the Parental Controls preference pane*

> **NOTE:** You may have discovered from our previous notes that I'm generally skeptical of most parental controls (especially the content-filtering stuff). This is because we've never seen one that worked well and couldn't be worked around by a clever kid wanting to break the rules (of course, maybe you actually want to train your kid to become a skilled hacker). That said, we think there is something to setting time limits. Seriously, there are days when we wish our computer would kick us out after a certain amount of time using it.

The Other tab (Figure 18–54) provides some additional options that one may wish to enable to a controlled account.

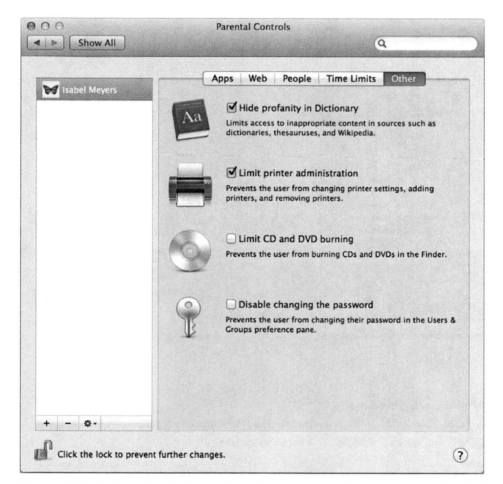

Figure 18–54. *The Logs tab on the Parental Controls preference pane keeps track of a user's activities.*

Date & Time

The Date & Time preference pane contains the system's date and time settings. These settings are broken up across three tabs: Date & Time, Time Zone, and Clock.

The Date & Time tab (Figure 18–55) simply allows you to either set the date and time of your system manually or set it automatically using one of Apple's timeservers. There are actually very few situations where you wouldn't want to set the time automatically (e.g., you have no Internet connection and thus the timeservers aren't available, or you want to fool your system into thinking the time is different than it actually is). If you choose to have the time set automatically, just select the closest Apple timeserver while connected to the Internet.

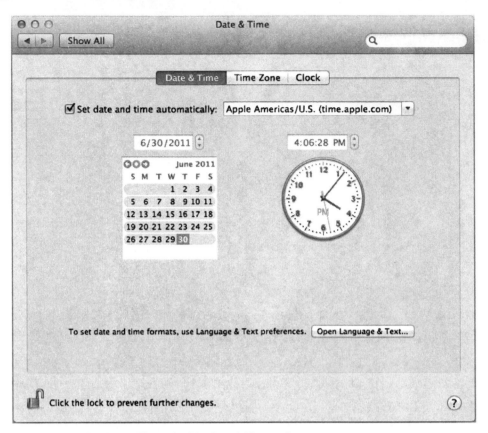

Figure 18–55. *The Date & Time tab of the Date & Time preference pane*

> **NOTE:** There are other timeservers available besides the Apple timeservers that are listed. In fact, many organizations have their own timeserver on their network. You can utilize any available timeserver by entering its network address in the timeserver text field.

The Time Zone tab (Figure 18–56) allows you to select what time zone you are in. You can do this by entering or selecting a city from the Closest City drop-down menu/text field or by clicking your location on the minimap. It's important to accurately set your time zone, even if you are manually entering your date and time information—otherwise, you may get incorrect time information.

The Clock tab (Figure 18–57) provides a number of options that affect how the clock appears in your menu bar. There is a further option that causes your computer to speak out the current time at designated intervals. These options are fairly explicit and shouldn't need much elaboration.

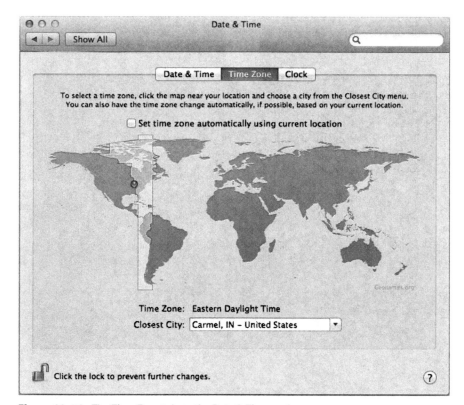

Figure 18–56. *The Time Zone tab on the Date & Time preference pane*

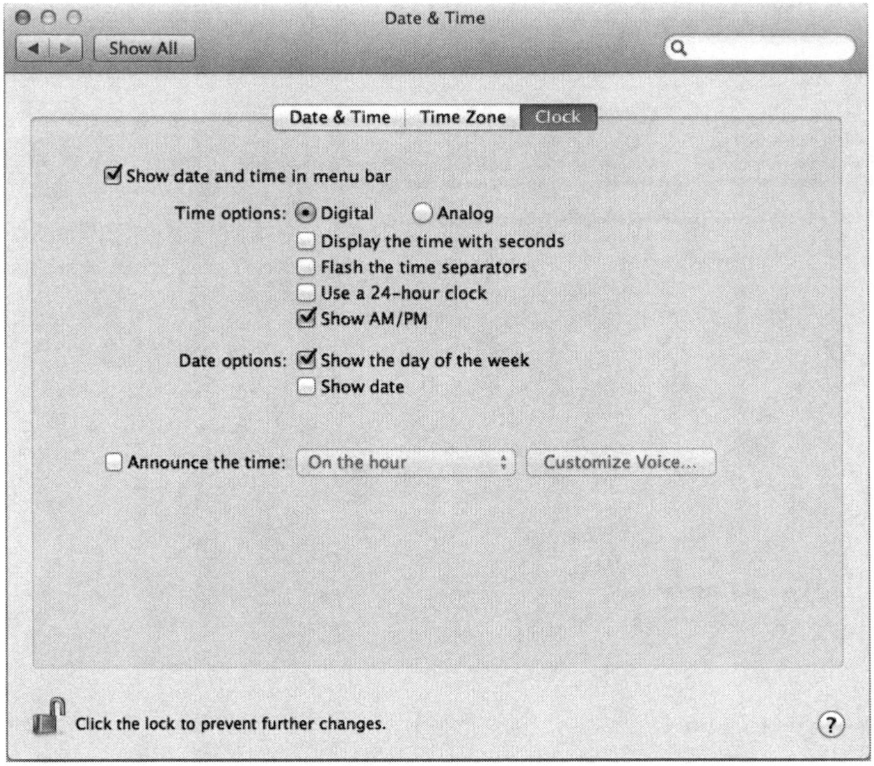

Figure 18–57. *The Clock tab on the Date & Time preference pane allows you to set options for the clock in the menu bar.*

Software Update

The Software Update preference pane (Figure 18–58) manages the Software Update features of OS X. This allows you to set the frequency that updates are checked for automatically, and it also provides a Check Now button to check for new updates manually.

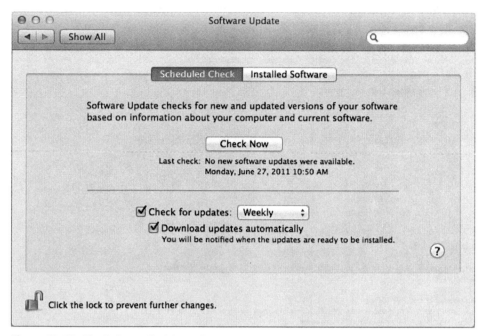

Figure 18–58. *The Software Update preference pane*

When you run Software Update (by clicking the Check Now button or using the Software Update item on the Apple menu), the Software Update window will open and check for the availability of updated Apple software. If updates are available, Software Update will let you now and allow you install them right away (by clicking Install) or later (by Clicking Not Now). To see the details of what software is available before you install click the Show Details button this will provide a detailed list of what will be installed (Figure 18–59). Certain updates may require authentication to install or require you to restart your computer to complete—in either of these cases, you will be prompted accordingly.

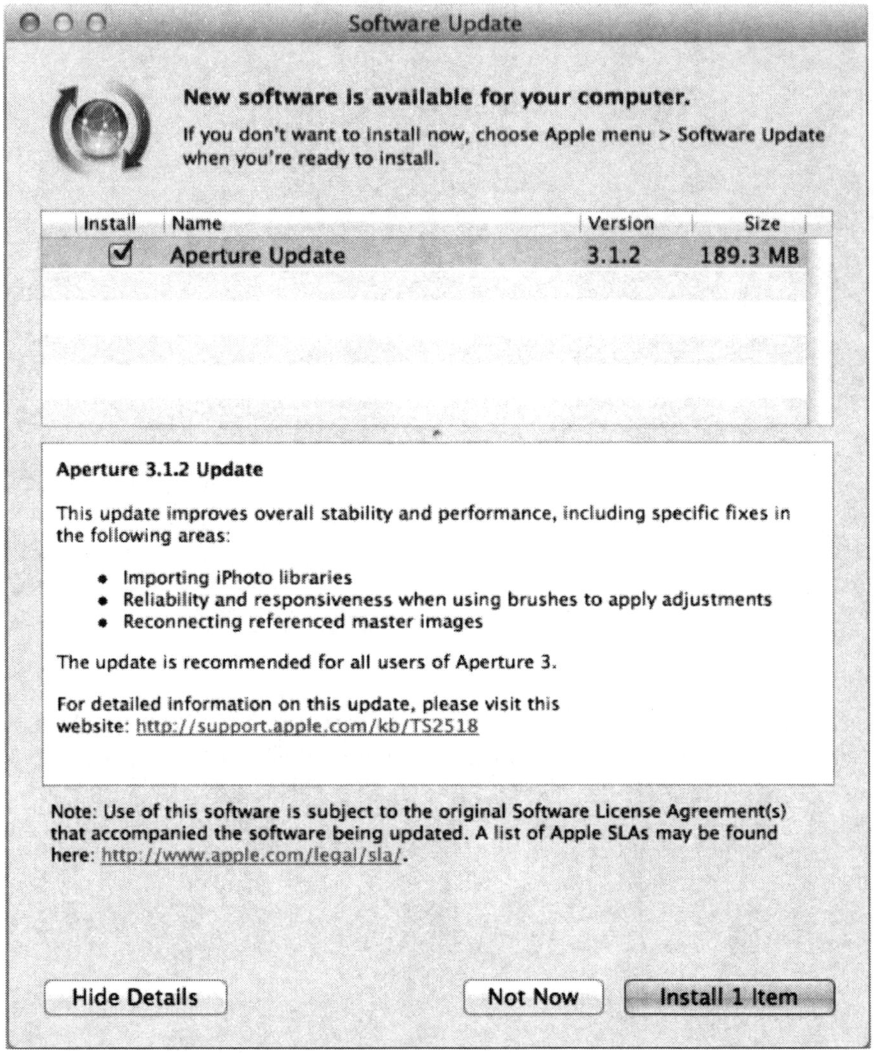

Figure 18–59. *The Software Update window*

The Installed Software tab of the Software Update preference pane lists all of your past software installs. Software Update tracks all the software listed here, but it's likely not all the software you have installed.

NOTE: Software Update checks for system updates and updates of Apple software that has not been installed through the App Store. Much of the general updating of Apps though is moving to the App Store updates

Speech

The Speech preference pane contains two tabs: Speech Recognition, which contains options for responding to speech; and Text to Speech, which contains settings for controlling how the computer speaks back to you.

The Speech Recognition tab (Figure 18–60) contains settings that control how to set up the computer to receive and respond to speakable items. To enable this feature, you first must set the Speakable Items option to On. Once the Speakable Items option is switched on, a small, roundish floating window with a microphone in it will appear. This provides visual feedback for your speakable items. By default, to speak a command, first hold down the Esc key and then speak your command clearly into the microphone. If the computer accepts your command, it will carry out the command requested and provide you with acknowledgment as set up under the Upon Recognition setting. The Commands subtab provides a list of active command categories. Any time speech recognition is active, you click the small inverted triangle at the bottom of the small, round, hovering speech window, and select Open Speech Commands Window to view a list of available speech commands as well as a log of previous spoken actions.

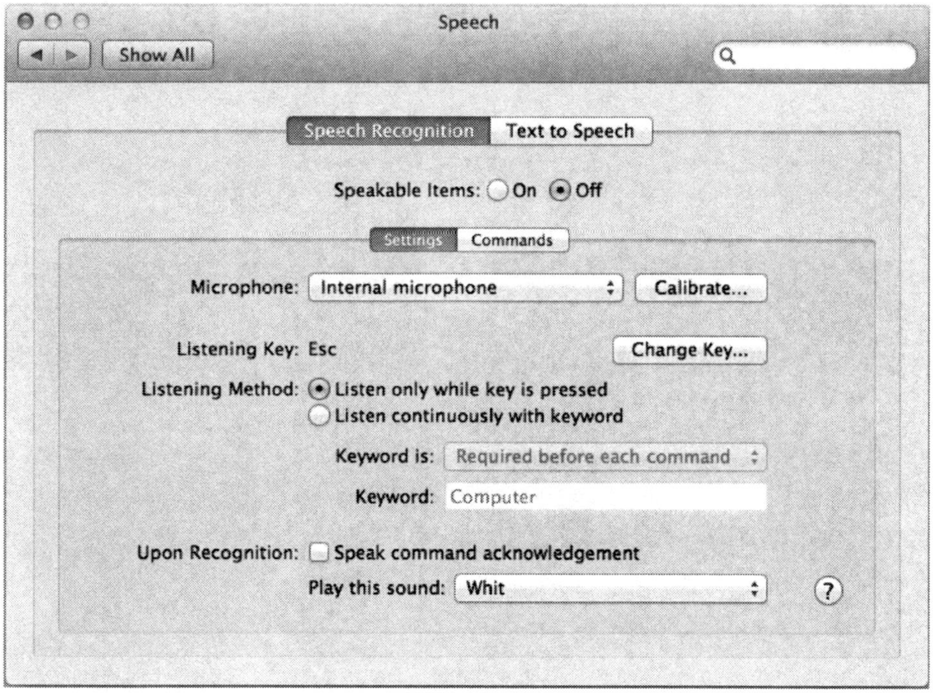

Figure 18–60. *The Speech Recognition tab contains settings that allow your computer to respond to spoken commands.*

> **NOTE:** Apple speech recognition technology has been around for years and has progressively gotten better; however, my results have always been mixed. While I find this fun to play around with sometimes (the chess game included in Mac OS X responds to spoken commands), I don't find it particularly useful. Maybe I just have a terrible voice. As they say, "Your mileage may vary."

The Text to Speech tab (Figure 18–61) controls how your computer speaks to you. Here you can change your computer's voice and the speed at which it talks. You can then set up options that will cause your computer to speak certain items:

- **Announce when alerts are displayed**: Causes your computer to read any alerts that pop up

- **Announce when an application requires your attention**: Causes your computer to tell you when an application is awaiting your input or has some message for you

- **Speak selected text when the key is pressed**: Allows you to set a key that causes any selected text to be read back to you

> **TIP:** The System Voice menu has a number of preinstalled voices for you to play around with to help you find the one you prefer, but if none of them will do, selecting Customize... will allow you to download a large selection of different voices (many for non-English languages).

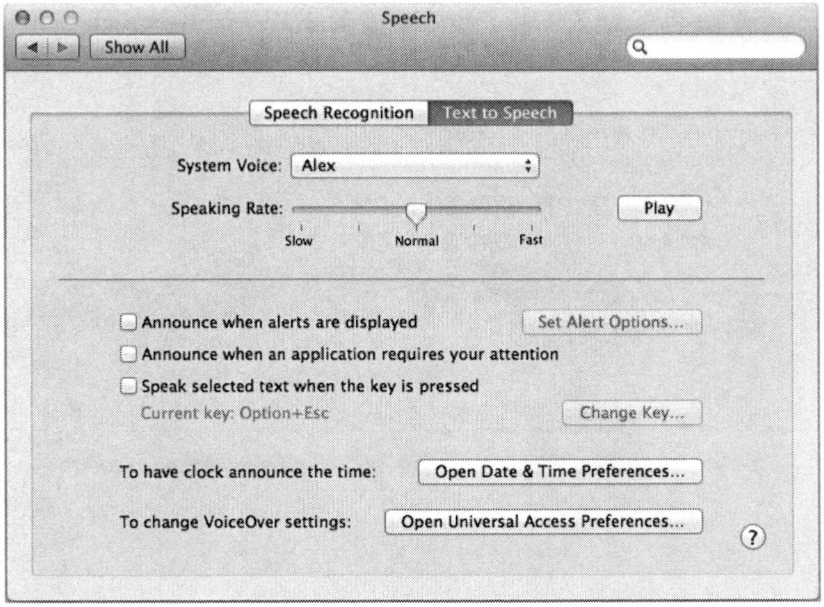

Figure 18–61. *The Text to Speech tab on the Speech preference pane*

Some applications have their own capability for reading back text as well. The important thing here is that the voice you pick on the Text to Speech tab will be the default voice used in all of the applications.

Time Machine

The Time Machine preference pane (Figure 18–62) allows you to set up and configure Time Machine. Time Machine is OS X's built in data backup utility that we will cover in Chapter 20.

Figure 18–62. *The Time Machine preferences provide a simple interface to configure Time Machine.*

Startup Disk

If you have multiple bootable volumes connected to your computer, the Startup Disk preference pane (Figure 18–63) will allow you to select which disk to default to when starting your computer.

Figure 18–63. *The Startup Disk preference pane controls which bootable volume the computer uses by default when starting up.*

The startup disk selected here can always be overridden by special startup key commands (holding the Option key while starting your computer allows you to choose to boot from any connected bootable hard drive), unless you've set a firmware password (discussed in Appendix A).

One interesting option here is the Target Disk Mode... option. This allows you to set up your computer so that the next time it's started, you can connect to another Mac via a FireWire cable and use it as a hard drive. This is a handy option for copying files from one computer to another very quickly. (You can also boot your computer in Target Disk mode by holding the T key while starting your computer.)

Summary

We have covered a lot of ground in this chapter, and while we have saved a few things that need more elaboration than was possible here for later in the book, you have hopefully learned a number of ways to help set up your computer to work in a way that suits you. Next, as promised, we will look at connecting and using a range of external devices with your computer.

Chapter 19

Printing, Peripherals, and Bluetooth

Today, more and more features are built into computers than ever before. Most new Macs (except the Mac Pro and Mac Mini) include features such as stereo speakers, decent microphones, and even video cameras all built in and ready to use. Still, oftentimes you need something else or want to improve on what you already have on your computer. Luckily for you, a range of hardware devices exist that can work wonderfully with your Mac (commonly referred to as *peripherals*). Since you have a Mac, you just need to plug in most of these items, and they work (i.e., they're plug-and-play, as it was intended). However, with the complexity and features available for some of these external devices, occasionally you need to do a little more to get the most out of them. Additionally, these days, many peripherals connect over a network or wirelessly, so rather than plugging something in, you often need to tell your computer to look for it. This chapter addresses all of this, including the following:

- ▓ Printing
- ▓ Bluetooth devices
- ▓ External storage
- ▓ Other external peripherals

Printing in Mac OS X

The world we live in is getting increasingly digital, yet we still haven't fully entered the paperless world of the future. Sometimes you may need to resort to actually printing things. To do this, you need to connect to and configure a printer. You can connect your computer to your printer in a number of ways, ranging from physically through a USB cable to over a wireless network. If it's over a network, whether wireless or wired, many protocols (the ways that your computer talks to the printer) are available, and each handles printing a little differently. Luckily, Mac OS X makes all of this easy (or at least as easy as possible).

How "Print" Happens

In very general terms, when you hit the Print button in an application, a few things happen:

1. You are often presented with a Print dialog asking you to choose which connected printer you want to print to and what printing options (if any) you'd like to utilize. When you have made your selection, you click the Print button to print your document.

2. Once you hit Print, the printing system in Mac OS X takes your document and puts it in a special block of memory called a *print spool* where print jobs are collected and then sent in order to a printer.

3. As the document leaves the print spool and is sent to the printer, the data stream passes through a *print filter* that translates the raw document data into data that the printer can understand.

4. The printer, as it receives this stream, usually starts printing the file as it receives it.

> **NOTE:** Because your computer can usually feed information to your printer faster than it can print, a lot of communication is necessary between your printer and your computer to regulate the flow of information. If your printer runs out of memory (and many less-expensive printers have very little to begin with) and your computer keeps sending the data, then data will get lost, and you'll end up with a garbled mess.

In a nutshell, that's it. It sounds like a lot of complicated stuff going on, and actually there is, but luckily for you, all you need to worry about is step 1 and occasionally adding more paper and ink/toner to your printer. Of course, before you can print, you need to set up your printer.

> **NOTE:** Mac OS X uses *CUPS (Common Unix Printing System)* to handle printing chores. CUPS was adopted by Apple in 2002 (and later purchased outright by Apple). The use of CUPS greatly simplifies the creation of print drivers for printers with the use of print filters, while at the same time providing the powerful network-printing and print management features of *IPP (Internet Printing Protocol)*. More information about CUPS is available at www.cups.org.

Setting Up a USB Printer

The most common printers, and the easiest to set up, are basic USB printers. In general, to set up a USB printer, plug in the printer power cord, and then plug in a USB cable from your printer into one of the USB ports on your computer. Unless your printer is a super-new model or a really strange off-brand, it's likely that's all you need to do. Your printer is ready to use. If in doubt, take a look on the Print & Scan pane of System Preferences (Figure 19–1); if you see the printer you just plugged in listed and correctly identified, you are good to go.

NOTE: The first time you plug in a printer to your computer, a Software Update dialog may pop up asking if you would like to download and install the software for your printer (Figure 19–2). Generally the answer is "yes you would" so click Install and let OS X take care of the rest.

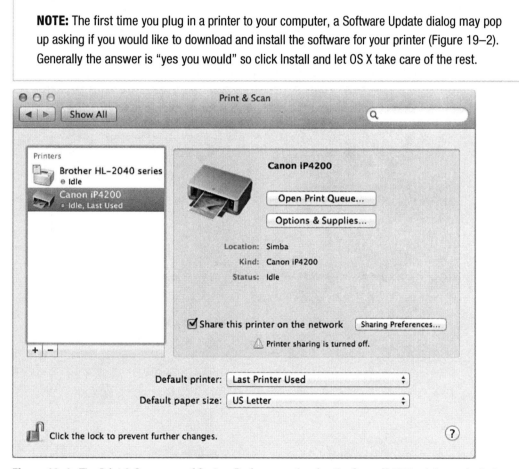

Figure 19–1. *The Print & Scan pane of System Preferences showing the Canon iP4200 printer we just plugged in*

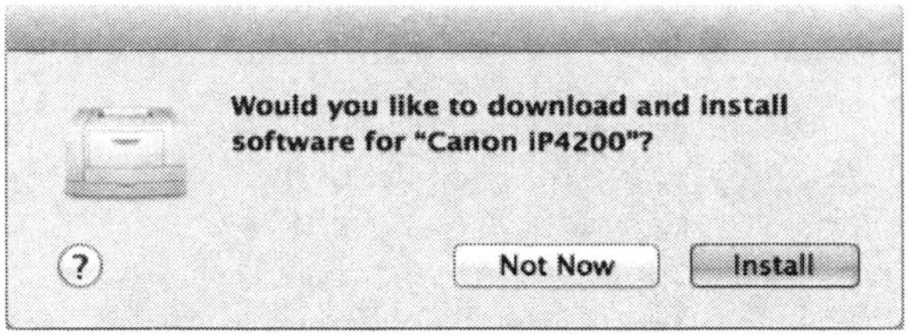

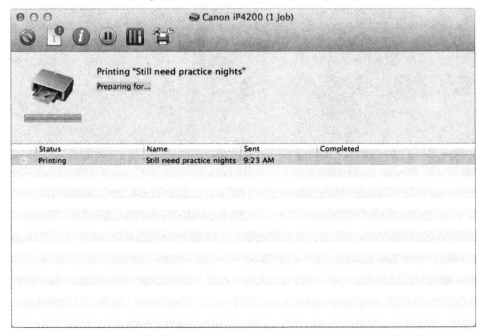

Figure 19–2. *When the Canon printer was first plugged in, Software Update automatically prompted us to install the latest driver software.*

At this point, you may be skeptical that everything worked; in other words, that was too easy, right? You didn't even need to insert the CD that came with the printer. If you double-click the printer icon in the Print & Scan preference pane, the printer's Print Queue window (Figure 19–3) will open. This window provides information about your printer, including information about any documents currently printing or waiting to be printed (documents waiting in the print spool to be printed are called *print jobs*). If you want to test your printer, you can select the **Printer > Print Test Page** command from the menu bar. If the test page prints, then all is well, and your printer is ready to use.

Figure 19–3. *The printer's Print Queue window provides information about a specific printer connected to your computer.*

Connecting to a Network Printer or Shared Printer

Printers in most companies as well as more and more homes are accessed through a network. These printers could be actual network printers, complete with network interfaces (either wired or wireless). Or they could be common USB printers attached to other computers on a network or a network print server (such as the ones built into Apple's AirPort and AirPort Express). The process of connecting to these printers ranges from almost as easy as connecting a USB printer to fairly easy if you know exactly what you are doing. We'll walk you through the general process using a real-life example of connecting to a networked Brother multifunction device (a fax/scanner/printer/copier).

The first step of adding a printer is to open the Print & Scan pane from System Preferences and click the + button at the bottom of the printer list. This opens a Printer Browser window (Figure 19–4).

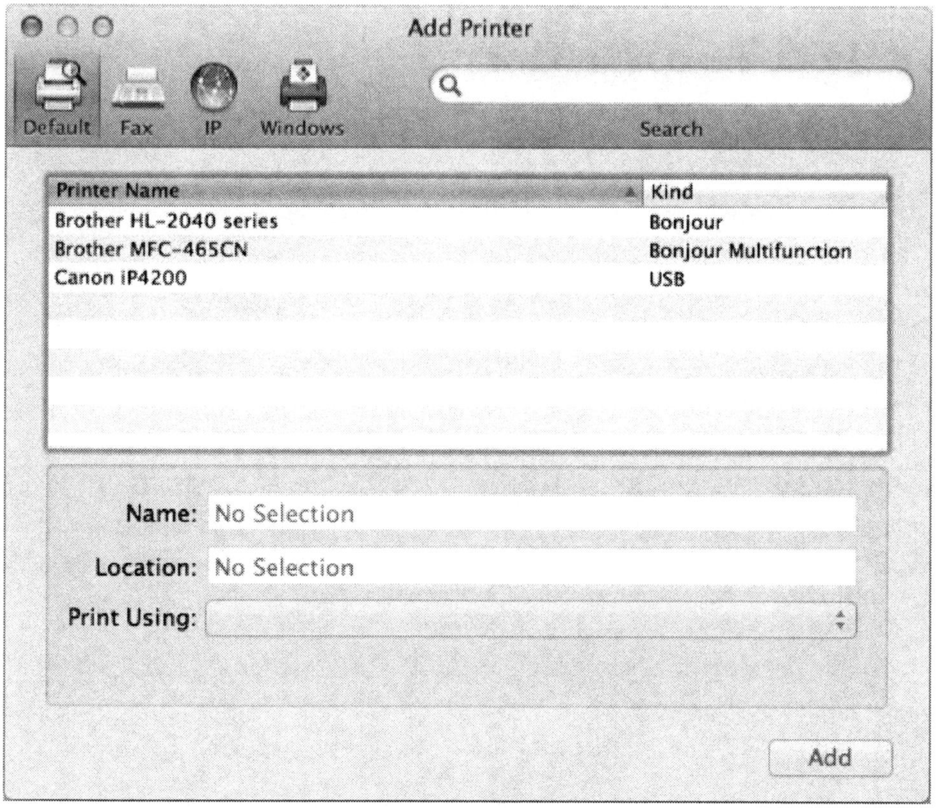

Figure 19–4. *The Printer Browser window allows you browse and pick various types of printers to connect to.*

As we look in the browser, we see Brother MFC-465 listed, which happens to be the printer we want. When we select it in the list, our computer will try to find the name, location, and driver automatically. In this case, it succeeded (Figure 19–5).

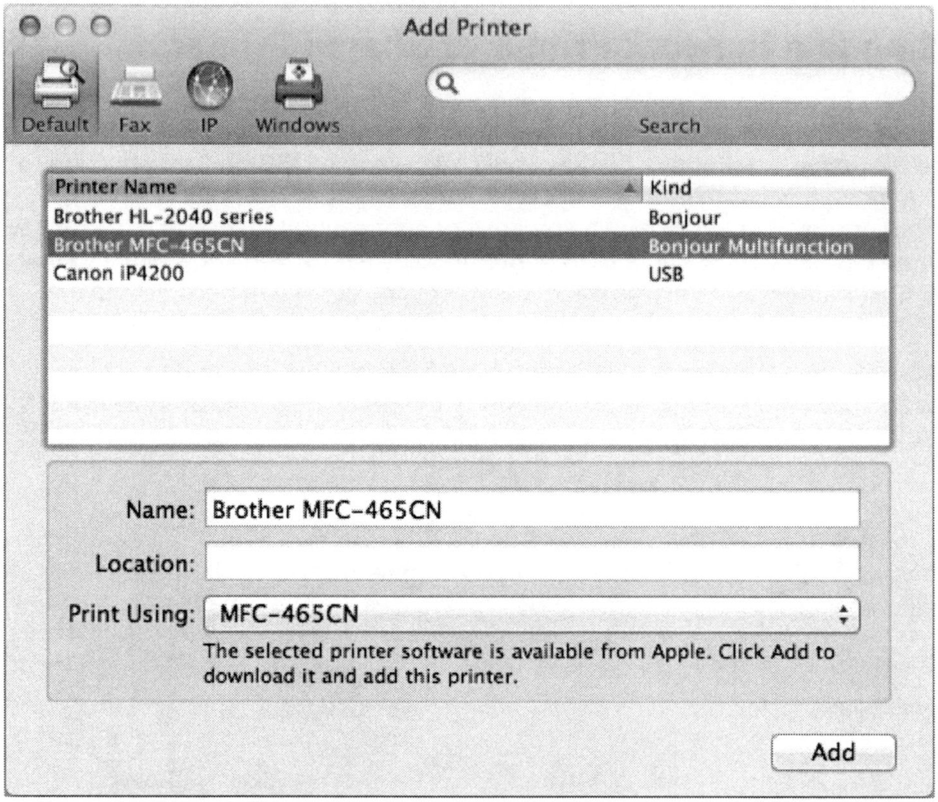

Figure 19–5. *After selecting the printer we want to add, Mac OS X automatically attempts to determine the name, location, and appropriate print driver.*

NOTE: You may notice that the Location field is blank; this is because the printer is connected using Bonjour. *Bonjour is* a special networking technology (which is also known in some non-Apple circles as *zeroconf)* that allows systems on a network to identify themselves and the services they offer in a flexible way without a central name server. Since this allows the location to be dynamic, it is not listed.

If the print driver is not found automatically, then you will need to select an appropriate driver manually for the printer. To do this, click the Print Using drop-down menu, and there you should first try "Auto Select," which will try to make a best guess. If that doesn't work then you may look for your driver in Select Printer Driver... dialog.

When your printer is selected and set up with the proper driver, click the Add button, and your printer will be ready to use.

Ninety-nine percent of the time adding a printer is quite easy. But what about the other times—the times when your printer just doesn't get automatically recognized?

NOTE: There tends to be a few ways to think about network printers. Some printers broadcast their presence (such as Bonjour printers), and they usually just show up in the default options of the Printer Browser window. Other printers, like those that use Windows networking, are browsable; that is, you can navigate around the network to find available printers in the various Windows workgroups or domains. Finally, there are other types of network printers, and basically, you have to know where they are located on the network, and usually some more information about them, to connect to them.

NOTE: Because I had previously installed the Brother Printer driver package for my Brother HL-2040 printer, there was no need to reinstall any software drivers.

When you are attempting to connect to a network printer at work or in a large computing environment or you are attempting to use a printer that is being shared by another computer, it might not just show up in the default printer listing in the Printer Browser window. When confronted with this situation, you need to find out what type of printer sharing is being used. The most common choice around homes and offices would be some sort of Windows printer sharing. Other less common network printer sharing protocols include the following:

- **Bluetooth**: There just aren't that many Bluetooth printers available right now, but if you happen to have one, the Bluetooth printer should be easily discoverable from the Bluetooth System Preference pane if it's in range, at which point you will need to pair the device and select a driver. Only the discovery and pairing should differ from the process of connecting a USB printer or a Bonjour printer.

- **IPP**: Actually, this is fairly common, since CUPS is built around IPP, it is the printing system used in Mac OS X, and it's the default printing system for many modern Unix and Linux systems. (Although an open source system, CUPS recently became an Apple product after acquiring the CUPS trademarks and hiring the original developer, Michael Sweet.) Microsoft also has IPP built into its printing services. Connecting to IPP printers within your local network is usually easy (in fact, that's what you are doing when you connect using Bonjour); however, occasionally the printer you are attempting to connect to isn't visible on the network, so in order to connect, you will need the printer's location (usually an IP address or even domain), and you may need to know the path to the printer (commonly called the *print queue*). IPP printers can be set up under the IP options in the Printer Browser window.

- **Line Printer Daemon (LPD)**: This is an older Unix printing system that has largely been replaced by CUPS. To connect with an LPD printer, you will need its network address, and you will need to know the name of the print queue. An LPD printer can be set up under the IP options in the Printer Browser window.

- **Others**: There are a handful of other, less common, mostly older, proprietary methods of connecting to a network printer. Mac OS X supports a number of these, including HP JetDirect, Canon IJ Network, Epson FireWire, Epson TCP/IP, and HP IP Printing.

> **NOTE:** Some newer printers also have built-in Wi-Fi capability. In general, these printers, if set up properly, will appear just like any other network printer. As a bonus, since these printers are fairly new, almost all of them will use Bonjour, making connecting to the printer a snap.

If you are connecting to a Windows network printer (shared or otherwise), click the Windows button, and then browse through the network until you locate the printer you want. It's unlikely that a driver will be selected for you automatically, so you will need to select "Select a driver to use" from the Print Using menu. When you select the appropriate driver, click the Add button.

Printer Options and the Print Queue

Once a printer is set up and working properly, there isn't much you need to do, but some options are available to you on the Print & Scan preference pane. When you select a printer on the preference pane, the view area displays some brief information about your printer and also has one check box and three buttons. The "Share this printer with other users on the network" check box will allow you to share this printer with other users on your network (provided that printer sharing is enabled on the Sharing preference pane). If sharing is not yet configured, you can click the Sharing Preferences... button to take you to the sharing preferences to configure it. The other two buttons are the Open Print Queue button, which will open the print queue (just like double-clicking the printer icon), and the Options & Supplies button.

Clicking the Options & Supplies button will open a dialog providing three or four tabs (depending on the driver, there may or may not be a Utility tab), as shown in Figure 19–6. The General tab provides basic information about the printer and the driver. The Driver tab lists your current driver in a drop-down list and allows you to select a new driver if you want. The Supply Levels tab can show you how much ink or toner is left in your printer; however, this relies on a number of variables and may not work accurately (or at all). The Supplies button at the bottom of this tab will take you to a web site to buy more printer supplies. It's also possible that there will be a Utility tab that contains tools specific for you printer; this is dependent on the driver, though.

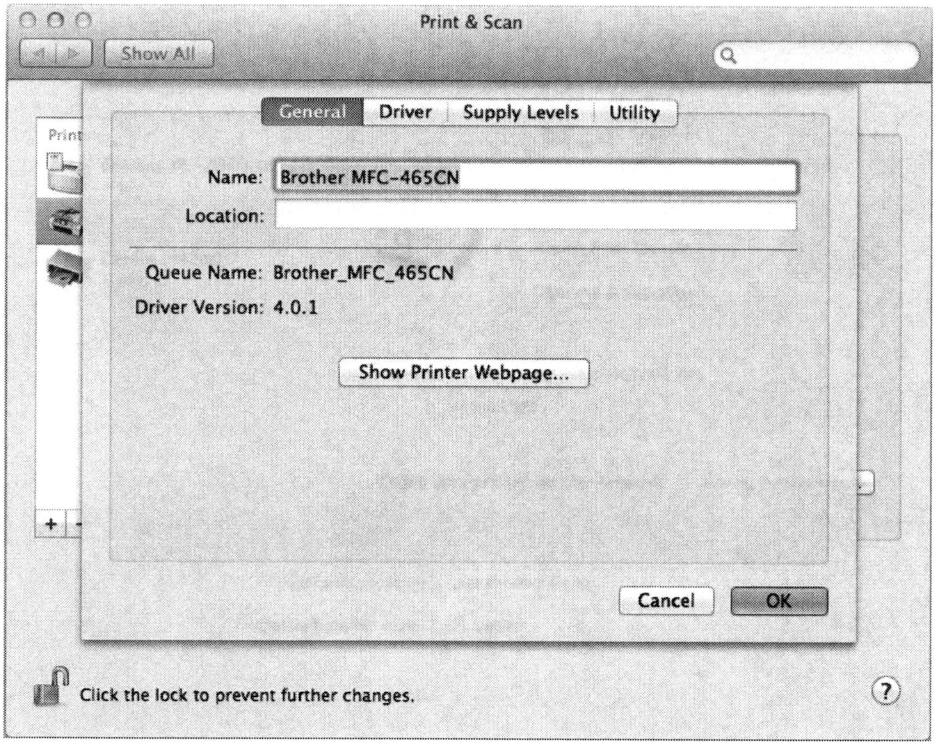

Figure 19–6. *The printer Options & Supplies dialog*

The Open Print Queue button will open the printer's print queue (shown earlier in Figure 19–3). As mentioned, this will provide information about what print jobs are being printed or waiting to be printed. This will also let you pause the printer, delete print jobs, and even rearrange the order of awaiting print jobs. The Supply Levels and Printer Setup buttons open the same dialog as the Options & Supplies button does.

In general, setting up a printer to work with your Mac is a fairly easy process. Even when it's not automatic, the features in Mac OS X tend to make it at least easier than may have been the case in the past (or is with other computer systems).

Printing from an Application

To use your printer, you usually just need to select **File > Print...** (Command-P) from the menu in any standard application. This will open a standard print dialog box that walks you through the printing process. The default Print dialog (Figure 19–7) is simple, with only a few options.

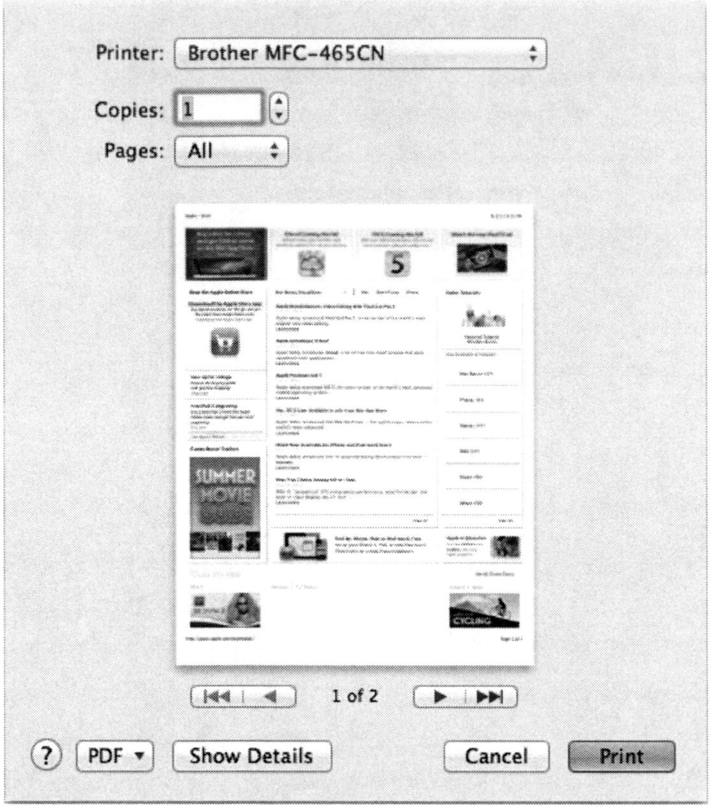

Figure 19–7. *The default Print dialog box asks which printer you'd like to print to and provides a preview of what will be printed.*

NOTE: Some applications will open the Print dialog as an attached dialog box, while others will open it as a floating window. Also, the Print dialog box may vary depending on the application because some applications provide special printing options.

If you have multiple printers connected to your computer, you can select the one you want to print to from the Printer drop-down menu (your default printer will be initially selected for you). The Presets button allows you to select any preselected print options you may want to use. For most printers, Standard is the only initial option unless you save your own print options; however, many photo printers include a few other options (different size prints, borderless options, and so on).

Along the bottom of the Print dialog box are four buttons. Print will send your document to the printer. Cancel will close the dialog box without printing. Show Details will expand the Print Dialog box to provide additional printing options (Figure 19–8). PDF will open a submenu that will provide you with various options for creating a PDF file from your document.

> **NOTE:** All of Mac OS X's display graphics are PDF based; as such, you will find that it can create a PDF out of any document from the Print dialog without any additional software.

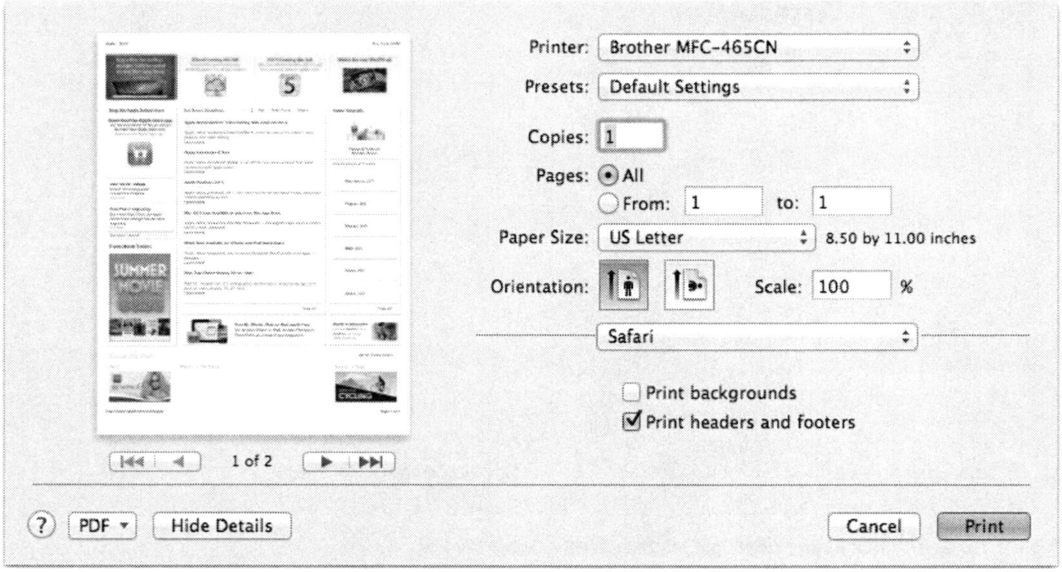

Figure 19–8. *An extended Print dialog box provides many more printing options, depending on the print driver and the application.*

The extended Print dialog provides a number of additional print options. The standard extended elements include a preview of the document, the ability to print multiple copies of the document, the ability to print only a range of pages rather than the entire document, the ability to adjust paper size and orientation, and the ability to scale the document up or down. However, numerous other options are available from the drop-down menu. This menu includes application options, options associated with your printer's features, color-matching options, advanced paper-handling options, scheduling options, fax options, and more.

Connecting Bluetooth Devices

Bluetooth is a technology that allows two devices, such as your mobile phone and your computer, to connect to each other. Unlike other common methods of doing this (USB and FireWire), Bluetooth does this wirelessly, and because of this, some additional work is necessary. The best place to begin connecting and setting up a Bluetooth device is from the Bluetooth preference pane in System Preferences (Figure 19–9).

Figure 19–9. *The Bluetooth preference pane, with no devices set up*

When no devices are set up, the preference pane will provide a Set Up New Device button right in the middle. There are various other areas in Mac OS X where you can set up Bluetooth devices as well. When you begin to set up a new Bluetooth device, Mac OS X will launch the Bluetooth Setup Assistant to help you through the process (Figure 19–10).

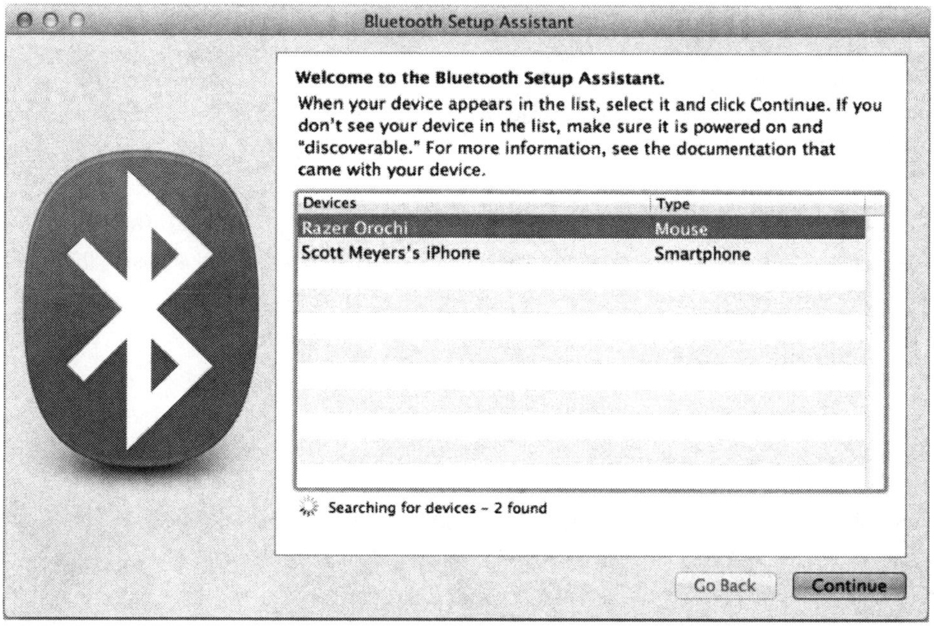

Figure 19–10. *The Bluetooth Setup Assistant will immediately try to detect any discoverable Bluetooth devices in range*

The first screen of the Bluetooth Setup Assistant is a welcome screen. Once the Bluetooth Setup Assistant launches, it will immediately begin scanning for any detectable Bluetooth devices. Any devices that are found will appear in the list on the left pane of the Bluetooth Setup Assistant window.

To continue setting up your device, simply select your device from the list and click Continue. If your device isn't recognized, make sure it is set up to be discoverable by other devices, and try again. Alternately, if you know the Bluetooth address of the device, you can click the Specify Device... button at the bottom of the window and manually enter the address there.

After you select your device and click Continue, the Bluetooth Setup Assistant will attempt to gather any information from your device to determine what services are available from your Bluetooth device. Once it has completed this, the assistant will walk you through pairing your device.

> **NOTE:** When the Bluetooth Setup Assistant first discovers a device, the initial name of the device may be a strange-looking string of digits. If you wait, this string will most likely become something a bit more familiar as the computer discovers more information about the device.

To pair your Bluetooth devices, you will usually be presented with a passkey to enter on your device, or alternately you will be prompted to enter a passkey that your device has generated. The theory behind passkeys is that since various types of information can be passed from one Bluetooth device to another, the connections between Bluetooth devices should occur only through paired devices. During the pairing process, each device must use the same passkey to assure a valid pairing. The complexity of the passkeys used to pair two devices tends to be consistent with the amount of risk involved with the pairing.

> **NOTE:** The default passkey for simple items such as headsets and mice is often 0000. The Bluetooth assistant, knowing this, will automatically attempt to pair with these devices using this passkey. If successful, the pairing will occur automatically, and you'll never need to enter a key. This also applies to most Bluetooth printers, which don't require a passkey at all.

> **TIP:** If you want to choose the passkey yourself, if you want to force pairings with no passkey at all (which is not recommended), or if the initial pairing didn't work (you have to be quick, because if the passcode isn't entered within a short period of time, the pairing will fail), a Passcode Options... button will appear. Clicking the button will open a dialog box, allowing you to choose many different options for selecting (or not selecting) a passcode.

Once the passkey is entered in to the appropriate device (if necessary), the assistant will continue making the connection, which results in a screen indicating that the pairing was successful.

Once you are done, when you take a look on your Bluetooth preference pane, you can see that it has changed to display your Bluetooth devices (Figure 19–11).

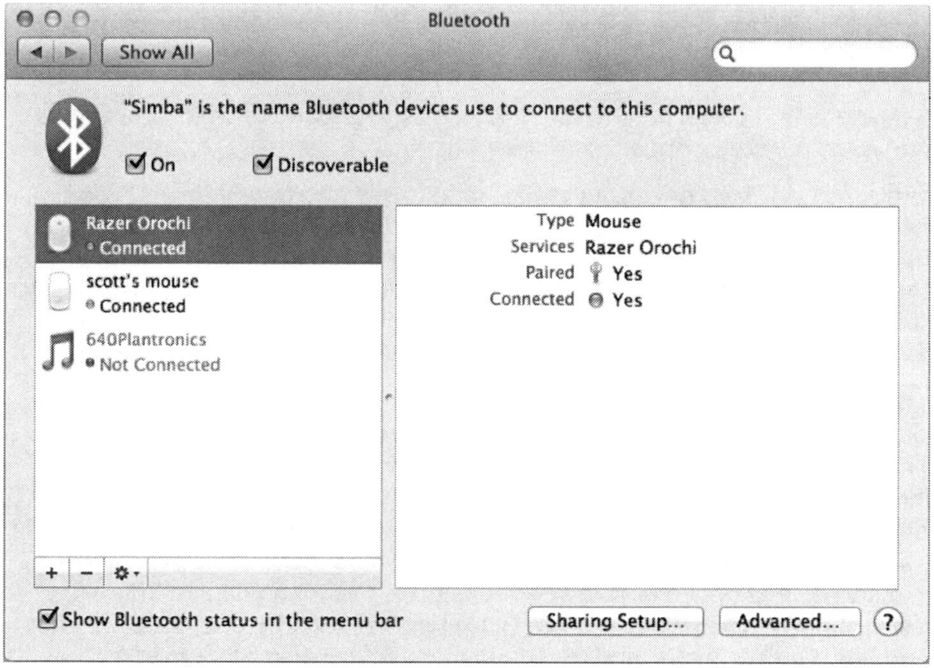

Figure 19–11. *The Bluetooth preference pane changes now that devices have been set up.*

Connecting External Storage

Ever since the advent of the floppy disk, and even the magnetic tapes before that, external storage has been a popular way of backing up and moving files, adding extra system storage, or even running entire operating systems. These days with the cost of large external hard drives dropping, the rampant use of thumb drives, and even media devices such as iPods being used for storage, this trend continues.

Like most things, connecting to external storage in Mac OS X is easy. In fact, you just plug in the external storage, and it shows up on your desktop alongside your primary hard drive and any other storage media you have connected to your computer. To remove it, you first tell your computer to "eject" the media and then unplug it. Still, a few things are worth knowing about: what the differences are between the different types of storage media and what all the available interfaces are and their advantages.

> **CAUTION:** To eject media in Mac OS X, you can either select Eject from the item's contextual menu, click the Eject button next to the item in the Devices section of a Finder window, or drag it into the Trash (to name a few ways you can do it). It's important to do this before you unplug the device, especially with external hard drives. If you forget to "eject" the device and you just abruptly unplug the external storage device, you may have unplugged the device while it was still writing data, thus causing data loss and corruption.

Storage Media

The storage media is that actual mechanism that stores your data, of which there are three popular types: magnetic, optical, and flash.

Magnetic media includes hard drives, as well as tape drives and floppy drives. Today that primarily means hard drives, though high-end tape drives are still in use for large-scale backup and archive purposes by many organizations and institutions. Magnetic media is generally fast, is stable, can store very large amounts of data, and, these days, is relatively inexpensive. On the downside, it can be fragile and susceptible to damage from outside radiation and magnetism; it also isn't the most energy-efficient media, since moving parts are used in almost all cases.

Optical media includes CDs, DVDs, and an array of both newer, emerging and older, deprecated media types. Advantages of optical media include the cost of storage and the durability and flexibility of the media. Because of this, optical media is perhaps the best, cost-effective media for archival for most users. On the downside, optical media is traditionally slower in both reading and writing data, and most optical media is write-once media, meaning that once the data is written, it can't be manipulated. There are today a number of rewritable optical formats; however, they tend to lose reliability after a number of rewrites. Optical media tend to require more power than other media types. Finally, although the technology exists (and is constantly under development) to increase the storage capabilities of optical media, the capacity is significantly less today than what is available with magnetic media.

Flash media, such as memory cards and flash drives, are becoming more and more popular. Flash media is popular in many electronic devices for digital storage, including digital cameras, media players, iPods, mobile phones, PDAs, and more. It's also more and more popular as external computer storage for moving files from place to place with thumb drives. It's fast, durable and energy efficient (no moving parts to break, just shuffling electrons), and small. Despite all the advantages, it's expensive and limited in capacity. Still, technologically, it has made the most gains of any storage media over the past few years. Capacity has increased, and costs have dropped dramatically.

> **NOTE:** Newer SSD hard drives, which come standard in MacBook Airs and optional in most other Macs, are also built using flash memory similar to other flash media, and while they share all the pros (and cons) of other flash media, they appear to the system like any other hard drive.

Storage Interfaces

Besides the different types of storage media, several interfaces are available. When choosing an external storage device, it's important to pick one with an interface that will fit your needs. Table 19–1 lists the common interfaces.

Table 19–1. *External Storage Interfaces*

Interface	Description
USB	The USB interface is one of the most common interfaces, not only for storage but for many external peripherals. USB comes in four flavors (or versions really): USB 1.0, 1.1, 2.0, and 3.0 (alternatively referred to as low speed, full speed, and high speed). These provide maximum data speeds of 1.5 Mbit/s, 12 Mbit/s, 480 Mbit/s, and 5Gbit/s. (Note the *bit* part. There are 8 bits per byte, so USB 2.0 really provides speeds up to 60 MB/s, for example.) Most USB ports, as well as most USB storage devices today, provide USB 2.0, but you really should check to be sure. USB 1.1 is sufficient for smaller thumb drives, but for hard drives, the performance would be excruciatingly slow. Finally, USB 2.0 ports and devices are backward compatible with older USB ports and devices. Currently Macs do not support USB 3.0, opting instead to incorporate the newer Thunderbolt technology.
FireWire 400 (IEEE 1934a)	FireWire 400, also known as IEEE 1934a and as i.Link by Sony, is a technology originally invented by Apple to provide an alternative to SCSI for high-speed data transmission. It was quickly adopted as a standard A/V interface for sending digital A/V data from one device to another (camcorder to computer). Because of its cost and simplicity, it's also choice for all but a few situations. FireWire 400 provides up to 400 Mbit/s transmission speeds, which in theory makes it similar to USB 2.0. However, FireWire, in the real world still tends to be faster than USB 2.0 devices, and it can support more devices on a single node than USB.
FireWire 800 (IEEE 1934b)	FireWire 800 doubles the performance of FireWire 400. The only issue with FireWire 800 is that while technically FireWire 800 is backward compatible with FireWire 400, it uses different connectors, which makes the physical connection incompatible. Today all new Macs with the exception of the MacBook Air include at least one FireWire 800 port.
FibreChannel	FibreChannel connections are available as an option only on Mac Pros and Xserves, but they provide a blazing 4 GB/s transmission (for comparison, that would be 32,000 Mbit/s). This is used for Apple's discontinued Xserve RAID system and other high-end storage systems. It's
eSATA	External Serial ATA (eSATA) is a technology that extends the SATA bus for external use. SATA is what all new Macs use on the inside to connect hard drives. For external connections, though, although eSATA promises high-speed throughput of data. eSATA is not included with any current Mac, though expansion cards may be available.

Interface	Description
Thunderbolt	Thunderbolt is the latest high-performance (10 Gbit/s per channel) data transfer standard to find its way into Mac systems. While at the moment the available external devices that support it are limited, the ones that are available demonstrate a massive increase in data throughput when using Thunderbolt over older technologies. In addition to external storage, Thunderbolt provides the speeds and features to send video signals across it, and Apple's newest displays allow Thunderbolt connections.

> **NOTE:** Currently Apple ships Macs with at least two different Thunderbolt controllers. While most Macs provide four data channels, some, like the 11-inch Mac Book Air, only provide two data channels.

The goal in choosing an interface is to pick the fastest one that provides what you want. If your new iMac supports Thunderbolt, FireWire 800, and USB 2.0, but you also have an older iMac that supports only FireWire 400 and USB 1.1, then a USB drive may be the best common denominator (though you could get the FireWire 800 drive and buy a FireWire 800-to-400 adapter for better performance).

> **NOTE:** Many external hard drives available today will include multiple interfaces. This is nice for maximum performance and connectivity, especially if you have computers of various ages.

No matter what interface or media is being used, it's important to remember that as long as the interface on your device matches up with an interface on your computer, you are good to go.

Connecting Other Peripherals

Besides printers, extra storage, and general Bluetooth devices, lots of other things are available to plug into your computer for various reasons. Although it's impossible to cover each possible device here, we'll end this chapter with some general advice, as well as a few specific instances where something unique will happen that relates to Mac OS X.

Whenever you connect a device to your computer, your computer must be able identify and communicate with the device. Most of the time your Mac OS X system will at least be able to identify the device; however, it may have no idea how to communicate with the device or how to make it work. A driver generally handles this communication process, and although Mac OS X ships with a large number of drivers and knows how to communicate with a large range of products, a large number of items will need you to install a driver for them to work correctly. Usually, any device you purchase will include not only any necessary drivers but also supporting software and instructions on how to get your device working with your computer.

Occasionally there will be a product that will work well without an additional driver but certain features won't work (common among certain multifeatured mice and keyboards). In such a situation, it's up to you whether to install the manufacturer's driver; in general, if you bought something for the features, then you probably want them to all work.

> **TIP:** If you happen upon a really nice mouse with lots of features, yet you find the drivers provided with the mouse to be lacking, there are a couple of third-party mouse drivers that are extremely flexible and that work with a large number of different brands of mice. My personal favorite is SteerMouse, available from `http://plentycom.jp/en/steermouse/`.

The following types of devices occasionally require a driver in order to function properly:

- Scanners
- Input tablets
- Audio/MIDI interfaces
- Screen calibration devices
- Multifunction mice and keyboards
- Certain video interfaces
- Some printers

On the other hand, a large number of devices should work immediately after plugging them in (though some configuration or special software may be needed to do much with them):

- Digital cameras
- Video camcorders with a FireWire or USB link
- Most Apple hardware
- Speakers and microphones (including USB headsets)
- Some USB/MIDI keyboards and controllers
- Storage devices
- Many standard mice and keyboards (including multibutton mice with a scroll wheel)
- Many printers

Occasionally some special action occurs when you connect a particular type of device.

Digital Cameras

Mac OS X has always recognized every digital camera I've ever plugged in. What you need to decide, however, is how you would like your computer to respond when you attach a digital camera. In OS X the standard application for dealing with importing images, Image Capture, has changed, and so has the default behavior when you plug in your camera. When you first plug in your camera, your camera will mount as a new drive on the desktop, and that's it (unless you have already set a preference in some other application such as iPhoto to open automatically when camera is attached)! If you don't have iLife and thus iPhoto, you can browse and download the images on your camera using Image Capture (Figure 19–12). Image Capture provides an easy way to preview and download images from your camera to your computer (by default it will download images to your Pictures folder.)

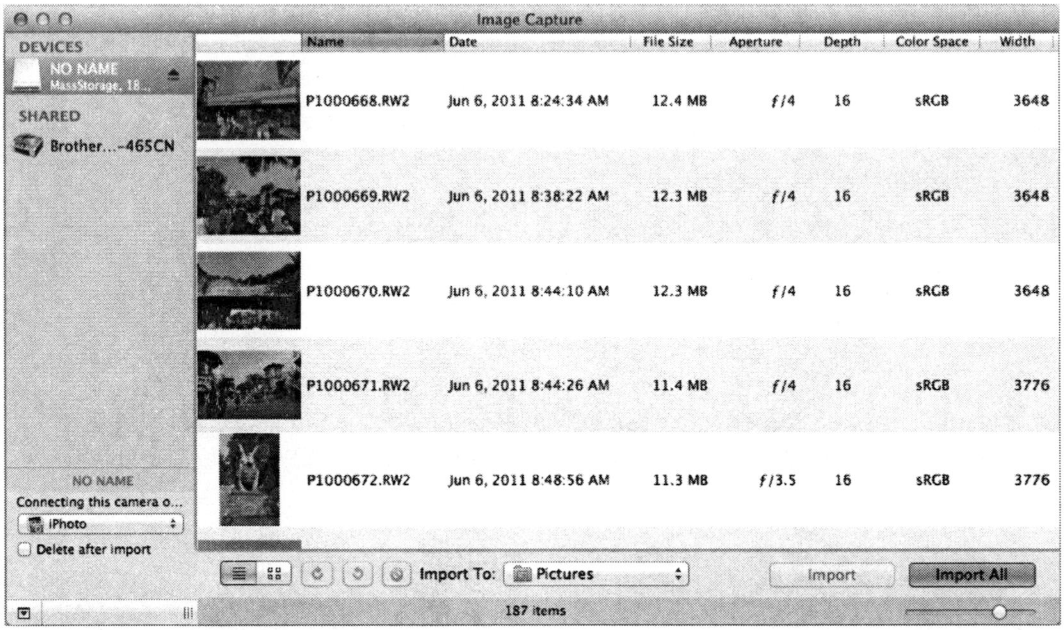

Figure 19–12. *The Image Capture application is a standard part of Mac OS X and is always available for importing images from a digital camera. Additionally Image Capture can be used to scan images from supported scanners.*

> **NOTE:** You can also use Image Capture to import images from devices other than cameras. In fact, you can use Image Capture to import images from a wide range of scanners without installing any additional software or drivers (Figure 19–13).

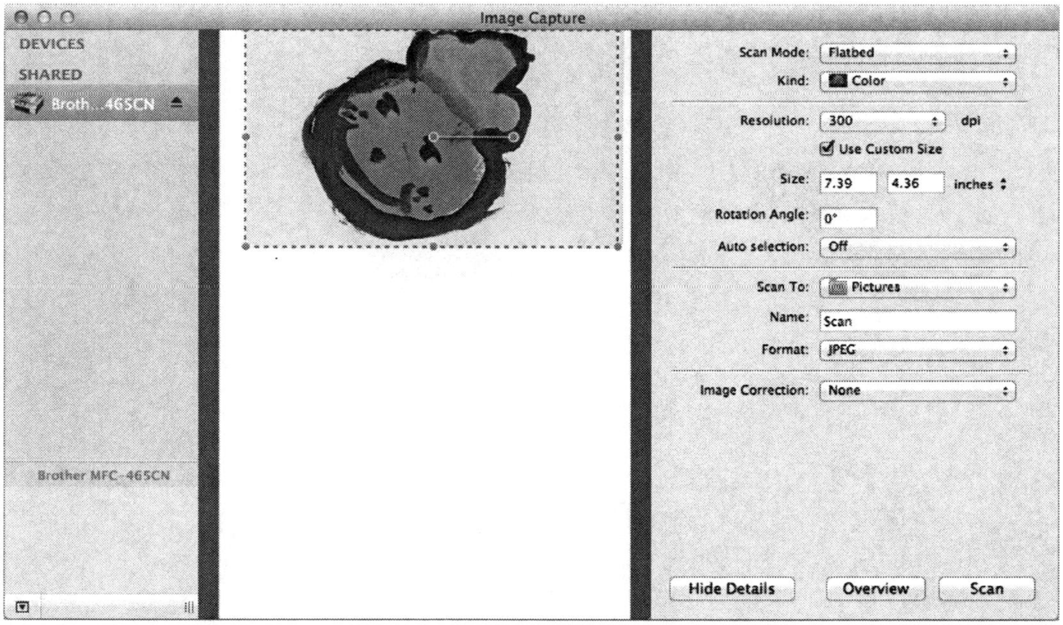

Figure 19–13. *The Image Capture application also provides basic scanning tools for supported scanners.*

If you've installed iPhoto or Aperture, you can choose to have these automatically launch to import images when you connect your camera. (In fact, when you first launch iPhoto, it will ask you whether you would like to do this. If iPhoto is your primary image application, then it's probably a good idea to do this.)

Input Tablets

Input tablets are another interesting input device, although they're generally used by graphic designers and artists with graphic applications. When you plug an input tablet into your Mac OS X computer, you will find that a new preference pane appears in System Preferences: Ink.

The Ink preference pane (Figure 19–14) provides options for the Inkwell feature introduced in Tiger (Mac OS X 10.4). Inkwell is a handwriting recognition technology that allows you to write text with your input tablet, which the computer will then (attempt to) convert it into editable type:

this is an example oftext entered withinkwell .

As you can see, it's still not perfect (or perhaps it's just my handwriting), but it's fun to play around with (and your handwriting may be better than ours).

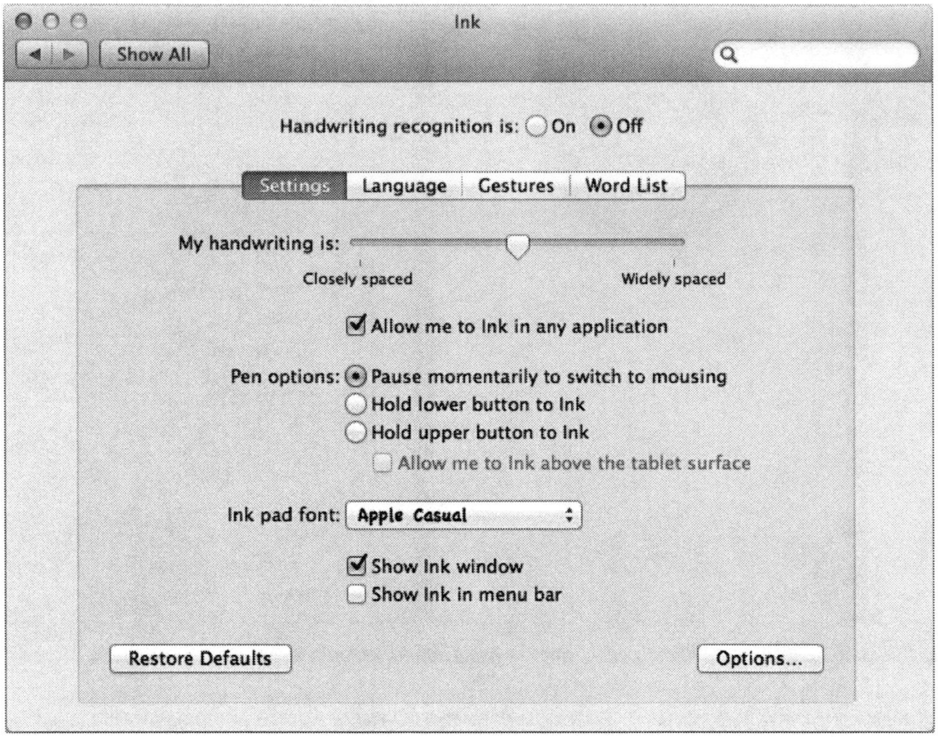

Figure 19–14. *The Ink preference pane appears when you have an input tablet connected to your computer.*

NOTE: The Inkwell preference will not work until the proper driver is installed for your input tablet and the tablet is plugged in.

Summary

Now you shouldn't have too much trouble getting any external peripheral to work with your Mac (provided it was designed to work with your Mac; getting non-Mac-compatible devices to work is often possible, but goes beyond the scope of this book). Next we will build on our discussion of external storage devices to talk about Time Machine, data backups, and recovery.

Chapter **20**

Time Machine Backup and Recovery

Most people who have been around computers for a long time have horror stories of disk crashes and data loss. And even if your story isn't horrific, you probably have an "Oh, $#!*!" moment or two when things go wrong and you lose an hour's or a day's (or more) worth of work. The thing is, the minute your hard drive was created, it started a countdown toward its *mean time before failure* (MTBF—a rating that measures the average amount of time before a hard drive fails); of course, more frequently, we tend to occasionally make mistakes (either as a user or as a developer), so we must make sure we have effective ways of backing up and syncing our data.

This chapter is dedicated to backing up and syncing data, not because it's a terribly long and complicated thing to explain (in fact, Mac OS X makes it relatively easy these days) but because it's such an important topic that it deserves to be treated on its own. In this chapter, we will cover the following:

■ The difference between backup and synchronization and what's appropriate in what circumstances

■ Keeping your computer's data backed up using Time Machine

■ Other methods of backup, syncing, and data recovery

The Difference Between Backups and Synchronization

Before we go too far, it's important to make some general differentiations between a backup and a sync. In overly simple terms, suppose you have two disks: disk A and disk B. When you *back up* disk A to disk B, you make an exact copy of disk A's data onto disk B. This assures that in the event that something undesirable happens to the data on disk A (or if disk A fails altogether), you can revert to the backup data on disk B. When you *synchronize* disk A with disk B, the information on each disk is usually copied to the other so that the data on each drive matches. One special feature of some backup applications is that they archive old information that has been deleted or changed. This can be known as an *archived backup* or *versioned backup*, but whatever it's called, it allows the added benefit of looking "back in time" to find files that may otherwise have been deleted (this is how Time Machine works). If you are more of a visual thinker, these differences are illustrated in Figure 20–1.

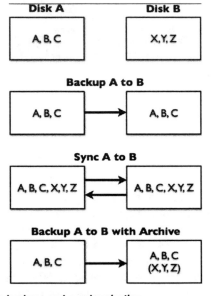

Figure 20–1. *Differences between backups and synchronization*

> **NOTE:** These descriptions of a backup and a sync, along with Figure 20–1, are meant to provide a simplified (perhaps overly simplified) differentiation between backups and synchronization. The reality can be much more nuanced. For example, while a backup only provides a one-way transfer of data (i.e., backing up one data source to another), synchronization can provide both a one-way and/or a two-way transfer of data, depending on settings. (In fact, when you first sync data, you're often asked if you want to copy source A to B, copy source B to A, or synchronize A and B. If data changes on both sources, most sync programs will ask you which change you want to use.)

DEFINING AN ARCHIVE

The word *archive* is a bit of a semantic battlefield and can mean different things in different applications. First the verb, *to archive*: some backup applications may ask, "Would you like to archive your data?" While this seems like a simple question, it could have two different results. In one scenario, the system could start keeping track of old files (this is the definition we're using and could—perhaps should—be referred to as *versioning*). In another situation, the system could ask you to insert a CD or DVD. In this case, the application is offering to help you create an offline archive or snapshot of your current data.

An *archive* (noun) could be many things: the physical CD or DVD you created when you made your archive, a single large file containing archived data in some proprietary format, a more general collection of files organized in a means for software to easily identify and retrieve it, or some combination of all of the above (or something in between). Archives aren't always backups, either (though often there is that connotation); they more generally are large collections of somehow related data. Confused yet? Don't worry, it's really not that bad. Generally, in any given situation, an archive means whatever makes the most sense for that situation, and if not, it's not too difficult to find out.

Generally, when you want to keep an extra copy of your important data in case something happens to your primary data store, then what you want is a backup. When you have two data stores that you need to keep current with each other, then what you want is synchronization. Either way, you are creating a redundancy that is important should one data source fail. One important note, though: creating a backup with archiving is the only way to effectively protect against file corruption. If you synchronize or simply back up a corrupted file, then you are just creating a new copy of a corrupted file, often overwriting an old, uncorrupted file.

Backing Up Your Data with Time Machine

Mac OS X includes a fantastic little backup utility called Time Machine. Time Machine provides data backups of all your information complete with a historical archive of data. The best thing about this is that Time Machine does all of its work automatically in the background, making it painless (in theory). However, like any good backup utility, in order to take full advantage of Time Machine, you will need an extra hard drive connected to your computer for Time Machine to back up data to.

> **NOTE:** When deciding whether to invest in an external hard drive for Time Machine to use, ask yourself how much the data you keep on your computer is worth. You can easily find a nice-sized external hard drive these days for less than $100, and in my opinion, our data is worth at least that.

NOTE: In the past some people would create a Time Machine backup to a different partition on their primary hard drive. Although this wouldn't help if your hard drive had a mechanical failure, it would provide archives of old files. Lion's new Versions feature (covered in Chapter 5) provides this for you (provided you are working with an application that supports it), so this is probably not necessary anymore.

NOTE: Time Machine will eventually use all the free space on the drive or partition you set for it. So, if you want to use a hard drive for both Time Machine and anything else, then you'll most likely want to partition the drive, dedicating one partition to just Time Machine. (I covered how to partition drives in the previous chapter.)

Setting Up Time Machine

To set up Time Machine:

1. Open the Time Machine pane in System Preferences (Figure 20–2).

Figure 20–2. *The Time Machine preference pane prior to setting up Time Machine the first time*

2. Click the Select Disk... button, which opens up a dialog box (Figure 20–3) allowing you to select the desired backup disk. Select the desired device and click the Use for Backup button. This selects the device automatically, turns Time Machine on, and starts a 120–second countdown until your first back up. Time Machine is now ready to go.

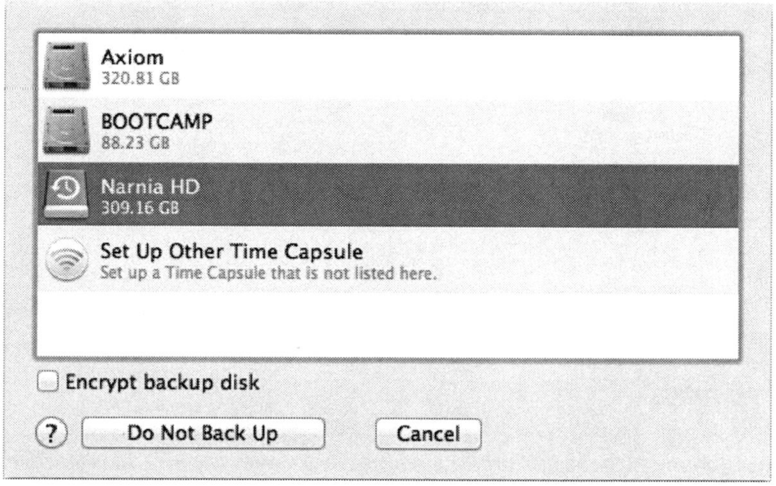

Figure 20–3. *The dialog box asks you which device you want to dedicate to Time Machine.*

> **NOTE:** If you haven't set up Time Machine already, when you first connect an external hard drive, you will be asked if you'd like to use that drive as a Time Machine backup. If you choose Yes, then you can bypass the previous steps.

> **NOTE:** If you are using one of Apple's Time Capsule network devices for backup, you may select the Set Up Time Capsule option. This launches the AirPort Utility to allow you to select the appropriate Time Capsule device to use. Once set up, using a Time Capsule will work as seamlessly as any other external backup device.

Once you've selected a backup device, the Time Machine preference pane changes to offer more information and options (Figure 20–4).

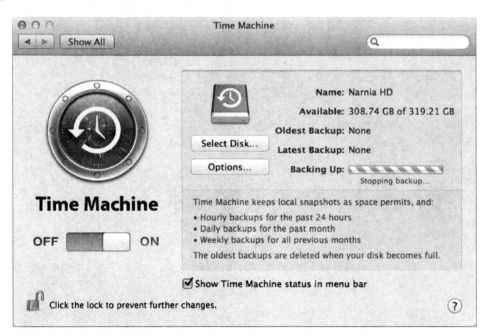

Figure 20–4. *The Time Machine preference pane changes to offer more options once you choose a Time Machine device.*

Selecting the Options... button opens a dialog box (Figure 20–5) that allows you to tweak a few options, the most important of which is the ability to select any folders or attached devices that you want Time Machine to ignore (and thus not back up).

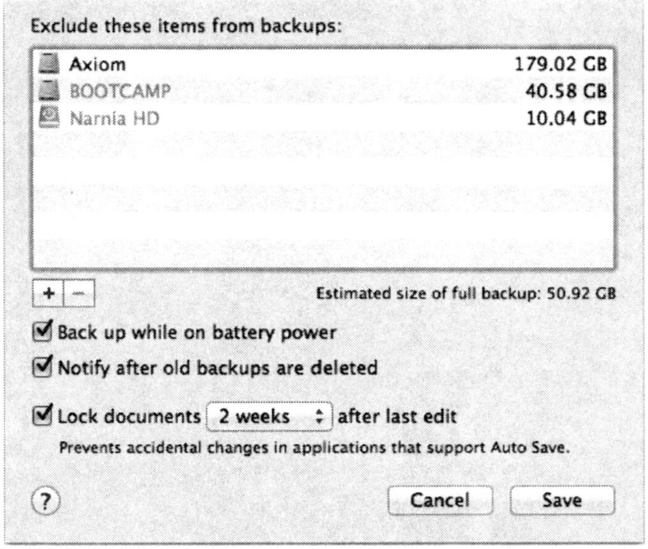

Figure 20–5. *The Options... dialog box provides some added options that affect how Time Machine works.*

This is particularly useful if you have large files or archives that are backed up with other methods, if you don't care whether they are backed up, or if you have folders containing sensitive data that you don't want archived.

> **NOTE:** You also may want Time Machine to ignore very large files that change often—for example, virtual disks from VMware Fusion or your Entourage database (no longer an issue if you updated to Outlook 2011 for Mac, though). However, if you do have Time Machine ignore these files, you may want to back them up manually (especially your Entourage database, if that's your primary e-mail and contacts tool). If you don't ignore these every time you make even a small change (which happens constantly when, in the case of the previous examples, a virtual machine is running or Entourage is open), then Time Machine will detect a change, back up the entire file, and archive the old. Not only will Time Machine be running constantly, but its drive will fill up with lots of large, slightly changed, archive files.

> **NOTE:** When you initially set up Time Machine or select a new Time Machine device, the initial backup may take a long time to complete. Once it completes, Time Machine will back up only new or altered items on your hard drive. These backups are generally quite fast unless you're doing manual or infrequent backups.

Using Time Machine Manually

When Time Machine is active, it makes automatic backups every hour. This keeps a rather complete record of changes to your system should anything minor or major occur, from the accidental deletion of a file to a dreaded hard-drive failure. If, however, you would like to forgo this level of detail and control your backups manually, simply turn Time Machine's OFF-ON switch to OFF. If you want to use Time Machine manually, it's handy to have the "Show Time Machine status in the menu bar" option selected. This allows you to select Back Up Now from the menu bar at any time and create a backup manually (Figure 20–6). Alternately, you can select the Back Up Now option by Control-clicking the Time Machine icon on your Dock.

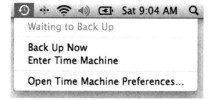

Figure 20–6. *The Time Machine icon in the menu bar allows you start a Time Machine backup manually.*

Using the Time Machine Interface to Recover Data

Once Time Machine is set up, it should begin keeping an up-to-date archive of the data on your system. Through the Time Machine interface (Figure 20–7), you can use Time Machine to recover past files that have been altered or deleted. Additionally, should your primary hard drive ever crash and you need to do a clean install of OS X (or you just want to do a clean install of OS X because you have some extra time on your hands), you can recover all of your data from your Time Machine backup either during the install process or at a later time using the Migration Assistant application.

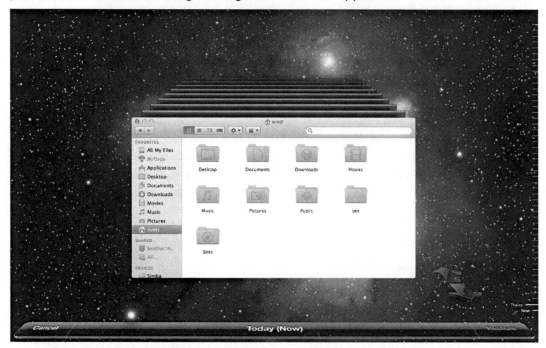

Figure 20–7. *Time Machine browsing Finder items as they were backed up through time*

You can enter the Time Machine interface by clicking the Time Machine icon, just as you would launch any other application. Alternately, you can select the Enter Time Machine option from the Time Machine menu icon (unless you've disabled it). To recover any data from the Time Machine archive, you may navigate through the single Finder window normally and then simply use the arrows or the timeline along the right side of the interface to navigate "back in time" and select the item you want to recover. Once you select the desired item, click the Restore button in the lower-right corner. This brings you out of the Time Machine interface and places the recovered file in its original Finder location. If an item of the same name already (or still) exists in that place, then you will be prompted to keep either or both files.

> **NOTE:** Time Machine assumes that the selected Time Machine disk or partition exists solely for Time Machine archives. It continues to fill up this drive with archives until the drive is full. When the Time Machine device is full, Time Machine begins to delete the oldest archived files to make room for the newer ones. If the "Notify after old backups are deleted" option is selected, you will be prompted after Time Machine overwrites old files.

If you want to leave Time Machine without restoring any items, just click the Cancel button in the lower-left corner of the Time Machine interface.

When you launch Time Machine, it usually opens up in the active Finder location; however, certain applications are also Time Machine–aware. One example of this is Apple's Mail application. Opening Time Machine with Mail active provides a Mail window in Time Machine so you can go back and find old deleted messages (unfortunately, you can't use Time Machine to go back and not send old sent messages).

> **NOTE:** Time Machine goes beyond just backup and actually provides a personal version control system as well. Version control tracks changes of items over time so that you can recover older versions if something critically wrong happens in a new version. For developers, version control (or source code management [SCM]) is essential for creating stable software, and support for a number of version control systems, including CVS, Subversion, and Perforce, are built into Xcode. For more general project version control, Versions (`www.versionsapp.com`), not to be confused with the Versions feature in Mac OS X, provides an easy-to-use interface for taking advantage of the Subversion version control system. One significant difference between Time Machine's version control and professional SCM is that the SCM tools are designed to keep track of changes made by a large number of different users, while Time Machine just tracks changes, not necessarily who's making them.

Other Methods of Backup, Sync, and Recovery

Besides Time Machine, you can use a range of other utilities, applications, and methods to protect your data. Some applications, such as Apple's Aperture, provide an integrated means of backing up and archiving their data.

If, however, Apple's backup tools don't quite fit your needs (or for whatever reason, you just don't like them), these other applications are worth a look:

- Decimus Software (`www.decimus.net`) makes two different backup applications depending on your needs: Synk Standard and Synk Pro. These apps range in cost from $40 to $60. Although the Standard version handles most common backup and synchronization tasks, the Pro version adds some nice features, and at $60, it offers the best bang for your buck.

▓   CrashPlan (`www.crashplan.com`) provides tools for backing up your data to multiple locations including online storage. The basic CrashPlan consumer application is free; however, with the CrashPlan+ options you gain online storage for additional security (10GB for $24.99 a year or Unlimited for $49.99 a year).

> **NOTE:** Two other backup utilities worth considering are SuperDuper! (`www.shirt-pocket.com/SuperDuper/SuperDuperDescription.html`) and Carbon Copy Cloner (`www.bombich.com/software/index.html`). What sets these apart from the others is their ability to keep up-to-date *clones* of your system; in other words, these backup utilities maintain a fully *bootable* copy of your system that can be swapped in for your primary system drive at a moment's notice, should the need ever arise.

What's most important—whether you use Time Machine, use Retrospect, or copy all your data onto thumb drives manually—is that you do *something* to back up your data. Just pick a system that works for you and go with it.

Summary

Now that you know how to protect your data from hard drive failures and accidental data loss, we'll move on to some general OS X maintenance tasks to keep your system running smoothly.

## Chapter 21

Common Mac OS X Maintenance

Mac OS X tends to do a pretty good job of taking care of itself; however, there are a few things that occasionally need attention or that Mac OS X leaves up to you to take care of. The issues that we will cover in this chapter include the following:

- Disk setup and maintenance
- Font management

Disk Setup and Maintenance

> **NOTE:** The most important thing about hard disks is that they will all fail in time. Sometimes it is a slow death where they start making a loud clicking that gets progressively worse until they just stop working; other times there is no warning. If you want to keep your data, back it up. Buy an external hard drive (or two) and use Time Machine or some other utility. Really. As the saying goes, "Pay now or pay more later."

Hard drives—both the primary hard drive that came in your computer and any extras, either internal or external—are essential parts of your computers. If things go wrong with a hard drive, your system may stop functioning, or more importantly, you may lose data. Luckily, apart from the very real worry that your hard drive may (and someday will) eventually physically stop working, Mac OS X tends to take care of things on your drive, limiting the amount of routine maintenance needed to keep your file system and hard drive (and thus your data) healthy. Still, occasionally there are routines that you may want to run to verify that everything is OK. Additionally, someday you may want to format, partition, or utilize a specific file system on one of the hard drives connected to your system. To manage your hard drives and take care of all these functions, Mac OS X includes the Disk Utility application (located in Launchpad's Utilities group).

NOTE: Two primary things can go wrong on a disk: there's physical damage, which is when the disk mechanism fails and possibly crashes, and there's file system damage, which is when the data on your disk gets mixed up or damaged. Tools like Disk Utility can often detect and repair file system damage before it causes data loss. Physical damage to the disk is more permanent and often irreparable (although in some cases the data can be recovered by special hardware and/or software).

NOTE: The term *disk crash* refers to the event when the arms that pass over the disk surface to read the data fall and literally crash into the disk's surface, causing irreparable damage. This used to happen with older disk mechanisms that would rely on the air force of the spinning disk to keep the arms up, so if the disks quit spinning suddenly before the arms could move back off the disk's surface (e.g., in a power failure), the arms would fall. Disk crashes like this don't happen often with today's hard drives, but mechanical issues still arise, and disks do get old and eventually wear out (usually after years of service, though).

Disk Utility divides its abilities into five panes:

- First Aid provides a couple of general maintenance tools that can help identify and repair both file system damage and issues in which the system's file permissions become altered.

- The Erase tab provides the necessary tools to partition and format a disk using various supported file systems.

- The Partition option appears if you select an entire disk, rather than just a volume in the list of devices on the left. The Partition tab allows you to split a single disk into multiple volumes (or create a single volume from multiple volumes).

- The RAID tab allows you to configure multiple disks to behave as one in various ways.

- The Restore tab lets you restore a disk image onto a disk. We'll cover each of these in the following sections.

NOTE: A disk is a physical device, whereas a volume is a file system written to a disk. The physical space on a disk can be divided up into different volumes (or even left as empty space). These divisions are referred to as *disk partitions*.

Performing First Aid

The First Aid tab (Figure 21–1) allows you to run a few tasks to help identify and fix certain problems with your disk's file system. If you seem to be having issues with your disk or notice anything unusual about how it's running or storing data, this is the first place to go to try to solve the problem.

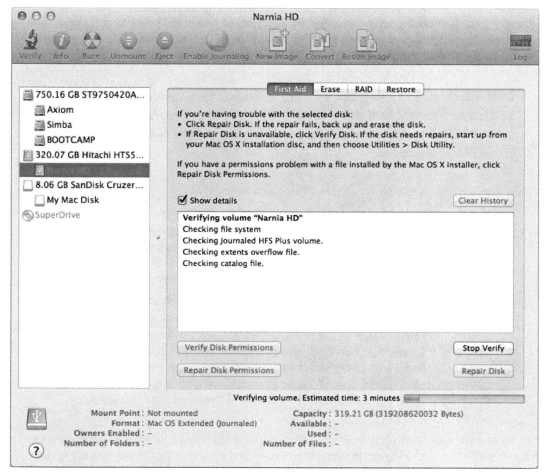

Figure 21–1. *Mac OS X's Disk Utility verifying a volume using one of the First Aid tools*

In the lower-right corner are two buttons: Verify Disk and Repair Disk. Clicking Repair Disk will scan the disk to identify and repair many common file system errors. Although most of the errors it may find are in themselves minor, they can often cause bigger issues down the road. One gotcha here is that you can't repair the boot volume—you can, however, click the Verify Disk button to see whether there are any problems with it, and if so, you can utilize the Repair Disk function from the Disk Utility application installed on your Lion recovery partition. Just boot from your recovery partition and run the Disk Utility from there.

> **NOTE:** To boot from Mac OS X's Recover partition, hold Command-R during a restart. (Alternately, you can hold the Command key during startup and choose the recovery partition from the list of bootable partitions.) More on the recovery partition will be covered in Appendix A.

On occasion, the Repair utility will come across an issue it cannot repair. At this point, you have two primary options (well, three if you are the type of person who can just ignore a problem until it's too late). Before you decide what you want to do, you should first make backup copies of everything you value on your hard drive. Even if you already have a copy, make another one.

> **CAUTION:** We've had a primary disk and a backup disk fail simultaneously, and it was not a happy moment. Luckily, I had another backup and lost only about a month of work; now I use a mirrored RAID, so I don't lose any data if a drive fails. I cover mirrored RAID in the "Using RAID" section later in this chapter.

Once that's done, you can do either of the following:

- **Erase, reformat, and reinstall everything on your disk**: This option takes a long time and will likely cause a few frustrating moments—and nothing will ever be quite the same. However, it should fix any file system problem, plus it can clean out some other gunk that can creep into your computer as you use it over a long period of time.

- **Purchase and try some other disk utility software**: There are three very good, easily obtainable disk utilities out there for Macs: TechTool Pro by Micromat (www.micromat.com), DiskWarrior by Alsoft (www.alsoft.com/DiskWarrior), and Drive Genius by Prosoft (http://prosofteng.com/products/drive_genius.php). Each of these come on a bootable CD or DVD, so you can boot them up and use them right away. The downside it that any of these will set you back about $100 (at least).

So, what happens if nothing works? Sadly, in that case it may be time to replace your hard drive. If it's your original internal hard drive and your computer is covered under warranty or AppleCare, you should be taken care of. Otherwise, you'll either have to order a new hard drive and install it yourself (easy with a Mac Pro; not so easy, but doable, with a portable, a Mac mini, or an iMac) or have to take it in and have someone else do it (a nearby Apple Store is a good choice, or ask around. Just make sure if you pay someone to do it that they are Apple certified).

> **NOTE:** You may wonder whether replacing a hard drive in your computer will void the warranty or interfere with AppleCare. The answer is no; however, if you are not careful, you could cause some collateral damage that would void your warranty. Also, we should mention that the replacement drive (or any damage it may cause, however unlikely) will not be covered under your warranty (though it may come with its own).

The other pair of buttons on the First Aid tab, Verify Disk Permissions and Repair Disk Permissions, do what they say. In OS X, each item in your system has a set of permissions that determine who can do what with the item and, in return, what that item can do (you can find a deeper look at Unix-style permissions in Chapter 17). Occasionally, permissions can get changed, and sometimes this causes applications to behave poorly or not work at all. In such a case, setting the permissions back to their defaults usually fixes the problem. To do this, just run Repair Disk Permissions and see whether that fixes the problem.

> **NOTE:** The Repair Disk Permissions option resets the permissions of certain Apple software to its original state. This can cure some runtime issues that occur when an application can't complete a task because of insufficient permissions. It's a fairly painless exercise, so if you are having issues, it's worth a try. It could just be the fix you need to solve your problem.

Erasing and Formatting a Volume

The Erase tab (Figure 21–2) allows you to erase all or part of a disk.

You will use this in the following scenarios:

- If you just want to zap all the data on your disk and start over
- If you want to change how a disk is formatted
- If you actually want to wipe the data on your hard drive clean

In the case of the first two scenarios, you basically do the same thing: choose a format from the Volume Format list (formats are explained in the next section), choose a name for your new volume, and click the Erase button. This effectively reformats your drive. A simple format, however, does not actually erase your disk; it just erases the existing directory information. With the directory information cleared, your computer has no record of anything stored on it, so it just assumes it's empty and starts writing over old content, keeping track of the new directory information.

If you want to actually erase the content on your hard drive so it cannot be recovered, you have two options. If you just want to assure that any files you have deleted in the trash are actually gone, then you can use the Erase Free Space button. If you want to assure that the entire volume is erased when you format it, click the Security Options button prior to formatting it. On the next screen, each of these buttons will allow you to choose between three different modes: zero out, 7-pass, or 35-pass of data. Each additional pass will assure that the data will be unrecoverable; however, it will also add a significant amount of time to the process (7 or 35 times the amount of time, to be specific).

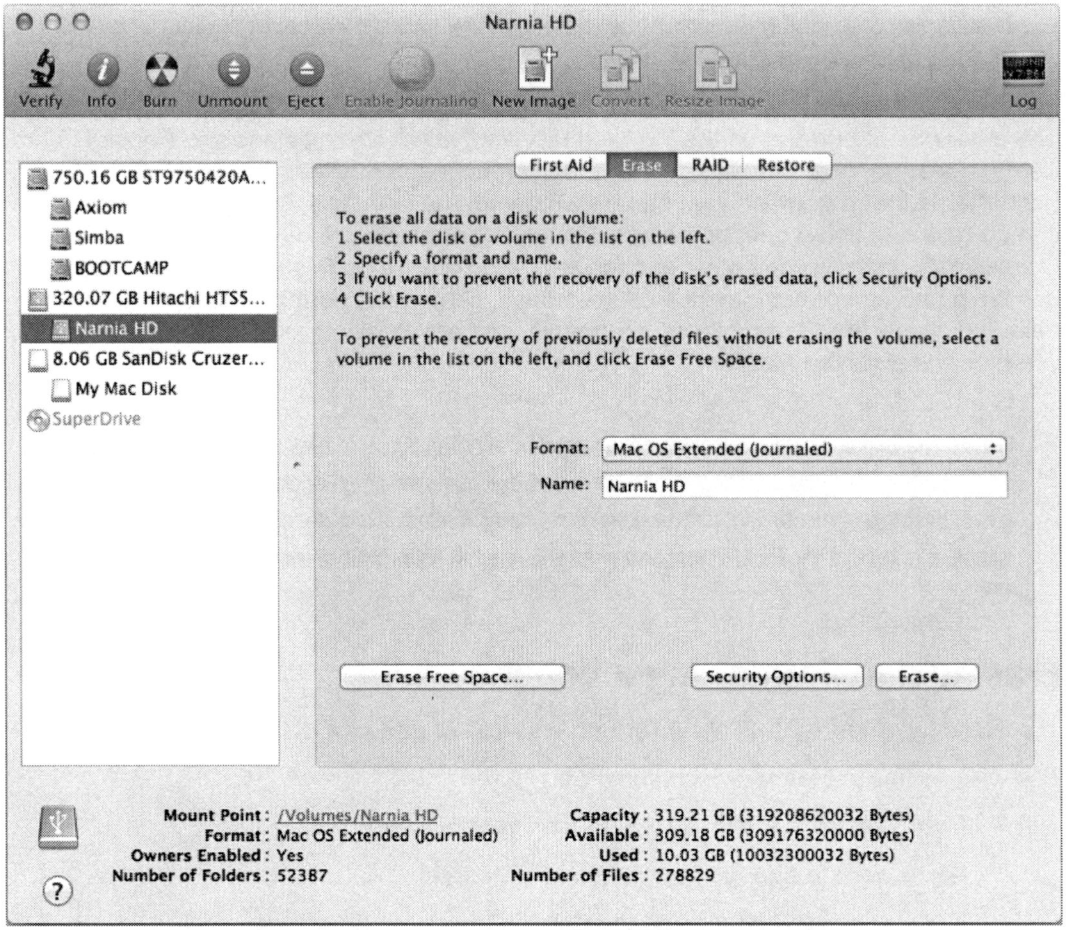

Figure 21–2. *The Disk Utility's Erase tab lets you erase and format disk volumes.*

NOTE: On a magnetic hard drive, even when you overwrite data, there may be magnetic remnants of old data that, using sophisticated data recovery tools, could be reassembled into the original data. Each time you pass over the disk, you tend to wipe out some of these remnants, so by writing over the drive multiple times, you ideally make the data more and more unrecoverable.

> **NOTE:** Researchers have pointed out that newer SSD hard drives provide different challenges. Not only is it more difficult securely wipe data from an SSD, but it's also more difficult to recover deleted data from an SSD. What this means is that zeroing out data may not actually zero out all data, while zeroed-out data is generally permanently gone.

Partitioning a Disk

Partitioning a disk is a similar process to formatting a volume; however, it allows you to create and format multiple volumes on the same disk at the same time. The Partition option (Figure 21–3) appears when you select a disk from the list at the left.

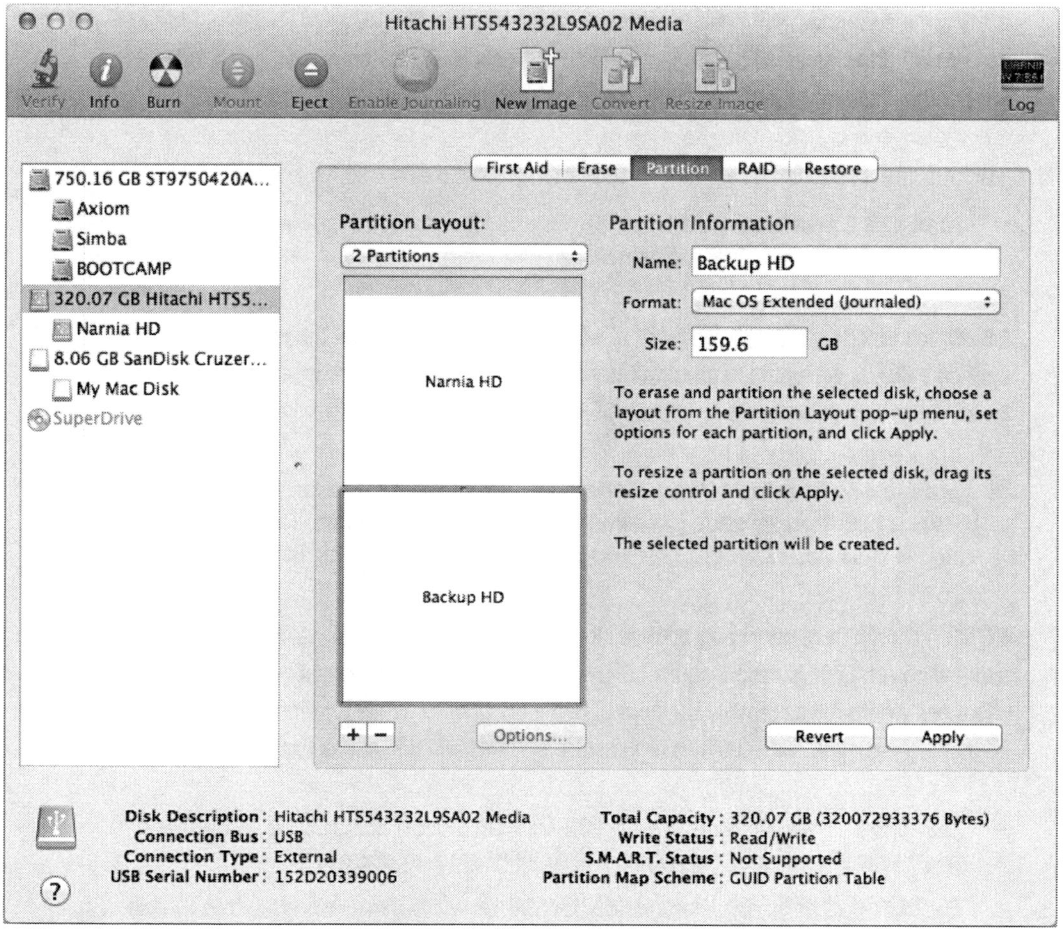

Figure 21–3. *The Partition tab allows you to create and format multiple volumes on a single disk.*

To partition a disk, first select the number of partitions you'd like to create on the disk from the Volume Scheme drop-down list. This will split the disk into the chosen number of partitions, each with approximately an equal size. To resize partitions, simply drag the separator between two partitions in the visual disk partition view below the Volume Scheme menu, thus shrinking one while increasing the size of the other. Alternately, you can select a partition and enter a size in the Size text field to the right (this will also change the size of surrounding partitions). When you have your partition sizes correct, you may enter a volume name in the Name field and choose a file system from the Volume Format list. If you are sure you are ready, click the Apply button, and your selected partitions will be created and formatted as you selected.

> **NOTE:** The file system you choose to install on a partition determines some of the types and capabilities of the systems that can be run on them. This is especially true when it comes to booting the computer. For example, through fancy software like VMware Fusion or Parallels, you can run Windows on an HFS partition, but you can only boot your computer into Windows (via Boot Camp) from an MS-DOS or NTFS formatted partition.

The various file systems available in the format fields are the following:

- **Mac OS Extended (Journaled)**: This is Mac OS X's current default file system (HFSJ or HFS+ Journaled).

> **NOTE:** Journaled partitions keep track of what the disk is doing at all times. In the event that data on a disk is corrupted, a journaled partition may be able to piece together what was going on when the failure occurred so you don't lose any data.

- **Mac OS Extended (Case-Sensitive, Journaled)**: This is the same as HFSJ, but it adds case sensitivity to the file system (so, for example, *Apple* and *apple* would be recognized differently in the file system).

> **NOTE:** Although case sensitivity sounds like a good thing, it's not always. It can make certain applications and computer functions behave poorly and therefore should be used only in situations where it's essential. The normal HFS+ file system, while it ignores case, preserves it so that any data you share with case-sensitive systems will behave as expected.

- **MS-DOS**: This will use the FAT32 format, which is useful if you intend to physically share the volume with Windows systems.
- **ExFAT**: ExFat is another option for Windows partitions. Use this if size of the disk exceeds 32GB.
- **Free Space**: This will leave the partition empty and unusable until you reformat it later.

Resizing Partitions

One other feature that Disk Utility recently added is the ability to resize partitions. To shrink an existing partition, grab the lower-right corner of the partition in the Partition pane of the Disk Utility, and drag it to the new desired size (or use the Size text field to enter the new size). When you click Apply, the partition will be resized, creating empty space on the drive for a new partition or for expanding an existing one. To increase the size of a partition, you can use the same technique, but instead of making the existing partition smaller, you can grow it into adjacent empty space.

While doing this, keep the following in mind:

- You can shrink only a partition's unused space, so if you have 2GB of data on a 3GB partition, you'll be able to reclaim (at most) 1GB of disk space.

- You can grow a partition only into empty disk space that is physically adjacent to the partition you want to grow.

- This isn't magic, and it won't create new space that didn't exist. Often the only way to effectively repartition a disk is to erase the existing ones. Still, in some situations, this is exactly what you need.

Using RAID

The RAID tab (Figure 21–4) allows you to configure multiple hard drives into a single volume (or RAID set name).

Disk Utility allows you to create three different types of RAID configurations:

- **Mirrored RAID set (a.k.a. RAID 1)**: This will configure two hard drives of the exact same size in a mirrored array. This means that any data you store on the resulting volume will be physically stored separately on each drive, thus assuring that the data will be safe in the event that one of the drives fails.

- **Striped RAID set (a.k.a. RAID 0)**: This option will take two hard drives of the exact same size and combine them into one larger volume (equal to the size of both of them together). It will do this in such a way that alternating data is fed to each physical drive (i.e., *striping)*, thus greatly increasing overall disk read and write speeds. This is very popular with people who work with large amounts of data and large media files. On the downside, if either drive fails, it will be difficult to recover any data from either drive.

- **Concatenated disk set**: This will take any number of hard drives and combine them into a single volume spanning all the drives.

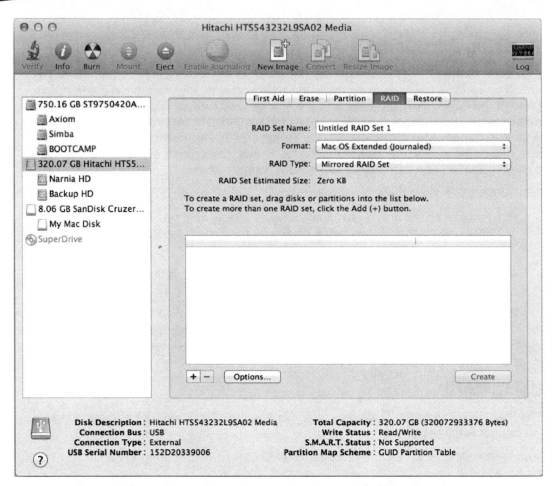

Figure 21–4. *The RAID tab allows you to combine multiple hard drives into a single volume.*

Besides these options, there are many other types of RAID configurations that are possible using third-party software or hardware. Many external drive enclosures that support multiple drives include hardware that makes different types of RAID configurations much more efficient.

NOTE: The RAIDs created in Disk Utility are *software* RAIDs. In this case, Mac OS X does the work in the background to accomplish the desired effect. Although this is highly effective, it's not as effective as a *hardware-based* RAID where the device in question has dedicated resources to create and manage the RAID.

Hardware-based RAIDs, though they are physically separate volumes, will many times appear as a single volume even in Disk Utility. Most software-based RAIDs, on the other hand, will show up as different devices in Disk Utility, even though they will appear as a single volume in the Finder.

Creating and Restoring Disk Images

A popular way of transmitting large files or applications from one computer to another, especially over a network, is to create a disk image. A disk image is essentially an archive of a disk volume that can be mounted like a disk. You can create a disk image using the Disk Utility application in a number of ways.

If you know you want to create a disk image of a certain size, you can click the New Image button on Disk Utility's toolbar (or select **File > New > Blank Disk Image...** from the menu bar or use the Option-Command-N shortcut). This will open a dialog box that allows you to name the image file, name the volume that the image file will expand into, and choose the size of the volume. Once you've filled out the information in the dialog box, click Create, and the system will create and mount the image. At this point, the image is writable, so you can copy any data you want to this image. When you unmount the disk, the data is still stored in the image file, so when you remount it, it will be available.

Another way to create a disk image is from an existing folder. To create an image this way, use the **File > New > Disk Image From Folder...** command from the menu bar (Shift-Command-N). This will open a dialog for you to select a folder. Once you select the desired folder, click the Image button, and a new dialog box will pop up asking you where to save the new image along with some other options.

> **NOTE:** If you select one of the encryption methods for your disk image, you will be prompted to create a password to decrypt the image before it is created. You will be prompted for this password before you can mount or restore this image file. If you forget it, your data will be lost.

> **TIP:** If you work with sensitive data, you can create a secure disk image containing this data and mount the disk when you need to work with the data. Then you can unmount the image when you are done with it, returning the data into a state of blissful encryption.

Clicking an image file will mount it to your desktop (you may need to enter the password for an encrypted image file first). Occasionally you may want to restore an image file to a disk or a partition. The Restore tab (Figure 21–5) allows you to re-create the image file onto a disk volume simply by selecting a disk image (as the source), selecting an available volume that the image will fit in (as the destination), and then clicking the Restore button. You should be aware that this will overwrite the destination volume entirely.

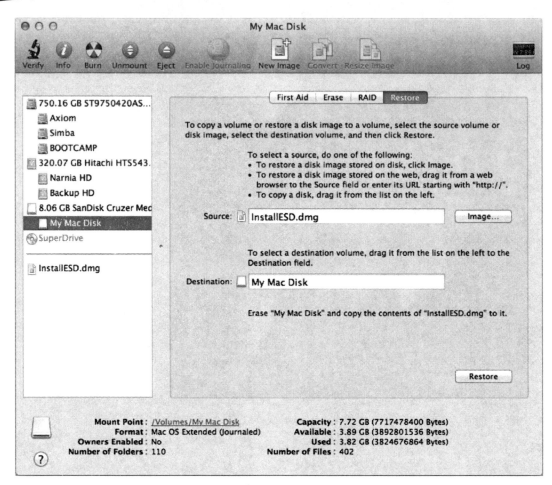

Figure 21–5. *The Restore tab allows you to restore a disk image to a disk volume.*

Burning an Image File to a CD or DVD

Certain disk images are actually images of CDs or DVDs, and as such, they (or any other appropriately sized image file) can, rather than be restored to a disk volume, be burned to a CD or DVD. To accomplish this, select Images > Burn... from the Disk Utility menu (or use the Command-B keyboard shortcut). This will first prompt you to select the appropriate image file from the standard open dialog, and then it will prompt you to insert the appropriate writable disk into your disk burner. It will then burn the image to disk.

Managing Fonts

Fonts may not seem like things that need to be managed too much, and in OS X, fonts don't tend to cause many of the issues that have been attributed to them in the past. Still, if you tend to accumulate lots of fonts, you may want to manage them for a number of reasons:

■ To be able to find the exact type of font you are looking for quickly and easily from a large list of installed fonts

■ To "turn off" unused fonts, since many applications (especially graphics apps and word processors) load all active fonts into memory when they launch (slowing up launch time and consuming memory)

Mac OS X, beginning with Panther, included an application named Font Book that helps you manage your fonts. Font Book (Figure 21–6) provides the ability to find, preview, organize, and switch on or off all the fonts installed on your system.

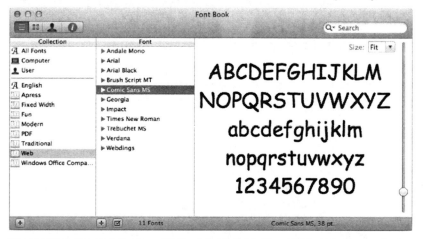

Figure 21–6. *The Font Book application is included in Mac OS X to help manage fonts on your system.*

The Font Book application is organized with two columns and a preview window. The first column, Collection, allows you to select and create sets, or *collections*, of fonts. The set you select in this column determines the specific font families that are displayed in the Font column. Selecting a font family or specific font from within a family will display that font in the view window.

> **TIP:** Font Book has the ability to identify and resolve duplicate copies of the identical font files that may be stored in different locations. (This commonly happens when applications, especially word processors and graphics apps, install font files that are already present.) To discover duplicate fonts, you may run **Edit > Look for Duplicates...** (Command-L) from the menu. If duplicates are discovered, you will be presented with options for dealing with them.

You can manage your fonts here:

- To create your own collection, click the + button at the bottom of the Collection column, and give your collection a name. Then you can drag fonts displayed in the Font column into your new collection. When you select your set, only the fonts you added to it will appear in the Font column.

- To add a new font, click the + button at the bottom of the Font column, and select the font file(s) to add.

- To deactivate a font or collection of fonts, right-click the font or collection, and select the Disable option from the contextual menu. Alternately, you can select fonts in the Font column and toggle them with the small check box button at the bottom of the column. When you deactivate a font collection, it will deactivate any fonts in that collection that are not present in any other activated collection. This prevents fonts from an active collection from becoming inadvertently disabled.

- Fonts may be reactivated in the same manner.

One nice thing about creating groups of fonts, beyond the ability to activate and deactivate entire groups easily, is that the groups appear in the standard Cocoa font selection dialog box (Figure 21–7), making it easy to find specific fonts that exist within a particular collection.

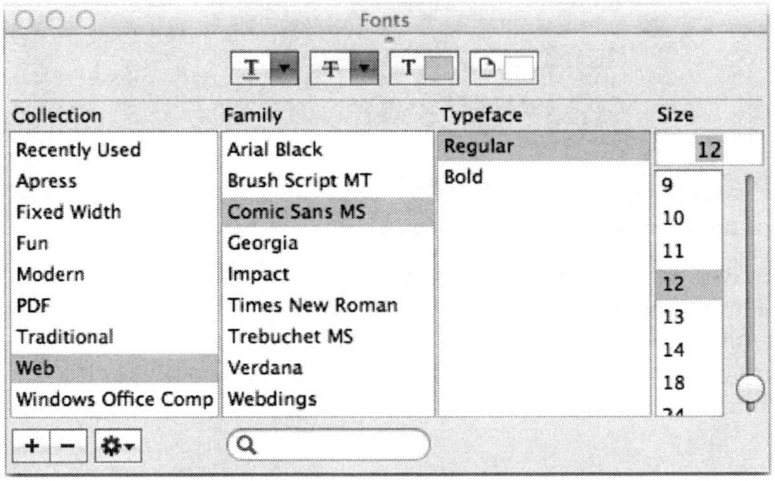

Figure 21–7. *Font collections appear in the standard font selection dialog box, making finding a particular font easy.*

NOTE: In Lion, Font Book provides **File > Restore Standard Fonts...** from the menu, which will reset the fonts on your computer to their original state. Running this command will reinstall any missing systems fonts while at the same time deleting any nonsystem fonts, thus restoring you font collections to Lion's default.

Summary

This chapter has covered a few basic housecleaning tasks that you are likely encounter at some point. The next chapter will focus one last general admin concern that, although last, may be one of the most important: security.

## Chapter 22

Mac OS X Security

Besides protecting your data from hardware failure and accidents, in today's world, where computers tend to be always connected, it's also important to protect your data from other users—both on your computer and outside of it. This chapter deals with security, including the following topics:

- Passwords and keychains
- Data encryption and FileVault
- Other security features

Passwords and Keychains

Passwords are used time and time again on your computer: logging in to your account, checking your e-mail, visiting certain web sites, logging in to connected servers, and more. You probably have so many passwords that it becomes a chore to keep track of them all. To help manage all your passwords, security certificates, and encryption keys, OS X includes a keychain feature to keep track of all this information.

The Keychain Feature

Whenever you enter a password into an application that takes advantage of the OS X keychain, you will be asked whether you want to save the username-password combination in your keychain. If you select yes, then the next time you log in, rather than getting a prompt to enter your username and password, the application will automatically use what's already saved in your keychain. Now, your keychain will use the passwords stored in it only under certain circumstances:

- The keychain will use data saved in the logged-in user's keychain only, so your keychain is protected from all other users (excepting shared keychains).

■ By default, passwords associated with a particular application allow only that application to access the password item in your keychain. Often when you update your application and attempt to use it, you will be prompted to update the key to work with the updated application (you will need to authorize the update).

■ The key in the keychain is valid and unexpired. Although this usually isn't a big problem for passwords, security certificates and encryption keys (which are also stored in the keychain) are generally set to expire after a certain amount of time.

The keychain data itself is stored in a number of keychain files located in various Library folders. For example, the System Roots keychain files (mostly security certificates for common root certificate authorities) are stored in /System/Library/Keychains, and the actual System Keychain (which stores common system level passwords and certificates) is stored in the /Library/Keychains folder. The login keychain, the keychain file of most interest to you as a user, is stored in your ~/Library/Keychains folder. It's in your personal keychain file that all of your sensitive data is stored in (safely encrypted from prying eyes). Should you ever need to view your keychain (or other keychains you have access to), Mac OS X includes the Keychain Access utility (in Launchpad's Utilities folder). The Keychain Access utility (Figure 22–1) provides a way for you to view, edit, and configure individual entries stored in your keychain.

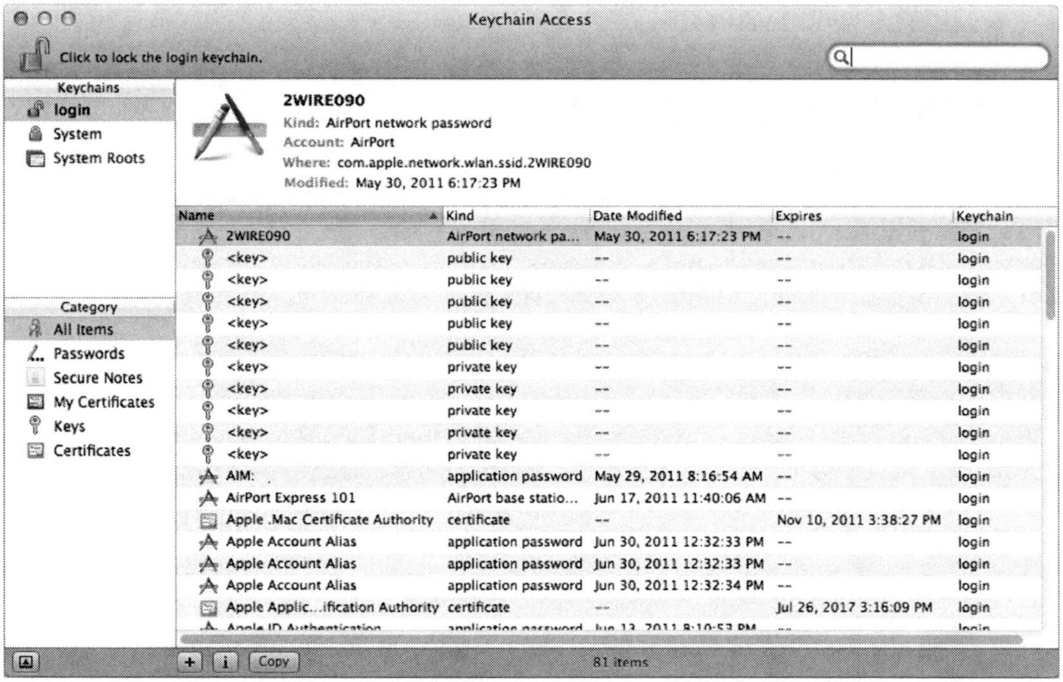

Figure 22–1. *The Keychain Access utility provides a way to view and alter your keychain items.*

The Keychain Access utility provides a column on the left where you can select the keychain you'd like to view (any available keychains will be listed there; your default keychain is the login keychain). Below the list of keychains is a list of categories of items that are stored in the keychain. Table 22–1 describes the categories and their descriptions. On the right side is the view area, where, at the bottom, the individual items stored in the keychain are listed. Above that is a view that provides some basic information about the selected item.

Table 22–1. *Categories of Items Stored in Your Keychain*

Category	Description
Passwords	These are your passwords, of which there are several kinds:
	▪ AppleShare: These are your passwords associated with file servers and other people's computers
	▪ Application: These passwords are associated with specific applications. They can be used for just about anything, including Internet sites, but rather than being associated with the site, they are associated with the application.
	▪ Internet: These are your Internet passwords, which include mail accounts and other Internet server credentials.
	▪ Web form: These are passwords and form data associated with web sites.
Certificates	Certificates provide a method of verifying a site, organization, or person's credentials, certifying that a service on the Internet (or network) is who it says it is. This is based on a method of trust: there are a number of certificate authorities who issue certificates—assuming you trust the authority, then you can trust all the certificates issued by that authority. A number of certificates from reputable issuing authorities are included with Lion (these are viewable from the System Roots keychain). Occasionally you may be prompted by a web site to approve a new certificate, which is of course at your discretion. If the certificate checks out, it will be categorized here.
My Certificates	The My Certificates category also stores certificates, but rather than certificates that verify others to you, these certificates verify you to others. Using certificates to verify you are who you say you are is becoming more common, especially in situations where data integrity is essential. These sorts of certificates can be used in lieu of a password or, more often, used in conjunction with a password. (If someone walks up to your computer, the certificate is available, but they may not know your password; on the other hand, if someone has your password, then they need physical access to your computer [or certificate] to do anything with it.)

Category	Description
Keys	Keys are used for encryption and digital signatures. In general, many forms of encryption use keys, but the essential idea is that communication on one end of the network uses one key to encrypt data that only a specific (and different) key on the other end of the network can decrypt. This is important because most bits of information passing through the Internet or a network can usually be viewed by many other computers and systems in between.
Secure Notes	Secure notes are different from most of the other items stored in your keychain, in that they are generally not used outside the keychain. Rather, they just provide a way for you to store confidential notes in your keychain. The information here could contain credit card information or any other personal information to which you decide to limit access.

> **NOTE:** Cryptography and encryption are very big, complicated topics. A great book that does a good job of introducing them, including keys and certificates, is *Cryptography Decrypted by* H. X. Mel and Doris Baker (Addison-Wesley Professional, 2000).

Double-clicking any of the items in your keychain will open a window providing detailed information about that item. For items such as passwords and secure notes, some details will be hidden, specifically the password and the actual content of the note.

The password items have a number of options spread out over two tabs: the Attributes tab and the Access Control tab.

The Attributes tab (Figure 22–2) provides the following information:

- **Name**: This is just the name of the keychain item.

- **Kind**: This indicates the type of information stored in the item.

- **Account**: This is the name associated with the account. Usually this field contains the username, but occasionally, especially for application passwords, it is used to represent something used similarly by the application.

- **Where**: This identifies where the password is valid; this is commonly a URI pointing to the online resource for which the item is valid, but occasionally it is something else (a protocol, for example, or just something that has meaning to an application).

- **Comments**: This field contains any comments associated with the item.

■ **Show password**: This is where the password is shown. However, by default it is empty to protect the password. To view the password, you will need to select the "Show password" option and then authenticate yourself. The key icon to the right of the password text field opens the Password Assistant, which can help you create strong passwords.

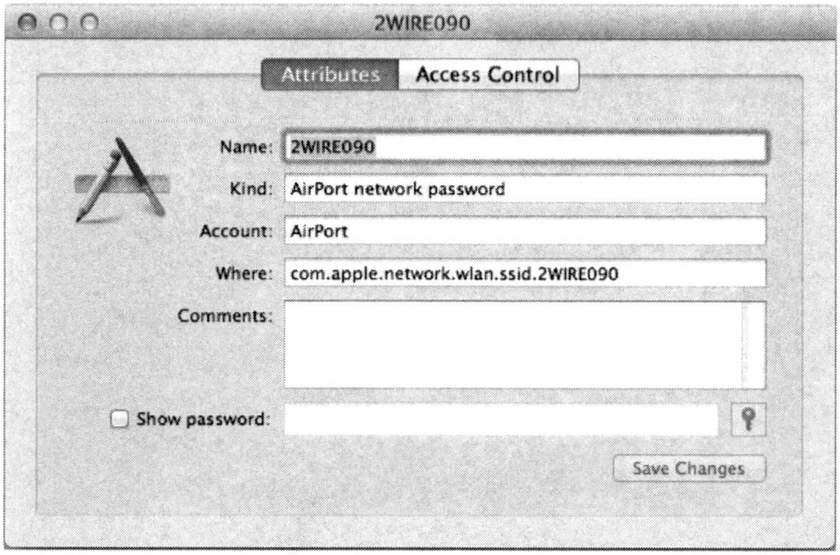

Figure 22–2. *The Attributes tab of a password keychain item*

NOTE: All the fields in the Attributes tab are editable. If you are storing items here for your own reference, you can certainly edit these—however, if the item is being used by an application, altering this information may interfere with the normal operation of the application.

The Access Control tab (Figure 22–3) allows you to delegate what applications can access the keychain item and whether you'll be prompted to approve any new application that wants to use the information.

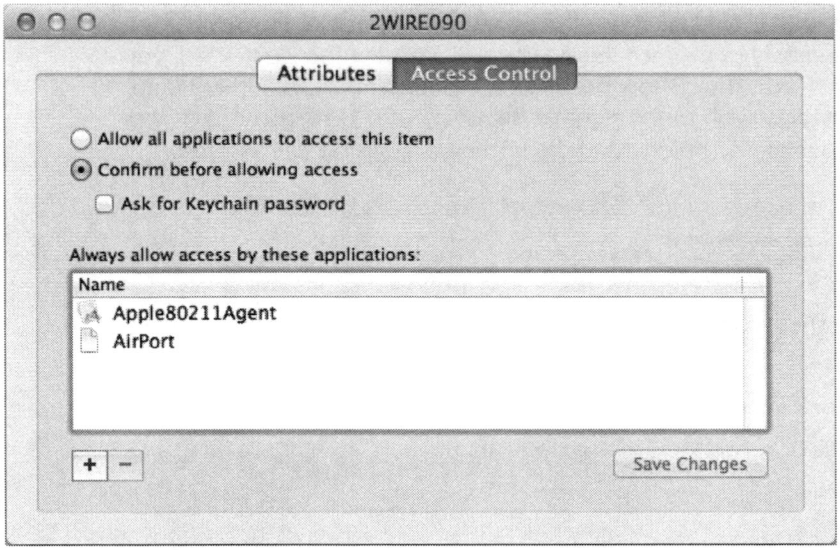

Figure 22–3. *The Access Control tab controls how the information in the item can be accessed.*

Creating Your Own Keychains and Keychain Items

While the keychain feature is designed to mostly run in the background to seamlessly manage passwords, keys, and certificates, it will also allow you to store your own information inside of it. You could store your own passwords and notes and even keep track of serial numbers for registered applications by creating secure notes.

> **NOTE:** Besides using the keychain, you can securely store password and application data using solutions provided by third parties. Some interesting applications include the $39.99 1Password (http://agilebits.com/products/1Password), which not only stores passwords and other encrypted information but also integrates with your web browsers to make using strong web passwords a snap (it even has a version for your iPhone, which allows you to keep your password data in sync and at your fingertips when you are away from your computer) and the donationware Pastor (www.mehlau.net/pastor/), which is a lightweight, easy-to-use password storage application.

To add a keychain item, you click the little + button at the bottom of the keychain window, and a dialog box will open so you can enter your information. By default, the dialog box will be geared toward passwords. If you want to create a note, select the Note group in the left column, and then click the + button. This will open a dialog box for entering your note. Alternately, you can select **File > New Password Item…** or **File > New Secure Note Item…** directly from the menu bar.

The password dialog box (Figure 22–4) is fairly straightforward; you enter a name for your item, the account name, and your password. There are some interesting points here, though. For one, the keychain item name determines what the type of item will be. If you enter a URL, the item will be created as an Internet password; otherwise, the item will be created as an application password. Finally, the bar at the bottom will extend to the right and change from red to green as you enter your password to indicate its strength.

Keychain Item Name:

Enter a name for this keychain item. If you are adding an Internet password item, enter its URL (for example: http://www.apple.com)

Account Name:

Enter the account name associated with this keychain item.

Password:

Enter the password to be stored in the keychain.

Password Strength: Weak

☐ Show Typing

Cancel   Add

Figure 22–4. *The password dialog box allows you to enter a password into a new keychain item.*

The strength of a password is determined by how hard it would be for a malicious user to crack it using various methods. This determination consists of many variables, including the length of the password, the uniqueness, and the type of characters used. Common names and words found in dictionaries are very weak, because a modern computer can run through a dictionary list of common words and passwords in a few minutes. Beyond that, short passwords take a relatively short amount of time to crack using brute-force methods (which basically means using every possible combination of every letter, number, and symbol for each space). The difficulty of brute-force cracking increases dramatically with each additional character. It's good practice to attempt to mix uppercase and lowercase letters, numbers, and, if possible, symbols, into your passwords. Additionally, passwords should be at least nine characters long.

> **NOTE:** Apple's Password Assistant (Figure 22–5) can help you craft secure, unique passwords based on various criteria. This utility will present itself as a dialog box when you click the key icon next to many password text fields in Mac OS X.

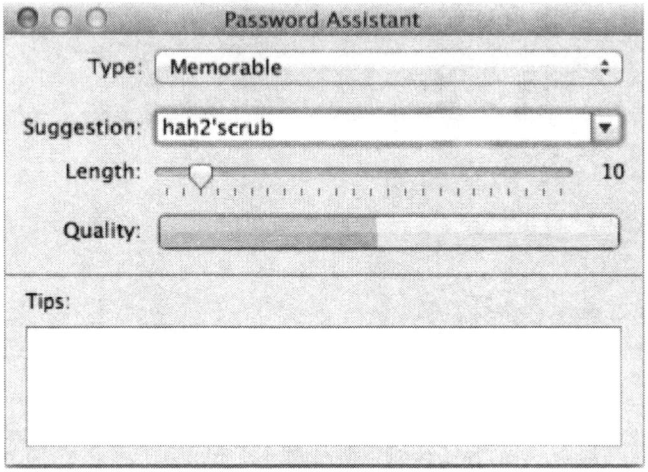

Figure 22–5. *The Password Assistant is available in many places throughout Mac OS X to help you create secure, unique passwords.*

> **NOTE:** Ten years ago, an eight-character password was considered strong. Today, that would be the minimum acceptable in most situations. As computing power increases, passwords become increasingly less effective, since as password lengths increase, it becomes increasingly hard to remember them and therefore less practical. For this reason, a number of password alternatives have been developed and are gaining in popularity. These alternatives may be used to complement a password system or eliminate passwords altogether. These alternatives include smart cards and other hardware authentication devices, as well as biometric security measures (such as fingerprint readers).

Besides storing passwords and security certificates, you can also securely store notes containing any information you choose in your keychains. If you select Secure Notes under the Category pane and click the + button, a dialog box will open asking for a name for your note item and showing a large text field for the contents of your notes.

If you intend to store lots of personal information in a keychain, you may want to create a keychain separate from your login keychain to store information; you can easily do this by selecting **File > New Keychain...** from the Keychain Access menu.

Other Keychain Options

A few other features associated with keychains are available from the Keychain Access utility. These are described in the following sections.

Keychain Passwords

By default, your keychain password (the password you will need to unlock data such as passwords and notes in your keychain) is the same as your login password. You can change this password for each keychain using the **Edit > Change Password for Keychain "***keychain***"...** command.

> **CAUTION:** When your keychain password is the same as your login password, your keychain is automatically unlocked when you log in. That means if you step away from your computer while you are logged in, someone could walk up and view your keychain contents fairly easily.

Keychain Settings

The **Edit > Change Settings for Keychain "***keychain***"...** menu item allows you to access some additional options for a particular keychain. These include the ability to lock your keychain after a certain amount of time or when your computer goes to sleep (you will need to enter your keychain password each time you or an application attempts to access a locked keychain).

Keychain First Aid

If your keychain gets mucked up to the point that it no longer functions correctly (for example, because of data or file corruption), the Keychain First Aid selection under the Keychain Access application menu can help solve a number of problems. Depending on what options are set on the First Aid tab in the Keychain Access utility's preferences, running Keychain First Aid will rebuild your keychain file and reset most settings to the defaults, including setting the keychain passwords back to the login password and setting the login keychain back to the default keychain.

Data Encryption with the FileVault

The keychain feature protects your passwords while keeping them easily accessible, and FileVault protects your data from others. FileVault, accessible from the FileVault tab in the Security preference pane (Figure 22–6), encrypts the contents of your disk, protecting it from anyone who attempts to access anything stored there when you're not logged in.

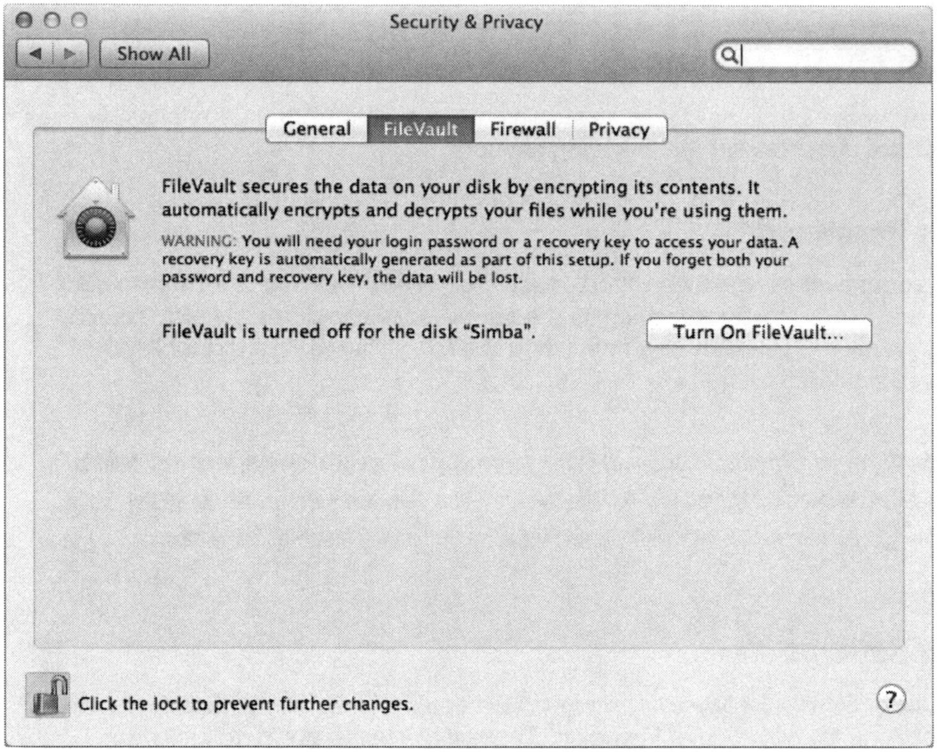

Figure 22–6. *The FileVault tab of the Security preference pane lets you turn FileVault on and off.*

When you first activate FileVault, you will be presented with a recovery key (Figure 22–7). Once FileVault is activated, the only way to access your information is by entering your password or using this recovery key. If both of these are lost and forgotten, then you data will be unrecoverable.

The recovery key is a "safety net" which can be used to unlock the disk if you forget your password.

Make a copy and store it in a safe place. If you forget your password and lose the recovery key, all the data on your disk will be lost.

KV6L-CFHT-JEYT-UYKV-ENJG-5QA4

(?)   Cancel   Back   Continue

Figure 22–7. *If you forget you password, you will need your recovery key to access your encrypted information.*

Once the security key is presented, you will be given the option to let Apple store your security key (Figure 22–8). If you choose this option, you will be prompted to enter three questions. To recover your key from Apple, the question must be answered exactly. The final step in setting up FileVault will prompt you to restart your computer and begin the encryption process.

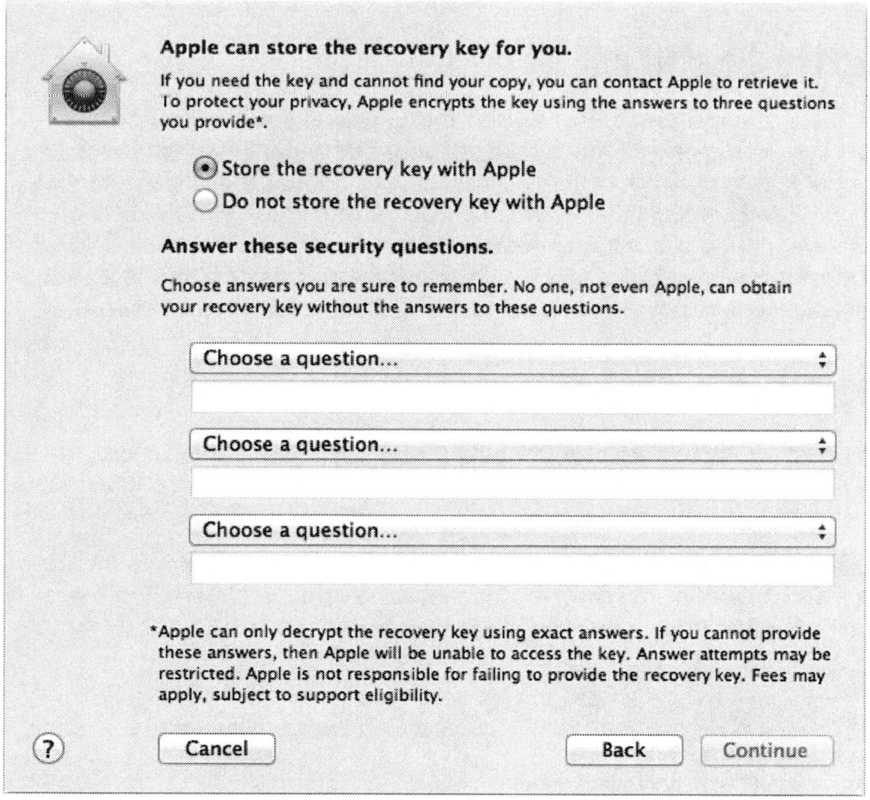

Figure 22–8. *If you'd like, you can store a copy of your recovery key on Apple servers. The key will be released only if you can answer your three security questions exactly.*

Once FileVault is set up, using your Mac will be pretty much the same, because your disk data will be decrypted as needed.

FILEVAULT CONSIDERATIONS: THE GOOD AND THE BAD

Besides what's already been mentioned, there are some serious considerations you should think about when deciding to use FileVault:

- Although, in general, passwords are required to access a user's data on a running system, there are ways to work around this, such as booting the computer in Target Disk mode. When using FileVault, your data is still encrypted, so even though someone may have access to it, they can't easily do anything with it.

- If you use FileVault, you should also keep in mind that any backups should be encrypted as well. It doesn't do any good to protect your information on your computer if your backups aren't equally protected.

If you should change your mind, you can turn off FileVault by repeating the same steps used in turning it on.

Other Security Features

In very general terms, computer security is divided into physical security and network security. Physical security represents the security of your computer when someone is sitting right in front of it, and network security protects your computer from a potential threat that could be halfway around the world. The trouble with these simple distinctions is that these days they tend to blur a bit, especially with multiuser systems like OS X. For example, remote desktop technologies (such as Apple Remote Desktop and VNC) allow many users to essentially have physical access to the system, even over a network.

The Security & Privacy Preferences

Many of the common security features for protecting Mac OS X are in the Security & Privacy System Preferences pane. The Security & Privacy preference pane contains four tabs: General, FileVault, Firewall, and Privacy.

The general security options (Figure 22–9) cover a wide range of options normally associated with physical security. Table 22–2 describes the options covered on the General tab of the Security & Privacy preference pane.

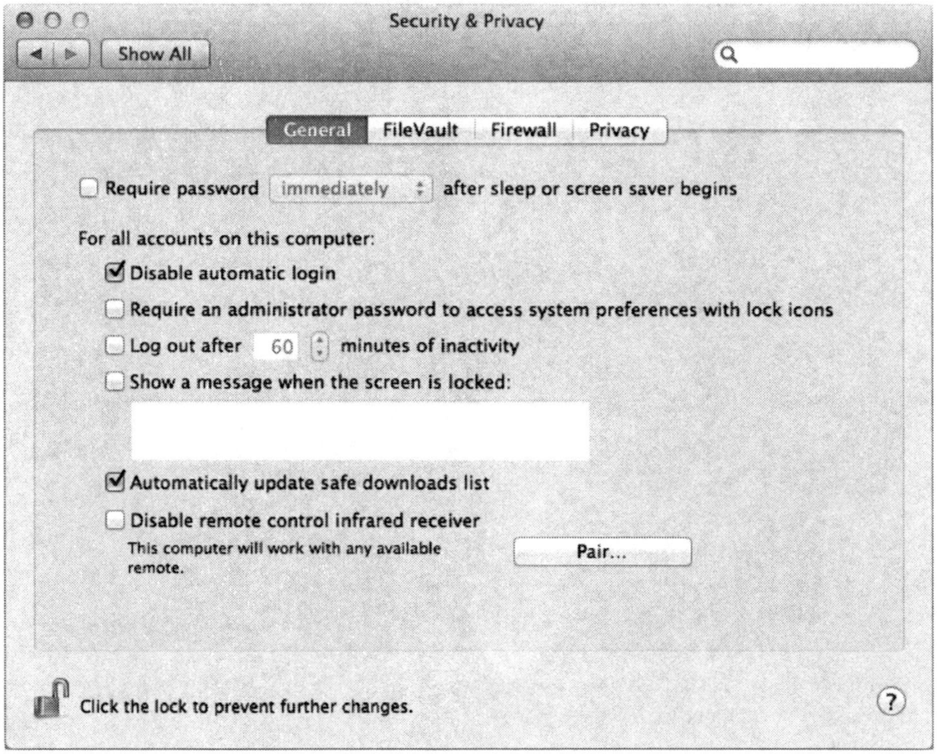

Figure 22–9. *The general security options in the Security preference pane*

Table 22-2. *General Security Options*

Option	Description
Require password X after sleep or screen saver begins	This option will prompt for a password when the computer is awoken from a period of inactivity. This protects your system if you step away for a bit, leaving your computer on but unattended.
Disable automatic login	This option requires a user to log in when the system is turned on.
Require an administrator password to access system preferences with lock icons	This will require an administrative password whenever someone attempts to adjust any system preferences (specifically the Mac OS X preferences listed under the System heading in System Preferences).
Logout after X minutes of inactivity	This will log out any user who is inactive for a certain period of time.
Show a message when the screen is locked	This will show the entered text message on the screen when the screen is locked.
Automatically update safe download list	Allows the list of file types that Apple considers safe to be updated.
Disable remote control infrared receiver	If your system includes an infrared receiver, this option will disable this functionality. Additionally, the Pair button will allow you to set up your system to work with a specified (paired) remote control only.

The Firewall tab (Figure 22–10) allows you to enable or disable Mac OS X's built-in firewall software. Mac OS X's firewall is a bit different than traditional firewalls that regulate access based on port numbers and protocols. In OS X, the firewall allows or denies access based on approved applications and services.

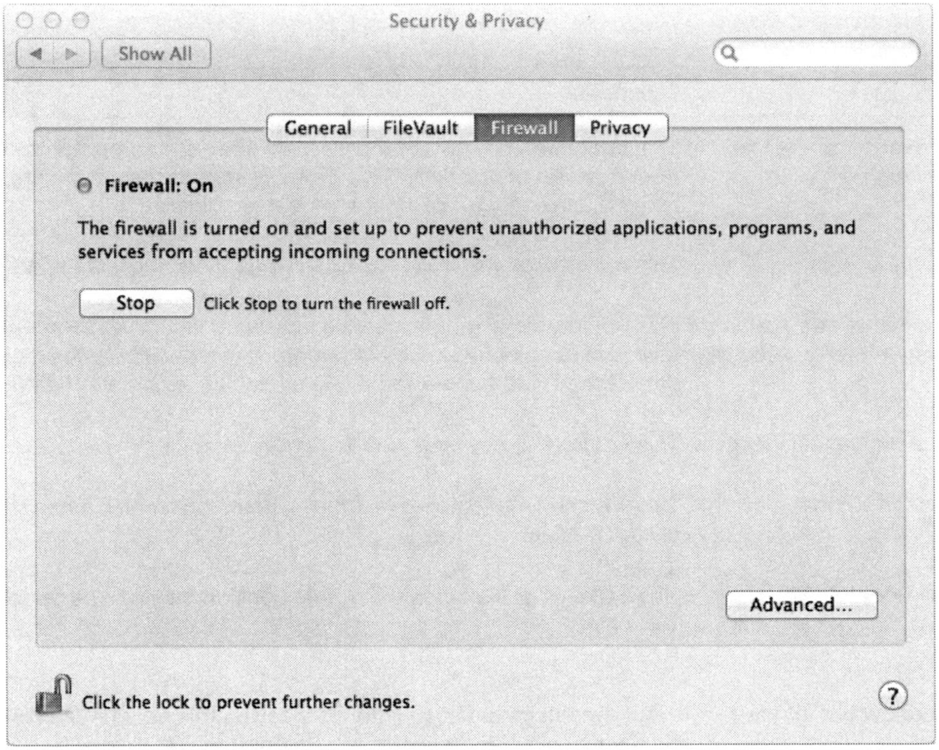

Figure 22–10. *The Firewall tab allows you to enable or disable the Mac OS X firewall.*

Clicking the Advanced... button will open a dialog (Figure 22–11) that allows you to control some additional options ranging from blocking all incoming network connection except those required for basic Internet services and to fine-tune or alter what services and applications can allow network connections.

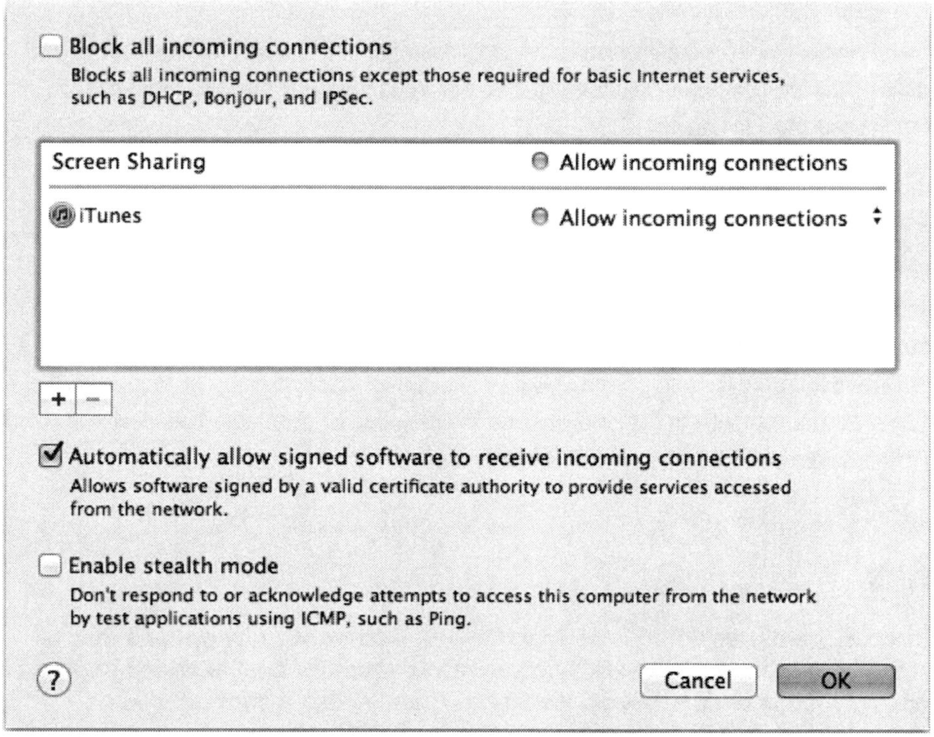

Figure 22–11. *The Advanced options allow you to fine-tune Mac OS X's firewall settings.*

By default basic Internet services, connections from signed software, and services that are enabled in the sharing preferences are allowed. All others are denied.

> **NOTE:** Lion ships with the firewall allowing all incoming and outgoing connections—however, all sharing services are turned off. This effectively eliminates most potential network security issues from the outside since no individual services are accepting any incoming communications. However, certain applications may open their own network ports and run services on them. Usually, if they're from a trusted source, you'll be OK; but if they're from an untrusted source, look out! Also, since no outgoing connections are being blocked, you should have no trouble using your web browser, e-mail, or other network-enabled applications unless you are on a network with its own dedicated firewall (and even most home cable and DSL routers have built-in firewalls these days). Again, caution should be used when using untrusted applications, since by default they would be free to transmit anything.

The final tab in the Security & Privacy preference pane deals with privacy. This allows you to select which applications (if any) are allowed to use Location services as well as select if you'd like diagnostic and usage information sent to Apple to help improve later versions of OS X.

> **NOTE:** When Location Services are enabled for an application, you are allowing that application to access the actual location of your computer. It does this using the same methods as Find My Mac (which I talked about in Chapter 14).

> **NOTE:** One other password option is setting a firmware password, which provides low-level system protection. To set a firmware password, you must boot up from the recovery partition and use the **Set Firmware Password Utility...** option. This will walk you through the process to set a password. Once a firmware password is set, it will be required for most special boot sequences, including booting your computer in Target Disk mode and selecting an alternative boot device at startup. For maximum protection this should be enabled.

Summary

Besides the security features noted here, Mac OS X has other security options that either lurk in the background to provide a secure environment or enable developers to implement security features into their applications. There is also a strong focus on network security that we will discuss more in Section VII of this book.

Mac OS X is built upon a naturally secure foundation and, coupled with a range of features, makes maintaining a secure system easy and without lots of the headaches and pain associated with security. This chapter covered mostly user-centric and basic system security, and later in the book we will cover network security in more detail. Additionally, we will continue to provide added security tips where applicable throughout the book.

The next part of the book will move on to additional advanced topics and look specifically at Darwin, OS X's Unix subsystem.

## Part VI

Introducing Darwin and the Mac OS X Command Line

Since the beginning of Mac OS X, a powerful Unix-based operating system has lurked beneath the wonderful, easy-to-use desktop and graphical elements. In a way, the graphical elements of OS X sit on top of the Unix environment referred to as Darwin.

In the next two chapters, you will get a quick introduction into the Darwin environment, the Unix shell, and the Terminal application so you can start to benefit from its vast abilities.

## Chapter 23

Introducing Darwin and the Mac OS X Command Line

Running behind the slick Mac OS X Aqua GUI is Darwin, the POSIX-compliant, UNIX-based environment that forms the foundation of Mac OS X. While the majority of Mac OS X users never find it necessary to use the command line, for those that are willing to learn there is whole new world of powerful computing awaiting.

In this chapter you will learn

- The basics of Darwin and the command line

- Common and useful command-line commands

- The power and pitfalls of working as root

- Editing files with Vim, Emacs, and Nano

- What file attributes are and how to change them

- Customizing your command-line environment

Darwin Basics

Included in Darwin is a collection of many powerful tools that are not only used by many functions of Mac OS X, but are also available for you to use. The most direct way to interact with Darwin and take full advantage of all these wonderfully powerful UNIX tools is through the use of the Terminal application (/Applications/Utilities/Terminal). When Terminal is launched, it opens up a terminal window running a shell program, as shown in Figure 23–1.

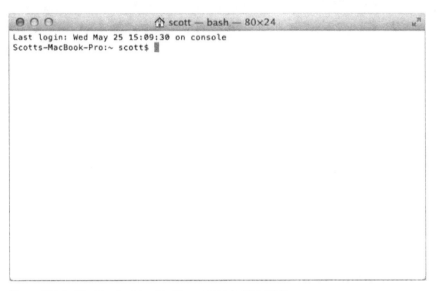

Figure 23–1. *The Terminal application running in Mac OS X*

Before we jump to far ahead of ourselves, though, there are a few things worth learning up front that will be helpful on your journey into the command line. The first thing you need to know when working with Darwin is some of the common language and terms used when talking about a command-line environment, in order to avoid confusion. Next, you need to know how files are organized; and finally, you need to know how to move around the file system.

> **NOTE:** When we talk about files here, we are not just talking about the last text file you created; Darwin treats everything as a file. For example, a directory (aka folder) is a file that contains other files. Each file has a number of properties that determine how the shell treats that specific file; if it's an application, the shell will launch it; if it's a directory, the shell will know that it can access other files contained in it. We'll cover file properties a bit later.

Darwin Semantics

To avoid confusion as the chapter proceeds, we should quickly go over some of the important terms used in Darwin and how they compare with terms used in the Finder. Table 23–1 defines a handful of terms used commonly in Darwin (and other UNIX systems), gives the Finder equivalent or alternate term, and adds any relevant notes. While there are many other terms you'll come across, these basics will be used repeatedly, so they are good to know.

Table 23-1. *Darwin Terms Explained*

Darwin Term	Finder or Alternate Term	Notes
File	File (and others)	Darwin treats all items, documents, directories, and applications as files; in the Finder, when we talk about a file, we are generally talking specifically about a document.
Directory	Folder	Folders are generally referred to as directories.
Root directory, or /	Top level of hard drive	Not to be confused with the root user, the root directory, which is represented by the / symbol, is the highest level of the Darwin file structure.
Root (user)	Administrator	In addition to the root directory, there is also a root user. The root user (also known as the *superuser*) has the ability to do just about anything in the Darwin environment, including irreparably destroying it. To maintain a secure system and avoid devastating problems, certain files require root privileges to read, write, and execute. While the administrator is the closest thing to root outside of Darwin, it's not quite the same, as root actually has more abilities.
Link (specifically a symbolic link)	Alias	A link in Darwin functions the same way as an alias does in the Finder (and appears as such when viewed in the Finder). While the function of a symbolic link and an alias behave similarly, it's worth knowing that they are implemented differently.
Alias	n/a	An alias in Darwin is a simple command set up in the shell that can trigger more complex commands or allow you to override the behavior of an existing command.
Directory path	Finder location	The directory path is a representation of where you are in the file system, beginning from the root directory. For example, if your username is scott, then the path to your home directory would be /Users/scott/ (your home directory can also be abbreviated to ~ , as you will see later). The leading / represents the root directory.
Executable command	Application or script	Any command that is issued at the command line and causes something to happen can be referred to as an executable.
Command arguments, arguments	n/a	Arguments are additional, sometimes necessary information added to commands. Arguments don't affect how the command is run in the way options do; instead, they generally target the command to affect specific items.

Darwin Term	Finder or Alternate Term	Notes
Command options or flags	Switches	Command options are special arguments (usually preceded by a - and immediately following the command) that can change how a command is run. This is similar to setting command preferences for a Cocoa application, but more flexible, as different preferences can be issued at runtime.
Process	n/a	A process is a running application or daemon (also known as a background process). In Mac OS X (and in fact most modern systems), there can be (and often are) hundreds of processes running at any one time.
Pipes	n/a	Pipes, represented by the | symbol, provide a way of stringing two or more commands together. Piping one command into another is a powerful way to accomplish some otherwise complex tasks. Pipes, along with redirection, are covered in more depth later in this chapter.

The File System

The Darwin file system shares the same folder structure found while navigating through the Finder. However, while navigating through Darwin, you will notice a few differences. First, there are quite a few more visible items in the Darwin view. Second, you will find that your additional volumes (added hard drives, CD/DVD drives, flash drives, etc.) are found a little differently.

The Darwin file system starts from root, which is symbolized by /. This is the highest level of the file system and is essentially the same as viewing your primary hard drive in the Finder. A quick look in our root directory reveals the following items (the trailing / and @ symbols that follow have special meaning and are only visible when you use them with the F flag: / indicates that the item is a directory [or folder], and @ indicates that the item is a link [or alias]):

```
Applications/    System/      cores/     mach_kernel    tmp@
Developer/       Users/       dev/       net/           usr/
Library/         Volumes/     etc@       private/       var@
Network/         bin/         home/      sbin/
```

As you can see, all the basic Finder folders—Applications, Library, System, Users, and Developer (provided you've installed the Xcode tools)—are there, along with a slew of other items. Some of these are merely system files that are of little interest to most people. Table 23–2 shows some common directory paths and describes what sorts of files are located in them.

Table 23–2. *Common Darwin Directories and Their Contents*

Directory Paths	Contents
/bin	The /bin directory contains the core user executables that are necessary for the OS to function normally.
/etc (/private/etc)	The /etc directory contains the primary configuration files for much of OS X and its services.
/sbin	The /sbin directory contains the core administrative executables necessary for the OS to function normally.
/tmp (/private/tmp)	The /tmp directory is where the OS and many services and applications store data that is only used briefly and then discarded.
/usr	The /usr directory is a metadirectory that contains a number of subdirectories. Historically, these directories have contained files that, while not necessary for the basic functioning of the system, are still often necessary for a system that functions the way one would expect it to. The truth is that these days, while the system would technically function without these files, most people would find this directory unusable.
/usr/X11 (/usr/X11R6)	X11 has historically been UNIX's primary graphical interface. While it's seldom used in Mac OS X, some people may have uses for specific applications that rely on it. For those needing to run X11-based applications, X11 is installed as part of Mac OS X.
/usr/bin	Like /bin, /usr/bin contains user-level command-line executables. Many of the most common commands you will use are found in this directory.
/usr/libexec	This directory contains a number of special executables. These include files that control tasks related to printing, networking, security, and the built-in web server.
/usr/local	This is yet another metadirectory. In the UNIX way of doing things, this is where one would install any add-ons to the system that didn't come with it by default. Many third-party additions will still install themselves here.
/usr/sbin	Like /sbin, this is a directory that contains administrative executables.

Introducing the Shell

The Terminal application (go ahead, fire it up) is essentially an empty window that can display and accept text input. In order for you to actually do anything, Terminal must run a shell program. Just as the Finder allows you to move around and interact with items in Mac OS X's GUI, the shell allows you to move around and interact with items on the command line. Bourne, Tcsh, and Zsh (the C shell is also listed as a shell—however, it is actually a link to Tcsh). Of the five, the shell Mac OS X uses by default is Bash.

> **NOTE:** Originally, Mac OS X used Tcsh by default, but switched to Bash with the release of OS X 10.3 Panther. If you are new to working with UNIX shells, I'd recommend sticking with Bash, at least while you are learning. The lessons in this book, unless specifically noted, are all given using the Bash shell.

The first time you launch Terminal, you'll be greeted by some text similar to this:

```
Last login: Wed May 25 15:09:30 on console
Simba:~ scott$
```

The first line tells you when you last logged into Darwin (even if you've never logged into Darwin before intentionally, you'll still get a message saying you did); the second line is the default prompt for Bash. The default prompt (which, like most everything else in Darwin, can be changed) gives you some important information. First, it gives you the name of your computer, which is either assigned by your network or taken from the Computer Name field in the system's Sharing preference pane. Next, following the :, the prompt gives you the name of your current directory in the file system (the ~ is a shortcut representing your home directory). Then the prompt gives you the username you are logged in as, followed by the $ prompt (which will change to a # if the user is logged in as the root user, otherwise known as the superuser). Finally, you get the cursor patiently awaiting your command.

As you will soon see, shells possess some hidden powers that can make your interactions with Darwin more pleasant and add a new level of power and flexibility to the command line. Before you look at the shell in more depth, though, you should first learn a bit about the Darwin file system, as well as a few basic Darwin commands.

Moving Around Darwin

One of the first things you need to learn about the shell is how to move around and view the file system. To do this, there are three basic commands to start with: ls, cd, and pwd.

ls

ls is the "list" command, and by default, lists all the visible files in a directory. If you're familiar with the Windows command line, it would be the replacement for dir. By default, the ls command looks something like this:

```
Simba:~ scott$ ls
Desktop         Downloads       Movies      Pictures
Documents       Library         Music       Public
```

The first thing you may notice is that by default all directories (folders), files, and executables (applications) look the same when using the ls command (of course, in this example, they all are directories). That's because, as we mentioned previously, Darwin treats everything as a file. To differentiate between the different types of files, there are two primary options:

- ls -F: Appends special files with a symbol to determine their type. It adds a / to directories, an * to executables, an @ to symbolic links (aliases), and a few other symbols for other special file types.

- ls -G: Colorizes the output using different colors for different file types as well as other file options. For example, by default most directories will appear blue; however, world-writable directories will appear black with a yellow background. Likewise, most executables will appear red, and most symbolic links will appear purple—however, if certain attributes are set, this will not always be the case.

> **NOTE:** One thing immediately noticeable to users moving to Darwin from Linux is that certain command-line commands are slightly different. For example, to colorize your output in Linux, one would traditionally use ls --color, and in some cases the output colors are different. This difference exists because UNIX comes in many different flavors, and occasionally there is slight deviation in commands from one to the other. For example, some UNIX tools are derived from the traditional BSD (Berkeley Software Distribution) camp, and they differ in some subtle ways from tools from the GNU camp. Linux almost always chooses its tools from the GNU camp, while Darwin tends to favor the BSD camp. While in general the tools will work the same, there are a few cases where there are minor differences—colorizing ls is one of those differences.

Like most command-line commands, the options can be combined. For example, you can use -F and -G together:

```
Simba:~ scott$ ls -FG
Desktop/    Downloads/ Movies/     Pictures/
Documents/ Library/    Music/      Public/
```

Other important ls options include the following:

- ls -l: Displays a long list that provides additional information about each file. We'll cover what everything here means later in the "File Permissions and Attributes" section of this chapter, but for now the results appear to be something like this:

```
Simba:~ scott$ ls -l
total 0
drwx------+  5 scott  staff    170 May 15 09:28 Desktop
drwx------+  8 scott  staff    272 May  6 15:13 Documents
drwx------+ 14 scott  staff    476 May 25 16:18 Downloads
drwx------@ 42 scott  staff   1428 May 15 18:29 Library
drwx------+  3 scott  staff    102 Apr 28 18:42 Movies
drwx------+  4 scott  staff    136 May  7 13:54 Music
drwx------+  5 scott  staff    170 Apr 30 13:53 Pictures
drwxr-xr-x+  5 scott  staff    170 Apr 28 18:42 Public
```

- ls -a **and** ls -A: Prints out a file listing that includes hidden dot files. There are two main types of files hidden on your computer: some that are hidden by default from the Finder but show up normally in Darwin, and others (the dot files) that are generally hidden in Darwin. These dot files (called that because they always begin with a .) are often preference or configuration files. They are usually hidden to reduce clutter, not for some nefarious purpose (although you may find that some Aqua applications utilize these hidden files to hide something they really don't want you to find). The main difference between ls -a and ls -A is that using ls -a will show two special files found in almost every directory—the . and the ..—which represent the current directory and the directory immediately above, respectively (these act the same as the . and .. files shown when issuing a dir command at the Microsoft Windows command prompt). A common ls -a on a home directory will produce quite a few more files than just a vanilla ls (three times as many or more is not uncommon):

```
Simba:~ scott$ ls -a
.                    .cups          Movies
..                   Desktop        Music
.CFUserTextEncoding  Documents      Pictures
.DS_Store            Downloads      Public
.Trash               Library
```

While there are significantly more options available for the ls command, those are the most common and should get you started on the right path. You may learn a few other options as you go along, and later you'll learn about the man command, which will allow you to learn more about the ls command (and most others) than you care to know.

Listing a Directory Other Than Your Current Directory

Besides ls's many options, ls will also accept a directory or file name as an argument. This allows you to view the contents of any directory without actually moving into that directory, or explore a single file's attributes (using the -l option). For example, if you're in your home directory but want to view the files in your Documents folder, your can do this by adding Documents as an argument—for example:

```
Simba:~ scott$ ls -F
Desktop/        Downloads/      Movies/         Pictures/
Documents/      Library/        Music/          Public/
Simba:~ scott$ ls -F Documents
About Stacks.lpdf/      Microsoft User Data/
Learn Lion              Snagit/
```

Furthermore, if you want to find out more about a specific file, you can enter a command like this:

```
Simba:~ scott$ ls -l Documents/Hello
-rw-r--r--  1 scott  staff  45 May 25 18:11 Documents/Hello
```

Now that you know how to list other directories, the next thing you may want to learn is how to move into them (virtually anyway).

cd

The cd command allows you to move from one directory to another (or as the command implies, it allows you to change directories). The cd command doesn't have any options, and it only accepts a path name as its single argument.

> **NOTE:** cd is kind of special in that, unlike ls, it is not an executable file—rather, it is a special type of command referred to as a *built-in command.* This command, along with a few others you will learn about, is a function of the shell and not traditionally a separate executable file. Although most common built-ins like cd exist in all common shells, it is possible that a built-in command in one shell will behave slightly differently from one in another (cd isn't one of these—it behaves the same way in every shell we've used over the past 20 or so years).

To issue the cd command, simply type cd followed by your destination, like so:

```
Simba:~ scott$ cd /
Simba:/ scott$
```

If no argument is given, then cd will take you back to your home directory:

```
Simba:/ scott$ cd
Simba:~ scott$
```

Finally, if cd doesn't recognize the argument as a file or directory, it will tell you so:

```
Simba:~ scott$ cd /blah
-bash:  cd:  /blah:  No such file or directory
Simba:~ scott$
```

This is an error statement, and most well-written functions and executables will provide some sort of error message if the information you provide doesn't make sense to them.

> **CAUTION:** Although well-written commands often give you an error message when you do something wrong, it's important to note that this only happens when the command has no idea how to parse the information you've given it. However, this will not prevent all erroneous commands from executing. If a command is recognized as valid, even if the information you enter isn't, the command will execute. While this is often harmless, it can have disastrous consequences (the rm command, as you will soon learn, deletes files immediately and permanently and can cause all sorts of badness if used poorly).

pwd

The final command in this section is the pwd command. The pwd command returns your current working directory, as this information is available by default in your prompt (after the :). You may not need to use this command too often—however, it is useful in illustrating the file structure of the system and can come in handy when you need to pass your current path into a script. Also, it's possible that you may find yourself stuck in a foreign shell on a foreign machine, where you may actually need this. The basic pwd command looks like this:

```
Simba:~ scott$ pwd
/Users/scott
```

In this case, pwd returns the absolute path of your home directory rather than the abbreviated ~ in the command prompt.

Being a rather simple command, pwd only offers two extra options:

- pwd -L: Prints the logical path to your working directory
- pwd -P: Prints out the physical path to your working directory, resolving any symbolic links

> **NOTE:** *Logical* paths and *physical* paths have to do with resolving symbolic links and aliases. For example, if you entered cd /etc and then entered pwd -L, the output would be /etc because that is where you are (logically); however, since /etc is a symbolic link, entering pwd -P would provide you with the actual physical location /private/etc.

Wildcards

Before moving on to more Darwin commands, we should have a quick lesson on wildcards and pattern matching. Wildcards are special symbols that, when used with other commands, can help limit or expand the results. Table 23–3 shows the three major wildcards and what they represent or match.

Table 23–3. *Darwin Wildcards*

Wildcard	Definition (Matches)
?	The ? used on the command line matches any single character.
*	The * matches any one or more characters in a file name.
[ ]	The [ ] matches any characters listed between the brackets; this can include a series of characters as well—for example, [1-p] would match *l*, *m*, *n*, *o*, and *p*.

To put this to use using what you learned previously, if you cd to /usr/bin and list out the contents using ls, you are struck with a rather large list of files (in this case, mostly executable commands). Wildcards allow you to selectively list out the directory contents in more manageable chunks. For example, if you just wanted to list the files that begin with *v*, you could use ls v*, like so:

```
Simba:bin scott$ ls v*
vacuumdb        vi              vimdiff         vm_stat
vers_string     view            vimtutor        vmmap
vgrind          vim             vis
```

If, for whatever reason, you wanted to expand the search to include *b* and *v*, you could use ls [bv]*:

```
Simba:bin scott$ ls [bv]*
banner          binhex          bzcmp           bzmore          vimtutor
base64          bison           bzdiff          vacuumdb        vis
basename        bitesize.d      bzegrep         vers_string     vm_stat
bashbug         bsdmake         bzfgrep         vgrind          vmmap
batch           bsdtar          bzgrep          vi
bc              bspatch         bzip2           view
bg              bunzip2         bzip2recover    vim
biff            bzcat           bzless          vimdiff
```

Note that like most things in Darwin, the characters used within the square brackets are case sensitive, so [bv] would not match any *B*s or *V*s.

Finally, if you wanted to list all files with two-letter names that begin with any letter in the alphabet from *b* to *v*, you could use ls [b-v]? and get the following:

```
Simba:bin scott$ ls [b-v]?
bc      cd      cu      ex      id      m4      nl      pl      rs      ul
bg      ci      dc      fc      ld      md      nm      pr      su      vi
cc      co      du      fg      lp      nc      od      ri      tr
```

Working with Files and Directories

While most people are perfectly happy and comfortable working with files and directories in the Finder, there are some times when it's either necessary or advantageous to work with files on the command line. Of course, like all things, before you are able to unleash the power of the command line, you need to learn a few basic commands for working with files and directories. These basic commands are shown and described in Table 23–4.

Table 23–4. *File and Directory Management Commands*

Command	Usage	Description
cat	cat *filename*	The cat command lists the contents of a file. This command was originally written to perform concatenation functions, so if used improperly, this could have unexpected results.
head	head [-n #] *filename*	The head command allows you to display just the beginning of a long file using the -n option followed by the number of lines you wish to view.
tail	tail [-n #] *filename*	The tail command allows you to display just the end of a long file using the -n option followed by the number of lines you wish to view.
cp	cp *filename filecopy*	cp creates copies of files.
mv	mv *filename newfilename*	mv is interesting in that it is used both to move files from one location to another and to rename files.
rm	rm *filename*	rm permanently and immediately removes a file (or files).
mkdir	mkdir *newdirectory*	mkdir is used to create new directories.
rmdir	rmdir *directory*	rmdir is a special command used to delete directories. It's a safer option than rm in that it will not delete a nonempty directory (which at times makes it more frustrating as well).
touch	touch *filename*	touch creates a new empty file. (However, if the file already exists, touch will merely alter the date it was last accessed.)

> **CAUTION:** Irresponsible use of `rm` can result in very bad things happening—for example, if you happen to be utilizing root privileges (which, in general, you probably shouldn't), and happen to type `rm -R /*` at the command line, your system will immediately begin to delete itself and everything contained within it until it deletes enough of itself that it can't continue . . . ever. (By the way, the `-R` option stands for recursive, a handy option found in many commands.) If you want to be extra careful you could use the `-i` option, which will ask for confirmation for each file to be deleted.

To illustrate how all of these work, we've created a test file named `soliloquy4` in a directory named Shakespeare.

First, you can use the `cat` command to view the file:

```
Simba:Shakespeare scott$ cat soliloquy4
Tomorrow,  and tomorrow,  and tomorrow,
Creeps in this petty pace from day to day
To the last syllable of recorded time,
And all our yesterdays have lighted fools
The way to dusty death. Out,  out,  brief candle!
Life's but a walking shadow,  a poor player
That struts and frets his hour upon the stage
And then is heard no more:  it is a tale
Told by an idiot,  full of sound and fury,
Signifying nothing.
```

Now, if you weren't sure what this file was (or how long it was), you could use head to view just the first three lines:

```
Simba:Shakespeare scott$ head -n 3 soliloquy4
Tomorrow,  and tomorrow,  and tomorrow,
Creeps in this petty pace from day to day
To the last syllable of recorded time,
```

Likewise, you could use `tail` to view the last three lines:

```
Simba:Shakespeare scott$ tail -n 3 soliloquy4
And then is heard no more:  it is a tale
Told by an idiot,  full of sound and fury,
Signifying nothing.
```

> **NOTE:** Like many OSs these days, OS X keeps rather long log files about many of the things happening on the system. While there are many dedicated viewers for many of these files, these files are often very, very long. For such files, `tail` can be a godsend. For example, if you run a busy web server for which you want to see the details of the last 50 hits, you could use `tail -n 50 /var/log/apache2/access_log`.

To make a copy of the file, you would use the cp command:

```
Simba:Shakespeare scott$ ls
soliloquy4
Simba:Shakespeare scott$ cp soliloquy4 macbethsolo
Simba:Shakespeare scott$ ls
macbethsolo     soliloquy4
```

You could then create a new subdirectory:

```
Simba:Shakespeare scott$ mkdir Macbeth
Simba:Shakespeare scott$ ls
Macbeth/        macbethsolo     soliloquy4
```

and then move one of the files into the new directory:

```
Simba:Shakespeare scott$ mv soliloquy4 Macbeth/soliloquy4
Simba:Shakespeare scott$ ls
Macbeth/        macbethsolo
Simba:Shakespeare scott$ ls Macbeth/
soliloquy4
```

You can also use the mv command to rename a file:

```
Simba:Shakespeare scott$ mv macbethsolo tomorrow
Simba:Shakespeare scott$ ls Macbeth/
tomorrow
```

Next, you could try to remove the Macbeth directory:

```
Simba:Shakespeare scott$ rmdir Macbeth/
 rmdir: Macbeth/:  Directory not empty
```

Oops, first you need to remove any files in there:

```
Simba:Shakespeare scott$ rm Macbeth/*
Simba:Shakespeare scott$ rmdir Macbeth
Simba:Shakespeare scott$ ls
tomorrow
```

Finally, you can create a new empty file with touch:

```
Simba:Shakespeare scott$ touch nothing
Simba:Shakespeare scott$ ls
nothing     tomorrow
Simba:Shakespeare scott$ cat nothing

Simba:Shakespeare scott$
```

More Essential Commands

There are literally hundreds of commands available at the command line, and it would take far more space than we have in this book to cover them all; however, as you progress through the rest of the book, you will learn a number of new commands when they are applicable to the topic at hand. In the meantime, there are a number of essential, or at least very useful, commands that you may want to know about that don't fit nicely in a future discussion in this book. They are covered here.

man

The man command is the command that explains all others. If you want to learn more about the ls command, enter man ls, and your terminal will open into a special mode (called a pager) for reading man pages, which will look something like this:

```
LS(1)                      BSD General Commands Manual                      LS(1)

NAME
     ls -- list directory contents

SYNOPSIS
     ls [-ABCFGHLOPRSTUW@abcdefghiklmnopqrstuwx1] [file ...]

DESCRIPTION
     For each operand that names a file of a type other than directory, ls
     displays its name as well as any requested, associated information.  For
     each operand that names a file of type directory, ls displays the names
     of files contained within that directory, as well as any requested, asso-
     ciated information.

     If no operands are given, the contents of the current directory are dis-
     played.  If more than one operand is given, non-directory operands are
     displayed first; directory and non-directory operands are sorted sepa-
     rately and in lexicographical order.

     The following options are available:

:
```

Now this is just the first page of the man page—you can scroll through the rest using either the arrow keys (to move up and down one line at a time) or the spacebar (to move through one page at a time). When you are done, you can exit the man page by pressing Q on the keyboard.

> **TIP:** Computers have come a long way since the man page system was created, and while reading a man page in the terminal is relatively easy for short and simple commands, it isn't ideal for more complex commands that can scroll through 100 or more screens. One neat trick (which we will revisit later in this chapter) is to use man -t *command* | open -f -a /Applications/Preview.app, which will open the entire man page of the command in Preview as a PDF file for immediate reading, printing, or saving. (The -t option converts the man page into a PostScript file, which you can then pipe into your Preview application, which converts the PostScript file into a PDF file as it opens it. Pipes are covered later.)

grep

The grep command searches through files or results for a specified string and then prints out the lines that contain a match. For example, using the preceding text file, you could print out all lines that contain "to" using the command grep to tomorrow. This is shown here:

```
Simba:Shakespeare scott$ ls
nothing   tomorrow
Simba:Shakespeare scott$ grep to tomorrow
Tomorrow, and tomorrow, and tomorrow,
Creeps in this petty pace from day to day
The way to dusty death. Out, out, brief candle!
```

> **NOTE:** grep is actually a powerful tool that can be used with *regular expressions*, expressions that allow you to specify specific patterns that can be matched in large collections of text. Wildcards, described earlier in this chapter, are just a taste of the pattern-matching capabilities available in regular expressions.

ln

ln is the command-line utility for creating links. While there are different ways of linking files, what we are most concerned with are symbolic (aka soft) links (more commonly referred to as aliases, or shortcuts in Windows). To create a symbolic link, you use ln with the s switch, followed by the name of the source file and then optionally the name of the linked file.

> **NOTE:** As mentioned earlier, while an alias you create in the Finder and a symbolic (soft) link created with ln will generally appear and behave the same, they are not technically the same thing. There may be situation where a symbolic link will work where a Finder alias won't.

> **NOTE:** ln by default creates a hard link, which is most likely not what you want, so it's important to remember the -s option. For the technically curious, a *hard link* essentially creates a new file that shares its data with another (the source). If you edit one, the data will change in the other. If you delete one, the other will still remain with all the data intact. A *symbolic link*, on the other hand (like an alias or shortcut), creates a special "path" file that always refers to the original. If this original is deleted, the path is broken unless a new file of the same name replaces the original. A big difference in use is that a symbolic link can refer to a directory or a file on a different file system, while a hard link cannot.

Let's look at ln in action:

```
Simba:Shakespeare scott$ ls
macbeth/ nothing
Simba:Shakespeare scott$ ls macbeth/
soliloquy4
Simba:Shakespeare scott$ ln -s macbeth/soliloquy4 tomorrow
Simba:Shakespeare scott$ ls -F
macbeth/     nothing      tomorrow@
Simba:Shakespeare scott$ cat tomorrow
Tomorrow, and tomorrow, and tomorrow,
Creeps in this petty pace from day to day
To the last syllable of recorded time,
And all our yesterdays have lighted fools
The way to dusty death. Out, out, brief candle!
Life's but a walking shadow, a poor player
That struts and frets his hour upon the stage
And then is heard no more:  it is a tale
Told by an idiot, full of sound and fury,
Signifying nothing.
```

who

The who command tells you who else is logged into the computer. Normally, this would just be you, since most personal computers would only allow one person to be logged in at a time (and this is how we still tend to use them). However, if you've turned on the Remote Login option on the Sharing control pane, it's possible for multiple users to actually be using one Mac OS system at a time. who also has a related command, whoami, which also tells you your username if you ever forget. (By the way, your Darwin username is the "short" username you picked when you created your account.)

Seeing these in action on your system isn't always that exciting:

```
Simba:~ scott$ who
scott     console   May 25 15:09
scott     ttys000   May 25 16:11
scott     ttys001   May 25 19:01
Simba:~ scott$ whoami
Scott
```

> **NOTE:** In the who example, you may notice scott (that's me) is listed three times as being logged in. Why is that? Well, because I am logged in three times. First I'm logged into Mac OS X (that's the console listing). Then I have two terminal windows open, and Mac OS X considers each of those a separate login (ttys000 and ttys001).

> **NOTE:** who is considered dangerous by many systems administrators who feel it's a potential
> security breach to disclose too much information about the system or its users; for this reason,
> on many servers, commands that provide information about users are either removed or
> disabled. Of course, the real cool (or if you're a systems administrator, real bad) command that is
> similar to who is `finger`. Historically, `finger` would allow you to find out all sorts of personal
> information about any user. Not only could you find information about users on your local
> machine, but you could actually "finger" anyone on any UNIX-type machine (and most other
> multiuser systems of the day). The `finger` command still exists on some computers and is even
> installed on your Mac (go ahead, finger another user or yourself)—however, it's unlikely that
> you'll be able to find many machines on your network or on the Internet that will allow you to
> finger them or any of their users (for aforementioned security and even privacy fears). By default,
> Mac OS X will not allow any remote machine to finger you.

ps

ps allows you to view what processes are running at any given time on your system. By
default, it shows limited information about all the services running from the terminal you
are using (i.e., only the current Darwin process that you've started from your current
terminal session). Until you really start digging into the power of Darwin, ps will likely just
return your shell as your only process:

```
Simba:~ scott$ ps
  PID TTY           TIME CMD
  276 ttys000    0:00.12 -bash
  503 ttys001    0:00.01 -bash
```

The important pieces of information here are the PID (process ID) and the CMD
(command). However, with a few options, ps can give you lots of information about
every command running on your system. The most common options are -a, -j, and -x
(so common, in fact, that you can issue them without the -). The ps command will most
likely give you a long scrolling list of processes (the following list has had a significant
chunk of the output removed for brevity):

```
Simba:~ scott$ ps -axj
USER         PID  PPID  PGID  SESS JOBC STAT  TT      TIME COMMAND
root           1     0     1 ffffff800beefe60   0 Ss    ??   0:16.08
/sbin/launchd
root          10     1    10 ffffff800beefba0   0 Ss    ??   0:01.45
/usr/libexec/
root          11     1    11 ffffff800beefa40   0 Ss    ??   0:00.80
/usr/libexec/
root          12     1    12 ffffff800beef8e0   0 Ss    ??   0:00.61
/usr/sbin/not
root          13     1    13 ffffff800beef780   0 Ss    ??   0:00.18
/usr/sbin/dis
root          14     1    14 ffffff800beef620   0 Ss    ??   0:01.80
/usr/libexec/
```

```
root            15    1    15 ffffff800beef4c0  0 Ss   ??    0:03.00
/System/Libra
root            16    1    16 ffffff800beef360  0 Ss   ??    0:00.33
/usr/sbin/sys
...
scott         1467 1466  1467 ffffff800beeede0  1 S    s001  0:00.03 -bash
root          1525 1467  1525 ffffff800beeede0  1 R+   s001  0:00.00 ps -axj
```

> **NOTE:** ps aux is one of the most popular ps commands. However, the -u option in the version
> of ps that ships with Mac OS X performs a different task. That said, if you are in the habit of
> typing ps aux, it will still work. The -u will filter the output based on a specific user, while u
> (without the -) will give you the traditional u output. I'm one of those people who habitually uses
> aux (plus, I prefer its output to the j option), so I tend to use that in many of my examples.

This gives you much more information besides the PID and CMD (which is the full path, and as shown, is often truncated by the width of the terminal), including what user is responsible for the process. By default, the information is sorted by the process ID. If you want to filter this to show only what tasks a specific user is running, you can use the -u option. For example, if you just wanted to see how many processes you are personally responsible for, you could use the following:

```
Simba:~ scott$ ps -jxu scott
USER   PID  PPID  PGID    SESS JOBC STAT  TT     TIME COMMAND
scott  123     1   123 ffffff800beed7e0  0 Ss   ??    0:01.21 /sbin/launchd
scott  126   123   126 ffffff800beed7e0  1 S    ??    0:00.85
/usr/libexec/UserEvent
scott  141   123   141 ffffff800beed7e0  1 S    ??    0:23.54
/Applications/Mail.app
scott  142   123   142 ffffff800beed7e0  1 S    ??    0:38.68
/Applications/Twitter.
scott  144   123   144 ffffff800beed7e0  1 S    ??    0:51.21
/Applications/iTunes.a
scott  145   123   145 ffffff800beed7e0  1 S    ??    0:03.59
/System/Library/CoreSe
scott  165   123   165 ffffff800beed7e0  1 S    ??    0:01.01
/System/Library/Privat
scott  189   123   189 ffffff800beed7e0  1 SN   ??    0:00.02
/usr/libexec/warmd_age
scott  199   123   199 ffffff800beed7e0  1 S    ??    0:00.03
/System/Library/CoreSe
scott  202   123   202 ffffff800beed7e0  1 S    ??    0:00.18
/Applications/iTunes.a
scott  203   123   203 ffffff800beed7e0  1 S    ??    0:02.79
/System/Library/Servic
scott  414   145   145 ffffff800beed7e0  1 S    ??    0:01.66
/System/Library/CoreSe
scott  469   123   469 ffffff800beed7e0  1 S    ??    0:01.10 /System/Library/Image
scott  543   123   543 ffffff800beed7e0  1 S    ??    0:00.08 /usr/libexec/lsboxd
scott  582   144   144 ffffff800beed7e0  1 S    ??    0:00.30
/System/Library/Privat
scott 1320   123  1320 ffffff800beed7e0  1 SN   ??    0:00.58
/System/Library/Framew
```

```
scott  1414    123   1414 ffffff800beed7e0      1 S        ??     0:06.26
/Applications/Utilitie
scott  1436    281    281 ffffff800beed7e0      1 S        ??     0:00.86
/System/Library/Privat
scott  1528    123   1528 ffffff800beed7e0      1 S        ??     0:00.04
/System/Library/Framew
scott  1529      1   1529 ffffff800beee2e0      0 Us        ??     0:00.05
/usr/libexec/xpchelper
root   1466    271   1466 ffffff800beeede0      0 Ss      s001     0:00.03 login -pf scott
scott  1467   1466   1467 ffffff800beeede0      1 S       s001     0:00.03 -bash
root   1530   1467   1530 ffffff800beeede0      1 R+      s001     0:00.00 ps -jxu scott
```

> **NOTE:** A similar command to ps is top. The primary difference between the two is that ps takes
> a snapshot of processes when you run the command, while top stays active and continually
> updates itself. The Activity Monitor application in the Utilities folder provides a nice GUI for the
> top command (and presents some additional information as well, including disk usage, memory
> usage, and CPU usage).

kill

kill is used to stop a specific process. This can be necessary if you have a task that is
running amok and you can't figure out how else to stop it (perhaps you are attempting to
write your own application or script, and it gets caught in a nasty loop).

To see this in action, you can intentionally create some nasty background tasks using
the yes command, which you will then kill.

> **NOTE:** The yes command by default prints out y indefinitely as fast as possible. If you want to
> find out just how hot your computer will get before a fan kicks in, you can open up a few terminal
> windows (or tabs) and run yes in each one. I'm not sure I'd recommend this if you are using a
> portable while it's sitting on your lap, though—you might not like the burning sensation it
> causes. To stop yes from running the "correct" way, just press Control-C.

To do this, first start running yes in the background twice, and then find out what the
process ID of each yes process is and kill it:

```
Simba:~ scott$ yes > /dev/null &
[1] 1535
Simba:~ scott$ yes > /dev/null &
[2] 1536
Simba:~ scott$ ps u
USER    PID %CPU %MEM      VSZ    RSS   TT  STAT STARTED      TIME COMMAND
scott  1535 99.3  0.0  2434788    420 s001  R     8:00AM   0:08.29 yes
scott  1536 97.8  0.0  2434788    420 s001  R     8:00AM   0:05.69 yes
scott  1467  0.0  0.0  2435492   1116 s001  S     7:40AM   0:00.03 -bash
Simba:~ scott$ kill 1535
[1]-  Terminated: 15          yes > /dev/null
```

```
Simba:~ scott$ kill 1536
[2]+  Terminated: 15         yes > /dev/null
Simba:~ scott$ ps u
USER    PID  %CPU %MEM     VSZ    RSS   TT  STAT STARTED      TIME COMMAND
scott  1467   0.0  0.0  2435492   1116 s001  S     7:40AM   0:00.04 -bash
```

There are a few things we should explain. The yes command you entered, yes >
/dev/null &, takes the output of yes and redirects it to /dev/null, which is a special
device in most UNIX systems that is a black hole of sorts. Everything sent to /dev/null
just goes away. The > is the redirect command, and the & tells the terminal to run this in
the background. We will cover background tasks and redirections later.

Finally, you may notice the ps command shows that one yes process is using 99.3
percent of the processor, and the other is using 97.8 percent, and these numbers don't
seem to add up. The reason for this is that the %CPU shows the percentage for a single
processor. Most Apple computers these days include at least two processing cores
(including ours shown here), so in this case, one yes command is using 99.3 percent of
one, while the other is using 97.8 percent of the other (your mileage may vary).

Occasionally, a simple kill still won't stop a process; in that event, you'll need to use
kill -9 to stop the process. The -9 signal runs kill in Kill mode, which means that the
process will force stop immediately.

> **NOTE:** kill will attempt to gracefully terminate a process. In a way, this is similar to the Quit
> command in a Cocoa application (though without the "are you sure" dialogs and versions to save
> any unsaved work). kill -9 is more like force quitting an application. Using kill -9 will stop
> the process immediately without warning. This can have unexpected results if you accidently kill
> the wrong process, so like many tools covered here, handle with care.

less (more)

less is a pager, which allows you to scroll through large amounts of text that may
normally scroll right by you in the terminal. You learned how pagers worked with the man
command, which automatically runs in a pager (which by default in Mac OS X is actually
less); however, sometimes it's useful to use a pager with other commands as well. For
example, when you use the ps aux command, you are presented with lots of information
scrolling right by; however, if you pipe the ps aux command into less, then you can
scroll around the output just as you scrolled around the man pages. An example of this
is the following:

```
Simba:~ scott$ ps aux | less

   RSS  TT  STAT STARTED      TIME COMMAND
235440  ??  S     3:09PM  20:20.55 /Applications/Microsoft Office 2011/Microso
 62636  ??  S     4:11PM   0:26.50 /Applications/Utilities/Terminal.app/Conten
144576  ??  Ss    3:09PM   6:19.10 /System/Library/Frameworks/ApplicationServi
  4200  ??  Ss    8:29AM   0:00.04 /usr/sbin/cupsd -l
  6812  ??  Ss    8:29AM   0:00.05 /usr/libexec/xpchelper
```

```
 2804    ??  Ss     8:28AM   0:00.03  /usr/sbin/ocspd
 1116  s001  S      7:40AM   0:00.04  -bash
 2820  s001  Ss     7:40AM   0:00.03  login -pf scott
42604    ??  S      7:36AM   0:00.87  /System/Library/PrivateFrameworks/WebKit2.f
27756    ??  S      7:18AM   0:06.27  /Applications/Utilities/Grapher.app/Content
25644    ??  SN    11:16PM   0:00.69  /System/Library/Frameworks/CoreServices.fra
 8028    ??  S     10:23PM   0:00.31  /System/Library/PrivateFrameworks/MobileDev
 3760    ??  S      7:03PM   0:00.09  /usr/libexec/lsboxd
42276    ??  S      7:03PM   0:07.48  /Applications/Preview.app/Contents/MacOS/Pr
  608    ??  S      6:47PM   0:00.00  /usr/sbin/httpd -D FOREGROUND -D WEBSERVICE
 1668    ??  S      6:46PM   0:00.00  /usr/sbin/httpd -D FOREGROUND -D WEBSERVICE
 5348    ??  Ss     6:46PM   0:00.41  /usr/sbin/httpd -D FOREGROUND -D WEBSERVICE
12732    ??  S      6:46PM   0:01.11  /System/Library/Image Capture/Support/Image
32164    ??  S      6:12PM   0:01.80  /System/Library/CoreServices/Dock.app/Conte
73716    ??  S      4:12PM   0:39.42  /Applications/Safari.app/Contents/MacOS/Saf
 1248    ??  S      3:11PM   0:00.04  /usr/sbin/distnoted agent
  800    ??  Ss     3:11PM   0:00.04  /sbin/launchd
:
```

Using the arrow keys, you can now scroll through your output, and when you are done, you can quit the pager and return to the prompt by pressing Q.

> **NOTE:** Another older yet extremely popular pager was called `more`. Although `more` was very popular, it was lacking in many ways—for instance, it would only allow you to scroll down (e.g., you couldn't go back once you scrolled past something). Because of this, `less` has largely replaced `more`; however, for backward compatibility, the `more` command has been linked with `less`, so the `more` command still works (although it will actually run `less`).

find and whereis

`find` and `whereis` are two commands that work very differently, yet are both used to the same ends: finding something in the Darwin file system.

`find`, by default, takes a path variable and presents a list of matches. Additionally, if a match is a directory, `find` will traverse that directory as well (`find /` will return every visible file on your hard drive!). Using regular expressions and wildcards can effectively narrow (or broaden) your search as needed. A simple `find` example may be something like this:

```
Simba:~ scott$ find "/Documents/Shakes*
/Users/scott/Documents/Shakespeare
/Users/scott/Documents/Shakespeare/macbeth
/Users/scott/Documents/Shakespeare/macbeth/soliloquy4
/Users/scott/Documents/Shakespeare/nothing
/Users/scott/Documents/Shakespeare/tomorrow
```

Listing directories is nothing new, but `find` becomes very useful with its ability to search for matches of specific file properties, the most popular being the name of the file. To use `find` this way, you give `find` the directory you wish to traverse, and then enter the -

name option, followed by your search string. For example, if you were looking for the soliloquy in your Documents folder, you could use the following:

```
Simba:~ scott$ find "/Documents -name "sol*"
/Users/scott/Documents/Shakespeare/macbeth/soliloquy4
```

Other properties that you can use as search parameters for find include the file's owner and its group.

> **NOTE:** When using find, it's best to have a good general idea of the location of the file you are looking for. While it's perfectly acceptable to do something like find / -name "sol*", find is not a fast command, so in addition to giving a number of false hits and warnings (mostly Permission Denied warnings from subdirectories that find isn't allowed to look in), it may take a relatively long time.

Unlike find, whereis is tailored specifically for finding executable files. It does this by specifically searching the common places where programs live (primarily the various bin and sbin directories for a specific program name you enter). For example, if you wanted to see where the whereis command is located, you could do this:

```
Simba:~ scott$ whereis whereis
 /usr/bin/whereis
```

While this may seem trivial on a certain level, there are a couple of good reasons to use this. First, if you occasionally compile or install your own Darwin software (which we'll talk about in the next chapter), at some point you may end up with two copies of the same program, and whereis will help you find them so you can deal with it. Second, scripts written in languages like Perl, Python, or Ruby often want to know where the language executable is, and whereis provides a quick way to determine that.

> **NOTE:** Two other commands worth mentioning here are locate and mdfind. locate searches its database, which contains a list of all publically readable files, for matches to your query, which makes it quite a bit faster than find. However, since the locate database is only occasionally updated, it's possible that what you are looking for isn't in the database. mdfind is a command unique to Mac OS X that actually searches on Spotlight's metadata. This makes it very fast and powerful—however, there is one minor setback in that Spotlight doesn't always index items until they are opened in the Finder. So, for example, our soliloquy4 text file may not show up in an mdfind search (or Spotlight search), at least until it is accessed by a non-command-line application. As such, mdfind wouldn't be a first choice for looking for something in the Darwin file system on the whole (however, it's an excellent choice if what you are looking for is visible in the Finder).

Pipes, Redirection, and Background Tasks

A few more things we should cover before we move on are the ability to pipe one command into another, the ability to redirect output (or input) to and from a command, and the ability to run tasks in the background. We've actually done each of these things in some of the preceding examples, yet as they are quite powerful, we'll give a bit more depth here.

Pipes

Piping one command into another is a great way to make even the simplest Darwin tools do powerful things. You saw this previously when you piped the ps command into the less command. The pipe symbol is the | (which is the tall line that lives above the \ on a normal US Mac keyboard). In practice, this takes the first command and sends the output into the second. For example, the ability to take commands that produce large amounts of output and pipe that content into a filter (like the grep command) can save lots of time and headaches.

Redirects

A redirect allows you to redirect the output of a command into a file, or alternatively direct the content of a file into a command. The symbols for redirection are < and >. A very simple use of a redirect is to create a text file using echo, like this:

```
Simba:~ scott$ echo "Hello my name is Scott" > name.txt
Simba:~ scott$ cat name.txt
Hello my name is Scott
```

The echo command normally would just print whatever you feed into it back to your terminal, but here we have redirected the output to name.txt (which may or may not have existed).

> **CAUTION:** If you are redirecting data into an existing file using >, all the contents of that file will be replaced with the new data. So be very careful with this command.

If you want to redirect additional data into an existing file (rather than replace the content, which the > always does), you can use >> to append the new data to the old:

```
Simba:~ scott$ echo " Hello Scott" >> name.txt
Simba:~ scott$ cat name.txt
Hello my name is Scott
Hello Scott
Simba:~ scott$ echo "Ooops" > name.txt
Simba:~ scott$ cat name.txt
Ooops
```

Background Tasks

Any Darwin command can be issued to run in the background with the & symbol tacked onto the end of the command. This is particularly useful when you want to start a command that may take a long time to finish, or when running a task that you want to keep running indefinitely. For example, if you want to use the find command to find something with the name profile somewhere on your system, knowing that this may take some time, you may want to run it in the background. Here's an annotated example of this:

```
Simba:~ scott$ find / -name "profile" > found 2> found_err &
[1] 358
```

Here you start the find command in the background. You are redirecting the output to a file named found. The 2> found_err part of the command will redirect any error messages to a file named found_err. Without the 2> found_err, even though the command is running in the background, error messages would still spam the terminal (2> is a special redirect in Bash that only redirects error messages).

```
Simba:~ scott$ jobs
[1]+   Running                 find / -name "profile"  >found 2>found_err &
```

The jobs command gives you a list of all of the background tasks and tells you their state (in this case, your only task is running).

```
Simba:~ scott$ fg
find / -name "profile"  >found 2>found_err
```

The fg command (fg for foreground) brings forward the first running task (which for now is your only task). Since the command is running in the foreground, you can no longer use the terminal unless you pause the process. You can do this using the Control-Z key combo.

```
[1]+   Stopped                 find / -name "profile"  >found 2>found_err
```

When you use Control-Z, you are giving the message that your task has stopped. You can now resume this task in the background using bg:

```
Simba:~ scott$ bg
[1]+ find / -name "profile"  >found 2>found_err &
```

While this task runs, let's start another background task:

```
Simba:~ scott$ (sleep 30; echo "done")&
[2]  359
Simba:~ scott$ jobs
[1]   Running                 find / -name "profile"  >found 2>found_err &
[2]+  Running                 ( sleep 30;  echo "done"  ) &
```

Now you have two jobs running in the background, your find command is still chugging along, and you have the new command (which will wait, or sleep, 30 seconds, and then run the echo "done" command). Notice that each job has been given a number. The find command is [1], and the sleep command is [2]. To pull the sleep command into the foreground, you must specify that you want job 2.

```
Simba:~ scott$ fg 2
( sleep 30;  echo "done"  )
done
```

Eventually, the `sleep` command will complete and echo "done" to the terminal. At this point, you can continue to use your terminal, and eventually you will get a message that your `find` command has completed.

```
[1]+    Exit 1                      find / -name "profile" >found 2>found_err
Simba:~ scott$ cat found
/dev/profile
/private/etc/profile
/System/Library/Tcl/8.4/tclx8.4/help/tcl/debug/profile
/System/Library/Tcl/8.5/tclx8.4/help/tcl/debug/profile
/usr/libexec/emacs/22.1/mac-apple-darwin/profile
/usr/share/devicemgr/backend/app/views/profile
```

Working As Root

In Darwin, the root user is synonymous with the administrator, superuser, or all-knowing, all-doing, grand poobah. Working as root is sort of like splitting the atom: great potential for good, great potential for total destruction. In the case of root, that which gets destroyed can vary from an important file to all of your data and the OS itself. Root has few boundaries and restrictions, and it can override all the security safeguards on the system. As such, you should never use it. Of course, sometime you may need to, or at least want to really, really badly.

> **CAUTION:** With root comes lots of responsibility. Nothing short of a very powerful magnet sitting on your hard drive can mess up your system quite like a misplaced root command. As such, we cannot stress enough that root should be used sparingly and only when absolutely necessary.

So, when should you run a command as root? When there is no other way to run it. For example, when we ran our `find` command on the whole hard drive, we received a number of Permission Denied warnings (take a look at our `found_err` file). If we in fact wanted to search those protected files and directories, we would have to do so as root (or as the owner of the specific protected files or directories). Additionally, while you may be allowed to see and use many of the files and directories in Darwin, you won't be allowed to alter them or add new files to the directories. If you need to alter a configuration file, or install a new Darwin application in a specific location, or do one of many other related tasks, you will often have to do so as root.

When the time comes to run a command as root, one generally doesn't log out and log back in as root (which Apple goes to great lengths to make very difficult to do anyway). Instead, the recommended way is to utilize the `sudo` command.

sudo

The sudo command (which means *substitute user do*) allows selected users (only users with administrator privileges, by default) to run any other command as the root (or any other) user, as specified in the sudoers file (located at /etc/sudoers).

To run a command as root (which is sudo's default nature), merely precede the command with sudo—for example, if you wanted to manually run the weekly maintenance script, you would do so like this:

```
Simba:~ scott$ sudo periodic weekly
WARNING:  Improper use of the sudo command could lead to data loss or the deletion of
important system files.  Please double-check your typing when using sudo. Type "man
sudo" for more information.
To proceed,  enter your password,  or type Ctrl-C to abort.
Password:
...
```

As you can see, the first time you use sudo, you are given a stern warning about the dangers of using sudo, followed by a prompt for your password. Upon entering your password, the command will execute. The preceding warning will only appear the first time you use sudo—however, each time you use sudo, you will be prompted for a password, with one caveat: by default, sudo will save your password for a period of time (5 minutes is the default), so you won't have to reenter it for any subsequent sudo commands within that time period.

> **NOTE:** The weekly maintenance scripts are among three script collections the system runs to maintain your computer. The other two are daily and monthly. These scripts are meant to run at their indicated intervals. However, this is based on the premise that your computer is always on! If you frequently turn off your computer (especially common for laptops), then it's possible that these scripts and their subsequent commands may never run. Thus, it may be beneficial to run these commands manually, as indicated previously, to help clean up and maintain your system. (The weekly and monthly scripts may take a few minutes to complete.)

By default, sudo allows root and any user in the admin group to utilize it. If a nonadmin user attempts to use sudo, instead of his or her chosen command being executed, that person will be presented with the following warning:

```
user is not in the sudoers file.    This incident will be reported.
```

To run a command as a user other than root, sudo offers the -u option, which you would use as follows:

```
sudo -u username command
```

On the slight chance that you really must execute a series of commands as another user and you'd like to maintain the user state for an extended period of time, sudo offers the -s option, which in effect starts the shell as the specified user. Since this command starts a shell as the specified user or root, no additional command is necessary. By default, this is the equivalent of using the older su command. If you must use this (and it's recommended that you don't), it's important to remember to quit (i.e., type exit) as soon as you are done—otherwise, you will remain in root state and are more likely to do something regrettable (or forget you are logged in as root and walk away from your computer for a cup of coffee or something and allow someone else to do something perhaps even more regrettable)!

> **NOTE:** Before there was sudo, there was su (substitute user). Rather than taking a command, su just dropped you into a shell as root or the specified user. For whatever reason, many old-time UNIX users still swear by the su command, and while these are generally intelligent people who can perform amazing computer tasks in their sleep, their stubbornness in regard to su is misplaced. You shouldn't use su on the Mac (and yes, it is there). su was written in a time of relative innocence, when mail servers didn't require passwords and spam filters didn't exist, when virus protection wasn't a billion-dollar industry, and when god was an appropriate (and sadly all too common) password for the root user. Anyway, those days are gone, and su just doesn't provide the features and, more importantly, the security that sudo provides (such as fine-grained per-user and per-group customizability, sophisticated checks on timestamps and files to assure that nobody has tampered with the file, and more).

The sudoers File

The sudo defaults are sensible and appropriate for most computer uses. However, for servers or other computers with many users, sudo can be coaxed into providing very specific, fine-grained privileges to individual users or groups. To do this requires editing the /etc/sudoers file. The catch is that to edit this file, you must have root privileges and you must use a special editor named visudo. visudo is really a special mode of the Vi editor—or more specifically, Vim, which stands for *Vi improved,* and is installed on Mac OS X in place of Vi. The easiest way to accomplish all this is to merely use the following:

```
Simba:~ scott$ sudo visudo
Password:
```

This immediately opens up the sudoers file to be edited (assuming you understand how Vi works, which if you don't right now, we will explain in the next section).

Sadly, a discussion of the many specific tweaks that can be made to this file would extend far beyond the confines of this book. However, typing man sudoers brings you to the man page for this particular file and explains in detail things like the extended Backus-Naur form, what exactly it means, and how to put it to use.

Editing Files

Editing files in Darwin is just one of those things that you'll eventually have to do to get the most out of it. For the most part, using a normal Mac OS X text editor like TextMate (€39, about $54), BBEdit ($49.99), TextWrangler (free), or one of the many other text editors, may be your best bet—however, at times it may be handy or necessary to edit a file on the command line. Mac OS X ships with four command line–based text editors: Ed, Vim, Emacs, and Nano. Ed is the original text editor for UNIX, but many newer text editors have surpassed it in both usability and features. Despite this, it is still included in most UNIX distributions, since it has found a small niche within certain shell scripts. Each of the remaining three has its advantages, and what it comes down to for most people is a matter of taste and habit (i.e., once you start using one, it becomes a bit frustrating to use another, since they vary quite a bit).

> **NOTE:** Since we mentioned some GUI text editors previously, it's worth noting that many of these come with a command-line executable as well, so that you may open any file in them from the command line. Specifically, BBEdit allows you to install the `bbedit` command-line executable, and TextMate allows you to install the `tm` command-line executable. Each of these will open the file in the GUI application when it's handy to do so from the command line. However, these applications won't help you much if you are accessing the machine remotely through a terminal window.

Vim

Vim is, as the name suggests, an *improved* clone of Vi (Visual Editor), which in turn is based on Ex, which is based on the aforementioned Ed (which was based on an even older text editor called QED). Vim can be baffling to people new to command-line editors because, like its predecessors, it is a dual-mode text editor. To get things done, you must switch between an insert or edit mode and a command mode. While this way of working with a text editor takes some getting used to, it's fairly easy once you get the knack of it. Also, Vim, Vi, or one of its clones is installed by default on almost every version of UNIX or Linux, so once you learn it, you can count on something like it to be installed on any UNIX (or UNIX-like) system you encounter.

> **NOTE:** Vim specifically has a special third mode—visual mode—which can be toggled by typing v in command mode. Once in visual mode, you can move the cursor around normally—however, the text you move over will be selected. This mode is very handy for selecting text for precise copying and pasting.

When you launch Vim, you can either open an existing file, create a new file, or just jump into the editor without creating a file. The syntax is fairly straightforward:

`vim [filename]`

where *filename* is either an existing file or one you wish to create.

> **NOTE:** In Mac OS X, `vi`, `view`, `vimdiff`, and `ex` all point to `vim`—however, they each cause Vim to exhibit different default behavior. `vi` and `vim` both launch in normal mode, `view` opens a file read-only, `vimdiff` allows you to open multiple files at the same time so that you can compare them, and `ex` opens Vim in ex mode (the `:vi` command returns you to normal mode).

Vim begins in command mode when opening a new or existing file; so, if you open the soliloquy file you've been working with in this chapter, you will be presented with the following:

```
Tomorrow, and tomorrow, and tomorrow,
Creeps in this petty pace from day to day
To the last syllable of recorded time,
And all our yesterdays have lighted fools
The way to dusty death. Out, out, brief candle!
Life's but a walking shadow, a poor player
That struts and frets his hour upon the stage
And then is heard no more: it is a tale
Told by an idiot, full of sound and fury,
Signifying nothing.
~
~
~
~
~
~
~
~
~
~
~
~
"soliloquy4"  10L,  409C
```

Some things to note here are the following:

- The cursor begins on the first letter of the first line.

- Lines on the screen beginning with ~ indicate that the line is empty (not just blank, but empty—in other words, it's not there).

- The line at the very bottom of the screen is the informational display. Initially, it displays the name of the file, how many lines the file contains, and how many characters the file contains.

In command mode, the keys and key sequences have special meanings. For example, you can move your cursor around the text using the arrow keys, or the H, J, K, and L keys (old UNIX keyboards didn't all have arrow keys). If you are searching for a particular word (e.g., *candle*), you could use the search function, which is / followed by your search term. /candle followed by the Return key moves the cursor to the first letter of the first instance of *candle* that it finds. If you want to continue to search for the next occurrence of your search term, you can use an empty / and then press Return. In this particular case, since there is only one occurrence of *candle*, the informational line at the bottom tells you the search hit BOTTOM, continuing at TOP. If there were more occurrences of your search term, / would continue to search forward in your text for them. To search backward, replace the / with ?.

> **NOTE:** Searching in Vim is case sensitive. Also, in its search, Vim has its own special characters—for example, the . character is a wildcard, so if you were to search for, say, the period at the end of a sentence, you would need to escape the . with a \ (backslash). Otherwise, it would match every character in the document.

To actually enter text, you need to enter insert mode. You can do this by typing i, which starts inserting at the point where your cursor is. Alternatively, typing I begins inserting text at the beginning of the line you are on, and o starts you at the beginning of a new line immediately below the line your cursor is on. In insert mode, you can type as you would normally. To exit insert mode and return to command mode, press the Esc key.

> **NOTE:** If in doubt about which mode you are in, you can always press the Esc key to return to command mode (pressing Esc in command mode has no effect). Additionally, the informational line at the bottom will present you with a big, bold INSERT message when you are in insert mode.

When you are done editing your file, you can save it (while in command mode) using :w followed by Return if you wish to save it with the name that you initially opened the file with. Alternatively, you can use :w *filename* to save the file with a specific name.

> **TIP:** To save some typing when saving files, you can use the % symbol to represent the initial file name. For example, if you opened a file named supertext, you could save it as supertext.new using :w %.new.

When your file is saved and you are ready to quit, you can quit using :q. Alternatively, you can save and quit in one shot using either :x, :wq, or (our favorite) ZZ.

> **NOTE:** Occasionally you will find that Vim won't let you simply save a file or quit for certain reasons—most commonly when you wish to quit and your file is unsaved, or you are attempting to save a file that was opened as read-only. In either of these cases, the informational line will tell you why Vim is acting ornery and give you the option of overriding its warnings by appending ! to the end of your command. For example, to force quit an unsaved file, you need to use :q! rather than just :q.

Once you get used to working with two modes in Vim, the next thing you'll want to do is explore the features of the command mode. To help, Table 23–5 lists common command mode keystrokes and what they accomplish (this is by no means a complete list).

Table 23–5. *Vim Command Mode Keystrokes Quick Reference*

Keystroke	Action
Moving Around	
k or up arrow	Move cursor up one line
j or down arrow	Move cursor down one line
h or left arrow	Move cursor one space to the left
l or right arrow	Move cursor one space to the right
e	Move to end of word
b	Move to beginning of word
$	Move to end of line
0	Move to beginning of line
(	Move back one sentence
)	Move forward one sentence
{	Move back one paragraph
}	Move forward one paragraph
:n	Move to line n
nG	Move to line n

Keystroke	Action
G	Move to last line in document
1G	Move to first line in document
Control-f	Scroll forward one screen
Control-b	Scroll backward one screen
Inserting Text	
i	Insert text before cursor
a	Insert text after cursor
I	Insert text at beginning of line
A	Insert text at end of line
o	Create blank line below cursor and insert text
O	Create blank line above cursor and insert text
r	Overwrite one character and then return to command mode
R	Begin overwriting text at cursor
Deleting Text	
x	Delete character under cursor
X	Delete character before cursor
dd or :d	Delete entire line
Searching and Replacing Text	
/*pattern*	Search forward for pattern
/ or n	Search forward for previous pattern
?*pattern*	Search backward for pattern
? or N	Search backward for previous pattern
:s/*orig*/*repl*	Replace *orig* with *repl* on current line

Keystroke	Action
:%s/*orig*/*repl*	Replace *orig* with *repl* throughout entire document
Copying and Pasting Text	
yw	Copy word
yy	Copy line
y	Copy selected text (from visual mode)
dw	Cut word
dd	Cut line
d	Cut selected text (from visual mode)
p	Paste text
:w [*filename*]	Save file as file name (if no file name is specified, the file will be saved with the current name)
:q	Quit Vim
:x, :wq, or ZZ	Save file and quit
:w!	Force save read-only file (if you have proper permissions)
:q!	Force quit changed file without saving
Other Commands	
Esc	Return Vim to command mode
u	Undo
J	Join two lines into one
:.=	Display current line number

> **NOTE:** Learning Vim takes some getting used to, but once you've grown comfortable with it you may find it indispensible. For those who love Vim but still enjoy a good graphical text editor, there is MacVim, a graphical Mac OS X native text editor built on Vim.

Emacs

Emacs (or GNU Emacs, as the faithful like to refer to it) is another popular text editor (perhaps it may be best described as a powerful runtime system with text-editing capabilities). Emacs can do wonderful things provided you take the time to learn a rather large number of mystical key combinations (and learning a little Lisp helps too). In fact, people who love and use Emacs (who really should have a name to describe them—like Trekkies or something, since they tend to share the same sort of devotion) won't settle for anything less.

Unlike Vim, Emacs is a single-mode text editor; so, in that way, it's probably similar to most GUI text editors you may have used. However, since it lacks a GUI, you can't use your mouse to access the fancy features. That's where the crazy keystrokes come into play. In general, these keystrokes use either the Control key or the Meta key plus some other key (in Emacs, the shorthand for this would be something like C-k for Control-K, or M-k for Meta-K). Usually, you would hold these keys at the same time. The gotcha here is that the Mac keyboard doesn't have a Meta key. You can fix this by selecting the "Use option as meta key" option in Terminal's Settings preferences (on the Keyboard tab, as shown in Figure 23–2).

> **TIP:** If you don't wish to remap the option key to meta, you can also use the Esc key to carry out meta commands. Pressing the Esc key and then x, for example, is the same as M-x. Keep in mind this is Esc first, then x; rather than Esc+x at the same time.

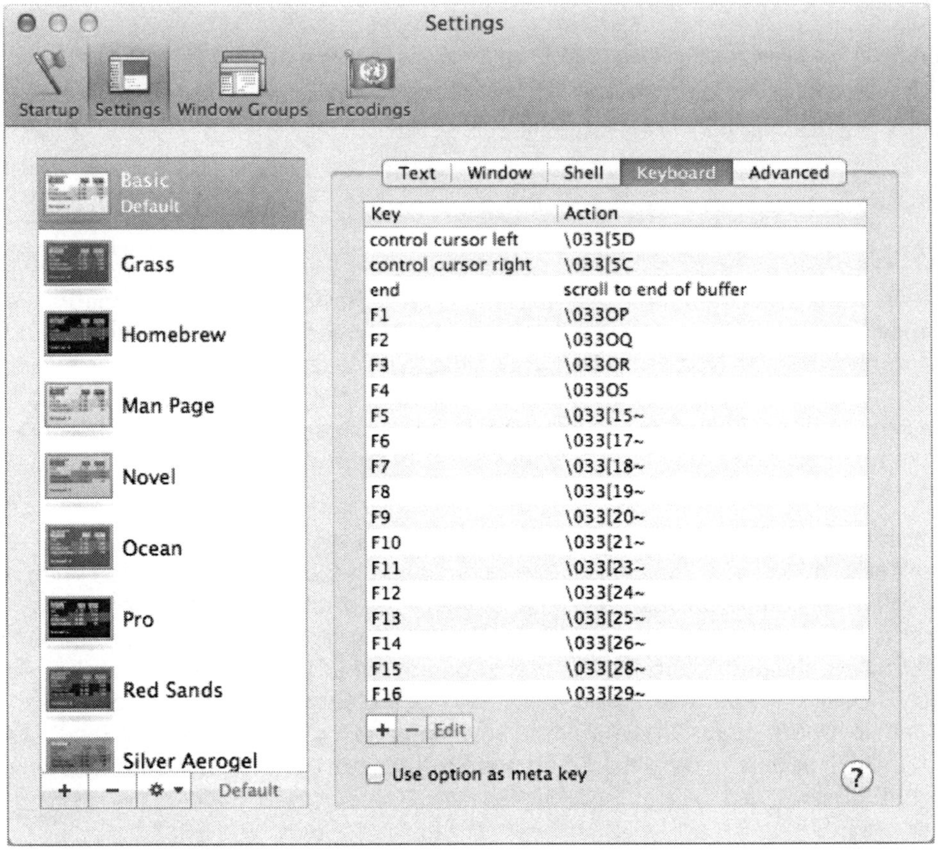

Figure 23–2. *The "Use option as meta key" option is found in Terminal's Settings preferences.*

As with Vi (described previously), you can either open an existing file, create a new file, or just start with a scratch buffer when you launch Emacs using the emacs [*filename*] command. Opening the soliloquy file produces the following output:

```
Tomorrow, and tomorrow, and tomorrow,
Creeps in this petty pace from day to day
To the last syllable of recorded time,
And all our yesterdays have lighted fools
The way to dusty death. Out, out, brief candle!
Life's but a walking shadow, a poor player
That struts and frets his hour upon the stage
And then is heard no more: it is a tale
Told by an idiot, full of sound and fury,
Signifying nothing.




-uu-:---F1    soliloquy4          All L1              (Fundamental)------------------
```

Once the file is open, it's immediately ready to edit. To move around in the file, you can use either the arrow keys or some C-n keystrokes (C-f, C-b, C-p, and C-n). The Delete key works as you would expect, and you can enter text at the cursor just by typing.

To save the file, you can either use C-x C-s to save the file with its existing name, or C-x C-w to save the file with a new file name. C-x C-c quits Emacs (it prompts you to save any changed files first). If you need to edit an additional file, you can use C-x C-f to open or create another file without quitting Emacs. Table 23–6 provides a handy list of a few common keystrokes and their effects.

Table 23–6. *Common Emacs Keystrokes and Their Effects*

Keystroke	Action
Moving Around	
C-f or right arrow	Move one character to the right
C-b or left arrow	Move one character to the left
C-p or up arrow	Move one line up
C-n or down arrow	Move one line down
M-f	Move one word to the right
M-b	Move one word to the left
C-a	Move to the beginning of the current line
C-e	Move to the end of the current line
C-v	Page down
M-v	Page up
M->	Go to the end of the document
M-<	Go to the beginning of the document
C-u *n* C-n	Move ahead *n* lines
M-g g *n*	Go to line *n*
Searching and Replacing Text	
C-s *pattern* Ret (Return)	Search forward for pattern
C-r *pattern* Ret	Search backward for pattern

Keystroke	Action
C-s Ret Ret	Search for next occurrence of previous pattern
M-% *orig* Ret *repl* Ret	Replace *orig* string with *repl* string (Emacs will prompt you for confirmation; press y to continue)

Copying and Pasting Text

Keystroke	Action
C-Spc (spacebar)	Set mark at cursor, which allows you to move the cursor anywhere in the document, thus "selecting" text between mark and cursor (called a *region* in Emacs lingo)
C-w	Cut region
M-w	Copy region
C-y	Paste last cut or copied region

Saving and Quitting

Keystroke	Action
C-x C-w *filename*	Save file as file name
C-x C-s	Save file under current file name (will prompt to confirm overwrite of existing file)
C-x C-c	Quit Emacs (will prompt to confirm if current document has changed)

Other Commands

Keystroke	Action
C-x C-f *filename*	Open existing or new file in current buffer
C-h t	Start a built-in Emacs tutorial
C-x u	Undo

NOTE: Emacs is big and powerful; we have just barely scratched the surface of all the features of Emacs here. For an example of how powerful (or perhaps how ridiculous) Emacs is, try this: Start Emacs and enter M-x doctor (press the Esc key and type "xdoctor"). Now, prepare yourself for a session of physiotherapy. Or for something else, try M-x tetris.

Nano

Nano is another handy command-line text editor in Mac OS X. What makes Nano special is that, compared to the others, it is relatively easy to figure out and use. The trade-off is that it lacks some of the more advanced (esoteric) features of Vim and Emacs, and while it's installed by default with Mac OS X (since Tiger), it's not as pervasive as Vim or Emacs.

> **NOTE:** Nano is a clone of the Pico text editor, which is part of the fabulous command-line mail reader Pine. If you've used Pine in the past (or still do), you will find Nano immediately understandable. As an additional bonus, while many UNIX and Linux systems may not have Nano installed, it's just possible that they do have Pine installed, which will mean you may find Pico available where Nano isn't. Before Tiger, OS X included Pico, and today the `pico` command is still there, it's just aliased to nano.

One advantage of Nano is that the most common commands, along with the keystrokes to invoke them, are listed at the bottom of the screen (and the ones that aren't listed are easily looked up with the short yet concise built-in help). While the keystrokes may seem similar to Emacs in practice, the actual keys are different. Also, the common shorthand is different—while in Emacs, Control-X is represented as C-x, in Nano, it's represented as ^x (the ^ [caret] symbol means Control).

Opening files in Nano is the same as opening them in VI or Emacs. Just type nano *filename* at the cursor, and it will open up. Once again, opening the soliloquy file, you would see the following:

```
GNU nano 2.0.6      File:  Documents/Shakespeare/macbeth/soliloquy4
Tomorrow, and tomorrow, and tomorrow,
Creeps in this petty pace from day to day
To the last syllable of recorded time,
And all our yesterdays have lighted fools
The way to dusty death. Out, out, brief candle!
Life's but a walking shadow, a poor player
That struts and frets his hour upon the stage
And then is heard no more: it is a tale
Told by an idiot, full of sound and fury,
Signifying nothing.



                        [ Read 10 lines ]
^G Get Help    ^O WriteOut   ^R Read File ^Y Prev Page ^K Cut Text  ^C Cur Pos
^X Exit        ^D Justify    ^W Where Is  ^V Next Page ^U UnCut Txt ^T To Spell
```

As you can see, at the top of the window Nano identifies the open file, and at the bottom it provides a list of common actions. The action list at the bottom will change based on circumstance—for example, when you go to save a file (using ^o), you will be prompted for the file name you wish to save your file as. The action list will also provide some other saving options (creating a backup, appending this file to another, etc.). With the short help file included with Nano, plus the adaptive action list shown, we're going to forgo the table of commands since it would largely be redundant.

File Permissions and Attributes

File permissions are a central concept found in UNIX systems. They allow one user to share files with everyone else on the system while still maintaining control of those files. The easiest way to view these permissions and attributes is with the ls -l command. For example, one line from an ls -l command may look like this:

```
-rw-r--r--    1 scott    scott       409 May 17 10:44 soliloquy4
```

The first string of 11 characters represents the permissions. Also of interest here are the file's owner (scott) and the file's group (also scott). The first ten characters are broken down as shown in Figure 23–3.

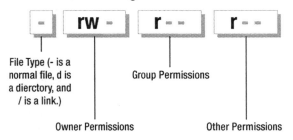

Figure 23–3. *Insert Figure Caption*

> **NOTE:** The 11th character is special and indicates additional file attributes or security applied to the file. We'll cover this in the "ACLs and Extended File Attributes" section.

The permissions are r, w, and x, signifying the ability to read, write, and execute, respectively (these are often referred to as bits). In the case of a directory, the execute bit signifies the ability to list files in the directory. The owner of any file can set these permissions as he or she sees fit using the chmod command. Additionally, the owner can reset the group to which the files belong to any other group the owner belongs to using the chgrp command.

The chmod command can be used one of two ways to set the permissions (also referred to as setting the mode): either literally or symbolically. The literal way is to specify the permissions as a string of numbers such as the following:

```
chmod nnnn filename
```

where *nnnn* is the combined value of permissions based on Table 23–7.

Table 23–7. *chmod Literal Number Values*

Value	Description
Basic Permissions	
400	Allows read by owner
200	Allows write by owner
100	Allows execute by owner
040	Allows read by group
020	Allows write by group
010	Allows execute by group
004	Allows read by everyone
002	Allows write by everyone
001	Allows execute by everyone
Advanced Mode Selectors(Optional, and Generally Not Recommended to Use Unless You Really Know What You Are Doing)	
4000	Sets UID on execution bit (execution of file will run with permissions of file's owner)
2000	Sets GID on execution bit (execution of file will run with permissions of file's group)
1000	Sets sticky bit

For example:

```
chmod 755 filename
```

would result in the file name having permissions -rwxr-xr-x.

The other, symbolic, way of setting permissions is to use chmod in the following way:

```
chmod [u][g][o]+/-[r][w][x] filename
```

where u stands for *owner*, g stands for *group*, and o stands for *other* (everyone);
followed by + (for adding) or - (for denying) permissions (r, w, and x).

For example, if you had a file with the permissions -rwxr-xr-x, but you wanted to allow anyone in its group to also write to the file, you could just use the following:

```
chmod g+w filename
```

This would effectively just add write permissions to the group for *filename*.

Suppose you create a file and then wish to give special permissions to a group of people. By default, any file you create will have both the owner and group listed as you. You can change the group file to any other group that you belong to using the chgrp command with the following syntax:

```
chgrp group filename
```

To find out what groups you belong to you (and thus what's available to you), you can use the id command, like so:

```
Simba:~ scott$ id
uid=501(scott) gid=20(staff)
groups=20(staff),402(com.apple.sharepoint.group.1),12(everyone),33(_appstore),61(localac
counts),79(_appserverusr),80(admin),81(_appserveradm),98(_lpadmin),100(_lpoperator),204(
_developer),401(com.apple.access_screensharing)
```

So in this case, if you want to allow anyone in the admin group to be able to write to your soliloquy4 file, you could do the following:

```
Simba:~/Documents/Shakespeare/macbeth scott$ chgrp admin soliloquy4
Simba:~/Documents/Shakespeare/macbeth scott$ ls -l
...
-rw-r--r-- 1 scott admin 409 May 17 10:44 soliloquy4
Simba:~/Documents/Shakespeare/macbeth scott$ chmod g+w soliloquy4
Simba:~/Documents/Shakespeare/macbeth scott$ ls -l
...
-rw-rw-r-- 1 scott admin 409 May 17 10:44 soliloquy4
```

ACLs and Extended File Attributes

ACLs (access control lists) and extended attributes were introduced to OS X in Tiger (OS X 10.4), but while they used to simply be an option available to those who wished to use them, they are now used by default.

> **NOTE:** ACLs will only be available on your system locally if you are using the HFS+ file system. For network shares, they can be used over AFP and SMB/CIFS.

ACLs allow fine-grained control of a file's access far beyond UNIX's historical owner/group/everyone permissions. With ACLs you can control specific permissions for specific users or groups, and you can treat each user and group differently.

Specifically, each file on your system has one ACL, and each ACL may contain an ordered list of entries. Each entry sets specific permissions for a single user or group.

> **NOTE:** If you have a user and a group with the same name, and you must differentiate these in an ACL, you may prefix the name with either user: or group: to specify which entity you are referring to.

Files with entries in their ACL will include a + in the 11th character in the permission listing when you use ls -l. If there are no ACL entries, but there are other file attributes for the given file, then the 11th character will contain an @. If there are no ACL entries or attributes, then the 11th character will be left off.

To view the ACL associated with a file, use the -e option with the ls command—for example, here's what one of our home directories looks like:

```
Simba:~ scott$ ls -le
total 32
drwx------+  5 scott  staff     170 May 15 09:28 Desktop
 0: group:everyone deny delete
drwx------+  9 scott  staff     306 May 25 18:11 Documents
 0: group:everyone deny delete
drwx------+ 14 scott  staff     476 May 25 16:18 Downloads
 0: group:everyone deny delete
drwx------@ 42 scott  staff    1428 May 15 18:29 Library
 0: group:everyone deny delete
drwx------+  3 scott  staff     102 Apr 28 18:42 Movies
 0: group:everyone deny delete
drwx------+  4 scott  staff     136 May  7 13:54 Music
 0: group:everyone deny delete
drwx------+  5 scott  staff     170 Apr 30 13:53 Pictures
 0: group:everyone deny delete
drwxr-xr-x+  5 scott  staff     170 Apr 28 18:42 Public
```

When you look at the ACLs attached to the default folders in your home directory, you'll see that they are set to deny everyone from deleting them. Don't be afraid to try it; if you try a rmdir, you'll get a Permission Denied warning, and if you try to drag the folders into the trash, you'll get a warning telling you that that directory can't be modified or deleted.

To view a file's attributes, use the -@ option with ls.

> **NOTE:** Most of the file attributes are strictly there for application and Finder support. You can add your own attributes for whatever reason you want, but for the most part in OS X they are there to support the Finder.

To add entries to or delete entries from an ACL, you use the chmod command with +a (to add an entry) or -a (to remove an entry). When you are adding an entry, the new entry will be added to the ACL. To remove an entry, you need to specify the entry number using # *n* directives. Here are some examples of working with ACL entries:

```
Simba:macbeth scott$ ls -l
total 8
-rw-r--r--   1 scott    staff   401 Sep   7 07:47 soliloquy4
```

```
Simba:macbeth scott$ chmod +a "staff deny write,delete" soliloquy4
Simba:macbeth scott$ ls -le
total 8
-rw-r--r--+ 1 scott    staff   401 Sep    7 07:47 soliloquy4
0: group:staff deny write,delete
Simba:macbeth scott$ chmod +a "scott allow read,write,delete" soliloquy4
Simba:macbeth scott$ chmod +a "nobody deny read,write,delete" soliloquy4
Simba:macbeth scott$ ls -le
total 8
-rw-r--r--+ 1 scott    staff   401 Sep    7 07:47 soliloquy4
0:  user:nobody deny read,write,delete
1:  group:staff deny write,delete
2:  user:scott allow read,write,delete
Simba:macbeth scott$ chmod -a# 1 soliloquy4
Simba:macbeth scott$ ls -le
total 8
-rw-r--r--+ 1 scott    staff   401 Sep    7 07:47 soliloquy4
0:  user:nobody deny read,write,delete
1:  user:scott allow read,write,delete
```

The types of actions you can control in ACLs depend on the type of file. The following actions are settable for any file:

- delete
- readattr
- writeattr
- readextattr
- writeextattr
- readsecurity
- writesecurity
- chown

The following actions are settable for folders/directories:

- list
- search
- add_subdirectory
- delete_child

Finally, the following are available for non-folder/directory items:

- read
- write
- append
- execute

More details about ACLs and controlling them are available in the chmod man page.

Customizing Terminal and the Shell

Once you start getting into using the command line, you may want to make a few tweaks to both the Terminal application and your shell environment to streamline how you work.

Terminal Setup

The Terminal application that Apple ships with Mac OS X is a nice, feature-rich application. It includes tabbed windows, which are handy for those who work with multiple shells or must access many remote terminals at the same time. It includes the ability to save different window settings that control the appearance and behavior of your terminal. The latest version that ships with Lion can be switched to full screen for a very retro-looking interface.

One of the first things you may want to do when working with Terminal is adjust how it looks and make a few other tweaks (such as remapping the Meta key if you are a big Emacs user). The options to control your terminal settings are listed under the Settings tab of Terminal's preferences (Figure 23–4).

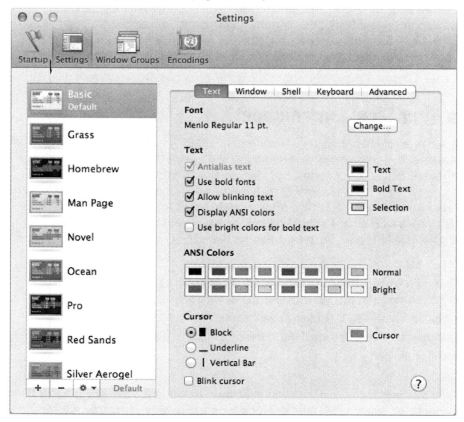

Figure 23–4. *The Settings tab of Terminal's preferences*

The Terminal Settings preferences provide a number of different possible terminal styles listed in the column on the left. In the preferences, you can set options for each setting individually using the five tabs: Text, Window, Shell, Keyboard, and Advanced.

The text settings control the font size, face, and colors. They also allow you to set the options for the terminal's cursor.

The Window tab allows you to set options for controlling the background color, title bar information, initial window size (set in character width and line height), and scrollback buffer.

The Shell tab allows you to set special shell startup commands, as well as options about what happens when you exit the shell or try to close the window while a shell is still running.

The Keyboard tab allows you to set up key bindings, and it lets you toggle the option to use the Option key as the Meta key.

The Advanced tab allows you to set a few other miscellaneous options pertaining to terminal emulation, bell actions, and text-encoding options for foreign languages.

The other main Terminal preference tabs include the Startup tab, which allows you to select the default settings to use when Terminal launches, as well as what type of shell Terminal should use upon launching; the Window Groups tab, which allows you to save the behavior of multiple Terminal windows together as a group; and the Encodings tab, which allows you to select which text encoding should be made available to Terminal's settings.

Setting Up Your Shell Environment

Every shell has what is referred to as an *environment*, which is basically made up of customized variables and commands that make the shell work the way you want it to. The Bash shell stores this info in a number of places. The variables that apply to everyone are stored in /etc/profile and /etc/bashrc. Additionally, you can make your own personal configurations to ~/.bashrc and ~/.bash_profile. As a general rule, things that affect your environment should go in the .bash_profile file, and things that affect the shell specifically should go in the .bashrc file.

> **NOTE:** On many UNIX systems, things in the profile files get read when you log into a terminal, and things in the .bashrc files get read each time you launch a new shell. This isn't exactly how these things work in Mac OS X (or some newer *nix systems), but it's still nice to keep the content of each separate especially if you'd like to share your Mac OS X command-line environment with other *nix systems.

One common environmental variable that you may want to set is the $PATH variable. The $PATH variable describes where your shell will look for executables when you attempt to launch one from the command line. By default, your $PATH is set to include /bin, /sbin,

/usr/bin, /usr/sbin, /usr/local/bin, and /usr/X11/bin (in the /etc/profile file).
However, if you begin to install new executables, or even write your own, you may find
that you need to add additional directories to your $PATH. The syntax to add a directory
to the $PATH is as follows:

```
export PATH=$PATH:/new/directory:/another/new/direcotry
```

> **NOTE:** Whether you add your own paths before or after the default $PATH is significant, since
> each path in $PATH is checked in order. When you enter a command, the first match found will
> execute.

You can add as many directories as you need, separated by a colon. The $PATH at the
beginning represents your existing path; without it, any of the default $PATH directories
will be removed from your $PATH. To have your path updated each time you launch a
shell, it's best just to put this info in your .bash_profile file. For example, the common
.bash_profile file may look like this:

```
###     .bash_profile     ###
#  a good place for environmental variables #

### $PATH ###

if [  -d ~/bin  ]  ;  then
    export PATH=~/bin:$PATH
fi

if [  -d /usr/local/bin ] ; then
    export PATH=/usr/local/bin:$PATH
fi

if [  -d /usr/local/mysql/bin  ]  ;  then
    export PATH=/usr/local/mysql/bin:$PATH
fi

if [  -d /opt/local/bin ]  ; then
    export PATH=/opt/local/bin:$PATH
Fi

if [  -d /opt/local/sbin ]  ; then
    export PATH=/opt/local/sbin:$PATH
fi

### include .bashrc if one exists ###
if [  -f ~/.bashrc  ];  then
    .  ~/.bashrc
fi
```

Any line beginning with # is a comment. Here, some of the built-in scripting functionality
is used to check if common executable directories exist—if they do, then they are
automatically added to the $PATH.

The last part checks to see if the .bashrc file is present; if it is, then it is included as well.

The .bashrc files generally contain variables and commands that are specific to the shell. For example, the default /etc/bashrc file sets the prompt variable. Other things that are generally included in the .bashrc files are common aliases and shell functions.

For example, a .bashrc file may contain the following:

```
###       .bashrc file     ###

#    This file is for shell-specific stuff                        #
#    $PATH and other env variables should go in the  .bash_profile   #

### aliases ###

alias ls="ls -FG"
alias la="ls -FGA"
alias ll="ls -FGAl"

### functions ###

function pman() {
    man -t "${1}"| open -f -a /Applications/Preview.app/
}
```

Again, the lines that begin with # are comments.

Creating Commands with Aliases and Functions

The preceding sample .bashrc file shows a few aliases and a function. Essentially, these are both ways to create simple command-line commands that carry out more complex commands. In general, an alias provides a way of creating a shortened version of a single command, while a function creates a command out of an actual shell script that may consist of many commands and simple logic.

Aliases are incredibly handy when you find you are using the same commands over and over and want to simplify them; you can even use them to essentially overwrite the default behavior of a command. Take the first alias listed previously:

```
alias ls="ls -FG"
```

This command creates the ls alias from the ls -FG command, effectively overwriting ls so that it will, by default, provide colored output and the benefits of the -F flag as well. The other two aliases in the previous .bashrc file example also create aliases to other common ls options.

> **NOTE:** You can create aliases at the command line using the alias command as well—however, if you don't save these to your .bashrc file, they will be gone once you exit that particular shell.

Functions, on the other hand, are more complex, as they are essentially simple shell scripts. Here's an example from the preceding `.bashrc` file:

```
function pman() {
    man -t "${1}" | open -f -a /Applications/Preview.app/
}
```

The first line defines `pman` as a function accessible from the command line, and everything between the curly braces defines what happens when we use the `pman` command. So, if you were to enter `pman ls` at the command line, the function would take the first argument, `ls`, and run `man -t ls | open -f -a /Applications/Preview, app/`, thus allowing you to open the man page of any command in the Preview application in one simple command.

Summary

Whew, there was lots of info in this chapter. While the aim wasn't to teach you everything about working with the command line (which would take an entire book in itself, and still leave out details), hopefully you now know enough to get around the command line comfortably, and more importantly, have a good base to build upon where you see fit. We will be using the info in this chapter to build upon in various upcoming parts of this book, beginning with the next chapter, where we will take a quick look at adding to the abilities of Darwin by creating our own simple scripts and adding new programs from other sources.

## Chapter 24

Extending the Power of Darwin

After the previous chapter, we hope you are at least somewhat comfortable working at the command line. In this chapter, we'll move on and show how to extend the power of Darwin by covering the following:

- An introduction to shell scripting

- An overview of Perl, Python, and Ruby, which are three powerful scripting languages included with Lion

- How to find and install a range of additional applications using MacPorts

- How to custom-compile a Darwin application from the source code

Getting Started with Shell Scripting

Shell scripting has been a staple in UNIX since the first shell was launched. In its most basic form, a shell script allows you to add a series of shell commands to a file so that these commands can be easily run over and over. You can see an example of the value of this by examining the startup process of Mac OS X. During the startup, the shell script /etc/rc.common is started; this file begins a series of processes that effectively start up, configure, and maintain many of the necessary OS and networking functions that occur during startup.

> **NOTE:** The `rc.common` file is a holdover from previous versions of OS X and has a strong UNIX heritage. Beginning with Mac OS X 10.4 Tiger, Apple introduced `launchd`, a startup daemon that standardizes the way processes start on OS X. In recent versions of Mac OS X, most of the old `rc`, `xinit`, and `initd` startup systems are gone or are no longer used very much, and it's likely that in future updates to Mac OS X they will be gone completely.

Writing a shell script can be as easy as just listing a series of any of the commands you may enter at the command line; however, shell scripts can also accept external variables and may contain simple `if...then` logic and loops. We'll briefly explain all of these things, but first let's take a look at a sample shell script (the line numbers are for reference and shouldn't be typed into your script):

```
01:  #!/bin/sh
02:
03:  # togglevis
04:  # A shell script to toggle the visibility of hidden files in the Finder
05:
06:  set `ps acx | grep Finder`
07:
08:  show=`defaults read com.apple.finder AppleShowAllFiles`
09:
10:  if [ $show -eq 1 ]; then
11:      defaults write com.apple.finder AppleShowAllFiles 0
12:      kill $1
13:  else
14:      defaults write com.apple.finder AppleShowAllFiles 1
15:      kill $1
16:  fi
```

> **NOTE:** For those of you who really hate line numbers in programs because they prevent you from copying the text out of an e-book and running it, later in this chapter there will be a Perl script that you should be able to tweak (when you are done with this chapter) to strip them out automatically.

This handy script will toggle the visibility of hidden items in the Mac OS X Finder, which is done by setting the hidden Finder preference `AppleShowAllFiles` to 1 (to show all files) or 0 (to hide hidden files) and then restarting the Finder to immediately enact the change.

> **NOTE:** Truth be told, this script doesn't restart the Finder. The script instead just kills the Finder, and since OS X depends on the Finder, it will automatically restart it.

> **NOTE:** When you first run this script, you may get an error mentioning that
> `AppleShowAllFiles` doesn't exist. This is fine; it will be created the first time you run the
> script, and you shouldn't receive any further errors any time you run the script afterward.

The first line, `#!/bin/sh`, often referred to as the *interpreter line*, is important for all
scripts because it points the shell to the executing script interpreter. This is often
referred to as the *shebang line*, for the #! combination that begins it. (The # resembles a
musical sharp, so "sharp" plus "bang" for the ! equals "shebang.")

> **NOTE:** Most shell scripts in OS X (and generally in UNIX) were written for the Bourne shell (sh) for
> compatibility across various UNIX platforms (of which almost all have the Bourne shell installed).
> The Bash shell itself (aka Bourne Again SHell) is 100 percent backward compatible with the
> Bourne shell, with some extra features borrowed from the C shell and Korn shell. The general
> scripting syntax we are covering in this chapter is mostly Bourne shell compatible; however,
> there may be certain commands issued inside a script that are specific to OS X.

> **NOTE:** There is no Bourne shell by default in Mac OS X; rather, `/bin/sh` is actually a Bash
> executable.

Lines 3 and 4, like all script lines beginning with # (except the shebang line), are
comments. These are included to provide a clue about what's going on for anyone
reading the script. Comments have no effect on how the script runs, and in this respect
are purely optional elements. It is a good habit to use comments, not only for others who
may be looking at your script but also for yourself should you have to look at a script
weeks, months, or even years after you wrote it. Here the first comment line gives the
name of the script, and the second comment describes what the script does.

Line 6 shows us two things: the use of the `set` command and the use of backticks (`` ` ``) in
scripts. In a shell script, anything within backticks is executed, and the result is passed
to the script (this is called *command substitution*). The `set` command sets the
arguments used in the script just as if they were entered at the command line. So, line 6
takes the results from the `ps acx | grep Finder` command (which would be something
like `261    ??    S         0:00.93 Finder`) and makes them our arguments (of
which there would be five). The importance of line 6 for the rest of the script is that it
specifically assigns the process ID of the Finder to our first argument, which can then be
accessed as the variable $1.

Line 8 sets the variable show to the result of the `defaults read com.apple.finder
AppleShowAllFiles` command. `defaults` provides a way to access and alter Mac OS X
user default settings from the command line. In this case, we use it to read the

AppleShowAllFiles value stored in the com.apple.finder preference to determine the existing setting (0 or 1) so we can then toggle the setting. If the AppleShowAllFiles value doesn't exist yet in your Finder preference file, you will get an error similar to this:

```
2011-05-30 09:58:09.195 defaults[473:60b]
The domain/default pair of (/Users/scott/Library/Preferences/com.apple.finder.plist,
AppleShowAllFiles) does not exist
./togglevis: line 10: [: -eq: unary operator expected
```

You can ignore this, since the script will continue and actually create this value. However, if you continue to get errors after this (or if you get a vastly different error), then something else is wrong, and you should check your script closely.

Lines 10 through 16 provide a conditional if...then...else statement and provide the expected actions based on the condition. First, in line 10 we check to see whether the show variable (which is the set value of com.apple.finder AppleShowAllFiles) is 1; if it is, then we move on to line 11 where we change com.apple.finder AppleShowAllFiles to 0. Then in line 12 we kill the Finder using $1, which we set in line 6. If the condition in line 10 is false (the show variable is not 1), then we move on to the else part of the script, and in line 14 we set com.apple.finder AppleShowAllFiles to 1 and then kill the Finder. Line 16 ends the if...then...else statement with fi (that's *if* backward).

The script ends when it runs out of things to do.

There are a couple ways to run this script: one is to pass the script to the shell executable as an argument, and the other is to make the actual script executable. Passing the script as an argument to the shell looks like this:

```
Simba:bin scott$ sh togglevis
```

> **NOTE:** This assumes a couple of things: First, I saved the file in a directory called bin located in my home folder (you may need to create this folder). Second, it assumes that I am currently "in" that folder.

If you want to have access to the script easily from anywhere, though, you must first make the script executable and make sure it's in a directory that is included in your $PATH (as discussed in the previous chapter). For example, we've placed this file in our own bin directory, which you can see is set in our path with the following statement:

```
Simba:bin scott$ echo $PATH
/Users/scott/bin:/usr/bin:/bin:/usr/sbin:/sbin:/usr/local/bin:/usr/X11/bin
```

To make it executable, we use the chmod command:

```
Simba:bin scott$ chmod u+x togglevis
```

Now, provided the script is in your path, you can use togglevis as you would any command from the command line.

Variables

Variables in shell scripts are generally reserved for use from within the script itself unless they are explicitly exported as environmental variables. Environment variables (which include things like $PATH) are variables that are available to all shell scripts and programs, while shell variables are available only within your script.

Setting a variable is quite easy; just create a variable name, and set its value like this:

```
aVariable=Value
```

> **NOTE:** The possible names a variable can have are virtually endless, but there are some rules. First, although the name can contain letters, numbers, or underscores, it's best that they begin with a letter (and they can't begin with a number, since that is reserved for command-line argument variables). Second, variables obviously can't share a name with a reserved word, which is one of the many words that have special meaning to the shell. Finally, by convention, environment variables are often written with all capital letters, and shell variables are traditionally written in all lowercase letters, but of late many people use camel case, which starts out lowercase but uses a capital letter where a new word begins. An example of camel casing is aVeryLongVariable.

> **NOTE:** Here's a list of standard shell reserved words (separated by spaces): ! case do done elif else esac fi for function if in select then until while { } time [[ ]].

It is important not to include spaces around the = when declaring your variables; if you do, you will get an error.

If you want to make your variable an environment variable (making it available everywhere), then you must export it using the export command. Usually this is done immediately after the variable is declared. This can be done all on one line, like this:

```
ENVAR=Value;  export ENVVAR
```

After the shell exports the variable, it will be immediately available for any program or shell script until the parent shell process exits. (In other words, every time you launch a new shell, you will need to redeclare and export the variable to use it again.) If you are planning on using an environmental variable over and over, it may be best to declare it in your .bash_profile file so it gets declared each time you launch your terminal or a shell.

Argument Variables

Some of the most commonly used variables are ones you don't need to declare at all. These are variables passed to the script as arguments from the command line when the script is called. For example, if you were to run an executable script called `ascript`, you could pass arguments to the script when you call it, like this:

Simba:~ scott$ **ascript arg1 arg2 arg3**

Here the `arg1`, `arg2`, and `arg3` values are automatically assigned to the variables $1, $2, and $3 so they can be used as needed in the script.

> **NOTE:** In many computer languages, counting begins with 0, not 1. Command-line arguments in scripts are no exception. In scripts, $0 is always the script itself and will return the complete path name of the executed script.

These special variables don't have to be passed in from the command line, though. Occasionally it may be advantageous to create and control these arguments from within the script. This can be done by using the `set` command (as we did in our example shell script earlier). The `set` command will replace all command-line arguments with the arguments provided.

> **NOTE:** `set` is a fairly complex command in Bash with lots of different capabilities. If you use `set` alone on the command line, it will list every environmental variable and function available to you in a nice, readable format. Used with options, `set` allows you to toggle many shell attributes. If you are interested, the gory details of all the possibilities for this command begin on page 51 of the Bash man page and continue until about three-quarters of the way through page 53. Also of note, `set` behaves differently in other shells; for example, in csh you would use `set` in place of `export` to create environmental variables. You can find a brief description of the built-in `set` command as it relates to Bash at http://www.gnu.org/software/bash/manual/htmlnode/The-Set-Builtin.html.

Command Substitution

Another way to assign a variable is through command substitution. This allows you to work with the result of any shell command by enclosing the command with backticks (the ` character below the Esc key on most Mac keyboards). This allows you to take advantage of any shell command, making up for most of the shell's natural shortcomings. For example, the Bourne shell doesn't have built-in capabilities for simple arithmetic; however, using command substitution, you can take advantage of command-line executables that do this for you anyway, like this:

```
#!/bin/sh
x=2
y=3
z=`expr $x + $y`
echo $z
```

This little script uses the `expr` executable to do the math for you and then prints "5," which is what you'd expect.

> **NOTE:** The Bash shell actually does have a built-in arithmetic capability facilitated by the `let` built-in, so if you were so inclined, you could replace the z=`expr $x + $y` line with `let` z=$x+$y and get the same results. (`let` specifically carries out arithmetic operations on variables.)

Controlling the Flow

The ability to control the flow of a script makes it much more adaptable and useful. There are two primary ways to control the flow of a script: using *conditionals*, which will execute commands if certain conditions are met, and using *loops*, which can repeat commands over and over a predetermined number of times.

Conditional Statements

Two common conditional statements are available in shell scripts: `if` statements and `case` statements. An `if` statement checks to see whether a condition is true or false. If the condition is true, then a block of code is run; if it is false, an `else` block is run (if else exists; otherwise, nothing else happens in the block). The whole thing looks something like this:

```
if [ condition ]; then
    condition is met block
else
    condition not met block
fi
```

The `fi` at the end signals the end of the `if` statement.

One other thing that can be added to respond to multiple conditions is the `elif` (else-if) condition. This allows you to create logic like this:

```
if [ condition1 ]; then
    condition1 block
elif [ condition2 ]; then
    condition2 block
else
    no conditions met block
fi
```

One thing to keep in mind is that once the condition is met, the script will execute that block and then exit the if block entirely, so if condition1 is met, the script will not check for condition2 or run the code in that block.

There are a number of ways to create conditional statements; one of the most common is to use a mathematical test condition, as listed in Table 24–1 (the Bash alternate expressions will work only with Bash, not a traditional Bourne shell).

Table 24–1. *Mathematic Test Expressions for sh and Bash*

Expression (sh)	Bash Alternate	Result
$x -eq $y	$x == $y	True if $x is equal to $y
$x -ne $y	$x != $y	True if $x is not equal to $y
$x -It $y	$x < $y	True if $x is less than $y
$x -gt $y	$x > $y	True if $x is greater than $y
$x -le $y	$x <= $y	True if $x is less than or equal to $y
$x -ge $y	$x >= $y	True if $x is greater than or equal to $y

Another common conditional statement is for checking on the existence of a file or directory. This is especially handy if you are creating workflow or other scripts that interact with the file system. An if statement that checks for the existence of a particular file would look like this:

```
if [  -e /path/to/file ]; then
    If file exists do this
else
    If file doesn't exist do this
fi
```

Here the -e option checks for the existence of the file. Table 24–2 lists some possible options.

Table 24–2. *Common Options for Testing File Attributes in Shell Scripts*

Option	Result
-e *file*	True if the file exists at all
-f *file*	True if the file exists and it is a regular file
-d *file*	True if the file exists and it is a directory
-r *file*	True if the file exists and it is readable
-w *file*	True if the file exists and it is writeable
-x *file*	True if the file exists and it is executable

> **NOTE:** In the UNIX landscape, where everything in the file system *is* a file, a regular file is most easily defined by what it isn't. Specifically, it's not a *block special file*, a *character special file*, a *directory file*, a *pipe*, a *FIFO special file*, a *symbolic link*, or a *socket*. Those are special files, while regular files (which generally contain binary or text data) are, well, not special.

It is also possible to test multiple conditions using logical *and/or statements*. This allows you to check either whether multiple statements are all true or whether one of many statements is true. This is done using either && or || (that's the long bar over the \ key) between the conditions. [*condition1*] && [*condition2*] will return true if both conditions are true, while [*condition1*] || [*condition2*] will return true if either condition is true.

One final common conditional is to utilize the exit status of a command. Every command you run will provide an exit status; that's usually a 0 if everything ran as expected and some other number if something special happened. Using the special $? variable (which contains the exit status of the last command), you can do some interesting stuff. For example, if we wanted to periodically see whether a user was running any processes on our computer, we could use the following:

```
#!/bin/sh
ps U scott >> /dev/null
if [ $? = 0 ]; then
    echo "Scott is working on something."
else
    echo "Scott's not doing anything here right now"
fi
```

The ps U scott >> /dev/null command simply lists all the processes being run by the user scott. Since we are not interested in the output of the command (just the exit status), we send the output to /dev/null. If there are any processes, the exit status will be 0. If the user doesn't exist or the user isn't running any processes, the exit status will be 1 (different commands may provide different exit statuses for different reasons). Although this example was fairly simple, with a few tweaks it could do some more interesting things. For example, if we replaced the user scott with the user www, we could check to see whether the default Apache web server is running. If it's not, we could use the else block to restart it.

Another way of dealing with multiple potential conditions is to use a case statement. A case statement looks at a variable and responds differently depending on its value.

A case statement is generally much easier to use then an if statement; however, it's a viable alternative only if you are dealing with multiple similar outcomes that may be stored in a singe variable. For example, if we wanted to check for different exit statuses using a case statement, we could write the following:

```
#!/bin/sh
shutdown
case $? in
    0) echo "Returned 0: The command executed successfully...goodbye." ;;
```

```
1) echo "Returned 1: The command or shell returned an error." ;;
127) echo "Returned 127: The command couldn't be found." ;;
*) echo "* is a wildcard, I'm not sure what happened" ;;
esac
```

> **NOTE:** `shutdown` allows for the automated shutdown of the system. There are some additional options available that can allow you to schedule a system shutdown at a later time and provide warnings to other computer users. This command isn't used much on Mac OS X, but if your find yourself using other *nix systems, it can be a useful one to know.

> **NOTE:** You need superuser privileges to run the `shutdown` command, so as long as you don't use `sudo` to run the preceding script, it should safely exit with an error and not shut down your computer.

As you can see, using `case` you can easily check for and respond to many different outcomes.

Loops

Now that you've learned a bit about how to selectively run or not run a command based on a condition, we will cover how you can run a command over and over with loops. There are three main types of loops for shell scripting: while, until, and for loops.

The `while` and `until` loops are similar in idea, but they do the opposite in practice. Each of them takes a condition (similar to the `if` statement); however, where the `while` loop will run a block of code as long as the condition is true, the `until` loop will run as long as the condition is false.

> **CAUTION:** Poorly written loops can have the adverse effect of running forever. If you are running a script from the command line, it's easy enough to stop such a runaway script with Control-C, but if this is part of a background or startup script, things can get more complicated. Therefore, it's a good idea to test your scripts from the command line before you place them in startup files and such.

A simple `while` loop could look like this:

```
#!/bin/sh
x=1
while [ $x -le 10 ]
do
    echo $x
    x=`expr $x + r`
done
```

This script will simply go through the while loop, printing the value of $x and then increasing the value of x by 1 as long as the value of $x is equal to or less than 10. If we switched while to until, the loop would be skipped entirely, since our declared value of x (1) would immediately be less than or equal to 10.

> **NOTE:** Like if statements, while and until loops can also evaluate multiple conditions using logical and (&&) and or (||) statements.

The other common loop is the for loop. Rather than relying on a true/false condition like the while and until loops, a for loop iterates over all the elements in a list. For example, a simple script to echo back the command-line arguments could look like this:

```
#!/bin/sh
echo "The command line arguments given to $0 are:    "
for x in $@
do
    echo $x
done
```

> **NOTE:** When you run the preceding script, any arguments you add will be echoed back to you. So, if you run it, make sure to add some.

> **NOTE:** $@ is a special variable that contains each command-line argument together in a single variable.

You may find that there is situation where you need to get out of a loop before it completes, which is accomplished with either the break command or the continue command. The break command will immediately stop the current loop pass and exit the loop process entirely (i.e., the script will continue immediately following the loop). The continue command will cause a halt in the current pass through the loop, but will continue the loop process if the conditions are still met.

Input and Output

Many scripts you write will need to provide output, and often you may want a script to prompt for input as well. In the previous chapter, you learned most of the basics you need in order to output text either to the terminal or to a file using the echo command (with redirection if you want to write the output to a file), but you can also use the printf command, which provides more options for how your output is presented. To get information into a script, you can use the read command, which will provide a prompt at the command line for input.

The following script (enhanced from the previous version) shows how read and printf work (line numbers have been added for reference):

```
01:  #!/bin/sh
02:
03:  printf "Please enter your input here: "
04:  read input
05:  set $input
06:  c=$#
07:  printf "You entered the following: "
08:  for x in $@
09:  do
10:  c=`expr $c - 1`
11:      if [ $c -gt 0 ]
12:      then
13:          printf "\"$x\", "
14:      else
15:          printf "and \"$x\".\n"
16:      fi
17:  done
```

When you run this script, you get something along the lines of this:

```
Please enter your input here:  hello goodbye dogcow
You entered the following:   "hello", "goodbye", and "dogcow".
```

The first thing you may notice is that unlike the echo command, printf does not automatically add a linefeed to each statement. By using printf in line 3, the prompt for the read statement appears on the same line rather than the line below.

The read statement is on line 4, and it's fairly easy: it's the read command followed by a variable to contain our input (cleverly called input).

In line 5 we set the input as our primary script arguments.

Line 6 starts a counter and starts it with $#, another special variable, which gives us the total number of arguments assigned by set in line 5.

Line 7 provides some text for our output.

Line 8 begins a for loop that will iterate through each of the arguments set in line 5. In this case, $@ and $input will contain the same values.

Line 9 starts the for loop.

Line 10 decreases the value of our counter by 1.

Line 11 uses an if statement to see whether our counter, c, is greater than 0. The counter is set up so that when it hits 0, the loop will be on our final input argument, so we continue the loop on line 13 until we reach the last of our inputs, and then switch over to line 15.

Line 13 uses the printf statement to print one of our arguments surrounded by quotes. To get the quote to print, rather than have it be interpreted as the closing or opening of the text we are printing, we need to escape the ". We do this by preceding the quote symbol with a backslash (\). printf knows a number of these formatting escape characters (which are actually borrowed from the C programming language) and will automatically expand them into their proper form when printing. Table 24–3 lists the common escape characters.

Table 24–3. *Escape Character Expansion*

Escape Character	Name	Output
\a	Alert (bell)	Activates the terminal's bell. Depending on your Terminal preferences (set on the Advanced tab of the Terminal Inspector), this will either flash the terminal screen or make an audible noise (or both or neither). By default the terminal window will flash.
\b	Backspace	Moves the cursor back one space.
\f	Form feed	Clears the screen. Historically, this was meant to eject the current sheet of paper and start a new sheet.
\n	Newline	Moves the input to the beginning of the next line (like pressing Return).
\r	Carriage return	Moves the cursor back to the beginning of the current line; any further input would overwrite what's already there.
\t	Tab	Moves the cursor one tab space to the right.
\v	Vertical tab	Moves the cursor down one line; however, unlike \n, it will not return to the beginning of the line.
\\	Backslash	Prints the backslash character.
\'	Single quote	Prints a single quote character.
\"	Double quote	Prints a double quote character.

If our counter is set up properly (and there aren't any other glitches in our script), line 15 will run on the last of our input values, also printing it surrounded by quotes. However, instead of placing a comma (as if to continue the list), it will then print out a . and then a newline character.

Line 16 then ends the `if` statement, and line 17 ends the loop and thus our little script.

One thing not shown here is that the `read` command can actually assign different variables to the input, where, for example, each input value would be assigned its own variable—well, that is if we assume that the number of variables and the number of words are the same. If we had the following `read` statement:

```
read a b c
```

and entered this:

```
one two three
```

then $a would be assigned the value one, $b would be assigned the value two, and $c would be assigned the value three. In the event we set read to accept three variables and we get four or more input terms, the last read variable ($c in this case) will absorb all the remaining values.

> **TIP:** If the integrity of your read variables is important and you want to protect against additional input, you could assign an additional read variables to suck up all the extra data. So, if you really wanted only three input values, you could set up read with four variables and then just use the first three, thus essentially ignoring all the excess input.

One final useful related tidbit is the ability to merge an entire file into a script. This is done quite easily with the dot (that is, period) command. If you paid attention, you saw this in our sample .bash_profile file toward the end of the previous chapter where we used this:

```
if [  -f ~/.bashrc  ];  then
   . ~/.bashrc
fi
```

Here, we first check to see whether our desired file (.bashrc) exists and is a normal file. If so, we include it with the . ~/.bashrc. And that's it. This is a handy way to create complex scripts where you can write entire parts as separate files and then include them all together to effectively run as one.

> **CAUTION:** If you combine scripts together, be careful with your variables. If two different script files use the same variable names and are then included together, unexpected (often bad) things can happen since the values of the named variables may get unexpectedly changed.

Advanced Scripting with Perl, Python, and Ruby

Shell scripting is very useful and fairly powerful for many things; however, there are a number of languages more powerful than the shell for writing scripts. Mac OS X comes with three of the biggest and most powerful scripting languages in use today: Perl, Python, and Ruby. Given the breadth of these languages (which are often referred to as *interpreted programming languages* or *very high-level languages* [VHLLs], rather than just scripting languages), it would be impossible to properly teach you how to use them in all their glory in this chapter. Although these languages are fairly easy to learn to use (some more so than others), the space (and time) needed to cover all of this goes beyond what is available in this book. Still, for those of you who are familiar with these languages, or are looking to expand your programming repertoire, we would be remiss not to talk a bit about them and how they work within OS X.

Each of these languages shares a number of benefits over compiled languages such as C, C++, Objective-C, and Java, including ease of use, portability, and immediate feedback (since there is no compilation). Since they are scripting languages, all you need to write them is a text editor. Finally, each of these languages is free and well supported across a wide range of platforms and devices. The other side of this coin is that interpreted languages such as Perl, Python, and Ruby (and shell scripts, for that matter) have a few disadvantages vs. their compiled brethren: they generally lack the performance of a well-optimized compiled program; they are not as well suited for low-level programming tasks; and if you choose to distribute your script, you are also revealing all your source code, which makes scripting languages less inviting for commercial applications.

> **NOTE:** Performance is a tricky matter. Although a well-optimized compiled program will always outperform an interpreted program (at least on the initial execution of the program), because of caching, the advanced subsequent execution of interpreted programs can easily match that of the compiled programs. Additionally, because of hardware advances, the real-time difference between the two is rapidly diminishing (though never quite reaching equality). Interestingly, certain programming technologies, such as Java and some .NET technologies, are both compiled and interpreted. This could lead one to assume that these would share the faults of both compiled and interpreted languages, such as added development complexity and time, and less-than-optimal performance. Although this may be true, they also gain a few benefits, such as portability and source code obfuscation. (That's not to say that if a language can be portable, it actually is.)

Perl

Perl (which stands for Practical Extraction and Report Language) is historically the leading interpreted language (though Python and Ruby have been gaining on it over the past few years). Perl, as its name seems to imply, was initially designed to work with large chunks of text: to read in information and to parse it and/or manipulate it in meaningful ways. Thus, when the World Wide Web came into being with all of its marked-up text, Perl, combined with CGI (Common Gateway Interface), which allowed scripts to be executed to produce output for the first dynamic web pages, was uniquely suited to work with all of this data and manipulate it in fun, interesting, and useful ways. As a web language, Perl's popularity began to grow rapidly.

As a language, one of Perl's greatest assets, and also one of its greatest weaknesses, is its fantastic flexibility. It prides itself on providing multiple ways to solve any given task—Perl's motto is TMTOWTDI ("There's more then one way to do it."). In the hands of a skilled programmer, this flexibility can unleash wonderful things, but it can also create a lot of unintelligible, unmaintainable code (thus giving Perl the unflattering reputation of a "write-only" language). The truth is that although Perl allows you to write some very ugly code, you can also write very clean, understandable code in Perl. Most importantly, though, when you have a problem, Perl usually can provide a way to solve it. For example, let's say we wanted to simplify numbering lines in source code (you know, because we're writing a book and sometimes it's nice to refer to line numbers). Rather than going through each code listing and manually entering numbers, we could easily whip together the following script in Perl:

```perl
#!/usr/bin/perl -w

foreach my $file ( @ARGV ) {
    my $n = 0;
    open  (OFILE, $file)   || die "Sorry, $file can't be opened: $!";
    open  (NFILE, ">num_$file");
    while ( <OFILE> ) {
        $n++;
        print NFILE sprintf("%3d:   ",$n), $_;
    }
    close OFILE;
    close NFILE;
}
```

This script allows us to enter any number of scripts as arguments at the command line, and it will go through each one of them, numbering every line and formatting the output back into another file with the same name prefixed with num_. For example, if we saved the preceding script as pnum and then ran the script with the following command:

```
./pnum pnum
```

the script would create a new file called num_pnum that would contain the following text:

```
1:    #!/usr/bin/perl -w
2:
3:    foreach my $file ( @ARGV ) {
4:    my $n = 0;
5:    open (OFILE, $file) || die "Sorry, $file can't be opened: $!";
6:    open (NFILE, ">num_$file");
7:            while ( <OFILE> ) {
8:                    $n++;
9:                    print NFILE sprintf("%3d:   ",$n), $_;
10:        }
11:        close OFILE;
12:        close NFILE;
13:    }
```

One other fantastic feature of Perl, which may be its ultimate strength, is that because of its maturity, it has built up a large collection of code libraries (called *Perl modules*) that can help you solve almost any task you can think of. Additionally, it has created a system around these libraries, the Comprehensive Perl Archive Network (CPAN), that provides an effective way of accessing these modules for your code. For the OS X user, included in CPAN are a number of modules for using Perl to manipulate Apple applications such as iTunes and iPhoto, as well as for accessing Apple events from Perl, and more.

For the ultimate in OS X/Perl programming, the Camel Bones project (`http://camelbones.sourceforge.net`) brings together a range of OS X/Perl-specific libraries, frameworks, and modules, allowing you to perform tasks such as creating Aqua interfaces for Perl scripts and using Perl instead of Objective-C in Cocoa applications.

Lion ships with version 5.12.3 of Perl, while, as of this writing, the latest official version of Perl is 5.14.0. Somewhere on the horizon is Perl 6, a complete rewrite of Perl that promises not only a new and improved interpreter, but also many updates to the language. For more information about Perl, the best place to start is the official web site: `www.perl.org`.

Python

Python, although not as well known as Perl, has been around for almost as long, but while Perl got to ride on the web wave because of its text-processing abilities, Python, being designed as a general-purpose scripting language, was often overlooked. Because of its more general-purpose beginnings, in many areas, especially surrounding math and science, Python was just the thing developers needed.

Python possesses a number of features that differentiate itself from Perl. First, Python was designed as an object-oriented scripting language (Perl gained reasonable object-oriented capabilities in version 5; however, on the whole, Perl is still used very much as a procedural programming language). Second, unlike Perl, Python script writing style is very strict. Proper indentation of code, whitespace, and line breaks have specific, essential meaning to Python. This often makes existing Python code much easier to understand than most Perl code, but dictating a strict style has also caused a few issues through Python's evolution (and of course has caused a few "free-thinking" individuals to shun the language).

Python has been around on the Mac for a while (beginning with MacPython even before Mac OS X). Today, like Perl, it's a standard part of Darwin. Unlike Perl, Python is developed as a framework, rather than many other Darwin applications, making Python available for Cocoa programming as well as Darwin development right out of the box.

Learning Python is fairly easy, as there are lots of books and online tutorials available. One of the best places to start is the Python tutorial at `http://docs.python.org/tut/`. One nice part about learning Python is that it comes with its own interactive interpreter, which will start when you type python at the command line without arguments. Not only is this a great tool for learning the language, but it can be very handy for unleashing the power of Python for common tasks. We use the Python interpreter all the time as a calculator (I find it much faster and more flexible to use than the GUI calculator for most things). A session with the Python interpreter could look like this:

```
simba:bin scott$ python
Python 2.7.1 (r271:86832, May  9 2011, 13:12:03)
[GCC 4.2.1 (Based on Apple Inc. build 5658) (LLVM build 2335.14.00)] on darwin
Type "help", "copyright", "credits" or "license" for more information.
>>> x=2
```

```
>>> for y in range(11):
...     y*x
...
0
2
4
6
8
10
12
14
16
18
20
>>>
```

> **NOTE:** Remember, Python uses tabs to indent code, not spaces. In the previous code sample, there is a singe tab between the first ... and y*x. There is simply a hard return after the second ....

As you may surmise from this, you can accomplish a lot of stuff with very little code. Once programmers learn the nuances of Python, they generally find themselves creating code at a significantly faster pace than with most other languages.

Ruby

Ruby is the new kid in the family, but it's making quite a showing, largely because of the buzz surrounding Ruby on Rails (RoR). RoR, which is included in Mac OS X, is a very nice web application framework written in Ruby. Ruby shares many similarities with Python in general and in Mac OS X. Both are object oriented (in Ruby everything becomes an object), both are relatively easy to pick up, and both include an interactive interpreter for playing around with code (Ruby's interactive interpreter is not built into the language in the same way that Python's is; to get to the Ruby interactive interpreter, you use the irb command). For OS X developers, the most important similarity is that they are both compiled as Cocoa frameworks, which makes them available for Cocoa development as well as Darwin development. Despite the similarities, Ruby is different from Python most noticeably semantically, but also syntactically.

Because Ruby is a newer language, it seems to have learned to avoid a number of issues and perhaps shortcomings that Perl and Python have had, while at the same time incorporating new ideas that weren't mature when Perl and Python were conceived. On the other hand, because of its relative newness, Ruby has not been tested as much as Perl or Python, and as such may not be as hardened as them. For example, there are those who think Ruby does not scale (in a performance sense) as well as Perl or Python.

> **NOTE:** Much of the performance talk about Ruby may be because, in the past, its use on a large scale was fairly limited. Today, you need only point to Twitter or Hulu to see that Ruby can in fact scale quite well, and as it matures, we can imagine it improving in this area.

If you are looking for specifics on developing Ruby Cocoa applications, documentation is included with the Xcode Tools installation (`/Developer/Documentation/RubyCocoa/`).

Installing New UNIX Software

Although scripting is a good solution for simple problems, or new problems, often it's easier to just use a program that someone else has already written. UNIX and related operating systems (such as Linux) have been around for a very long time and continue to be popular, so for many of the tasks you may want to accomplish, an existing application or program may already be available. Best of all, many of these programs are available for free and are waiting for you to install them. Some are available simply by downloading an OS X installation package and installing it like any other OS X app (MySQL is a popular database that is available in many formats, including an official OS X installation package), but many more are available as a precompiled binary (i.e., a ready-to-run program), or more commonly (and often preferably) as a source package. This gives you some options. You could download the source package, configure it for your specific needs, and then compile the source code into an application optimized for your computer. You could try to locate a precompiled binary and install that (and hope that it works right). Or you could take advantage of MacPorts (formerly known as DarwinPorts), which provides a relatively easy way of finding, installing, and maintaining third-party Darwin applications. This ultimately boils down to preference, but if you haven't already formed your own, we suggest you try the following, in this order:

1. An official binary release, if available, would be the first choice. This should make installation trivial and effective, and should make for easy upgrades if needed. Additionally, any other applications that may rely on the application would probably assume the official release.

2. If an official version is not available, check MacPorts to see whether the application you are after is available. MacPorts, once properly set up, will provide you with a way to download and install the application. MacPorts will also assure that any other applications or libraries that the application depends on are installed as well, and will provide an effective way to upgrade the apps or uninstall them if you no longer need them.

3. If you need a highly customized version of an app, or want to sidestep MacPorts for whatever reason, then you can download the source code and compile the application yourself. This will assure that the app is good to go; however, if you go this route, you will need to manually assure that all dependencies are covered, and all further maintenance of the package will need to be made manually.

4. Installing a random precompiled binary should be a last resort and should generally be avoided, unless the binary comes from a trusted, reliable source and was compiled for your specific system; that is, an application compiled for Tiger (OS X 10.4) might not work right on Lion (OS X 10.7). There are very few cases where this is recommended.

> **NOTE:** A good source of finding official binaries, or at least reputable ones, is on Apple's web site, at `www.apple.com/downloads/macosx/unix_open_source/`. Here Apple provides lots of UNIX and open source software and utilities to download.

> **NOTE:** Much of the software available for Darwin has come from other UNIX and Linux roots; however, binary applications from Linux or other UNIXes will not just work in Mac OS X. First they must be specifically compiled and occasionally significantly changed to work correctly (if they will work at all).

MacPorts

As mentioned, one excellent way to get a large amount of Darwin goodness is through MacPorts. MacPorts (`www.macports.org`) originated as the DarwinPorts project at Apple as the quasiofficial way to manage additional Darwin applications. As such, it was rumored that sooner or later DarwinPorts would be integrated into Mac OS X. As of yet this has not happened; instead, the project was renamed to MacPorts. MacPorts is part of Mac OS Forge (`http://macosforge.org`), which is a larger project that hosts many of the open source projects specific to OS X. Other Mac OS Forge projects include Bonjour, the Darwin Streaming Server, WebKit, xnu (Darwin's Kernel), and Calendar Server. Apple sponsors all of these projects.

MacPorts does not have an option to install precompiled binaries, so to use MacPorts, you must have the latest version of the Xcode Tools installed. Many MacPorts applications also assume you have installed the X11 packages and the X11SDK.

MacPorts by default installs itself, and all the packages you install with it, in the `/opt/local` directory, so to effectively use MacPorts, you'll need to add `/opt/local/bin` and `/opt/local/sbin` to your $PATH. Additionally, if you decide at some point to use any of the X11 applications from MacPorts, you should add the line `export DISPLAY=:0.0` to your `.bash_profile` as well.

Once all of that's out of the way, you can download and install the latest MacPorts binary installer from `www.macports.org`.

Once the installation is complete, the first thing you should do is to make sure everything is up to date. To do this, run the following command in the terminal:

```
sudo port selfupdate
```

> **NOTE:** Why would you need to update something you just downloaded? Well, the binary installer is packaged together only at certain intervals, while the updating of software is constant. By performing a self-update, you ensure that you are catching any new packages that have been added since the binary package was assembled.

This will update the entire ports system. Once you start using MacPorts, you should continue to periodically run this command to make sure you are working with a current version of MacPorts and that you have a list of all the current applications.

Once your environment is set up and you have the latest updated version of MacPorts installed, it's quite easy to use MacPorts with the commands listed in Table 24–4.

> **NOTE:** Many of the commands needed to successfully install and manage MacPorts require root privileges. As such, some of the commands require the use of sudo. Please keep in mind all the cautions regarding the use of sudo covered in the last chapter.

Table 24–4. *MacPorts Commands*

Command	Action
port list	Returns a list of all available ports.
port search *searchstring*	Returns a list of available ports whose name matches *searchstring*.
port info *appname*	Returns information about the port named *appname*.
port variants *appname*	Occasionally a port will have multiple options; if so, this command will list the additional port options available for the port *appname*.
sudo port install *appname*	Installs the base *appname* port.
sudo port install *appname* +*option1* +*option2*	Installs the port *appname* with *option1* and *option2*.
port installed	Returns a list of installed ports.
sudo port selfupdate	Updates the base port package as well as the list of ports.
sudo port outdated	Lists outdated installed ports.
sudo port upgrade *appname*	Upgrades port *appname*.
sudo port upgrade outdated	Upgrades all outdated installed ports.
sudo port uninstall *appname*	Removes the port *appname*.
sudo port clean *appname*	Removes the build files for *appname*, which is a good way to free up disk space after you install a port.

FINK: AN ALTERNATIVE TO MACPORTS

Another popular system for installing and managing additional Darwin and open source software is Fink (www.finkproject.org). While much of the software available from MacPorts and Fink is the same, there are a few notable differences between the two.

First of all, the command-line tools are different. MacPorts is based on the BSD ports system, while Fink uses the Debian-based dpkg (see www.debian.org) and apt-get tools. This provides a notable advantage to Fink in that many of the available packages come precompiled for your version of Mac OS X, saving you time when you want to install something and also alleviating the need to have the Xcode developer tools installed.

Second, Fink will, by default, install into the /sw directory, while MacPorts will install into the /opt directory. This tends to be rather arbitrary; however, because of this difference, both Fink and MacPorts can coexist on the same system without too much trouble.

The bottom line is that either one of these provides a nice way of adding some really cool extra software to your system. And in the end, the primary difference comes down to what you are most comfortable with. You can't go wrong with either of them.

Compiling Software from the Source Code

With the maturity of Darwin in Mac OS X combined with the availability of most popular open source software through MacPorts (or Fink), it's rare that you would ever need to compile software from source code (unless of course you are actively developing software, in which case you probably know all the information we're about to relate, plus a good bit more). Still, if you really want to try a bleeding-edge program that hasn't found its way to Fink or MacPorts, or you think you must compile an application with just the right options, then you'll want to compile your own application from source code.

> **CAUTION:** Compiling your own software from source code is not for the weak. Things will often just not work as they should, and it could take some time and research to figure out how to get something built correctly on your computer. Sometimes, things won't work at all (unless of course you want to dig into the code yourself and tweak it). If you are easily frustrated, then we suggest that the benefits of compiling your own program might not outweigh the mental anguish you could be setting yourself up for.

Compiling your application from source code generally requires three steps: configuring, building, and installing. Usually these steps are fairly automated, and with the exception of the configure stage, are usually pretty much the same.

> **NOTE:** To be honest, there is often a fourth step: figuring out what went wrong when one of the three primary steps fails.

Before you start any steps, though, you need to get the source code. This can usually be found on a project's web site or through a source repository such as SourceForge (www.sourceforge.net).

Step 1: Configure

For users building an application for their own use, the configure stage is the most important part of the whole build process. This is where you can customize the application for your specific needs and your specific system. The first part of configuring your build is to see what configure options are available. You do this by going into the primary source folder and typing the following:

```
./configure --help
```

This will return a whole list of configure options. Most of these options either have sensible defaults or are automatically set during the configure stage. The things you want to look at are the optional features to see whether any of them would be useful to you.

> **NOTE:** One configure option you may want to pay special attention to is where things will get installed. Traditionally, all software you install yourself would (should) be installed in the /usr/local/ subdirectory. In UNIX file systems, things in / are necessary for the system, things in /usr/ are part of the default system, and things in /usr/local/ are things that are added on or customized for the system. Maintaining this sort of hierarchy assures that essential files aren't adversely affected by any incompatibilities or errors.

> **NOTE:** Certain programs require that your system provide specific libraries or other applications to compile correctly, and this is especially true for certain options you may want to build into your application; these are what are referred to as *dependencies.* MacPorts and Fink will usually solve dependency issues automatically when you install apps using them, but when you are compiling things yourself, you need to make sure these dependencies are satisfied.

If you think you don't need any options, you can usually configure your build by just typing this:

`./configure`

If you want to include options, then you would type something like this:

`./configure --with-option1 --with-option2 --enable-feature-x [...]`

Either way, when you press Return, the configure script will run and attempt to create a *makefile*, which will guide the actual build and install processes (together referred to as the *make process*). For a complex program, the configure script can take a few minutes or even longer to do its work, during which time lots of text will scroll by, letting you know what's happening. Upon successful completion, the text will often issue a message saying that the configure completed successfully, and perhaps giving some additional build advice. If something goes wrong, the text may or may not give you a clue as to what needs to be fixed.

> **NOTE:** If something goes wrong, it's not always going to be easy to fix. Scrolling through the configure text may reveal a missing library, or it may indicate it cannot figure out what to do with your system. A missing library can usually be found and installed (sometimes it's there but the configure can't find it, in which case you may need to specify the library path as a configure option). Sometimes there is a specific issue, and if you poke around support forums, you can get an answer. Sadly, sometimes it's just not going to work on your system.

Step 2: Build

If the configure stage went without issue, the next step is to build the app. This should be as easy as typing the following:

`make`

Yep, that's it. Now go get a cup of coffee, stretch your legs, or play a game on your Wii while your computer compiles your program. Although these days it could take your computer anywhere from a few seconds to a few hours to compile a program, for a moderately complex application it usually takes only between 5 and 30 minutes depending on your computer.

Here's one trick to significantly speed up this process. Since even the lowliest Mac mini has at least two processor cores, you can use them both simply by adding `-j 2` to the end of `make`. `make -j 4` will work if you have four cores, and so on.

> **NOTE:** Again, occasionally things will go wrong. Unfortunately, an error during the build process is usually even more difficult to track down than during the configure stage. If you notice the build failing in a specific that you identify with a configure option, you may try not enabling (or disabling) that particular option. If you really aren't using any strange options (or if you're not using any at all), and this is a fairly popular program, then it's likely someone else is having the same issues, and if enough people are having these issues, then it's possible someone out there has a solution.

Step 3: Install

Usually, if you are dealing with a stable version of a popular application, things go smoothly and your configure and build stages happen without issue (or without major issues anyway), after which it comes time to install your program. This is also a very easy process; just type the following:

```
sudo make install
```

That should do it.

Most software compiled this way will install software in the /usr/local/ directory. By default this directory doesn't exist in Mac OS X, so you may want to create it. If, however, you want to install your software (or parts of it) somewhere else, this can usually be configured as a configure option (though this isn't highly recommended).

To sum up, the quick way to compile a program you downloaded as source code is often as easy as this:

```
./configure
make
sudo make install
```

Summary

We covered a lot of material in this chapter, from writing to shell scripts to compiling an application from source code. The point here wasn't to make you an expert at any of these things, but to familiarize you with some of the power that Darwin brings to the Mac world. The most important parts of this chapter were the ones on MacPorts, though, since MacPorts provides the path of least resistance to the world of great new software. Then, should you ever need to install and use something like, say, figlet, you'll be just a few commands away from being able to do this:

```
simba:~ scott$ sudo port install figlet
Password:
---> Fetching figlet
---> Attempting to fetch figlet-2.2.4.tar.gz from
http://ykf.ca.distfiles.macports.org/MacPorts/mpdistfiles/figlet
---> Attempting to fetch figlet-2.2.4.tar.gz from http://distfiles.macports.org/figlet
```

```
---> Attempting to fetch figlet-2.2.4.tar.gz from
ftp://ftp.figlet.org/pub/figlet/program/unix/
---> Verifying checksum(s) for figlet
---> Extracting figlet
---> Applying patches to figlet
---> Configuring figlet
---> Building figlet
---> Staging figlet into destroot
---> Installing figlet @2.2.4_0
---> Activating figlet @2.2.4_0
---> Cleaning figlet
simba:~ scott$ figlet neat huh?
```

Part VII

Lion Networking

Although most modern computing devices are quite capable of accessing common network services such as e-mail and the Web, Mac OS X with its Unix underpinning can dish out a packet just as well as it can take one. Part VII covers Mac OS X networking, beginning with advanced network configuration and then moving on to talk about sharing files and other resources over a network. Part VII concludes with an overview of the web-serving prowess that is included with Lion.

## Chapter 25

Networking Beyond Connecting to the Internet

Earlier in this book (Chapter 8) we discussed the basics of connecting to a network with the goal of connecting to the Internet. For many people, that was all the networking knowledge one would need; however, Mac OS X being Mac OS X, it has lots of networking power for those who want or need it. In this chapter we are going to

- Provide a basic overview of networking and network terminology

- Look at some advanced networking options offered on the Network System Preference pane

- Explore additional networking tools offered by Mac OS X, including Network Utility and AirPort Utility

Networking Defined

When you send an e-mail message from your computer to a friend's computer, across town or halfway around the world, a whole bunch of stuff happens behind the scene to make sure it gets there. First, your message is broken up into *packets* or *datagrams* (small organized collections of data and metadata that can be reassembled as your complete message when it reaches each destination). The way these packets are created and reassembled is defined by a protocol, in this case TCP (Transmission Control Protocol). These packets are then sent from your computer using another protocol, usually SMTP (Simple Mail Transfer Protocol), to your outgoing mail server, which will forward your message using yet another protocol, IP (Internet Protocol), on a journey around the Internet until it reaches your friend's mail server. There, your friend's computer will use another protocol, such as IMAP (Internet Mail Access Protocol), to query its mail server and download the message. Sounds like a lot of work to send a simple message. In fact, this little example glosses over a number of other stops and protocols that likely were used along the way.

> **NOTE:** As in the preceding example, I'm going to try to keep this discussion somewhat oversimplified. My goal is to provide an understanding of how things work if you're interested, at which point you can go seek it out. For everyone else, you could probably skim over this section (or this whole chapter) and be perfectly content.

To add to the complexity, there are different ways of describing networking: there is the OSI (Open Systems Interconnection) model, which defines seven different networking protocol layers, and there is the Internet Protocol Suite (know more often as TCP/IP), which defines four. For our purposes we are going to focus on the Internet Protocol Suite, not only because it's simpler, but also because this is all most people in most situations today will need to know.

The Internet Protocol Suite (TCP/IP)

The Internet Protocol Suite, as mentioned, defines four layers of protocols that work together to send all manner of information from one point to another over a network, These layers are:

- **The Link Layer**: This is the lowest layer in the Internet Protocol Suite; it covers protocols that cover the connections between physical devices or hosts. For example, a Wi-Fi connection between your computer and a wireless router would fall into the link layer. Common protocols in the link layer include PPP, MAC (Media Access Control), DSL, ISDN, and IEEE 802.11 (Wi-Fi) (many of these were mentioned in Chapter 8).

- **The Internet Layer**: This layer defines protocols that define how datagrams and packets are sent from one location to the next through the use of gateways. In other words, this defines how data on one system is accurately routed to the system or systems where it is intended. The most common protocol for this layer is IP (IPv4 and IPv6).

- **The Transport Layer**: The transport layer protocols work with the application layer to assure that data is reliably transported from end to end in a network. That is, while the Internet layer assures that the data moves from system to system, the transport layer assures that the data is accurately moved from the application on one system to the appropriate application process on the other. The most common transport protocols are TCP and UDP (User Datagram Protocol).

- **The Application Layer**: Using the transport layer, the application layer contains protocols that allow one application to talk to another application over a network. This layer contains a long list of common protocols, including DNS, SMTP, IMAP, POP, Telnet, and HTTP.

All four layers work together, often at the same time, to make networks and network applications work as expected.

> **NOTE:** Internet Protocol Suite gets its name from the Internet, which, as you may have guessed, is built and functions using this protocol suite. While there are other networking protocols in use that aren't covered here, they are extremely rare, as most networking technology today has evolved from the Internet.

Common Networking Terms and Protocols

Of the few common protocols just mentioned, some you may have heard of; others maybe not. One thing you may have noticed is that most of them are acronyms that aren't very descriptive of what they do or why you would care about them. Table 25–1 provides a list of some of the protocols and other networking-related terms that are fairly common, along with definitions.

> **NOTE:** You may encounter most of the terms mentioned following if you decide to manually configure a traditional port-based firewall. While Mac OS X uses an alternative socket-based firewall, many routers contain firewalls that can be highly configured based on the type of packet being sent or received.

Table 25–1. *Common Networking Terms and Protocols*

Name	Definition
Protocols	
TCP (Transmission Control Protocol)	This is the most common transport layer protocol in use today. It and IP form the two major protocols that made the Internet possible. While TCP is essential for modern networking, users will likely never need to deal directly with TCP on any level.
IP (Internet Protocol)	This is largely responsible for data being accurately routed from one system to another. Most computers on a network are required to have an accurate IP address. Today IPv4 address are the most common; however, IPv6 is becoming more widespread.
UDP (User Datagram Protocol)	This is an alternate transport layer protocol that is more lightweight than TCP because it foregoes built-in handshaking and error correcting (duplicate packets and packets arriving out of order are common). Despite its lack of built-in data integrity, because of its lack of overhead UDP is very common for streaming services and online games where lack of latency overrides the need for 100 percent data integrity.

Name	Definition
DHCP (Dynamic Host Configuration Protocol)	DHCP allows a primary server or router to automatically assign and manage the network configuration of any client computer. Because of this you will rarely, if ever, need to configure the networking on your computer for basic use.
DNS (Domain Name System)	DNS is a system that maps domain names to IP addresses. This is useful because apple.com is easier to remember than 17.172.224.47.
FTP (File Transfer Protocol)	FTP is a traditional method to upload and download files to and from a server. While still in wide use, it has been loosing popularity for other methods of file transfer.
HTTP (Hypertext Transfer Protocol)	HTTP it the primary protocol for the World Wide Web (hence the http part of a web address like http://www.apple.com).
IMAP (Internet Mail Access Protocol)	IMAP provides a method of accessing e-mail messages from a client while the messages are stored on the server. Managing messages on the server allows your e-mail to be accessed from multiple clients.
POP (Post Office Protocol)	POP is a slightly older protocol for accessing one's e-mail from a server. Unlike IMAP, with POP, messages are downloaded and managed on the client, not the server.
SMTP (Simple Mail Transfer Protocol)	While POP and IMAP are both options for retrieving mail from a server, SMTP is primarily for sending e-mail and routing it to its intended destination.
SSH (Secure Shell)	SSH is a popular method of securely accessing a remote system. While traditionally used for remote command-line access, SSH has features that allow its use for other types of connections, such as SFTP for file transfer.
TLS/SSL (Transport Layer Security and Secure Sockets Layer)	These protocols are part of the transport layer that allow the connection between two system to be secure (i.e., data passed between the two layers is encrypted). Today it is very common to use one of these protocols along with IMAP, SMTP, POP, and HTTP (i.e., a secure web connection).

Other Common Network Terms

Name	Definition
VPN (Virtual private network)	A VPN allows a client system to form a direct connection with a remote host or server separate from any other network that the client system has access to. This allows the client to securely join a private network from a remote location over the Internet. *VPN* is a generic term; the actual protocol used to create a VPN connection can be L2TP over IPSec, PPTP, and Cisco's proprietary (yet very popular) version of IPSec. (All three of these protocols are built in to OS X.)

Name	Definition
Proxy server	A proxy server is a special server that acts as an intermediary between a client and another server. The most common proxy used today is a web proxy, which may allow one to access information on a remote server that may otherwise be blocked.
802.1X	802.1X (not be confused with 802.11, or Wi-Fi) is a standard for network access control. Users who use their Macs in a corporate setting may need to add an 802.1X certificate to access network resources.
WINS (Windows Internet Name Service)	WINS is a Microsoft implementation of the NetBIOS name service. This allows the name of your system to be broadcast on a network, which is useful for many sharing services on a Microsoft network.
MAC (Media Access Control) Address	A MAC address is a unique identifier for a network interface. The manufacturer usually assigns a MAC address to a network interface. It is possible to override the assigned MAC address using a technique referred to as MAC spoofing. While there are legitimate uses for this, usually MAC spoofing is used to either bypass security or impersonate another device on a network.

This is by no means an all-inclusive list of networking terms; however, these are the terms that you are most likely to encounter for certain more advanced yet common network configurations.

Advanced Mac OS X Network Configuration

In Chapter 8 we discussed connecting to the Internet. There, we relied on DHCP to handle most of the configuration of our network connection. Here we'll look behind the curtain to see what must be done if we are in a situation where DHCP either isn't available or isn't enough.

The Advanced Networking Options

To enter the advanced network configuration dialog, select the network interface you wish to configure on the Network System Preference pane and click the Advanced button in the lower-right corner. This will open up a dialog with six or seven tabs: Wi-Fi (only for Wi-Fi interfaces), TCP/IP, DNS, WINS, 802.1X, Proxies, and Hardware.

TCP/IP

The TCP/IP tab (Figure 25–1) gives you a number of options for configuring your all-important IP address, which, as described previously, is necessary for data on the network to successfully reach your system. Here you can configure IPv4 and IPv6 independently.

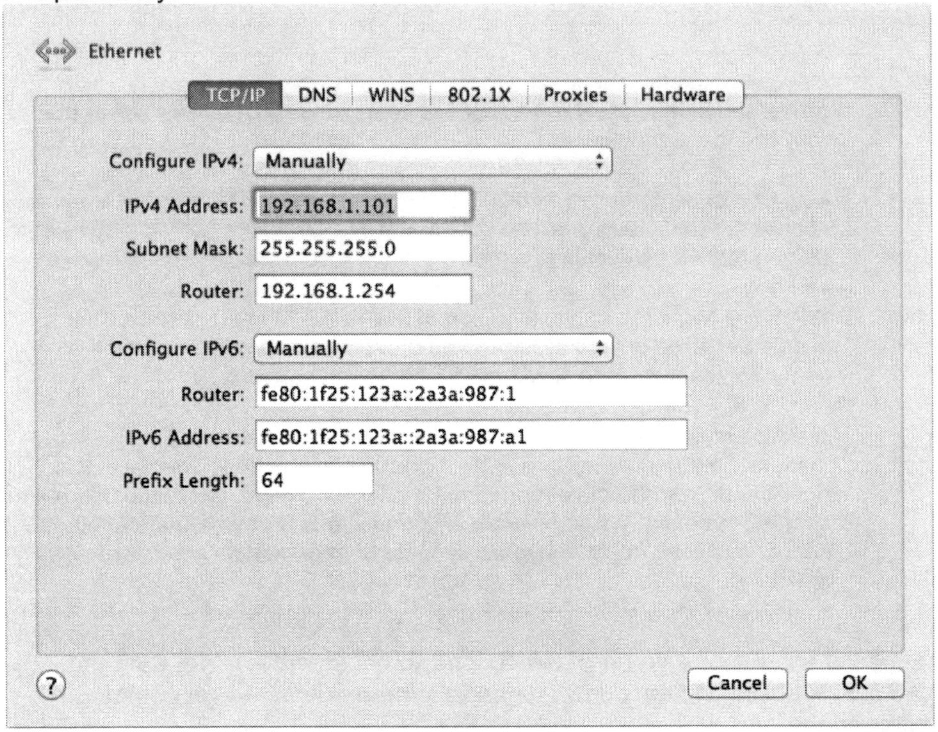

Figure 25–1. *The TCP/IP tab on the Network Preference pane's Advanced dialog allows you to change your IP address and related networking information.*

Configuring IPv4 has four options: Using DHCP, "Using DHCP with manual address," BootP, and Manually. If you should have to manually configure your network, you will need to first collect a few bits of information: the IP address assigned for you computer (which must be unique, at least within your network), the router or gateway address, the subnet mask, and the IP address for your DNS server(s) (which will be covered later).

> **TIP:** The "Using DHCP with manual address" option allows you to manually set your IP address while otherwise having the benefits of DHCP. This is very useful if you must have a set IP address for whatever reason (i.e., you are using your computer as a server and need a static IP address). Keep in mind if you choose this option that you must choose an unassigned unique IP address. Generally, a DHCP server will only assign IP address within a range, leaving valid IP addresses unassigned. These unassigned IP address are a good place to look for available IPs.

CAUTION: IP addresses must be unique. You should not randomly pick an IP address for any system, or you could cause some real network issues, not only for yourself, but also for others. If a static IP address is assigned to you from a network provider, that is what you should use. If you are running you own local network, you can use NAT (Network Address Translation) to set up a private network behind a router (this is what most local networks and Wi-Fi routers do). There are certain blocks of IP addresses that you are free to use within your private network within IPv4. These address spaces are 192.168.0.0 to 192.168.255.255, 10.0.0.0 to 10.255.255.255, and 172.16.0.0 to 172.31.255.255. With IPv6 the range is FC00::/7 (anything beginning with FC). If you want to experiment, experiment within that range.

NOTE: Only certain servers and routers should ever have to manually configure IPv6. If you find yourself in this situation, it's assumed that you know what you are doing, so other than showing you where to enter the information I'm not going to dwell on the specifics.

DNS

The next tab in the advanced network dialog is the DNS tab (Figure 25–2). The DNS tab has two columns: one for listing your preferred DNS servers and the other for listing your preferred search domains. A DNS server is a service that will help resolve domain names, so when you type in a domain name (like apple.com), your request will make it to the proper IP address associated with the domain name.

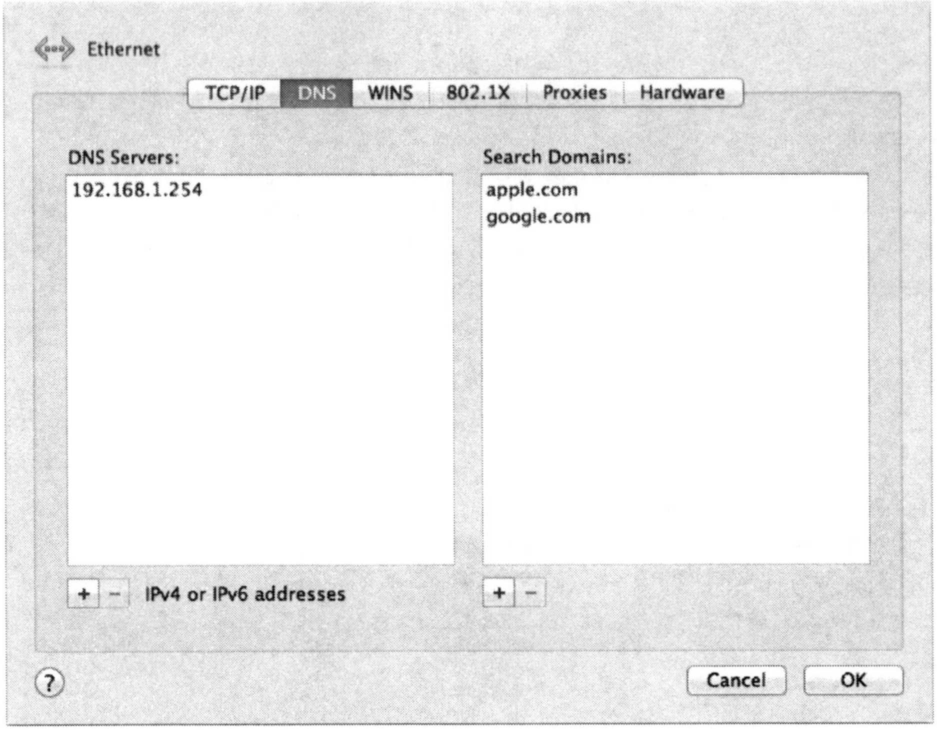

Figure 25–2. *The DNS tab allows you to set up your preferred DNS servers and search domains.*

TIP: Usually DHCP will automatically configure a DNS server (or servers) along with the rest of the network information, and if you are given information to manually configure your network settings, the proper DNS servers will be included. That said, you are not limited to these DNS servers; if you'd like to add to (or replace) your designated DNS server, you can. There are a number of public DNS servers that you are able to include here, including 8.8.8.8 and 8.8.4.4, two of Google's public DNS servers (for IPv6, use 2001:4860:4860::8888 and 2001:4860:4860::8844).

NOTE: DNS, while relatively simple in terms of networking on the whole, is still fairly complex—too complex to describe in detail here. If you are deeply interested in networking, it is definitely a topic worth fully understanding. A good place to start for a more complete explanation is www.howstuffworks.com/dns.htm.

The Search Domain column allows you to add a list of domain names that allows you to enter any number of domains that will be appended to names you type in Internet applications. For example, if apple.com and tumblr.com are added there (with apple.com listed first—order here is important), and then you type developer in the address field of Safari, you will be taken to http://developer.apple.com. If you type theatlantic, you will be taken to http://theatlantic.tumblr.com since theatlantic.apple.com doesn't exist.

> **NOTE:** By default, if a term doesn't match anything in your Search Domain list, Safari will make a last-ditch attempt to add .com to the term; however, certain domains are "hungry" and will swallow all matches. tumblr.com is one such domain, so any terms that don't match *.apple.com or *.tumblr.com will result in a tumblr page-not-found screen.

WINS

The WINS tab (Figure 25–3) allows you to configure your Mac to work with Microsoft Windows name services. The NetBIOS name is the name your computer is given on Windows networks. Workgroup is the workgroup your computer will be assigned to, and the WINS Servers field is for a list of dedicated WINS servers that serve a purpose similar to a DNS server for Windows networks.

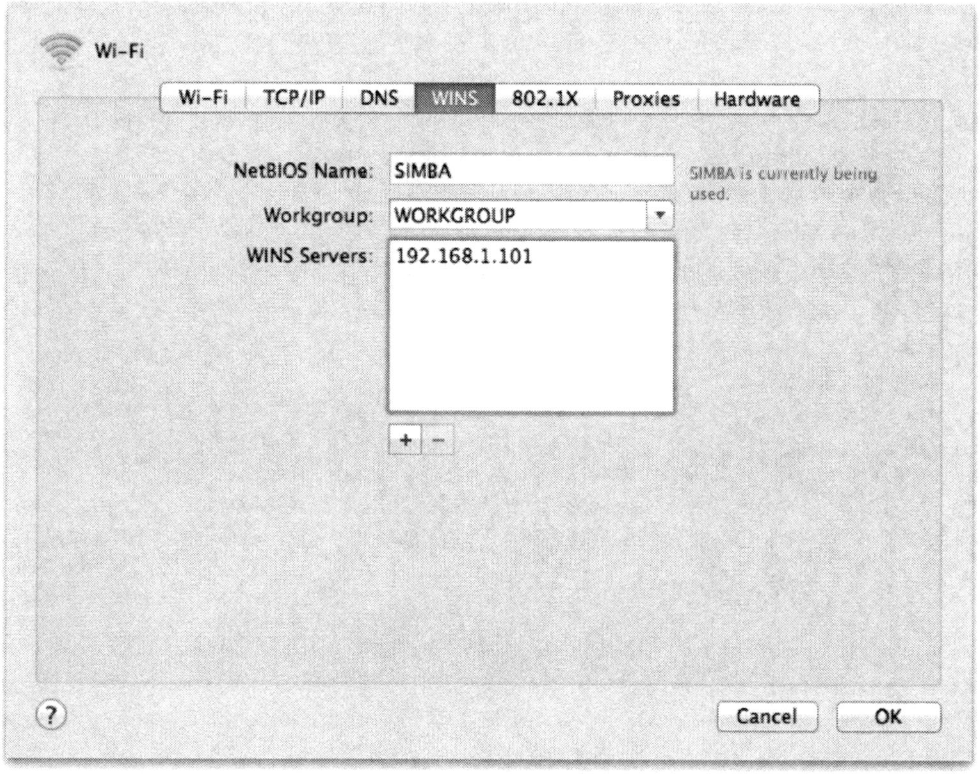

Figure 25–3. *The WINS tab allows you to configure your Mac to behave on Windows networks.*

802.1X

As mentioned, 802.1X is an access control standard that is enabled on many networks (especially in corporations and other large organizations). If you are required to connect to such a network, you will need to add a valid certificate to this tab. (The certificate helps certify the validity of the connection between your computer and the network). There will also be some additional configuration and authentication steps required to connect to the network. After your first successful connection, all the information will be stored, so you shouldn't need to reenter it each time. Selecting the "Enable automatic connection" option will automatically initial the network connection whenever you are attached to the protected network.

Proxies

Certain local networks are protected by a firewall that requires users to access the Internet through a proxy. A proxy is a server that sits between a computer and the Internet, ensuring all Internet traffic passes through the it. The proxy can be used for filtering, administrative control, and caching.

Occasionally, proxies will only be necessary for certain services, while other times all Internet services will need to pass through a proxy. Should your local network require a proxy, you should be given the proper configuration information from your administrator.

> **NOTE:** While proxies are generally used to help secure a network, proxies can also be used to circumvent some network protections. For example, a common use of proxies is to circumvent web filtering (e.g., a student may use a proxy to circumvent a block on Facebook at school). It should be noted that utilizing such proxies could be used to capture personal information from unsuspecting users, and as such their use is not recommended. (A crafty student could, however, set up his or her own proxy servers for such purposes, though.)

Hardware

The Hardware tab provides information about a particular network interface, including the assigned MAC address. You can also make some adjustments to how the interface will behave; however, the Automatic settings are almost always adequate.

Wi-Fi

The Wi-Fi tab (Figure 25–4) (only shown on Wi-Fi interfaces) provides some useful options for dealing with Wi-Fi connections.

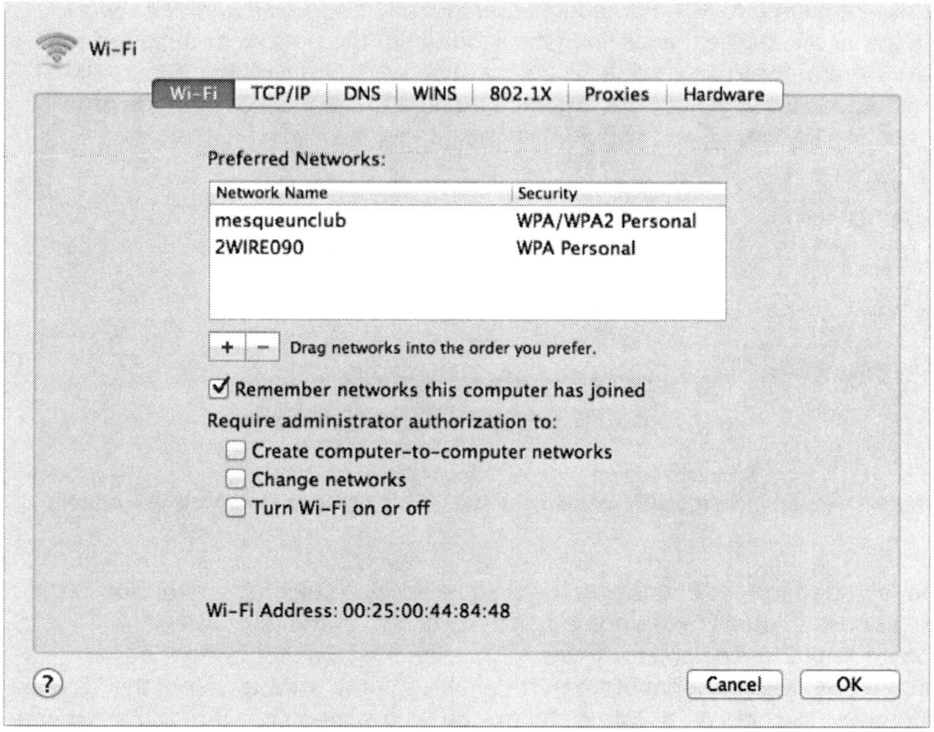

Figure 25–4. *The Wi-Fi tab provides a number of options for working with Wi-Fi networks, including the ability to manage your preferred Wi-Fi networks.*

One of the most useful options here is the ability to manage your preferred networks. If the "Remember networks this computer has joined" option is checked, every Wi-Fi network you connect to will be listed in the Preferred Networks field. You can also manually add or remove Wi-Fi networks using the + and – buttons under the Preferred Networks field. Networks listed as a preferred networks will be joined automatically when your computer comes into their range. If you work or live within range of many different networks, this assures that you will always connect to the network of your choice. If none of you preferred networks are in range, you will be prompted to connect to any available Wi-Fi networks.

Below the Preferred Networks options are some additional options for making changes to your Wi-Fi network; these will require an administrator's password.

Connecting to a VPN

One other common task that may be handled from the Network System Preference pane is setting up a VPN connection. The ability to connect to various types of VPNs is already built into Mac OS X; however, this isn't immediately evident from the network preferences. To configure a VPN connection, you must first add a new VPN network interface. This is accomplished by clicking the + button at the bottom of the interface list on the Network preference pane. Clicking the + button will open a dialog (Figure 25–5) where you should select VPN from the Interface menu and then select the type of VPN you are connecting to. Finally, you should give the interface a name.

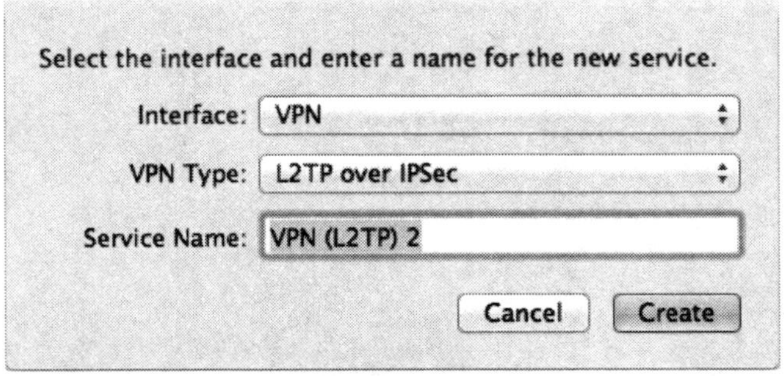

Select the interface and enter a name for the new service.

Interface: VPN

VPN Type: L2TP over IPSec

Service Name: VPN (L2TP) 2

Cancel   Create

Figure 25–5. *The first step in setting up a VPN connection in Mac OS X is adding an appropriate VPN network interface.*

Once you have added the VPN interface, it will show up as a selectable interface in the network preferences (Figure 25–6). At this point you can fill in the appropriate configuration information. To connect to the VPN, click the Connect button. If you frequently connect to and disconnect from the VPN, you may want to select the "Show VPN status in menu bar" option to add a status icon on the menu bar that will allow you to control the VPN connection.

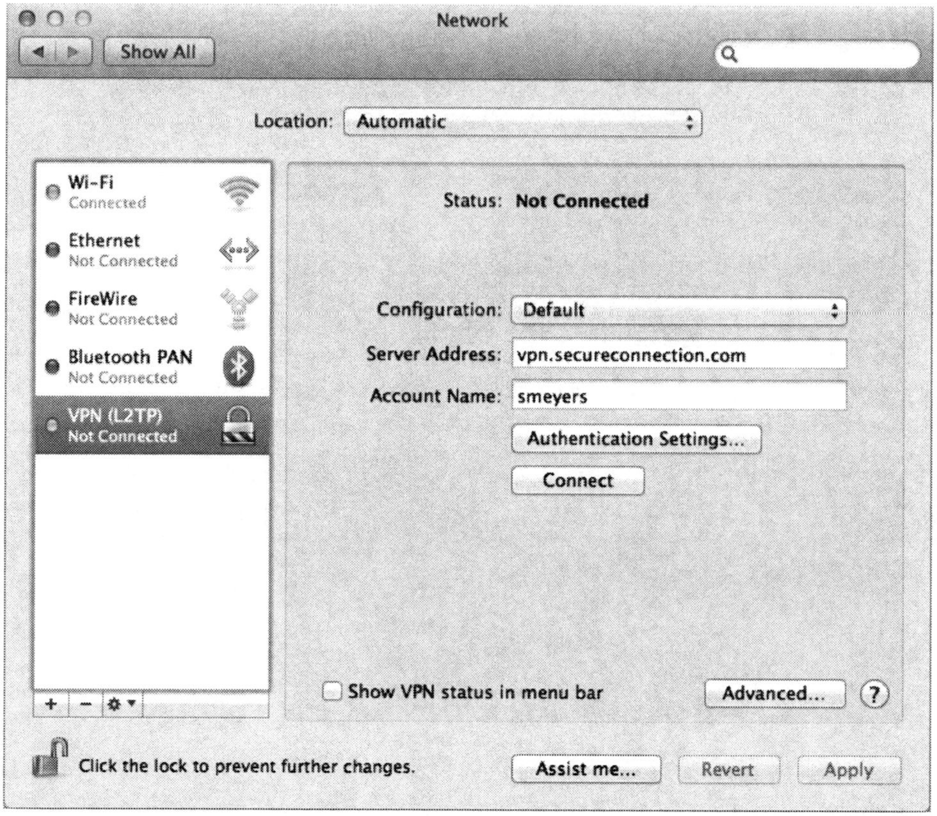

Figure 25–6. *Once you have added a VPN interface, you can configure it to connect to the desired VPN server.*

NOTE: Because of the many VPN types and various options for each, the details of setting up a specific VPN connection fall well outside the scope of this book. A network administrator should be able to provide you with the necessary details to accurately configure you VPN connection.

TIP: In most situations, organizations with a reasonable administrator will be able to provide you a configuration file to automatically set up your VPN interface and configuration. If such a file is available, you may import it directly into the network preferences by selecting Import Configurations... from the action menu at the bottom of the Network Interface list (the menu has a gear icon on it).

Networking Utilities in OS X

Besides the many network configuration options in the System Preferences, Mac OS X provides a number of additional tools for network configuration and monitoring. This includes Network Utility, which provides a graphical front end to common command-line networking tools, and AirPort Utility, which is used to configure Apple's range of AirPort devices.

Network Utility

Apple's Network Utility (Figure 25–7) provides a number of network information and monitoring tools. Located in the Utilities folder accessible from Launchpad, Network Utility has eight tabs, each representing a specific network utility.

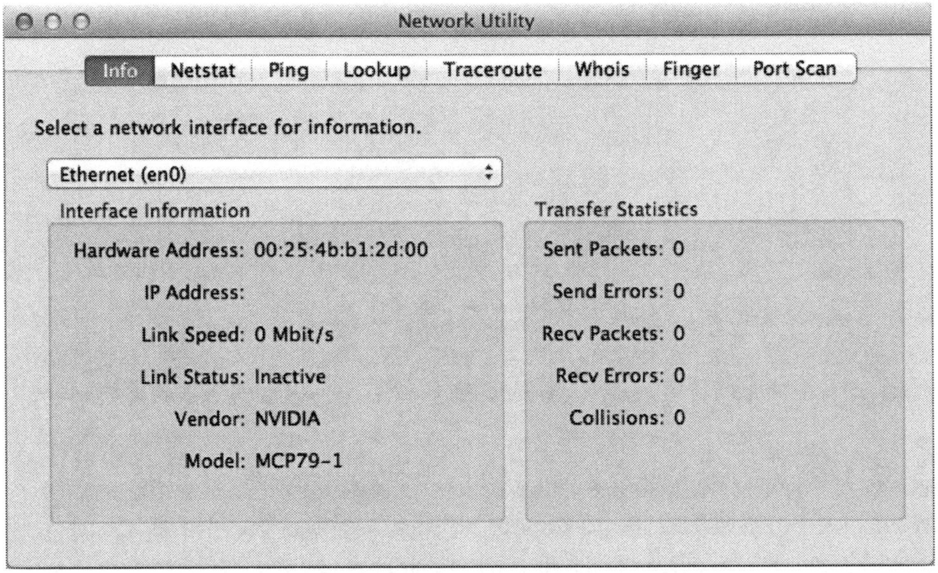

Figure 25–7. *Network Utility provides eight different tools that provide network information. The Info tab shown here provides information about the selected network interface.*

Info

Chances are your computer has several network interfaces. Most Macs have an Ethernet port, an AirPort card, and a FireWire bus, all of which are capable of connecting to a network.

The Info tab lets you get statistics on all your network interfaces, such as their hardware (MAC) and Internet (IP) addresses, their make and model, whether they're active, and at what speed they're connected. You can also see how many packets they've sent and received, and how many errors and collisions they've logged.

Netstat

Netstat, as its name implies, provides network statistics in four varieties (selectable by the radio buttons):

- **Routing table**: This is a map of known nodes from which your packets can begin their long trek across the Internet. This is not unlike a list of your local post offices.

- **Statistics**: This is a comprehensive list of statistics by protocol. This is the long version of the simple numbers displayed by Activity Monitor and the Info tab. If you're curious to know how many inbound IPsec/IPv6 packets failed because of insufficient memory, here's where you can find out.

- **Multicast**: This many-to-many communication protocol is used primarily by enterprise networks, though it's also used by mDNS, peer-to-peer technologies, and Internet Relay Chat (IRC). If you want to monitor your multicast memberships or packet statistics, Netstat is there for you.

- **Socket states**: Every connection on the Internet uses a socket, which is the combination of your computer's IP address and a port. It's not a bad idea to see who's connecting to your machine and what they're doing.

> **NOTE:** For more information about the information shown here (or for more information about what Netstat is capable of), type man netstat from Terminal's command line.

Ping

Ping is a diagnostic tool that uses the Internet Control Message Protocol (ICMP) to determine your ability to reach a given IP address, be it another computer or something like a router. The theory behind Ping is that any machine that receives a ping is supposed to echo it back. Unfortunately, Ping has been abused by malware in the past—hence stealth mode.

> **NOTE:** Stealth mode is an option in the Advanced Firewall settings on the Security & Privacy System preference pane. When stealth mode is enabled, your computer will no longer respond to ping requests, and will not answer any connection attempts to closed network ports. This has the effect of hiding your computer on a network, providing you aren't hosting any network services.

To use Ping in Network Utility, enter an IP address or domain name. Ping will then list the pings as they return, along with how long it took them to traverse the network. This can be useful in a variety of ways.

For example, if your web site goes down but your web host responds to pings, you can deduce that the host program crashed but that the server is OK. If the server does not respond to pings, you can assume something is wrong on a hardware level.

Similarly, if your server responds by IP address but doesn't respond by domain name, you can deduce that something is wrong with DNS. Further investigation would be needed to determine whether the domain name has expired or whether there is something else going on. This can be determined elsewhere in Network Utility.

Lookup

The Lookup tab combines the nslookup and dig tools to query DNS, which converts human-readable web addresses to the numerical IP addresses used by computers. The information returned by Lookup varies by host, but at the very least you can use it to get the IP address of a given server name.

Traceroute

Traceroute maps the path of packets as they travel to a given server address. Aside from being kind of interesting, it's a useful diagnostic tool. When a server is unreachable, you can use Traceroute to figure out where the packets are being stopped and who you need to call to get traffic flowing.

Like Ping, Traceroute has been abused by nefarious forces, so some servers will block Traceroute requests. Even so, you can usually get to the outer bounds of a given network, which will certainly tell you something, so Traceroute remains a good thing to have in your toolbox.

Whois

As opposed to the tools in Lookup, which convert domain names into IP addresses, Whois queries domain registries to determine who owns them. There are a couple of reasons why you might want to know this.

If your site is down and your server is reachable by IP address, but not by domain name, one possibility is that your domain name has expired or has been stolen. Checking the Whois information will let you know for sure. If Whois checks out OK, you can begin suspecting something is wrong with the name server itself.

Should you find your packets are being stopped at a certain node via Traceroute, Whois will tell you who you need to call about it. It's also a good way to see whether a domain name is available, and if it's not, to see when it expires.

As with many parts of the Internet, Whois registries have been abused. Putting your name, e-mail address, home address, and telephone number where anyone can get them is a potential privacy concern.

As such, some registrars now offer anonymous registration, whereby they will register the domain in their own name on your behalf, preventing people from getting any useful information about you. As with any such tactic, this certainly improves security by some degree, while breaking the Internet by another.

Finger

In the halcyon days of yore, when spam was just a delicious luncheon meat and the Internet was just a military research project, a computer scientist named Les Earnest wrote a program that would take an e-mail address and "point out" who it belonged to by giving you the person's name, whether they were logged on, and where their home directory was.

When the Internet opened for general use, people soon found less earnest uses for Finger, and the protocol was eventually abandoned. The tool still exists, but mainly as a way to generate the words the "connection refused."

Port Scan

You should probably be noticing a theme with Internet tools. That is, they can be used for good or evil. Of all the tools in Network Utility, nothing fits this profile as well as Port Scan.

In a nutshell, Port Scan tries every port on a given machine and reports which ones are open. This is handy information for potential attackers, which makes it handy information for potential victims.

It's also useful for figuring out, say, why a particular Internet service is not working, because having its port closed will render any Internet application silent.

> **NOTE:** Besides the tools here, some good command-line network utilities to read up on would be `ifconfig`, which lets you configure your network interfaces, similar to the Network panel in the System Preferences; and `tcpdump`, which lets you examine the contents of network packets and replaces the popular `tcpflow` application (which is always available via MacPorts).

AirPort Utility

I would be remiss not to mention a very important networking tool that comes in a pretty graphical package—AirPort Utility—which also lives in Launchpad's Utilities folder.

AirPort Utility replaces the old AirPort Setup Assistant and AirPort Admin Utility programs with a single, attractive, easy-to-use application. AirPort Utility also adds several features and makes it easier to manage multiple AirPort base stations.

At its most basic, AirPort Utility will show you which AirPort base stations are operating in your area, their names, and their IP and AirPort addresses, as well as which standards and firmware versions they support, as shown in Figure 25–8.

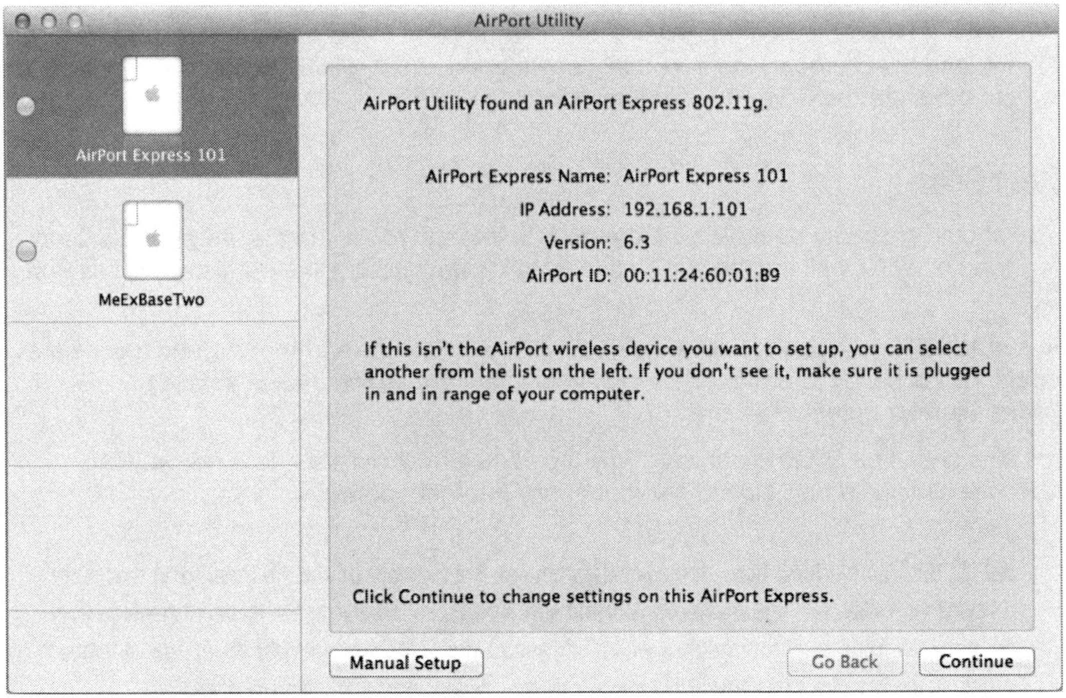

Figure 25–8. *Apple's lovely graphical AirPort Utility*

If one or more of the base stations in range belong to you, you can rename them and change their settings by double-clicking the device listed in the left column and clicking the Manual Setup button (or, for a more basic, step-by-step configuration, click the Continue button).

The availability and usefulness of settings in AirPort Utility will vary depending on which model of AirPort base station you have, its firmware version, and the peculiarities of your Internet provider. There are, however, a few notable groups of settings you should pay particular attention to:

■ **Wireless Security**: To access this setting, select AirPort and then the Wireless tab from a selected device's setup screen (see Figure 25–9). Unless you're intentionally running an open access point, you need to protect your network by setting up encryption and a password from the Wireless tab of the AirPort panel. Several encryption standards are in common use, but you should probably choose one based on Wi-Fi Protected Access (WPA), such as WPA2 Personal. AirPort's recommended setting is WPA/WPA2 Personal, which supports the older version of WPA for backward compatibility. If you have machines that do not support WPA2, you can use this setting, but in general, you want to limit the abilities of your AirPort base station to those needed by machines you own.

> **CAUTION:** If at all possible, avoid using a standard based on the Wired Equivalent Privacy (WEP) protocol. It's better than nothing, but at this point, even a moderately competent attacker can crack a WEP key with ease. If you have to use WEP to support older hardware, make it habit to frequently change your password. You should also steer clear of WPA2 Enterprise, which requires a special RADIUS server far beyond the means and needs of the everyday user.

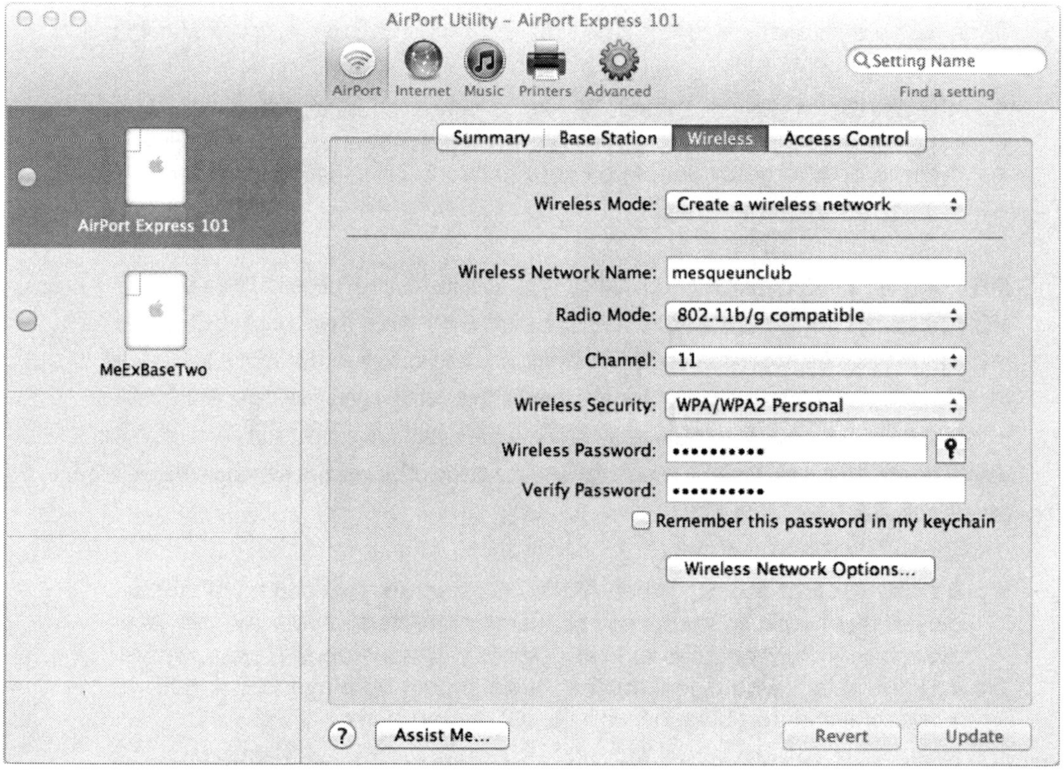

Figure 25–9. *Besides setting the wireless network name (SSID), radio mode, and channel, it's always advisable to set up reliable wireless security.*

■ **Radio Mode**: This single setting resides right above the security options on the Wireless tab. Because an AirPort base station will support up to four wireless standards, you should check this to ensure you're using the smallest, fastest set of standards that will meet your needs. For example, if all your machines have an 802.11n AirPort card, supporting the a, b, or g standards could needlessly slow the network down, besides making it all the more usable by uninvited guests.

■ **MAC Access Control**: This setting is located on the Access tab when AirPort is selected. It lets you filter access by hardware ID. This can be used to close a network to guests or to impose time limits on certain machines. This should be used only for convenience, not security. Unlike a password, a MAC address is easily spoofed.

■ **Remote Printing (Select Printers)**: By connecting a printer to your AirPort base station, you can allow any machine on the network to use the printer. This is an improvement over standard printer sharing because it doesn't require a host computer.

NOTE: While your Mac computer will immediately detect a printer set up on an AirPort device, to share the printer with a Windows computer you will need to download Bonjour Print Services for Windows. You can learn more about this here: `http://support.apple.com/kb/DL999`.

■ **AirPort Disks (Select Disks)**: Similar to printer sharing, you can connect USB hard drives to your AirPort base station, which will allow them to be shared by people on your network. This is also used for Apple's Time Capsule disk.

NOTE: Sharing a disk connected to an AirPort base station—known generically as *network-attached storage (NAS)*—is a really cool feature, particularly if you have a laptop. Shared disks host files that can be accessed over your network, or, used in conjunction with iCloud's Back to My Mac feature, the Internet. Unlike printers, hard drives contain personal data, which raises privacy issues. Apple lets you set up user accounts, password protection, and permissions on shared drives. That way, multiple people can use the same drive without having access to each other's data.

■ **AirPlay (Select Music)**: When AirPlay is selected, you can have music played from your computer to speakers connected to your AirPort. Any available AirPlay-enabled AirPort devices will show up in iTunes, where you can select what speakers the music should be played from (this works great in combination with the iOS Remote app).

Beyond these, one other AirPort feature deserves some additional explanation: *Connection sharing.*

AirPorts have three options for sharing an Internet connection (located under the Internet Connection tab when Internet is selected): "Share a public IP address"; "Distribute a range of IP addresses"; and Off (Bridge Mode).

> **NOTE:** Depending on what connection-sharing option is selected, different tabs will appear under the Internet and Advanced panes in AirPort Utility.

"Share a public IP address" is the option you will want to select if you are only provided (or assigned) a single IP address, yet you want to connect multiple devices to the Internet through your AirPort. This will set up your AirPort device to use NAT to distribute private IPs to all connected devices via DHCP.

"Distribute a range of IP addresses" is the option you can use if you have been given a range of valid IP address to use for your devices. With this option selected, the AirPort will use DHCP to distribute that range of addresses to devices connecting to your AirPort.

Off (Bridge Mode) is the option you should select if you want to bypass the router features of your AirPort. This is common if you have a router that already assigns IP addresses to your network, but you wish to add wireless access points to the network using AirPort devices.

Summary

This chapter provided a closer look at Mac OS X's network configuration options, as well as some of the included network utilities. While what we covered here should cover 99 percent of all networking situations that anyone may face, there are situation where some additional research and configuration may be necessary. Keep in mind that much of the networking in Mac OS X is descended directly from its UNIX roots, and that most of the common networking features and tools found in most UNIX systems are also available in OS X (though they may require some command-line work to install, set up, and configure).

That said, now that we can set up our network, in the next chapter we will take a close look at sharing resources over our network.

## Chapter 26

Remote Access and Sharing

Chances are you connect to remote servers and networks every day without really thinking about it. When you open your favorite web browser to read the news, check the weather, or catch up on Facebook, you're sending out packets of information requesting data. Those packets adhere to a particular protocol, in this case the Hypertext Transfer Protocol, and they traverse networks around the globe seeking the particular port at the particular address of the particular server that has your requested content.

The server will consider your request and, if all goes well, package the information you've requested and send it flying through the vast network of networks until it ends up back at your machine. Most people probably never realize how much work they're doing just by slacking off on the Web!

In this chapter we are going to look more closely at not only how you can access remote services and files but also how you can share files and services right from your Mac. While we probably won't talk too much about the Web (we'll cover that in the next chapter), we will cover the following:

- Connecting to file servers over a network (and the Internet)
- Creating small private networks
- Sharing files through AirDrop
- Activating and configuring formal sharing services on your Mac

Making the Remote Connection

The Web is just one part of the Internet, which is in turn just one type of network. There are as many ways to connect to another machine as there are reasons to do so, which has resulted in an alphabet soup of capabilities, methods, and protocols. Fortunately, Mac OS X has integrated, easy-to-use networking built right in. In fact, it's quite possible that, as with surfing the Web, you won't even have to think about the fact you're accessing a remote machine.

Accessing Remote Systems from the Finder

The easiest way to browse your local network is in the Finder. Machines that have enabled an appropriate type of sharing, such as file sharing, will be listed in the Finder window under the Shared category, as if they were part of the system.

If the selected resource has guest (or public) sharing available, those folders or resources will be presented in the Finders view window (Figure 26–1). If guest sharing is not available or you want to access other resources not available to guests, click the Connect As... button to open a dialog allowing you to sign in as a registered user (Figure 26–2).

Figure 26–1. *If guest sharing is enabled on the remote system, you will be able to view publicly shared items as a guest user.*

Figure 26–2. *If you want to connect as a registered user on a remote system, click Connect As... and enter your user info in the dialog.*

If the machine has screen sharing enabled, the Share Screen… button will appear to the left of the Connect As… button (unless you are in column view, in which case it will be below the Connect As… button). Clicking the Share Screen… button lets you activate screen sharing (Figure 26–3) once you enter your user information in the resulting dialog. The Screen Sharing application descends from the Apple Remote Desktop application, which has roots going all the way back to Mac OS 8. The upshot is Lion's screen-sharing feature can connect to machines running previous versions of Mac OS X. Even Tiger (10.4) and Panther (10.3) come with the necessary client software already installed.

Figure 26–3. *Screen Sharing allows you to remotely access another Mac as if it were right in front of you. Screen Sharing even allows you to access systems running previous version of Mac OS X.*

The Screen Sharing application has a few preferences worth checking out. By default, the remote screen is scaled to fit your screen, data is minimally encrypted to improve network performance, and drawing quality is adjusted on the fly depending on the quality of your connection. You can instead elect to view the screen at full size, to encrypt all data, or to draw the screen at full quality regardless of performance.

NOTE: This section deals only with connecting as a client to machines that already have a network service available. We'll discuss how to enable your machine as a server in the "Sharing" section later in this chapter.

> **TIP:** Like many applications in Lion, the Screen Sharing application can be run full-screen to make the remote screen seem much less remote.

Connecting to Other Remote Servers

The Finder's network browsing is limited to machines on your local network, but the Finder can connect to any machine, local or remote. As long as you know the IP address or a domain name to the resource, you can connect to it directly using the Finder's Connect to Server window, as shown in Figure 26–4.

Figure 26–4. *Connecting to a server by name in the Finder*

Launch the Connect to Server window from the Finder's menu bar by selecting **Go > Connect to Server** (Command-K). To connect to a machine, type its address in URL form into the Server Address text field. If you intend to connect to the machine on a regular basis, click the + button to add it to the Favorite Servers list.

Earlier, we connected to a machine using the Connect As… button in the Finder. We could have also established that connection directly by typing the machine's URL, like so:

```
afp://10.0.1.5
```

Connecting to a machine in the Finder will use the default protocol. Connecting directly allows you to explicitly specify the protocol. Valid protocol declarations include the following:

- **afp**: The Apple Filing Protocol is the standard protocol used for addressing remote volumes in the Finder. Although it is Apple's standard, AFP support is available for many operating systems, including Windows, NetWare, and several flavors of Unix and Linux. If you do not specify a protocol, afp is assumed.

- **at**: AppleTalk is an obsolete networking protocol that is included for backward compatibility. Previous versions of AFP used AppleTalk behind the scenes, but modern AFP uses the Virtual Network Computing (VNC) standard on top of standard TCP/IP.

- **nfs**: The Network File System protocol is a remote file access protocol developed by Sun Microsystems. It is similar to AFP and is available for several flavors of Unix, as well as for operating systems such as NetWare, Windows, and, of course, Mac OS X.

- **smb**: The Server Message Block protocol is the Windows equivalent to AFP. From within Windows, it's referred to simply as Microsoft Windows Network. The SMB protocol is sometimes called Samba, though technically Samba is a free reimplementation of SMB and not simply another name for the same thing.

- **cifs**: The Common Internet File System, despite its name, is actually just a rebranding of SMB to reflect changes Microsoft made to the protocol since its invention at IBM. It was submitted, but not accepted, as an Internet standard. It can be considered to be the same as SMB.

- **http**: The Hypertext Transfer Protocol is the standard protocol of the World Wide Web. Taking advantage of the ubiquity of the Web, HTTP is used for transporting more than web pages. For example, the WebDAV standard is used to mount remote file systems over HTTP.

- **https**: The secure version of HTTP is not a true protocol. Instead, it simply refers to the use of standard HTTP over a connection that has been encrypted by either the Secure Sockets Layer (SSL) protocol or the Transport Layer Security (TLS) protocol.

- **ftp**: The File Transfer Protocol is a very old standard for moving files from one computer to another. Because of its age and that it's compatible with every known operating system, it's in widespread use all over the Internet.

- **ftps**: Analogous to HTTPS, FTPS refers to the use of regular FTP over an SSL or TLS connection.

The list of protocols supported by the Finder's Connect to Server window is impressive but not all-encompassing. Absent are sftp, the Secure Shell File Transfer Protocol; svn, the Subversion file transfer protocol (although Subversion can be transacted over other protocols, such as HTTP); and file, as used in standard file URLs. The absence of file URLs is notable not because they have much meaning in a dialog intended for connecting to servers but because they are used extensively throughout the system. Using them in the Connect to Server window simply returns an error.

Connecting Remotely from the Command Line

Although using a computer's graphical interface via screen sharing is relatively new, the concept of using one computer to log in to and control another computer remotely is anything but. Unix is, by its very nature, a remotely controllable operating system, and old-fashioned shell-to-shell networking is very much alive in Terminal.

To connect remotely to another machine, open Terminal, and from the command line, invoke ssh with the username and address of the machine you want to connect to, separated by the "at" sign. For example, to connect to a machine at the local IP address 10.0.1.5 with the username booksystem, you would type this:

```
ssh booksystem@10.0.1.5
```

> **NOTE:** You don't have to use a local IP address or an IP address at all. Anything that can be resolved on the Internet is valid, including standard and local domain names.

> **NOTE:** Secure Shell (SSH) isn't the only way to connect to a remote server. Other services exist to accomplish a remote connection through the command line including Telnet and rsh. These other technologies generally lack sufficient security safeguards, and using them could open up the possibility of having your account compromised. As we will soon see, granting remote access on your Mac OS X system defaults to SSH (though it would be possible, but not recommended, to allow Telnet and other connections through some command-line configuration).

If you are connecting to a machine for the first time, you will be asked whether it is safe to proceed. Confirm this by typing **yes**. Unlike most Unix programs, you have to type the entire word. You will then be prompted for a password, and then, assuming you can authenticate properly, you'll be presented with a welcome message and the command prompt.

From this prompt you can create, delete, and alter files and folders, as well as list, run, and kill processes. You can even launch new shells and Secure Shell sessions in other servers. It's the same as if you were sitting at the remote machine typing into a Terminal window.

This can have unexpected consequences. For example, any DNS resolution will be in terms of the remote machine. If you have domains listed as default, a custom hosts file, or discrepancies in the closest name server's routing table, the remote machine might behave differently than would your local host.

To log out of the remote server, type **exit**. This is the same as exiting any shell, so bear in mind that if you've launched a new shell from within Secure Shell, typing **exit** will not log you out. Fortunately, when you log out of a Secure Shell session, Secure Shell will let you know the connection is closed. If you don't get that confirmation, assume you are still logged in.

Remote login via Secure Shell can be enabled from System Preferences, as discussed in the "Sharing" section later in this chapter.

The command line also includes an FTP program for using the File Transfer Protocol to move files between machines. As opposed to shell access, which allows for all manner of shenanigans, FTP access is much more limited, restricting user privileges to basic file operations.

To use FTP from the command line, simply type **ftp**. Unlike Secure Shell, FTP can be invoked without actually opening a connection. To connect to a remote machine, type **open**, and then, when prompted, enter the address of the machine, your username, and your password.

Unlike the Finder's Connect to Server menu, by default there is no `ftps` command available from the command line, but there is an `sftp` command, which works just like the regular `ftp` command. However, although opening a connection and supplying your username at invocation time are optional in `ftp`, they are required in `sftp`.

`sftp booksystem@10.0.1.5`

> **NOTE:** `sftp` is actually an extension of `ssh` specifically for file transfer.

Enter your password when prompted and then proceed as normal.

Whatever the advantage to using sftp, moving files back and forth in the terminal is almost too complicated to make it worthwhile, but if you really want to know, type **man ftp** or **man sftp** in the terminal to read all about it. A much better idea would be to use a dedicated FTP client.

> **NOTE:** You may think here, "Well, while I may not want to use `ftp` or `sftp` directly from the command line, I imagine they could come in handy if I was willing to create scripts that needed to access these services." It's a reasonable thought; however, in such cases you would much better off using the `curl` command, which is also included in Mac OS X. cURL is a command-line utility for libcurl and acts as sort of a Swiss Army knife of moving files to and from remote servers. Type **man curl** from at the command line for more info about cURL.

Third-Party Graphical Clients

As mentioned earlier, FTP and SFTP from the command line are not particularly intuitive or user friendly, so when you hit the limitation of what the Finder can do, it's time to go shopping for third-party solutions.

While there are quite a few clients to choose from, three of them get my recommendation: Fetch, Transmit, and Cyberduck.

- Fetch ($28.99 from the App Store) has a long history as the FTP client of choice for Mac users. Originally developed at Dartmouth College in the pre–Mac OS X, since then it has spawned its own company, Fetch Softworks (http://fetchsoftworks.com), and has been constantly maintained and updated to provide all the features one could expect from a file transfer client. Fetch supports FTP, SFTP, and FTPS.

- Transmit ($33.99 from the App Store) is a beautiful, feature-rich file transfer client from Panic Software (http://panic.com). Although it's the most expensive client here, for many people it's worth it. In addition to supporting FTP and SFTP, Transmit also supports transferring to and from WebDAV and Amazon's S3 cloud.

- Last but not least is Cyberduck ($23.99 from the App Store). Cyberduck is an open source file transfer client that supports connecting to the widest range of services including FTP, SFTP, FTPS, WebDAV, Amazon S3, Google Storage, Google Docs, Windows Azure, and Rackspace Cloud files. While it lacks some of the graphical flair and Finder integration that Transmit has, it is certainly capable.

> **NOTE:** You may be wondering, if Cyberduck is open source, why is it $23.99 on the App Store? The simple answer is the developer decided that $23.99 is fair price to pay for an excellent piece of software delivered to you through the convenience of the App Store. That said, if you are adamant about not paying the $23.99 for this piece of software, you can download the application or the source code from Cyberduck's official web site (http://cyberduck.ch/), or you can even download and compile the source code from MacPorts and use it for free. Once for each version you will be asked if you'd like to donate to the development, but other than that, it is free to use.

Besides these excellent dedicated clients, many pieces of software include built-in file transfer capability. Applications such as BBEdit, Coda, and Espresso have built-in FTP and SFTP capabilities. Jumping back to Apple software, Xcode has built-in support for remote SVN (Subversion) and Git repositories (which we will talk about in Chapter 32).

Creating Local, Private Networks

It wasn't that long ago when there was no Internet to which regular people could connect. Back then, setting up a local area network in your house was far too expensive to be feasible, and wireless networking wasn't even something most people could fathom. Yet, whenever two people had a file they wanted to exchange that wouldn't fit on a 1.44 MB floppy disk or they wanted to play some head-to-head Doom, they were always faced with the same problem—how the heck do we connect these two computers?

Even when the Internet was well established and routers were cheap, creating a small, informal network between two or three computers was always a big challenge. Fortunately, the modern Macintosh makes these arrangements, known as *ad hoc networks*, extremely easy to set up and use.

Target Disk Mode

The first question you have to ask yourself is, why would I want to connect two computers? A lot of times it's to exchange files. Whether it's to copy some work from a laptop to a desktop or to move some videos from a desktop to a TV server, people are forever connecting two machines just to facilitate getting files from computer A to computer B.

> **NOTE:** It should be noted that Target Disk mode provides an alternative to standard network sharing. The connection you are making, however, would fall into a different category of networking than what we are talking about in the rest of this chapter.

In this case, a network is not actually necessary. Any two Macs with FireWire or Thunderbolt ports can take advantage of a special trick called Target Disk mode. To put a computer into Target Disk mode, hold the T key while booting, or select Target Disk Mode... from the Startup Disk pane of System Preferences. The machine will start, but instead of a login screen, the computer's monitor will display the FireWire (or Thunderbolt) symbol.

When it's in Target Disk mode, a computer is treated as just another FireWire or Thunderbolt peripheral. That means if you plug it into another computer, that machine will mount the targeted machine's drives as if they were regular external drives. This includes the hard drive, as well as connected drives such as the DVD drive.

To copy, move, or delete files, just do so in the Finder as you would with an external drive. You can also read or eject removable media in the usual way. A direct connection with a FireWire 800 cable is much easier and just as fast as a Gigabit Ethernet connection, which is theoretically faster, and it's hard to beat the performance of two Macs connected via Thunderbolt.

> **NOTE:** Somewhat counterintuitively, the proper way to bring a computer out of Target Disk mode is to hold down its power button until it shuts down. However, like any other external drive, you must remember to eject it from the other machine first.

Target Disk mode can do some pretty interesting things. For example, you can boot your computer as a different machine by putting that machine in Target Disk mode. That means you could put your laptop into Target Disk mode and boot your Mac Pro from its drive so you'd be using your laptop, except it would be your Mac Pro. Then you put the Mac Pro into Target Disk mode and use it from your laptop.

Why would you ever do that? Well, maybe your laptop got run over by a car and the screen is busted but the mechanics are still good. That sounds far-fetched, but it's actually a documented occurrence. Or maybe your friend brings over a Mac mini and you want to boot it up but you don't have a monitor. As long as you have your laptop, Target Disk mode is all you need.

AirPort

If you want to connect machines that all have AirPort cards, it's easy to connect them. One machine can create a computer-to-computer (or ad hoc) AirPort network if you simply select the Create Network… option from the AirPort menu bar item and fill in the information in the resulting dialog (Figure 26–5). After you give it a name and an optional password, other people can join the network from the AirPort menu bar item as well.

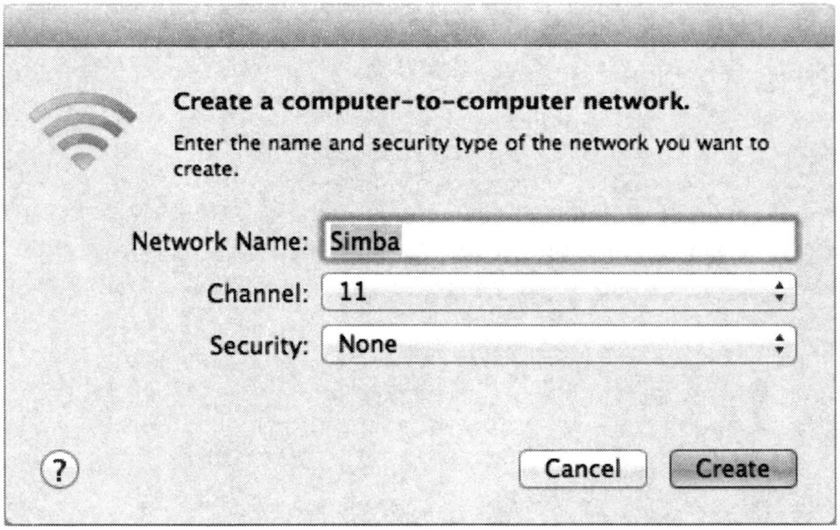

Figure 26–5. *Creating a computer-to-computer network with AirPort*

If you don't use the AirPort menu bar item, you can accomplish the same thing through the Network pane of System Preferences. Simply select the AirPort icon on the sidebar, and then, from the Network Name drop-down menu, select Create New Network. Other AirPort users can connect the same way.

I've never had a lot of luck setting up Wi-Fi on non-Macintosh computers, but since AirPort is just Apple's brand of Wi-Fi, it's at least theoretically possible to connect to Windows machines the same way.

> **NOTE:** Unfortunately, AirPort's ad hoc networking doesn't support WPA, so you're stuck with easily cracked WEP encryption instead. Try not to talk about too many state secrets over an ad hoc network.

FireWire and Ethernet

If you don't have AirPort or want a faster way to connect, you can always plug the two machines together with FireWire. Aside from Target Disk mode, FireWire is actually a full network interface. After connecting the two machines, open the Networking pane of System Preferences.

> **NOTE:** One big advantage of creating a network between two computers over a FireWire connection rather than using Target Disk mode is that with the network connection there is no need to restart either computer, and both computers will still be fully functional while connected.

You will have a self-assigned IP address. It doesn't really matter what it is, as long as the other person's self-assigned address is not the same. If it is the same, one of you should edit the last number so it's different.

> **NOTE:** As long as you have an appropriate adapter, it's fine to create a FireWire network when one computer is using a FireWire 400 port and the other using a FireWire 800 port.

Ethernet works the same way. Connect two machines, check the IP addresses, and change one if necessary. With Ethernet there is a trick, however. Some types of Ethernet cables are specially designed for connecting two machines directly. These so-called crossover cables are typically green in color.

If you're both using Macs, it doesn't matter whether you're using a crossover cable. If you connect two Macs with a standard cable, they will automatically cross over their Ethernet connections, so it makes no difference at all. If you're trying to connect to a machine that isn't a Mac or the machine is a Mac that's too old to run Mac OS X, be aware that you might need the special cable.

Assuming you have the latest versions of each and the proper cables, there's no particular advantage between FireWire and Ethernet as network adapters. There is, however, an advantage to having two network adapters.

You can connect your computer to another computer using one and then connect your computer to a different computer using the other. By switching off between the two, you can chain together any number of computers into an arbitrarily long daisy chain.

AirDrop

Lion introduces a new way of sharing files wirelessly with a feature called AirDrop. AirDrop is a feature that is built into the Finder and allows you to identify other AirDrop-capable Macs and transfer files to them by dragging and dropping files on their systems through the AirDrop view in the Finder (Figure 26–6).

Figure 26–6. *AirDrop makes sharing files with nearby Macs very easy, even if no network is available.*

NOTE: AirDrop relies on the hardware capabilities of newer AirPort cards to create a special ad hoc network between computers. Currently, not all AirPort cards possess the capabilities required for AirDrop. Because of this, some systems that support Lion will not support AirDrop unless Apple can make changes to how AirDrop works or there is a firmware update that would enable these features in older AirPort cards.

> **NOTE:** A computer will show up in AirDrop only when AirDrop is selected in the Finder. So, to share a file, both computers must have AirDrop selected in a Finder window. The idea is that all parties involved must be knowing participants in an AirDrop file transfer.

As mentioned earlier, to share a file over AirDrop, simply select the desired destination system from the AirDrop view in Finder and drag the file or files you want to share to the appropriate icon of the system you want to share the files with. Once you have dragged your files to the icon, a dialog will pop up asking to confirm that you want to share the selected files.

If you are on the receiving end of an AirDrop share, a dialog will pop up letting you know that someone is trying to share a file with you and asking you what you would like to do with it. Your options are to save and open, decline, or save (Figure 26–7).

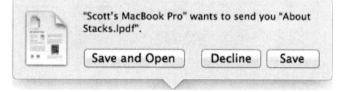

Figure 26–7. *When someone is attempting to share a file with you over AirDrop, you will be asked what you want to do with the files.*

Sharing Services in Mac OS X

If this chapter has taught you anything, it should be that there are a lot of different ways to connect to another computer. Even though the standard version of Mac OS X is different from the Server version, in Unix the line between client and server is tenuous at best. With Mac OS X, if you can be a client, you can probably be a server. To see this for yourself, open the Sharing pane in System Preferences, and read the long list of services you can offer, as shown in Figure 26–8.

Selecting a service from the list on the left will open status and preference information on the right. To activate or deactivate a service, toggle the check box next to its name. System changes, such as opening the relevant port and making necessary adjustments to the firewall, are done for you.

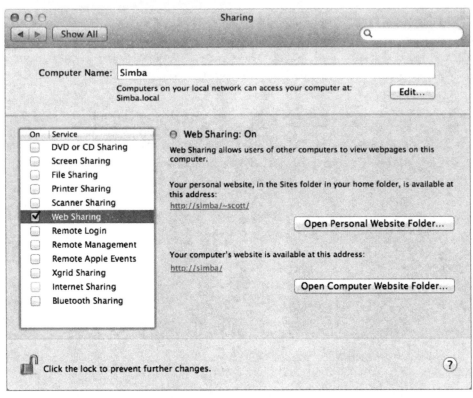

Figure 26–8. *Many ways to share your Mac in System Preferences*

Although each type of sharing has a description, it's not necessarily obvious exactly to which protocols or services they relate. Make sure you have the right service before you check the box and run out the door, or you might be in for an unpleasant surprise.

DVD or CD Sharing

Optical drives are such anachronisms, or so the MacBook Air would have you believe. However, if you have an optical drive and want to share the contents of a disk in it, Mac OS X provides DVD or CD sharing. You wouldn't want to use this to watch a movie, but for installing software once in a while, it gets the job done.

Screen Sharing

This allows people to connect to your machine using Mac OS X's built-in screen sharing but not Apple Remote Desktop. It bears noting that screen sharing is more than just being able to see your machine. People who share your screen can actually use your computer as if they were sitting at it, as shown in Figure 26–3. It's the graphical equivalent of logging in with ssh.

Options include explicitly naming which users can connect using this protocol, whether people can request to control the screen, and whether to protect screen control with a password. Note that turning on screen sharing will cause your computer to become browseable from your local network, so don't turn it on unless you need it.

When might you use screen sharing? Traditionally, its primary purpose is administrative. Apple Remote Desktop is, above all, a tool to help system administrators manage a network of machines. By bundling screen sharing with Mac OS X, Apple is expanding it to more informal uses. For example, if your mom calls you for tech support, you can just show her how to create a new album in iPhoto instead of trying to describe it over the phone.

File Sharing

When you connect to another machine in the Finder, you are using file sharing. In some previous versions of Mac OS X, different protocols were listed separately. In Snow Leopard, AFP, FTP, and SMB are all covered by the same service. You can decide which protocols are allowed by clicking the Options button.

In addition to the protocol list, you can decide which folders you'd like to share and explicitly list which users should be allowed to connect to your machine. As with screen sharing, enabling file sharing will make your machine visible on the local network, so make sure you need it before activating it. Also, SMB requires storing passwords in a less-secure way than Mac OS X prefers, so make double sure you need to let people connect to you with SMB before activating it.

Access to folders and files on your machine is determined by the permissions and access lists you've already set up. If you'd like to exchange files with other people on the network without having to worry about all that stuff, you can use the default Public folder, which is set up automatically on each new account.

By default, people who connect to your machine can read files from the Public folder, but they cannot edit or delete them, and they cannot put files in the Public folder itself. Within the Public folder, there's a folder called Drop Box, which works in the opposite way. People can put files in the Drop Box folder, but they cannot open the Drop Box folder to access the files it contains.

If you have a file you want people to access, simply put it in the Public folder. If someone else needs to give you a file, they can simply drop it in the Drop Box folder. It doesn't get much easier than that!

Printer Sharing

When printer sharing is enabled, printers connected to your machine are also connected to the network. Other machines on the network can see the printer in the printing system and negotiate the protocol on their own, typically via Bonjour. If you have a desktop machine hooked up to the printer, this a great way to print from your laptop.

Scanner Sharing

Many, if not most, of the printers sold these days are multifunction machines that also serve as scanners. Scanner sharing is a case in point. It's just like printer sharing but for scanners.

Web Sharing

This simple, ambiguous name covers a lot of ground—so much ground, in fact, the entire next chapter is devoted to it. In a nutshell, though, web sharing means you will host web sites from your machine.

Remote Login

Unlike file sharing, which covers all manner of file transfer protocols, remote login specifically enables SSH connections to your system. Although Remote Login is conceptually similar to screen sharing (and sounds similar to Remote Desktop), as far as the Sharing pane is concerned, they are completely unrelated. The only option is an access control list.

Remote Management

Not to be mistaken for Remote Login or screen sharing, Remote Management controls whether people can connect to your machine using Apple Remote Desktop. The options are almost identical to screen sharing.

Traditionally, a given protocol used a given port, so enabling access to a particular service was an all-or-nothing affair. As discussed in the previous chapter, Mac OS X's firewall is able to route or block requests at the application level. As such, even though Apple Remote Desktop and screen sharing use the same protocols, they can be enabled, disabled, and configured separately.

Remote Apple Events

The Apple Events system underlies interapplication communication, as used by AppleScript. To control a remote machine with AppleScript, therefore, a machine would have to respond to remote Apple Events. This would be useful if you were trying to use AppleScript to automate some administrative task over a network.

For example, if your remote machine were at IP address 10.0.1.5, you could make it sleep with the following bit of AppleScript:

```
tell application "Finder" of machine "eppc://10.0.1.5"
sleep end tell
```

You can scale this technique to do amazing things with scriptable applications such as iTunes. For an example, check out the remote access section of Doug's AppleScripts for iTunes (http://dougscripts.com/itunes/itinfo/remcontrol.php). We talk more about Doug, and AppleScript, in Chapter 31.

Xgrid Sharing

If you have a bunch of Macs and a copy of Mac OS X Server, you have a supercomputer. Mac OS X includes Xgrid, the same cluster computing software used in university supercomputers. The Xgrid Admin application bundled with Mac OS X Server makes it easy to set up computing clusters using Bonjour.

Internet Sharing

Contrary to what you might be led to believe by its ambiguous name, enabling Internet sharing does not allow you to connect to your computer from other computers on the Internet. Rather, it allows you to share the Internet from your computer with other computers.

The typical Mac has at least three network interfaces: Ethernet, FireWire, and AirPort. At any moment, only one of those interfaces is usually connected to the Internet, while other interfaces could be connected to another computer or even an entirely different network. By enabling Internet sharing, you're able to let the computers on one network interface connect to the Internet on another.

For example, a typical setup might have the Internet coming into your home via a cable or DSL modem, which, in turn, is connected to an AirPort base station. All the computers in your home would then be connected to the AirPort base station, sharing its Internet connection.

With Internet sharing, you could instead plug one computer directly into the modem via Ethernet and then use that machine's AirPort card to create an ad hoc network that other computers could use to share the Internet connection, eliminating the need for the AirPort base station altogether.

This kind of setup is particularly convenient when you are away from home. If your hotel room has an Internet connection via Ethernet, several people can share that connection without having to pack an AirPort base station or other network hardware.

Bluetooth Sharing

Although it's usually associated with headsets and other simple gadgets, Bluetooth is a general short-range wireless standard that can connect two machines with file systems, such as two computers, or a computer and a phone. To move files around over a Bluetooth connection, you'll need to enable Bluetooth sharing, though connecting a Bluetooth device will usually activate Bluetooth sharing for you.

Summary

When it comes to connecting to remote machines, you have a lot of options. Networking is built into the Finder, integrating the entire web publishing experience into the Mac's legendary interface. Third-party applications expand this integration by offering direct connections to the Internet, through technologies such as FTP and Secure Shell.

In the next chapter, we will focus on one specific form of sharing, web sharing.

## Chapter 27

Lion as a Web Server

Lion makes doing everything with the Web as easy as doing it on Mac OS X. We talked about surfing the Web with Safari in Chapter 9 and about generating content for the Web throughout the book. There's one thing left to do: become part of the Web itself by hosting a web server.

To some that might sound complicated, but it doesn't have to be. Getting started is as easy as clicking a button. For the hardcore Net geeks, don't be fooled by Mac OS X's cuddly appearance. When you want to get fierce, there are fangs and claws to go around.

So, whether you'd like to host a home page for your neighborhood bridge club, build an intranet for your home or office, or develop and stage web applications for production and profit, keep reading. In this chapter, we will do the following:

- Introduce the Apache web server
- Start basic web sharing in Mac OS X
- Serve our own web page from Mac OS X
- Delve into advanced Apache configurations
- Introduce PHP
- Introduce SQLite, MySQL, and PostgreSQL
- Cover some other important details for hosting your own web site from your Mac

Apache and Mac OS X Web Sharing

Mac OS X's built-in web server is the Apache HTTP server, a web server which traces it's linieage back to the NCSA HTTPd server, one of the first web servers ever written. Today the Apache HTTP Server (often reffered to as just Apache) is the most popular web server currently used today (in May 2011 it was estimated that approximately 63% of all website were run using Apache). For Mac OS X users, this means that they can easily replicate most web servers on thier Mac for development purposes and then seemlesly deploy thier finished web sites and web applications to larger servers. Of course it's not unheard of for websites to be hosted directly from a Mac.

Apache's current incarnation, Apache 2, stands ready to host your personal home page right from you own computer, as shown in Figure 27–1.

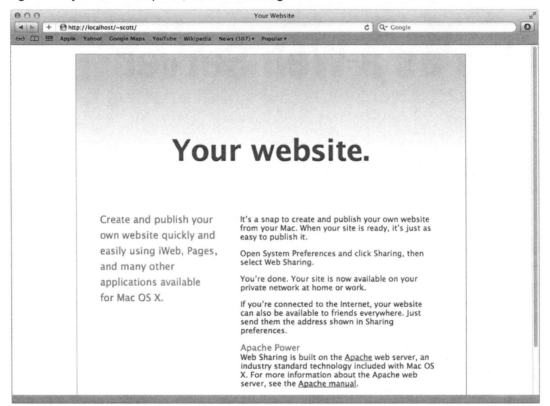

Figure 27–1. *Mac OS X's default personal home page shown in Safari*

To enable all this goodness, you need to turn on web sharing in the Sharing preference pane in System Preferences. Select the Web Sharing box, and you may imagine your computer shuddering slightly as Apache rumbles to life. Once the check box is tamed, the dialog helpfully explains where everything is, as shown in Figure 27–2.

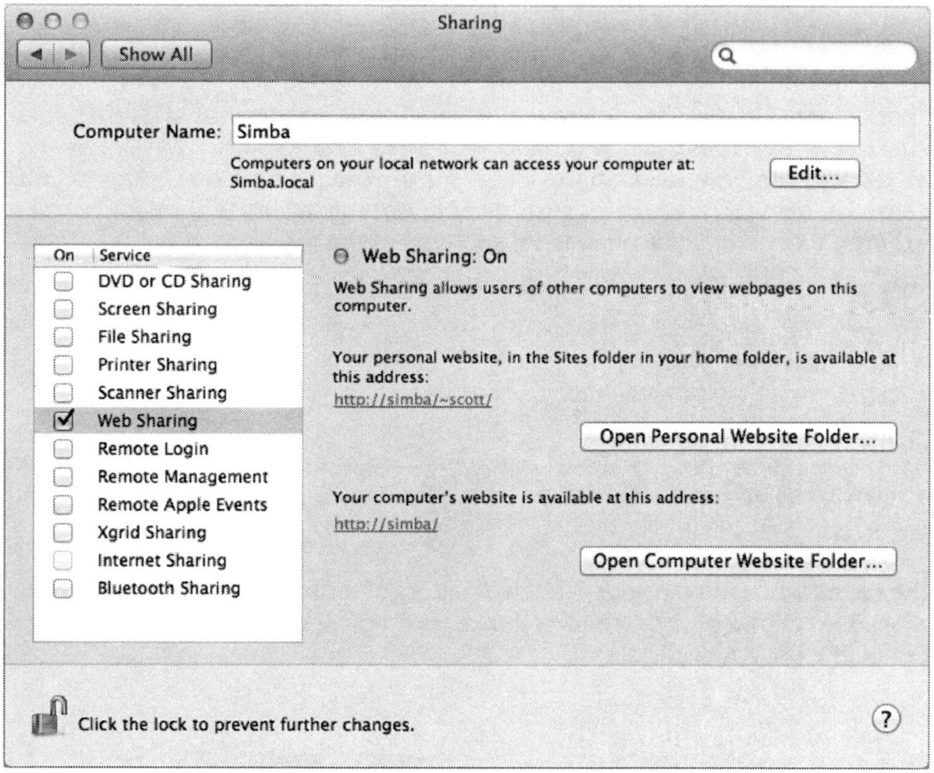

Figure 27–2. *Activating web sharing from System Preferences*

NOTE: If your site doesn't show up, see the "Tips and Tricks" section later in this chapter.

CAUTION: Turning on web sharing is an all-or-nothing proposition. If you turn web sharing on for one account, it will be on for all accounts. To change this behavior, see the "Configuring Apache" section later in this chapter.

Customizing Your Site

As the information panel in the Sharing preferences explains, your personal home page is kept in your user Sites directory. The items in your Sites directory are what will be served when you visit the personal web site link. For example, using a text editor or your choice (you can use Mac OS X's built-in TextEdit app, but make sure you select **Format > Make Plain Text** from the menu if you choose to) and type in the following:

```
<!DOCTYPE html>
<html lang="en">
<head>
    <title>A very simple web page</title>
</head>
<body>
    <h1>My new personal home page</h1>
    <p>By learning a little HTML, or using your web development tool of choice, you can
easily build and serve your own website right from your Mac OS X computer!</p>
</body>
</html>
```

Then save the file as index.html in your ~/Sites directory (it's okay to replace the default index.html file). Then reload your personal web site, and you should see a new, very simple web page (Figure 27–3).

Figure 27–3. *A customized personal home page shown in Safari*

NOTE: The web page example in Figure 27–3 is about a simple as you can get with Hypertext Markup Language (HTML), the original and most prominent language of the Web. Combined with Cascading Style Sheets (CSS) to format your content, you can build some very nice-looking web pages. Teaching HTML and CSS goes beyond the scope of this book, but there are numerous books and online resources that can get you started. Learning at least the basics of HTML and CSS (if not continuing on to JavaScript, PHP, and other web development languages) is a very useful and highly recommended endeavor.

NOTE: For creating HTML pages, I strongly recommend a decent plain-text editor (not TextEdit). There are many to choose from; however, for getting started, you can't go wrong with Bare Bones' TextWrangler, which is both free and easily available from the Mac App Store. As you progress in web development, you may want to look into more advanced text editors such as TextWrangler's big brother, BBEdit, or look into full-featured web development tools such as Coda or Espresso.

NOTE: For creating HTML pages, I strongly recommend a decent plain-text editor (not TextEdit).

TIP: Don't forget that you have access to both Vim and Emacs from the command line, either of which make excellent editors for web development.

In addition to the user sites located at ~/Sites, your machine also has a main system site, as shown in Figure 27–4. This site's content is located in the Apache server's document root. Unlike the logical ~/Sites location, the default document root is /Library/WebServer/Documents/. On a single-user machine, these two sites can be combined, as discussed in the "Tips and Tricks" section later in this chapter.

Figure 27–4. *If everything is working right with your web server, visiting http://localhost/ will let you know.*

ACCESSING YOUR COMPUTER'S WEB SITE

There are many ways to access your web site depending on where you are accessing it from.

The easiest way to access your web site from your computer or elsewhere on your local network is to use the IP address assigned to your machine (viewable from the Network System Preferences pane). Additionally, you can use your .local domain name, which is the computer name set in your sharing preferences with .local added to the end.

If you want to just access your web server from the computer it is running on, you can use a *loopback* name or address. A loopback does just what it says: it loops the network connection right back to the computer it originates from. The default loopback name is localhost, and the default loopback address is 127.0.0.1.

Finally, if you are planning on hosting a web site from your Mac for the world to see, then things may get more complicated. If you have a dedicated public IP address, you can use that (and you could set up a domain name to point to that IP address as well). Most computers aren't accessible directly from the Internet, though, but rather are assigned a private IP address from a router using NAT and DHCP. In this case, many routers enable port forwarding that will allow you to select a computer on your network to pass information through to (that is, all incoming network requests sent to the router's IP address are sent to a specific computer on the private network behind the router). You will need to check the documentation for your router to determine whether and how you may do this. On your Mac, though, you may want to choose the "Using DHCP with manual address" option in the network preferences so you have a consistent IP address to route the information to.

Most people serious about serving web pages will look to a web-hosting provider to handle the hosting. If your provider uses Linux or Unix running Apache, it's likely that the server configuration either will be or can be similar enough to your Mac's configuration that you can develop web sites locally on your Mac and then deploy them to the web host without modification.

Customizing Apache

Since Apache is a Unix application, it doesn't have a convenient GUI preference pane, and it doesn't use a standard Macintosh property list. Rather, it has its own configuration file in its own directory using its own peculiar scheme.

> **NOTE:** Actually, there are third-party applications that provide a GUI to Apache's configuration file; however, none of them really simplifies the process too much, and there are some obscure important details. As such, we won't cover any of these and generally don't recommend them. Additionally, Mac OS X Server provides its own very nice GUI for Apple's web server.

Fortunately, the configuration file, like everything else about Apache, is well documented and, honestly, not that complicated. Links to the Apache manual, as well as a dire warning instruction you should read and understand, is at the top of the httpd.conf configuration file. To begin, you should keep the link to the Apache documentation home page handy: `http://httpd.apache.org/docs/`.

By default Apache's configuration files live in the `/etc/apache2` directory, which in Mac OS X is actually located in `/private/etc/apache2` (though `/etc/apache2` will work). Unless you've turned on the ability to see invisible files in the Finder, you'll have to navigate there in Terminal. Listing the contents of the directory shows the primary file we've come here to see: httpd.conf.

> **NOTE:** Although it's called Apache, the name of the Unix executable is httpd, which reflects its role as a background process (daemon) that serves the Hypertext Transfer Protocol.

Open `httpd.conf` in your text editor of choice. Again, TextWrangler or BBEdit are excellent for this. With BBEdit, you can use its disk browser to easily navigate here, since it can see the hidden folders. It will also take care of overwriting the old file, which is read-only. You can also use Nano, Emacs, or Vim, as detailed in Chapter 23.

> **NOTE:** In Lion all the Apache configuration files are protected as unwritable. Before you make any changes to a conf file, you must chmod it so it can be written to. Otherwise, you will be unable to save any changes. The easiest way to do this is from the command line by issuing this: `sudo chmod u+w httpd.conf`. When you are done editing the file, you should reverse the process with `sudo chmod u-w httpd.conf`. The chmod command was covered in Chapter 23.

The configuration file is very long, but don't be scared. Lines that start with the number sign are comments, which is to say they are ignored. The file mainly consists of hints explaining what the various sections do. There's very little actual content here, and even less you have to worry about. We will work through the file and describe the essential sections as they appear.

> **NOTE:** Prior to Apache2, the httpd.conf file was generally a single self-contained file that contained all the configuration options in one place. With Apache2, it became customary to break out certain configuration options into other files that are then pulled into `httpd.conf` when the file is read. As we encounter areas where information is stored in separate files, I will let you know.

ServerRoot

Much as Unix considers ~ to be a shortcut for your user directory, the ServerRoot command tells Apache where it should look for any files that are not explicitly named. Since these files are all for its internal use, there's really no need to change the default value.

Listen

Like any server process, Apache listens on a particular port or socket. Normally, it answers any incoming calls on port 80. If you need to change the port for some reason or you want to bind to a specific IP address, you can edit this.

One particular use for Listen is to limit who can see your page. Remember how we said you could load your page by one of several means? What if you don't want people to be able to load your page elsewhere on the network? By binding Apache to 127.0.0.1:80, you will be able to view the page locally only. Dialing in to the actual IP address would simply return an error page.

Another use for the Listen directive is to use a port other than the default. For example, your ISP may block access to port 80 in an effort to prevent you from running a web server from your home. You could instead bind to port 8080.

You can bind to multiple ports and sockets by issuing multiple Listen directives. So, for example, to view the site locally on the standard port but to let others see it only on a secret port, you could say this:

```
Listen 127.0.0.1:80 Listen 1984
```

You could then load your site by simply pointing to 127.0.0.1, but someone else on the network loading your site would get an error unless they knew to append the correct port to the end of your IP address. So, for example, if your IP address were 10.0.0.1, they would have to point their browser to http://10.0.0.1:1984.

Dynamic Shared Object (DSO) Support

Dynamic Shared Object (DSO) is a fancy name for the LoadModule directive. As the name may suggest, LoadModule loads . . . modules, which are plug-in software products that extend the functionality of Apache. Several modules are loaded by default. We will come back to LoadModule when we are ready to add PHP to our web server.

> **NOTE:** You may notice here sections that are wrapped in tags such as <IfDefine MACOSXSERVER> </IfDefine>. If the IfDefine directive is met, then the commands within the tags are run; otherwise, they are ignored. Here you may notice that one set of commands is run for Mac OS X Server (<IfDefine MACOSXSERVER>) while another is run if the system is not Mac OS X Server (<IfDefine !MACOSXSERVER>). Later we will see the similar IfModule used in a similar manner depending on whether a specific module is loaded.

User/Group

Since Apache operates on your system, it needs to be able to access files. You could run it as root, but that would be a security risk. Instead, Apache runs as the user _www as part of the group _www. Should you want to change this, you would do that here. Honestly, though, you probably don't need to do that.

VirtualHost

If you have a web site running on a host somewhere, chances are you're not on a dedicated server. Lucky for everyone involved, you can run multiple sites on a single machine using a feature called *virtual hosting*.

Virtual hosting is off by default, but if you want to configure multiple sites to run on your machine, perhaps because you work on multiple sites and would like to access them all separately, you can do so.

Incidentally, the different user sites built into Mac OS X, while similar to virtual hosting, are actually a different feature; they're user directories, provided by Apple's UserDir module. User directories are for multiple users on one site, while virtual hosts are for multiple sites on one machine.

ServerAdmin

One of the nice things Apache does is automatically generate index and error pages for you. Since these pages may require action by the server administrator, they will include an e-mail address. That address is given with the ServerAdmin directive.

ServerName

Similarly, the ServerName directive is how the server refers to itself. This would typically be the domain name and port, or possibly the IP address. Since this information can be determined automatically, it's commented out by default. Should you find yourself actually serving web pages to the public, you should define it explicitly.

DocumentRoot

This directive tells Apache where to start serving pages from. That is to say, it defines which directory on the host machine is represented by / in the web address. Directories attached to / will be similarly mapped to directories on the host machine.

By default, the document root is set to /Library/WebServer/Documents, so loading http://127.0.0.1/ loads the contents of/Library/WebServer/Documents. Loading http://127.0.0.1/Site/Welcome.html loads the file /Library/WebServer/Documents/Site/Welcome.html (if such a file exists).

If you wanted to change the document root to your user directory, you could change the DocumentRoot directive to the following:

```
DocumentRoot  "/Users/username/Sites"
```

You can also redirect the document root using symbolic links, as discussed in the "Tips and Tricks" section later in this chapter.

Permissions

There's no actual Permissions directive, but that's the best term we can think of to describe the several entries that follow. These define the options for directories and files on the system. A notable entry is the Options FollowSymLinks directive, which is on by default and which allows our symbolic link trick to work.

There are several more entries that block web visitors from being able to see certain types of files, such as hidden files that begin with a dot or the Mac OS X resource files.

One thing to keep in mind is that there are permissions entries for every known directory, including the document root. If you change a directory elsewhere in the configuration, you will have to be sure to change its permissions entry as well. This is one of the reasons why using symbolic links is easier than editing the configuration file.

DirectoryIndex

Easily missed amid all the permissions directives, the DirectoryIndex directive defines the default index file name. That is to say, when a user simply points to a directory, which file do they get? The default is index.html, which is why you don't have to type index.html all the time when you're surfing the Web.

If you decide to start using PHP or some other technology that requires you to use a different file name or extension, you can edit this. By including multiple listings, you can give several possible defaults. Apache will serve up the first one it finds. For example, to serve index.html by default but then serve the old Microsoft FrontPage standard, welcome.html, as a backup, you would say the following:

```
DirectoryIndex index.html welcome.html
```

If nothing listed in DirectoryIndex exists, visitors will see a listing of everything in the directory. To prevent that, you can put a failsafe at the end of the DirectoryIndex directive, such as a reference to a file in your root directory telling people to stop poking around in your directories:

```
DirectoryIndex index.html welcome.html /lost.html
```

> **NOTE:** It's actually possible (and more common) to remove the ability to present an index of everything located in the directory without the reference file; you just remove the indexes from the directory options earlier in the configuration file.

Logging

Several directives are related to logging. You can customize where logs are kept, how much logging Apache should do, and what format log messages are in. These are best kept to the default values, but if you spend a lot of time reading your logs and you develop an opinion on some aspect of logging, here is where you can flex your will.

Redirects

Much like the DocumentRoot directive, the Redirect, Alias, and ScriptAlias directives let you map the URLs people request to your file system.

Redirect will actually cause the browser to request a new location. This is useful if you've permanently moved a file to elsewhere on the system. Alias will cause a given path to look outside the normal document root hierarchy.

For example, you might want to give the outside world access to your Pictures directory (for some reason) by mapping requests to www.yoursite.com/pictures to /Users/*username*/Pictures. You could, of course, also accomplish this with symbolic links, assuming you allow FollowSymLinks on the directory.

ScriptAlias is like Alias, but it applies specifically to directories that contain executable scripts, rather than simple documents.

DefaultType

Most of the Internet uses MIME types to determine how it should deal with files. Since most web servers serve web pages, it's appropriate to leave this set to the default, text/plain.

> **NOTE:** MIME stands for Multipurpose Internet Mail Extensions. Like most of the Internet, it has been expanded beyond its original purpose.

What makes this directive interesting is actually the list of AddType and AddHandler directives, which allow you to add support for certain types of files. The list starts with a TypesConfig directive that points to an external list of types, stored by default in /private/etc/apache2/mime.types.

Most webmasters meet the types section when adding PHP support, because the traditional .php file extension is not handled by default; however, on Mac OS X this is handled for you in the PHP configuration file (/private/etc/apache2/other/php5.conf).

ErrorDocument

If you ever go poking around the coolest sites on the Net, they always seem to have these sexy custom error pages, so pulling a 403: Access Denied doesn't jar you from the overall design of the site. The ErrorDocument directive lets you point to custom pages and scripts.

If you define a custom error document, be sure to actually implement it, lest your users not only be treated to a generic error page but also be blighted with the ever-embarrassing "Additionally, a 404 Not Found error was encountered while trying to use an ErrorDocument to handle the request."

Include

Apache configuration is typically split into multiple files. External files are referred to using the Include directive. For the purposes of scope, you can consider the entire text of an included file to be inserted where the Include directive is used.

This is important, because the general rule with Apache is that the last word is the one that's obeyed. So, if an included file disagrees with the main file, the one farther down the list is going to win. If you find some configuration detail is not working, despite being clearly documented, make sure you're not being overridden by another file.

Of particular importance is this line:

```
Include /private/etc/apache2/extra/httpd-userdir.conf
```

Editing the httpd-userdir.conf file reveals two things. First, it uses the `UserDir` directive to tell Apache that every user's personal root is their Sites directory. If, for example, you are old-school and you'd prefer this directory to be called publichtml, this is where you'd set that up.

Second, this file in turn includes all conf files contained in the directory /private/etc/apache2/users. Listing that directory reveals a series of files of the form *username*.conf, where username is a username on the system.

Each of these files contains a permissions directive.

```
<Directory "/Users/username/Sites/">
Options Indexes MultiViews
AllowOverride None
Order allow,deny
Allow from all </Directory>
```

Again, *username* refers to the actual username dealt with by the file.

By default, all directories on your system are forbidden, except for those explicitly named. This directive makes the named user's Sites folder readable and sets up a few options. Were this file to be missing, you would not be able to access your site, regardless of system-level permissions.

When you turn on web sharing, these files are created by default. By editing the files, you can disallow certain users the ability to host sites. You could even remove the main include, disabling all user sites, while giving yourself the document root.

> **NOTE:** Although disabling the explicit permissions on a user directory will do the job in a roundabout way, the proper way to enable or disable users is with the `UserDir` directive. See the Apache documents for more information.

Activating Changes to the Apache's Configuration

Whenever you change Apache's configuration file, you will need to restart Apache. The easiest way to do this is with Terminal, using the special Apache control program, apachectl.

```
sudo apachectl graceful
```

This will restart Apache gracefully, which is to say it will let it finish what it's doing, shut down, and then restart.

If you try to restart Apache but it's not already running for some reason, it will just start. If you've messed up the configuration file, it will usually let you know on restart. Otherwise, you should be ready to test your changes.

PHP

PHP is the weapon of choice for many developers for creating dynamic web pages and applications. PHP is a dynamic scripting language that can be embedded in web pages. PHP is processed by the server, outputting normal HTML. Unlike client-side technologies such as JavaScript, PHP developers know their scripts will run with the capabilities they need.

Since it is open source, PHP is the preprocessor of choice on Unix systems running Apache. Indeed, PHP has been implemented as an Apache module and comes installed, but not activated, by default on Mac OS X.

To properly ensure PHP is installed, you need to have a PHP page. The best test page is a simple PHP Info page. It relies on PHP to be working, so it's a good test, and it gives you a lot of information about your PHP installation, so it's actually useful.

Create a PHP Info page in your favorite text editor, and save it to your document root as index.php. All you need to include is a single call to PHP's built-in phpinfo function:

```
<?php phpinfo() ?>
```

Then, load the page in your browser of choice by pointing to http://localhost/index.php. You have to point to the page explicitly, because otherwise you'll get the default index page, index.html.

> **NOTE:** You can, of course, also save the PHP Info page to your home Sites directory.

Loading the page in your browser, you're greeted with the entirety of its source, as written. That's because Apache doesn't know what a .php file is, so it's serving it as its default MIME type, text/plain.

To enable PHP, you simply need to uncomment a single line of text from the Apache configuration file:

```
#LoadModule php5_module                    libexec/apache2/libphp5.so
```

Since it starts with #, it's a comment and is ignored. Delete the # and save. Back in the day, you'd also have to tell Apache how to handle the file type and look for index.php by default, but all that stuff is now handled automatically by the included php5.conf file. Just restart Apache, and, as the saying goes, there is no step 3. The PHP Info screen should now display properly, as shown in Figure 27–5.

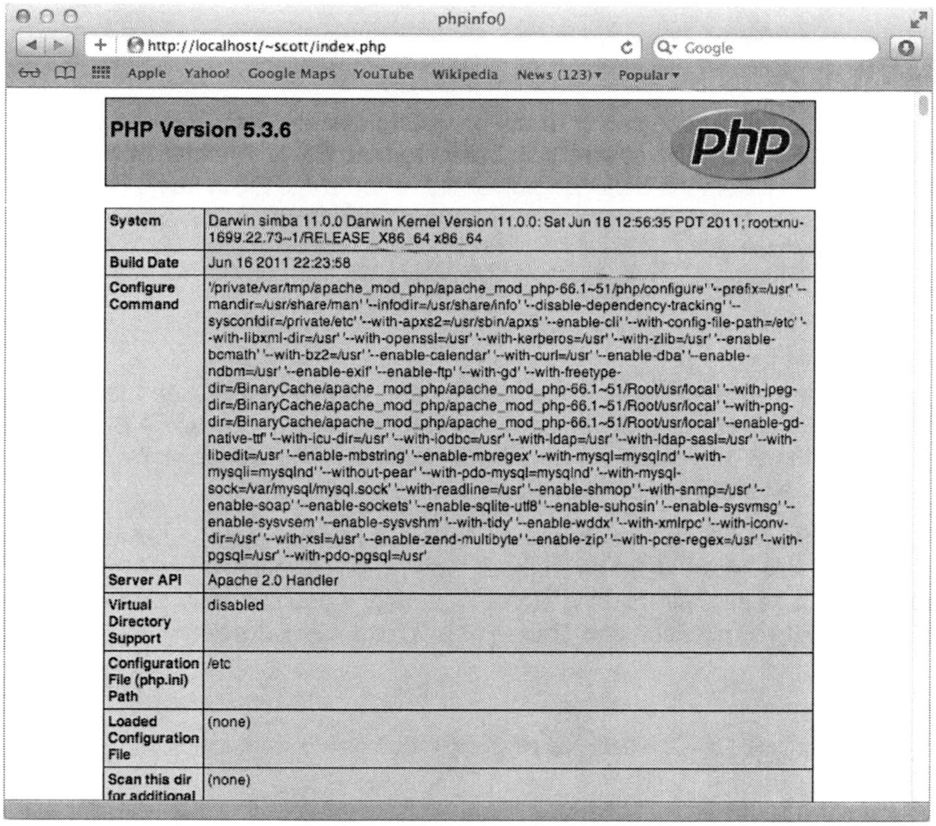

Figure 27–5. *PHP Info page provides the details about the version of PHP installed on your computer.*

Examining the PHP Info page will tell you a lot about how your server is set up. It's a good idea to run it on both your local machine and your remote host so you can be aware of any differences between versions, features, or configuration options that might affect you.

To learn more about PHP, including an extensive manual with installation and integration guides, visit PHP's official web site at php.net.

NOTE: PHP certainly isn't the only game in town for server-side web development on your Mac. All the common open source web scripting languages are there including Perl, Python, and Ruby, and newer web frameworks are generally easily available. For example, installing Ruby on Rails is a simple `sudo gem install rails` away.

Databases

Many web servers add a database server to the operating system, web server daemon, and scripting engine. You can add several databases to Mac OS X, Apache, and PHP. Choosing a database is a balance between power and effort. Mac OS X has a database server running and ready, but if you need more features than the default setup provides, it's going to take some doing.

SQLite

Mac OS X's default database manager is the fast, simple, lightweight SQLite that is quickly gaining popularity with web developers. It's compatible with the same Structured Query Language (SQL) used by nearly every other database in the world. More important, it's directly addressable from PHP.

Aside from the fact that SQLite is already set up for you, it has the major advantage of being the same database server used throughout the system. Applications written with CoreData can use SQLite as their backing store. That means you can share a database between your Core Data application and your PHP web site without ever having to touch SQL.

> **Note:** For more information on Core Data and other application development topics, see Chapter 33.

If you're serving web pages from your machine or if your remote host has SQLite (and the requisite PHP modules) running, you're good to go. Run sqlite3 from the command line to access the included management program. You can also learn more by visiting http://sqlite.org/.

MySQL

When it debuted in 1995, MySQL was the scrappy alternative to the Tyrannosaur-like Oracle. What it lacked in features and polish, it made up for by being fast and small. It helped that it was free, open source software, quickly establishing itself next to Linux, Apache, and PHP in the standard LAMP (Linux, Apache, MySQL, and PHP) stack, which is one of the more popular setups for web hosting these days.

As time went on, MySQL added features to better compete with the name-brand databases. This meant giving up its spot as everyone's favorite nimble, lightweight database to SQLite. If, however, you want to be like everyone else and run MySQL, you're going to have to install it yourself. Fortunately, MySQL maintains a Mac OS X installer package on its web site, http://dev.mysql.com. To install MySQL, simply download the disk image that matches your architecture and run it.

Although it's available in more traditional tarball format, I downloaded the more Mac-like disk image installer package. This contains an installer for the database server itself and a separate installer if you'd like MySQL to start automatically. If you're running a web server, that's probably a good idea.

Once it's installed, you can start the MySQL server from the command line. It's installed in /usr/local/mysql, which is not in the default path, so to run any MySQL tools you will have to actually go into the directory or use the full path:

```
sudo -b /usr/local/mysql/bin/mysqld_safe
```

> **TIP:** If you included these lines into your `.bash_profile` as shown in Chapter 23:
>
> ```
> if [ -d /usr/local/mysql/bin ]; then
>     PATH=/usr/local/mysql/bin:"${PATH}"
> fi
> ```
>
> then you can omit the `/usr/local/mysql/bin/` part since that should already be in your $PATH.

After entering your password, the server will start. The -b flag on sudo invokes the server as a background process. You can eliminate the background flag on your first run just to make sure everything is copacetic.

Alternately, if you installed the startup item, you can use it to start the MySQL database:

```
sudo /Library/StartupItems/MySQLCOM/MySQLCOM start
```

Finally, the installer includes a MySQL preference pane for System Preferences, as shown in Figure 27–6. Double-clicking the MySQL.prefPane will install it after asking you whether to install it just for you or for all users. The preference pane tells you whether MySQL is running, lets you start and stop MySQL, and includes a setting to automatically start MySQL at boot time.

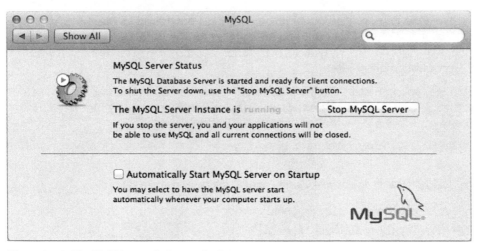

Figure 27–6. *The MySQL pane in System Preferences*

By default, MySQL sets up a root user with full access and no password. In other words, until you do something about it, your MySQL installation is completely unsecured. The first thing to do after starting the server is to lock down that root account. The easiest way to do this is with the MySQL command-line admin tool:

```
/usr/local/mysql/bin/mysqladmin -u root password "newpwd"
```

where *newpwd* is your new password.

> **NOTE:** Aside from the root user, there are also two anonymous accounts with unsecured root access. However, these accounts can access only those databases whose names start with test_, and only from the localhost, so they are not much of a risk. Still, if you are actually planning on serving pages professionally, you should lock or remove these accounts. See the online MySQL manual for more details.

Once it's installed, the default MySQL client program can be invoked from the command line, like so:

```
/usr/local/mysql/bin/mysql -u root -p
```

The -p flag will cause MySQL to prompt you for your password. Once you enter it, the command-line client program will launch. Type **help** to get a list of available commands, and type **quit** to exit.

```
                 GETTING PHP AND MYSQL TO PLAY NICE IN MAC OS X
```

There is one frustrating issue with getting PHP and MySQL to play nice together in Mac OS X: the location of mysql.sock. mysql.sock is a Unix socket file that allows a bidirectional communication between MySQL and any other local application. In this case, we want PHP and MySQL to talk to each other, but if we look at our PHP info (using our `<?php phphinfo() ?>` file shown earlier), we see that PHP is looking for `mysql.sock` in `/var/mysql` while the actual `mysql.sock` file is by default in `/tmp/`. What to do?

There are four ways to fix this:

1. Create the /var/mysql directory (`sudo mkdir /var/mysql`) and then create a symbolic link from /tmp/mysql.sock to /var/mysql/mysql.sock (with `sudo ln -s /tmp/mysql.sock /var/mysql/mysql.sock`).

2. Edit the /etc/php.ini file (it may not exist, in which case just `sudo cp /etc/php.ini.default /etc/php.ini`) so that pdo_mysql.default_socket = /tmp/mysql.sock (by default line 1065), mysql.default_socket = /tmp/mysql.sock (by default line 1219), and mysqli.default_socket = /tmp/mysql.sock (by default line 1278).

3. Edit (or create) /etc/my.cnf by adding the following lines: `[mysqld]` `socket=/var/mysql/mysql.sock [client]` `socket=/var/mysql/mysql.sock`   . This will tell MySQL to create its socket where Mac OS X's default PHP is looking for it. Next, you also need to create the /var/mysql directory *and* `sudo chown mysql /var/mysql` it or MySQL won't start since it wont be able to create the socket. (Various sample my.cnf files can be found in /usr/local/mysql/support-files.)

4. Recompile PHP for your version of MySQL (a PIA, but not a terrible idea at all).

Of these, #1 is easiest but a bit of a hack. #2 is the easiest *real* way. #3 isn't too bad but could cause issues with other MySQL clients that look for the socket in /tmp/mysql.sock. #4 is ultimately the best fix but is clearly neither very fast nor particularly easy.

PHP and MySQL are expected to run together, so once you have MySQL running, PHP will notice immediately. Reloading your PHP Info page will confirm this. Beyond that, accessing MySQL in PHP, setting up user accounts in MySQL, and the sometimes maddening/sometimes magical world of database programming are beyond the scope of this book. Fortunately, there is no end of online resources, and there are several excellent books, including *Beginning PHP and MySQL* by W. Jason Gilmore (Apress, 2010), *PHP and MySQL Web Development* by Luke Welling and Laura Thomson (Addison-Wesley, 2008), and *MySQL* by Paul DuBois (Addison-Wesley, 2008).

PostgreSQL

While SQLite concentrates on pure performance and MySQL maintains a good mix of performance and added support for advanced features, PostgreSQL has always been conceived as an enterprise-level solution. It has more advanced capabilities (e.g., multiple indexing algorithms) and can be hooked up to the enterprise directory and authentication servers, LDAP, and Kerberos, but it is still free, open source software.

For more information on PostgreSQL, visit its official home page at `www.postgresql.org` where you can get information for downloading and installing the latest version on Mac OS X.

> **NOTE:** PostgreSQL is actually installed by default on Mac OS X Lion Server, and some PostgreSQL client tools are accessible from the Client command line. Despite the existence of pieces of PostgreSQL on the Client version of Lion, PostgreSQL isn't there; however, it certainly will run well once installed.

Tips and Tricks

The joy of running a web server on a personal computer is in mucking around with things. Sometimes a little hackery makes things more convenient; other times, it's just good, clean fun, like mixing chemicals together to see what happens. If that seems to imply a little tingle of danger, so be it. Make of these what you will.

Making Sites the Document Root

If you're developing web content, you want your local server setup to mirror your remote setup as closely as possible. Since ~username sites went out of fashion with Geocities, that means working out of the document root. Compared to the user Sites directory, working out of/Library/WebServer/Documents seems so un-Mac-like.

If you're the only user on your machine, you can unify your Sites directory (or a root-level Sites directory you'd create) with Apache's document root. There are a couple of ways to do this.

The Unix way is to edit Apache's configuration file, as discussed in the earlier "Configuring Apache" section. The nice thing about setting the document root in httpd.conf is that it's portable. As long as you use the same username, your configuration file will work on any machine. It also doesn't rely on file system trickery, which makes it seem more pure.

The Mac way is to replace the file that the configuration file points to with a symbolic link. This uses the file system to fool Apache into loading a site different than it expects.

This is the same method Mac OS X uses to bridge the Finder's view of things to the Unix beneath.

Creating a symbolic link leaves the configuration file untouched, which makes it that much harder to mess up, but at the end of the day, it really doesn't matter which one you use.

> **NOTE:** A symbolic link is similar to an alias on Mac or a shortcut on Windows. In Mac OS X, links are Unix file system constructs, while aliases belong to the Finder. Using an alias to redirect your document root will not work.

To redirect your document root using symbolic links, navigate to the /Library/WebServer directory. Move aside the original Documents folder. You could delete it, but simply renaming it to something like OldDocuments will do the trick.

Launch the Terminal application and invoke the following command:

```
sudo ln -s ~/Sites /Library/WebServer/Documents
```

This means, "Using superuser privileges (sudo), create a link (ln) that is symbolic (-s) from my local Sites directory (~/Sites) to the path /Library/WebServer/Documents." If your user account does not have administrator privileges, you can invoke your admin user via the -u flag, as follows:

```
sudo -u yourAdminUserName ln -s ~/Sites /Library/WebServer/Documents
```

Since you're using sudo, this will prompt you for your password. After entering it, invoking ls on /Library/WebServer will show a file called Documents. In the Finder, it will appear to be a shortcut. Loading the root site in your browser of choice should show your personal home site.

> **TIP:** Your browser may have the old page cached, so you might need to reload or even empty your cache to see the change.

Troubleshooting Permissions

On a clean installation of Mac OS X, getting your home page to load really is as simple as selecting a check box, but if you've been lugging the same home directory around since 10.0, things can get a little weird. The same is true of site contents. A new site should have no problems, but importing an old site from who-knows-where might leave things broken.

One of the most common problems is seeing a 403 Forbidden message instead of a page on your site. This is caused by having improper permissions settings on Sites or its contents. In general, folders serving web sites need to be readable and executable by everyone, while web documents and files should be readable by everyone.

You can check and fix permissions on your Sites folder and its content using the Finder's Info panel by selecting the folder or file and pressing Command-I. You can also use the chmod command from the Terminal.

Domain Name Tricks

Were you so inclined, you could set up a DNS server, but why? Chances are your registrar has a name server, so providing you have a static outside IP address, you can simply have them point to it and start welcoming visitors to your self-hosted web site.

However, not everyone has the need to spend the money on a static IP address, especially when you consider that the cost of getting one is greater than the cost of professional web hosting. If you're setting up a web host just because it's fun, because you want to save money, or because you're doing local development, paying for a static IP address is overkill.

Custom Domains Without DNS

You can actually override DNS at a local level. Mac OS X maintains a list of known hosts in a file called /private/etc/hosts. Editing this file will let you map web addresses to IP addresses. Why would you do this?

First, looking at IP addresses all day is boring. That's why DNS was invented, after all. It's much more fun to give your local network machines fun names at imaginary top-level domains. Then you can surf over to http://i.am.awesome.

Second, if you are developing web pages locally, you might run into a problem with absolute paths. That is to say, if you have a link pointing to www.mydomain.com/somefile.php, your browser will want to go to the remote version, rather than the local version you're developing.

The hosts file is the first place your machine looks when it tries to resolve a domain. Rerouting calls to mydomain.com or www.mydomain.com to your local machine is easy. Just open /private/etc/hosts in your favorite text editor, and then add the following line:

```
127.0.0.1 mydomain.com www.mydomain.com
```

Just remember to edit the hosts file back to normal before trying to surf the Web, or strange things might happen. On the other hand, maybe you want strange things to happen. One technique for blocking web content from unwanted domains is to route them to a blank page. Here's an example:

```
128.0.0.1 doubleclick.com
```

For more information on the hosts file, invoke man hosts in Terminal.

> **CAUTION:** It's OK to add things to the hosts file, but don't edit any of the existing entries. The system has that stuff there for a reason.

Dynamic DNS

If you've configured port mapping to reach your machine from the Internet but don't want to spend the money on a static IP address, you can use a dynamic DNS service to keep your domain name pointed to the right place.

There are many cheap to free services, such as No-IP (www.no-ip.com) and FreeDNS (http://freedns.afraid.org/), that will let you point a domain name to your dynamic IP address. Unlike a standard name server, dynamic DNS services keep a very short refresh time on their name servers, so changes propagate quickly.

Other Considerations

Here are a couple more things worth checking out:

- **Mac OS X Server**: If you're running a site as a hobby or as a small business, the standard version of Mac OS X is all you need, but Apple does produce a server version of Mac OS X, aimed at the enterprise. It has some additional administrative features that, while available in Unix form, have been wrapped in that great Mac OS X user experience. If you're using Mac OS X as a server, you might look into it. Visit www.apple.com/server/macosx/ for more details.

- **Ruby on Rails**: Although PHP is a popular way to create web applications, it's far from the only game in town. One platform that's rising fast is Ruby on Rails. Ruby is an object-oriented programming language, not unlike PHP 5. Rails is a development framework written in and for Ruby.

Summary

With its open source and Unix roots, Mac OS X is built from the same stuff as the Internet itself. It's no wonder the Mac is such a great platform for web development. Whether you're serving web pages to the public right from your desktop or just building a development environment on your laptop, Mac OS X comes with everything you need, and adding more is easier than ever.

Part **VIII**

Cross-Platform Solutions

Unless you live in a utopian environment where all the enlightened people use Macs and other Apple products exclusively, you will occasionally have to deal with other operating systems, including Microsoft Windows and maybe a flavor of Linux or Unix. This of course is entirely possible with Mac OS X, so this part will share some of the cool ways you can work with or even work *on* other OSs right from your Mac.

Chapter **28**

Working with Microsoft Windows and More

Not everyone can, or even chooses to, use a Mac. As a Mac user, you can scoff at them, you can make fun of them, and you can even pity them (though more often than not you should refrain from this behavior because it's undignified). But no matter what you do, there may come a day that you need to work with them and their foreign operating system with their strange files. Luckily, as a Mac user, this usually isn't a problem. In this chapter, we will look at the following:

▓ Working with a Mac in the enterprise

▓ Dealing with foreign files and file systems

Using a Mac in the Enterprise

Since businesses and organizations first started widely adopting computers, they have been brainwashed into thinking the only way it would work was if everything was standardized, which meant the same hardware and the same software for everyone. Not too long ago this was the only way things *would* work well if at all, so it's a perfectly reasonable assumption that things would be the same today. Of course, making this assumption today would mostly be wrong, at least from a technological perspective. Still, for reasons both good and bad, many organizations today rely heavily on Microsoft for a large part of their computing needs. For efforts on both Apple's and Microsoft's part, this hardly causes a hiccup for Mac users who find they must work in a Windows environment.

Let's take a look at common enterprise technologies and see how our Mac works with them.

Microsoft Exchange Server

We've already touched upon this one earlier in the book. Apple's suite of Mail, Address Book, and iCal can all work just fine with Microsoft's Exchange Server. Just configure your Exchange Server in the Mail, Contacts & Calendar System Preferences pane, and you should be good to go on all accounts.

Microsoft Networking

Again, this is something we have talked about previously. Microsoft Networking is built in, and all resources on a Microsoft network should be immediately available from your Mac. You may need advice on configuring your WINS server if necessary.

Active Directory

Active Directory is a popular directory service created by Microsoft. Among other things, a directory service provides a central server where user account information is stored. This would be like taking the user information found in the Users & Groups System Preferences pane and storing it on central server rather than on your computer; then, when you tried to sign in to your computer, the central server (aka the directory service), you would be queried to fetch your user information. The advantages of using a directory service are that administrators have a central location where they can manage all users and permissions (which is a big deal for administrators) and users can log in from any available workstation and be assured proper access to available resources.

In the Users & Groups System Preferences pane, by selecting Login Options at the bottom of the left user and group column and clicking the Network Account Server: Join... button, you can add an Active Directory domain to Mac OS X that will be queried when users attempt to log in.

> **NOTE:** Besides supporting Active Directory, you can also configure an Open Directory server using this same method. Open Directory is the directory service used by Apple in its Mac OS X server. Both it and Active Directory are based on LDAP directory services.

SharePoint

Microsoft's SharePoint Server and SharePoint Services are growing in popularity across all sizes of organizations. SharePoint provides a centralized web application that performs a number of services including intranet and extranet services, web sites, document and file management, collaboration, and much more into a single web-based platform.

Unlike the countless web sites created by third-party "developers" using Microsoft tools that require you to use Internet Explorer to access them, SharePoint works equally well in the latest versions of Safari (as well as Firefox and Chrome) as it does in Microsoft's Internet Explorer. Additionally, Office:mac 2011 provides the same feature as the Windows counterpoint for accessing and working with documents stored on SharePoint servers.

Working with Foreign Files and File Systems

Of course, allowing computers to access the same services isn't quite the same as being able to work with files created from or for another operating system. Years ago, working with files created on another operating system was troublesome. First, the files created by one application were often unreadable in any other application, so if an application were available only on one operating system, that file would be unreadable on another. Second, each operating system stored files in a way that made it difficult to move a file from one operating system to another. (This was back in the days when the most popular way to move a file from one computer to another was with a good ol' floppy disk.)

The types of files you can easily share without much concern are fairly vast and inclusive of most situations. For business productivity files, Microsoft Office formats tend to work fine on both Macs and Windows computers with one of the major office suites installed, including, of course, Microsoft Office, but also iWork and OpenOffice.org (or one of its spin-off projects). Any standard graphics formats, such as JPEG, GIF, PNG, and TIFF files (along with numerous others), will transfer from one system to another just fine. PDF files are also common among most operating systems. When it comes to audio files, MP3, AAC, and WAV are all just fine (FLAC and a number of other audio formats are equally cross-platform but require third-party software to play them).

Video is a bit trickier since video is generally comprised of mixing both audio and video formats. Apple's QuickTime is the best option for cross-platform video with a few important considerations. First, some QuickTime movies created on a Mac must be *flattened* (which means the audio and video are combined in the file in such a way that any external dependencies are removed) to work on the Web or on a Windows computer. This is done by using the **Save As...** command in QuickTime or using the Lillipot utility (`www.qtbridge.com/lillipot/lillipot.html`). Movies exported from iMovie and most other video-editing software will be flattened automatically. Second, QuickTime must be installed for them to play back properly. This isn't a big issue for most Windows computers, because many computer manufacturers include QuickTime by default, and it's a free and easy install for any Windows computers that don't already have it. QuickTime, however, isn't available for Linux or other alternative operating systems. MPEG-4 files (which is the default video format for QuickTime movies these days) work just fine too.

> **NOTE:** Windows Media files are popular; however, they pose a number of tricky problems. First, you will likely need a third-party QuickTime plug-in or stand-alone application to play them on your Mac. Filp4Mac WMV (www.flip4mac.com) is a third-party QuickTime plug-in that today is endorsed by Microsoft for playing Windows Media files, and VLC media player (www.videolan.org/vlc) is an open source stand-alone media player that supports many formats, including WMV. The bigger problem is that at this time neither of these products will support Windows Media protected by DRM (which is quite popular).

> **NOTE:** A QuickTime plug-in called Perian (http://perian.org) will greatly enhance QuickTime's abilities to play back a number of media types. QuickTime, combined with Flip4Mac and Perian, should enable you to play back the majority of video files you find on the Internet with the notable exception of protected Windows Media files.

Once you have your file, transferring it from one computer to another is the next trick. Transferring your file over a network circumvents most file system problems. By enabling file sharing on your Mac, you can allow a Windows user to simply browse your shared directory and copy the file from your Mac to a Windows computer. Also, your Mac can utilize any Windows file servers or shared directories. If, rather than using the network, you want to use a physical means of file transfer (such as external hard drive, thumb drive, and so on), then you will likely want to format the drive using the FAT32 file system, which will work with both Macs and Windows computers.

> **NOTE:** Windows computers do not support Apple's default file system (HFS+) without special third-party software. Additionally, Mac OS X currently supports NTFS (the Windows default file system) as read-only, which makes it a bit limiting for file sharing (without the use of a third-party add-on like MacFUSE or Paragon's NTFS for Mac OS X). The FAT32 file system, however, is the old Windows default file system and has had good Mac support for many years (though FAT32 can't be used for Boot Camp partitions running Vista or Windows 7).

> **NOTE:** In the past, iDisk would be a recommended method for transferring a file from one computer to another, but with iDisk seemingly going away along with MobileMe, it's not a good time to start using it. That said, a number of excellent services provide a similar service. These include Dropbox (www.dropbox.com) and SugarSync (www.suagrsync.com), as well as Microsoft's Windows Live SkyDrive service (which is accessible from a Mac using a web browser with Silverlight).

Summary

In general, computers today tend to play nicely with each other because both businesses and individuals have demanded that computer companies become more open and standardized about these things. Still, sharing files and accessing network services is one thing. Actually running an application designed from another operating system is another case, one that we will deal with in the next chapter.

## Chapter 29

Running Other OSs on Your Mac

In the previous chapter we looked at how easy it is these days for Macs to work with other operating systems. Even when placed in a Windows environment, Mac OS X can connect to network resources, access web services, manage documents, and work with most file formats you can throw at it. There is still one thing Mac OS X can't do, and that's run all the software that was written natively for another operating system. For this problem too there are solutions: emulation, virtualization, and Boot Camp.

In this chapter, we will look at a number of ways to run other operating systems and to run applications designed for other operating systems, including the following:

- Boot Camp
- Parallels Desktop, VMware Fusion, and VirtualBox
- CodeWeavers Crossover
- Windows Remote Desktop

A Brief History of Emulation on the Mac

More than ten years ago, a highly innovative company called Connectix created a product called Virtual PC that allowed your Mac to run an emulated x86 system as a separate application. This x86 system allowed Mac users to run Microsoft Windows on their Macs. Although the performance was notably slow, it worked and ushered in the era of emulation on the Mac. Eventually, Virtual PC was purchased from Connectix by Microsoft (which continues to support Virtual PC but only for running on other Windows systems).

NOTE: Besides Virtual PC, Connectix also invented the QuickCam, which it sold to Logitech. After selling off QuickCam and Virtual PC (as well as selling its Virtual Game Station product to Sony, which promptly killed it), the company effectively called it quits in 2003. During its 15 years of existence, the company also introduced innovative techniques for taking advantage of virtual memory on the pre–OS X Mac platform.

NOTE: Emulation and virtualization seem similar in many cases but are quite different. Emulation (like the original Virtual PC) requires that the code being run actually be translated before being used. (Virtual PC used dynamic recompilation to translate x86 code to PowerPC code before the code could be run.) Virtualization, on the other hand, allows concurrent computer processes to run using the same hardware by partitioning the hardware's memory and processing power so that each process runs entirely independently of every other. Common "virtualization" software that runs on your Mac today actually is a hybrid of both virtualization and emulation.

NOTE: From Mac OS X Tiger up through Mac OS X Snow Leopard, Mac OS X actually contained its own emulation software that, like the original Virtual PC, used dynamic recompilation. This software (called Rosetta) did the opposite, though. Rather than translate x86 code into PowerPC code, it allowed old PowerPC code on your Mac to run on the new x86 architecture. Beginning with Lion, however, Rosetta is no longer available.

Upon switching to an Intel-based platform, Apple changed everything. Today not only is it possible to run Windows natively on your Apple computer, but a new range of virtualization products are now available to Mac users that run extremely well with little performance loss.

As a Mac user, you have a number of options for running Windows on your computer. We'll quickly go over each of these and point out the pros and cons of each of them.

Boot Camp

Shortly after Apple started shipping Intel-based computers, it released a utility called Boot Camp (which you had to seek out on its web site and download as a beta). Beginning with Leopard, Boot Camp was included along with Mac OS X. To get it up and running, you can use the Boot Camp Assistant, which is located in the Applications/Utilities folder.

Running Boot Camp allows you to effectively turn your Mac computer into a full-fledged Windows machine. The advantage of this is that all your Mac's hardware will become dedicated to running Windows. One significant advantage here for most people, which is not available through any current virtualization or emulation methods, is that running in Boot Camp gives you full video acceleration, which is a must for certain applications (including most Windows gaming).

Boot Camp has a few disadvantages as well, though:

- You must reboot your computer to switch between OS X and Windows (though some virtualization software can access Boot Camp partitions from Mac OS).

- You must create a dedicated partition on an internal hard drive to install Windows on, and this drive may (by default) have only two partitions: a primary Mac Partition and a Boot Camp partition.

> **NOTE:** You cannot install Windows on an external hard drive using Boot Camp.

- You must have a *full* version of Windows XP SP2 or newer to install Windows with Boot Camp.

> **Note:** When you begin to install Boot Camp with the Boot Camp Assistant, you will be prompted to print an installation and setup guide. We strongly recommend printing these 26 pages (or at least keeping them handy in an electronic format), because they contain step-by-step installation instructions as well as valuable troubleshooting, usage, and upgrade advice. Also, keep in mind that this information won't be available during the installation process unless you print it, since your computer will be otherwise occupied (with the installation and all that).

> **NOTE:** Boot Camp is very particular about the partition scheme of the drive it's installed on. For systems like a Mac Pro with more than one internal hard drive, this is easy to deal with, but if you have only one internal hard drive, the only supported configuration is for you to have a hard drive with two partitions: one for Mac OS X and one for Boot Camp.

> **TIP:** If you try to install Boot Camp on a drive with more than two partitions, it won't install. If you must have three partitions, then once you install Boot Camp, you can resize (shrink) the primary Mac partition and create a new partition from the newly empty space. It should be noted this is *not* supported and could cause data loss on any and all partitions, could cause your system not to boot, or could damage or make it impossible to install a Mac OS X recovery partition.

> **NOTE:** Depending on the model of computer you are installing Boot Camp on, Boot Camp may require you to have the original Mac OS X install disc for you to install it; this is because certain drivers are contained there that are necessary for Boot Camp to operate. With some new Mac models, Boot Camp can download the drivers from the Internet that then must be burned to CD or DVD or copied to a flash drive, but I've found this process unreliable at best (at least for my particular system.

Parallels Desktop, VMware Fusion, and VirtualBox

Shortly after the release of Intel-based Macs, the buzz started increasing about a company called Parallels (www.parallels.com/products/desktop) that was making a virtualization product for the new Macs that would allow one to run Windows and other x86 operating systems on the new Macs under OS X with exceptional performance. Sure enough, when Parallels Desktop (Figure 29–1) for the Mac was released, it did what it said it would. Soon, VMware, a company that has a long history of virtualization, announced it too was building a product for the Mac; VMware has since released Fusion with similar capabilities to Parallels Desktop. These two products, although slightly different, work (from a user's perspective) so similarly that it's hard to pick one to recommend over the other.

> **NOTE:** One other virtualization option available today is Oracle's (formerly Sun's) VirtualBox (Figure 29–2) (www.virtualbox.org). Although it's currently not as feature-rich as either Parallels Desktop or VMware Fusion, it's actively in development and improving at a fast pace. Also, it's an open source product that is free for personal use.

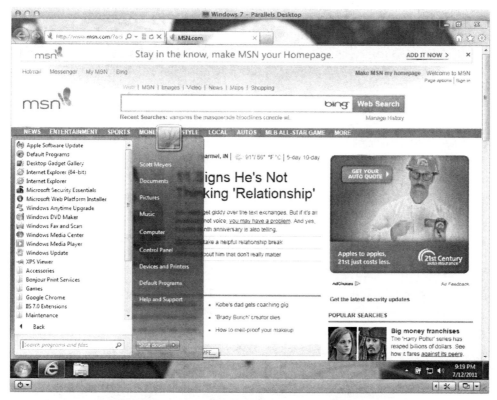

Figure 29–1. *Microsoft Windows 7 from a Boot Camp partition in Parallels*

Running either Parallels Desktop or VMware Fusion has some obvious advantages:

- They run on top of Mac OS X, providing you with the ability to switch quickly and easily from one environment to another without rebooting; in fact, both Parallels Desktop and VMware Fusion have modes that allow you to run Windows applications alongside of Mac OS X applications.

- They can both run other operating systems besides Windows, allowing you to run Linux, FreeBSD, Solaris x86, and many other operating systems.

- You can run multiple instances of one or many operating systems at the same time.

- They are both reasonably priced, well-supported, easy-to-use products that are quickly evolving with new features and better performance.

- Both are able to boot a Boot Camp partition, making Windows available in virtualization mode when needed quickly or from Boot Camp when performance is a factor.

Despite the overwhelming advantages, there are a few disadvantages to both of these virtualization products:

- To allow them to run on top of Mac OS X, many hardware devices need to be emulated. Although this largely doesn't affect performance much for most devices, it has a very big effect on video acceleration performance.

NOTE: VMware Fusion and Parallels Desktop both support DirectX, making it possible to use applications that require it. However, there is still a rather significant performance hit. As both of these products evolve, it is likely that video performance will continue to improve, but it's still a big consideration for some (i.e., gamers!).

- You will need a copy of Windows or whatever operating system you choose to run. However, unlike Boot Camp, Parallels Desktop and VMware Fusion allow you to use older products and upgrades.

- You may need to reactivate Windows on your Boot Camp partition if you boot your Boot Camp partition in either Fusion or Parallels Desktop.

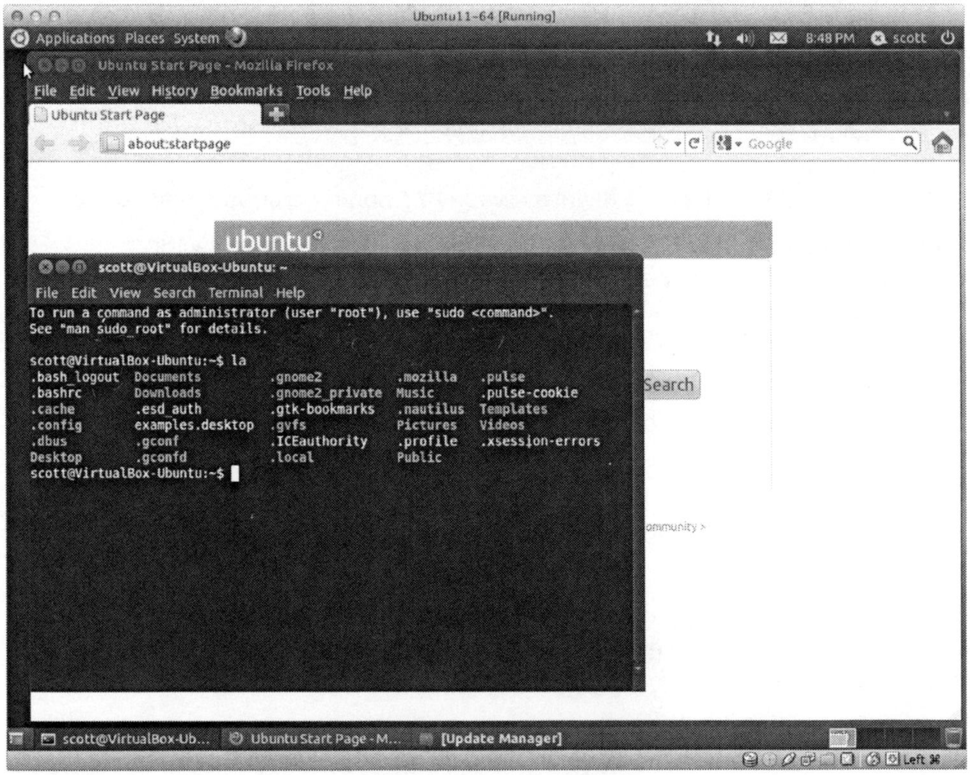

Figure 29–2. *Ubuntu Linux running in the free VirtualBox application*

CodeWeavers CrossOver (and Wine)

One other option for running Windows applications (without Windows) is CodeWeavers CrossOver (`www.codeweavers.com/products/cxmac`). CrossOver is a commercially enhanced and supported product based on the open source Wine (Wine Is Not an Emulator) project (`www.winehq.org`). What's interesting about this is that rather than rely on Windows to run Windows-based applications, Wine attempts to duplicate the underlying libraries and frameworks used by the applications in order to run them natively on a different host operating system. The advantages of CrossOver over other options are as follows:

- It's a less expensive option that doesn't require you to purchase Windows.
- Nothing is emulated, so the overall performance is very good, even for applications requiring video acceleration.
- It's fairly easy to install and use.

> **NOTE:** The ease-of-use claim is made specifically for the commercial CrossOver product. Wine requires some work to get up and running, and it isn't as easy to use once it's set up (but it is free and does work).

That said, it has some significant disadvantages. The biggest one is that not all Windows apps will work with CrossOver, and some that do exhibit some significant bugs. So, if you need to run one or two Windows applications that are supported by CrossOver (or Wine), then this is a good way to go; if, however, you need to run a wide range of Windows applications, one of the other solutions is likely a better option.

Accessing a Windows Computer Remotely

Another, very different way of using Windows on your Mac is to actually connect to another computer running Windows using Microsoft's Remote Desktop Connection (RDC). With RDC (available for free from `www.microsoft.com/mac` and included with Office installs), you can actually use a remote Windows computer from your Mac as if you were sitting right in front of it (Figure 29–3).

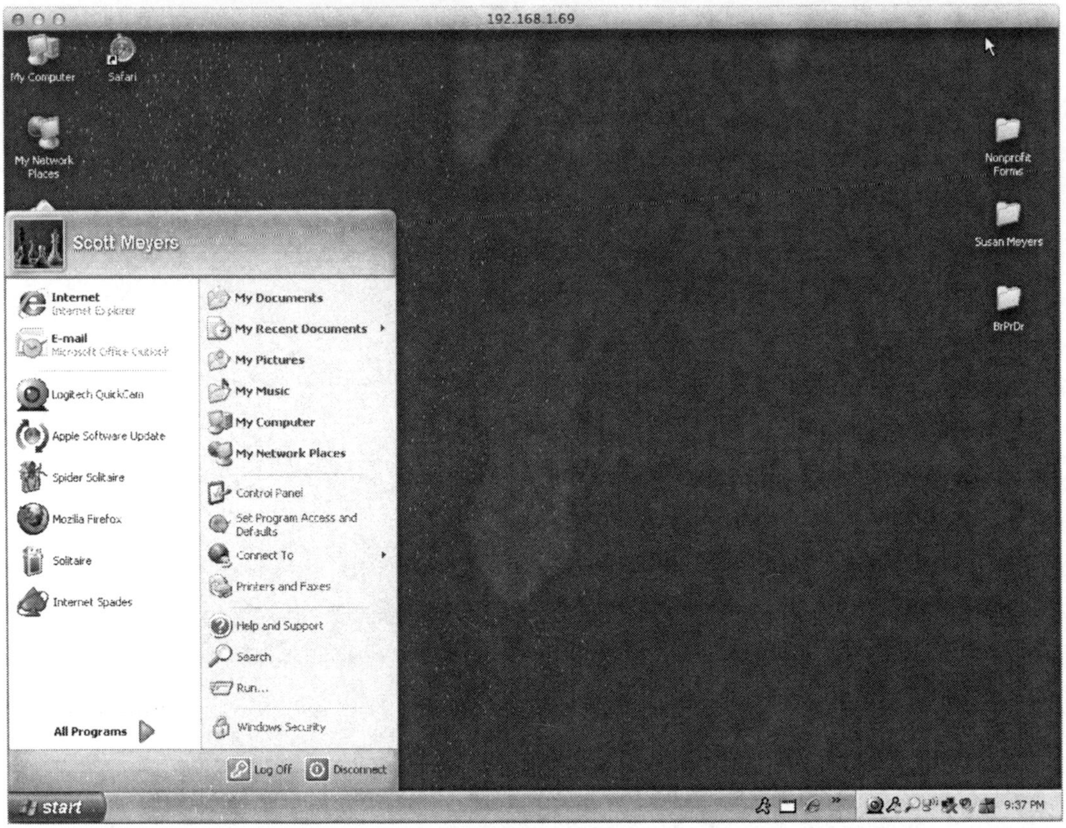

Figure 29-3. *Windows computer accessible from a Mac using RDC*

Not only does RDC allow you to access a remote Windows computer, but it allows you to copy and paste files and move them back and forth from your Mac to the connected Windows computer. You can even print items on your connected Windows computer to the printer connected to your Mac. Of course, you can also take full advantage of any application installed on the remote Windows computer.

The downside to RDC is that you need to have access to a computer running Windows. And of course, depending on the network connection between your Mac and the Windows computer, your performance may vary.

Summary

Not only do apps such as Boot Camp, VMware Fusion, and Parallels Desktop provide compatibility when necessary, but for people switching from Windows computers to Macs, they provide a way to maintain your investment in Windows software while you discover the advantages of using a Mac.

Part

Mac OS X Development: An Introduction

By this part of the book, it's assumed you are on your way to mastering everything about using Mac OS X that there is to know. Now maybe you'd like to consider tinkering with development. Your Mac provides a wonderful platform for development whether you are doing Unix shell scripting and web development or you creating the next must-have iOS or Mac OS X application.

Part IX provides an overview of the technologies and tools available on Mac OS X for the seasoned or aspiring developer.

## Chapter 30

An Overview of Mac OS X Development

Mac OS X makes an excellent development platform for a wide range of development. Not only are there tools and technologies available that allow you to create new Mac OS X applications, but you can also get your feet wet by extending the capabilities of the applications you already have. Mac OS X also is a great platform for developing services and applications for other platforms outside of Mac OS X.

In this chapter, we will take a wide look at the development landscape and provide a glimpse of the development platforms and technologies that fall outside of Apple's core development tools. We will broadly cover the following:

- The types of software you can develop on Mac OS X

- The types of platforms (other than Mac OS X and iOS) you can develop for

- The types of third-party tools and technologies available for various types of development

> **NOTE:** AppleScript, Automator, and Xcode will be covered in the following three chapters.

Scripts, Applications, and More

Most people think about development in terms of application development. That is, they assume developers write apps and nothing else. A typical daily conversation for a developer goes along these lines:

> Person: "So, what do you do?"
>
> Developer: "I'm a software developer."

Person *[excitedly]*: "Oh, really? You know I had this idea for an app that will do this and that. Do you think you could create something like that?"

Developer *[attempting to maintain their cool, but knowing where this is going]*: "Well, yeah, maybe, but that's not really the sort of development I do."

Person *[puzzled expression appears on face]*: "Oh, so what kind of apps *do* you make?"

Developer: "Well, not really apps; I develop business logic compon...*blah blah blah....*"

Person *[backing away slowly]*: "Oh... ummm... cool... well nice meeting you...."

The truth about development is that a large number of developers don't create apps (or at least they don't create *just* apps). This begs the question, what do developers develop? Well lot's actually:

Applications: For our purposes, an application is computer software that is written for a computer user to accomplish one or more specific tasks. This is a fairly broad term, and it is usually useful to further divide apps into smaller categories such as native apps, web apps, and widgets.

Utilities: A utility is computer software that performs one or more specific maintenance or general-purpose computing tasks that are designed to help analyze, configure, optimize, or maintain the computer system itself.

> **NOTE:** Applications and utilities are occasionally confused. A good way to differentiate them is to consider that an application is designed so the computer can help accomplish a task for a user, while a utility is designed so a user can help accomplish a task for the computer.

Scripts: Scripts are generally user-created programs that are written to customize or automate the execution of another command or series of commands.

Frameworks or libraries: Frameworks and libraries are collections or reusable code that developers can use to simplify the development process.

Plug-ins: Plug-ins are pieces of software that can enhance the features of other software.

Components: Components are modular pieces of software in which related data or functions are encapsulated. Components can then be strung together to create custom applications.

NOTE: While the component model is quite popular in computing today, with it being used in many web and enterprise development technologies, it's not a model that is popular at Apple for development these days. Apple was once a big proponent of application-based component technology and even helped develop OpenDoc, a framework where individual, task-specific software components (i.e., a text component, a web component, a bitmap component) would be tied together to create a document-centric application environment. OpenDoc had a number of major problems and was scrapped, and while components are still used here and there (mostly on the OS level), Apple has never brought component technologies like OpenDoc back to applications

> **System software**: System software includes operating systems (like Mac OS X) and software that helps govern computing resources. Some consider large-scale web-based systems to also fall into this category.

> **Device drivers**: Device drivers control specific hardware components in modern computing systems. For any hardware to work with your computer, a device driver must be written for it.

Beyond the types of software listed here, there are many others, including embedded programming, firmware, and language development. While some forms of each of these software types can be (and are) regularly developed on Mac OS X, what we are going to concern ourselves with in the later chapters of this book are applications and scripting.

Platform Targeting

When you create any software, you need to choose a target platform; that is, you need to decide what computing environment you want your software to run in. Depending on the specific project, sometimes this is decided for you; other times you can choose. The most common platforms for development on Mac OS X are Mac OS X itself, iOS, and various web stacks. (A *stack* in this context is a collection of technologies that work together to create a development platform; a common stack is Apache, MySQL, and PHP (*X*AMP, where the *X* can be "L" for Linux or "M" for Mac). Of course, other platforms may be targeted from Mac OS X, including Java and even Android.

We will cover the Mac OS X and iOS stuff in the next three chapters (with a focus on Mac OS X, but many of the tools and frameworks apply for iOS as well). We touched a bit upon web development in Chapter 27. Let's take a quick look at some other platforms you can target from Mac OS X.

Java

Mac OS X and Java have an interesting history. Originally Java was an integral part of Mac OS X development, and Java was a fully supported alternative to Objective-C for Cocoa development. At the same time, though, there was often a discrepancy between the latest versions of the official Java SDK, Java Runtime Engine (JRE), and Java Virtual Machine (JVM) and what was available on Mac OS X (with Java for Mac OS X often lagging behind). To help solve the discrepancy, Apple started developing and maintaining Java releases for Mac OS X and managed to largely keep Mac OS X on par with other Java-enabled platforms.

With the release of Mac OS X 10.4 (Tiger), Apple announced that new additions to Cocoa would be written specifically for Objective-C, effectively signaling the end for Java as an official language for Cocoa development; however, Apple continued to support native Java development with frequent JDK releases.

In October 2010, Apple made yet another switch in its Java support stating that as of Mac OS X 10.6.3, Apple would deprecate its own version of Java and instead rely on Oracle, which now controls Java, for Mac OS X versions of Java. Since that time, however, Apple has continued to supply and update Java, at least for now.

Beginning with Lion, Java is no longer included with Mac OS X at all. Rather, the first time you attempt to access Java you will be prompted to install it through Software Update (Figure 30–1).

Figure 30–1. *The first time you try to use Java in Lion, you will be prompted to install Java from Software Update.*

NOTE: While Java is still available from Apple, the question seems to be when, and not if, it will finally pull the plug on releasing Java. So, until Oracle gets on board with its own Mac OS X releases of Java, what can you do? Well, there are options; one of the most promising is the OpenJDK project that is a fully supported open source version of JDK Standard Edition (SE). OpenJDK is available either from http://openjdk.java.net or from MacPorts.

NOTE: Apple also has Java downloads available for registered developers from its Developer website.

Once Java is installed, it's ready to use for both running and developing Java applications (Figure 30–2).

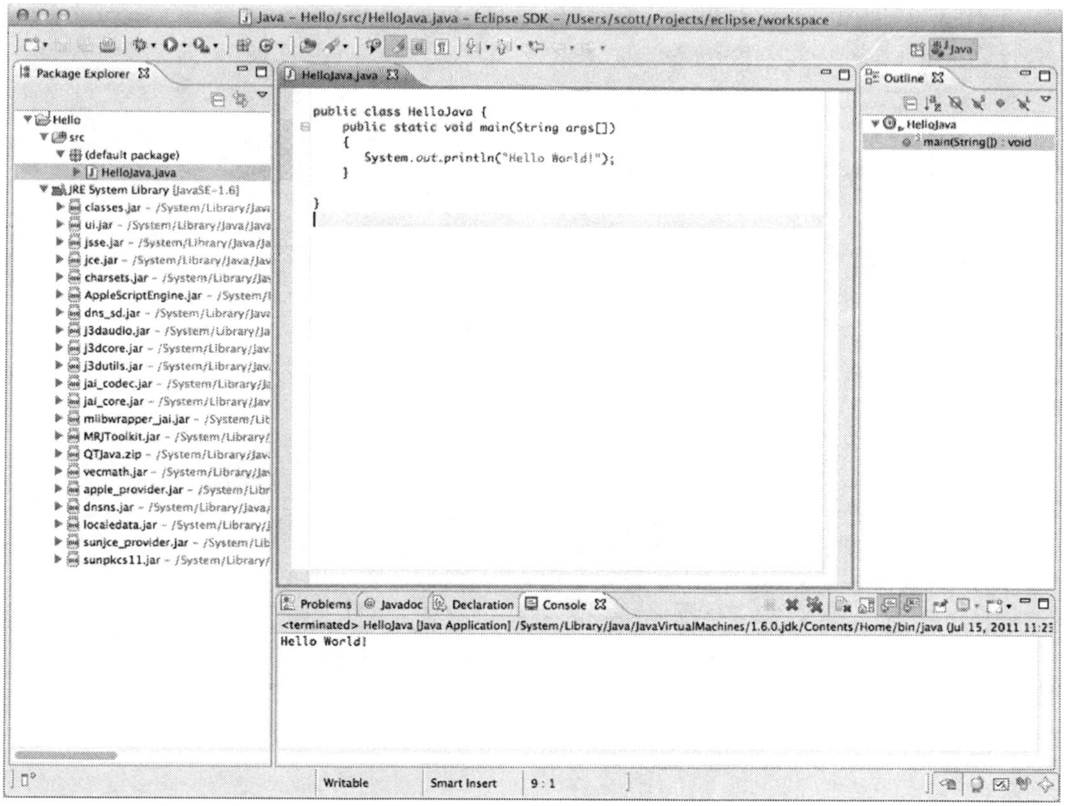

Figure 30–2. *Eclipse is a popular development IDE written in Java. Here it is shown with a simple "Hello World" Java project open.*

Despite the second-class status that Java seems to be receiving from Apple in Mac OS X these days, it's still a compelling platform since a native Java app should run on any platform with a Java runtime. Also, Java has found a strong niche in both enterprise and embedded systems development.

Android

Because Mac OS X is the only platform for native iOS development, countless mobile developers rely on it daily for their needs. Of course, iOS isn't the only mobile platform, and many mobile developers like the option of being able to develop for other platforms as well. Luckily, once you have Java installed, adding the necessary tools for Android development is a snap (especially if you have Eclipse, a Java-based IDE, shown in Figure 30–2, already installed). Not only can you develop android applications in Mac OS X, you can even run them using the Android emulator included with the developer tools (Figure 30–3). For details on how to get started with Android development, head over to http://developer.android.com.

Figure 30–3. *Mac OS X is an excellent platform for developing and testing Android applications. Here an Android tablet is being emulated to test applications.*

POSIX Development

Portable Operating System Interface for Unix (POSIX) is a specification that allows developers to create applications on one POSIX-compliant platform and then easily port them to another POSIX-compliant platform. Along with systems like Solaris, AIX, HP-UX, and many other Unix and Unix-like OSs, Mac OS X is fully POSIX compliant.

> **NOTE:** Most flavors of Linux, FreeBSD, NetBSD, and other popular open source platforms are not officially certified as such but are in fact largely POSIX compatible as well.

POSIX development usually revolves around the Unix tools available on Mac OS X that we covered in Chapters 23 and 24.

NOTE: In POSIX terms, portability is based on source code compatibility, not application compatibility. This means POSIX-compliant programs written in scripting languages should work unaltered from one POSIX platform to another (though certain path names and locations may very). However, compiled applications written in languages like C and C++ will need to be recompiled on each various platform. The recompilation, though, should be fairly pain-free. It is largely because of POSIX compliance that so much software is readily available from projects such as MacPorts.

Third-Party Tools and Technologies

A developer relies on their tools to help create applications, and Mac OS X has a large selection of tools for developers. Let look at just a sampling of some developer tools available from third parties.

NOTE: The next three chapters will cover Apple-branded development tools that are included either with Mac OS X line or as part of Xcode.

Text Editors

For a developer, a good general-purpose text editor can be a life-saver. Even though most integrated development environments (IDEs) have text editors (or text-editing capabilities) built in, sometimes you just want to quickly open a text file to make changes. Here are some of my favorites:

- **BBEdit ($49.99 in App Store)**: BBEdit is one of my all-time favorite tools for development. Not only has it been a top choice for web development for years, but its disk browser and Unix scripting support combined with unmatched text-editing capabilities make useful for any text editing you can throw at it.

- **TextWrangler (free in App Store)**: This is BBEdit's little brother (in fact, it was once BBEdit Lite). It lacks the features of BBEdit, but it's still a capable text editor.

- **TextMate (micromates.com)**: I hesitate to mention this app since it's been stuck at version 1.5.*x* for years (the last release was version 1.5.10, a minor update in November 2010) and little official word has been released about version 2 (which has allegedly been in development for more than four years). However, TextMate was at the time of its release an excellent highly customizable text editor that has attracted a large following. I can't really recommend running out and buying the current version; however, if TextMate 2 ever does appear, it should be worth checking out (after all, Duke Nukem Forever shipped, so at least there's hope).

Web Development Tools

Traditionally web developers just needed a good text editor, but today a number of extra tools are available that either provide a good addition to a text editor or provide a full-fledged web development environment with text-editing capabilities as well as much more. A few of the most interesting include the following:

- **Coda ($99.99 in App Store)**: Coda combines text editing, a visual CSS editor, file upload and download capabilities (including Subversion source control), a terminal, and more into a single application.

- **Espresso ($79.99 at macrabbit.com)**: Espresso is similar to Coda, yet it has some unique features. The current 1.1 release is solid, but there isn't much to recommend over Coda. The 2.0 release, which at the time of this wiring is in testing, promises to be excellent.

Mobile Development

Besides the native mobile development kits provided by Apple for iOS and Google for Android, there are a number of other ways to build native mobile Apps on Mac OS X. Two products (of many) that allow developers to use the latest web-based technologies to create native mobile applications are PhoneGap and Titanium Mobile.

> **NOTE:** There has been discussion about Apple's policy of allowing third-party development tools for creating applications that can be distributed through the App Store. There are currently a large number of approved apps created by both of these products available on the iOS App Store, and to my knowledge no apps have been disapproved because they were built using either of these products.

PhoneGap (www.phonegap.com) is a framework developed by Nitobi Software that allows developers to create applications using HTML5 and JavaScript to leverage the native APIs and hardware features of mobile devices that can then be compiled into applications suitable for multiple mobile platforms including iOS, Android, BlackBerry, and webOS. Because this is a add-on framework (along with a custom JavaScript library), iOS development can take place in Xcode for easy iPhone testing and App Store deployment.

> **NOTE:** To compile and deploy your application for various mobile platforms, you must be working in a native deployment environment. This includes iOS and Xcode, Android and Eclipse, and webOS with its SDK, which are all accessible from Mac OS X. BlackBerry development, however, requires Windows, so you will need a Windows system (or virtual machine) if you want to deploy your application to BlackBerry.

PhoneGap is released under either a BSD license or an MIT license, which makes it free to use and extremely flexible. (There are of course commercially available add-ons and support available.)

Titanium Mobile is developed by Appcelerator (`www.appcelerator.com`). Like PhoneGap, Titanium Mobile starts at the irresistible price of free and goes up for different add-ons and support options. Also like PhoneGap, developers use web-based technologies such as HTML and JavaScript to create the app that Titanium then converts to a native app. Unlike PhoneGap, Titanium uses its own IDE from development rather than each platform's specific tools, which makes cross-compiling much easier. Also unlike PhoneGap, while Titanium supports only iOS and Android for mobile apps, the Titanium platform extends to provide desktop application development for Mac OS X, Windows, and Linux.

Summary

If it's not immediately obvious, this is just a small smattering of the development tools and technologies available for developers who use Mac OS X as their primary development platform. The goal was to cover a range of what's available and let you fill in the gaps where necessary. Next, however, we will start to take a more detailed look at the development tools that Apple provides for Mac OS X, beginning with AppleScript and Automator.

## Chapter 31

Mac OS X Automation with Automator and AppleScript

If you've been using a computer for a while, you've probably figured out a few basic workflows for getting things done. You even may have committed them to muscle memory because you do them over and over. This is ironic, because computers were designed to spare you from boring, repetitive tasks. It's like tidying your hotel room.

Of course, if the hotel room is in another country and you don't speak the language, what are you going to do? You could be at the nicest hotel in the world with a staff of thousands standing by 24 hours a day to satisfy your every need, but if you don't know how to ask for help, you may end up tidying your own room, to say nothing of reusing your towels and foraging for coffee.

If you ever find yourself saying things like "Why can't I make a single iTunesPhotoshopSafari App?" then it's time to meet Otto, the friendly automation robot built into Mac OS X, shown in Figure 31–1. Otto isn't like your computer. Otto understands you. You can tell Otto things you want to do with your applications, and he'll do them for you.

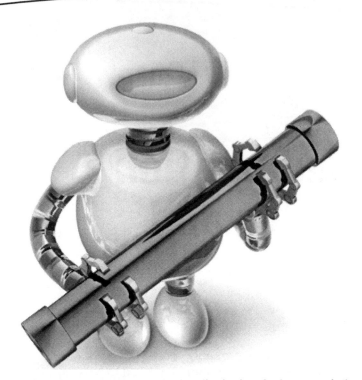

Figure 31–1. *Otto, the mascot and application icon for Automator, is there to serve.*

Otto is the mascot for Automator, an application that allows you to graphically tie together functions of Mac OS X and various applications into workflow. To test-drive Automator, let's build something original and cool and kind of dangerous. Mac OS X ships with an amazing photo-slideshow screen saver, but using it to show the same boring vacation photos over and over seems like a waste. Let's solve this problem by asking Otto to build an Automator application that fills our screen saver with fresh pictures it downloads through Google based on some keyword we can change with our mood.

Just to make sure we're on the same page, let's create a folder to keep our images in and set up the screen saver to use it. Using the Finder, create a new folder in your Pictures folder called Keyword Screensaver, as shown in Figure 31–2.

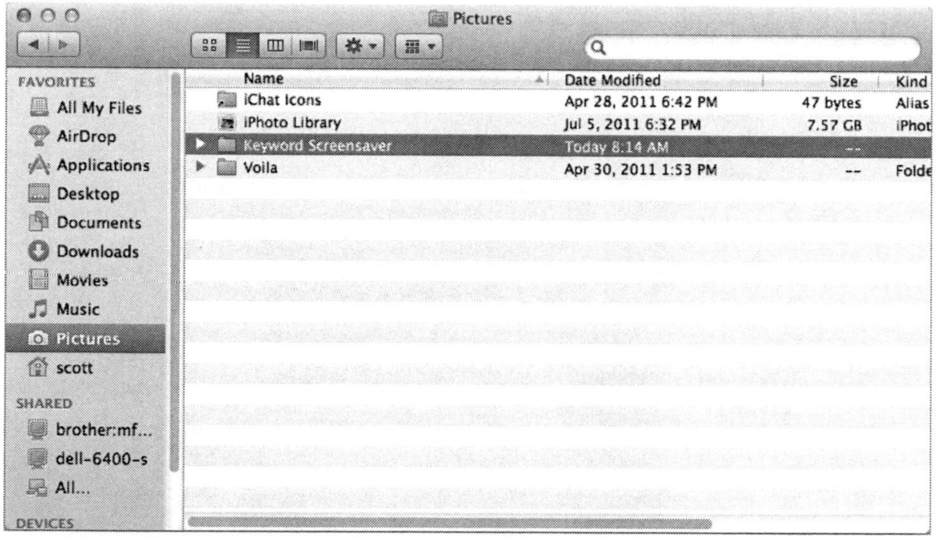

Figure 31-2. *Creating your Keyword Screensaver folder in the Finder*

With the folder in place, open your System Preferences, select the Desktop & Screen Saver preference pane, and then select the Screen Saver tab. Click the plus button beneath the list of screen savers and then select Add Folder of Pictures..., as shown in Figure 31-3. This presents you with a standard open sheet. Select the Keyword Screensaver folder, and click the Choose button. Select the "falling pictures" display style, which is the second of the three style buttons under the preview.

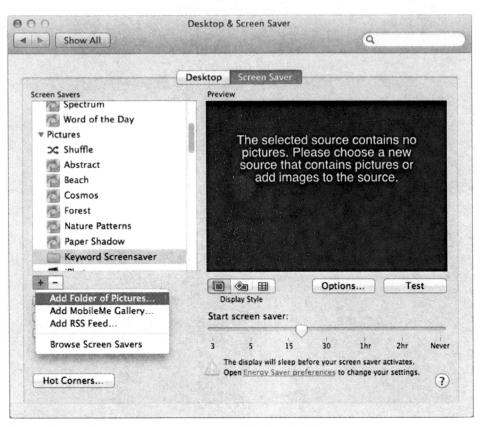

Figure 31–3. *Setting up your photo screen saver in System Preferences*

With the screen saver set up and the Keyword Screensaver folder in place, you can start working on the application. Click Otto in Launchpad to launch Automator.

Automator

Like all good document-based applications, Automator greets you with a template picker, as shown in Figure 31–4. The template picker is Otto asking you what you want to do with your workflow. You want an application you can launch from the Dock whenever you want fresh photos, so select Application, click Choose, and then save the project as Keyword Screensaver, Application.

> **NOTE:** We'll talk about the other types of Automator projects in the upcoming "Advanced Automator Shenanigans" section.

Figure 31–4. *Automator's template picker showcases the various types of projects you can create with Automator.*

Actions

Automator lets you describe your workflow as a step-by-step list of simple actions, using a graphical, drag-and-drop interface. Actions are the basic unit of work in Automator. The typical action takes some piece of data, asks an application to perform some task with that data, and produces the results. The results can then be fed into the next action until the work is done.

All the actions available to you are contained in the Actions library on the left side of your new workflow, as shown in Figure 31–5. You can browse actions, which are grouped in a browser view on the left. Selecting an action pops up a description view that describes what the action does, what the action needs as input, and what the action produces as a result. You can also search for an action using the search field atop the browser view.

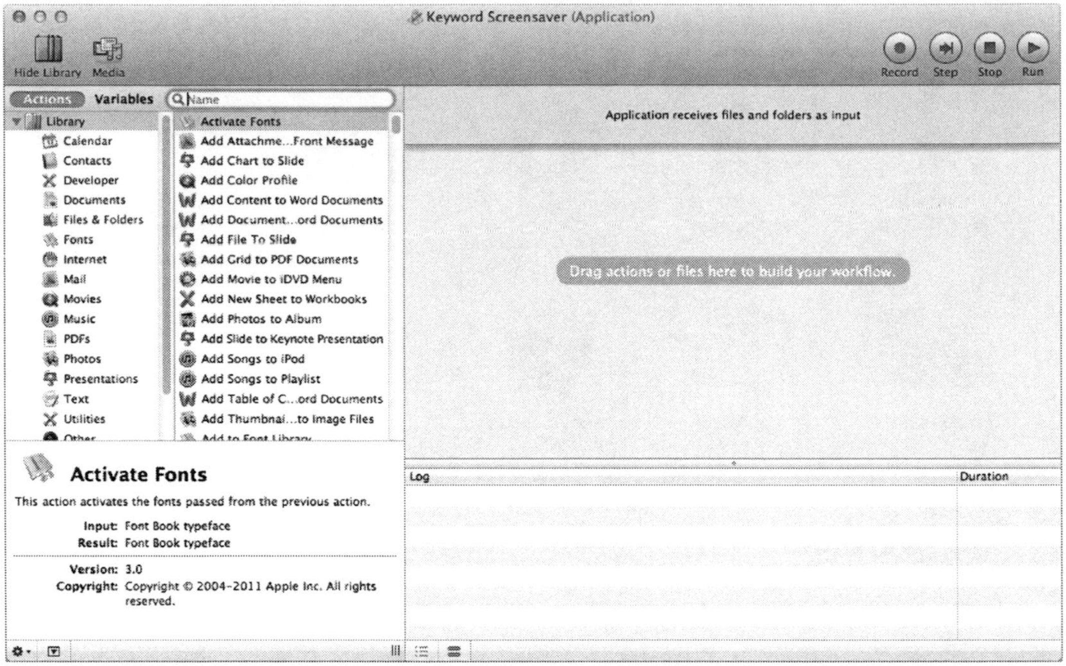

Figure 31–5. *The Actions library gives the empty shell of your new Automator application an air of possibility.*

You can create your own groups and smart groups from the group view's shortcut menu or from the action (gear) menu in the lower-left corner of the Automator window. The default groups are based on the types of data the actions work upon:

- **Calendar**: iCal calendars, events, and to-do items.

- **Contacts**: Address Book contacts and information.

- **Developer**: Xcode, SQL, CVS, and other developer tools.

- **Files & Folders**: Finder items and tasks, including moving, copying, and deleting items; setting the desktop picture; and setting Spotlight comments.

- **Fonts**: Font Book management tasks and metadata.

- **Internet**: Web and RSS data, including extracting, filtering, and loading URLs.

- **Mail**: Mail tasks, such as getting, filtering, displaying, and sending e-mail messages.

- **Movies**: QuickTime, iMovie, iDVD, and DVD player actions.

- **Music**: iTunes and iPod actions, as well as the cool Text to Audio File action.

- **PDFs**: Preview actions for creating, controlling, or extracting data from PDF documents.

- **Photos**: iPhoto, Preview, and QuickTime actions for getting, manipulating, and organizing photos. This also includes actions for controlling digital cameras and the iSight /FaceTime camera.

- **Presentations**: Keynote actions for controlling slide-show presentations.

- **Text**: TextEdit actions for creating, editing, and working with text documents.

- **Utilities**: System services and Automator control actions, such as burning a disc and presenting different kinds of dialogs, as well as the powerful Run AppleScript, Run Shell Script, and Run Workflow actions.

- **Other**: Theoretically, this group would contain actions that somehow don't fit into other groups. In practice, it's up to developers to define which groups their actions should be sorted into. If this information is not provided, the action ends up here.

NOTE: Your categories may differ based on which applications you've installed. For example, the Developer category won't exist unless you have installed the developer tools, and if you have Microsoft Office installed, a Documents category will be present.

Workflows

On the other side of your Automator document, the workflow editor exhorts you to "Drag actions or files here to build your workflow." Heed this advice with a simple exercise to warm up for the Keyword Screensaver app. Find the Get Specified Finder Items action from the Files & Folders group and drag it into the workflow view. As you drag the action from the sidebar to the workflow editor, it will expand into a small window with its own title bar, a content view, and a tabbed details view, as shown in Figure 31–6.

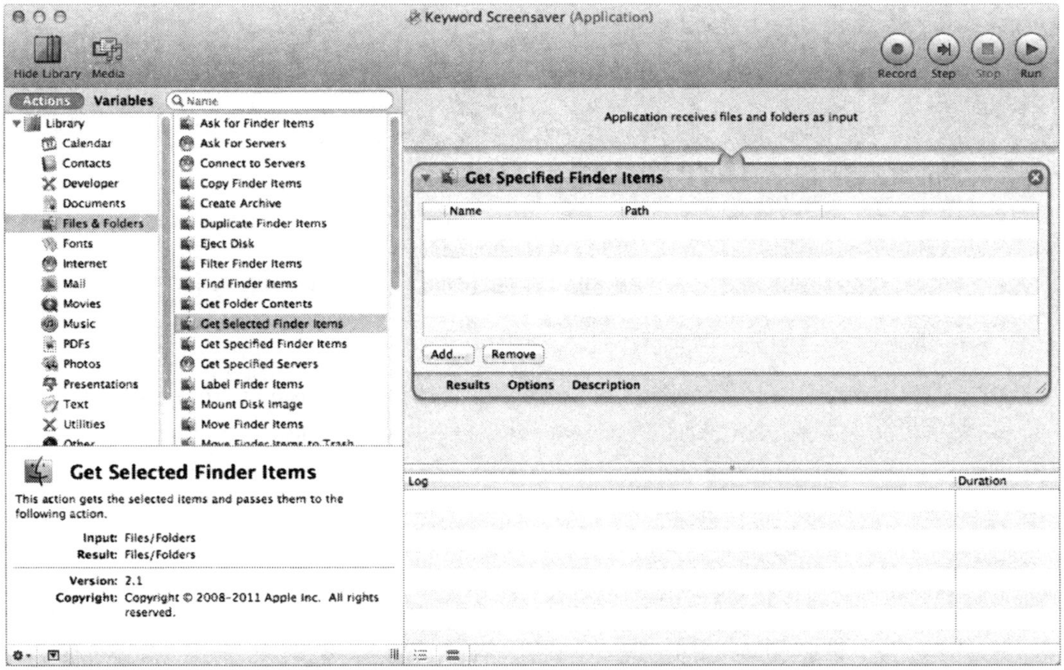

Figure 31–6. *Your first Automator action as it appears in the workflow editor*

NOTE: A common question at this point is, "What's the difference between the Get Specified Finder Items and Get Selected Finder Items?" Although these two items sound like they do the same thing (and the descriptions aren't that enlightening), they have a significant difference. The Get Specified Finder Items action allows you to select specific Finder items that Automator will use in the workflow every time it is run. The Get Selected Finder Items action will tell the Automator workflow to use items selected from the Finder when you run the workflow.

The title bar, which has the action's name and icon, has a disclosure triangle on the left that collapses and expands the action. Double-clicking the title bar has the same effect. On the right side of the title bar is an X icon. Clicking this icon removes the action from the workflow.

CAUTION: Clicking the X icon removes the action without warning or confirmation. You can undo this by selecting **Edit** > **Undo** or by pressing Command-Z.

The action's content view typically contains preferences or other configuration options in the form of drop-down boxes, text fields, table views, and so forth. The Get Specified Finder Items action contains a list of folders or files you specify, which it returns as its result. To specify the Keyword Screensaver folder, click the Add... button and then navigate to the Keyword Screensaver folder you created earlier.

TIP: To rearrange actions within the workflow, simply drag them around.

To run this simple workflow, click the Run button in the toolbar. Click the Results tab below the content view to see the result of running your first Automator action, as simulated in Figure 31–7.

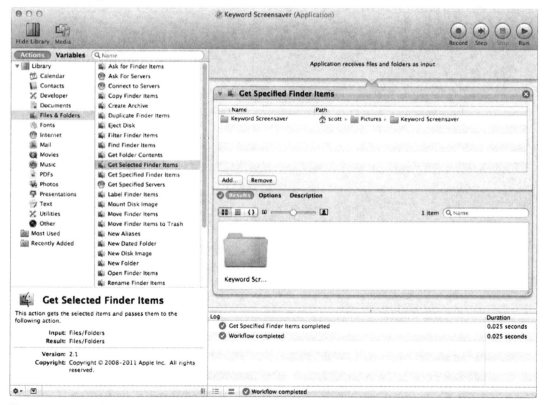

Figure 31–7. *Examining the results of running your first Automator action*

Aside from the Results tab, all actions should have a Description tab. This is the same description you see when you click an action in the Library browser. Some actions have an additional Options tab. One option you see a lot is "Show this action when the

workflow runs." This is for those actions where you'd rather leave the configuration up
the user. If this option is checked, the workflow will pause to present the user with more
or less the same interface as the workflow editor, as shown in Figure 31–8.

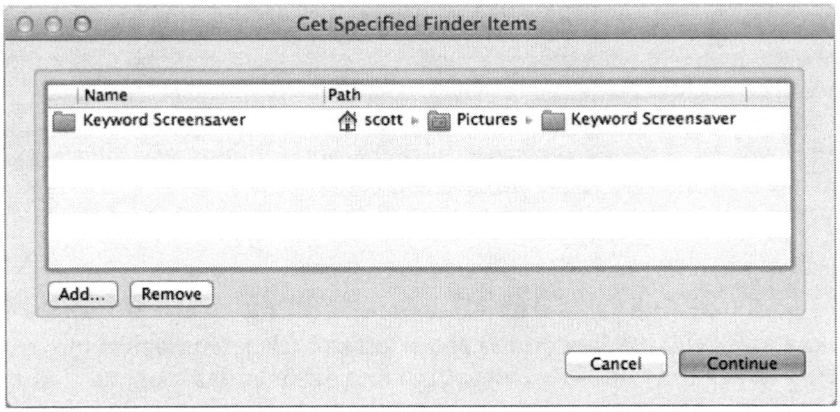

Figure 31–8. *Automator's runtime interface for the Get Specified Finder Items action*

One action isn't much of a workflow, since there's nowhere for the work to flow to. The
magic is in connecting the result of one action to the input of another and combining
their effects to perform a complicated task. You have a folder; it's time to look inside.
Drag the Get Folder Contents action from the Files & Folders group to above the Get
Specified Finder Items action. Automator connects these actions automatically, as
shown in Figure 31–9.

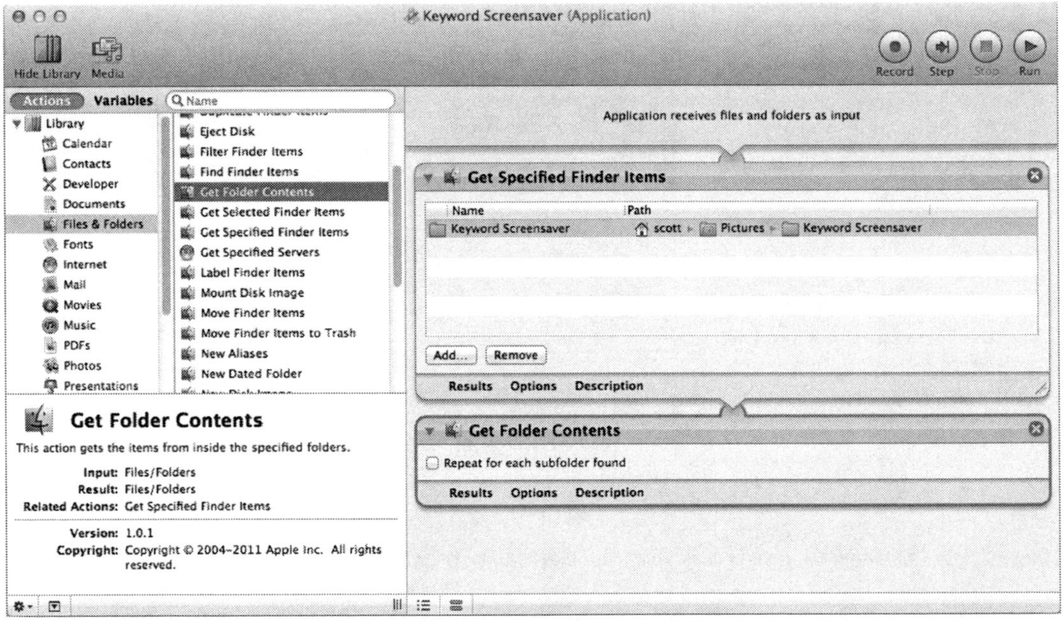

Figure 31–9. *Connecting a second action to your Automator workflow*

This connection indicates that the result of the Get Specified Finder Items action will be the input of the Get Folder Contents action. The Get Folder Contents action takes the folder you specified in the Get Specified Finder Items action and produces a list of the files and folders it contains. Next, drag the Move Finder Items to Trash action from the Files & Folders group to below the Get Folder Contents action. This takes the list of files produced by the Get Folder Contents action as input and deletes them.

Running the workflow produces a warning, as shown in Figure 31–10.

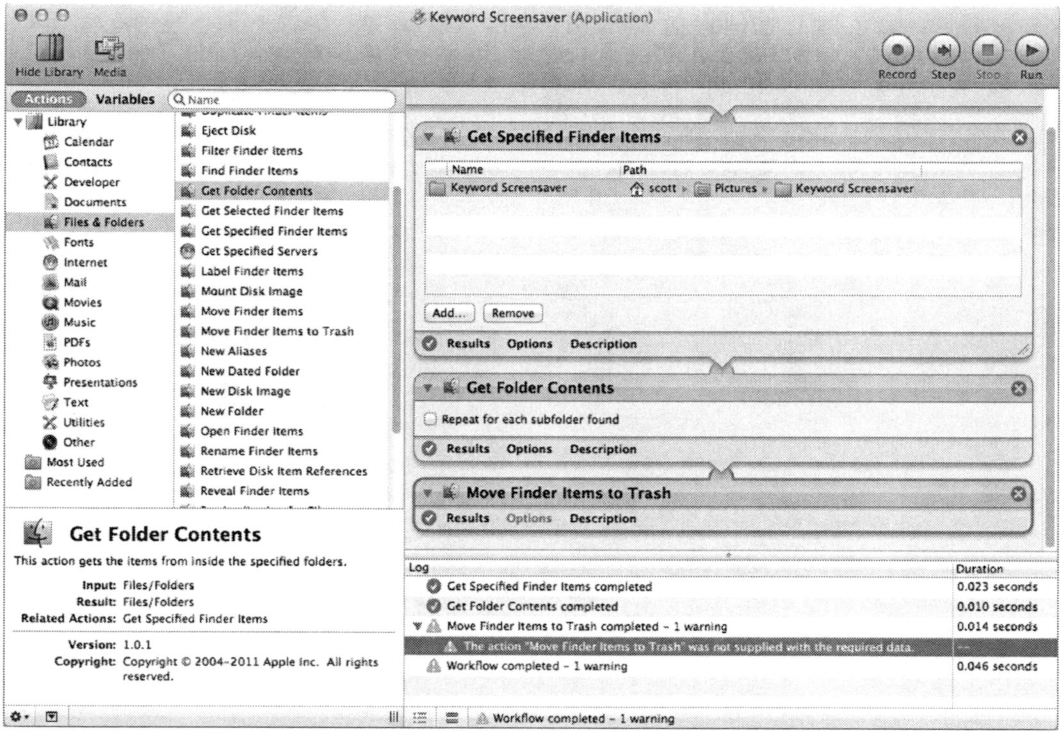

Figure 31–10. *Emptying a folder in Automator*

The warning that the Move Finder Items to Trash action was not supplied with the required data makes sense. You just created the Keyword Screensaver folder, so it doesn't contain anything. If you want to verify that it works, stick some random file in there and run the workflow again. It should run without warnings, and checking the Keyword Screensaver folder should verify that its contents have been deleted.

Deleting the contents of a folder may not seem very exciting, but there's a Mr. Miyagi moment here. Not only have you managed to build something useful, if prosaic, in Automator, but it's actually a necessary component of the Keyword Screensaver application. The first thing the application has to do is remove the old images before it downloads new ones. This forms the second, somewhat more complicated, part of the application.

Using Actions

The first action in the second part of the workflow prompts the user for a keyword. The fact that this requires user interaction should complicate things, but Automator will take care of the details. All you have to do is drag an Ask for Text action (from the Text category) below the Move Finder Items to Trash action. Notice that Automator does not connect these two actions. That's because the Move Finder Items to Trash action destroys its input, so it doesn't produce a result. This broken connection means no data flows between these actions. It does not affect the way the workflow runs. The actions will still run sequentially, regardless of whether the actions are connected.

The Ask for Text action displays a dialog box asking the user a question, and it provides a text area for the user to type an answer, which is this action's result. Fill the Question field with **What keyword shall I search for?** Leave the Default field blank, and leave the button text as it is, but check the "Require an answer" option, as shown in Figure 31–11.

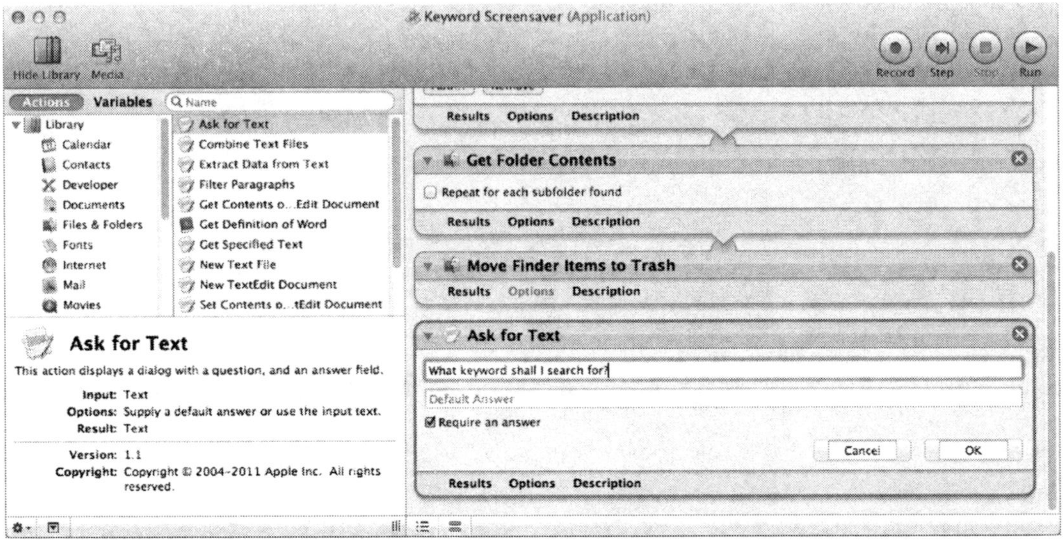

Figure 31–11. *The Ask for Text action in your workflow*

Running the workflow should display a dialog box, as shown in Figure 31–12. The workflow pauses while it waits for an answer. Type a keyword and click OK. The workflow will resume, and the result of the Ask for Text action will be the text you typed.

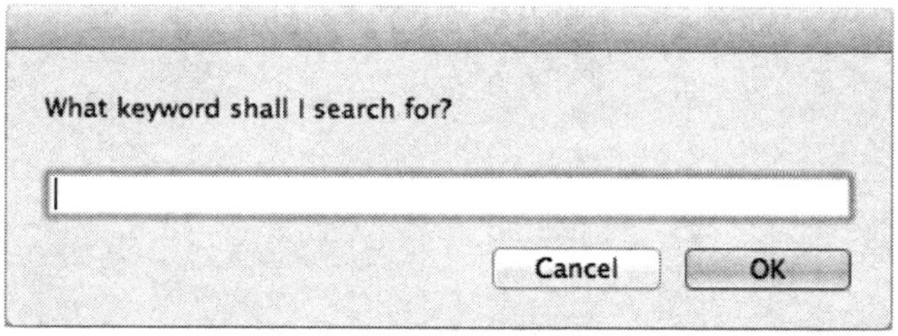

What keyword shall I search for?

Cancel   OK

Figure 31-12. *The Ask for Text action in action*

At this point, you have a keyword, but what you really need is a URL to search for that keyword on Google Image Search. This reveals the major difference between using Automator vs. a full programming language. It takes a lot of code to generate a user interface that can ask the user for new input and then convert that input into a usable form. With Automator, that comes free with the template. On the other hand, combining two strings to create a URL—among the most basic of programming tasks—is apparently impossible, because there's no "concatenate string" action in the standard Actions library.

Luckily, Automator includes actions like Run Shell Script that let you perform arbitrary tasks. Drag the Run Shell Script action from the Utilities group to below the Ask for Text action. This uses the text the user entered as input to its shell script, and it returns the result of running the script.

The Run Shell Script action has two options. The **Shell** drop-down lets you select which shell you are scripting for, which affects subtle linguistic differences, analogous to choosing between the U.S. and Canadian keyboard layout. Because Bash is perhaps the most common shell, select **/bin/bash** from the **Shell** drop-down. The **Pass input** drop-down lets you decide whether you want the incoming data (from the Ask for Text action) to arrive as arguments or via standard in. In this instance, it's easier to have the data as arguments, so select **as arguments** from the **Pass input** drop-down.

As for the shell script itself, all you're doing is taking the URL to Google Image Search and appending the first piece of input, represented in Bash as $1. You don't need any processing or anything. You just want the shell to read it back to you, so use the command echo. Altogether, that looks like the following, which you should enter in the action's main text area:

```
echo "http://images.google.com/images?q="$1
```

The output will be the full URL to query Google Image Search, which you can confirm by running the workflow and comparing it to Figure 31-13.

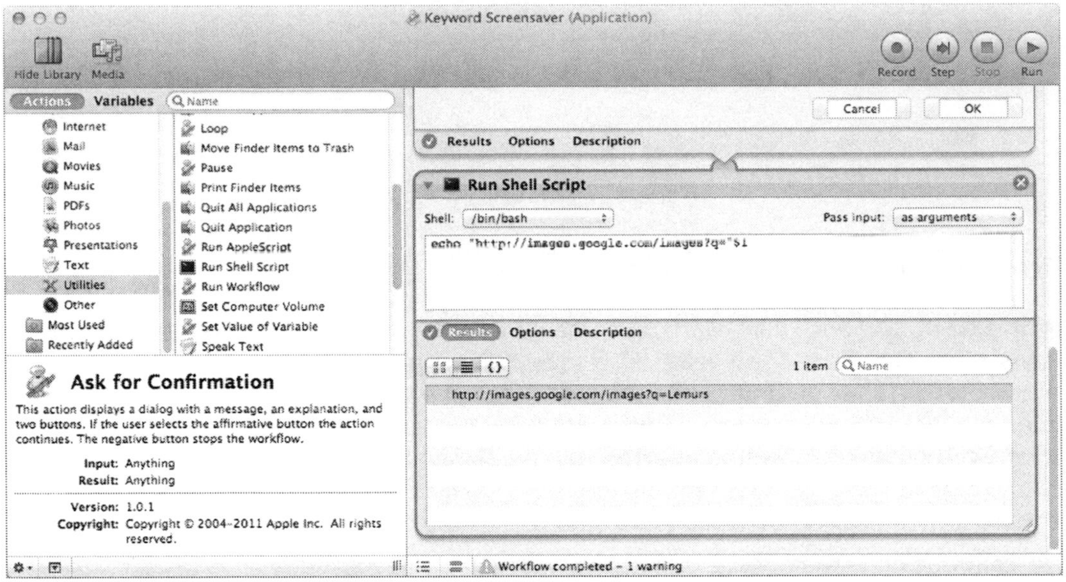

Figure 31–13. *Running a shell script as part of your Automator workflow*

> **NOTE:** Shell scripting is covered in Chapter 24. Apple also provides a shell scripting primer,
> available at
> `http://developer.apple.com/documentation/OpenSource/Conceptual/ShellScri`
> `pting/`.

Of course, the URL alone is no good. You need to actually load the URL to run the
search and then retrieve the results: a list of URLs pointing to images on the Web.
Automator includes the Get Link URLs from Webpages action in the Internet group,
which can load the search URL and extract the resulting URLs in one step. Drag the Get
Link URLs from Webpages action to below the Run Shell Script action. You're not
interested in links to ads or other non-Google content, so check the "Only return URLs
in the same domain as the starting page" option. Run your workflow and check the
results, as shown in Figure 31–14.

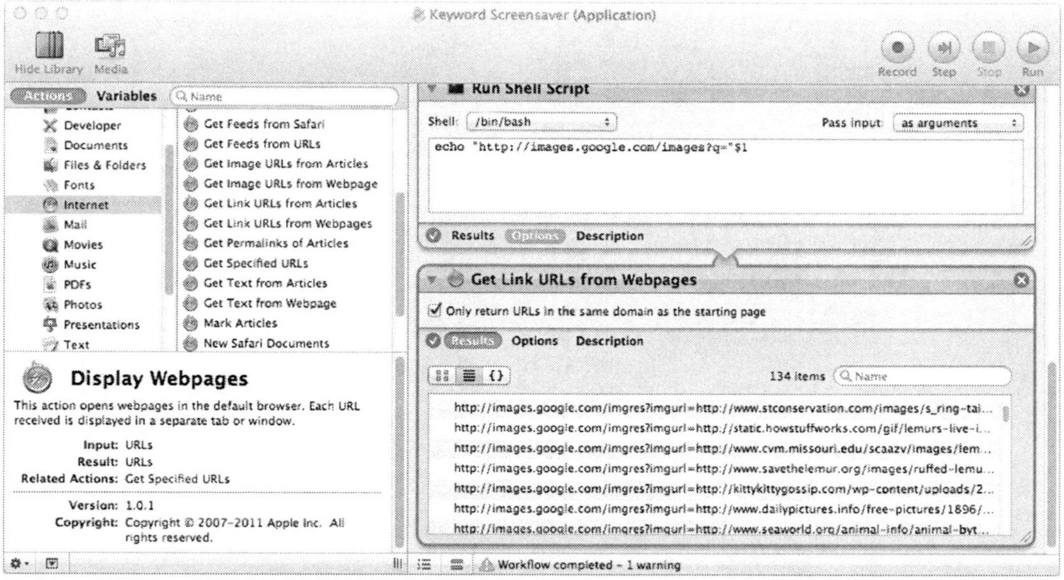

Figure 31–14. *Downloading a page and extracting its link URLs in your Automator workflow*

The Get Link URLs from Webpages action's result contains a few different types of URLs, but you're only interested in the ones that start with `http://images.google.com/imgres?imgurl=`. Automator includes a Filter URLs action in the Internet group. This uses a rule editor, similar to the one used in Mail. The rule you want to define is Entire URL "begins with" http://images.google.com/imgres?imgurl=. To do so, drag in the Filter URLs action and then select **Entire URL** from the first drop-down and **begins with** from the second drop-down. Then enter the text **http://images.google.com/imgres?imgurl=** in the text area.

Running the workflow should show a much smaller collection of URLs, as shown in Figure 31–15.

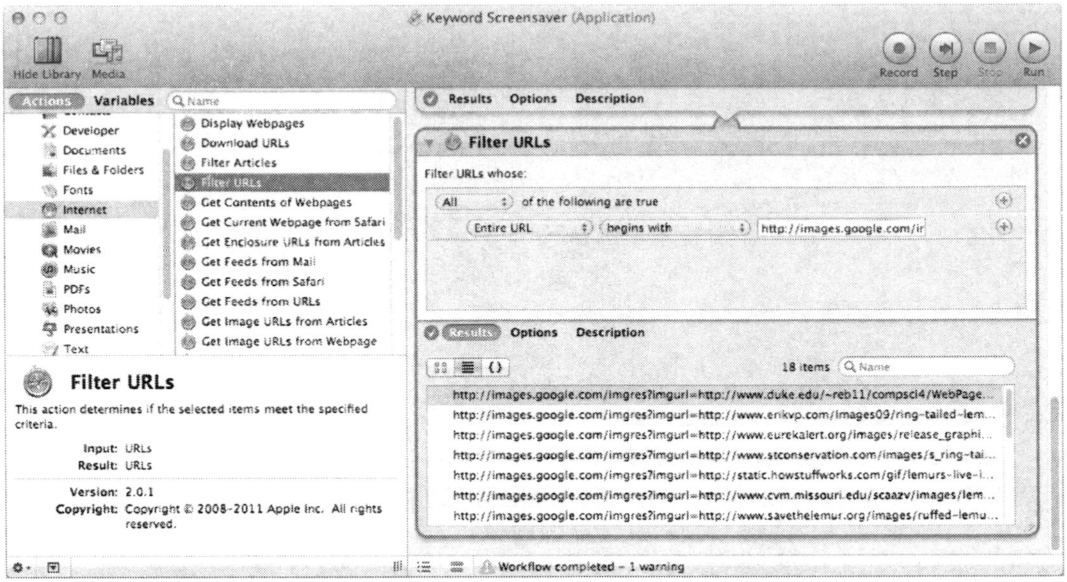

Figure 31–15. *Filtering URLs in Automator*

Frustratingly, plugging one of these URLs into Safari doesn't load the image directly. Rather, it leads to a multiframe Google results page that requires some clicking to get the image. The URL of the image itself is contained within the URL from Filter URLs, but extracting it means going back to the shell for more string manipulation. Drag in another Run Shell Script action, below the Filter URLs action, and enter this script:

```
for url in $@
do
    url=${url##*imgurl=}
    url=${url%%&*}
    echo $url
done
```

This script is a bit more complicated than the previous one. Instead of $1, the first argument, you refer to $@, another built-in variable that represents the list of all arguments. The for... in... do... done construct loops through the arguments, performing the logic between do and done for every item in the list of all arguments. The three cryptic lines of string manipulation code extract the text between imgurl= and &, which is the direct link to the image result, and return it as its result, as shown in Figure 31–16.

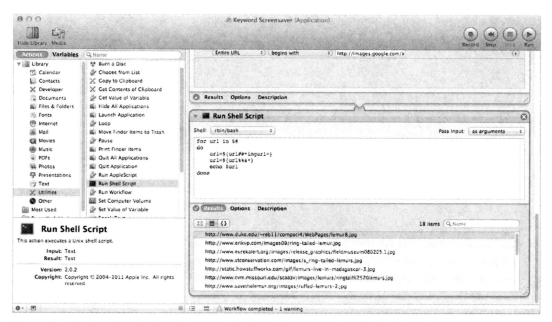

Figure 31–16. *Extracting the direct links from the Google links with a Run Shell Script action*

> **TIP:** If you find it confusing having two actions called Run Shell Script, you can rename any action from its contextual menu.

Running the workflow now produces a list of URLs, each one a link to an image. All that's left is to download the images each URL points to. Automator includes the Download URLs action in the Internet group for just this sort of thing. Drag this into your workflow, as shown in Figure 31–17.

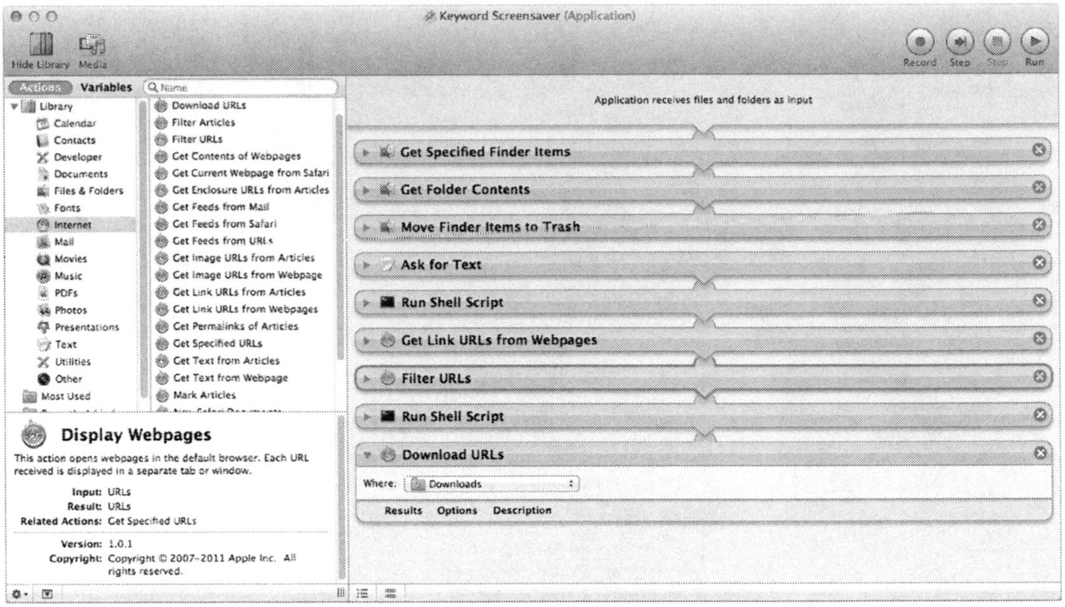

Figure 31-17. *The Download URLs action at the end of our workflow in Automator*

You could set the download folder directly to Keyword Screensaver, but what you'd really like is the same folder reference used way back in the Get Specified Finder Items action. That way, if the folder ever changes, perhaps by user action, you would already know about it. Unfortunately, that information is no longer in the flow, and there's a big separation between the Move Finder Items to Trash and Ask for Text actions. What you really want is for the Get Specified Finder Items action to store its value someplace where you can retrieve it later in the workflow. In the next section, we'll show you how to use Automator's variables to do just that.

Variables

Variables in Automator, as with other programming languages, are a way to store values. Automator provides a wide variety of variables in its Variables library, shown in Figure 31-18. Some are containers for different types of data you provide, but most are values of interest provided by Automator as a convenience for your workflow. To reveal Automator's variables, click Variables at the top of the library view.

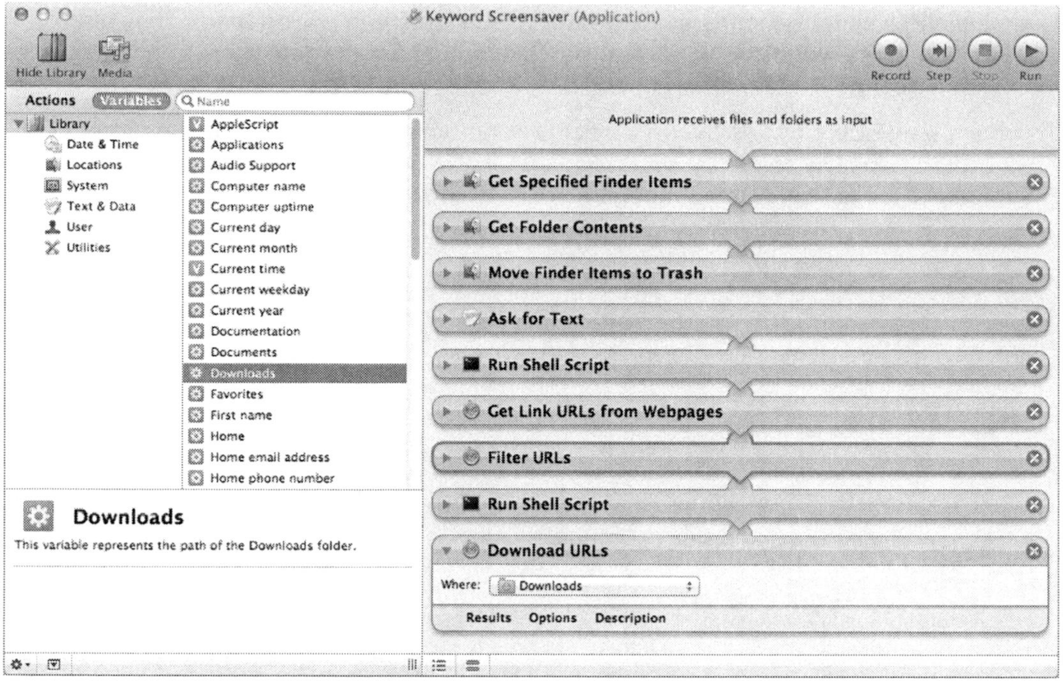

Figure 31–18. *Automator's Variables library shares space with the Actions library.*

Like actions, variables are grouped by category:

- **Date & Time**: The current year, month, day, day of the week, and, of course, the date and time

- **Locations**: Known folders such as Applications, Documents, Downloads, and the current user's home directory

- **System**: System information such as the computer's name, IP address, and operating system version

- **Text & Data**: Generic variables for storing text and data

- **User**: User information such as username, first name, last name, e-mail address, and MobileMe account name

- **Utilities**: Other useful values such as an AppleScript variable or a random number

NOTE: Recall that actions can, by user preference, be sorted by the applications that provide them. Variables are not considered part of any application but rather of Automator itself. Therefore, there is no "group by application" option for variables.

User-definable variables in the sidebar have a blue icon with a *V* on them. They also appear blue in the workflow. Variables whose contents are predetermined have a purple icon with a gear on it in the sidebar, and they appear purple in the workflow.

There are a number of ways to use variables in Automator. Create a variable to hold the Keyword Screensaver folder by selecting **New variable...** from the **Where** drop-down of the Download URLs action. Name it Image Folder, as shown in Figure 31–19.

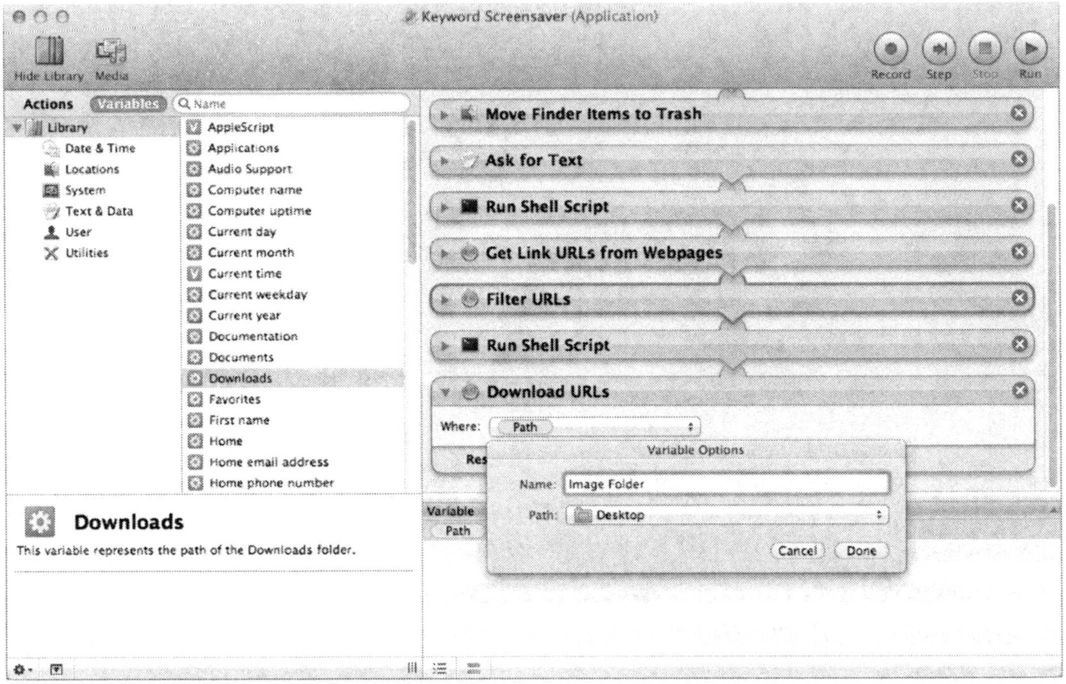

Figure 31–19. *Setting the download folder to a variable in your Automator workflow*

Creating a new variable pops up the variable list below the workflow editor. This list contains every variable in your workflow. You can interact with variables directly in the list, and you can drag variables into this list from the Variables library or out of this list to use in your workflow. To save the Keyword Screensaver folder in a variable, drag in a Set Value of Variable action from the Utilities group to between the Get Specified Finder Items action and the Get Folder Contents action. These two actions move apart to make room, as shown in Figure 31–20.

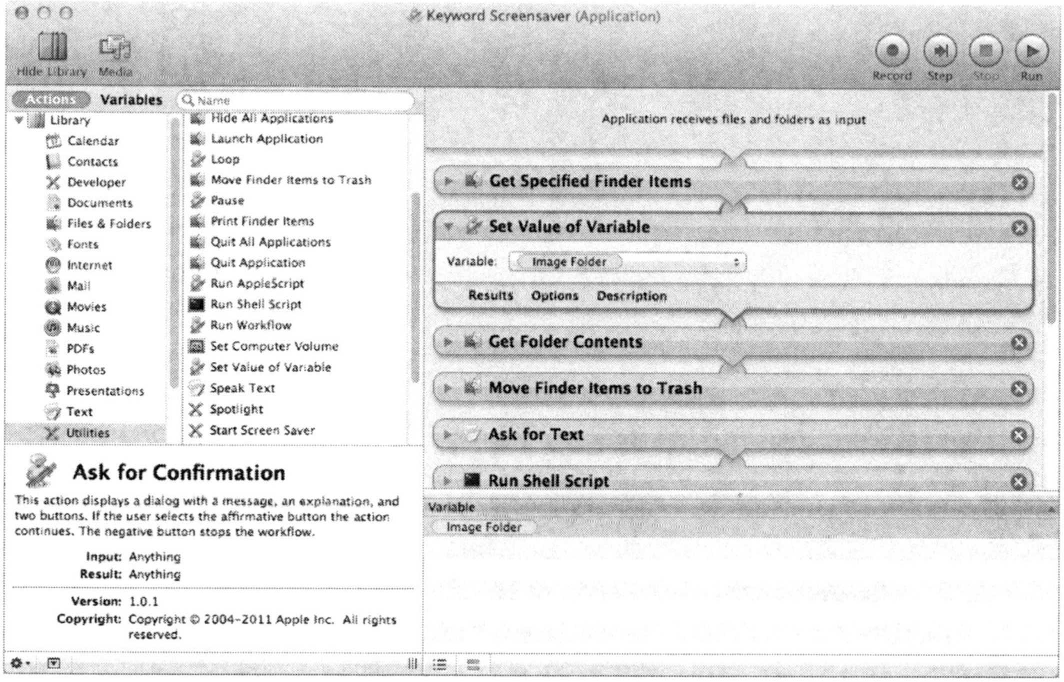

Figure 31–20. *Inserting a Set Value of Variable action in your Automator workflow*

The Set Value of Variable action should automatically set its single option, the Variable pop-up, to the Image Folder variable. If it doesn't, set it manually. The connections between actions are automatically reestablished to this inserted action. The result of the Set Value of Variable action will be the value the variable is set to, which is the same as the action's input. In other words, it just passes the value through, so the deletion actions work the same.

Running the workflow now will automatically download the images to the Keyword Screensaver folder. The only thing left to do is to actually start the screen saver. Drag a Start Screen Saver action to the end of your workflow to complete the application, as shown in Figure 31–21.

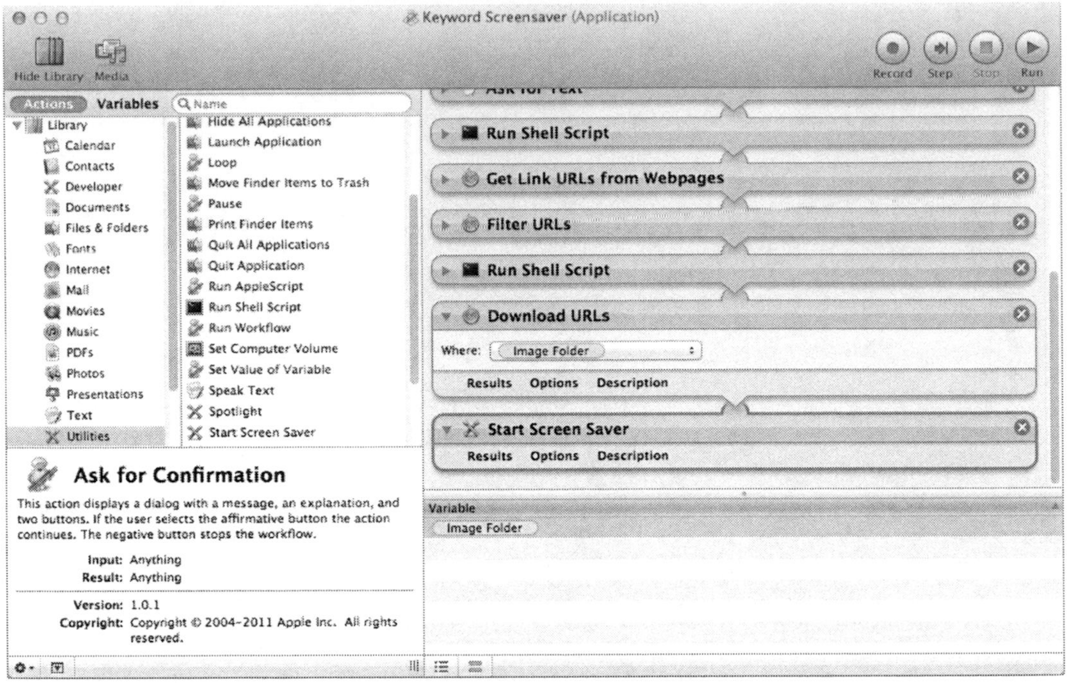

Figure 31–21. *The final action in your Automator workflow launches the system screen saver.*

You can run the workflow from Automator, but since you've built an application, you can also run it from the Dock. Drag the title of your newly minted application directly from the Automator window's title bar into the Dock and then click the Dock icon to launch the application. You may notice that, without the feedback from Automator's workflow editor, it's hard to tell what the application is doing. When you run your new application, check out the status (and Stop option) in the menu bar.

Advanced Automator Shenanigans

This brief sojourn into Otto's world is one of an endless array of projects you can build with Automator. It's not just that there's more to Automator than fits in this chapter; there's more to Automator than fits in Automator. There are as many potential workflows as there are types of work, so Automator lets you extend its capabilities by adding new actions.

Extending Automator

Anyone with a modicum of programming skills can write an Automator action. Many software developers include Automator actions with their applications. As you add applications to extend your Mac's abilities, Automator will automatically import their included actions, expanding in turn. If your favorite application lacks the actions you need to incorporate it into your workflows, petition the developer to provide them. Most developers are happy to help you find ways to make their product an indispensable part of your life.

Automator actions don't have to come with an application. You can download new actions individually or in "action packs," as well as whole workflows, from the Internet.

If you're programmatically inclined, Xcode provides templates for creating Automator actions. If you whip something up for yourself, consider making it available to others. If you wind up shipping an application for the Mac, make sure you include a good set of Automator actions. If you're not programmatically inclined, you may still find a home with AppleScript, but we'll get into that in a moment.

Embedding Automator

Automator is like bacon. It's great on its own, but it's even better when it's combined with other things. Automator started picking up a certain embeddability in Leopard with the introduction of the Automator framework. This lets developers use the step-by-step user interface of Automator's workflow editor in their own applications.

Today Automator makes it easy to extend applications with workflows. Automator now contains templates for creating a folder action, an iCal alarm, a Print plug-in, or an Image Capture plug-in. Most interestingly, however, you can create a service.

A service is an Automator-like construct dating all the way back to NeXTSTEP. The idea was for applications to provide parts of their functionality from anywhere in the system via the **Services** menu, which is part of the standard main menu set, next to **Preferences**, **Hide**, and **Quit**.

The **Services** menu now uses contextual information to show only the services that are relevant to what you're doing in an application. If you select some text in Safari, for example, the **Services** menu will contain only services that make sense given that text.

Services Made Simple

Your new Keyword Screensaver workflow would make a great service to add to this set. To complete this bonus project, follow these steps:

1. Create a new Automator workflow using the Service template. The workflow's input should be "Service receives selected text in any application," as shown in Figure 31–22. This will allow us to set our keyword based on text selected in any application.

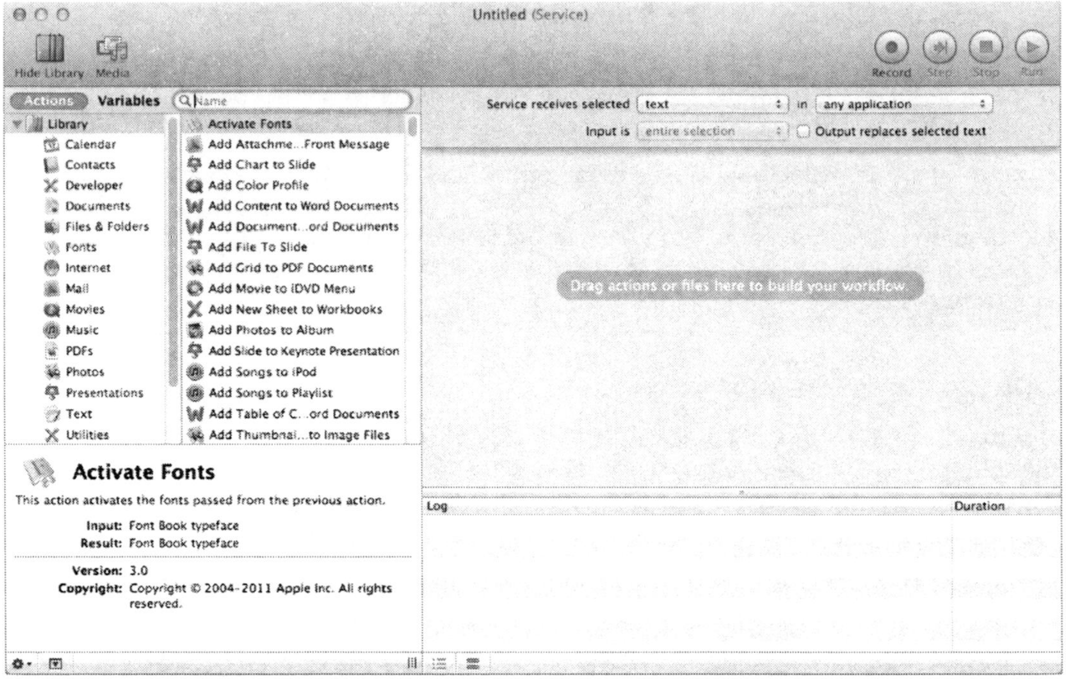

Figure 31–22. *Automator makes it easy to create context-aware services.*

2. Copy the workflow from Keyword Screensaver application and paste it into this workflow.

3. Store the value of the selected text by dragging in a Set Value of Variable action and creating a new variable named Keyword, as shown in Figure 31–23.

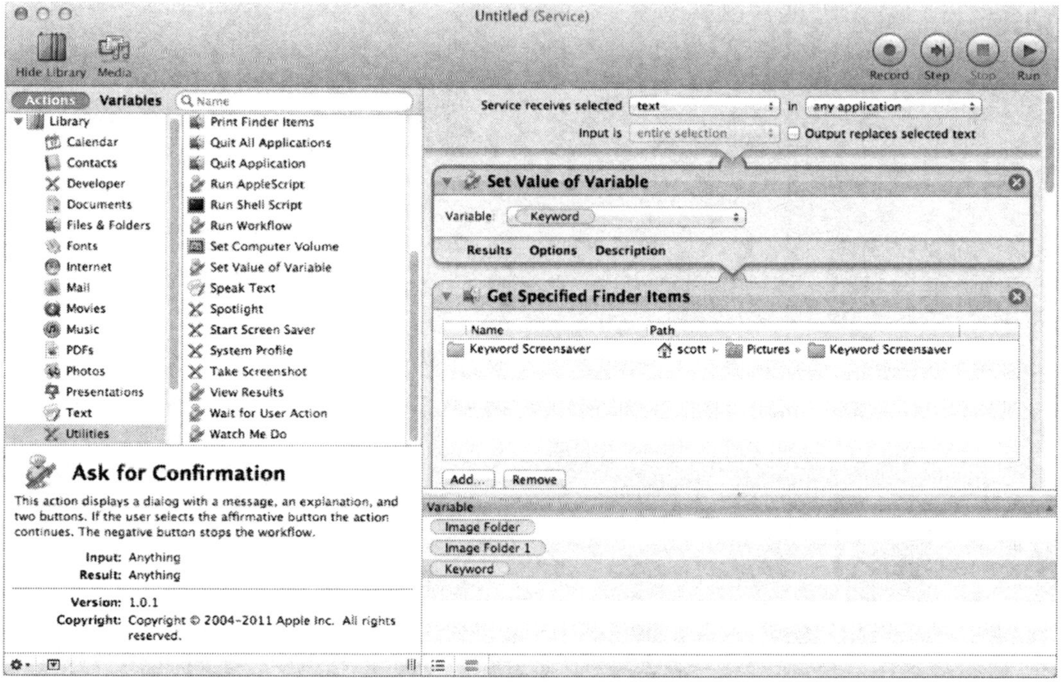

Figure 31–23. *Automator's variables make it easy to make large changes without changing the actual flow of actions.*

4. Select Ignore Input from the Get Specified Finder Items action's contextual menu to disconnect it from the new Set Value of Variable action.

5. Replace the Ask for Text action with a Get Value of Variable action using the same variable created in step 2, as shown in Figure 31–24.

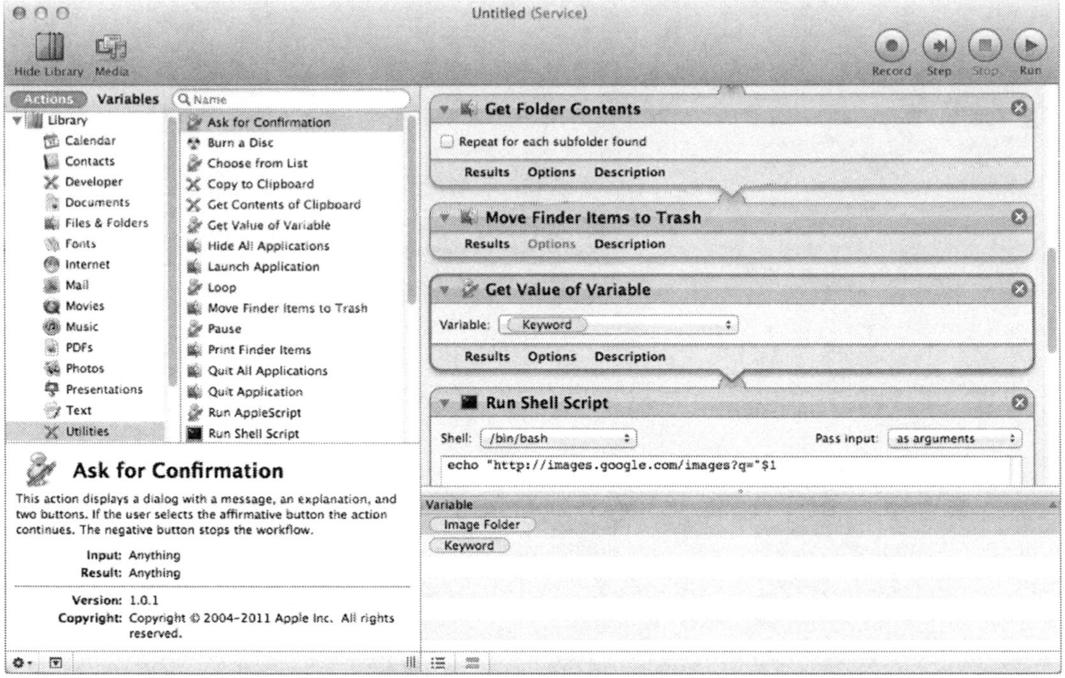

Figure 31–24. *As a service, the Keyword Screensaver gets the keyword as input, instead of asking the user.*

Saving the workflow automatically adds your new service to the Services menu.

How Automator Works

Every Automator action is actually a tiny application. Developers can implement new actions as shell scripts or even full-fledged Objective-C programs. However, many, if not most, of the included Automator actions are simply a drag-and-drop interface on top of some behind-the-scenes voodoo the system uses for controlling other applications. Automator serves as a friendly abstraction from AppleScript, the quirky scripting language that lets you tap into the aforementioned system voodoo.

To look at it from the other direction, controlling other applications from Automator is cool and useful, but more than that, it's easy. That ease of use is inherently limiting. AppleScript is like Automator as a programming language. Learning AppleScript is like putting down your Speak & Spell and learning to type.

> **TIP:** We're going to show you AppleScript, but we're not really going to do it justice. For ultimate power, check out the "More Information" section or just pick up a copy of *Learn AppleScript: The Comprehensive Guide to Scripting and Automation on Mac OS X by* Hamish Sanderson and Hanaan Rosenthal (Apress, 2010).

AppleScript

AppleScript is a simple programming language for controlling applications among other things. Although AppleScript and Automator are different around the edges, it's not a bad metaphor to think of AppleScript as writing Automator workflows in longhand.

To demonstrate that point, here is a close facsimile of the Keyword Screensaver application written entirely in AppleScript:

```
--Remove any existing images
tell application "Finder"
    set _imageFolder to path to pictures folder
    set _imageFolder to folder "Keyword Screensaver" of folder _imageFolder
    delete every file in _imageFolder
end tell
--Ask for Text
display dialog "What keyword shall I search for?" default answer ""
set _keyword to text returned of result
set _queryURL to "http://images.google.com/images?hl=en&sout=1&q=" & _keyword
--Query Google
tell application "Safari"
    open location _queryURL
    set _timeoutInSeconds to 20
    delay 2
    repeat with _waitInSeconds from 1 to _timeoutInSeconds
        if (do JavaScript "document.readyState" in document 1) is "complete" then
            exit repeat
        else if _waitInSeconds is _timeoutInSeconds then
            number -128
        else
            delay 1
        end if
    end repeat
    set _searchResults to source of document 1
end tell
--Extract image URLs from page source, then download them
set AppleScript's text item delimiters to "\\x"
set _rawResults to text items in _searchResults
set AppleScript's text item delimiters to ""
repeat with _text in _rawResults
    if _text starts with "3dhttp://" and _text ends with ".jpg" then
        do shell script "cd ~/Pictures/Keyword\\ Screensaver;
        curl -s0 " & quoted form of (text 3 thru (length of _text) of _text as string)
    end if
end repeat
--Activate screen saver
tell application "ScreenSaverEngine"
    activate
end tell
```

To use this script, open the AppleScript Editor application from the Utilities folder in Launchpad. The AppleScript Editor is a basic application that provides a text editor for composing your scripts, simple controls for testing your scripts, and syntax coloring and formatting, which make it easier to read your scripts. Below the text editor is a console for observing the results of running your script.

> **CAUTION:** In the AppleScript for the Keyword Screensaver application, the do shell script command has a carriage return as part of the command. If the shell script portion of the script fails, select the whitespace between the semicolon and the command curl, and hit the Return key to replace it with a single carriage return.

AppleScript is a strange language. It tries to look as much like English as possible, which includes having several different ways of saying the same thing. This makes AppleScript readable even by nonprogrammers. However, many programmers find AppleScript hard to write in, because it's not actually English. You can't just write English and expect AppleScript to understand you. Not only do you still have to deal with the limited comprehension of a programming language, but now you also have to deal with the vagueness of English.

The upshot of all this is AppleScript needs to be written line by line. Don't just rush in, write it all down, and expect it to work. AppleScript Editor is a far cry from the professional tools in Xcode, discussed in the next chapter. Instead, you must write a line, save it, test it, and then write another and repeat.

Analyzing the Code

Although AppleScript and Automator accomplish similar things, they don't exactly translate back and forth, so you have to do some things a little differently. It's probably best to just run through the code sample and point out some sights along the way. Comments in AppleScript are preceded by --, like so:

```
-Remove any existing images
```

Since AppleScript is mainly concerned with telling applications what to do, AppleScript programs revolve around the tell block:

```
tell application "Finder"
```

Every scriptable application contains a dictionary that lists its vocabulary, which is to say, the functionality it makes available to AppleScript. To examine an application's scripting dictionary from within Script Editor, select **File > Open Dictionary…** or press Shift-Command-O and then navigate to the application whose dictionary you would like to view.

To set a variable to a certain value, use the set ... to construct:

```
set _imageFolder to path to pictures folder
```

Although AppleScript is meant to read like English, programmers may find it convenient to use a special prefix, or *sigil*, to mark which words represent variables. I like an underscore combined with standard CamelCase, but this is a personal preference. AppleScript Editor's syntax coloring also helps.

To find the user's Pictures folder, use the *path to* construct shown here. Note that the literal names of things are enclosed in quotation marks:

```
set _imageFolder to folder "Keyword Screensaver" of folder _imageFolder
```

When something is inside of something else, AppleScript says it is "of that thing." You can talk about the third word of a sentence, the last page of a document, or a certain subfolder of a given folder. As in English, this can turned into a possessive relationship by using an apostrophe and then the letter *s*:

```
set _imageFolder to _imageFolder's folder "Keyword Screensaver"
```

In a way, everything in AppleScript is a list. A folder is a list of documents; a document is a list of pages; a page is a list of paragraphs, which are lists of sentences, which are lists of words, and so forth. Anyone familiar with the programming language Lisp will recognize this paradigm. When you think of a folder as a list of files, it makes sense to use a construct like this:

```
delete every file in _imageFolder
```

Like most major languages (except, for example, Python), AppleScript doesn't care about whitespace such as tabs and carriage returns, which are used to give code a readable format. However, it expects sentences to end when you hit Return. This doesn't always work; for example, tell blocks may need to encompass several other lines of code. For this case, you can end the block of code by using an end statement:

```
end tell
```

As a testament to the flexibility of the AppleScript language, you also could have written the entire first tell block as a single line:

```
tell application  "Finder" to delete every file in  (path to pictures folder)'s  folder
"Keyword Screensaver"
```

It's a bit awkward but still understandable. Note the use of parentheses to clear up syntactical ambiguities and the lack of end tell for the single-line version.

Displaying a dialog to ask the user for input uses the following quite understandable form:

```
display dialog "What keyword shall I search for?" default answer ""
```

The dialog presents the user with a text field, prefilled with the text appearing after the default answer clause. Since you've defined that text as an empty string, the text area will simply be blank. Simply removing the default answer clause would cause the dialog to appear without any text area at all.

> **NOTE:** Popping up dialogs is part of AppleScript's default functionality. Since you're only telling AppleScript, you don't have to use a `tell` block.

When a dialog returns, any input from the user appears in a variable named `result`, which you read and store:

```
set _keyword to text returned of result
```

To combine, or *concatenate*, the Google search URL with the user's keyword, use the & operator:

```
set _queryURL to "http://images.google.com/images?hl=en&sout=1&q=" & _keyword
```

As before, this block could have been rendered as a single line:

```
set _queryURL to "http://images.google.com/images?hl=en&sout=1&q=" & text returned of
(display dialog "What keyword shall I search for?" default answer "")
```

> **NOTE:** The `sout=1` in the URL tells Google to display images using its older "basic" interface. While the newer interface provides more user features, it is much more difficult to parse programmatically.

Automator is a little more polished when it comes to dealing with common Internet tasks, such as fetching results in the background and returning a list of links. Let's start with fetching the results, which is a whole problem in and of itself. Use Safari to load and render the page:

```
tell application  "Safari" open location _queryURL
```

Using other applications is what AppleScript does best, but there are some problems inherent to this cooperation that remain prosaically manual. For example, the script has to wait for Safari to finish loading the URL. Apple's recommended method is to use a polling loop to ask Safari if it's done loading. Since it might never actually load, start by setting a timeout of 20 seconds:

```
set _TimeoutInSeconds to 20
```

Loading will take at least a couple of seconds, so the script will pause for 2 seconds right off the bat:

```
delay 2
```

AppleScript has several ways it can loop. Using the `repeat` commands with a <number> to <number> construct with a 1-second pause between attempts creates a nice, predictable bit of control logic. The script will poll Safari once per second for 20 seconds, after the initial 2-second pause:

```
repeat with _waitInSeconds from 1 to _timeoutInSeconds
```

To ask the question, use Safari's do JavaScript command. This powerful command lets the script speak to Safari in its native scripting:

```
if (do JavaScript "document.readyState" in document 1) is "complete" then
```

If loading is complete, the script will stop looping and continue building the screen saver:

```
exit repeat
```

If loading is not complete, the script will see if it has timed out, in which case it will return an error:

```
else if _waitInSeconds is _timeoutInSeconds then error number -128
```

Error -128 means "User canceled." This basically clicks the Cancel button for you after 20 seconds. If the script has not been running for 20 seconds, it will wait for a second, after which time execution will return to the top of the loop:

```
else
delay 1
end if
end repeat
```

Novice scripters should pay attention to how the logic flows: "If something is true, do something, or else if something else is true, do something else, or else do something else entirely." This is reflected in the code using the if...else if...else construct common to most programming languages.

With the power of do JavaScript, you could almost write the rest of the script in JavaScript (in fact, if given the choice, that may be the better solution). Navigating a page, finding links, and simple parsing are well within the reach of JavaScript. This being the AppleScript section, we're going to craft a solution using AppleScript:

```
set _searchResults to source of document 1
```

The HTML source of the Google results page is basically one big string. Recall that a string is a list of paragraphs, words, characters, and text items. Wait, text items? What are text items? It turns out text items are kind of complicated.

When you think of a list, you may think of a comma-separated list, where each list item is separated by a comma, followed by a space. This is distinct from the words in the list, which are separated only by a space. Were this list an AppleScript string, the comma-separated list items would be the text items. The comma and space between those items would be the "global text-item delimiter."

Sometimes list items may themselves contain commas, in which case you can use semicolons to separate the list items. In AppleScript, this would be equivalent to changing the global text-item delimiter from a comma and space to a semicolon and space.

The power of the global text-item delimiter is that you can set it to anything you want and then ask the string for its text items and get custom results based on the delimiter. In the source of the Google results page, the links you want are separated by a \x followed by either 3d or 26, which makes the delimiter. Since we can pick only one delimiter in Apple Script, we will use \x and deal with (or ignore) the trailing characters later. AppleScript will be confused by the \ inside the quotes, so we will use \\, which tells AppleScript to use a single \.

```
set AppleScript's text item delimiters to "\\x"
```

> **NOTE:** Although there is technically a list of delimiters, it's a list of one. Thus, we talk about the text-item delimiter, but the actual keyword is pluralized. We set the delimiter to a single string, but behind the scenes, AppleScript coerces the string into a single-item list.

Retrieving the text items from the string _searchResults now yields a list of substrings, separated by the delimiter you set previously:

```
set _rawResults to text items in _searchResults
```

Since the global text-item delimiter is global and all, it is considered good form to set it back to the default, which is the empty string, "":

```
set AppleScript's text item delimiters to ""
```

Now all that's left to do is loop over the items in the list and decide which ones are URLs. Use the repeat command again, but this time with the form "with <item> in <list>":

```
repeat with _text in _rawResults
```

The strings in the list that are URLs will start with the substring "3dhttp: //" and end with .jpg (which would indicate it's a JPEG image file). Since the URLs start with \x3d and end with \x26 and we used \x as the delimiter, we need to include the 3d here (we can ignore the 26 since we aren't concerned with what's after the URL).

```
if _text starts with "3dhttp://" and _text ends with ".jpg" then
```

To download the images that the filtered URLs point to, you can use another cool AppleScript command, do shell script. Like the Safari do JavaScript command, do shell script lets AppleScript talk to the Unix shell in its own language. You can even run Unix programs, like the URL-downloading utility curl:

```
do shell script "cd ~/Pictures/Keyword\\ Screensaver;
curl -sO " & quoted form of (text 3 thru (length of _text) of _text as string)
```

The (text 3 thru (length of _text) of _text as string) part does something interesting. The text 3 thru (length of _text) part specifically uses the text beginning from the third character of _text and continues through the length of _text. This effectively gets rid of the pesky "3d" at the beginning of our URL (which would cause curl to complain causing our script to exit with an error).

Because the name of the directory has a space but Unix uses spaces as separators, it has to appear in the shell script as Keyword\ Screensaver. This is the same use of the backslash as AppleScript, which will confuse AppleScript. As such, you must escape the backslash with another backslash, appearing to AppleScript as Keyword\\ Screensaver.

The script will pause while the pictures download to the folder your screen saver is set to, so all that's left is telling the screen saver to activate:

```
tell application "ScreenSaverEngine"
    activate
end tell
```

AppleScript in Context

Given the choice between Automator and AppleScript for your automation needs, which one should you choose? These two tutorials should give you a pretty good idea of the strengths and weaknesses of each. In general, I'd say Automator is easier to use, but AppleScript is more powerful. Even with such features as variables and basic looping, Automator's drag-and-drop ease of use comes at the expense of the flexibility and power that a full written language like AppleScript provides.

Still, for our dollar, we'd pick Automator if at all possible. You can pass things off to shell scripts, just like in AppleScript. You can also call AppleScript from Automator, giving you the best of both worlds. We have to admit a certain bias: when we want to program, we'd rather use Objective-C, which we'll get into in the next couple chapters.

For nonprogrammers, AppleScript may be much more approachable, and even programmers can find AppleScript convenient. Just as C is optimal for communicating with hardware, AppleScript is optimal for communicating with other applications. AppleScript can be used within Objective-C applications, and Xcode has a template for building an entire application out of AppleScript.

For the AppleScript party to continue, developers must make their applications scriptable. If you're developing an application, implementing scriptability lets users incorporate your application into their workflows. Snow Leopard's Scripting Bridge framework uses your scripting interface to provide interaction with other programming environments, such as Automator, Ruby, Python, and Objective-C.

Automation saves people time and eliminates wasted effort, and the foundation of automation is interapplication cooperation. The more developers and users can leverage existing applications, the more our platform becomes extensible, flexible, and—that most important of attributes—usable. That makes application developers who write scriptable applications a boon to the platform.

More Information

If you think there's something to the phrase "Cult of Mac," you should see the zealots in the Mac automation community. I don't think I've ever written an AppleScript or a halfway decent Automator action without consulting at least one of the following sources:

- **Automator home page (http://automator.us)**: Sal Soghoian is Apple's product manager for automation and is generally recognized as a, if not the, foremost expert on AppleScript and Automator. I can also personally attest that he is a character. All that aside, Sal's Automator page has everything you need to know, from the whys and wherefores of Automator to a massive collection of free Automator actions and links to other great Automator sites on the Web.

- **Automator Programming Guide (http://developer.apple.com/documentation/AppleApplications/Conceptual/AutomatorConcepts/)**: This is Apple's official documentation on developing Automator actions. There's less here for the casual user, but the barrier to becoming a power user who can bust out custom actions is really not all that high. If you have any scripting or programming experience, you're practically there already.

- **Apple Training Series: AppleScript 1-2-3 by Sal Soghoian and Bill Cheeseman (Peachpit Press, 2009)**: Sal Soghoian's long-awaited book is the ultimate resource for mastering AppleScript. Together with Bill Cheeseman, Sal gives you an understanding of the language that comes only from a lifetime of dedication. Start here, and the rest of these resources will be all the more useful.

- **Learn AppleScript: The Comprehensive Guide to Scripting and Automation on Mac OS X by Hamish Sanderson and Hanaan Rosenthal (Apress, 2010)**: This is a definitive reference book on AppleScript. Hamish and Hanaan's critically acclaimed work walks you step by step from automation neophyte to AppleScript master. It also makes a great footstool, on account of being huge.

- **AppleScript Essential Subroutines (www.apple.com/applescript/guidebook/sbrt/)**: This page of useful AppleScript functions is the first place we turn when we get stuck trying to figure out how to do something. There's not a lot here, but what is here is solid gold.

- **AppleScript Language Guide (http://developer.apple.com/library/mac/#documentation/AppleScript/Conceptual/AppleScriptLangGuide/introduction/ASLR_intro.html)**: This is Apple's official documentation on AppleScript.

- **AppleScript Users Official Mailing List (http://lists.apple.com/mailman/listinfo/applescript-users)**: Another official channel for all things AppleScript, the official mailing list is always a good place to get and give help.

- **Doug's AppleScripts for iTunes (http://dougscripts.com)**: It sounds really specific, but iTunes is probably the most scriptable, and the most scripted, application in the world. As such, Doug's page may well be the largest repository of practical AppleScript on the Web. Having a simple relationship with iTunes, I don't think I ever actually used one of these scripts for its intended purpose, but I've studied dozens of them. The people who write Doug's scripts are truly some of the cleverest, to say nothing of most dedicated, AppleScript users around.

Summary

If you find yourself doing the same task over and over again, it's time to stop and think about automation. Using Automator or AppleScript might seem like a lot of trouble the first time, but once you learn how to use these powerful tools, your productivity will skyrocket, and you will truly earn the laurels of a power user.

If you've already mastered automation, need more than the OS can provide, or want to contribute to the platform by writing applications, plug-ins, or Automator actions, read on. In the next couple chapters, we'll talk about the tools used by professional Macintosh application developers.

## Chapter 32

Introducing Apple's Xcode and Developer Tools

The very tools that are used by software engineers, both inside and outside Apple, to develop applications for Mac OS X and iOS are available to you to download and use. Some of these tools are behemoth environments whose brambles are crisscrossed with the narrow paths cut by tutorials. Some are utilities useful to programmers and nonprogrammers alike. And some of these tools defy a simple explanation yet invite exploration. Whether you've bought your Mac to write the next big iPhone game or whether you're an avid novice looking for more toys to play with, the developer tools for Mac OS X are ready to flex your imagination.

In this chapter, we will cover the following:

- Downloading and installing Xcode (and related tools)

- An overview of the big four Apple developer apps: Xcode, Instruments, Dashcode, and Quartz Composer

- A quick description of some of the many additional utilities and application included with Xcode

Getting and Installing Xcode

With all previous versions of Mac OS X, Xcode was included either on the Mac OS X install DVD or on an included CD. Beginning with Lion, however, there is no media to include Xcode with. So, beginning with Lion to install Xcode, you will have to download it first.

Xcode is available from two places, Apple's developer web site and the App Store. The easiest path to downloading Xcode is to open the App Store, search for *Xcode*, and download it. Now, unlike most other apps you get from the App Store, with Xcode you aren't actually downloading the Xcode app but an installer (Figure 32–1) that will allow you to install Xcode.

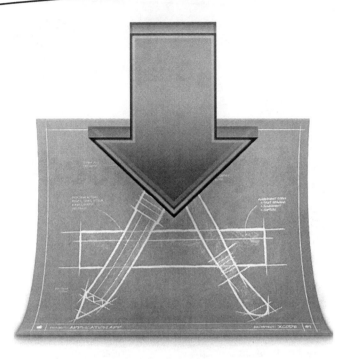

Install Xcode

Figure 32–1. *When you download Xcode from the App Store, you are actually downloading the Xcode installer that must be run before you can use Xcode.*

> **NOTE:** Downloading from the App Store will always provide you with the current version of Xcode and tools. When a new version is released, it will show up as an update for you to install. If you sign up for either the iOS or Mac developer programs and are working on prerelease versions of either iOS or Mac OS X, then you may need a prerelease version of Xcode as well, and for this you will likely need to go to http://developer.apple.com to download the version of Xcode you need.

Once you have the Xcode installer from the App Store (or from http://developer.apple.com if you downloaded it directly from there), then you will click it to start the installation. A dialog box will walk you through the installation (Figure 32–2). Depending on whether you are installing Xcode for the first time or upgrading an older version, just follow along to get Xcode and all the associated apps, utilities, SDKs, and documentation you will need to develop for Mac OS X and iOS installed.

Figure 32–2. *A dialog will guide you through the installation or update of Xcode and associated tools.*

Once the installation is complete, the four primary developer apps—Dashcode, Instruments, Quartz Composer, and Xcode—will show up in Launchpad under the Developer folder (Figure 32–3). On your disk you will find these as well as many other utilities and tools installed in the Developer folder in the root of your primary disk. Let's now take a look at the big four developer apps beginning with Xcode.

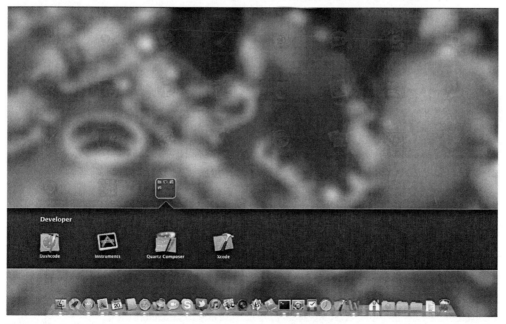

Figure 32–3. *Once installed, Dashcode, Instruments, Quartz Composer, and Xcode will show up in the Developer folder in Launchpad.*

Welcome to Xcode

Xcode is Apple's main integrated development environment (IDE) for Mac OS X and iOS native development. Xcode combines text editing, graphical UI tools (which prior to Xcode 4 were part of a separate application named Interface Builder), source code repository management, build tools, debugging tools, and more, into a single application.

When you first launch Xcode, you are presented with the Welcome to Xcode window (Figure 32–4) that will either allow you to quickly start a new project, open a recent project, connect to a *repository* (a local or remote collection of project files), browse development documentation, or head over to Apple's developer web site.

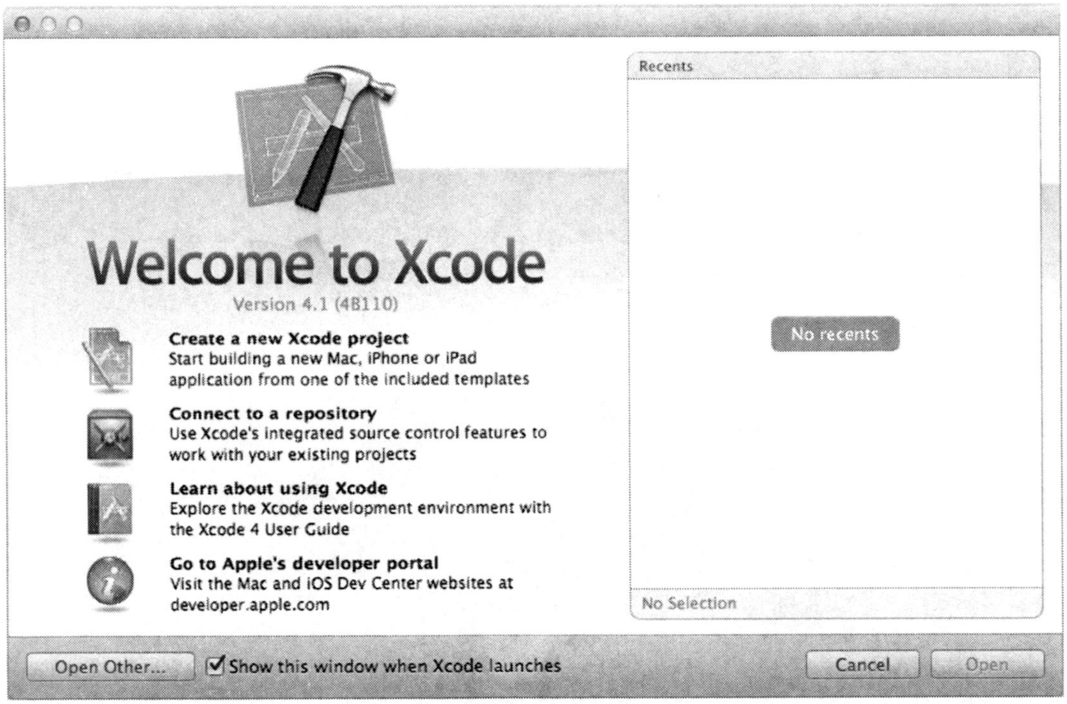

Figure 32–4. The Welcome to Xcode window provides a good starting point for working with Xcode.

Usually at this point the first thing you'll want to do is get started creating a new project, so we will look at that first.

> **NOTE:** Although jumping in and getting started is the most temping thing to do, it may not be a bad idea to click the "Learn about using Xcode" option. This will open the Organizer window to the included documentation that not only covers all the features of Xcode but also provides extensive detailed documentation on all facets of Mac OS X and iOS development.

Creating a New Project in Xcode

Clicking the "Create a new Xcode project" option in the Welcome to Xcode window (or selecting **File** > **New** > **New Project...** or pressing Shift-Command-M) will open a new workspace window with a new Project Template dialog (Figure 32–5), allowing you to select the type of project you want to develop. As you can see, there are a wide range of options to choose from (more than we could adequately explain in the space we have here).

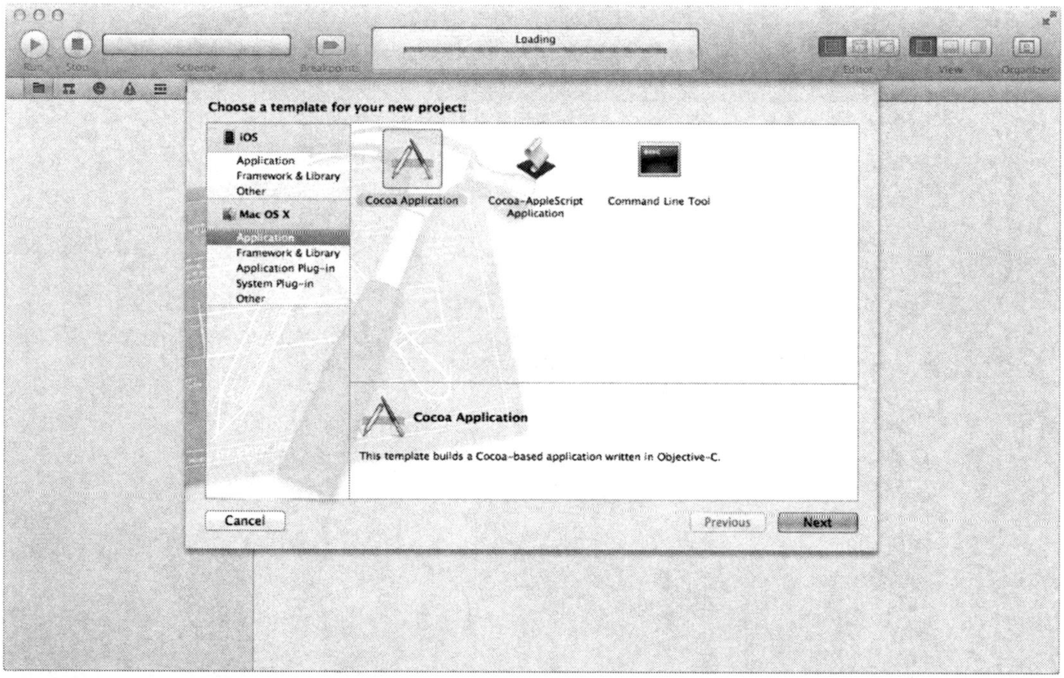

Figure 32–5. *When you start a new project, you are presented with a number of templates for possible project types to get you started.*

Once you select the type of project you are building, click the Next button where you will be prompted to fill out some basic information about your project (Figure 32–6). The options listed here will depend on the type of the project.

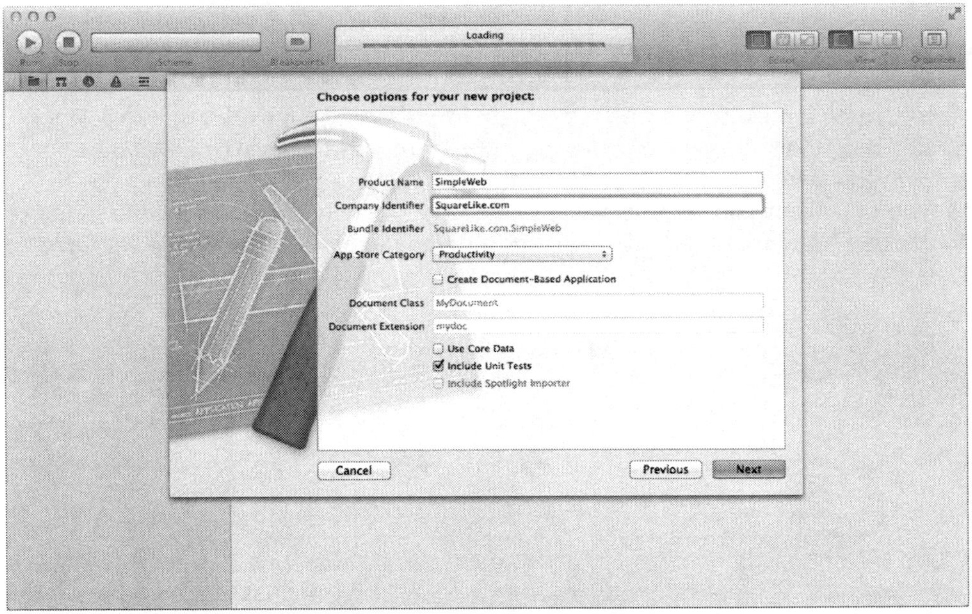

Figure 32–6. *After you select your project type, you will be asked to fill in some basic information about your project. Here we see the information requested for a Mac OS X Cocoa application.*

Once you fill out the requested information and click Next, you will be prompted for a location to create your project and store all project-related files (Figure 32–7). By default Xcode will create a git repository for your project.

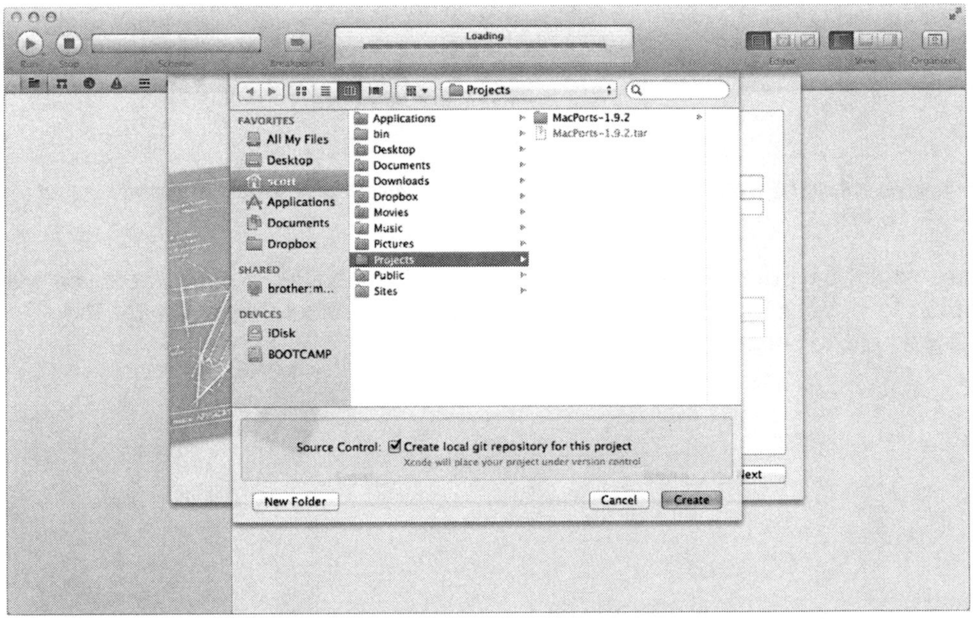

Figure 32–7. *After you fill in the basic details for your project, you will need to select a location to store your project files.*

NOTE: Git is a type of distributed version control system that helps organize projects, as well as tracks changes to the project. More importantly is that it facilitates the organization and tracking in a way that allows multiple developers to work on the same project efficiently. For more information on Git, take a look at http://git-scm.com.

NOTE: Prior to adding support for Git, Xcode used Subversion as its default source control repository. Xcode still supports Subversion if you have a need or preference for it.

After selecting the location for your project, Xcode will create a folder in that location and populate it with a number of sensible files to get you started with your project. Then Xcode will close the dialog and open your new project in a new workspace (Figure 32–8), which will provide you with the interface to accomplish most of your development needs.

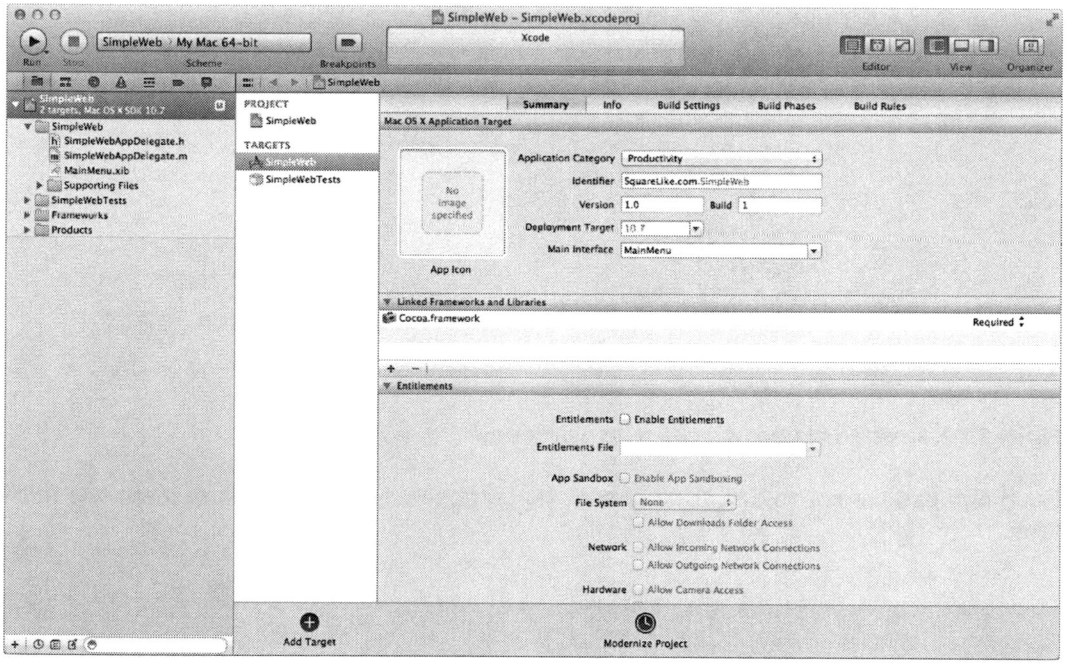

Figure 32–8. *A default workspace is showing a summary of the selected project.*

The Workspace

The workspace in Xcode is designed to provide you with all the features and tools you need to develop and build your project. The workspace is divided into four primary areas: the navigator, the editor, the utilities, and the debug area (Figure 32–9). While the editor area is always visible, the other three areas' visibility can be toggled using the View controls on Xcode's toolbar. You can access more control over the visibility, as well as the content, of each of these areas from Xcode's View menu and via its associated keyboard shortcuts.

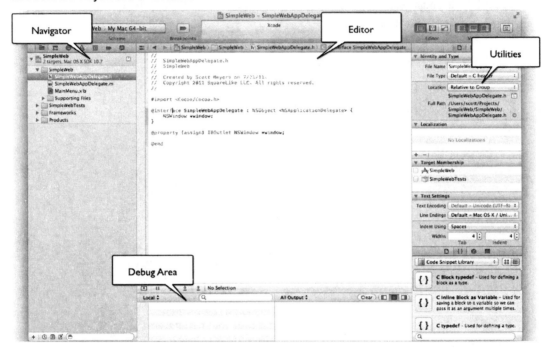

Figure 32–9. *Xcode's workspace with all four main areas visible*

Each of these areas has one or more specific purposes, so we will look at them one at a time.

The Navigator

The navigator (Figure 32–10) that appears on the far left of Xcode workspace provides a number of ways to navigate through your project, source code, debugging information, and more.

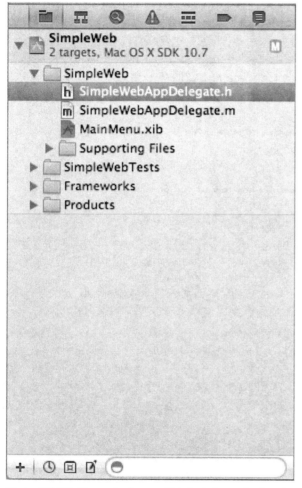

Figure 32–10. *The navigator provides tools for navigating through your project in various ways. The Project navigator shown here is the most common view.*

Along the top of the navigator area is a small toolbar that allows you to view different navigators in the navigator area. The navigators available are as follows:

- *The Project navigator*: The Project navigator allows you to view the various components that make up your project in an adaptable, hierarchical form.

- *The Symbol navigator*: The Symbol navigator allows you to browse for specific symbols in Xcode. In this case, a *symbol* is a specific type of code feature such as a specific class, function, or variable.

- *The Search navigator*: The Search navigator does what you think it does; you enter some text in the field on the top, and Xcode will search for that text in the current project and provide matches below.

- *The Issue navigator*: When you first attempt to build you project, it's not uncommon for the build to fail the first time (or second time...). When a build fails, Xcode will attempt to identify the issue preventing the project from building and list the identified issues here.

- *The Debug navigator*: The Debug navigator allows you to select specific threads and symbols during a debugging session to view and control some details of that specific item.

- *The Breakpoint navigator*: When you are building a complex application, it's often useful to stop the execution of the program at certain points to see what's going on. That's what breakpoints are; they will stop a program so you can peek at the debugging information to see whether everything is working correctly. Here you can view and edit any breakpoints in a project.

- *The Log navigator*: The Log navigator will allow you to view logs created during a project's development.

Often whatever you select from the navigator will appear in the editor view so you may immediately work with the item you selected.

The Editor

The editor area, as the name implies, is where you do the editing of your source files, nibs, and project information. The editor itself will adapt and present itself in a manner most appropriate for the type of item that requires editing. For example, if you have the main project file selected in the navigator, then the editor will provide forms allowing you fill out project information ranging from including an application icon to fine-tuning the build processes and adding linked frameworks and libraries (Figure 32–8). If you have a source file selected, then the editor will display a text editor to edit the file. If you have a nib file selected, then the editor will provide the Interface Builder view to design and hook together your interface (Figure 32–11).

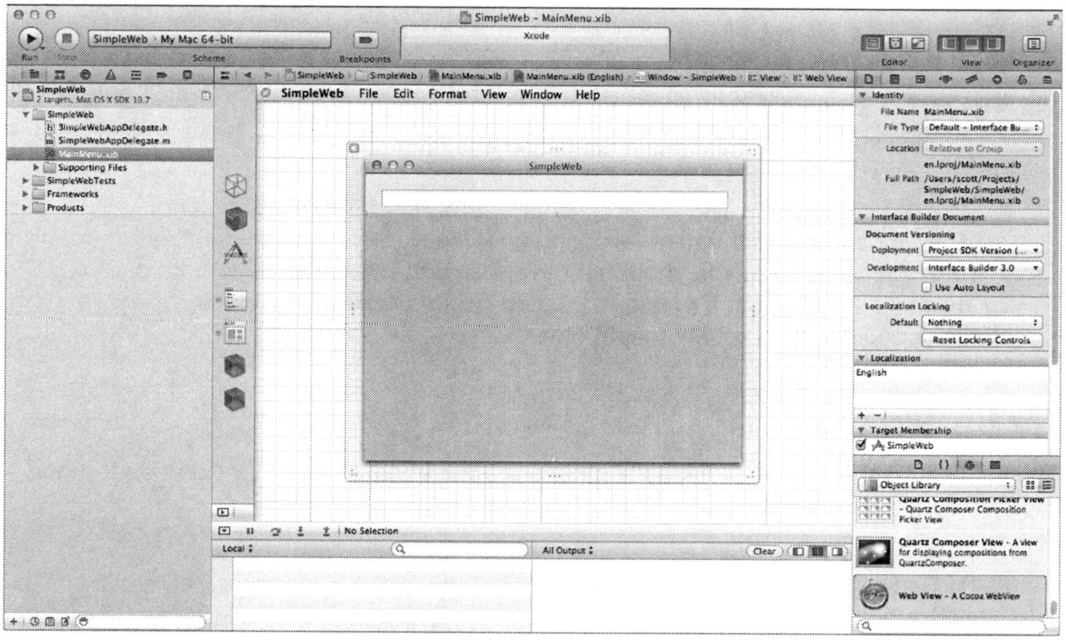

Figure 32-11. *The editor area in Xcode will adapt itself to provide the most appropriate features needed for editing the selected item. For a nib file, it will take on the features of the old Interface Builder application.*

> **NOTE:** Nib files are files with the extension `.xib`, which stands for Xcode Interface Builder. Not so long ago these files were given the `.nib` extension, which stood for NextStep Interface Builder, and they are still commonly referred to by that historic name.

> **NOTE:** A nib file is a special resource file that contains an archive of the objects in an interface. They were traditionally created in Interface Builder, which beginning with Xcode 4 no longer exists as a separate application, but rather its functions are now part of Xcode.

Besides taking on different roles for different types of project items, there are three distinct editor modes available from the toolbar (or the View menu):

- *The Standard editor*: The Standard editor view is what we have seen so far up to this point; it presents a single area ready for editing.

- *The Assistant editor*: The Assistant editor divides the editing area into multiple areas so that multiple related items can be shown at once. For example, if you have a *header* file open, then the Assistant editor will also display the source files that import it. This is handy to make sure that your @interfaces and @implementations match up.

> **NOTE:** In Objective-C, an `@interface` provides a class declaration or defines a class and sets it up. A class is like a blueprint for an object. An `@implementation` is where you create a specific object to use in your project from the class.

- *The Version editor*: The Version editor compares different versions of the same item, so if you are working on a file all day, but accidentally change something you shouldn't have, you can compare the results of your edited file from a previously saved file to discover what was changed and correct any destructive edits.

The Utilities Area

The utilities area in Xcode provides two separate panes, the Inspector pane on top and the Library pane on the bottom.

> **NOTE:** The utilities area is hidden by default. To show it click the Hide or Show the Utilities button in the View controls on the toolbar. Other buttons there will toggle the visibility of the navigator and the debug area.

The Inspector pane provides editable details about a selected item that can be very different depending upon the item. For example, if you have a source file selected, then a File inspector will appear that provides information about the source file, and a Quick Help inspector will be available that will provide any available help on the selected text in the file. If a nib file is selected, though, the inspector will provide many additional inspectors (Figure 32–12) to deal with customizing the behavior of the objects used in the nib.

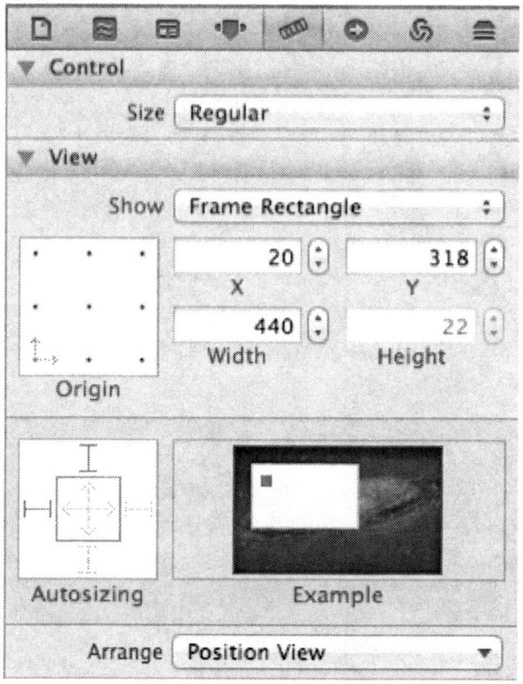

Figure 32–12. *The Inspector pane on the utilities area provides various inspectors for getting information or customizing various project items. The Size inspector, shown here, determines the size of an object relative to its container in a nib file.*

Unlike the Inspector pane, the Library pane is fairly static, presenting four different libraries:

- The *File Template Library* makes a number of different file templates available. You can drag a file template from the File Template Library into the Project navigator to add a file to your project.

- The *Code Snippet Library* provides code snippets that you can drag into your source files to simplify the addition of common code segments.

- The *Object Library* provides common objects that you can use to construct interfaces. This is essentially the same Object Library that was part of Interface Builder.

- The *Media Library* provides a list of all media (images, movies, and so on) imported into your project.

The Debug Area

The final area we'll talk about here is the debug area that opens below the editor area. The debug area displays detailed information about what's happening inside your program when it's running. Whenever a program reaches a breakpoint or you manually pause execution of a program running from Xcode, the debug area will automatically appear.

The debug area is divided into two side-by-side panes: the Variable pane and the Console pane. The Variable pane will display all the program's variables and their current values. If a program seems to be running fine but it's presenting the wrong (or odd) output, this is a good place to see whether a variable is picking up some wrong information (or not picking up the right information) during the program's execution.

The Console pane displays the raw debugger output. Xcode has two debuggers: GDB and LLDB. LLDB is part of the LLVM compiler project (LLVM is the default compiler in Mac OS X). Depending on which debugger you choose, the output here will be similar but different.

> **NOTE:** Debugging is as an important topic because it a big topic. Luckily, it's a topic that you can ease into. As you start developing, usually you begin with simple projects where the errors are fairly easy to track down. As your projects increase in size and complexity, though, your reliance on the debugger grows. As you become more reliant on the debugger, you can gradually learn more and more about it.

The Organizer

The Organizer (Figure 32–13) is another important part of Xcode. The Organizer provides five tabs to help you keep track of resources of great value to a developer.

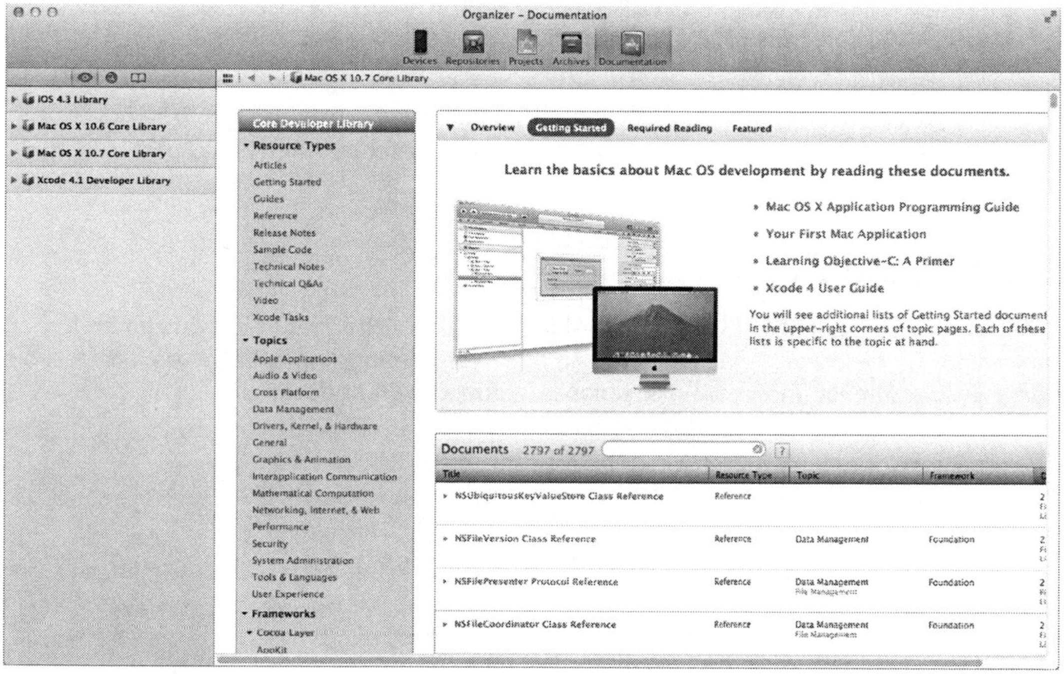

Figure 32.13. *The Organizer keeps track of documentation, repositories, projects, archives, and devices.*

■ The Devices tab in the Organizer keeps track of devices such as iPhones and iPads that you use for development, as well as some important profile information that you'll need to distribute iOS applications. Besides keeping track of your devices, you can view lots of information from them including crash reports and console data.

■ The Repositories tab lets you manage your source code repositories. This includes any local projects you've created with the Source Control option checked, but it also allows you to add remote Git or Subversion repositories to work with.

■ The Projects tab provides a list of all your local projects.

■ The Archives tab allows access to application archives. Once you've successfully developed and built an application in Xcode, the next step is to archive it (using **Product > Archive** from the menu). Once archived, the application will show up here where you can save you app for sharing or submit it to the App Store (provided you are a registered developer).

■   The Documentation tab provides an easy way to search for and read the developer documentation included with Xcode.

NOTE: Much of what we've covered here is covered in this documentation, along with a whole lot more. A good starting point if you are really interested in Mac OS X development is selecting Mac OS X 10.7 Core Library in the Documentation tab and selecting Getting Started.

This concludes our brief overview of Xcode for the moment. (We will return to Xcode in the next chapter where we build a simple application just to get a taste for Mac OS X development.)

Instruments

When developing programs for Mac OS X and iOS, the debugger in Xcode can be a fantastic help; however, it has its limits. To push your debugging capabilities further, you can use Instruments (Figure 32–14),which is included with Xcode.

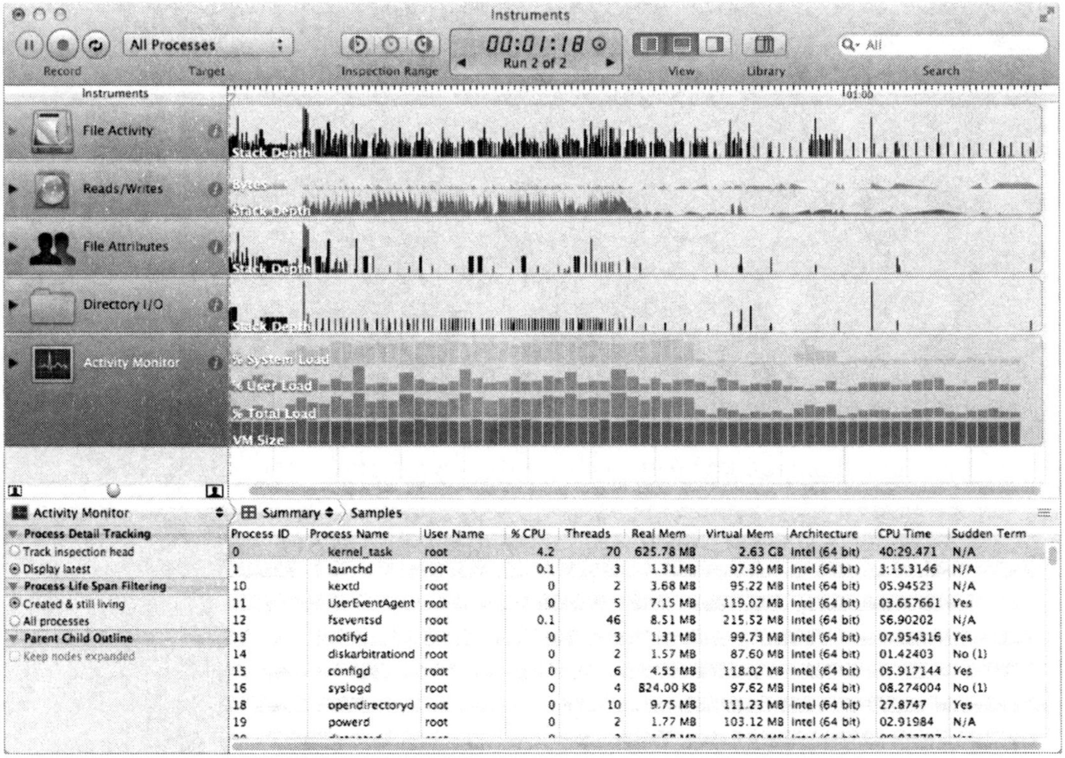

Figure 32–14. *Instruments provides tracing tools that allow you to study specific traits of a program while it is running.*

Instruments provides a wide selection of *tracing instruments*, or tools that can log specific information about the behavior of a running program, all wrapped together in a single program.

Each individual instrument traces a specific trait in a single process program or in the system on a whole. There are all types of instruments available ranging from "Leaks" and "Allocations," which together help discover memory leaks in a single process, to "Read/Writes," which provides details of disk activity.

Besides providing tracing on your Mac, Instruments can be used on connected iOS devices and the iOS simulator, so you can get details on the performance of your iOS apps and identify areas where your app's performance and behaviors can be improved.

When you are just getting started in development, it's often a victory just to get your app to run. Once you've gotten beyond that stage, though, learning to use tools like Instruments to further improve the end user's experience makes the difference between an app and a great app.

Dashcode

While Xcode is used primarily for developing native Mac OS X and iOS programs, Dashcode (Figure 32–15) is an IDE for creating web-based applications and widgets. First released along with the developer tools included with Mac OS X Leopard, Dashcode was primarily designed for developing dashboard widgets.

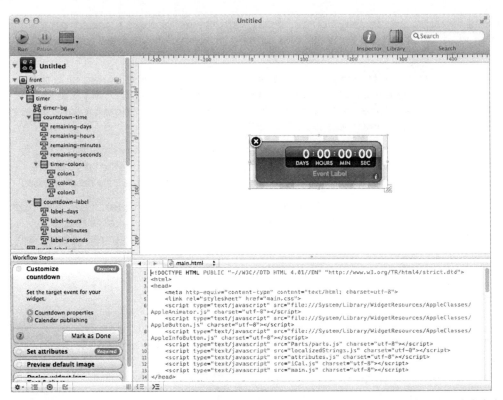

Figure 32–15. *Dashcode is an IDE for creating web-based application and widgets for Dashboard, Safari, or Mobile Safari.*

As Dashcode evolved, it has grown beyond a tool just for creating dashboard widgets (though it still of course can be used for that) and into a tool that can be used for creating full-fledged web applications for both Safari and Mobile Safari.

Quartz Composer

The final main app included with Xcode is Quartz Composer (Figure 32–16). Quartz Composer is an interesting application used for processing and rendering graphical data.

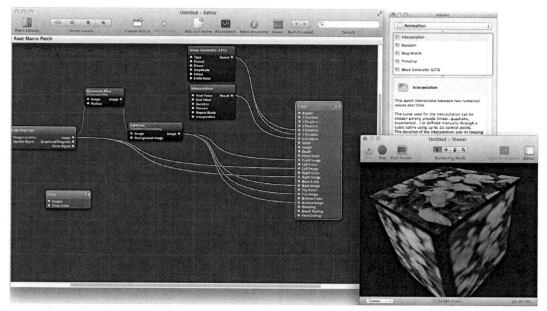

Figure 32–16. *Quartz Composer provides a visual programming environment for rendering and processing graphical data.*

> **NOTE:** Quartz is the name given to Mac OS X's graphics layer. Quartz uses a combination of other rendering technologies including OpenGL, Quartz 2D, Core Image, Core Animation, Core Video, Color Sync, and QuickTime.

Unlike traditional programming, a developer does not write code to build projects in Quartz Composer; rather, *patches*, special elements used for building compositions, are added from a library to the editor and then configured and connected to create graphical scenes.

In addition to being a fun way to learn about some of the graphical capabilities in Mac OS X, Quartz Composer can be used to create screen savers, iTunes music visualizers, and custom image filters.

Other Developer Utilities and Tools

Besides the four apps that show up in Launchpad, when you install Xcode, a number of additional tools and utilities are installed. To explore them, take a look in the /Developer/Applications folder. There, in addition to Xcode, Instruments, Dashcode, and Quartz Composer, are four additional folders containing other programs that may come in handy for developers.

The Audio folder contains two applications: AU Lab and HALlab. AU Lab can be used for testing audio units (a plug-in technology provided by Core Audio), and HALlab is used for testing audio hardware.

The Graphics Tools folder contains a number of applications for monitoring and working with OpenGL and Quartz as well as Core Image Fun House, which is an application that allows you to apply Core Image filters to an image, and Pixie, a screen area magnifier.

The Performance Tools folder contains Quartz Debug, a tool that provides a number of ways to help debug graphic issues with your applications, and Spin Doctor, which can help identify where applications may throw up the dreaded spinning rainbow wait cursor.

The Utilities folder contains a number of useful developer utilities for handling specific tasks such as creating icons from images and making traditional Mac OS installer packages.

Summary

Although this chapter by no means provided a complete look at Xcode and the included developer tools, it gave you a passing familiarity with the development environment that Apple provides. Apple's developer documentation provides a significant amount of additional information about all of these tools and how they are used. However, the best way to learn is to start using the tools and then discover new features as a need arises. In the next (and final) chapter, we are going to give you a taste of actual Mac OS X development to get you started on your path.

## Chapter 33

A Taste of Cocoa Development

In the previous chapter, you got a quick look at Xcode along with many of the other tools Apple provides for development. Learning about the tools is important, but it's all for naught if you don't know how to use them; after all, it would be cool to have a jet plane but less so if you don't know how to fly. With that in mind, in this chapter you will do the following:

- Build a simple Cocoa application in Xcode
- Discover what you still need to know to do real Cocoa programming
- Look at where to go to learn more

While this chapter won't earn you your wings, it will get you off the ground.

> **NOTE:** Cocoa is one of Apple's primary application programming interfaces (APIs) for Mac OS development. Often mistakenly referred to as a framework, Cocoa is actually two separate frameworks: Foundation Kit and Application Kit (or App Kit for short). These two frameworks provide a wide range of prebuilt functions, utilities, and UI elements that can be used in any Cocoa application to simplify the development process. In this chapter, you will rely 100 percent on available frameworks to build your sample application.

Building a Cocoa Application

The best way to learn something is to just do it. So, let's get started by building a little application in Cocoa called SimpleWeb (Figure 33–1). Don't worry if you have never programmed before; you can do this.

Figure 33–1. *SimpleWeb is a very simple but fully usable web browser.*

Creating Your Project in Xcode

To begin with, you must first create your project in Xcode, so open Xcode; in the Welcome to Xcode window, select "Create a new Xcode project" (Figure 33–2).

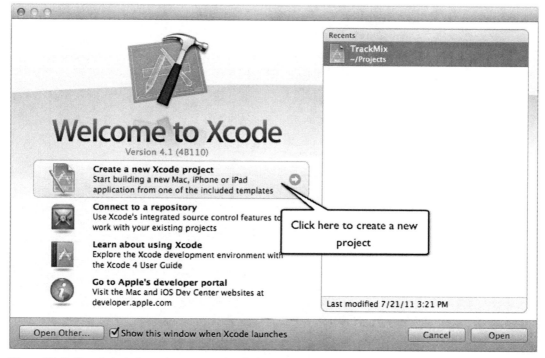

Figure 33–2. *To get started, create a new project in Xcode.*

NOTE: If Xcode is already open or the Welcome screen doesn't appear, you can start a new project by selecting **File > New > New Project...** from the menu bar.

When you choose to select a new project in Xcode, a new workspace will open with project template dialog. In the dialog, select Mac OS X Application in the left column and select the Cocoa Application template (Figure 33–3); then click Next.

Figure 33–3. *You will start your project with the Mac OS X Cocoa Application template.*

After you choose your template and click Next, the dialog will prompt us for some important project options (Figure 33–4). In the Product Name text field, enter **SimpleWeb** (or whatever you would like to call your final program). The company identifier is a unique name to represent you or your company; traditionally, this is you or your company's Internet domain name with the top-level domain (TLD) first (i.e., com.mydomain). All other fields and check boxes should be left blank or unchecked (though if you'd like, you can select the App Store category, which in this case would be Productivity. When you are done, click Next.

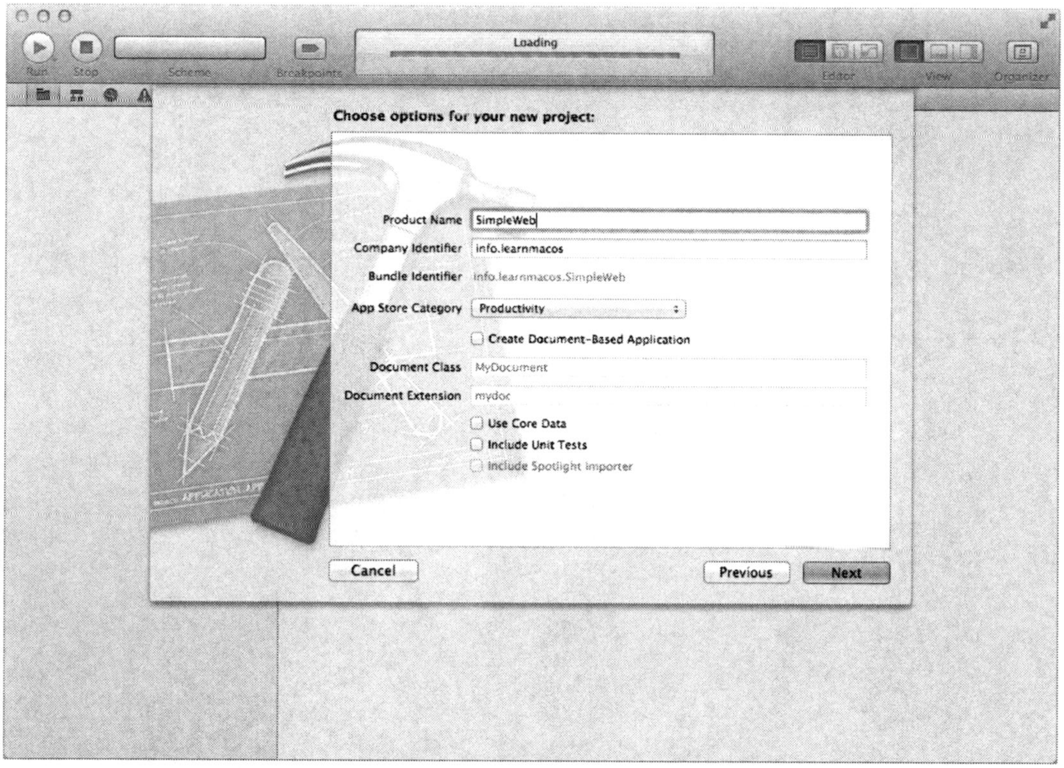

Figure 33–4. *After you select your project template, you must fill in some additional information about your project.*

> **NOTE:** The App Store category determines how your application will be classified in Apple's App Store. While some of the categories are fairly specific, others are quite vague. Categories like Productivity, Life Style, Business, and Entertainment tend to be catchalls where a more specific category is not available.

When you click Next, you will be asked for a location to save your project file. Any suitable location will be fine; a common location is your Documents folder, or occasionally developers will create a separate Projects folder in their home directory. When you've chosen a location, click Create to create your project. Once you've created your project, the dialog box will disappear, revealing the workspace with your project open and ready (Figure 33–5).

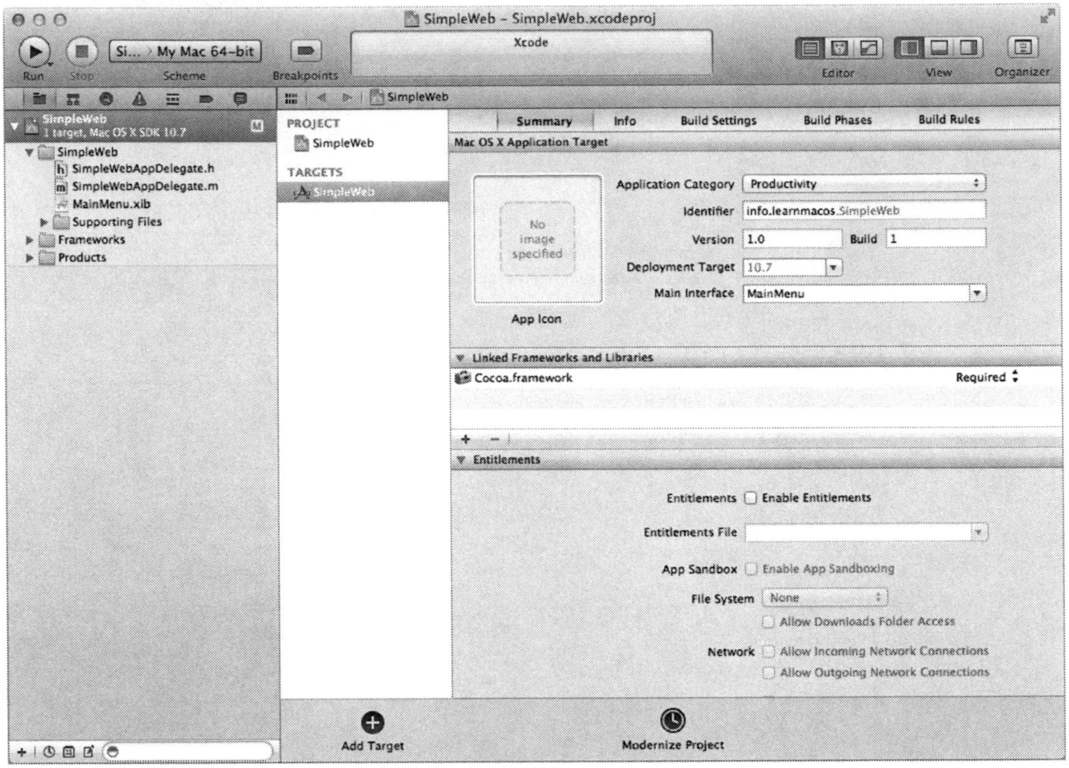

Figure 33–5. *Once you've successfully created your project, it will open in the workspace window.*

Building Your Application's Interface

When your project is first created, the project will be selected in the Project navigator, and a summary of your project will appear in the editor. Feel free to look around, but for now don't change any of your project's settings here. Rather, turn your attention to the Project navigator, where you will see a number of folders listed under your SimpleWeb project. The item that you are initially concerned with is in the SimpleWeb folder: MainMenu.xib. MainMenu.xib holds your application's interface, and it is in this file that you are going to do almost all of your work.

Select MainMenu.xip from the Project navigator, and the editor should switch into its Interface Builder mode with placeholders and objects along the left side of the editor view and just a toolbar in the main editor area (Figure 33–6).

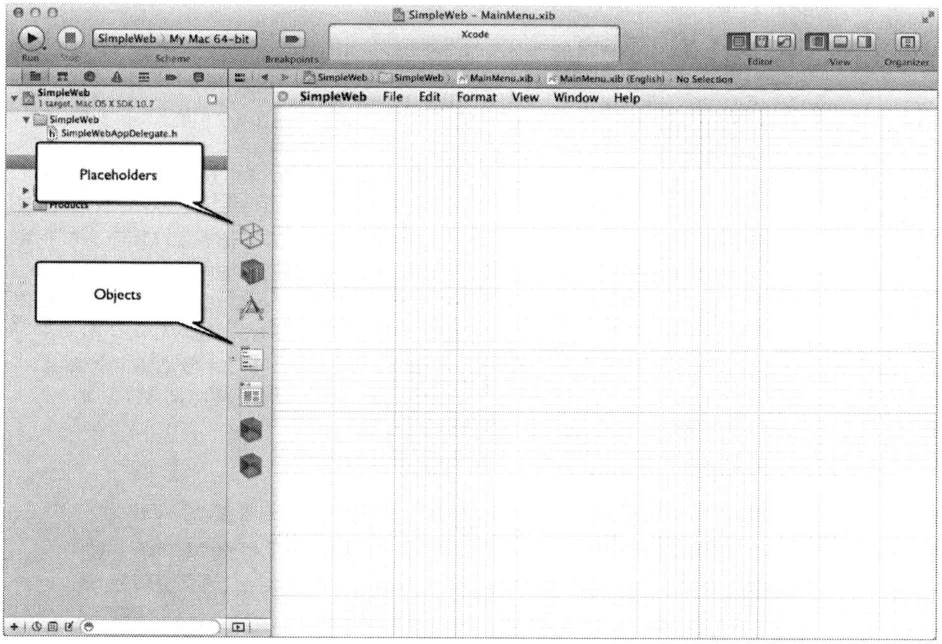

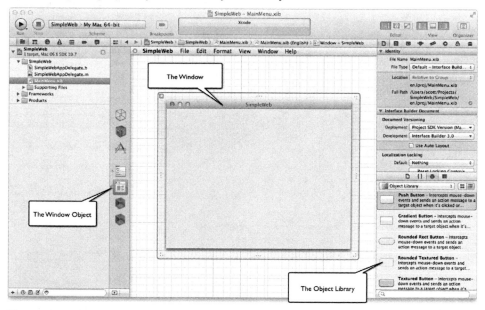

Figure 33–6. *Your first look at MainMenu.xib in Xcode*

To build your interface, you need to select the Window object from the Object list in the editor and open your Object Library in the utilities area of Xcode (Figure 33–7). Once you have everything open, you are ready to build your interface.

Figure 33–7. *With your Window object selected and your Object Library open, you are ready to build your interface.*

Adding Objects to Your Window

Your SimpleWeb application needs at least two things to be effective. It needs a way for to tell it what web page to display, and it needs a way to display them.

Taking a look through your Object Library, you may get a few ideas on how to get a web address into your application, but the most flexible one is the Text Field option, which is actually an NSTextField object (just like the "n" in nib, NS stands for NeXTSTEP). To add a text field to your window, simply select Text Field from the Object Library and drag it to your window. In building your application, you'd like your Text Field to start in the top-left corner, so drag your Text Field there until blue guidelines appear, letting you know you have reached the ideal location for your object (Figure 33–8). The blue guidelines appear as you position elements to help size and locate them in your windows with spacing consistent with Mac OS X Human Interface Guidelines.

> **NOTE:** The Mac OS X Human Interface Guidelines provide advice for building a great user experience in a manner consistent with Mac OS X and other great Mac OS X applications. If you open the Documentation in Xcode's Organizer window, you can browse to *Mac OS X 10.7 Core Library > User Experience > Apple Human Interface Guidelines* to read the guidelines in full.

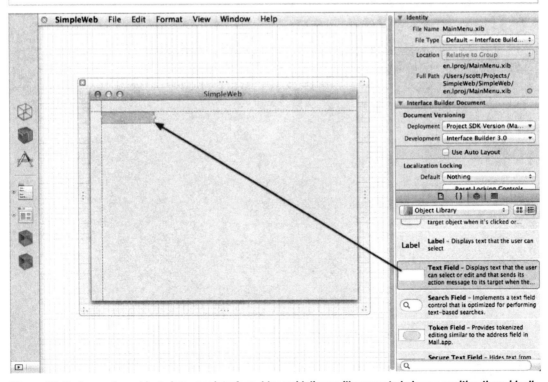

Figure 33–8. *As you drag objects into your interface, blue guidelines will appear to help you position them ideally.*

Once you have your Text Field positioned, position your cursor over the right edge of the selected text field until the pointer changes to a horizontal size cursor (a vertical line with small arrows pointing out to each side), click and drag to resize the Text Field across the width of the window until the guidelines show up on the right side of the window (Figure 33–9).

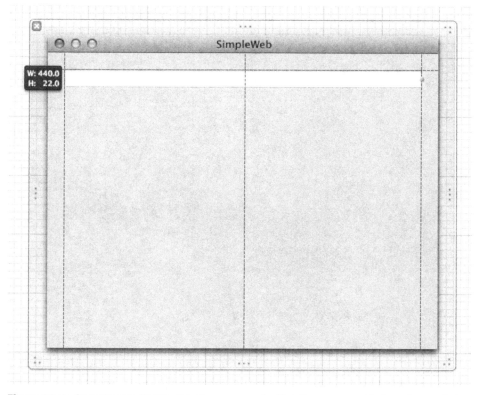

Figure 33–9. *Once the text filed is placed, you can resize it so it goes across the top of your window.*

Now that you have your Text Field, you need something that can display a web page. It just so happens that your Object Library contains the perfect object. Scroll all the down to the bottom of the Object Library until you reach the Web View and then drag the Web View onto your window and resize it to fill all of the window below your Text Field. Pay attention to the guidelines to leave a nice space between the bottom of the Text Field and the top of your Web View; you can also choose whether to pay attention to the guidelines to leave a border around the sides and bottom on the Web View or to extend it to the edge of the window. I prefer to extend the Web View all the way to left, right, and bottom edges, which is just how the Web View object is positioned in Safari. When you are finished, you have a very simple interface (Figure 33–10).

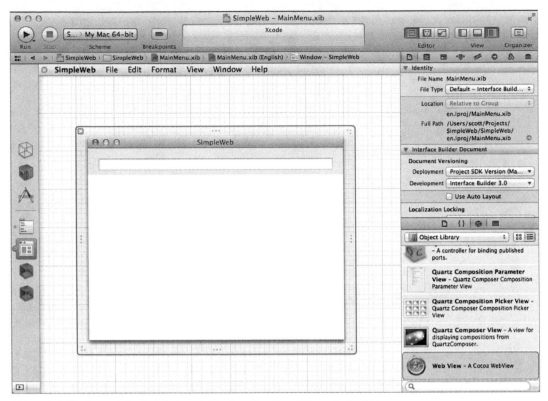

Figure 33–10. *Your window's interface in Xcode with a Text Field and a Web View*

Testing and Tweaking Your Interface

To see how your interface will look in the finished application, you can simulate your layout by selecting **Editor > Simulate Document** from Xcode's menu. This will open your layout in its own window so you can see how the elements appear. When your window first opens, everything looks like you expected, but if you resize your window, things start looking ugly real fast (Figure 33–11). What you neglected to do is configure your objects to resize along with the window, so let's go back and do that.

Figure 33–11. *Not configuring your objects to resize when the window size changes gives us undesired results.*

To set up your object to resize with the window, you need to select each object and configure it in the Size inspector (Figure 33–12). In the Size inspector, you will use the Autosizing control to control how your object resizes.

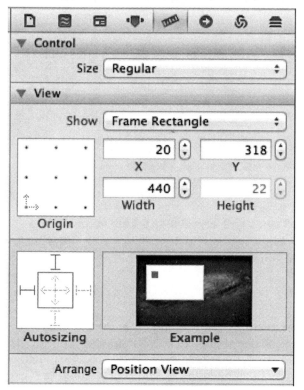

Figure 33–12. *You can adjust the sizing properties of your object using the Size inspector.*

The Autosizing control has two concentric squares. The outer square determines what sides the object is pinned to. The object will seem to "stick" to the sides it's pinned to when its container is resized. The inner square determines vertical and horizontal resizing of the object in proportion to the size of the container it's placed in. The red "I" bars in the outer square determine what sides an object is pinned to. Clicking one side on the outer square will toggle the pinning on that side.

> **NOTE:** When pinning, objects the left and bottom sides have precedence. That is, if you have an object pinned to the top and bottom, if the object needs to choose, it will stick to the bottom.

> **NOTE:** I referred to containers rather than windows, while in your application a Window is your primary container. If I were to add other NSView objects inside of my window (such as a Box), the size and location of any items placed in it would be relative to the size and location of the NSView object it's contained in.

With this in mind, select your Text Field and pin it to the top, left, and right and set it to resize horizontally. This will cause your Text Field to stretch across the top of your window when it is resized.

> **NOTE:** To see the effect your selections have, take a look at the example animation to the right of the Autosizing control.

> **NOTE:** Your Text Field object cannot be resized vertically. This is because the Text Field object you chose is always one line high. If you wanted a flexible text area, you could have used a Wrapping Text Field.

Turning to your Web View, let's pin it to all sides and have it resize both vertically and horizontally. Once you have made the appropriate selections, simulate your document again and make sure everything is scaling correctly.

Connecting Your Objects

Right now you have a perfectly good interface that does nothing other than display a couple of objects in a window. If you were to successfully build your application now (ignoring that it would currently result in an error), you could enter text in the Text Field and resize the window, but do little else. What you need to do now is connect your objects so they can communicate with each other. Specifically, you want to connect your Text Field to your Web View so that when you enter a web address in your Text Field and hit Return, the web address is sent to the Web View where the address will be opened. Luckily, your objects come equipped with all the underlying code to accomplish this already self-contained, so all you need to do is make the proper connection.

To make the connection, select your text field object; then, while holding the Control key, click and drag from the Text Field to the Web View. As you drag, a faint blue connection line will follow your mouse movement. When the line is complete between the Text Field and the Web View, release the button, and a menu will pop up asking you which action you want to make the connection to (Figure 33–13). Select takeStringURLFrom: from the menu and—*presto*—your connection is made.

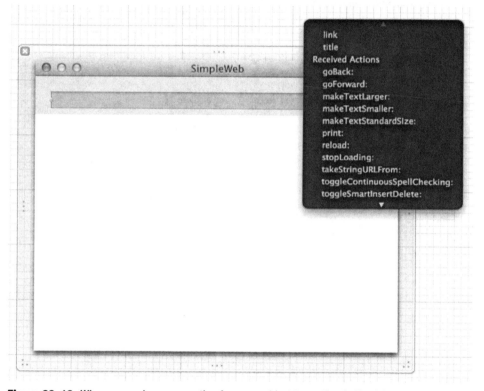

Figure 33–13. *When you make a connection from one object to another in Xcode's Interface Builder, a menu of available connections will appear. Select the desired action to complete the connection.*

Looking through the list of available actions that you can connect to in your Web View should give you some ideas for other options you could add to your application without much trouble (i.e., connecting a Button object to goBack:), but for now you are going to stop and see whether your application in its current state works.

> **NOTE:** You may be curious about the two SimpleWebAppDelegate files in your project. To provide an example with the minimum of complexity, your sample application doesn't require us to write any code, so you really don't need to deal with these files. This doesn't mean these files don't do anything; in fact, they do. These two files form the basis of your application's delegate object. Delegation is an important concept in Cocoa programming that allows a single delegate object to keep events happening in the interface in sync with events happening within the rest of the program including other interface elements. The applicationDidFinishLaunching method in the SimpleWebAppDelegate.m file is a good example of how this works. This method receives a message from your interface when it is finished launching, allowing a developer to run any code at startup. Without delegation, you could still inject code into the startup, but you may have no way of knowing when all aspects of your program have successfully loaded.

Building and Debugging Your Application

The process of building and testing an application is quite easy *if* everything goes according to plan. To build and test an application, save all of your files and click the Run button in Xcode's toolbar. This will cause all of the files to start compiling, and if everything is successful, your application will launch.

In your case, if you attempt to build and run your application, while everything seems to build OK, your application will not run; rather, the debugger will open up with all sorts of cryptic errors and stack dumps (Figure 33–14). Most of this probably isn't very helpful, but delving through the debugger console for something you can understand does reveal this: cannot decode object of class (WebView). While this in and of itself may not provide the specific answer to your problem, it at least gets us looking in the right direction.

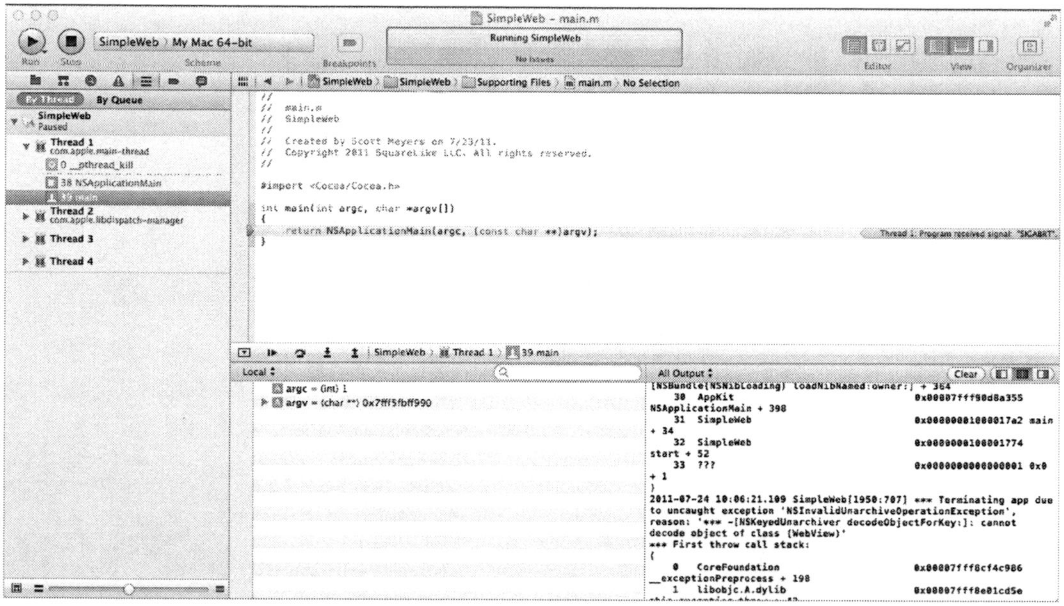

Figure 33–14. *Your first attempt at building and running your application failed. While much of the information in the debugger may be cryptic, there could still be clues to what went wrong.*

To help figure out what went wrong, let's take another look at the Web View object in your Object Library (Figure 33–15). Reading the description, you should notice that the WebView class is part of the Web Kit Framework. Looking back at your project summary, you notice the only linked framework in your project is the Cocoa.framework, so maybe your solution is to add the Web Kit Framework.

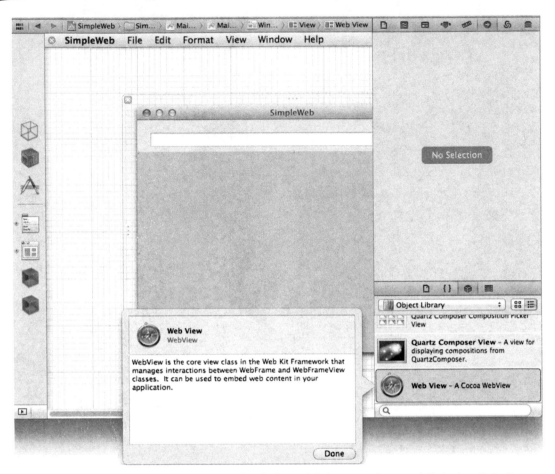

Figure 33–15. *The summary of the Web View object indicates it belongs to a framework that currently isn't included in your project.*

To add a framework to your project, go back to the project summary view in Xcode (by clicking the root project item in the Project navigator), and under the Linked Frameworks and Libraries area, click the + button to add a framework to your project. When you click the + button, a dialog will appear, providing us with a list of all libraries and frameworks that Xcode can detect on your system (Figure 33–16). Scrolling down, you can select WebKit.framework to add it to your project.

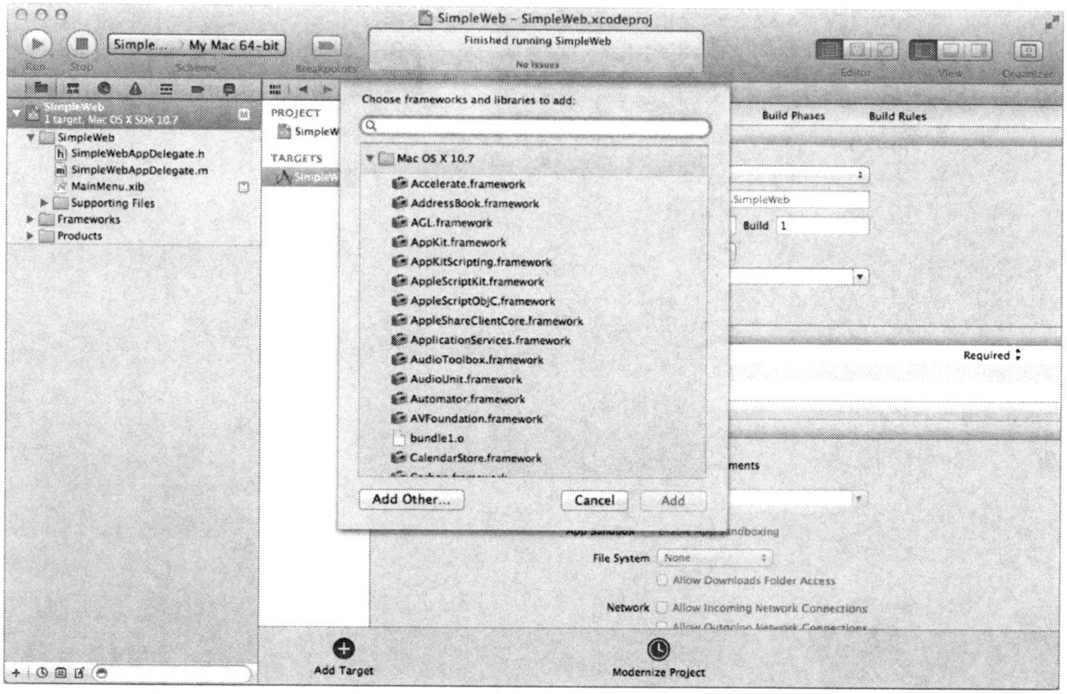

Figure 33-16. *In your project summary, you can choose from a list of any additional frameworks or libraries you need for your project.*

Now that you added the Web Kit Framework when you try to build and run your application, everything should work splendidly. Type a URL in the Text Field and hit Return to load a web page in your new app.

NOTE: Remember to stop any versions of your app you already have running before you try running the app again. If you don't, you will be prompted to do so.

Archiving and Distributing Your Application

Now, your SimpleWeb application isn't going to win any "great app of the year" awards as is, so at this point, if you were creating anything other than an example app, you'd probably want to go back and continue development. Supposing your app was finished, though—and by finished, I mean it builds, it runs, you've checked it for memory leaks and performance issues in Instruments, and so on—you now want to share it with the world. To get you app out of Xcode, the first step is to archive it, which is done by selecting **Product > Archive** from Xcode's menu. Once archived, the app should appear on the Archives tab in Xcode's Organizer (Figure 33–17).

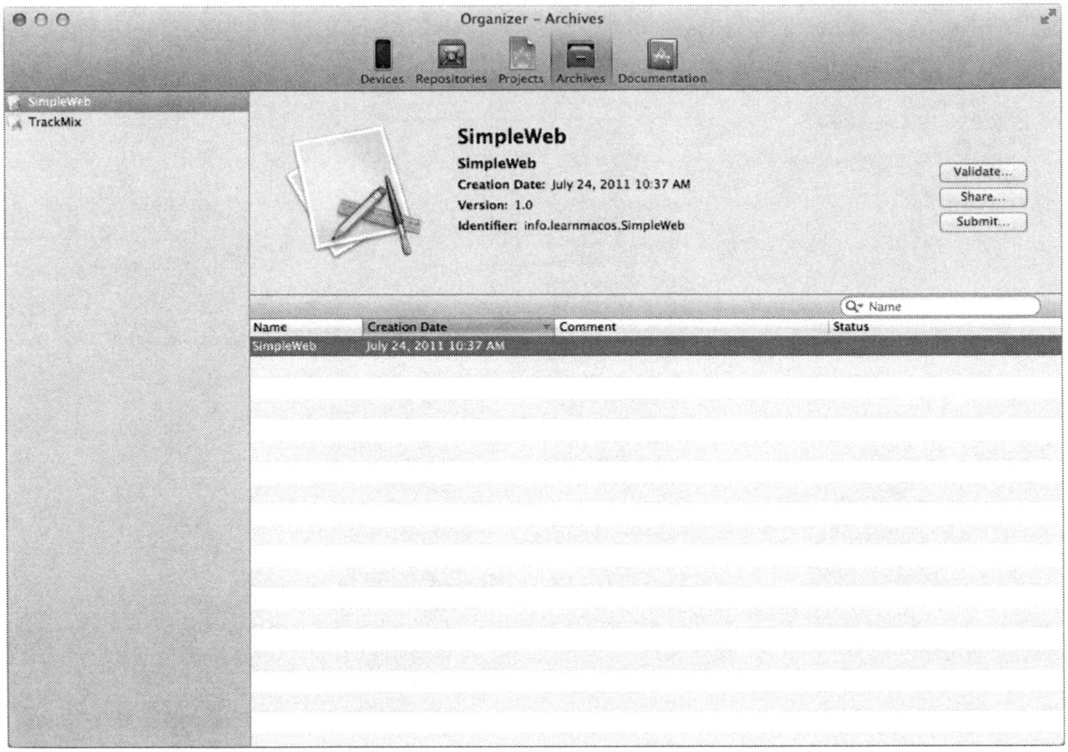

Figure 33–17. *From the Archives tab in Xcode's Organizer, you can prepare and submit your app to the Mac OS X App Store or share your app by other means.*

The easiest way to share your application with others once you have archived your app is to click the Share... button. This will bring up a dialog asking you how you'd like to share your application. The options are as follows:

- Mac OS X App Store Package (.pkg) will create a package that allows a simple double-click install of your app.

- Application will just export the final application itself, which can be double-clicked to launch right away.

- Archive will create an archive of your actual project that can be shared with other developers.

To distribute your app on the Mac App Store, you have to go through a number of additional steps, the first being you need to be a registered member of the Mac Developer Program. You can find more information about Apple's developer programs on the `http://developer.apple.com` web site.

NOTE: Since the developer tools are free to download, there is no urgent reason to run out and join one of Apple's developer programs as you are learning to develop. Once you've reached a level where you think you have an application worth sharing, it's definitely a worthwhile endeavor, though. The Mac and iOS developer programs each cost $99 to join (that's $198 for both); they allow you to sell you apps via the respective App Stores and give you access to many other features including access to prerelease software and additional developer support options.

What You Still Need to Know

Building your application should have helped with a few things. First, it should have helped you familiarize yourself with Xcode a bit more by actually walking you through using the tools rather than just looking at them. Second, it should have illustrated that with the available frameworks and libraries, you get a lot of features built in for free, making it easier and faster to create a great application. Finally, you should have realized, wait a second, there has to be more to it than this, and of course there is.

To be a great Cocoa developer, you will need to learn a whole lot more than what I discussed here. Let's look at just few things.

Objective-C

Objective-C, Cocoa's native programming language, is sort of a mash-up of C and Smalltalk into a single language. Technically Objective-C is a superset of C with additional Smalltalk-inspired syntax added to it to allow object-oriented programming features. The bond between C and Objective-C is such that if I wanted to provide a valid "Hello World!" example written in Objective-C, I could refer to the original "Hello World!" program written in Kernighan & Ritchie's *The C Programming Language*.

NOTE: *The C Programming Language* is often referred to as just the K&R book. It is one of the best programming books ever written. While there are some great books that start right off teaching you Objective-C that may be better suited to novice Mac and iOS developers, starting with K&R will do nothing but help you.

For a quick introduction to Objective-C, Apple provides both a short *Learning Objective-C: A Primer* document as well as a longer *The Objective-C Programming Language* document. The first is suitable for developers already familiar with C, and the latter is a more in-depth introduction to Objective-C. Each of these documents is included with Xcode's developer documentation.

Some other excellent resources for learning Objective-C that may be more suitable than Apple's documentation for some include *Learn Objective-C on the Mac* by Mark

Dalrymple and Scott Knaster (Apress, ISBN 978-1430218159) and *Programming in Objective-C, 3rd Edition* by Stephen Kochan (Addison-Wesley, ISBN 978-0321711397).

Cocoa Programming

We barely scratched the surface of Cocoa and didn't even begin to go into many of the important topics necessary to build more interesting Cocoa applications.

Many useful documents to help explain Cocoa programming are included with Xcode's documentation. Some good documents to start with include *Your First Mac Application* and the *Mac OS X Application Programming Guide*.

There are also a number of books available to help you learn Cocoa, including *Learn Cocoa on the Mac* by David Mark, Jeff LaMarche, and Jack Nutting (Apress, ISBN 978-1430218593), as well as *Cocoa Programming for Mac OS X, 4th Edition* by Arron Hillegass and Adam Preble (Addison-Wesley ISBN 978-0321774088).

> **NOTE:** Many introductory books on Cocoa programming also include some basic introduction to Xcode and Objective-C, thus making them a good place to start.

Frameworks and Technologies

Once you've learned the basics of how to program in Cocoa, it pays to start delving into the various frameworks available for Cocoa development. Besides the all-important AppKit framework, there are a host of other frameworks to make your life as a developer simpler. Some standouts include the CoreData, WebKit, Quartz, and Foundation frameworks, but there are many more that are important and useful.

> **NOTE:** The Cocoa framework is an umbrella framework that includes the AppKit, CoreData, and Foundation frameworks, so by including the Cocoa framework in an application, you gain access to each of these frameworks automatically.

You will find many of the most common features of the most common frameworks covered in many general Cocoa and Mac OS X programming books, with a few minor exceptions, but the best place to find up-to-date information about the various frameworks is Apple's developer documentation.

> **NOTE:** One additional thing that developers should take into account when writing applications is security. This is a topic with growing importance, especially as more applications share resources and work over the Internet. One of the best security resources for Cocoa developers currently available is *Professional Cocoa Application Security* by Graham Lee (Wrox, ISBN 978-0470525951).

Summary

With this chapter you got a taste of Mac OS X development. You also learned that while Mac development is relatively easy, there is a lot of information you need to absorb to become a competent programmer. The difference between a competent programmer and a great programmer is the ideas you bring to the table.

Part **X**

Appendix

Installing Lion and Recovery Options

There are two primary ways to get Lion on a Mac: either you buy a new Mac with Lion preinstalled or you purchase Lion from the Mac App Store and download and install it. This appendix will walk you though the initial installation process of Lion using the App Store purchase and then discuss using Lions recovery options if you ever need to fix or reinstall Lion at a later time.

What You Need to Install Lion

To install Lion on an existing Mac, your Mac must have a few things:

- Your Mac must have a 64-bit Intel processor including Intel Core 2 Duo, Xeon, and Core i3, Core i5, and Core i7 processors. (Macs with Intel Core Duo or Core Solo processors will not be able to run Lion.)

- You Mac must have at least 2GB of RAM (memory) and 7GB of free disk space.

- Your Mac must have Snow Leopard installed and updated to Mac OS X 10.6.6 (10.6.8 is recommended).

> **NOTE:** Beyond these base requirements, certain features may not be available to some Macs depending on how they are configured. One notable example is that depending on the AirPort card that came with your Mac, AirDrop may not work. (This includes MacBook Airs and Mac Minis built as recently as 2010.)

Installing Lion

Provided you meet the hardware and software requirements, you are ready to install Lion. Let's walk you through the process:

1. The first step is to open the App Store application and purchase and download Lion. Lion is available for $29.99 from the App Store (using the App Store is covered in Chapter 6). Once you complete your purchase, the Install Mac OS X Lion installer (Figure XA–1) will download to your Applications folder and automatically launch, starting the installation.

Figure XA–1. *The Install Mac OS X Lion application will start automatically after the download is complete. Upon successful installation and creation of a recovery partition, this application will be deleted.*

NOTE: Besides purchasing Lion from the App Store, Lion is available for purchase on a USB key from Apple for $69. The steps for installing Lion from the USB key are similar to the steps here. One significant difference is that the USB key install does not install a recovery partition, so for maintenance and recovery, you will need to keep the key handy.

2. Upon the launch of the installer, you will be greeted with a welcome screen (Figure XA–2) that will start walking you through the installation process.

Figure XA–2. *When the Lion installer launches, you will be presented with a screen that will walk you through the installation.*

3. Clicking Continue on the initial installer screen will take you to the next screen where you will be asked to accept the software license agreement. You must accept this by clicking Agree to continue. (Once you click Agree, a dialog box will appear asking you to verify your agreement.)

4. After you agree to the license agreement (twice), you will be presented with the next screen that will ask you what disk you would like to install Lion on (Figure XA–3). The disk the installer is installed on will be chosen by default. If you would like to install Lion on another disk or partition, click the Show All Disks... button to be presented with a list of all available partitions.

Figure XA–3. *After you accept the license agreement, you will be asked to confirm the disk you would like to install Lion on; to view all available partitions, click the Show All Disks... button.*

5.   Once you have selected the disk and clicked the Install button, you will then be prompted to enter your administrator password, after which the installation will begin immediately. The actual installation happens in two parts. First the installer will prepare the installation (Figure XA–4). After a couple minutes of this, your computer will restart, and the actual installation will take place. (This can take from ten minutes to an hour to complete.)

Figure XA–4. *When you start the installation, the installer will first prepare the installation and then restart to complete it. The total installation time seems to average about 30 to 45 minutes, but this will vary on your hardware and whether you are installing over an existing system or on a clean partition.*

6. Upon successful installation, you will be greeted by the Mac OS X Setup Assistant. If you have installed Lion on top of an existing Snow Leopard partition, the Assistant will present you with some informational screens (Figure XA–5). If you installed Lion on a new drive or partition, it will ask if you'd like to use the Migration Assistant to transfer your settings from another partition, Time Machine backup, or another computer (you can even transfer information from a Windows PC). If you choose not to transfer settings from elsewhere, you will be walked through some basic setup screens where you will be asked to create a new user, set up networking, and register with Apple.

Figure XA–5. *After successfully installing Lion, the Setup Assistant will start. The screens you are presented with will vary based on whether you installed Lion over an existing Snow Leopard system or whether you installed Lion on a clean disk or partition.*

THE MIGRATION ASSISTANT

The Migration Assistant is a utility that can transfer user accounts, files, applications, and settings to your Mac from another startup disk, from a Time Machine backup, or from another Mac or PC over a network. If you installed Mac OS X on a clean partition (a disk or partition that has been formatted prior to installation) or when you first turn on a new Mac with a fresh copy of Lion, one of the first decisions you will have is whether you want to transfer users, files, and settings from another partition, drive, or system .. This is awesome if you have purchased a new Mac and are worried about transferring your existing data to your new computer.

If you decide not to transfer any information when you are first setting up Lion, then you need to manually add a new user and configure your networking when you are first getting started with Lion. After that, you can use Migration Assistant (which is located in the Launchpad Utilities folder) at any time to transfer information to your computer with one caveat: once a username is created in Lion, Migration Assistant will overwrite that account, so if you create an account named "Scott" on Lion and then try to copy a user named "Scott" to the system using Migration Assistant, these accounts will not merge.

With Lion, Migration Assistant will even transfer user data from a Windows PC to a Mac (though not applications). This allows documents, videos, music (MP3s or existing iTunes library), contacts, calendars, and even e-mail (from Outlook and Windows Mail Live) to be moved from a Windows PC and installed on your new Mac, all ready to go.

Mac OS X Recovery

When Lion is installed, it will automatically create a recovery partition on the boot disk of your hard drive. By booting into this partition, you will be able to reinstall Mac OS X Lion as well as access additional utilities that previously were commonly found on Mac OS X install media.

To boot your Mac using the recovery partition, you may hold Command-R when you start or restart your computer to boot directly to the recover partition; alternately, hold the Option key and select the Recovery HD from the resulting list of bootable partitions.

> **NOTE:** The recovery partition will not be created on systems with unsupported partition schemes (e.g., you have added extra partitions to a startup disk that has a Boot Camp partition). If you find yourself in situation, you will need to alter your existing partitions to a supported scheme prior to installing Lion; otherwise, you will need to either *manually* create a recovery disk on your own (covered next) or do without a recovery option.

Upon booting into the recovery partition, you will be presented with a simple window (Figure XA–6) offering you four common recovery options: Restore From a Time Machine Backup, Reinstall Mac OS X, Get Help Online, and Disk Utility.

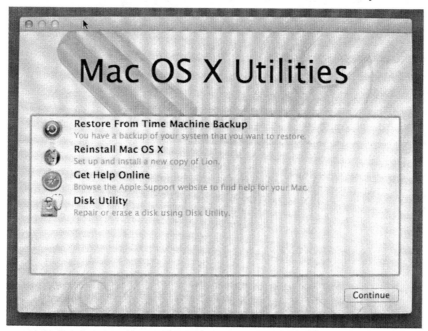

Figure XA–6. *When you boot into the recovery partition, you will be presented with a window giving you access to common recovery options.*

The Restore From Time Machine Backup option will allow you to recover your system to a previous Time Machine backup state. The Reinstall Mac OS X option will launch the

Mac OS X installer to allow you to install or reinstall Mac OS X Lion. The Get Help Online option will open Safari to Apple's Support web site (you could of course continue to browse to any other web site if you so desired). The Disk Utility option will launch the Disk Utility (covered in Chapter 21) so you can manage and repair a disk or disk partition.

SETTING A FIRMWARE PASSWORD

Besides the recovery options, the booting from the recovery disk reveals one other unique feature: setting a firmware password. Setting the firmware password provides additional security for your Mac OS X system by requiring a password to be entered when attempting to boot your system from any nonstartup disk or when attempting to use special startup commands.

To set a firmware password, launch the Firmware Password Utility (Figure XA–7) by selecting **Utilities > Firmware Password Utility** from the menu. From there you can click the Turn on Firmware Password... button to set and activate the firmware password.

Figure XA–7. *The Firmware Password Utility allows you to set and activate a password that will be required when you try to boot your computer using any volume other than the selected startup disk.*

Without this option, anyone with physical access to your system and an external bootable disk could use their disk to boot your computer and access any unencrypted files on your drives.

> **NOTE:** Besides the Firmware Password Utility, the Terminal app and Network Utility are also available from the recovery Utilities menu.

Lion Recovery Disk Assistant

Although having a recovery partition on your primary disk is useful for a quick repair or recovery, it won't help you if your hard drive fails entirely. Because of this, it's not a bad idea to create a separate recovery option on an external disk or flash drive. And while creating a stand-alone recovery drive on your own isn't too hard, Apple has made the Lion Recovery Disk Assistant available to make this process very easy. Using the Lion Recovery Disk Assistant is a simple three-step process.

NOTE: Before you begin, you will need an external disk to create the recovery disk on. A 4GB flash drive will make a lovely external recovery HD.

1. Download the Lion Recovery Disk Assistant from Apple. For information and a link to the download, visit http://support.apple.com/kb/dl1433.

2. Once you have downloaded the Lion Recovery Disk Assistant, copy it from its disk image to somewhere on your hard drive, and launch it.

3. When launched, the Assistant will ask you to select the external volume to create a recovery disk on. Once the external drive is selected, the assistant will do its thing and turn the external volume into a recovery HD.

When the Assistant finishes, you should have a new bootable recovery option. To use your new recovery disk, plug it in to your computer and hold the Option key when you start or restart you computer. When it's starting up, you should be presented with a list of bootable volumes, and the external recovery HD should be among them.

MANUALLY CREATING A RECOVERY DISK

If you want, or need, to create a bootable recovery disk without using the Lion Recovery Disk Assistant, you can, but you must follow these steps:

1. Once you have downloaded the Lion installer from the App Store, cancel the installation. (You may of course continue with the installation at any time, but upon completion, the Install Mac OS X Lion application will be deleted, and we need that.)

2. Go to the Applications folder and locate the Install Mac OS X Lion application. Control-click it and select Show Package Contents from the shortcut menu.

3. Navigate through the contents Contents/SharedSupport folders until you find the InstallESD.dmg file. This is a recovery disk image.

4. Using Disk Utility (see Chapter 21 for details), restore this disk image onto your desired external drive or partition.

Presto, you should now have a bootable recovery disk.

Now, what if you already installed Lion and the Install Mac OS X Lion application is no longer in your Applications folder? In this case, open the Mac App Store, and hold down the Option key while you click the Purchased tab at the top. Provided you previously purchased Lion, this should cause the Installed button to change into an Install button, allowing you to redownload it.

Index

A

A private server option, 222–223
About This Mac information window, 11
About This Mac option, 10
About This Mac window, 10
access
    remote, of Microsoft Windows
        computers, 579–580
    Universal Access pane, in Personal
        preferences, 307–311
access control lists (ACLs), 464–466
Account Setup dialog, 228
accounts
    e-mail, adding, 186–194
    in iCal, 223–224
Accounts submenu, 230
ACLs (access control lists), 464–466
actions, 597–599, 604–610
Active Directory service, 568
Activity option, 158, 186
Activity window, 158
Actual Size option, 156
Add Account... option, 181, 186, 251
Add Bookmark Folder option, 158
Add Bookmark For These [n] Tabs
    option, 158
Add Bookmark menu, 160
Add Bookmark... option, 157
Add Buddy... option, 232
Add Field option, 212
Add Folder of Pictures... option, 595
Add Group... option, 232
Add RSS Feeds... option, 181, 205
Add Sender to Address Book option,
    185

Address Book, 207–214
    contacts in
        creating, 208–212
        editing, 208–212
        sharing, 213
    groups in, creating, 212–213
    printing labels and envelopes, 213
    setting up card, 212
    shared contact lists, viewing, 213
Address Panel option, 186
Adjust tools, in iPhoto, 265
Administrator option, 339
Advanced Options dialog, 340
AFP (Apple Filing Protocol), 526
AIM (AOL Instant Messenger), 227, 233,
    238
AIM option, 228
AirDrop feature, 534–535
AirPort networks, 532–533
AirPort Utility, 383, 518–521
aliases
    in Finder, creating, 49–50
    and functions, commands with,
        470–471
All Messages in this Thread option, 182
All My Files option, 36
Allow access to only these websites
    option, 343
Allow guests to connect to shared
    folders option, 340
Allow guests to log into this computer
    option, 340
Allow unrestricted access to websites
    option, 343
Always Insert Attachments at End of
    Message option, 182

S

CPSIA information can be obtained at www.ICGtesting.com
Printed in the USA
LVOW050059141011

250462LV00006B/4/P